Migrating to Oracle8*i*™

David Austin

Meghraj Thakkar

Kurt Lysy

SΛMS

A Division of Macmillan USA
201 West 103rd St., Indianapolis, Indiana, 46290 USA

Migrating to Oracle8*i*™
Copyright© 2000 by Sams Publishing

International Standard Book Number: 0-672-31577-7

Library of Congress Catalog Card Number: 99-63645

Printed in the United States of America

First Printing: October 1999

02   01   00   99   4   3   2   1

Trademarks

Warning and Disclaimer

EXECUTIVE EDITOR
Tim Ryan

DEVELOPMENT EDITOR
Songlin Qiu

MANAGING EDITOR
Jodi Jensen

PROJECT EDITOR
Gretchen Uphoff

COPY EDITOR
Rhonda Tinch-Mize

INDEXER
Sharon Hilgenberg

PROOFREADERS
Jill Mazurczyk
Megan Wade

TECHNICAL EDITOR
Dave Thompson

TEAM COORDINATOR
Karen Opal

INTERIOR DESIGNER
Anne Jones

COVER DESIGNER
Aren Howell

COPY WRITER
Eric Borgert

PRODUCTION
Jeannette McKay

Overview

Contents

About the Authors

David Austin has been in the data processing profession for almost 25 years and worked with many database architectures, including hierarchical, network, and relational, before becoming an Oracle DBA over 10 years ago. For the past six years, David has worked for Oracle Corporation where he is currently employed as a senior principal curriculum developer. His previous positions at Oracle include senior principal consultant and senior principal instructor. David, author of *Using Oracle8* published by Que/Macmillan, and a contributor to two *Special Editions* in the Que *Using* series, is a certified Oracle8 database administrator. He obtained both of his degrees—a B.A. with a double major in Mathematics and English and a minor in Computer Science, and an M.S. in Applied Mathematics—from the University of Colorado. He can be reached by email at daustin@us.oracle.com.

Meghraj Thakkar currently works at Quest Software. Before this, he worked as a technical specialist at Oracle Corporation and has been working with various Oracle products for the past seven years. Meghraj has several certifications including OCP, MCSE, Novell Certified ECNE, SCO UNIX ACE, and Lotus Certified Notes Consultant. He has presented at the Oracle Openworld (Australia), UKOUG (Birminghan, UK), and ECO (New York, USA). He has also taught several courses at the University of California, Irvine. He is the author of *Sams Teach Yourself Oracle8i on Windows NT in 24 Hours* published by Macmillan Computer Publishing and has also coauthored several other books, including *Special Edition Using Oracle8, Oracle8 Server Unleashed, C++ Unleashed, COBOL Unleashed, Oracle Certified DBA,* and *Using Oracle8.* He can be reached at mthakkar@bigpond.com.

Kurt Lysy is a senior principal instructor with Oracle Corporation and has worked in the information systems industry since 1982. Over his career, Kurt has been responsible for the administration and tuning of large databases in the aerospace, commercial, and health care industries. Kurt has over 15 years experience with Oracle as a database administrator, developer, and consultant. As an Oracle seminar presenter, Kurt has presented numerous technical seminars in Latin America, Europe, Asia, and Australia. His areas of technical expertise include database performance tuning and optimization, database recovery, distributed database tuning, replication, data warehousing, and system administration. Prior to joining Oracle, Kurt presented on-site courses on database tuning and administration for a number of large corporations worldwide. Kurt holds a B.S. in Computer Science from Brigham Young University. He can be reached by email at klysy@us.oracle.com.

Dedication

I would like to dedicate this book to my son, Alton "Monty" Austin.

—David Austin

This book is dedicated to the two amazing women in my life: my mom, who always encourages me to make my dreams a reality and my wife, Komal, who makes my life complete.

—Meghraj Thakkar

This book is dedicated to my wife, Shannon, and my sons: Matthew, Jeffrey, Jon, Michael, and Brett.

—Kurt Lysy

Acknowledgments

Thanks to the many professionals who have helped and encouraged me in my career, particularly my various managers, instructors, and colleagues at Oracle including Vijayanandan Venkatachalam, Chris Pirie, Deborah West, Nick Evans, Larry Mix, Beth Winslow, Bruce Ernst, Sue Jang, Scott Gossett, Scott Heisey, Erik Peterson, and Charles Rozwat. I would also like to say thank you to some of my earliest mentors in this business: Bob Klein, Donald Miklich, David Aichele, and Roland Sweet.

I would also like to thank my coauthors and the editors at Macmillan who have supported my work on this book.

—David Austin

Writing this book was very demanding considering the various changes going on in my life at the time and I would like to acknowledge the much needed support and strength provided by my wife for whom it was an equally difficult journey.

I would also like to thank all the folks at Macmillan Computer Publishing, specially Angela Kozlowski, Tim Ryan, Songlin Qiu, and Gretchen Uphoff for pulling everything together for this book.

—Meghraj Thakkar

Taking on the task of writing this book has been a major undertaking for me and my family. I would like to thank my coauthors for allowing me the opportunity to assist in the development of this book, and to Tim Ryan and his editorial staff at Macmillan for their assistance. I would also like to thank Terri Cobb and Carrie Anderson at Oracle for inspiring me to take on this project.

Finally, I wish to thank my wife Shannon for her sacrifice, love, patience, and support while I was writing this book. Without her assistance, I would never have been able to complete this book.

—Kurt Lysy

Tell Us What You Think!

As the reader of this book, you are our most important critic and commentator. We value your opinion and want to know what we're doing right, what we could do better, what areas you'd like to see us publish in, and any other words of wisdom you're willing to pass our way.

As an executive editor for Sams Publishing, I welcome your comments. You can fax, email, or write me directly to let me know what you did or didn't like about this book—as well as what we can do to make our books stronger.

Please note that I cannot help you with technical problems related to the topic of this book, and that due to the high volume of mail I receive, I might not be able to reply to every message.

When you write, please be sure to include this book's title and authors as well as your name and phone or fax number. I will carefully review your comments and share them with the authors and editors who worked on the book.

Fax:	(317) 581-4770
Email:	tryan@mcp.com
Mail:	Tim Ryan, Executive Editor
	Sams Publishing
	201 W. 103rd Street
	Indianapolis, IN 46290 USA

Introduction

Our initial intent for this book was to be a detailed guide for Oracle DBAs who never before have had to perform a migration between major releases. We know that this can be a daunting task, and we wanted to offer as much help as we could, based on our experience with such migrations across many releases of Oracle. As work progressed, we realized that many features are available in Oracle8*i* that could be of benefit to any Oracle customers. So we expanded the scope of the book to introduce you to these features. For those of you who have already upgraded to Oracle8, release 8.0, we added a chapter to help you with an upgrade to Oracle8*i*. We also included detailed scripts in the migration section of the book, which you will find useful in many other contexts. We believe these changes have produced a general handbook for Oracle8*i* without diluting its value as a migration guide.

*Migrating to Oracle8*i is designed so that you can easily find a topic of interest through the use of many topic headings in each chapter. Each topic is written to be as self-contained as possible, reducing the need for you to continually switch back and forth between chapters and sections. We believe you will find this feature particularly useful as you follow the step-by-step instructions to complete a migration or upgrade to Oracle8*i*. Of course, whereas a subject is covered in extensive detail in a section, we will use cross-references from other sections to help you locate this information and to avoid repeating material unnecessarily. When a topic is beyond the scope of this book, we include a reference to the specific item in the Oracle documentation library where you can read more.

We hope that you will find this book a handy reference, whether this is your first migration of an Oracle database or simply one more upgrade out of many. You should also find it valuable to help you identify those features that you or your users might want to investigate after you have completed your migration to Oracle8*i*. In fact, Part II, "Using the Oracle 8*i* Features," of the book can be read as a primer on the new features offered in this version of the database even if you don't intend to use all of them at this time.

Who Should Use This Book

This book is written primarily for Oracle Database Administrators who have not had to perform a migration from one version to another, such as from Version 6 to Version 7, but who now face the onerous task of moving from Oracle7 to Oracle8*i*. It is also written to help DBAs experienced with migrations to identify and understand the features that have been introduced or enhanced by Oracle in release 8.1. Application developers can also find useful information about the features offered in this latest release in Part II of this book.

We do expect that readers will have some experience with Oracle database management, including knowledge of the basic Data Dictionary tables and the tools used to perform database startups, shutdowns, backups, and exports. Familiarity with the SQL language, Server Manager, and SQL*Plus scripts would also be useful, particularly for readers who might be interested in adapting the SQL-generating scripts included in a number of the chapters to other uses.

Data processing professionals, particularly Database Administrators, without any Oracle experience might find this book useful, although more so if you have access to the Oracle documentation that we reference as necessary. It walks you through a typical Oracle installation and gives you examples of the basic commands needed to manage an Oracle database.

How This Book Is Organized

*Migrating to Oracle8*i is divided into two distinct parts. The first part contains a task-oriented, cookbook-like approach to the various steps required to install Oracle8*i* and migrate or upgrade a database to this release. Each chapter covers a major task and includes examples of the GUI screens and commands needed to complete it along with detailed instructions and suggestions. In the second part of the book, you will find discussions on the benefits and uses of the new and enhanced features offered in Oracle8*i*.

In Part I, "Migrating," a number of general chapters cover activities needed to be addressed by anyone performing a migration from Oracle7 to Oracle8*i*. These include chapters on installing the new release, on preliminary steps to prepare your database for the migration, and on troubleshooting the migration process should you encounter problems. Additionally, Chapter 9, "Upgrading from Oracle8 to Oracle8*i*," is included for readers who are already running a release 8.0 database. Chapter 13, "Downgrading," covers downgrading from Oracle8*i* to an earlier release in case some of you decide to do that.

Four different methods of completing the migration are covered in this part of the book. Chapter 1, "Steps to Perform Migration," compares these approaches, discusses their capabilities, and compares their advantages and disadvantages. Each of these migration methods is covered in its own chapter. These four chapters, Chapter 4 through Chapter 7, are deliberately organized along similar lines. They include topics relating to the specific pre-migration activities, installation requirements, migration and post-migration steps, and troubleshooting techniques specific to the migration method being described. If you are not sure which is your best migration strategy, this structure allows you to easily compare the actual work and resources required at each step of the process, which should help you reach a decision. The structure of these chapters should also prove useful for you after you begin the migration process using your chosen method.

Part II, "Using the Oracle8*i* Features," contains a separate chapter on each product, option, or feature that is new in Oracle8*i* or that has been significantly modified. It is intended as a practical guide on how and when to use these specific capabilities of Oracle8*i*. If you are already using one of the features covered by a chapter in this part of the book, you will find information on what changes have been made and how you can incorporate them into your environment. If you see a new feature that interests you, the related chapter will provide you with sufficient background so that you can decide how valuable it might be to you, either immediately after you migrate, or as part of a longer-term strategy.

The chapters in this section do not have the same regularity of structure as the migration chapters in Part I because of the dissimilarities between the products and features being discussed. They are intended to be read for background information as well as serve as basic documentation on the use of the new features.

Now we suggest that you examine the full table of contents and decide which topics you need to read right away and which you can defer until you have completed your migration to Oracle8*i*.

Migrating

PART
I

IN THIS PART

Steps to Perform Migration

IN THIS CHAPTER

The time has come to migrate your Oracle7 database to Oracle8*i*, version 8.1. You might have made this decision because you or your users need one or more of the features provided by the more recent versions of Oracle. Or you might be like many Database Administrators (DBAs) who are facing the loss of Oracle support for your current version of the database. Those of you in the first category are probably very motivated to complete the conversion and to move on, enabling the new features and improving the database environment for you and your user community.

But for many DBAs, a database migration is probably yet another task in an already-busy schedule. You want to get it done with the least amount of trouble and interference with your regular work. You want it to be invisible to your customers as well as to you, as far as that is possible, and you want to put as little effort into the task as you can get by with. That was certainly my first reaction on learning that I would have to migrate an Oracle database. Back then, we had fewer options and fewer tools to help us—I'm talking about a migration from Oracle version 4 to version 5—and not many experienced DBAs to help guide us.

This book should help DBAs who have performed migrations in the past as well as those to whom this is a brand-new venture. You should start with this chapter, which shows you the basic steps you need to complete a successful migration. You can then select which chapters you need to read to increase your knowledge about the steps that are not familiar or completely clear to you. After you are done, you can take your time reviewing the contents of the final two sections of the book and learn about any new features that could be of benefit to you and your users.

For those of you with prior experience in database migrations and upgrades, you might only need a few of the chapters in this first section; for others, this whole section may be required reading. You be your own judge, and good luck with your conversion.

Introducing the Migration Steps

Very briefly, the steps needed to plan, execute, and test a database migration consist of the following:

1. Choose a migration method—During this step, you will evaluate the various options available to you to migrate your Oracle database from a version 7 release to a version 8*i* release.

2. Design a test plan—This is a critical step that will help you no matter how you decide to perform the conversion. It can even help you succeed if you have chosen less than an optimal migration strategy, either by allowing you to identify weaknesses very early on or by providing you a set of steps that you can follow no matter what might go wrong.

3. Build a migration plan—As with any other project, you need to have a plan to help you control the resources as well as the timetable to complete it successfully. The plan should include the test steps defined in step 2 because this can involve more time and people than the migration itself. Remember to share your plan with all the people who will be impacted by the migration.

4. Perform the migration—We will work together to complete this step, without which the remainder of this book is superfluous.

5. Complete post-migration tasks—Although this step might appear to be essential only for those of you who intend to avail yourselves of the new features immediately, it can be critical to maintain continuity for any database and its applications. Of course, during the life of the post-migrated database, any of the features offered by the current releases of Oracle can be incorporated if they seem useful and appropriate. Such work can also be considered part of an ongoing post-migration task.

In the remainder of this chapter, you will learn a little more about what each of these steps is intended to achieve. You can then decide how much of the detailed information you need to explore in more depth from the rest of the chapters in this section.

In addition to a migration from Oracle7 to Oracle8*i*, this section of the book also discusses how you could downgrade from version 8.1 back to 8.0. For most of you, this topic will not be of great importance. You should be aware that it is there in case you need it in a future project when you thought you were done with this book.

Choose a Migration Method

You have a number of options when it comes to performing an Oracle migration. Which is best for you and your database depends on a number of different factors. I advise you to look over all the options before you make a decision based on just one or two positive characteristics of any one method. In some cases, it might even be beneficial to combine different methods, particularly if you have a number of databases to migrate.

The migration approaches I will explain in detail are

- Oracle's Migration Utility
- The Oracle Data Migration Assistant
- Database Export and Import
- Data Copying

In the discussion of the last option, using the SQL*Plus COPY command, I will also introduce some related approaches that use standard SQL commands. In some cases, these might be a better choice if you decide to adopt this type of migration approach. To help you with your decision, I describe the various options in detail in the following sections.

Oracle's Migration Utility

The main component of Oracle's Migration utility is a computer program that builds a control file to support the new physical structure. The command, ALTER DATABASE CONVERT, then uses the contents of this precursor control file to modify the internal database structures and the data dictionary contents. The utility is rounded out by a number of other scripts and additional SQL commands.

Although it consists of a number of components that have to be used carefully to avoid damaging your database, it does perform a migration quite efficiently. If you migrated to Oracle7 from Oracle Version 6 using the Oracle7 Migration utility, you will already have used many of the components. Much of the utility was converted from the previous release to support a migration to Oracle8*i*.

The most important feature of the Migration utility is that it performs all of its work on the existing database. You don't have to create a new database and move the data into it. As a consequence, the resources needed to complete the migration are not as dependent on the database size as for other methods. In particular, the time taken to complete the migration is not directly related to the size of your database. This makes the utility a good option if you want to minimize your downtime, or if you have such a large database that other methods would simply take too long to complete. Anyone who has had to export and import large tables knows how frustratingly slow that can be.

Of course, for a data processing tool to minimize the use of one resource, it has to make heavy use of one or more alternative resources. In the case of the Migration utility, the time savings comes at the cost of disk space. As you already know, the utility converts your database in place. Although it can do this without expanding the size of your physical files themselves, it does require space in the SYSTEM tablespace beyond the normal size.

Specifically, it needs to be able to store both the Oracle7 and the Oracle8*i* versions of the data dictionary at the same time as it converts one to the other. This is one reason that some of you might not be able to make use of the Migration utility. If you have very limited disk space, you might not be able to accommodate two versions of the data dictionary simultaneously. Further, because an Oracle8*i* data dictionary itself is larger than its Oracle7 equivalent, your SYSTEM tablespace will need almost three times its current storage requirements.

Even if you can temporarily find disk space to add datafiles to the SYSTEM tablespace while the migration is in process, you might not be able to reclaim the space afterward. When the old version of data dictionary is dropped, the freed blocks will not be in the newly added datafiles, but in the current files. You might not be able to drop these files, however, because parts of the new data dictionary might be stored in them. Although you could defragment the tablespace free space in any other tablespace, you can't do that with the SYSTEM tablespace. The typical tools used to defragment an Oracle database rely on export/import tools, but these do not work for the objects owned by SYS. Unless you have a third-party product that can defragment the SYSTEM tablespace, therefore, you will not be able to coalesce the free space. This, in turn, will prevent you from shrinking or removing any of the datafiles.

In Table 1.1, I summarize the benefits and limitations of the Migration utility for you. The main ones have just been discussed, and I will briefly examine the others in the rest of this section.

TABLE 1.1   Benefits and Limitations of the Migration Utility

Benefits	*Limitations*
Performs migration on the database itself, not on a copy	Requires additional space inthe SYSTEM tablespace
Time is a factor of thenumber of objects, not on the overall database size	Space needed for the migration might not be available again after the migration
The steps are easy to execute and reasonably automatic	You can't perform a partial migration
	You cannot make other changes to the database as part of the migration task
	The utility is only valid for migrating forward from major release to major release

Other than the SYSTEM tablespace storage issues, the items listed in the limitations column of Table 1.1 are not pertinent to many databases. The first of these is that you can't perform a partial migration. In other words, you must migrate everything in the database, even if there are some users, segments, or other objects you won't need after you start using your Oracle8*i* database. This should not be a major concern. After all, you can always drop the unneeded items following the migration, and the migration itself shouldn't be impacted unless there are many objects of this type. The process will waste time converting the dictionary references to these objects, a poor use of resources if they are going to be dropped.

One reason you might be disappointed that you cannot complete a partial migration is that you would like to test the process without committing your whole database to run under Oracle8*i*.

Of course, you can do this if you have a test database that contains just the items you would like to test, and you might be able to easily build such a test database. However, if you really want to migrate only some components of your production system and not others, this limitation of the Migration utility might be a reason to use a different approach.

Another limitation to the Migration utility is somewhat related to the one just discussed. Because the whole database is processed as is, you can't combine the migration task with other database maintenance chores. One common benefit from performing a migration in the past was that you had to use Export and Import to move the data from the old to the new version. In so doing, you also rebuilt the database segments in new, empty tablespaces. Consequently, you also accomplished a database reorganization and space defragmentation at the same time.

Along with the inability to rebuild your segments in the new database, you will obviously not be able to make even more drastic changes using the Migration utility. I am talking about such changes as altering the base character set or moving the database to a new hardware platform or operating system. One physical feature that can be changed when using the utility when you are migrating to Oracle8*i*, version 8.1 or later, is to switch between a 32-bit and a 64-bit architecture. This word-size change, of course, is only relevant if it is made on the operating system where the database resides.

A final point to note about the Migration utility is that it is built to support migrations only from a major release to the next major release level. If you want to use a tool for your migration from Oracle7 to Oracle8*i* that you can also use for a downgrade back to Oracle7 or for upgrading between intermediate releases, you must choose something other than the Migration utility. I suspect that most of you have already built scripts and tools to help you with installing and upgrading Oracle point releases and patches so this will not be a significant concern. As for downgrading again, you should seriously consider whether this is likely scenario before choosing your upgrade method based on this factor. For those of you who plan to implement Oracle8*i* features as soon as you upgrade, a downgrade to Oracle7 can be very difficult no matter what technique you use because you will have to back out all of those features first.

Oracle Data Migration Assistant

The Oracle Data Migration Assistant is a newer feature that became available with Oracle8*i*. The tool provides a GUI front end to the steps performed by the Migration utility. By guiding you through the steps in the correct order and running many of the commands automatically, it helps ensure a successful migration. You will not accidentally miss steps and you will not have to enter as much unfamiliar syntax as a user of the Migration utility.

When you perform a complete installation of Oracle8*i*, the Oracle Data Migration Assistant is started automatically. You can then perform the migration immediately by following the

directions from the assistant. If you want to wait until a later time, you can start the Oracle Data Migration Assistant from the operating system.

Given that Oracle Data Migration Assistant is just a front-end to the Migration utility, it has basically the same benefits and limitations, just as you might expect. For completeness, and because there are a couple of minor differences, I have summarized the characteristics in Table 1.2.

TABLE 1.2 Benefits and Limitations of the Oracle Data Migration Assistant

Benefits	*Limitations*
Performs migration on the database itself, on a copy	Requires additional space in the SYSTEM not tablespace
Time is a factor of the number of objects, not on the overall database size	Space needed for the migration might not be again available after the migration
Look and feel is simple and standard across other Oracle GUI tools	You can't perform a partial migration
	You cannot make other changes to the database as part of the migration task
	The utility is only valid for migrating forward from major release to major release
	You cannot migrate Parallel Server

As noted already, the major benefit of the Oracle Data Migration Assistant over the Migration utility is the interface. Being a GUI front-end tool, it hides the details of the syntax from you and ensures that each step is performed in the correct sequence. Other than that, it doesn't do anything particularly differently from the Migration utility. Therefore, it has the same pattern of space usage in the SYSTEM tablespace and allows only a complete migration with no physical changes to the database, other than switching between a 32-bit and 64-bit word-size.

There is one other restriction imposed by Oracle Data Migration Assistant, as noted in Table 1.2. You cannot migrate a database with this tool if it has Oracle Parallel Server installed. There are some hardware platforms, such as the IBM RS/6000 SP, on which all Oracle installations include Oracle Parallel Server. For most of you, however, you will have installed Parallel Server only if you really intended to use it for failover or scalability. Either way, the restriction applies whether or not you are running multiple-instance databases. If you have Parallel Server installed, you cannot use the Oracle Data Migration Assistant front-end tool, although you can still use the standard, manual version of the Migration utility.

Migrating with Export and Import

I suspect that using Oracle's Export and Import utilities is historically the most-used technique to migrate databases to newer versions. This is because no other tools were available until the more recent releases and Export and Import were reliable tools with which most DBAs were very familiar. Even now, Export and Import provide some useful features that make them an important tool in any DBA's kit. For example, as an adjunct to database backups, they can provide a recovery mechanism for single tables that is typically much more efficient, and less intrusive, than performing full database restore and recovery operations. They can also be used to build a test database from the structure or contents of a production system as well as offering a simple method to move the objects from one user's schema to another.

Over time, however, databases have grown in size to a point where the time to perform full exports followed by full imports has become prohibitive in many cases. At the same time, users have become more demanding in their requirements for database access. A multi-megabyte database can take a week, or longer, to fully export and re-import. If you are expected to provide a service level of 99% database availability, a week of downtime while you migrate between releases misses your target by almost 1% over the period of a year. Even if you can use the DIRECT option for your Oracle7 export, there is no equivalent direct import option and you are still likely to miss your conversion target.

But Export and Import do have some advantages, otherwise I wouldn't expect you to spend your valuable time reading about it. In general, the benefits relate to the topics which we considered limitations for the Migration utility, whether it was used in its standard form or through the Oracle Data Migration Assistant. Table 1.3 lists the benefits and limitations of using these utilities for your migration. As you read on, you will find more detailed explanations about these characteristics.

TABLE 1.3   Benefits and Limitations of Migrating with Export and Import

Benefits	*Limitations*
You can perform a partial migration, or multiple partial migrations	Slow, and overall time increases with database size
You can make concurrent physical changes to the database	Full export files are large and might cause disk or tape storage problems
Allows migration between any supported versions, with either higher or lower version numbers	Requires a new database at the required release level
Can be completed without additional disk space during the conversion	

Depending on your perspective, any one of the benefits in Table 1.3 could be the most important to you. I have organized the benefits in what I consider to be the general order of most importance, with the partial migration capability being the prime benefit. If you know anything about Oracle's Export utility, you know that it can be used to export the entire database, a list of one or more specific users, or even a single table or a list of tables. By using this tool to migrate from one release to another, you can choose which level of Export to use and, hence, just what database contents you want to include.

This capability allows you not only to ignore old objects that you no longer need in the migrated database, but it offers one other great capability. You can stage your migration over time. If you have completely independent applications, or sets of users and sets of tables, you can export them one set at a time. That way, you can complete all the tasks associated with migrating one application before tackling the next one. Although this sounds as if you have to perform many migrations, it might not be as daunting as having to deal with all your applications and users at once, which you have to do when using the Migration utility. It can also help alleviate one of the other problems with a large database export, namely, having to support a very large export dump file on disk or on tape.

Another benefit is that you can run some tests on a new Oracle8*i* database without having to migrate your entire production system. You can extract an appropriate subset of information using Export, use Import to load it into your Oracle8*i* database, and test it thoroughly without impacting any of your production users.

The second important benefit is that you can make structural and physical changes to your database in conjunction with the migration. These changes could be as simple as coalescing extents and free space, or as complex as moving to a new hardware platform and operating system. Other structural changes you can make that are not possible with the Migration utility or Oracle Data Migration Assistant, include the following:

- Character set
- Block size
- Tablespace structure
- Segment storage allocation

The last point might need some further clarification. You can use Export and Import to transfer the data between the versions, but you are not prevented from building some, or all, of the segments in the new, Oracle8*i* database before you begin the import step. This allows you to change the storage and space utilization characteristics of the segments from how they are defined in your current, Oracle7 database. If you want, you can even build your tables using

the Oracle8*i* partitioning option. This is particularly useful if you intend to use partitioning for certain tables and you know what partition ranges you need. The Import utility will insert the rows into the correct partitions even though they were exported from a nonpartitioned table.

A final benefit to using Export and Import as a migration technique is that after you have created and tested the method, you can use it for any future conversions. These can be future migrations, from Oracle8 to Oracle9, for example, or upgrades to newer versions of Oracle8*i*. You can also use the Export and Import utilities to downgrade your database to a lower version number than it currently uses. You could even reverse the migration process and restore your data to an Oracle7 database if you needed to, as long as you had not implemented too many new Oracle8*i* features.

The biggest limitation—the time it takes to migrate a large database with the Export and Import utilities—has already been discussed, as has the need for large files to store the Export dump file. However, you might see one possible solution to this. You can possibly migrate the database a piece at a time. Each piece, such as an application or a set of related schemas, can be exported and imported reasonably quickly, regardless of the overall size of the database. Further, it will not require anything as large a dump file as an export of the complete database would need.

Of course, you must be prepared to execute multiple migrations to use this approach, and your database must amenable to partial migration. If all your tables are interrelated, you can't use this approach. In such cases, you may be able to use a variant of the Export/Import method.

If your restriction on the use of Export/Import is the space required for the dump file, you can split the work up into multiple files, just as you would if you were migrating a piece at a time. Instead of waiting between each step, however, you can execute them all simultaneously, generating a number of small Export dump files as you go and importing them as soon as they are complete. You can delete a used file to make room for a new one as soon as the import is finished.

On the other hand, if you are concerned about the time it might take to perform a migration with Export/Import, you can possibly use different tools. You will need one tool to create your own dump files containing your Oracle7 table data in a structured format. Then you can use Oracle's SQL*Loader utility to move the data into your Oracle8*i* database. In general, SQL*Loader outperforms Import and can be made to run very quickly if you use its direct path and parallel load options. For unloading your data, you can use the SQL*Plus SPOOL command, or else write a program with one of Oracle's precompilers. You might even have access to a third-party vendor's unload utility.

If you use one of these methods to move your table data—multiple concurrent exports or unloads along with multiple concurrent imports or SQL*Loader sessions—you can still use the

Export and Import utilities to transfer your other database objects. You simply have to perform a full database export and full import, but select the options to prevent rows from being exported and imported.

A final limitation to using Export/Import is that you need to build a brand-new database under Oracle8*i* before you can complete the migration. For a large database, this itself can be a time-consuming process, although it is likely to take much less time than the data transfer. It also requires that disk space be available, which could be a problem for some of you. Although I recommend that you don't destroy your Oracle7 database until the migration is completely tested, you could possibly make yourself a little more disk space, if you need it. Simply back up the Oracle7 database when you have completed the export step, and then remove its files. If you use tape for your exports, you will never need to have space for more than one database at a time on your disks.

Be careful if you decide to perform a migration this way. If the backup you make is not readable, you will not be able to restore your Oracle7 database should you need to do so. This could be a serious problem if one or more of the export files is also unreadable, or if the Oracle8*i* database fails one of its acceptance tests. The other issue you need to consider is the time needed for this type of migration. By using tape for your backup and your export dump file (or files if you choose to execute multiple exports or data extracts), you will require much more time than someone doing exactly the same work, but using disks.

Migrating Using Data Copying

In some ways, this approach to migration is similar to using Export/Import. It involves moving the data from your Oracle7 database to your new Oracle8*i* database. The differences lie in the tools and commands you use to move the data and in the resources required by Oracle to process them. This approach involves creating a new, Oracle8*i* database and moving the contents from your Oracle7 database in real time. Unlike performing the migration with Export/Import, you must have both databases up and running concurrently. The major benefits to this approach are that you can make the same type of changes as with Export/Import, but you don't need to find the space taken by Export dump files, nor do you have to process each record twice, once to take it out of your Oracle7 database and once to insert it into Oracle8*i*.

The only database objects you can readily copy using real-time techniques are the user tables and their contents. You will have to supplement these copies with data from the data dictionary about users, indexes, constraints, stored PL/SQL, privileges, roles, and all the other objects that your database contains. Your best tool to use for this is Export/Import. Using these tools, however, should not cause significant drawbacks to using the copying technique. The Export dump file will not include any table data, just the definitions of the tables along with all the other objects that need to be migrated. The resulting file will not be particularly large and

should not take long to import once it is built. This is exactly what I suggested in the previous section if you wanted to use an unload and reload method, rather than a full Export/Import.

If you decide to use this approach, you also need to choose a method for copying the data between the old and the new databases. The two simplest methods are the SQL*Plus COPY command and the SQL CREATE TABLE...AS SELECT command. You can also use an INSERT INTO...AS SELECT SQL command if the table structure is already in place. The COPY command in SQL*Plus is the more restrictive command and you should only consider using it if you have small tables and small records. The CREATE TABLE...AS SELECT command provides you with all the same capability as the COPY command, but also lets you assign a degree of parallelism to the steps and include some datatypes that COPY might not be able to handle.

Table 1.4 summarizes the benefits and drawbacks of this migration strategy.

TABLE 1.4   Benefits and Limitations of Migrating with Export and Import

Benefits	*Limitations*
You can perform a partial migration, or multiple partial migrations	Manually intensive with lots of steps
You can make concurrent physical changes to the database	Slow, and overall time increases with database size
Allows migration between any supported versions, with either higher or lower version numbers	Requires a new database at the required release level
Requires no intermediate files for the data	Typically requires a "no rows" Export and Import to complete the migration

The limitations listed in Table 1.4 are the main reasons why Oracle no longer discusses this methodology in its documentation set. However, if you cannot use the other methods for some reason, this might still be your best option. For example, you might need to change some of the physical characteristics of your database but lack the operating system resources to perform a full Export and Import.

The biggest problem with this approach is the fact that you need to create and execute a SQL*Plus COPY command or a SQL statement for every single table you have to migrate. This leads immediately to the second limitation listed in Table 1.4; the more tables you have, the more statements you have to create and execute, so the longer the overall process will run. You can use SQL-generating SQL to do some of the work for you. Listing 1.1 is a SQL*Plus script that will build a migration script. The script, MIGACCT.SQL, will contain all of the CREATE TABLE...AS SELECT commands for the tables in the ACCTS schema.

In addition to working with the individual statements needed, you will also need to configure SQL*Net or Net8 to allow the two databases to communicate with each other across database links. After that is done, you need to build the required database links. Finally, you might well have to perform an Export and then an Import to transfer the non-table objects between the Oracle7 and Oracle8*i* databases.

LISTING 1.1   Sample SQL*Plus Script to Generate Table Migration Statements

```
REM Script to build CREATE TABLE...AS SELECT
REM commands for all tables in the ACCT schema.
REM This script builds the commands to execute
REM with parallel degree 10.
REM
REM The commands will be stored in file,
REM called MIGACCT.SQL, which should be executed
REM in the Oracle8i database after the database
REM link, V7.WORLD, has been built to point to
REM the ACCT schema in the Oracle7 database.
REM
REM Set SQL*Plus options:

SET PAGESIZE 0 FEEDBACK OFF AUTOTRACE OFF

REM Open output file and execute query to
REM build required statements

SPOOL migacct.sql
SELECT 'CREATE TABLE /*+ PARALLEL (' || table_name ||
   ', 10) */ ' || table_name || chr(10) ||
   ' AS SELECT /*+ PARALLEL (' || table_name ||
   ', 10) */ * ' || chr(10) || 'FROM ' || table_name ||
   '@V7.WORLD;'
FROM dba_tables
WHERE owner = 'ACCT'
/

REM Close output file

SPOOL OFF
```

Another possible drawback is that, in order for this approach to work, both versions of your database will have to be online concurrently. Unlike the pure Export/Import method, you can't drop the Oracle7 database to make room for the Oracle8*i* database. You will also need to configure the SQL*Net or Net8 files and run a listener process for the database links to use.

Selecting a Migration Method

If you have read the preceding sections carefully, you are probably wondering just which methods might or might not work for your migration. If you have already done that, you might need to decide between two or more methods. To help you with both of these tasks, I have created Table 1.5. You can use a copy of this table, or even reproduce it in a worksheet if you want, to help you decide which method should be your best option.

TABLE 1.5 Analysis of Migration Methods

	Data Migration Assistant	*Migration Utility*	*Export/ Import*	*Data Copying*
Database Size	+1 per MB	+1 per MB	−1 per MB	−1 per MB
Number of Objects	+1 per 10	+1 per 10	−1 per 10	−1 per 10
Time Limitations	+1 per datafile	+1 per datafile	−1 per MB	−1 per 10 tables
Parallel Server Installed	+1	−1000	+1	+1
No Space on Disk	0	0	−10 or −20	−10 or −20
No Space in SYSTEM	−15	−15	+2	+2
Need to Restructure	−5 per change	−5 per change	+5 per change	+5 per change
Can or Need to Use Stages	−10	−10	+2 per subset	+2 per subset
Totals				

The purpose of this table is to help you derive a numeric value for each of the methods based on your database and your migration requirements. To fill out the table, use these guidelines:

1. Add the sizes of all your datafiles and determine the number of megabytes they consume. Show this as a positive number in the entries in the first row (*Database Size*) where there is a +1 and as a negative number where there is a −1.

2. Determine the number of objects in your database by querying the DBA_OBJECTS view. Because you need this number divided by 10 to complete the table, you can use the following query:

```
SELECT COUNT / 10 FROM dba_objects;
```

As with the previous row, store the result of this query as positive number in row 2 (*Number of Objects*) where there is a +1 and as a negative number where there is a −1.

3. Add the number of datafiles to the first two columns in the third row (*Time Limitations*). You can find the number of datafiles in your database by issuing the following SQL statement:

```
SELECT COUNT FROM dba_data_files;
```

For the third column in this row (*Export/Import*), you can simply use the same value as in the first row. And for the fourth column, you need to divide the number of tables in your database by ten and record this as a negative number. You can use this query to get the value you need:

```
SELECT COUNT / (-10) FROM dba_tables;
```

4. The fourth row (*Parallel Server Installed*) is included only to ensure that you do not choose the Oracle Data Migration Assistant method if you have Parallel Server on your system. Use the following query to determine whether your database has this option installed:

```
SELECT * FROM v$option
WHERE parameter = 'Parallel Server';
```

If the VALUE column contains TRUE, you should subtract a large enough number from the *Data Migration Assistant* column to ensure this method is not selected.

5. To fill out the fifth row requires a little more thought. If you have absolutely no free space on your disks, you can't perform a migration. Even if you could magically overlay your Oracle7 database with its equivalent Oracle8*i* version without any migration overhead, your attempt would fail because the Oracle home directory structure as well as the SYSTEM tablespace in Oracle8*i* is larger than its Oracle7 predecessor. Choose the values for this row, *No Space on Disk*, using the following criteria:

a) If you have space to support a full export and simultaneously run your Oracle7 and Oracle8*i* databases, put zeroes in every column.

b) If you have room for either a full export or both versions of Oracle, but not both, use the values shown in Table 1.5 (0, 0, −20, and −10, respectively).

c) If you don't have room for both Oracle versions running concurrently, reverse the values shown in columns three and four, giving the values 0, 0, −10, and −20 in columns one through four, respectively.

d) If you have room, and are prepared to perform a staged export or an export to tape rather than disk, add 5 back to the value in the *Export/Import* column.

6. Find out how much space you would need in the SYSTEM tablespace by issuing the query:

```
SELECT 2 * SUM(bytes) FROM dba_extents
WHERE tablespace_name = 'SYSTEM';
```

The values you assign to the sixth row, *No Space in SYSTEM*, depend on whether your SYSTEM tablespace has room, or can be expanded, to hold this much additional storage. If it can, set all values for the row to zeroes. If it can't, but you have space elsewhere, use the values shown in the table, −15, −15, +2, and +2, for each column, respectively.

7. If you need to restructure your database as part of the migration task, add five points for each change you'll make to the last two columns in the seventh row (*Need to Restructure*) and subtract the same value from each of the first two columns.

8. If staging your migration is a requirement, you will have to use either Export/Import or data copying, so the values in the first two columns should be sufficiently negative to preclude the Oracle migration tools from consideration. If it is an option you could use, apply the values shown in Table 1.5, with an additional two points in the last two columns for each subset of data you could migrate separately.

9. After you sum up the numbers you have entered, the column with the highest score should be your best option for migration.

You should use the numbers in Table 1.5 as guidelines. If you have a very fast system, for example, the numbers related to time should be reduced in magnitude. Similarly, if your structural changes could be accomplished before or after the migration without much difficulty, you can set all the values in the row, *Need to Restructure*, to zeroes. Before you make a final decision, I recommend you look over the description of the selected option earlier in this chapter, as well as the detailed migration steps covered in the later chapters on the specific migration options. You might see something that alerts you to an unforeseen problem that the calculations above were too simplistic to recognize.

Design a Test Plan

After you have selected a method to use for your migration, you should be able to complete the process using the detailed information in the chapter devoted to that method. After you complete the migration process itself, you will need to test the results before turning the database over to your users. A test plan can consist of many steps and various types of test. In a highly visible database, you might want to use every test to ensure you have a valid and usable database after the migration. For less-critical databases, you may choose to skip some of the tests.

Here is a list of the types of tests that Oracle has proposed would be appropriate to use following a migration. I will discuss just how to implement each type in the next chapter.

- Migration test
- Minimal test
- Functional test
- Integration test
- Performance test
- Volume/Load stress test

Build a Migration Plan

You might already be familiar with project planning tools and techniques. You might even work for a company that has a formal task planning and tracking system in place that will you use for your database migration. The critical issues for migration planning, which might or might not be obvious when you sit down with a formal planning tool, is that the migration itself is only a very small part of a migration project. In fact, if you consider only the migration steps, your whole project probably only involves one person, yourself, and will take a relatively short amount of time.

When you plan your migration project, you must also remember that the migration will impact all of your users, even if only for the amount of time the database will be unavailable during the migration steps. You must, therefore, include your users' needs in your migration plan. For example, you don't want to schedule downtime for the migration during a weekend when your user community is planning to test a new version of a key application.

If you intend to perform post-migration testing on your migrated database, you will need additional time. You might also need the help of the application developers or the end users, either to assist in the test design or even to help you run the tests. Of course, if you are performing tests, you also need to leave time to fix any problems that are uncovered and then to perform the tests over again.

It should be clear that your migration plan is really everyone else's migration plan who uses your database. Make sure that you develop your plan in sufficient detail that anyone who will be impacted can determine what role he or she has to play, if any. Then distribute it to everyone who will be participating or who will be affected by downtime or other changes in the normal environment. To amplify this last point, consider the case of a DBA who is upgrading in order to provide some new features to the application developers. The whole exercise becomes pointless if those developers are never told when the new features will become available and so will never use them.

Perform the Migration

The specific steps required to perform your migration depend on the migration method you use. A chapter on each of the four common methods is provided later in this section of the book, and I invite you to turn there when you are ready to work on your migration details. There are some general issues that you should consider, however, no matter what method you employ.

As just discussed, you should have a migration plan in place, meaning it has been seen, and even possibly approved, by all the organizations in your company that could be impacted. Use this plan when you perform the migration and the related steps so that nobody gets unwanted surprises.

Another point that you should take to heart, and one that I will mention again and again, is that you should always protect your current database before beginning your migration process. This means making at least one cold backup and ensuring that it is kept safely, in case it is needed should your migration activities end with a non-reversible error.

Finally, after the migration, make sure that all the tests you decided were appropriate to run, are run. You might not run all of these tests yourself, but you should still take responsibility for their execution. You know that, somehow, any problems that turn up later will come back to haunt you as will, in all probability, the blame for causing them in the first place.

Complete Post-Migration Tasks

There are four specific tasks that you should perform following a database migration:

1. Perform a full, cold backup of the migrated database
2. Complete the test suite you designed
3. Tune the database
4. Add or modify your administrative procedures and tools

Some of these tasks might be needed in a different order than shown in this list. For example, you might have to modify your backup script, an administrative tool, in order to make the initial backup of the migrated database. You should simply make sure that each of the items required to complete these steps is included in your project plan so that you can track which you complete and which are still to be done. Some of them, it might turn out, you won't do until well after your migration is over with and you have had time to work with your new version of Oracle. For instance, if you intend to implement a backup and recovery strategy using the Recovery Manager, you might want to wait until you have checked out its functionality on a test database. Meanwhile, you can continue to use the backup strategy, and even tools, you used for your Oracle7 version of the database.

As mentioned, there are a number of components in these tasks, and Chapter 8, "Post-Migration Issues," is devoted to covering them in detail later in this section.

Be sure you identify those items that could be critical to the well-being of your database if they are not addressed and include those in your test plan. Make sure that you allow time in your migration schedule to address these issues and that you will have the support of anyone else who might be needed to work on them with you. Take it from me: It can be very frustrating to complete what appeared to be a successful migration, and then have to return to an earlier release because you couldn't complete all the follow-up steps in the assigned time.

Summary

You should now be ready to select a migration method that will meet your specific requirements to upgrade to Oracle8*i* and have some understanding of what type of resources you need to accomplish your migration. In particular, you should be able to rule out any of the migration options—Oracle's Data Migration Assistant, the Oracle Migration utility, Export/Import, and data copying—that will not be of use to you. You should be aware of why you can and can't use these options and also have selected an alternative approach in case your first choice doesn't work for some unforeseen reason.

You should also have some ideas about how you will proceed to put together a plan to perform the migration and which of the other chapters in this book will be helpful as you start the whole planning and migration process. For those of you who have performed migrations from earlier releases to Oracle7, you should have noted the few additional considerations and options made available for the migration to Oracle8*i* that you have not seen before.

If you are still feeling uncomfortable with the whole migration concept, I invite you to sit down and reread this chapter. It will not answer all of your questions, but it should help you locate the items you need to concentrate on in the remainder of this section. If this still doesn't help, you should plan on reading all of the chapters in this first section of the book, along with the Migration manual that Oracle provides with Oracle8*i*.

PreMigration Issues

IN THIS CHAPTER

This chapter discusses some of the key issues that you need to consider before starting a migration. These are items that need to be included in your migration project plan. Please note the word "key" in the first sentence. I am not going to be able to give you every single item that belongs in your plan. Too many different systems and management styles are out there for me to presume to be able to cover all possible requirements for a plan. Similarly, because you might all be using different tools to manage your projects, I am going to concentrate on content, not format.

I have grouped the issues under three topic headings:

- Assess Resource Requirements
- Assign Duties
- Build a Test Plan

As with so many categorized topics, you might not be able to work on these one by one in the order shown, but you might be switching back and forth as an item in one topic requires a correlated item in another topic. You should be developing a project plan as you work on the various issues discussed in this chapter. If you record everything you think of in the plan, or in adjunct materials, the order you do that shouldn't really matter.

Assess Resource Requirements

In this section, I will try to help you identify the physical resources you will need, or might need, to complete a successful migration. Depending on how you document your project plan, you can possibly include these items in your plan. On the other hand, you can simply create a checklist of the resources you will need and maintain it as you confirm that each is in place.

Should you discover that you are short of a necessary physical resource, you will need to include the acquisition of that resource as part of your migration plan. In some cases, you will not be the person responsible for the actual acquisition of the resource even though you need to have the step in the plan. The next section discusses how to include other staff members in your plan and in the execution of the plan. You must ensure that you have communicated the need for the resource to the party or parties responsible for obtaining it and that the plan includes the time for the acquisition plus any installation, configuration, and testing by the appropriate people.

Next, take a look at the computer requirements for your upgrade. Table 2.1 shows the size requirements for version 8.1 of Oracle8*i*.

TABLE 2.1   Oracle8*i* Enterprise Edition Size Requirements

Resource Type	Size
RAM for Kernel	100MB
RAM for Server Processes	5+ ×Oracle7
RAM for Legato Storage Manager	40MB
Disk Space for Oracle Home	800MB
Disk Space for Oracle Intermedia, Spatial, Visual Information, Time Series	80MB
Disk Space for Each of the Other Options	5-20MB
Disk Space for Legato Storage Manager	64MB
Disk Space for SYSTEM Tablespace Contents	2 × Oracle7

I have just mentioned the human resources you might need to complete the hardware acquisition, if needed, of your migration plan. This is probably a good place to continue my discussion of required resources with a more in-depth look at the people components. If you read the first section of this chapter, I suggest ways to include people from other departments, or even from your own department, in your project. Here, I will look at who these people could be.

We believe that the end users of your database comprise the most important group for you to consider. Hopefully, this has been made clear to you as you've read through this book to this point. Whether their involvement is simply passive—that is, they will be logging on to a new version of the database one day with no other changes to their software or routines—or active, they must be informed of the project. If your test plan calls for their participation, you must also ensure that they know the timetable and be apprised of any changes to it. Also, as mentioned earlier, you might be required to work through intermediaries, such as department heads, to authorize their time. In such cases, you should try to elicit feedback from these intermediaries on a regular basis to confirm that the commitment of their staff to the project is still in place.

We have already mentioned the system and network staff who might be involved in any upgrades and additions to the hardware or system software. Oracle8*i* can consume from two to ten times the RAM needed for Oracle7, depending on which options and configurations you use. Similarly, it will need two to three times the disk space for the base products and options plus double your Oracle7 SYSTEM tablespace time. You need to ensure that these staff members are going to be able to commit the time needed for their work, including the procurement and installation of any additional hardware components. Remember that they, too, might need to develop and execute a test plan after the upgrades are in place, so make sure that you have their input before basing other milestones in your plan on their activities.

The software developers who are responsible for the applications that run on your system will also be part of the migration effort in all likelihood. They will almost certainly want to ensure that their applications are tested, and they should be included in the migration test planning and probably in its execution. And you should determine whether the application developers or the database administration staff will relink the applications.

There are a number of other groups you might also need to involve in your migration efforts. These include

- your Oracle support or sales contacts to ensure you obtain the required release, or your network staff if you plan to download it from an Oracle site
- the shipping or mailing department if you need to obtain materials being shipped by Oracle in a timely fashion
- your Security Administrator if you will need additional privileges to install the software
- your disaster plan administrator so that the new version of the Oracle software can replace the current version after the migration is completed
- other Oracle DBAs in your company who might have already performed a migration to the new version or who will be planning a migration some time in the future; you can learn from the first and provide assistance to the latter

Along with the hardware requirements shown in Table 2.1, you should also confirm that the operating system on your database servers is at the appropriate level for the version of Oracle to which you will be upgrading. If you do need an upgrade, you might need to involve the same level of system support that we discussed in relation to required hardware upgrades.

You might also have to upgrade any third-party software that runs against the Oracle database. This upgrade might be the responsibility of any number of departments. We have worked in academic environments, for example, where certain divisions acquired software for research purposes and took the responsibility for performing any upgrades after new releases were installed. As the DBA, you should be aware of all third-party applications and products that use your database. If you are not certain of what these are, you should attempt to get an audit of the database server performed. This is something you might be able to complete yourself, or it might again require assistance from the system staff. As an extension of the audit, you will also need to identify the users of any software that is identified in order to include them in the project plan. As with your other users, they should be informed of the pending migration, including key dates when the system will be unavailable, and they should be invited to participate in migration testing.

Assign Duties

I have included this section to emphasize that you cannot work on a database migration in isolation. Well, unless you are planning to migrate your own, personal database, of course. For a production environment, you will need to get others involved. In the previous section, I identified the types of people these could be, from your user community to your shipping department clerks.

Hopefully you realize by now that you will need to contact your users as part of the migration process, even if they won't have any task to perform. And this is not just because for some period their database will be unavailable. As well as a courtesy, and as a way to validate that your timetable is not conflicting with someone else's, sharing your migration plans with your users can have some benefits to you directly. I'm sure you have been in a situation in which you have been told on Friday that there will be a whole new process, procedure, computer interface, or network protocol in place when you come back to work on Monday. If you are like me, your heart sinks as you contemplate the problems you will have, in all likelihood, just trying to get your work done the following week. Even if everything runs smoothly, you expect to be spending time learning the ins and outs of the new whatever-it-is.

Your users have the same reaction to change. Just telling them, directly or indirectly, that the database is going to be down for some "maintenance" is going to leave them fretting about just what that will mean to them. If you have a plan in place that you can distribute, your users will have more time to get used to the idea that the change is coming. And if your plan is detailed enough, they will be able to see that their concerns are being addressed. For instance, an extensive testing program following the migration, particularly if it involves members of the user community, will really help them feel comfortable that they won't get any nasty surprises.

There is a strong likelihood that some of your users will be needed as active participants in the migration project. If your test plan includes confirming that the user interface acts and feels the same way after the migration as before, you might want this tested by the end users who are the most familiar with the interface. They might also be the best judges of whether the reports produced by the system are still producing the required results accurately.

Your other users, the application developers, will also probably be part of the migration process. As with end users, they might help with the testing steps. In particular, they can help identify any performance problems with programs that don't meet service level agreements and might even be able to help resolve them with some coding changes. In addition, they might be needed to relink the applications for which they are responsible.

Other people in your organization who might have a key role in the migration are the system and network administrators. You might need to work with the system staff to plan for disk space requirements, either temporarily during the migration work, or permanently because

of the increased storage needs of Oracle8*i*. The network staff might be involved if you decide to upgrade some or all of your servers to Net8 from SQL*Net or if you want to take advantage of some of the more advanced networking features of Net8.

Depending on the structure and size of your organization, other individuals or groups might be directly or indirectly affected by the migration. I tried to identify the potential candidates for you in the preceding section of this chapter. You might think of even more as you start your detailed planning, and you should include the steps to be performed by anyone else besides yourself. Even if you don't contact these other people when you initially develop the plan, by including the steps they will be responsible for, you will remember to involve them before you finalize the project time table.

In some cases, you might need to have approval from your management and the managers involved with other departments who will be impacted as you develop the migration plan. Having steps that identify not only the actions, but also the responsible parties, will help to ensure that the appropriate managers are involved. This will prevent the sort of scheduling conflict that we have seen when projects haven't been fully coordinated. One example that comes to mind is a database upgrade that was scheduled for the same weekend that the system administrators had planned a hardware upgrade, and the database server was going to be down.

Even if you are not required to have your migration plan reviewed by anyone outside of your department, you should work with your managers to ensure that it is shared with the managers of the groups who will be impacted or involved. This will help avoid the type of problem discussed previously and prevent you from having a project fail because of someone else's schedule.

As your plan evolves, you should continue to keep the other departments and involved parties informed of the changes. This will not only prevent other, conflicting projects from being overlooked, but will also help make your project more prominent. Other groups are less likely to schedule themselves or their resources without checking against your plan. As mentioned earlier, the visibility of your plan will help users overcome the fear of change. They will feel that they are part of the process and not just uninvolved recipients of your changes. This might not seem like an important issue, but we suspect that you have heard of at least one data processing project that failed because the users were not willing to accept changes that they felt were being forced on them.

Although the spreadsheet information shown in Table 2.2 might not conform to your specific planning tools, it is intended to show you one example of how you might work manage the process of ensuring that everyone involved in the project is aware of the requirements you have and the role they will take. It even provides a method for you to track who has been contacted and has committed the necessary time to perform their part of the migration.

TABLE 2.2 Project Plan and Personnel Assignments for Migration from Oracle7, Version 7.3.4, to Oracle8i, Version 8.1.5

Step ID	Step Name	Dept	Contact Name	Wk 1	Wk2	Wk 3	Wk 4
1	*Prepare Plan*						
1.1	Choose method						
1.1.1	Review resource requirements	System Admin	R. Satayan	A			
1.1.2	Downtime analysis	User Community	B. Harris	A			
1.1.3	Select method	DBA Staff	D. Austin	A			
1.2	Develop Test Plan						
1.2.1	DBA tests	DBA Staff	D. Austin	A			
1.2.2	Developer tests	Development	T. Bridges	R			
1.2.3	User tests	User Community	B. Harris	R			
1.3	Develop plan and timetable						
1.3.1	Create plan and timetable	DBA Staff	D. Austin	A			
1.3.2	Plan and Timetable acceptance	MIS Management	H. Zien	R			
2	*Acquire Resources*						
2.1	Acquire Hardware	System Admin	R. Satayan	A	A	A	
2.2	Test Hardware	System Admin	R. Satayan		A	A	
2.3	Acquire/Install Software						
2.3.1	System Software	System Admin	R. Satayan			R	R
2.3.2	Oracle Software	DBA Staff	D. Austin			A	A
3	*Test Migration*						
3.1	Build Test Database	DBA Staff	D. Austin		A		

continues

TABLE 2.2   Continued

Step ID	Step Name	Dept	Contact Name	Wk 1	Wk2	Wk 3	Wk 4
3.2	Migrate Test Database	DBA Staff	D. Austin		A		
3.3	Review test results						
3.3.1	DBA review	DBA Staff	D. Austin		A		
3.3.2	Developer tests	Development	T. Bridges		R		
3.3.3	User tests	User Community	B. Harris		R		
4	*Reverse Migration Plan*						
4.1	Modify plan	DBA Staff	D. Austin		A		
4.2	Modified Plan Acceptance	MIS Management	H. Zien		A		
5	*Perform Migration*						
5.1	Preparation						
5.1.2	Database backup	DBA Staff	D. Austin			A	
5.1.3	Other preparations	DBA Staff	D. Austin			A	
5.2	Migrate production database						
5.2.1	Migrate database	DBA Staff	D. Austin			A	
5.2.2	Backup migrated database	DBA Staff	D. Austin			A	
5.3	Test Migration						
5.3.1	DBA tests	DBA Staff	D. Austin				
5.3.2	Developer tests	Development	T. Bridges			R	
5.3.3	User tests	User Community	B. Harris			R	
5.4	Follow-up Activities						

Step ID	Step Name	Dept	Contact Name	Wk 1	Wk2	Wk 3	Wk 4
5.4.1	Revise production scripts	DBA Staff	D. Austin			A	
5.4.2	Revise applications	Development	T. Bridges			R	

Key: R   Contact has been requested to provide assistance
*   A   Personnel have been assigned to provide assistance*

The sample spreadsheet information shown in Table 2.2 is not necessarily complete, but it does include the key steps you should consider in your migration planning. You can, of course, add more details, such as the name or names of individuals assigned to each task or subtask, as they become known. You can also put specific dates on the tasks as you refine your plan and complete the detailed timetable. The whole plan might also take much longer than four weeks, but we condensed it in order to show you the more critical elements rather than a complete timeline.

Build a Test Plan

Software development and maintenance efforts should always include a good test plan as part of the acceptance strategy. Your migration from Oracle7 to Oracle8*i* is no different. Indeed, because you already have a working production database, you need to devise a test strategy to ensure that the end results of the migration contain the same, or better, production capabilities. This means testing not only the capabilities, but also the performance and data validity.

You can apply a number of types of tests to help assure you, the application developers, and your users that everything is working properly at the end of the migration. In this section, you'll see what types of tests you can use and when to use each type. From these selections, you can build a test plan and identify the resources needed to complete the tests. We strongly recommend running all of these tests before concluding the migration.

Identifying Types of Tests

You can perform six basic types of tests to validate the migration:

- Migration test
- Minimal test
- Functional test
- Integration test
- Performance test
- Volume/load stress test

Migration Test

This test validates your migration strategy, whether you were planning to use the Migration Utility or one of the methods to transfer the data from your Oracle7 to your Oracle8 or Oracle8*i* database. It's intended to help you determine whether you've allotted sufficient resources for the migration, including disk space, time, and personnel. If you are not sure about the migration strategies mentioned here, you can find further details in Chapter 1, "Steps to Perform Migration."

If your migration test fails, you might need to rethink the chosen migration strategy and possibly choose another method, depending on the nature of the failure. For example, if the time taken is greater than your users are willing to allow, you might need to plan a staged migration, or, if you were hoping to use Export/Import, you might need to consider the Migration Utility instead.

To run a migration test, you need to perform the following steps:

1. Prepare a test database
2. Execute a migration on the test database
3. Upgrade the tools used by your test application

The following sections describe these steps in more detail.

Prepare a Test Database

For the most foolproof test, you should use a copy of your complete production database. You will need to use Export/Import or some type of data unload and reload facility to create such a database. In some cases, you can perform an adequate test using a subset of the data in your production system. You can use the same techniques to build this partial database as you use for a complete test copy. If you do decide to use an incomplete copy, you should make sure that the objects you include represent a valid subset of your production work and will allow the users to test some of their key applications as part of the test. Don't use the smallest tables and indexes just because they are faster and easier to copy to your test system.

If you are planning to use a migration method other than the Migration Utility or the Data Migration Assistant, you might not need to create a separate test database. You can migrate the production database as a whole, or in part, when it is not in use without changing its contents. Users can continue to work on the Oracle7 version of the database while you continue tests on the migrated data. Should you be responsible for a database that is never quiescent, you need to decide whether you can rely on data that is not time consistent, in which case you can perform the transfer to Oracle8/Oracle8*i* in stages, or whether you need truly consistent data in order to complete application testing. In the latter case, you will have to build a read-consistent test copy of the production database containing those components you want to test. This, of course, might encompass the entire database.

Before starting the migration testing, you should consider creating a full backup of the test database, if you have built one. This will allow you to re-create it should the testing fail before attempting a revised migration process. Having a stable starting point can make further migration testing easier because you can see exactly which results change between subsequent runs. If you are not using a test database, you might not be able to restore the system to its pretest state without losing the work that was processed during your test period.

Execute the Migration Steps

If you are using your production system instead of a test database, consider the production system to be your test system in the following discussion. You should use as many steps as you can from your migration plan to complete the migration of your test database. This will ensure that your test results will resemble as closely as possible the actual migration results. This includes performing all the other tests, if possible, on the migrated database.

As you perform this test, you should be noting how much time, memory, disk space, and other resources the migration consumes. Pay particular attention to those resources that are in short supply or have specific limitations. Refer back to Table 2.1, "Oracle8*i* Enterprise Edition Size Requirements," to remind yourself of system resources you are likely to need.

If you are not testing your complete database, you should estimate the total resource requirements for your production migration from these test results. Remember that not all resources grow in a linear fashion when you perform these calculations. For example, the Migration Utility might not take twice as long to process if you double the number of tables to be migrated, but an Export/Import probably will. This is because the Migration Utility only has to change the physical structure of the major database components, not the individual tables. The Export/Import processes have to manipulate the rows in every table, so doubling the number of rows tends to double their execution time. On the other hand, the Migration Utility will need double the additional space for table information in the SYSTEM tablespace if you double the number of tables to be migrated.

As always when estimating and extrapolating resource requirements from a test system, allow a fudge factor so that you are more likely to over-, rather than under-, estimate the values. You should also take into account any time that might be needed to upgrade the operating system or any tools, such as the C compiler or third-party products, that might be required by Oracle8*i*.

1. Create a test copy of your whole database, or a subset if you don't have the resources to test the complete database migration. You don't have to complete this step if you're using Export/Import or copying data using some other method.

2. Execute the migration with the utility you plan to use when migrating your production database.

3. Upgrade the tools used by your application.

Minimal Test

Resolving problems with minimal tests

A failure of a minimal test typically indicates problems with the migration itself, such as missing tables, synonyms, views, or stored procedures. It's most likely to fail if you've tried a partial database migration or if you're using one of the data-transfer strategies rather than the Migration Utility.

This type of testing involves migrating all or part of an application and simply attempting to run it. No changes are made to the application, and performance and value testing should not be attempted. This test simply confirms that the application can be started against the migrated database; it's not intended to reveal all problems that could occur.

You should perform this test after a successful migration test before moving on to the more rigorous tests. It might require relinking the tools used by the applications, in which case, you'll need to maintain a separate copy of such applications if the users still need to continue to use the production Oracle7 database. Some application packages will continue to work without any changes, such as those written in Perl or Java. Part of this test will be to determine which software will need relinking and ensuring that the relink will succeed.

Running a minimal test

1. Complete the migration.
2. Have users, developers, or a test suite run selected programs from the applications.
3. Record any anomalies.

The results of this test are only intended to show that the resources were adequate to allow the migration to complete with the application objects intact. Of course, if you only tested the migration on a subset of the database, you can only test the application areas that depend on the migrated objects. At this point, you should only consider the test a failure if the migration doesn't complete or the application test fails because it cannot find a specific table or other object.

Functional Test

The functional test follows the minimal test and ensures that the application runs successfully. This test requires that a user, or a test suite that simulates a user, executes the application command and confirms that the results are identical to what they would have been in the pre-migrated database. During this test, you should ensure that all database components of the application are tested unless you only migrated a subset of the database. In such a case, you should confirm that all the functions related to the migrated portion perform correctly.

This test only requires that the SQL and PL/SQL components be tested, but in order to compare results, you might need to run other parts of the application, such as batch reporting programs, to confirm that data stored through SQL commands is no different when being output through the same processing as before. In some cases, it might be necessary to execute the different SQL and PL/SQL commands, or complete components, under different users to validate that data flows through the system correctly. If the application requires multiple users to test different aspects of the application, your test should also involve this mix of users or simulated users.

In some rare cases, you might need to make changes to employ certain Oracle8 features before you can complete this test. For example, if your application uses tables with ROWID datatypes, you will have to convert their contents to conform to the extended ROWID format in Oracle8 before they can successfully access data stored prior to the migration. ROWID conversion is covered in Chapter 11, "Upgrading Applications," so you might need to refer to this information if you run into this situation. Other than such situations, however, you should not make any changes to the application or try to introduce Oracle8 features while performing this test.

Conducting a functional test

1. Complete the migration and minimal tests.

2. If you need to modify the database with Oracle8 features, such as stored ROWIDs, make these changes or have the developers make them.

3. Have users, developers, or a test suite execute the applications, testing all functions and features.

Tracking the cause of errors detected during functional testing might involve close cooperation between the DBA and the application developers. It's important, therefore, to ensure that the development organization is apprised of this testing phase and can commit the necessary resources. If you're running third-party application software, you might need to get help from your vendor should this test fail.

> ## Testing third-party applications
> Some vendors might not be aware of all the changes made in Oracle8. If you're using third-party applications, you shouldn't commit to a completed migration until the functional tests have been rigorously completed.

The easiest way to confirm results in this test is to run the same application steps on an Oracle7 version of the database, saving the results as the work progresses, and then check that the Oracle8 results are identical. Although you could prevent some Oracle8 features from being invoked in the testing by setting the COMPATIBLE initialization parameter, you can't avoid them all, such as ROWIDs as mentioned earlier. Be aware that discrepancies might occur if you are using some part of the product that has changed between releases. If the results are not identical, be sure to make any necessary changes to the application or the data before concluding that the test is a failure.

You shouldn't be concerned about how efficiently the application runs during this test. The performance aspect of the migration will be examined later. Your only concern should be whether the application produces the correct results, not how long it takes it to accomplish this.

Integration Test

Resolving problems with integration tests

Should you run into problems with these tests, you'll have to isolate whether the cause is in a single component, such as Net8, or whether it's part of the overall migration. Generally, if you've completed the functional testing successfully, the likelihood is that the problem is just with one component, or the interface between a pair of components.

Integrated testing involves executing the application just as you did in the premigrated database. This includes establishing client/server connections, using any GUI interfaces, and testing online and batch functions. This test ensures that all components of the application continue to work together as before. The difference between this test and the functional test is that instead of isolating individual SQL statements and PL/SQL blocks, the application code written around them is also executed.

Running an integration test

1. Complete the migration, minimal, and functional tests.
2. Install and configure any communication software, such as Net8, for client/server or multitier architectures.
3. Install and configure any drivers, such as ODBC drivers, that the applications use.
4. Have the users, developers, or a test suite run the applications across the network, using the same front-end tools and middleware that are now planned for database access.

This test should produce exactly the same results as the functional tests so, once again, having a set of results from your Oracle7 database is a useful tool. Failing that, your results from the functional test should be a basis of comparison for these test results.

Performance Test

> ### Resolving problems with performance tests
>
> In some ways, this might be the most difficult test for the DBA because it can be very difficult to determine what is causing any perceived performance degradation. SQL statements that have hints to make them work with Oracle7's optimizer might not be taking advantage of new Oracle8 optimizer features because of the hint and need to be rewritten. Similarly, parameters in the initialization file might no longer be set optimally to support new Oracle8 database and instance structures. On the other hand, the database might have been damaged during one of the migration steps and is causing the performance problems.

Although the kernel code tree has been optimized in Oracle8, you might discover that some parts of your applications aren't running as well as before the migration. This could be because of a number of factors, such as tuning efforts that were made to avoid a problem in the earlier release. You need to run the performance tests to ensure that overall processing throughput is at least the same as, if not better, than the Oracle7 performance.

Conducting a performance test

1. Complete the previous tests to ensure that you're running the equivalent of a full production system.
2. Have users run their interactive and batch programs as they would in a production environment.
3. Monitor and record the database performance by using queries against the various dynamic performance tables or by using such tools as the UTLBSTAT.SQL and UTLESTAT.SQL scripts.
4. Solicit feedback from users as to their perceptions of performance and response times compared to the current production system.

If you've been monitoring your Oracle7 database with the various analytic and diagnostic tools, you can easily make comparisons by using the same tools on the migrated database. Should you find you are not getting the performance you expected or required, you might need to perform standard tuning on the applications or the database rather than conclude that the migration is a failure. In some cases, you might have to move on to the next test to see if you can resolve what is causing lowered performance. This is because some types of operations in Oracle work better when there is a true load on the database and testing an application all by itself might not produce the best possible results. Oracle8 has introduced some performance features specifically to support large user populations and can, therefore, exacerbate the performance problems of such operations.

Volume/Load Stress Test

Ideally, you should be able to test your migrated database against a realistic workload. This includes the amount of data being processed (volume) and the concurrent demands on database (load). To perform such testing, you might need to set up automated procedures rather than expect your user community to test your database under realistic conditions while continuing work on the unmigrated production version. This test will ensure that the database is ready for the workload intended for it and should also reveal any other problems that the other tests didn't uncover.

Also, as mentioned in the discussion of the performance testing, there might be some situations in which this test is needed to allow the applications to run at their peak performance. If you have deferred judgment on the results of the performance tests, you should pay specific attention to the results you achieve in volume and load tests. Unless you do get acceptable results from this test, you might have to consider performing the migration over again, or find more ways to tune the migrated database.

Building a load test

If you have software that can capture the keystrokes entered during an interactive session, you can use this to collect the session work completed by the users in earlier tests. You can use these to build scripts that emulate those sessions. Run multiple concurrent copies of these scripts to simulate different levels of system load.

Performing volume/load stress tests

1. Assemble a workforce or automated scripts to represent a normal, everyday workload.
2. Exercise the system by having the users or scripts execute the applications concurrently.
3. Monitor and record the system performance as you did in the performance testing.

Because of changes in the structure and use of internal structures—such as the data dictionary, rollback segments, and ROWIDs—you might find that the behavior of the database changes differently from the way it did in Oracle7. Although most resources won't reach a performance threshold as quickly as they might in Oracle7, you can't depend on this. It's therefore inadvisable to assume that if you achieve performance equal to, or better than, Oracle7 with a small number of concurrent sessions manipulating a few tables, this performance level will be maintained under full volume and load.

Setting Up a Test Program

> ## Ensure the integrity of your test environment
> There's no point performing a test for validity after migration if the original version is flawed. Similarly, if you plan to test just part of your database, you need to ensure that you'll get a valid subset of the data. For example, if you're going to test a function that adds new records to a table and a sequence generator is used for the primary key values, you'll have to ensure that the sequence generator is available in the premigration set of objects.

Keeping in mind the various tests you need to perform, your test program should address the when, where, what, who, and how questions associated with each test. The test program should also address the methods you'll use to compare the actual results with what should be expected if the test is successful. This might include creating test suites that can be run on the current production database and on the Oracle8 test database, or simply recording the sizes of such objects as temporary segments and rollback segments in the test database so that you'll be prepared to size the associated tablespace appropriately when the migration is performed for real.

When to perform the tests depends on the resources you need and their availability. For example, DBAs are used to working on major database changes during periods of low activity, such as late night, weekends, and holidays. If your test needs the participation of developers or end users, however, you might have to plan the test during normal working hours.

Where to perform your tests depends on your computer environment. Ideally, you want to test as much of the database as you can: all of it if possible. This might require using a separate machine if one is available. A test or development machine is probably the best place to run the various tests. Remember, however, that you might have to schedule this machine if it's regularly used by the developers because some tests might require shutting down the Oracle7 database(s) running there.

What to test will depend on the test you're performing. By using the descriptions of the different tests in the previous section, make sure that you have the resources to complete the test and record the findings in a meaningful way. For example, you won't learn anything about whether the Oracle8 performance is equal to, better than, or even worse than the Oracle7 performance if you don't have a method to record the performance characteristics you want to measure in each environment.

Who to involve in the testing also depends on the type of test. The earlier test descriptions should help you identify the type of personnel needed for each one. You might want to form a migration team with members from your system support, developer, and end user communities

if you're going to migrate a large database. This team can help you schedule the tests in such a way that they don't cause major conflicts with other groups. For example, you would want to avoid running a test needing input from the users during times of heavy workloads, such as month-end processing. The team can also help you find the best resources within their respective groups to help with the tests and can act as your communication channel back to the various groups regarding the progress of the migration.

How to complete the tests depends on your environment as well as the test type. You need to decide if you'll run tests on the whole database or on partial applications. This, of course, depends on the resources you have available. Similarly, you need to ensure that you have the resources, including people and tools, to fix any problems encountered during the testing so that you can keep the migration project on track. The individuals needed to fix a problem might not be the same as those involved in the test itself.

The how question also needs to address how you'll obtain your test data. If you want to test against the entire database, you'll need a method to create an exact copy of it, possibly on a separate machine. This could involve an Export/Import or some form of Unload/Reload utility. If using the latter, you need a verification test suite to ensure that the copy was successful.

After your test plan is in place, you can begin the process of fully testing a migration. Ideally, you'll run every test on a complete test version of the migrated database before tackling the migration of the production system.

Summary

For a successful migration, you must ensure that you have the cooperation of everyone who will be needed to help you complete the project or who will be impacted by the process. Part of the project will be to test the migration. The testing will incrementally examine the success of the migration and the ability of the migrated database to support the current workload, application processes, and user complement.

The purpose of the testing is to ensure that the database will support the same load after migration as it did before. Although it might be important to incorporate some of the new features of Oracle8*i* into your production database after you have completed the migration, during testing you should only make those changes necessary to obtain the same functionality and performance as your current system.

Some of the changes necessary to make the system work successfully under Oracle8*i* might involve hardware upgrades, application changes, and network reconfiguration as well as database structure and instance configuration. Your migration plan must include the resources—time, people, and hardware—necessary to be successful.

Installing and Configuring Oracle8*i*

IN THIS CHAPTER

The installation process in Oracle8i is very simple; however, you must understand the various alternatives available to you to configure the environment. In this chapter, we will look at the various options you have for installing Oracle8i including silent-mode installation. Oracle8i provides the software packager and the Oracle universal installer that will help you in automating the installation process.

System Requirements

You should check the Oracle8i installation guide and release notes for operating system–specific hardware and software requirements. Tables 3.1 and 3.2 describe the system requirements needed to install Oracle8i Enterprise Edition on Windows NT, whereas Table 3.3 describes the products that can be installed.

TABLE 3.1   Hardware Requirements

Component	Requirements
CPU	100 percent IBM-compatible personal computer with a Pentium processor or higher. DEC ALPHA or any other system that runs Windows NT can also be used. Multiple processors are supported.
Memory	64MB minimum for server installation. If you plan to use the Oracle Enterprise Manager, you should use an additional 20MB.
Disk space	300MB of available hard disk space (typical); 35MB of available hard disk space for server installation. Depending on the option chosen, you will need additional space as follows:
	Oracle8 Context Cartridge (1MB),
	Oracle8 Spatial Cartridge (6MB),
	Oracle8 Parallel Server Option (5MB),
	Oracle8 Partitioning Option (1MB),
	Oracle8 Objects Option (1MB),
	Oracle8 Advanced Networking Option (1MB),
	Oracle8 Time Series Cartridge (6MB),
	Oracle8 Audio Data Cartridge (1MB),
	Oracle8 Image Cartridge (1MB),
	Oracle8 Visual Information Retrieval Cartridge (1MB).
	Oracle8 Recovery Manager requires a media management layer such as Legato Storage Manager, which requires 32MB of RAM, 64MB available hard disk space, and a tape drive.

TABLE 3.2   Software Requirements

Component	Requirements
Operating system	Windows NT 4.0 Workstation or Server with Service Pack 3
Web browser (to view online documentation)	Netscape Navigator 3.0 (or higher) Internet Explorer 3.0 (or higher); browser should be frames- and Java-enabled
16-bit color video	

TABLE 3.3   Products That Can Be Installed with Oracle8i

Product	Release	Purpose
Assistant Common Files	8.1.5.0.0	Collection of files used by all the Oracle Assistants
Java Runtime Environment	1.1.6.2.0	Required to run Java applications
Oracle AppWizard for Microsoft Visual C++	8.1.5.0.0	Allows applications to be written to access the database
Oracle Data Migration Assistant	8.1.5.0.0	Migrates Oracle7 databases or upgrades previous Oracle8 releases to the current Oracle8i release
Oracle Database Configuration Assistant	8.1.5.0.0	Used to create and delete Oracle databases
Oracle Documentation	8.1.5.0.0	Both HTML and PDF formats are available
Oracle Universal Installer	1.5.0.4.0	Used to install, update, and remove Oracle products
Oracle Intelligent Agent	8.1.5.0.0	Manages jobs scheduled with the Oracle Enterprise Manager
Oracle Connection Manager	8.1.5.0.0	Allows the multiplexing of multiple logical client sessions to Oracle database using a single physical connection
Oracle Software Packager	1.5.0.4.0	Packages software in a format that can be used by the Oracle Universal Installer
Oracle Home Selector	8.1.5.0.0	Allows editing the environment path to select the Oracle home directory
Oracle Installation Libraries	1.5.0.4.0	Used during installation
Oracle Names	8.1.5.0.0	Naming service used during the setting up of global client/server networks

3

INSTALLING AND
CONFIGURING
ORACLE8*I*

continues

TABLE 3.3   Continued

Product	Release	Purpose
Net8 Assistant	8.1.5.0.0	Used to configure sqlnet.ora, listener.ora, tnsnames.ora, and Oracle Names Server
Net8 Client	8.1.5.0.0	Allows client connections to the databases to occur over the network
Net8 Server	8.1.5.0.0	Allows the network listener to accept client connection requests coming across the network
Oracle Advanced Networking Option	8.1.5.0.0	Provides enhanced network security and authentication
Kerberos authenticatiom	8.1.5.0.0	Enables authentication with the Kerberos authentication method
RADIUS authentication method	8.1.5.0.0	Enables authentication with RADIUS-compliant devices
SecurID authentication method	8.1.5.0.0	Enables authentication with SecurID authentication method
Named Pipes Protocol	8.1.5.0.0	Enables client/server communication through Named Pipes and Net8
SPX Protocol Support	8.1.5.0.0	Enables client/server communication through SPX and Net8
TCP/IP Protocol Support	8.1.5.0.0	Enables client/server communication through TCP/IP and Net8
Object Type Translator	8.1.5.0.0	Allows the creation of C- Struct representations of Abstract Data Types (ADTs)
Pro*C	8.1.5.0.0	Allows the embedding of SQL Statements in a C/C++ program to manipulate an Oracle database
Oracle Objects for OLE	8.1.5.0.0	Provides an OCX or ActiveX custom control with OLE in-process server that allows the placement of Oracle database functionality into Windows applications
Oracle Services for Microsoft Transaction Server	8.1.5.0.0	Allows the development and deployment of COM-based applications by using Microsoft Transaction Server against an Oracle database
Oracle Parallel Server Manager	8.1.5.0.0	Manages an Oracle Parallel Server environment
Oracle Web Publishing Assistant	8.1.5.0.0	Allows the query and publishing of data via a Web page

Product	Release	Purpose
Oracle8 Enterprise Edition	8.1.5.0.0	Oracle database server
Oracle Parallel Server Option	8.1.5.0.0	Allows multiple instance to share a single database
Oracle8 ConText Cartridge	8.1.5.0.0	Allows client tools to manipulate text in an Oracle database
Oracle8 Image Cartridge	8.1.5.0.0	Allows the storage, retrieval, and processing of two-dimensional, static, bitmapped images
Oracle8 Objects Option	8.1.5.0.0	Allows the use of object technology
Oracle8 Partitioning Option	8.1.5.0.0	Allows the use of partitioning techniques
Oracle8 Spatial Cartridge	8.1.5.0.0	Allows the storage, retrieval, and processing of spatial data
Oracle8 Time Series Cartridge	8.1.5.0.0	Allows the storage, retrieval, and processing of time-stamped data through object datatypes
Oracle8 Visual Information Retrieval Cartridge	8.1.5.0.0	Allows the storage, retrieval, and processing of digital audio data
Oracle8 ODBC Driver	8.1.5.0.0	Supports ODBC connections from Windows 95/98 and Windows NT clients to an Oracle8 database
Oracle8 Performance Monitor	8.1.5.0.0	Monitors the performance of local and remote Oracle databases
Oracle8 Utilities	8.1.5.0.0	Provides a suite of database administration tools including SQl*Loader, Export, Import, Recovery Manager, OCOPY, Instance Manager, TKPROF, DBVERIFY, Migration Utility, and Password Utility
Oracle Call Interface	8.1.5.0.0	Allows C/C++ programs to make calls to Oracle database
Oracle8 Database Server-Managed Video Cartridge	8.1.5.0.0	Allows the storage, retrieval, and processing of video data
Oracle8 Enterprise Edition Release Notes	8.1.5.0.0	Last-minute, important information about the installation and use of the Oracle database
SQL*PLUS	8.1.5.0.0	Client tool that enables the use of SQL and PL/SQL to manipulate the database
Oracle COM Cartridge	8.1.5.0.0	Allows the manipulation of COM components by PL/SQL developers
Pro*COBOL	8.1.5.0.0	Allows the embedding of SQL statements in a COBOL program to manipulate an Oracle database
Net8 Easy Config	8.1.5.0.0	Java-based tool that allows the configuration of tnsnames.ora

3

INSTALLING AND
CONFIGURING
ORACLE8*i*

Starter Database Components

You can choose to install a starter database during Oracle8*i*'s installation. The starter database on Windows NT contains the following:

- User accounts

  INTERNAL (password ORACLE)

  This is not a true account. It is an alias for the SYS account and SYSDBA privilege. It can be used for database startup and shutdown in addition to other database administration tasks.

  SYS (password CHANGE_ON_INSTALL)

  This is a DBA account with the following privileges: CONNECT, RESOURCE, DBA, AQ_ADMINISTRATOR_ROLE, AQ_USER_ROLE, DELETE_CATALOG_ROLE, EXECUTE_CATALOG_ROLE, EXP_FULL_DATABASE, IMP_FULL_DATABASE, RECOVERY_CATALOG_OWNER, SELECT_CATALOG_ROLE, SNMPAGENT, CTXADMIN, CTXAPP, and CTXUSER.

  SYSTEM (password MANAGER)

  This is an account with the DBA database role.

> **NOTE**
>
> For security reasons, you should change the password of the SYS and SYSTEM accounts.

  Username SCOTT (password TIGER)

  This is a user account with CONNECT and RESOURCE privileges.

  Username DEMO (password DEMO)

  This is a user account with CONNECT and RESOURCE privileges.

  Username DBSNMP (password DBSNMP)

  This is an Oracle Enterprise Manager account with the CONNECT, RESOURCE, and SNMPAGENT database privileges.

  Username CTXSYS (password CTXSYS)

  This is an Oracle Context Administrator account with the CONNECT, RESOURCE, and DBA database privileges.

- Tablespaces

  System tablespace containing the data dictionary

  User-data tablespace containing application data

Temporary_data tablespace contains the temporary tables or indexes created during the execution of SQL statements

Rollback_data contains the rollback segments

- Datafiles located in the %ORACLE_HOME%\ORADATA\ORCL directory. For the starter database, Oracle8*i* provides the SYSTEM01.DBF, USERS01.DBF, TEMP01.DBF, and RBS01.DBF datafiles in the system, user_data, temporary_data, and rollback_data tablespace respectively.

- The INITORCL.ORA initialization file in the %ORACLE_HOME%\ORA81\database directory

- The Redo01.log, Redo02.log, Redo03.log, and Redo04.log redo logs in the %ORACLE_HOME%\ORADATA\ORCL directory

- The CONTROL01.CTL and CONTROL02.CTL control files in the %ORACLE_HOME%\ORADATA\ORCL directory

Installing Oracle8*i*

Installation of Oracle8*i* software is operating system specific and you should see the version 8 operating system–specific installation documentation and the version 8 README for your operating system. Using the instructions in your OS-specific manual, start the Oracle Universal Installer and follow these steps:

1. In the Welcome dialog box (see Figure 3.1), click Next to proceed with the installation.

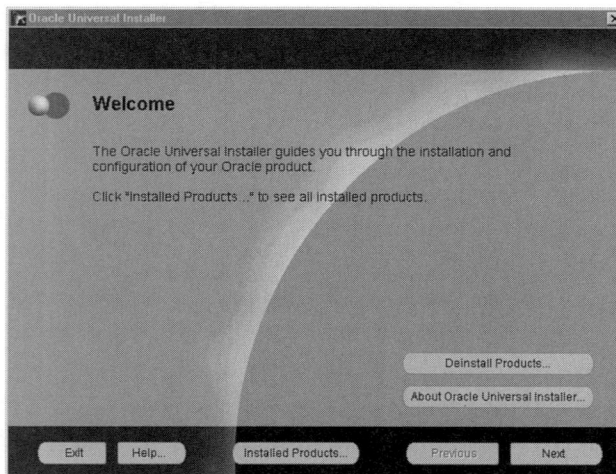

FIGURE 3.1
The Welcome screen of the Oracle Universal Installer.

3

INSTALLING AND
CONFIGURING
ORACLE8*I*

2. In the File Locations dialog box (see Figure 3.2), make sure that the source files are located in the source location indicated. In the Destination section, type the location where you want to install Oracle8*i*. Click Next.

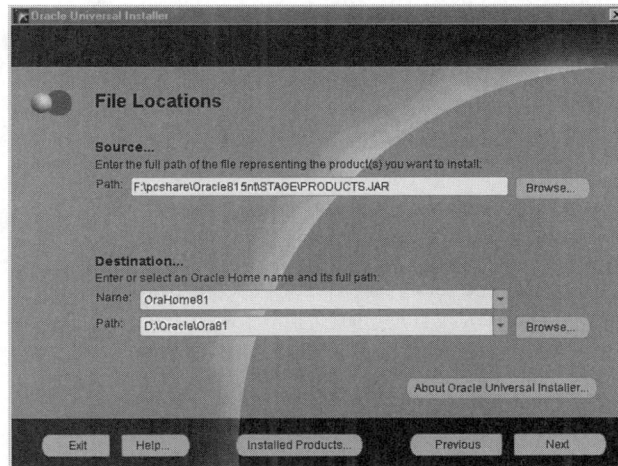

FIGURE 3.2
Specify the location of ORACLE_HOME.

3. From the Available Products dialog box (see Figure 3.3), select the product you want to install and then click Next. The following options are available:

Oracle8 Enterprise Edition 8.1.5

Oracle8 Client 8.1.5

Programmer 8.1.5

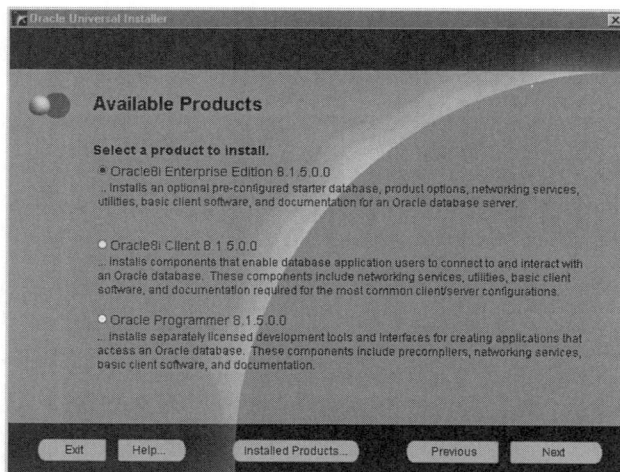

FIGURE 3.3
Select the product to install.

4. Select the type of installation and then click Next (see Figure 3.4):

- *Typical* installs the most common components.
- *Custom* allows you choose the components you want to install.
- *Minimum* installs the minimum component srequired to use Oracle8*i*.

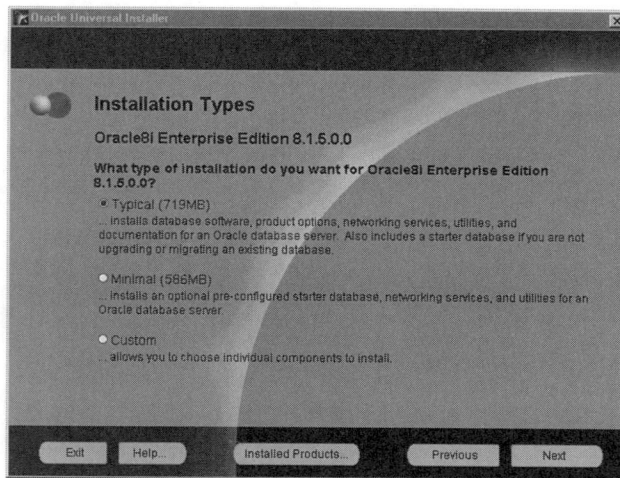

FIGURE 3.4
Choose the type of installation.

5. Select the location where the Oracle documentation is to be installed. This can be on the hard disk or you can leave it on the CD-ROM to save space (see Figure 3.5). Click Next.

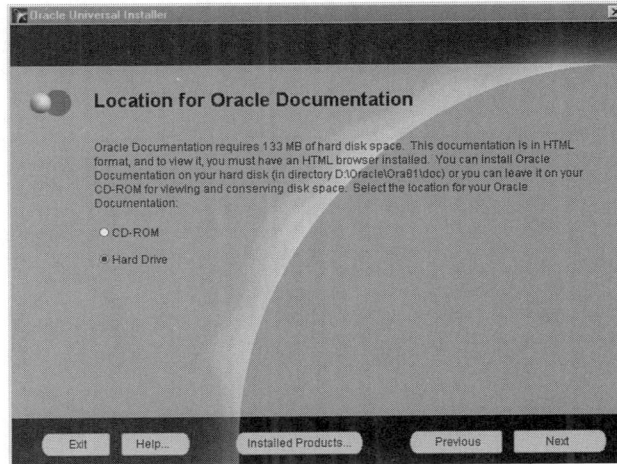

FIGURE 3.5

Choose the location of the Oracle documentation.

6. Specify the database name (see Figure 3.6), and click Next.

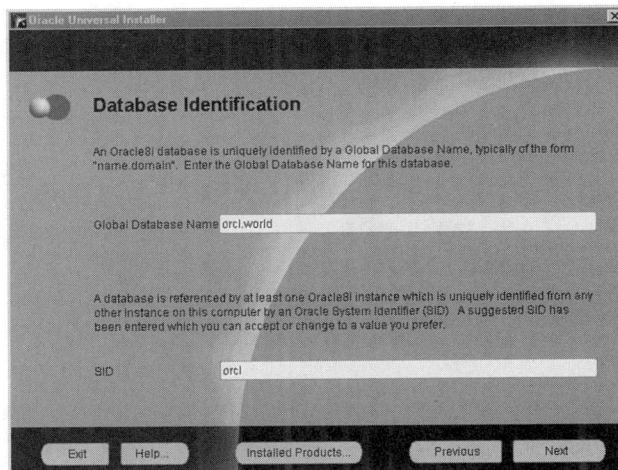

FIGURE 3.6

Specify the name of the database.

7. The Summary dialog box shows the options you have chosen so far. Verify these choices and click Install (see Figure 3.7).

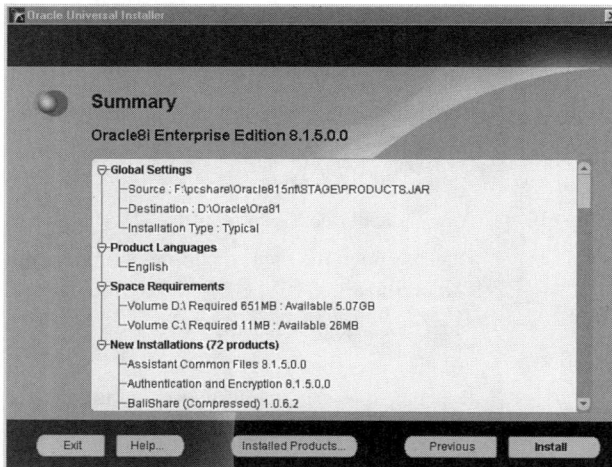

FIGURE 3.7
The Summary page shows the options you have chosen.

8. Installation proceeds and the starter database is created.

9. The Net8 Configuration Assistant is automatically run during installation. Configure Net8 by using the Net8 Configuration Assistant.

10. The Oracle Data Migration Assistant is automatically run if an earlier version of an Oracle database is detected on your system and you choose to migrate it.

NOTE

When migrating from Oracle 7.3.x to Oracle8*i*, the appropriate version of SQL*Net should be installed in the Oracle7 home directory before using the Oracle Data Migration Assistant.

11. When the installation completes, click Exit to exit the Oracle Universal Installer.

Options configurable during the installation are shown in Table 3.4.

3

Table 3.4   Options Configurable During the Installation of Oracle8*i*

Product Option	Configuration
Net8 network software	Automatically configured for server, but must be done manually for client
Oracle Enterprise Manager	Must be configured separately
Oracle Cartridges	Depends upon the options chosen during the installation of Oracle Server Software
Oracle8 objects	Automatically configured
Oracle8 partitioning	Automatically configured
Oracle8 parallel server	Depends upon the options chosen during the installation of Oracle Server Software
Oracle Services for Microsoft Transaction Server	Must be configured separately
Oracle support of Multi-Threaded Servers	Depends upon the options chosen during the installation of Oracle Server Software
Oracle Advanced Replication	Depends upon the options chosen during the installation of Oracle Server Software

Configuring Oracle8*i* Cartridges

Oracle8*i* allows the use of various features such as spatial data, as well as image and audio data. Use of these features requires the installation of the appropriate cartridges. The following steps show how cartridges can be installed (also refer to Table 3.5, which shows the various scripts that need to be run in order to install the particular cartridge):

1. Connect to Server Manager using the internal account.
2. Start the database.
3. Run the ORDINST.SQL script:

   `Svrmgr> @ORDINST.SQL`
4. Run the script for the desired cartridge (see Table 3.5).
5. Exit Server Manager.

Table 3.5   Scripts to Run to Install Cartridges

Cartridge to Install	Script to Run
Oracle8 Audio Data Cartridge	AUDINST.SQL
Oracle8 Video Cartridge	VIDINST.SQL
Oracle8 Image Cartridge	IMGINST.SQL

Cartridge to Install	Script to Run
Oracle8 Spatial Cartridge	MDINST.SQL (must be run in connection with the system account)
Oracle8 Time Series Cartridge	TSINST.SQL
Oracle8 Visual Information Retrieval Cartridge	VIRINST.SQL (must configure the Oracle8 Image Cartridge before configuring this cartridge)

Removing Oracle8*i* from Windows NT

The following steps can be used to remove Oracle8*i* from Windows NT:

1. Log on to Windows NT as administrator.
2. From Control Panel, stop all Oracle services.
3. Choose Start, Programs, Oracle8 for Windows NT, Oracle Universal Installer.
4. In the Welcome dialog box, click the Installed Products button.
5. In the Inventory dialog box, select the components that you want to uninstall. For a complete uninstall, choose all components.
6. Confirm the removal of the selected products.
7. Close the Inventory dialog box, and then exit the Oracle Universal Installer.

3

INSTALLING AND
CONFIGURING
ORACLE8*I*

NOTE

Oracle8*i* software must be installed in a directory that is separate from your version 7 $ORACLE_HOME.

Noninteractive Installation

The Oracle Universal Installer is usually run in the interactive mode. However, advanced database administrators might choose to run it in the noninteractive mode (also referred to as silent mode) to perform multiple unattended installations. When run in the noninteractive mode, a response file is used to specify the answers to the questions that are normally asked during an interactive install session. A response file is a text file containing variables and values used by the Oracle Universal Installer during the installation process. In order to run the installer in the silent mode, it is launched with the `-responseFile` flag that indicates the location of the response file.

A response file can be created by modifying a response template provided under the \RESPONSE folder in the Oracle8*i* server CD-ROM. Values that are not supplied in the response file are set to their default values by the installer. The following steps can be followed to perform a silent-mode installation:

1. Copy one of the response files (typical815.rsp or custom815.rsp) from the \response folder on the Oracle8*i* server CD-ROM to your hard disk.

2. Using any editor such as Notepad, edit this file to indicate your choice of values and save the file.

3. Run the installer in the silent mode by specifying the response file created in the preceding step. For example,

```
C:\> setup.exe -responseFile c:\rspfiles\typical815.rsp
-silent -nowelcome
```

The syntax of the silent-mode install is as follows:

```
Setup.exe -responseFile X:\pathtoresponsefile\responsefilename.rsp [-silent]
[-nowelcome]
```

Where,

- `responseFile` indicates the location of the response file.

- `silent` indicates that a log file is to be created to specify success or failure of the install process. This log file is created in the directory specified by the TEMP user variable and the name of the log file is silentInstall.log. Also, all user interface feedback including installation progress is suppressed.

- `nowelcome` indicates that the welcome screen should be suppressed.

NOTE

Setup.exe is located in the \install\win32 directory from the root of the Oracle distribution CD-ROM.

A sample response file for a custom install of Oracle8*i* server is shown as follows:

LISTING 3.1   A Sample Response File for Installing Oracle8*i* on a UNIX System

```
##############################################################
## customprod.rsp                                           ##
##                                                          ##
##   PLEASE VERIFY (CUSTOMISE) THE VALUES FOR THE FOLLOWING ##
##   VARIABLES BEFORE USING THIS FILE FOR SILENT INSTALL.TKX! ##
```

```
##                                                          ##
##   1) UNIX_GROUP_NAME                                      ##
##   2) ORACLE_HOME && ORACLE_HOME_NAME                      ##
##   3) s_GlobalDBName                                       ##
##   4) s_dbSid                                              ##
##   5) s_mountPoint                                         ##
##                                                          ##
##   ALSO, MAKE SURE /var/opt/oracle/oraInst.loc EXISTS.     ##
##   TYPICAL ENTRY IN "oraInst.loc" LOOKS LIKE -             ##
##   inventory_loc=/home/dba/oraInventory                    ##
##   BASICALLY, WHEREVER INVENTORY NEEDS TO BE LOCATED.      ##
##                                                          ##
##   AT THE END OF SILENT INSTALL LOOK UP THE FOLLOWING LOGS: ##
##   - oraInventory/logs/installActions.log                 ##
##     (for $ORACLE_HOME/root.sh execution, etc.)           ##
##   - /tmp/silentInstall.log                               ##
##                                                          ##
##############################################################

[General]

RESPONSEFILE_VERSION=1.0.0.0.0

[Session]

#This entry is not used on Windows platforms
#UNIX_GROUP_NAME;String;Used in Dialog
#Group that the current user is part of, for ownership of the install files.
#UNIX_GROUP_NAME="dba"

#FROM_LOCATION;String;Used in Dialog
#Full path for the products.jar file.
FROM_LOCATION="/dev/stage/products.jar"

#ORACLE_HOME;String;Used in Dialog
#Enter the path to your oracle home.
ORACLE_HOME="/mercury/home/oracle/product/8.1.5"

#ORACLE_HOME_NAME;String;Used in Dialog
#Enter the name of this oracle home.  The name will be used to identify this
#home.
ORACLE_HOME_NAME="OraHome81"

#TOPLEVEL_COMPONENT;StringList;Used in Dialog
#Choices: "oracle.server", "8.1.5.0.0"
TOPLEVEL_COMPONENT={"oracle.server", "8.1.5.0.0"}
```

3

INSTALLING AND
CONFIGURING
ORACLE8*i*

continues

LISTING 3.1   Continued

```
#SHOW_COMPONENT_LOCATIONS_PAGE;Boolean;Used in Dialog
#Some components are flexible in where they are installed, although all have
# default locations.
#Set this to FALSE if you want to accept the default locations
# and not show this page.
SHOW_COMPONENT_LOCATIONS_PAGE=false

#SHOW_SUMMARY_PAGE;Boolean;Used in Dialog <---------------
#MUST be <false> for "silent" install
SHOW_SUMMARY_PAGE=false

#SHOW_INSTALL_PROGRESS_PAGE;Boolean;Used in Dialog <---------------
#MUST be <false> for "silent" install
SHOW_INSTALL_PROGRESS_PAGE=false

#SHOW_REQUIRED_CONFIG_TOOL_PAGE;Boolean;Used in Dialog
SHOW_REQUIRED_CONFIG_TOOL_PAGE=false

#SHOW_OPTIONAL_CONFIG_TOOL_PAGE;Boolean;Used in Dialog
SHOW_OPTIONAL_CONFIG_TOOL_PAGE=false

#SHOW_END_SESSION_PAGE;Boolean;Used in Dialog <---------------
#MUST be <false> for "silent" install
SHOW_END_SESSION_PAGE=false


[oracle.server_8.1.5.0.0]
#COMPONENT_LANGUAGES;StringList;Used in Dialog
# US-ENGLISH, JAPANESE, FRENCH, GERMAN
# {"EN","JA","FR","DE"}
COMPONENT_LANGUAGES={"EN"}
#INSTALL_TYPE;String;Used in Dialog
# Custom - for selecting components of one's choice
INSTALL_TYPE="Custom"
#DEPENDENCY_LIST;StringList
#These are the list of optional dependees you want to select for this
#component. # You can specify this in a string list as a component version
➥pair.
#Eg {"CompA","1.0","CompB",1.0}
DEPENDENCY_LIST={"oracle.networking","8.1.5.0.0","oracle.rdbms",
➥"8.1.5.0.0","oracle.cartridges","8.1.5.0.0","oracle.doc.unixdoc",
➥"8.1.5.0.0","oracle.assistants","8.1.5.0.0","oracle.options",
➥"8.1.5.0.0","oracle.java","8.1.5.0.0","oracle.install","8.1.5.0.0",
➥"oracle.emprod","8.1.5.0.0","oracle.p2k.p2kprod","8.1.5.0.0",
➥"oracle.utilities","8.1.5.0.0"}
```

```
# This is to be used when doing a silent install for "Client" software
#[oracle.client_8.1.5.0.0]
#COMPONENT_LANGUAGES;StringList;Used in Dialog
#COMPONENT_LANGUAGES={"EN"}
#INSTALL_TYPE;String;Used in Dialog
#Choices are Typical and Custom
#INSTALL_TYPE="Custom"
#DEPENDENCY_LIST;StringList
#DEPENDENCY_LIST={"oracle.networking","8.1.5.0.0","oracle.doc.unixdoc",
➥"8.1.5.0.0","oracle.assistants","8.1.5.0.0","oracle.java",
➥"8.1.5.0.0","oracle.install","8.1.5.0.0","oracle.emprod",
➥"8.1.5.0.0","oracle.p2k.p2kprod","8.1.5.0.0",
➥"oracle.utilities","8.1.5.0.0"}

# This is to be used when doing a silent install for "Programmer 2000" software
#[oracle.p2k_8.1.5.0.0]
#COMPONENT_LANGUAGES;StringList;Used in Dialog
#COMPONENT_LANGUAGES={"EN"}
#INSTALL_TYPE;String;Used in Dialog
#Choices are Typical and Custom
#INSTALL_TYPE="Custom"
#DEPENDENCY_LIST;StringList
#DEPENDENCY_LIST={"oracle.p2k.proc","8.1.5.0.0",
➥"oracle.p2k.procob","8.1.5.0.0"}

[oracle.cartridges_8.1.5.0.0]
#DEPENDENCY_LIST;StringList
DEPENDENCY_LIST={"oracle.cartridges.ordsmv","8.1.5.0.0",
➥"oracle.cartridges.ordvir","8.1.5.0.0","oracle.cartridges.ordts",
➥"8.1.5.0.0","oracle.cartridges.ordimg","8.1.5.0.0",
➥"oracle.cartridges.spatial","8.1.5.0.0",
➥"oracle.cartridges.context","8.1.5.0.0"}

[oracle.networking.netcltprod_8.1.5.0.0]
#DEPENDENCY_LIST;StringList
DEPENDENCY_LIST={"oracle.networking.netclt","8.1.5.0.0"}
#OPTIONAL_CONFIG_TOOLS;StringList
OPTIONAL_CONFIG_TOOLS=

[oracle.utilities_8.1.5.0.0]
#DEPENDENCY_LIST;StringList
DEPENDENCY_LIST={"oracle.utilities.util","8.1.5.0.0",
➥"oracle.utilities.plus","8.1.5.0.0"}

[oracle.install_8.1.5.0.0]
#DEPENDENCY_LIST;StringList
DEPENDENCY_LIST={"oracle.swd.oui","1.5.1.4.3","oracle.swd.osp","1.5.1.4.3"}
```

continues

3

INSTALLING AND CONFIGURING ORACLE8*I*

LISTING 3.1 Continued

```
[oracle.java_8.1.5.0.0]
#DEPENDENCY_LIST;StringList
DEPENDENCY_LIST={"oracle.java.javavm","8.1.5.0.0",
➥"oracle.java.javavm.javatools","8.1.5.0.0","oracle.java.jdbc",
➥"8.1.5.0.0","oracle.java.sqlj","8.1.5.0.0"}

[oracle.assistants_8.1.5.0.0]
#DEPENDENCY_LIST;StringList
# Oracle Database Configuration Assistant, Oracle Database Migration Assistant
DEPENDENCY_LIST={"oracle.assistants.dbca","8.1.5.0.0",
➥"oracle.assistants.dbma","8.1.5.0.0"}

[oracle.emprod_8.1.5.0.0]
#DEPENDENCY_LIST;StringList
DEPENDENCY_LIST={"oracle.emprod.oemagent.cmp","8.1.5.0.0"}

[oracle.networking_8.1.5.0.0]
#DEPENDENCY_LIST;StringList
DEPENDENCY_LIST={"oracle.networking.netclt","8.1.5.0.0",
➥"oracle.networking.netsvr","8.1.5.0.0","oracle.networking.cman",
➥"8.1.5.0.0","oracle.networking.names","8.1.5.0.0"}
#OPTIONAL_CONFIG_TOOLS;StringList
OPTIONAL_CONFIG_TOOLS=

[oracle.p2k.p2kprod_8.1.5.0.0]
#DEPENDENCY_LIST;StringList
DEPENDENCY_LIST={"oracle.p2k.ott","8.1.5.0.0","oracle.p2k.oci","8.1.5.0.0"}

[oracle.java.jdbc_8.1.5.0.0]
#DEPENDENCY_LIST;StringList
DEPENDENCY_LIST={"oracle.java.jdbc.thin102","8.1.5.0.0",
➥"oracle.java.jdbc.thin111","8.1.5.0.0","oracle.java.jdbc.oci102",
➥"8.1.5.0.0","oracle.java.jdbc.oci111","8.1.5.0.0"}

[oracle.swd.oui_1.5.1.4.2]
#PROD_HOME;String
PROD_HOME=

[oracle.swd.osp_1.5.1.4.2]
#PROD_HOME;String
PROD_HOME=

[oracle.options.ano.ssl_8.1.5.0.0]
#s_walletPassword;String
```

```
#When using global security, you need the Oracle Wallet Manager.
➥This password allows
# access to this tool, which allows you to create wallets to
#identify entities on
# your network.
s_walletPassword="sys"

[oracle.options.ops.cic_8.1.5.0.0]
#userNodeList;String
#This is only used if the current node is on a cluster.
#This variable contains a list of nodes
# on the cluster onto which the current install should be done,
#for Oracle Parallel Server.
# It's a list of node names, separated by ¦.
#userNodeList="oraclesun1¦oraclesun2¦oraclesun3"
userNodeList=

[oracle.options_8.1.5.0.0]
#DEPENDENCY_LIST;StringList
DEPENDENCY_LIST={"oracle.options.ano","8.1.5.0.0",
➥"oracle.options.partitioning","8.1.5.0.0",
➥"oracle.options.ops","8.1.5.0.0"}

[oracle.rdbms_8.1.5.0.0]
#OPTIONAL_CONFIG_TOOLS;StringList
OPTIONAL_CONFIG_TOOLS=

#s_GlobalDBName;String
#This is the name of the database which will be created
#as part of the custom install.
#You should modify this string to use an appropriate name.
s_GlobalDBName="acme.us.oracle.com"

#b_createDB;Boolean
#set to TRUE if you want a starter database, set to FALSE if not.
b_createDB=true

#This entry is not needed for Windows installations
#sl_dbaOperGroups;StringList
#This is the name of the group which represents the database operators.
#Must have 2 values ONLY. Repeat the first one if there is just one.
#sl_dbaOperGroups={"dba", "sys"}
#sl_dbaOperGroups={"dba", "dba"}

#sl_migrateSIDDialogReturn;StringList
#This list will contain the (SID, Home) pair of the DB to migrate,
```

continues

LISTING 3.1 Continued

```
#or ("<None>", "<None>") if
#no migration is desired at install time.
#Note that migration is a complicated process, so if you plan on
#doing silent migration you
# should be sure you have read all of the migration documentation in advance.
sl_migrateSIDDialogReturn={"<None>","<None>"}

#s_ORACLEBASE;String
#Replace this value with the correct path to the oracle base.
#You need only change the
#drive letter if you kept the default oracle home path.
s_ORACLEBASE="/home/oracle"

#This entry is not needed for Windows installations
#s_mountPoint;String
#Database file location: directory for datafiles, control files, redo logs
#s_mountPoint="/home/oracle/dbs"

#s_dbSid;String
#Value for ORACLE_SID. Change this to an appropriate SID.
s_dbSid="ORCL"

[oracle.networking.netclt_8.1.5.0.0]
#OPTIONAL_CONFIG_TOOLS;StringList
OPTIONAL_CONFIG_TOOLS=
```

Oracle Software Packager

Oracle8*i* allows installation developers to generate installation package using a Java-based object-oriented tool called Oracle Software Packager. The Oracle Software Packager provides wizards to simplify the packaging of products into components that can later be installed by the Oracle Universal Installer. Each component is the basic object that can be installed by the Universal Installer. Several wizards are provided:

- Component Wizard—Used to specify the installation properties of the components such as the component name, version number, files, or groups of files to install as part of the component, dependencies, sequence of dialogs, and actions that make up the installation plan and so on. These dialogs and actions can be implemented in one of two ways:

  Predefined dialogs and actions by using the packager's Java class libraries

  Creating custom Java classes and then importing them

- Verify Wizard—Used to verify the component's integrity.
- Staging Wizard—Used to move the component from the development area to a distribution medium such as CD-ROM, Internet Server, or NFS system.

Summary

The new Java-based Oracle Universal Installer is used to install Oracle8*i* with the same look and feel across all platforms. The Oracle Software Packager can be used to package products into components and prepare a staging area that can be interpreted by the Oracle Universal Installer. Silent-mode installations are possible by creating response files and passing them as a parameter while starting the installer. Dependencies between components is automatically resolved and the software packager can specify that postinstallation tools such as Database Configuration Assistant be automatically launched upon the completion of installation.

Migration Using the Migration Utility

IN THIS CHAPTER

The Migration utility (MIG) is a command-line utility that can be used to migrate Oracle7 databases to Oracle8i. It converts files and structures to the Oracle8i format by changing the file headers. If necessary, the definition of the data in the files will also be changed.

> **NOTE**
>
> The version 8 Migration utility cannot be used to migrate a database to a computer system that is on a different operating system. For example, you cannot migrate a version 7 database on Windows NT to a version 8 database on Sun Solaris. For situations such as these where you are migrating to a different operating system, you have to use the Export/Import utilities to export the database from the source machine and import it to the destination machine.

Reviewing the Migration Process

Irrespective of which technique you use to perform the migration from Oracle7 to Oracle8i, several general steps need to be performed:

1. Choose a migration strategy by making the following decisions:
   - Which migration method will you use?
   - Depending upon the method chosen, do you have the necessary resources available?
   - Several Oracle7 features have become obsolete in Oracle8i. Are you familiar with these?
   - Become familiar with the new Oracle8i features you're planning to use.
   - Develop a testing plan for the migrated database.
   - Make sure you have a backup and recovery strategy that can be quickly used to fall back to the Oracle7 database in case the migration fails.
2. Use a test Oracle7 database to perform a test migration.
3. Using the test strategy developed in step 1, test the migrated database and verify that there are no errors or problems during the migration.
4. Prepare the source database for migration. This step includes taking a backup of the database, scheduling downtime for the database, making sure that there isn't any user with the name MIGRATE, checking space and resource availability, and so on.
5. Migrate the database by using the strategy decided in step 1.

NOTE

The following checklist can help you during the planning stage of the migration:

- Become familiar with the migration steps from the Oracle migration guide.
- Prepare a list of the hardware, software, and other resources you need.
- Contact Oracle Support Services and obtain a list of any gotchas regarding the migration.
- Talk with peers who have performed similar migrations.
- Schedule downtime for the migration process.
- Choose a backup strategy.
- Roll out the new features of the new version.

6. Back up the database again so that you have a baseline for your backups.
7. The database parameters used for the Oracle7 database might not necessarily be ideal in the Oracle8*i* environment. Tune the migrated database by revisiting the initialization parameters used and make any desired changes.
8. Migrate the applications.

NOTE

The extent of planning and testing of the migration depends on the number of applications used. The migration time using MIG utility will vary with your system, but the suggestions discussed this chapter can be used to minimize it.

Changing Word Size

Oracle8*i* allows you to change the word size of your Oracle database during upgrade, downgrade, or migration. Changing the word size allows you to perform several tasks:

- You have a 32-bit Oracle software installed on a 64-bit hardware and want to change to 64-bit Oracle software in order to take advantage of it.
- You have a 64-bit Oracle software installed on a 64-bit hardware and want to change to 32-bit Oracle software.

Manual Migration with MIG

The Migration utility is provided by Oracle to perform fast and automatic migration of Oracle7 databases to Oracle8/8*i* databases. The MIG utility changes the file headers and the data definitions, but does not change the actual data. The MIG utility has the following features:

- It migrates a complete Oracle7 database to Oracle8/8*i*.
- It does not copy the data.
- It is automatic and doesn't require much interaction from the DBA.
- It is faster than other migration strategies because the Data Dictionary objects are the only objects that are changed. As a result of this, the migration speed is not dependent on the database size.
- Compared to other migration strategies, it uses less additional disk space.
- It can be used only to migrate an Oracle7 database.
- After the migration is complete, you cannot downgrade back to Oracle7 without using the backups.
- It cannot perform release-to-release upgrades for the same major version, for example, from Oracle 8.0.3 to Oracle 8.1.5.
- It cannot migrate to a different operating system.
- It cannot migrate to a different hardware platform.

> **NOTE**
>
> For databases of large size and large datatypes, the MIG utility might be the only practical method of migrating your Oracle7 databases.

- It makes use of several simple and standardized steps.
- At any point prior to migrating the Oracle7 database, it can be opened and accessed by using a version 7 instance. However, after the migration is complete, the only way to go back is to restore from a good Oracle7 backup.

MIG is a command-line utility provided by Oracle to help during the migration process. The following must be true in order to perform manual migration using the MIG utility:

- You are at Oracle release 7.1.3.3.6 or greater before the migration.
- The DB_BLOCK_SIZE for the Oracle7 database and the migrated Oracle8 database must be the same.

- The character set on the Oracle7 database and the migrated Oracle8 database must be the same.
- The database is to be migrated to the same operating system.

If the above steps are all true, the following steps can be used to migrate an Oracle7 database by using the Migration utility:

1. Back up the Oracle7 database.
2. From Server Manager, create a spool file that will contain a list of database files that have been backed up. This will allow you to fall back to the appropriate files in case the migration does complete successfully:

   Svrmgr> **spool backup.lst**

NOTE

You should also backup the init.ora file for the appropriate database instance.

The following commands can be used in Server Manager to generate the list:

select * from v$datafile;	List of datafiles
select * from v$logfile;	List of redo log files
select * from v$controlfile;	Control files to back up

3. Make sure that you have enough disk space for the Oracle8 binaries (at least three times the space required for Oracle7 binaries). Depending upon other utilities installed, such as Pro*C/C++, Developer, and so on, the space requirements might be more.
4. Run the MIG utility with the CHECK_ONLY command-line option to make sure that there is enough space for the Oracle8 Data Dictionary.
5. Set the optimal setting of the SYSTEM rollback segment to NULL.

   SVRMGR>Alter rollback segment system storage (optimal NULL);

NOTE

The optimal setting of rollback segments can be verified by executing the following from the Server Manager prompt.

```
Select a.usn, a.name, b.optsize
From v$rollname a, v$rollstat b
Where a.usn = b.usn;
```

6. Verify that there is no user or role with the name MIGRATE. This can be done by executing the following from the Server Manager prompt:

```
Select username from dba_users where username = 'MIGRATE';

Select role from dba_roles where role = 'MIGRATE';
```

To drop the user MIGRATE:

```
Drop user MIGRATE;
```

To drop the role MIGRATE:

```
Drop role MIGRATE;
```

7. Make sure that all the datafiles and tablespaces are online or offline normal. None of the datafiles should be in need of recovery. You can query the Data Dictionary views v$recover_file and dba_data_files to check the status of the files.

8. Query dba_2pc_pending view to verify that no in-doubt transactions exist. In-doubt transactions should be resolved by committing or rolling them back. In-doubt transactions can be identified by querying dba_2pc_pending for transactions that have a state of collecting. For example:

```
Select global_tran_id from dba_2pc_pending
Where state = "collecting";
```

> **NOTE**
>
> The MIG utility can be used in the check-only mode to verify that you have enough space to perform the migration:
>
> ```
> mig pfile=c:\orant\database\init<SID>.ora check_only = true
> ```
>
> where pfile is set to the initialization file associated with the Oracle7 database to be migrated.

Migration Utility Command-Line Options

There are several command-line options that you can use with the Migration utility:

- CHECK_ONLY, when set to TRUE, performs check of the space usage so that you can determine whether there is enough space available for the migration to go through successfully. It checks only the space and doesn't perform an actual migration. When set to FALSE, it performs both a space usage check and an actual migration.

> **NOTE**
>
> The CHECK_ONLY option is mutually exclusive with the NO_SPACE_CHECK option. If one option is TRUE, the other is FALSE.

- DB_NAME specifies the name of the database to migrate.
- MULTIPLIER specifies the factor by which the version 7 I_file#_block# index is increased to obtain the initial size of the version 8 I_file#_block# index. For example, a MULTIPLIER of 20 will double the initial size when the index is created. The default value of MULTIPLIER is 15.
- NEW_DBNAME specifies a new name for the migrated database.
- NLS_NCHAR specifies the National Language Standard (NLS) character set for the version 8 database. The default is to use the character set of the version 7 database.
- NO_SPACE_CHECK, when set to TRUE, means the migration doesn't perform a space usage check.
- PFILE specifies the initialization file to use during the migration.
- SPOOL specifies the spool file for the migration. This serves as the migration log file and should be checked for errors during migration.

> **NOTE**
>
> On UNIX, the path used for the PFILE and SPOOL options must be enclosed in double quotes and masked by a backslash.

Step-by-Step Migration

When performing a migration from Oracle7 to Oracle8*i*, you have to perform several steps on both the environments as discussed below. Also, the installation of Oracle8*i* should be done with the following considerations:

- Install the Oracle8*i* software into a different ORACLE_HOME than the Oracle7 ORACLE_HOME.
- When prompted for the database you want to migrate, choose NONE.
- Choose not to create a database because we will actually be migrating.

> **NOTE**
>
> If you are migrating from an Oracle6 database, you have to first migrate to the latest version of Oracle7 and then use the techniques discussed in this chapter to migrate to Oracle8*i*.

Let us consider a migration on the Windows NT platform. As mentioned earlier, you have to perform several steps in both Oracle7 as well as Oracle8*i* environments. Perform the following steps on the Oracle7 environment:

1. Log on to Windows NT as administrator.
2. Run the Registry Editor (regedt32.exe).
3. Set the ORACLE_HOME variable to the Oracle7 home.
4. Make sure that the NLS_LANG variable is set to the character set used by the Oracle7 database.
5. Using the environment tab of the system icon in the Control Panel, set the PATH environment variable so that the first entry points to the Oracle7 executable.
6. From the command prompt, set oracle_sid=oracle7_sid.
7. Connect to Server Manager as internal.
8. Shut down the database normally (or immediately).
9. Run the Oracle8*i* Migration utility:

   ```
   C:> mig pfile=c:\orant\database\initO7_sid.ora spool=
   c:\orant\database\mig.log
   ```

   A convert file (convert.ora) will be created by the Migration utility. This will be used later in the migration to convert the database to Oracle8*i*.

> **NOTE**
>
> After you have run the Migration utility and the convert file is created, don't open the database with the Oracle7 executables; otherwise, it might become corrupted.

10. Using the Control Panel, stop the Oracle service for the Oracle7 database.
11. Using the Instance Manager (oradim), delete the Oracle service for the Oracle7 database

    ```
    C:> oradim7x -delete -sid Oracle7_sid
    ```

    where *x* represents the Oracle7 major version number.

The preceding steps have prepared the Oracle7 database for migration. The Oracle8*i* installation should be performed now if it has not yet been done. After the installation of Oracle8*i* is complete, the following steps must be performed in the Oracle8*i* environment:

1. Run the Registry Editor (regedt32.exe).
2. Set the ORACLE_HOME variable set to the Oracle8*i* home.
3. Using the Environment tab of the System icon in the control panel, set the PATH environment variable so that the first entry points to the Oracle8*i* executable (c:\oracle\ora81\bin).
4. Create the Oracle8 service by using the Oracle7 SID and init.ora file:

```
oradim –new –sid <Oracle7_sid> -intpwd <internal_password> -
startmode auto -pfile c:\orant\database\init<Oracle7_sid>.ora
```

5. Rename the database's control files.
6. Edit the init.ora file as follows:
   - Set compatible to 8.1.5.0.0
   - Remove the init.ora parameters that have become obsolete from Oracle7 to Oracle8*i*

NOTE

The following Oracle7 parameters are obsolete in Oracle8*i*:

CCF_IO_SIZE	OPTIMIZER_PARALLEL_PASS
CHECKPOINT_PROCESS	PARALLEL_DEFAULT_MAX_SCANS
GC_SAVE_ROLLBACK_LOCKS	PARALLEL_DEFAULT_SCAN_SIZE
GC_SEGMENTS	SEQUENCE_CACHE_HASH_BUCKETS
GC_TABLESPACES	SERIALIZABLE
IO_TIMEOUT	SESSION_CACHED_CURSORS
INIT_SQL_FILES	SNAPSHOT_REFRESH_INTERVAL (renamed to JOB_QUEUE_INTERVAL)
IPQ_ADDRESS	SNAPSHOT_REFRESH_PROCESS (renamed to JOB_QUEUE_PROCESSES)
IPQ_NET	UNLIMITED_ROLLBACK_SEGMENTS
LM_DOMAINS	V733_PLANS_ENABLED
LM_NON_FAULT_TOLERANT	

7. From the command prompt, set oracle_sid=*Oracle7_sid*.

8. Connect to Server Manager using the internal account.

9. Start up the Oracle8*i* database in nomount mode.

   `Svrmgr>startup nomount`

10. Create new control files and use the ALTER DATABASE CONVERT command to convert the file headers of the files to the Oracle8*i* format:

    `Svrmgr> alter database convert;`

CAUTION

Running ALTER DATABASE CONVERT is the point of no return. If the migration fails from this point onward, you will have to rely on your Oracle7 database backups to recover the Oracle7 database.

---

11. Open the database and reset the logs:

    `Svrmgr> alter database open resetlogs;`

12. A spool file should be created to hold the results of running the scripts in steps 13 through 15:

    `Svrmgr> spool migdb.log`

13. Run U0703040.sql:

    `Svrmgr> @c:\oracle\ora81\rdbms\admin\U0703040.sql;`

14. Run catrep.sql if you're using the advanced replication option:

    `Svrmgr> @c:\oracle\ora81\rdbms\admin\catrep.sql`

15. Run catparr.sql only if you're using the Oracle Parallel Server option:

    `Svrmgr> @c:\oracle\ora81\rdbms\admin\catparr.sql`

16. Turn off spooling:

    `Svrmgr> spool out`

17. Shut down the database.

18. Back up the database.

19. View the contents of migdb.out spool file to make sure that the scripts ran successfully. Troubleshoot and fix any problems indicated by the script.

20. Start the database.

> **NOTE**
>
> When the ALTER DATABASE CONVERT command is executed, it creates a new control file based on the convert file generated by the Migration utility, converts all online datafile headers to version 8 format, and mounts the version 8 database.

> **NOTE**
>
> When the ALTER DATABASE OPEN RESETLOGS command is executed, it converts all objects and users to version 8 specifications. The rollback segments are also converted to version 8 format.

Abandoning the Migration Process

It is possible to run the Migration utility multiple times and still be able to return to your version 7 database provided you have not passed the point-of-no-return in the migration process. Returning to the version 7 database requires the re-creation of the catalog views because when the Migration utility is run, it will eliminate the version 7 catalog.

> **NOTE**
>
> The Migration utility upgrades version 7.1 and 7.2 to version 7.3. Therefore, if you abandon a migration from a pre-version 7.3 database to Oracle8*i*, the version 7 database will be left with a version 7.3 Data Dictionary.

The following steps can be used to restore the version 7 database if you abandon the migration to Oracle8*i*:

1. Using the Server Manager, start up the version 7 database:

   Svrmgrl

   ```
   SVRMGR> connect internal
   SVRMGR> startup
   ```

2. Drop the migrate user

   ```
   SVRMGR> drop user migrate cascade
   ```

3. Rerun catalog.sql and catproc.sql

   ```
   SVRMGR> @catalog.sql
   SVRMGR> @catproc.sql
   ```

NOTE

If you have installed Parallel Server, you will also have to rerun catparr.sql. If you have installed Advanced Replication, you will also have to rerun catrep.sql.

Post-Migration Steps

After the migration process completes, you should check several files to make sure that the process was a success. Table 4.1 shows that files that need to be checked for errors.

TABLE 4.1 Errors During Migration Might Be Contained in These Files

File	Description
Oradim73.log	Instance Manager log for Oracle7
Oradim81.log	Instance Manager log for Oracle8
Alert.log	Alert log
Windows NT Event viewer logs.	Application and System logs of the Event viewer
*SID*nls.log	Character set migration information
*SID*checkspc.log	Verification of space availability in SYSTEM tablespace
*SID*mig81.log	Migration log
*SID*altdbs.log	ALTER DATABASE CONVERT places its output in this file
*SID*cat8000.log	cat8000.sql places its output in this file
*SID*pupbld.log	v8pupbld places its output in this file
*SID*summary.log	Contains the summary of the migration process

Several post-migration tasks might be needed in order to take advantage of the full capabilities of the Oracle8*i* database:

- *Precompiler applications:* In order to use Oracle8*i*'s new features, you might need to modify the application code, and then recompile and relink the code. At a minimum, you should relink the applications to the SQLLIB runtime library provided by the Oracle8 precompiler before running them against the Oracle8 database.

- *OCI applications:* Oracle7 OCI applications can be run against an Oracle8*i* database without making any changes. If the OCI applications make use of constraints, you should relink the applications by using Oracle8*i*'s OCI library (OCILIB).

> **NOTE**
>
> When relinking applications by using Oracle8*i*'s OCI library, if you use the non-deferred mode of linking, you will receive error messages immediately after the bind and define operations. However, if the deferred mode of linking is used, the error messages are seen later in the execution, for example during DESCRIBE, EXECUTE, and FETCH calls. Performance with the deferred mode is better than with the non-deferred mode.

- *SQL*Plus Scripts*: SQL*Plus scripts should run without any problems after you have changed the compatibility from Oracle7 to Oracle8*i*.

Troubleshooting the Migration Process

When performing a migration using the Migration utility, you might encounter various types of errors. These errors can be categorized as

- General migration errors
- Migration utility errors

General Migration Errors

Incorrect database configuration might cause errors during migration of an Oracle7 database. Some of the common errors include

- Incorrect setting of the audit_trail parameter may return the following errors:

  ORA-00604: error occurred at recursive SQL level *num*

  ORA-01552: cannot use system rollback segment for non-system tablespace '*name*'

  ORA- 02002: error while writing to audit trail

  The preceding error indicates that either the SYS.AUD$ tables is located in a non-SYSTEM tablespace or the initialization parameter AUDIT_TRAIL is set to DB or TRUE. The following steps can be used to resolve this problem:

  1. Shut down the database.
  2. Edit the initialization file and set AUDIT_TRAIL=NONE.
  3. Rerun the Migration utility.

- Using the optimal setting of the SYSTEM tablespace might give you error ORA-01562 because the optimal setting will dynamically deallocate extents that are no longer needed, resulting in insufficient space for migration purposes.

  ORA-01562: failed to extend rollback segment (id = 0)

This problem can be resolved by setting the optimal parameter to NULL for the SYSTEM rollback segment and rerunning the Migration utility.

- Using a small value for the MULTIPLIER option will result in

    ORA-01632: max # extents (%s) reached in index %s.%s

    By default, the Migration utility uses the MULTIPLIER value of 15. This might not be enough for this particular migration and you need to specify a larger value.

- Errors during alter database convert command

    You may get various errors during the execution of the command ALTER DATABASE CONVERT:

    If version7 control file(s) exist, you might get

    ORA-00200: cannot create control file name

    ORA-00202: controlfile: name

    ORA-27038: skgfrcre: file exists

    Action: Remove or rename the old control file(s), and then reissue the ALTER DATABASE CONVERT command.

    If the convert file is not found in the proper location, you might get

    ORA-00404: convert file not found: name

    ORA-27037: unable to obtain file status

    Action: Move the convert file (convSID.dbf) to the $ORACLE_HOME/dbs directory and re-run the ALTER DATABASE CONVERT command

    If the database is using a password file and the REMOTE_LOGIN_PASSWORD parameter is set to EXCLUSIVE, you will receive an ORA-600 [kzsrsdn: 1] error.

    Action: Take the following steps to resolve this issue:

    1. Shut down the database.
    2. Edit the init.ora file and set REMOTE_LOGIN_PASSWORD to NONE.
    3. Startup mount the database.
    4. Issue the command ALTER DATABASE OPEN RESETLOGS to reset the redo logs.
    5. Continue the migration process with the step following the ALTER DATABASE CONVERT command.

Migration Utility Errors

During the migration process, the Migration utility might generate various errors and informational messages. Let us look at some common errors and messages along with their cause and corrective actions:

- cannot create conversion file, records exceed number bytes

  This error indicates that a valid convert file could not be created using the version 7 control file. In order to resolve this problem, you should check the control file for possible corruption. If corruption exists, you should recover from this problem using the steps described in Chapter 28, "Performing Backups and Recovery." After you have recovered from the lost control file, you can rerun the Migration utility.

- CHECK_ONLY and NO_SPACE_CHECK are mutually exclusive options

  This error indicates you have tried to run the migration utility with both the CHECK_ONLY and the NO_SPACE_CHECK options set to TRUE. Only one of these options can be set to TRUE simultaneously. Therefore, you should rerun the Migration utility after deciding whether you want to check the space (using CHECK_ONLY) or not (using NO_SPACE_CHECK).

- client nls_characterset does not match server nls_characterset—check that NLS_LANG environment variable is set

  This error indicates that the NLS_LANG character set does not match the character set in PROPS$. You should check the character set in PROPS$, and then set NLS_LANG to that value.

- command line argument value must be TRUE or FALSE (string)

  This error indicates that an incorrect value was used for a command-line argument. Verify the syntax of the MIG utility and make sure that a valid value is used for all arguments.

- command name not found (string)

  This error indicates that the migrate.bsq script might be corrupt. Make sure that the Migration utility and the migrate.bsq are compatible with the target version 8 software.

- command not of form CMD(arg1, arg2,..)

  This error indicates that the migrate.bsq script might be corrupt. Make sure that the Migration utility and the migrate.bsq are compatible with the target version 8 software.

- copy long command must be of the form COPYLONG(U1, T1, C1...)

  This error indicates that the migrate.bsq script might be corrupt. Make sure that the Migration utility and the migrate.bsq are compatible with the target version 8 software.

- could not find single contiguous extent of *number* bytes for c_file#_block#

  This error indicates that the SYSTEM tablespace might be fragmented and you do not have enough contiguous free space. Add more space to the SYSTEM tablespace and rerun the Migration utility.

- could not find single contiguous extent of *number* bytes for c_ts#

  This error indicates that the SYSTEM tablespace might be fragmented and you do not have enough contiguous free space. Add more space to the SYSTEM tablespace and rerun the Migration utility.

- current version: str—Database must be version 7.1 or later

  You are trying to migrate an Oracle database that is prior to version 7.1. You will have to first migrate the source database to the latest release of Oracle7 and then rerun the Migration utility.

- data type must be long for column *name*

  This error indicates that the migrate.bsq script might be corrupt. Make sure that the Migration utility and the migrate.bsq are compatible with the target version 8 software.

- datafile is offline while tablespace is online—apply media recovery and bring datafile online before migration—*datafile*

  You have an offline datafile in a tablespace that is online. You should apply media recovery to the datafile, bring it online, and then rerun the Migration utility.

- error closing file *name*

  Indicates problems with the disk or user permissions. Verify that you don't have any problem with the space or quota on the disk, file access permissions, or bad disks. Fix any problem found and rerun the Migration utility.

- fixed portion of control file does not fit in *number* bytes

  Check the control file for possible corruption. If corruption exists, you should recover from this problem using the steps described in Chapter 28, "Performing Backups and Recovery." After you have recovered from the lost control file, you can rerun the Migration utility.

- insufficient space for new dictionaries, *number* bytes needed, *number* found

  The SYSTEM tablespace might be fragmented and you do not have enough contiguous free space. Add more space to the SYSTEM tablespace and rerun the Migration utility.

- migration can't proceed—database blocksize is less than Oracle8's minimum block size 2K

  Oracle8*i* requires that the blocksize be at least 2KB. The Oracle7 database that you are trying to migrate has a blocksize that is less than 2KB. You should rebuild the Oracle7 database and use a blocksize of at least 2KB, and then rerun the Migration utility.

- migration cannot proceed with active transaction or offline tablespaces with outstanding undo

  One or more tablespaces was not offlined cleanly. Resolve the in-doubt transactions, make sure that the tablespaces are offlined cleanly, and then rerun the Migration utility.

- MULTIPLIER value must be at least 2

  Oracle8*i* requires that the multiplier value be at least 2. This value is used to determine the initial size of the version 8 I_file#_block#. Rerun the Migration utility with a MULTIPLIER value of at least 2.

- NEW_DBNAME name too long—maximum length is 8 characters

  Rerun the Migration utility after specifying a new database name of 8 characters or less.

- ORA-number

  Resolve the particular Oracle ORA error and rerun the Migration utility.

- parameter buffer overflow

  Reduce the size of the initialization file by removing any obsolete parameters and rerun the Migration utility.

- unable to allocate buffer space to copy longs

  Make sure that you have enough memory on the system.

- V8 catalog space requirement: *number*

  This error specifies the amount of additional space required in the SYSTEM tablespace so that the Migration utility runs successfully.

Summary

Planning is a very important step in performing a migration from Oracle7 to Oracle8*i*. Several methods can be used to migrate, such as using the MIG utility, the Oracle Data Migration Assistant, and Export/Import. This chapter discussed how the migration can be performed by using the MIG utility.

Just like other strategies, migration using the MIG utility can be involved and it depends on the project scope and depth. One of the benefits of the MIG utility is that it can perform a check for the available space to ensure that the migration will complete smoothly.

4

MIGRATION USING
THE MIGRATION
UTILITY

Migration Using the Data Migration Assistant

IN THIS CHAPTER

The Oracle Data Migration Assistant is available only for migrations from Oracle7 to Oracle8*i*, version 8.1. It automatically performs many of the steps you would otherwise have to execute manually if you used the Oracle Migration Utility, discussed in the previous chapter. You cannot use this tool if you are migrating to Oracle8, version 8.0, and you might not be able to use it if your current database is not at a sufficiently high release level of Oracle7. On some operating systems, for example, your database must be at release level 7.1.4 or higher in order to use the Oracle Data Migration Assistant. On other systems, the cut-off release might be 7.1.3, or even 7.2, instead of 7.1.4. You need to check your operating system–specific documentation to determine whether you can migrate your database with this tool.

CAUTION

If you are using the Oracle Parallel Server option, you cannot use the Oracle Data Migration Assistant to migrate your database. Oracle does not support such a migration, and you must choose an alternate method. We recommend that you read Chapter 1, "Steps to Perform Migration," and review the migration options listed there to help you decide which is the best method for you to migrate your database.

Suppose that you don't have a supported version of Oracle7, but you still want to use the Oracle Data Migration Assistant to migrate to Oracle8*i*. First, you must upgrade your database to a supported version, and second, use the Oracle Data Migration Assistant to upgrade to Oracle8*i*. To perform the initial upgrade, you will have to install a supported release of Oracle7—we recommend that you choose release 7.3—and then upgrade to this release. You can find details of how to perform such an upgrade in the Oracle7 migration documentation.

Like the Migration Utility, the Oracle Data Migration Assistant performs a migration of your database *in situ*. In other words, the database you migrate will begin as your Oracle7 database and end up as your Oracle8*i* database. No files will be moved and no copies of your database files will be needed. In general, the time taken to complete a migration this way depends on the number of datafiles and rollback segments you have, because the headers of these objects have to be modified, and on the size of your Data Dictionary. The latter influences the migration time because it is completely rebuilt during the migration processing.

If you think about this, it should be obvious that either the entire database will be migrated or none of it will, should there be a problem along the way. If you need to migrate only a portion of your production database, either for testing your migration strategy or because you don't need everything from your current production system, you must create a temporary Oracle7 database to hold just that portion. You will then apply the migration processing to this temporary database only. Throughout this chapter, I will assume that the database you are migrating

is a complete database, regardless of whether it represents your complete production database or a subset thereof.

We have broken down the migration process using the Oracle Data Migration Assistant into the following six main steps:

1. Define system resource requirements for Data Migration Assistant
2. Prepare the Oracle7 database for Data Migration Assistant
3. Install Oracle8*i* for Data Migration Assistant
4. Migrate the database using Data Migration Assistant
5. Complete the migration using Data Migration Assistant
6. Troubleshoot and abandon a migration with Data Migration Assistant

Each of these steps is covered in its own section of this chapter. Generally, you will perform the two activities listed in step 3—install Oracle8*i*—and step 4—migrate the database—as part of a single session. It is possible that some of you might install Oracle8*i* before deciding to use the Oracle Data Migration Assistant. For example, you could complete the installation with the intent of migrating using the Migration Utility and then change your mind. For those of you who are in such a situation, or find yourselves with Oracle8*i* already installed for any reason whatsoever, you can, of course, skip step 3. However, you still need to check that you have the required resources and prepare your Oracle7 database before applying the contents of that section to your database.

The Oracle Data Migration Assistant completes the majority of the conversions required to prepare your database for Oracle8*i*. It changes the physical contents of your datafile header blocks and redo file header blocks and it prepares a new control file structure. It also begins the process of replacing your Oracle7 Data Dictionary with an Oracle8*i* Data Dictionary. In many cases, it is this last operation that causes the most problems with migration projects. This is because the program builds a second version of your Data Dictionary inside your SYSTEM tablespace. The Oracle8*i* version, which is typically almost twice the size of your Oracle7 Data Dictionary, has to reside in the free space of your current SYSTEM tablespace. As you might guess, the process fails if there is insufficient space for Oracle to build this new version of the Data Dictionary.

If you install Oracle8*i* independently of running the Oracle Data Migration Assistant program, you can use an option of the migration program to check the space you have available in the SYSTEM tablespace. Execute the migration program, as explained in the section of Chapter 4 titled "Migration Utility Command-line Options," using the CHECK_ONLY option. The program will inform you whether you have sufficient space to hold the new Data Dictionary. The program takes very little time to run with this option and takes the guesswork out of sizing your SYSTEM tablespace.

System Resource Requirements for Data Migration Assistant

You will need diskspace in two different locations to complete the migration using the Oracle utility. First, you will need a SYSTEM tablespace large enough to hold both your current and your new Data Dictionary. Second, you will need space for your new version's Oracle home directory structure. Although your Oracle7 diskspace can be used to store some of the new Oracle home—there won't be room for all of it—we don't recommend replacing your Oracle7 directory contents until after the migration is fully completed, which will require you to maintain both versions concurrently for a time.

The amount of space required for the Data Dictionary depends on the number and type of objects defined in the database. In general, you should expect the size of the new Oracle8*i* dictionary to be almost twice the size of your Oracle7 dictionary. As mentioned previously, if you do install Oracle8*i* independently of running the Oracle Data Migration Assistant, you can use the migration program to determine if you have sufficient space in your SYSTEM tablespace. The command you need to execute is covered in Chapter 4, under the section heading "Migration utility command-line options."

Should you determine that you need more space for your Data Dictionary to hold the Oracle8*i* Data Dictionary alongside your current Oracle7 dictionary, you need to add a new datafile, sized to provide the additional space. This can be done by using the command

```
ALTER TABLESPACE system     ADD DATAFILE 'filename' SIZE size_in_bytes;
```

issued by the user SYS from a Server Manager or a SQL*Plus session. Use a fully qualified directory and filename for *filename*, such as this Windows NT example:

```
    e:\orant\v7.3\database\sys02.dbf
```

For the *size_in_bytes* value, you can supply a simple number, such as 50000000, for 50 million bytes (note that there are no commas), or you can use the letter M to indicate megabytes, as in 50M. If you don't have a sufficiently large extent of free space on your database disks to support a single new file, you can add as many smaller files as you need. The following example, from a UNIX environment, shows how to add three files with a total space of 60 megabytes to your SYSTEM tablespace:

```
ALTER TABLESPACE system ADD DATAFILE
```

➡   `'/disk1/oracle7.3/database/syst02' SIZE 20M,`

➡   `'/disk1/oracle7.3/database/syst03' SIZE 20M,`

➡   `'/disk1/oracle7.3/database/syst04' SIZE 20M;`

There isn't a program to define how much space will be required by your new Oracle home directory. However, you can determine the approximate size by reading the installation manual

for your specific hardware and software environment. You should find a chapter in that manual that lists the space requirements for the basic installation and the various options. As a very rough guide, you should expect the installed Oracle8*i* binaries to require about three times the space of your current Oracle7 binaries, depending on the specific version of Oracle7 you are using. The total space for your Oracle8*i* home directory structure, excluding your database files, could approach one gigabyte.

One other change in your space requirements is of particular importance if you are using raw devices for your control files. Because of additional information stored in Oracle8*i* control files, they can be up to 100 times larger than their Oracle7 counterparts. Additionally, control files in Oracle8*i* are no longer fixed in size. They can grow dynamically as a result of changes in your parameter file or simply through the automatic generation of backup and recovery information. Although you should ensure that you have the required space for the new control files on whatever type of file system you are using, you need to take particular care if you are using raw devices because raw partitions cannot grow to accommodate expanding file sizes.

Prepare the Oracle7 Database for Data Migration Assistant

When you are ready to prepare your database for migration, we recommend that you modify it to prevent users from accessing it. To do this, you need to drop all current connections and place it into restricted mode. This allows only users with the RESTRICTED SESSION system privilege to make new connections. If you have assigned your privileges correctly, this will prevent anyone but you or your immediate colleagues from accessing the database until the migration is complete and you are ready to allow users to log in again.

NOTE

To place your database in restricted mode, you need either to shut it down and restart it in restricted mode or modify the current instance to be in restricted mode. If you are using Enterprise Manager, you can perform the shutdown and startup commands using its instance management screens, remembering to select the RESTRICT option for the startup. If you are using Server Manager, you use the STARTUP RESTRICT command following the shutdown command. If you use the SHUTDOWN command, you will automatically disconnect all users except the one used to perform the shutdown. If, on the other hand, you simply alter the instance, with the ALTER SYTEM ENABLE RESTRICTED SESSION command in Server Manager, any current users will remain connected, regardless of whether or not they have RESTRICTED SESSION privilege. To ensure that you have exclusive access to the database, you should terminate all other sessions but your own, using repeated executions of the ALTER SYSTEM KILL SESSION command.

You might even want to change the database to a restricted status before you perform the SYSTEM tablespace space check discussed in the previous section. This will prevent user activity from adding to the contents of the Data Dictionary, for example, by issuing commands that add new extents to a segment, after you check whether you have sufficient space.

Complete a Database Backup

Before you begin the migration process, you should protect your Oracle7 database and its contents by performing a full, cold backup. This means shutting down the database with the NORMAL or the IMMEDIATE option and then copying all the database files—datafiles, online redo log files, and at least one copy of your control files—to the backup media. If things go wrong with the migration process, or you decide you need to use Oracle7 for a little longer, this backup might be your only way to retrieve your production system. Therefore, you might also want to include your parameter file and archived log files in this backup, along with any key scripts you might need to use if you restore your Oracle7 database for any reason.

If you create your backup before proceeding with the remaining preparation steps, you will be able to restore your database to its current operating functionality. However, if you expect to attempt another migration, you will have to repeat all the preparation steps you apply after taking the backup. If you have time, therefore, you might consider making a backup at this point in the process and then making an additional one after you have completed your preparations. Of course, if you decide, after reading the rest of this section, that the changes you might need to make would not significantly impact the use of your database, even if you restore it as a production Oracle7 database, you only need to make a post-preparation backup.

Confirm Release Number Compatibility

Next, you need to confirm that your database release number is the same as, or higher than, the earliest release number supported by the Oracle Data Migration Assistant. If it is lower than this release, which will be documented in your operating system–specific manuals, you will need to upgrade it to at least the minimum-supported release number. We recommend that you upgrade to release 7.3 if you have to perform such a preliminary step. Of course, you can choose to migrate using a different method if you don't want to take the time to perform this initial upgrade.

Enable and Confirm Procedural Option Capability

Another item you need to check and, if necessary, address, is to confirm that you have the Procedural Option (as it is known in Oracle7) installed. The easiest way to check for this is to start up SQL*Plus or Server Manager and see whether the banner lines, following the Copyright line displayed when the product starts up, contain a line beginning with the words

"PL/SQL Release…" followed by a release number and production status. If you don't see such a line, you need to install the option by running the Oracle7 installation program and selecting the Procedural Option product. We suggest that you refer to your Oracle7 installation documentation if you are not sure how to perform such an installation.

Restore Offline Tablespaces and Datafiles

Next, you should check for any tablespaces that are offline. You can execute the command

```
SELECT tablespace_name, status FROM dba_tablespaces
```

to find this out. You should then bring all your offline tablespaces back online unless you're certain that they were taken offline by using the NORMAL option.

Any tablespaces taken offline with the TEMPORARY or the IMMEDIATE option will be unavailable after migration to Oracle8/Oracle8*i*. If you cannot get them back online, therefore, you might as well drop them. If you leave tablespaces offline because they were taken offline normally, or if you return them to offline status with the NORMAL option after getting them online, the datafiles for these tablespaces will not be converted as part of the migration. However, Oracle will convert them as they are brought back online without any problems.

NOTE

If you are using a later release of Oracle7, you can use the dynamic performance view, V$RECOVER_FILE, to check the status of your datafiles and their tablespaces. Issue the query:

```
SELECT * FROM v$recover_file;
```

and look for any rows with values other than OFFLINE in the ONLINE column and OFFLINE NORMAL in the ERROR column. These rows represent datafiles, or the tablespaces they belong to, which need to be brought back online prior to migration. You can use the V$DATAFILE view to match the file number from V$RECOVER_FILE with its filename. When online, a tablespace can be taken offline again as long as this is done with the NORMAL option.

If the query produces no rows in its output, all your files and tablespaces are online, and you can continue with your migration preparation without any further concern about offline tablespaces or datafiles.

Similarly, you must also ensure that all your datafiles are online. You can check the DBA_DATA_FILES view for the status. If any are offline and you can't bring them back online because they need recovery, the Migration Utility will fail with errors. When you have

all your datafiles online, make sure that the physical files are named and located in the correct directories. Also, if your redo logs are stored on raw devices, make sure that they are accessible to the server in which you plan to run the Oracle Data Migration Assistant.

Remove Special Users and Roles

The migration process will create a temporary user called MIGRATE. Because this user eventually will be dropped along with the Oracle7 Data Dictionary objects, ensure that you don't already have a database user, or a role, with this name. If you do have a user with this name, create a new schema to contain the MIGRATE user's objects, or use a user-level export and plan to re-import the user's schema following the migration. In either case, remember to drop this MIGRATE user, with the CASCADE option, before continuing with the Migration Utility processing.

If you have a role called MIGRATE, you must drop it or rename it temporarily until after you complete the migration. To rename it, you will have to create a new role and grant it all the privileges from the MIGRATE role. You should grant the new role to the same roles and users to which MIGRATE was granted. Even if you don't do this, you might need to record the information about the MIGRATE role's granted privileges and the roles and users to which it has been granted. When this is done, you can drop the MIGRATE role. After the migration, you will need to reverse the steps to restore the role to its initial state.

> **NOTE**
>
> To determine whether you already have users defined with either of the names that are needed for the migration to Oracle8*i*, you can issue the following query:
>
> ```
> SELECT username FROM dba_users
> ➡WHERE username IN ('MIGRATE', 'OUTLN');
> ```
>
> This query will return no rows if you don't have any users with a problem name, or else will list the name or names of such users. Similarly, you can check for roles with the same names by issuing the following command:
>
> ```
> SELECT role FROM dba_roles
> ➡WHERE role IN ('MIGRATE', 'OUTLN');
> ```
>
> As with the query for usernames, this will return no rows if you don't have a role with one of the reserved names, or will list the names of the roles that do exist.

You will also have to check for, and remove, any user or role with the name OUTLN. This is because a schema called OUTLN is created automatically as part of every Oracle8*i* database.

Unlike the MIGRATE user discussed previously, the OUTLN user will remain in the database after the migration. You must therefore take steps to remove the OUTLN schema or role permanently. Presumably, you will want to move it to a new name before dropping it.

If OUTLN is a user, you can create a new user and export the OUTLN user's schema, and then import it again using the FROMUSER and TOUSER options of the Import command. If OUTLN is a role, you will have to perform the same steps as described previously to "rename" a MIGRATE role. That is, you need to create a new role and grant it the same privileges as the OUTLN role. You will then have to grant the new role to the same users as those who had been granted the OUTLN role. When you have made all the necessary changes, whether OUTLN is a userid or a role, don't forget to drop the OUTLN object.

Set SYSTEM Rollback Segment Storage Options

The next set of changes you might need to make in your Oracle7 database are related to your SYSTEM rollback segment. First, you need to ensure that your SYSTEM rollback segment does not have an OPTIMAL value set. To check this, you can issue the following query:

```
SELECT n.name, s.optsize
➡  FROM v$rollname n, v$rollstat s
➡  WHERE n.usn = s.usn
➡  AND n.name = 'SYSTEM';
```

The column OPTSIZE should not contain a value indicating that OPTIMAL was not set for the SYSTEM rollback segment. If it does contain a number, you need to change the rollback segment's storage. You can change it back again to its current value after you complete the migration. To expedite this, you should make a note of the current value shown under OPTSIZE.

Use the following command to remove the OPTIMAL setting from your SYSTEM rollback segment:

```
ALTER ROLLBACK SEGMENT system STORAGE (OPTIMAL NULL);
```

You might want to confirm that the command was successful by repeating the query used earlier and checking for a NULL entry in the OPTSIZE column. If you want to restore the previous value after the migration, you can use the same ALTER ROLLBACK command, substituting the value from OPTSIZE that you (hopefully) recorded in place of the NULL keyword.

The second change you might have to make to the SYSTEM rollback segment is to allow it to acquire the largest possible number of extents supported by a single segment header block. This value will depend on your database block size. Table 5.1 shows the typical number of extents allowed per segment by database block size. You can confirm that the number is valid

for your database by issuing the following command and comparing the results with the values in Table 5.1:

```
SELECT DISTINCT max_extents FROM dba_segments;
```

In the query results, you should see one value that is the same as, or very close to, one of the default maximum extent counts from the table.

TABLE 5.1   Default Maximum Extent Counts by Database Block Size

Oracle Database Block Size (in Kilobytes)	*Default Maximum Extent Count*
2	121
4	249
8	505
16	1,017
32	2,041

Use this value to set your SYSTEM rollback segment's maximum extent count, using a command similar to the following:

```
ALTER ROLLBACK SEGMENT system STORAGE (MAXEXTENTS 249);
```

If you already know your default maximum extent count, you can combine both of the SYSTEM rollback changes in one command, should you need to make them both. For example, if you needed to set your OPTIMAL storage value back to NULL and change your maximum extent count to 505, you could execute the single command:

```
ALTER ROLLBACK SEGMENT system

➥    STORAGE (MAXEXTENTS 505 OPTIMAL NULL);
```

If you want to check your current setting for the maximum extents assigned to the SYSTEM rollback segment, either so you can decide if you need to make any changes, or to be able to reset it after the migration, you can use the following query:

```
SELECT max_extents

➥    FROM dba_rollback_segments

➥    WHERE segment_name = 'SYSTEM';
```

Remember to execute this query before you issue the ALTER ROLLBACK SEGMENT command and to record the value if you want to be able to change back to it after the migration.

Modify the Initialization Parameter File

Certain parameters in an Oracle7 initialization parameter file, commonly known as the *init.ora* file, have to be set to specific values, or removed, for the migration to be successful. Check your current parameter file for the following parameters and reset the values if necessary.

JOB_QUEUE_PROCESSES

If your database uses snapshots that are updated automatically, you probably have this parameter set to the number of SNPn background processes you need to perform these updates efficiently. These background jobs must be terminated for the duration of the migration. The easiest way to do this is simply to comment out the parameter in your init.ora file, using the hash symbol "#" at the start of the entry. This way, you can easily restart the jobs after the migration by deleting the hash symbol.

LARGE_POOL_SIZE

Oracle8*i* can automatically size the large pool based on the setting of SHARED_POOL_SIZE and a new parameter, PARALLEL_AUTOMATIC_TUNING. To avoid problems during the final steps of the migration process, you might want to resize your shared and large pools. We recommend that you comment out the LARGE_POOL_SIZE parameter, if you have it set, and add its value to your SHARED_POOL_SIZE parameter value. The migration processing will only need to make use of the shared pool, so these settings should ensure that you don't run into space limitation problems during the migration.

You can restore your original values after the migration completes, or you can examine the behavior of the shared and large pools along with the setting of PARALLEL_AUTOMATIC_TUNING and determine if you want to use new values. To help you return to your current settings, you should include a comment in your parameter file to identify what they were.

DB_DOMAIN

Oracle8*i* no longer applies a default value to this parameter if it is not set, unlike all previous releases of Oracle where DB_DOMAIN was a valid parameter. For this reason, you should ensure that your parameter file includes this parameter and has a value assigned to it. This will allow any database activity that relied on the setting, even if it were the default setting, to continue throughout the migration process. If your init.ora file does not include this parameter, add it with the value of .WORLD as shown here:

```
DB_DOMAIN = .WORLD
```

If you already have a value for DB_DOMAIN set, leave it as it is during, and even after, your migration to Oracle8*i*. If you have set the value as shown previously, you might or might not need to leave it set after the migration. That will depend on how your applications access the database through SQL*Net/Net8.

IFILE

If you are using an included parameter file, you need to check it for the same parameters as you do your main init.ora file. Note that if the same parameter appears in both files, the last one processed will be the one established for the instance. For example, if your primary init.ora file contains the value .WORLD for the DB_DOMAIN value, and the file identified by IFILE contains the value .PROD_SYS for the parameter, only one of these values will be used. If the IFILE entry in init.ora precedes the DB_DOMAIN entry, the value for DB_DOMAIN will be .WORLD, but if the DB_DOMAIN entry comes first, followed by the IFILE parameter later in the file, PROD_SYS will be the value for DB_DOMAIN.

CAUTION

If you are using an included parameter file with the IFILE parameter, don't get caught out if you are trying to comment out a parameter. Commenting out a parameter in either the main init.ora file or the included file will not automatically negate a value if the parameter is repeated in the other file with a value. This is true whether the commented-out line is logically before or after the uncommented line. To ensure that the parameter is not given a value, you must comment it out wherever it occurs in either file.

If you make changes to either the primary init.ora file or to the included file, remember to save the changes before proceeding with the migration.

Resolve Pending Transactions

If you've used distributed transactions in your Oracle7 database, you need to check that none are still pending because of problems with the two-phase commit mechanism, such as lost network connections or offline databases. You can find such transactions by examining the DBA_2PC_PENDING table. If you have any such transactions, you need to commit or to roll them back manually. You can find the instructions on how to do this in your Distributed Database documentation, including details on how to determine if you should commit or roll back.

When these steps are complete, you should perform a database shutdown. You must use the NORMAL or IMMEDIATE option; a SHUTDOWN ABORT command can leave the database with outstanding transactions that would leave data integrity compromised following the migration. This is because two structures needed to resolve an aborted shutdown are modified by the migration process—redo log files and rollback segments.

After the database is shut down, you might want to make a full backup. You should definitely do this if you decided not to make a backup before you prepared your database for migration, as discussed at the beginning of this section. You can skip this step if you are content with the backup you made prior to making any changes in preparation for the migration. The important

thing to remember is that you might have to resort to restoring your database from an Oracle7 backup if the migration process encounters an unrecoverable problem.

Hot backup option before migration

If you don't have the time to complete an offline backup, you can complete an online backup immediately before shutting it down for the migration. Remember that, as soon as it's closed, you should back up the online redo logs as well. If you need to restore the Oracle7 version for another migration attempt, you have to recover the backup to a stable point, which requires the contents of the online redo.

Install Oracle8*i* for Data Migration Assistant

To begin the installation process, you will need to follow your operating system–specific directions to start up the Oracle Universal Installer. This product is provided as part of your Oracle8*i* distribution. When you have stared the Universal Installer, you should respond to the installation prompts using the suggested items listed in Table 5.2. During execution of the Universal Installer, you can see additional help about the product or the screen on which you are working by clicking on the Help button at any time.

TABLE 5.2 Screens and Responses for the Universal Installer with Oracle8*i*

Universal Installer Screen	*Your Response*
Welcome Screen	Click the Next button
File Locations Screen	Enter the full pathname for your desired Oracle8*i* home directory in the Destination block
Available Products Screen	Select the Oracle8*i* Enterprise Edition or the Oracle8*i* option
Installation Types Screen	Select the Custom or Minimal installation to avoid creating a starter database
Custom Installation Screens	If you selected Custom on the previous screen, be sure to choose the options you used in Oracle7 if you want to continue their use in Oracle8*i*
Upgrading or Migrating and Existing Database Screen	Complete the following three actions: 1. Check the Upgrade or Migrate an Existing Database selection box 2. Choose your Oracle7 database name 3. Click the Next button
Summary Screen	Confirm that all the settings are correct; then click the Install button

The installation itself might take some time, so you need to be patient (or go for a cup of coffee, or something). When it completes, the Oracle Data Migration Assistant, possibly along with other assistants, will be started. You can use this assistant to migrate your Oracle7 database to Oracle8*i*, as explained in the next section. Note that an alternate method to invoke the Oracle Data Migration Assistant is explained at the beginning of the section, so you can still perform the migration if something prevented it from starting during your installation procedure.

Migrate the Database Using Data Migration Assistant

If you have just completed the installation steps described in the previous section, you should be able to navigate directly to the Oracle Data Migration Assistant Welcome screen. If, for any reason, you are unable to do this, follow the instructions in the next paragraph to get started.

For those of you who have already installed Oracle8*i* at another time, you can start the migration using the Oracle Data Migration Assistant by invoking the program directly from the operating system. How you do this depends on your operating system, and should be covered in your operating system–specific documentation. For UNIX and Windows NT users, we have provided what should be the appropriate command here.

On UNIX, type the following command at the operating system prompt:

```
odma
```

On Windows NT, select:

```
Start > Programs > Oracle (for the Oracle8i release) >
```

```
➥Migration Utilities > Oracle Data Migration Assistant
```

This should bring up the Welcome window of the Oracle Data Migration Assistant that the installation process can also invoke automatically.

> **NOTE**
>
> On most systems, the Oracle Data Migration Assistant Welcome screen has a check option that allows you to bypass the screen if you invoke the assistant a second, or subsequent, time. Therefore, you might not see the Welcome screen if you, or possibly a colleague, have already started the assistant once before and chosen to bypass it.

Table 5.3 lists the various screens that you will encounter while running the Oracle Data Migration Assistant and provides suggestions on how to respond to each screen. If you need further help, either overall documentation or specific to the screen you are working on, you can click the Help button that is available on each screen. Running the Oracle Data Migration Assistant will relocate certain files and will modify the content of your online datafile header blocks, your online rollback segments, and your control files.

CAUTION

To complete its work, the Oracle Data Migration Assistant will have to ensure that the database is shut down. If, for any reason, it is still open, any connected users will have their sessions terminated without their work being saved—the assistant uses the IMMEDIATE option of the SHUTDOWN command.

TABLE 5.3   Screens and Responses for the Oracle Data Migration Assistant

Screen Identifier	Suggested Response
Before You Migrate or Upgrade screen	1. Check, and correct if necessary, the conditions of your Oracle7 database 2. Click the Next button
Select a Database screen	1. Select the name of the instance used for your Oracle7 database 2. Click the Next button
Database Password and INIT.ORA File screen	1. Check, and correct if necessary, the pathname to your Oracle8*i* home directory (it should be the same as the one named on the File Locations screen during the installation) 2. Check, and correct if necessary, the full pathname to your Oracle7 parameter file, *initSID.ora* 3. Check, and correct if necessary, the pathname to your Oracle7 home z directory 4. Click the Next button
Choose Migration Type screen	1. Choose a migration type. Note that a CUSTOM migration will require you to answer a number of additional questions; do not choose this option if you are not certain you are prepared to do this
Various Custom Migration screens	1. Fill out the necessary information on each screen 2. Click the Next button
Confirm Backup screen	1. If you have not completed a backup of your Oracle7 database, click the Cancel button to exit from the assistant; make a cold database backup before repeating the program 2. If you have completed a backup of your Oracle7 database, either before or after preparing it for the migration, click the Next button

continues

TABLE 5.3 Continued

Screen Identifier	Suggested Response
Start the Migration or Upgrade screen	1. Confirm the specifications and, if necessary, click the Back button on each successive screen until you can correct any errors; then click the Next button until you return to this screen 2. If the specifications are correct, click the Next button
Listener.ora Migration Confirmation screen	1. If you plan to use Enterprise Manager, click Yes to allow the assistant to make necessary modifications to your *listener.ora* file 2. If you do not plan to use Enterprise Manager, click No to prevent the assistant from making changes to your *listener.ora* file

NOTE

When you click the Next button on the Start Migration or Upgrade screen, the Oracle Data Migration Assistant will display a status bar showing the progress of the migration steps. These steps might take some time to complete.

Some of you might be concerned about what changes the final steps of the Oracle Data Migration Assistant might be making if you choose to let it modify your *listener.ora* file. This is the option you choose on the last screen of the assistant program, as shown in Table 5.3. Very simply, the changes involve expanding the SID_DESC entry to include the global database name (consisting of the database name and its domain name) and the pathname to the Oracle8*i* home directory. If a global name was already included, the assistant replaces it with the new one and includes both the old and the new names in the SERVICE_NAMES parameter. Also, if the instance name is not the same as the database name, the assistant will replace it with the database name.

To give you an example, suppose that a database called ACC1, with an Oracle7 instance name of ACCG and a domain of .ACC_PROD, had the following SID_DESC as part of its *listener_ora* entry:

```
(SID_DESC =
        (GLOBAL_DBNAME = acc1.acc_prod)
        (SID_NAME = ACCG)
)
```

Assuming that the new Oracle8*i* home directory is /disk2/oracle/v8.1 and the domain was reset to .WORLD, the assistant would add a new entry defined as follows:

```
(SID_DESC =
        (GLOBAL_DBNAME = acc1.world)
        (ORACLE_HOME = /disk1/oracle/v8.1)
        (SID_NAME = ACC1)
)
```

In addition, the assistant would add an entry to the SERVICE_NAMES parameter, resulting in the following:

```
SERVICE_NAMES = acc1.world, acc1.acc_prod
```

On some operating systems, such as Windows NT, the assistant will remove the entry for the Oracle7 version of the database, leaving just the replacement entry. On other systems, such as UNIX, both the new and the old entries are left in the *listener.ora* file. In either case, the last step performed by the Oracle Data Migration Assistant is to start up the listener using whichever version of the *listener.ora* file is available.

Complete the Migration Using Data Migration Assistant

Now that the Oracle Data Migration Assistant has completed its work, you should be able to start up an instance to run some scripts needed to finish the migration. We suggest that you start Server Manager in line mode and execute the following commands to start up your instance in the correct mode:

- CONNECT INTERNAL
- STARTUP RESTRICT

NOTE

In order to start your database after running the Oracle Data Migration Assistant, you might have to locate your parameter file and then use the PFILE option of the STARTUP command to identify it to the instance. In some cases, the file will have been moved to its default location in the Oracle8*i* home directory structure.

You can now complete your remaining database migration activities from this Server Manager session. In the following, I list the specific steps for you to implement:

1. Open a log file to track the remaining conversion tasks performed on the database by issuing the command SPOOL *filename.log*, where you can choose whatever filename and extension you want.

2. If you want to watch the statements being executed on your terminal screen as you run the various scripts, you can issue the SET ECHO ON command.

3. If you have installed Advanced Replication, you need to run two scripts, CATREP.SQL and R0703040.SQL. Make sure that you run them in the order listed because R0703040.SQL performs an update to the information loaded by CATREP.SQL.

4. You might want to run the script UTLRP.SQL. Although optional, this script will recompile any invalid PL/SQL modules in your database. We recommend that you run it, as does the Oracle documentation, in case there are any problems. It is better to find these as early as possible rather than continuing on with further steps.

5. Terminate your logging activity by issuing the command SPOOL OFF and check the contents of your log file (which you named in step 1) for any errors. You might want to re-run any procedures that failed or recorded errors.

6. If you issued the SET ECHO ON command in step 2, you might want to terminate command echoing with the SET ECHO OFF command.

7. Issue the SHUTDOWN command to close the database normally and allow it to complete any other cleanup activities needed to finalize the migration process. You can use either the SHUTDOWN NORMAL or SHUTDOWN IMMEDIATE syntax. However, you must not use the SHUTDOWN ABORT command; doing so might corrupt your Oracle8*i* database.

Some of you might experience slow performance when running the scripts discussed in step 4. If this is the case, check the size of your large pool by issuing the command

```
SELECT value FROM V$PARAMETER
WHERE name = 'large_pool_size'
```

Should your log file, which you should examine in step 5, indicate that you have problems with the scripts discussed in steps 3 and 4, you can re-run them as many times as needed until the problems are fixed. Be sure to run them all in the same order as discussed in step 3 and 4 if dependencies exist between them. For example, if you have to re-run CATREP.SQL, you must run R0703040.SQL again afterwards. You are advised to re-run UTLRP.SQL any time you re-run any of the other listed scripts.

You might want to start another log file to store the results if you need to re-run one or more of the scripts. Use the SPOOL command, ideally with a different filename each time, to start a new log file, and the SPOOL OFF command to end the logging activity. If you cannot resolve some of the problems, you should consider abandoning the migration, as discussed in the following section, "Troubleshooting and Abandoning a Migration with Data Migration Assistant."

When you have successfully run the scripts and performed a normal (or immediate) database shutdown, your database should be ready for your post-migration testing. Before you can open it, however, you might need to modify your parameter file. Appendix B of the Oracle8*i* Migration manual, distributed as part of the release documentation set, contains a list of parameters that have become obsolete in each release since Oracle7. You need to remove all such parameters from your *init.ora* file. Additionally, you should verify that you have set appropriate values for parameters with changed meanings or defaults as described in the aforementioned Appendix. You might also want to change the COMPATIBLE parameter value to an Oracle8*i* release number—the Oracle Data Migration Assistant sets it to 8.0.5 automatically. Of course, until you are ready to make use of release 8.1 features, and add any new parameters to your parameter file to support them, you don't need to reset the COMPATIBLE parameter.

When you have edited and saved a valid Oracle8*i* parameter file, you should try to open your database. Use the STARTUP command, which you can issue from Server Manager or from SQL*Plus. When the database is open, confirm that you have a working Oracle8*i* database by looking at the banner displayed when you initiate your Server Manager or SQL*Plus session or by querying the V$VERSION dynamic performance table.

One final word of advice before you leave this chapter. It would be a very good idea to preserve your new Oracle8 database by performing another backup before you begin your testing. You should shut it down, again with the NORMAL or IMMEDIATE option, and create a cold backup. If you have problems with your tests, you can at least restore this version of the database and not have to repeat any of the migration steps unless, of course, you determine that this is what is required to fix the problems.

Troubleshooting and Abandoning a Migration with Data Migration Assistant

There are a number of reasons that a migration might fail. The most common are faults in the preparation and setup steps, or performing one or more steps in the wrong sequence. In some cases, the particular step being executed will simply fail, typically providing an error message to explain why. We will examine the different types of failures and the methods you can use to solve them in detail in Chapter 14, "Troubleshooting the Migration Process."

If you have run the Oracle Data Migration Assistant, you can still return your database to its Oracle7 state. The easiest way to do this is probably to restore the backup you made before you ran the program. However, if you don't have a usable backup for some reason, you need to execute the following steps:

1. Ensure that your environment is set to point to the Oracle7 home directory, using your Oracle7 installation guide if you are uncertain how to do this

2. Start the Oracle database using Server Manager

3. Drop the user called MIGRATE, if it has already been created, by issuing the command DROP USER MIGRATE CASCADE

4. Re-run the CATALOG.SQL and CATPROC.SQL scripts from the Oracle7 home directory structure

5. Run the following optional scripts: CATSVRMG.SQL if Server Manager is installed and CATREP.SQL if the Advanced Replication option is installed

> **CAUTION**
>
> When executing step 4, be sure that you execute the scripts from the Oracle home directory structure belonging to your Oracle7 installation. If you accidentally run the scripts from the Oracle8/Oracle8*i* installation, any subsequent attempt to migrate the database will fail again.

If you simply intend to re-run the Oracle Data Migration Assistant at this point, you should be able to do so, following the same steps as discussed earlier in this chapter. If you want to continue to use your database with Oracle7, this should also be possible. However, if you restored your database from a backup taken after you made the changes to prepare for the migration, you might need to back out those changes in order for your database to act exactly as it did before. For example, you might need to restore the OUTLN or MIGRATE user or role, or put certain datafiles or tablespaces offline again.

Summary

The Oracle Data Migration Assistant is a GUI tool that performs many of the tasks required to migrate to Oracle8*i* with minimal input from the database administrator who is performing the migration. I describe the input required for each screen of the assistant to complete a migration to Oracle8*i*. I also discuss the additional tasks you need to complete when migrating with the assistant, as well as some of the values that the assistant will store in various files in your Oracle8*i* environment.

I also discuss the situations in which it is not possible to use the Data Migration Assistant and suggest other options for you, when they exist, to complete your migration. Finally, as in other chapters where we discuss specific migration processing, I outline the troubleshooting steps that you might need to employ if the migration using the assistant should fail.

Migration Using Export/Import

IN THIS CHAPTER

The Export/Import tools are probably the most used tools for Oracle migrations since version 5 of the database. Unlike the migration tools provided with Oracle7, Oracle8, and Oracle8*i*, which are designed to migrate a database from one major release to the next release level and nothing more, Export/Import tools are generic in nature. They can be used to migrate database contents between many versions of Oracle, even from a higher release level to a lower release level. But migrations are not the only activities that Export/Import tools can perform. They are used to supplement database backup and recovery strategies, to reorganize the physical structure of a database, to change ownership of database objects, and to move databases between different operating systems, character sets, block sizes, and similar activities.

As a result of the tools' flexibility, which makes them very useful in a number of different ways, they are also less focused than the migration tools when it comes to the process of migrating your Oracle7 database to an Oracle8 or Oracle8*i* database. Consequently, they might not be quite as straightforward to use as either the Migration Utility or the Oracle Data Migration Assistant. The other issue is that the migration tools tend to work about as fast no matter how large the database happens to be. The speed of the Export/Import tools is very dependent on the database size. In this chapter, I will try to help you use the Export/Import tools for migration purposes as simply and as efficiently as possible.

One of the first issues to consider when planning to use Export/Import for a migration is to decide whether you will use just these tools, or supplement the activity with other tools. Of course, using just the tools themselves makes the process simpler, but might not be the most efficient approach. In fact, for DBAs with very large databases to migrate, the time required to run full exports and imports can be so great as to make this option impossible to use. By combining Export/Import with other tools, you can perform an efficient migration and gain some of the other benefits that are not available with the migration tools. These benefits include the ability to migrate portions of your database and to restructure the physical layout of the data. Even if you intend to migrate your entire database, the option to migrate parts of it can be useful for testing purposes prior to a complete migration.

The most useful approach to supplement Export/Import is to extract the data from the tables into files that can be used by the Oracle SQL*Loader utility. This places the most time-consuming part of the process—that of importing masses of data—onto SQL*Loader, which is able to run much more efficiently than Import by using its direct path mode and its parallel options. Although Oracle does not provide a utility to perform the data unload, it is reasonably easy to use SQL*Plus and its SPOOL option to create flat files that can be used by SQL*Loader.

Define System Resource Requirements for Export/Import

The main system resource you need to perform a migration with Export/Import is the space to store the information extracted from your Oracle7 (or even, for that matter, your Oracle6) database. You can use a disk, a tape, or a mixture of both for this storage. Of course, a disk will be

faster, but tape generally offers greater capacity. You can reduce disk space requirements if you use some form of compression. This can be done efficiently by using a pipe, if your operating system supports it, to take the Export output and direct it to the compression tool.

As with the Migration Utility, you can also reduce the need for disk space by removing the Oracle7 version before you perform the installation of the Oracle8*i* software when you use Export/Import. As with the other option, this can slow down the overall migration effort if there is a problem with the migration and you need to drop back to Oracle7.

The second resource you need is the Export program for your current release of the database. This should be readily available from the Oracle home directory used with the database you want to migrate.

> **NOTE**
>
> If you are still running a database earlier than version 6, you will need to upgrade it to at least version 6 before you perform an export in readiness for a migration to Oracle8*i*. This is because the entire kernel of the Oracle product was rewritten for version 6, and even the export files cannot be guaranteed to be read with complete certainty by the Oracle8*i* Import program.

If you want to use Export/Import along with tools to perform an unload and reload of the data, you will also have to develop or acquire such tools. A number of products are available from various vendors and also from free sources, such as the Internet, that will provide such capability. Of course, you can develop your own tools too.

Using SQL*Plus, you can build a SQL-generating SQL script to identify and save the contents of the tables you want to export. This will then allow you to export just the table definitions, which you can then import, followed by the reloading of the table contents. A sample SQL*Plus script is shown in Listing 6.1, which builds another script to save the rows from the tables that are identified in the listing.

LISTING 6.1   SQL*Plus Script to Generate Unload Script

```
REM Script to produce a script to copy the contents
REM of one or more tables into a flat file. After
REM this script completes, the script that will build
REM the output file containing table contents will
REM be in a file called "unload.sql" which you can
REM execute directly from the same SQL*Plus session
REM that you use to run this script, or you can edit
```

continues

LISTING 6.1   Continued

```
REM it first and then run it from SQL*Plus.
REM
REM Stop output of titles, page feeds, and row count
REM feedback to the script file. . .
REM
SET PAGESIZE 0 FEEDBACK OFF

REM Start the output to the script file,
REM "unload.sql" . . .
REM
SPOOL unload.sql

REM Query to produce name of table followed by list of
REM row contents for selected tables; the CHR(10) may need
REM to be modified if this does not produce the desired
REM linefeed plus carriage-return.
REM
REM You can insert any desired delimiter before or after
REM the table name field in the following statement, such
REM as the angle brackets around the table name as follows:
REM SELECT 'SELECT ''<' || table_name || '>'' FROM dual;'
REM
REM Similarly, you can write your own predicate to choose
REM which tables you want to dump if it would be easier than
REM listing them all, in a comma-delimited list of quoted
REM table names in response to the SQL*Plus prompt. . .

SELECT 'SELECT ''' || table_name || ''' FROM dual;'
|| CHR(10)
|| 'SELECT * FROM ' || table_name || ';'
FROM dba_tables
WHERE table_name IN (&list_of_tables)
/
REM Stop the output
SPOOL OFF

REM If you are not going to use the "unload.sql" file
REM immediately, you may wish to reset the PAGESIZE and
REM FEEDBACK values.
```

Assuming this script is saved in a file called *unload_table.sql*, a sample execution might look like the following:

```
SQL> @unload_table
Enter value for list_of_tables: 'CUSTOMERS','ORDERS'
```

```
old    5: WHERE table_name IN (&list_of_tables)
new    5: WHERE table_name IN ('CUSTOMERS','ORDERS')
SELECT 'ORDERS' FROM dual;
SELECT * FROM ORDERS;

SELECT 'CUSTOMER' FROM dual;
SELECT * FROM CUSTOMERS;
```

As noted in the script comments, you can modify the query that stores the table names and contents in the output file. For example, if you don't want to see the table names in front of each table's contents, you can omit the query from DUAL. On the other hand, you can identify the table name with any prefix, suffix, or both as shown with the angle bracket example in the script. You can also include additional line feed characters before or after the table name and contents. Also, as noted in the comments, you can add a list of tables based on a coded list of table names, or on the schema they belong to, or any other selection criteria you can code. For example, the following query will select tables belonging only to user ACCTING with no foreign key constraints:

```
SELECT table_name
FROM dba_tables
WHERE owner='ACCTING'
AND table_name NOT IN
  (SELECT table_name FROM dba_constraints
    WHERE constraint_type = 'R');
```

You could substitute the WHERE clause from the previous query, or any other clause that you might desire, into the WHERE clause of Listing 6.1.

Continuing my previous example, here I show you the output from the execution of the *unload.sql* file that was created from the *Customers* and the *Orders* tables:

> **NOTE**
>
> When creating SQL-generating SQL scripts, the script file that is created with the SPOOL command will typically contain lines of feedback from the original script. These will generate error messages if you execute the output file without editing them out first—as you see in the example—but they will not cause the required statements in the script to fail.

```
SQL> @unload
unknown command beginning "Enter valu..." - rest of line ignored.
unknown command beginning "old    5: W..." - rest of line ignored.
unknown command beginning "new    5: W..." - rest of line ignored.
```

```
ORDERS
        1487 26-FEB-99        116 FILLED


        1488 26-FEB-99        414 FILLED


        1489 26-FEB-99        712 FILLED


        1490 26-FEB-99        472 FILLED


        1491 26-FEB-99        308 FILLED


        1492 26-FEB-99        606 FILLED


        1494 26-FEB-99        203 FILLED


        1495 28-FEB-99        502 FILLED


        1496 28-FEB-99        801 FILLED


        1497 28-FEB-99        472 FILLED
This is a special rush order
        1499 28-FEB-99        700 FILLED


        1500 28-FEB-99        472 FILLED


        1501 28-FEB-99        300 FILLED


CUSTOMERS
        116 Ryan's Roofing
12232 Peralta Drive
Anaheim, CA 92611
```

```
        203 J.A.General Carpentry
1181 W Katella Avenue
Laguna Hills, CA 92623


        300 Majestic Glass
PO Box 138
Riverside, CA 93128


        308 Keifer-Riley Window Tinting
312 Big Springs Road
Garden Grove, CA 92625


        414 Abba Patio & Spa
20243 Pacific Coast Highway
Laguna Hills, CA 92622


        472 Homestead Garage Door Co
961 Saint Tropez Court
Dana Point, CA 92618


        502 A-Nelson Sectional Garage Door
19271 Irvine Boulevard
Mission Viejo, CA 92626


        606 California Entry Systems Inc.
91162 San Remo
Tustin, CA 92758


        700 H.J.Garrett Leather
23332 Mill Creek
Mission Viejo, CA 92626


        712 Furniture Warehouse
16133 Camino Capistrano
Laguna Hills, CA 92623


        801 Dayne's Home Furniture Center
7651 E 25th Avenue
Los Angeles, CA 90113
```

Typically, you would execute *unload.sql* with a spool file open so that the data is saved, as well as being displayed on the screen.

You will need to extract the rows belonging to each table, in turn from this spooled file and create a SQL*Loader control file to load these rows into your migrated database. Extracting the rows can be done simply with an editor, as can constructing the required control files. However, if you want, you can use another SQL-generating script to build the basic SQL*Loader control file for each table using the data from the DBA_TAB_COLUMNS data dictionary table.

Prepare the Oracle7 Database for Export/Import

You need to do very little to prepare your Oracle7 database if you are going to perform a complete migration using Export/Import. You don't even need to run a backup to preserve your current database, as long as you can recreate the SYSTEM tablespace easily because everything else should be in the Export dump file or, if you are unloading the data for use with SQL*Loader, in the export file and the data extract files. Of course, if you have a fast way to perform a backup, you might want to do this anyway because it can be a faster option than rebuilding your database from scratch should there be problems. As always, you should shut your database down with the NORMAL or IMMEDIATE option before making a premigration archive copy.

If you are going to migrate only a part of your database, either for test purposes or because only part of it will be needed after the migration, you need to do a little more preparatory work. For running a test migration on partial contents, you will need to build a separate database to hold only the objects you intend to migrate. This can be done while the production remains open and in use, as long as you don't need static data for your testing. Remember that unless you ask for it, an export file will not contain data that is all consistent at a single point in time. If you do want data that is internally consistent, you need to prevent access by the users while you make the export dump file, or use the Export option, CONSISTENT=Y, when you run it. This latter option might cause the export to fail unless you have sufficient rollback segment space to hold all the before images generated by users for the duration of the export process.

To migrate parts of the database and ignore the remainder, you have two options. You can either remove the unwanted objects before you run the Export command, or you can build a new database and move the required objects into it, as explained in the preceding paragraph. In either case, you should perform these steps after the database has been brought up-to-date by the users and all further activity will cease until the migration is complete. Anything not included in the export, or in the specially-built database, won't be available in the Oracle8*i*

database. To prevent further use of the database, you should shut it down and restart it in restricted mode by using the command STARTUP RESTRICT. This will prevent anyone without the RESTRICTED SESSION system privilege from logging into the open database.

If you decide to remove objects from the production database rather than build a new database to migrate, we really encourage you to make a backup before you begin. You should also seriously consider a backup if you intend to drop the database after you complete your new database with just the required objects. How you drop the objects you don't need or move the ones you do need is up to you. You have seen an example of SQL-generating SQL in Listing 6.1 that might be of use to you in this type of activity. In fact, to build a new database, you can use exactly the same techniques we suggested for performing the migration itself. That is, use Export/Import to move the object definitions and an unload routine plus SQL*Loader to transfer the table data.

When you have completed your preparations and your database is ready for migration, you should ensure that nobody can log on and make any further changes until you complete the migration. You can do this in the manner suggested earlier in this section—shut down and restart the database in restricted mode—or use some other technique. For example, you can remove all your users' privileges, which allow them to connect to the database, or you can set the total number of processes allowed by the instance to the background processes and your own session to perform the export and other tasks.

Install Oracle8*i* for Migration Using Export/Import

I suggest that you complete this step before you begin the export/unload of your Oracle7 database. This will enable you to quickly test the software before committing your resources to perform the migration. It will also reduce the period between the time you shut down your production Oracle7 database and restart it as an Oracle8*i* database. However, if you need to remove the Oracle7 database, software, or even both, from your system before installing Oracle8*i*, you will first need to complete the export, which I describe in the next section. Whether you complete the installation and prepare your Oracle8*i* database before or after you extract your Oracle7 data, you will need to execute the same steps to install your new release of the Oracle software.

To begin the software installation, you will need to follow your operating system specific directions to configure your server and to start up the Oracle Universal Installer, provided as part of your Oracle8*i* distribution. The specific instructions for the previous steps can be found in the *Oracle8i Installation and Configuration* manual for your system. Then respond to the installation prompts using the suggested items listed in Table 6.1.

TABLE **6.1**   Installation Options for Oracle8*i*

Installer Screen	*Your Response*
Welcome Screen	Click the Next button
File Locations Screen	Select a directory path separate from your Oracle7 Oracle Home
Available Products Screen	Select the Oracle8*i* Enterprise Edition or the Oracle8*i* option
Installation Types Screen	Select the Custom or Minimal installation to avoid creating a starter database
Custom Installation Screens	If you selected Custom on the previous screen, choose the options you used in Oracle7 and want to continue to use in Oracle8*i*
Upgrading or Migrating an Existing Database Screen	Click the Next button WITHOUT selecting the Upgrade or Migrate an Existing Database selection box
Create Database Screen	Select the No radio button, and then click the Next button
Summary Screen	After confirming that all the settings are correct, click the Install button, and then click the Exit button after the installation completes

NOTE

If you are using Oracle Parallel Server and want to use this option in Oracle8*i*, you must choose the Oracle8*i* Enterprise Edition from the Available Products screen and the Custom option from the Installation Types screen. You will also be presented with a Cluster Node Selection screen. You should select the nodes on which you want to install Oracle8*i*.

The installation itself generally takes a fair amount of time, so you need to be patient or find something else to do, such as surf your favorite Web sites (but don't tell your boss I told you to do that). At the end of the Universal Installer session, your Oracle8*i* installation will be complete. However, you will not have a database built if you followed the suggestions in Table 6.1. I recommended this approach because the installer is unlikely to be able to identify all the requirements to build a database that exactly matches the structure of your production system. In the next section, I will explain how to build your Oracle8*i* database.

Prepare the Oracle8*i* Database for Migration Using Export/Import

You will need to build a database using the Oracle8*i* installation to reflect your Oracle7 production database structure. If you have a script you used to build and maintain that database, you can use it to build its Oracle8*i* equivalent. Remember to increase the SYSTEM tablespace by roughly 50 to 70 percent of its Oracle7 size.

You might also want to build the tablespaces for your database instead of letting the import program build them for you. This is particularly important if you want to prevent Import from overwriting your Oracle7 datafiles. You might also need to increase the sizes for tablespaces holding indexes and rollback segments because of the increase in the length of the ROWID fields. I recommend about a ten percent increase in such tablespace sizes.

TIP

If you want to preserve your Oracle7 database and you are migrating to Oracle8*i* on the same machine, you will need to prevent the import program from creating the tablespaces as discussed in this section. You should also set the DESTROY option to NO in your import command. See the next section, "Perform the Export/Import" for details of the command options. This setting will prevent accidental loss of your Oracle7 datafiles should your new database not have all the required tablespaces defined.

If you don't have a script to build your equivalent database structure, you can obtain the information you will need for it as long as your Oracle7 database is still available (or you can restore it from the backup I recommended you make). The following statement will produce a listing of the names and sizes of the datafiles that comprise your SYSTEM tablespace:

```
SELECT file_name, bytes
FROM dba_data_files
WHERE tablespace_name = 'SYSTEM';
```

Similarly, you can find the names and sizes of the members of each of your online redo log groups using this query:

```
SELECT l.group#, l.thread#, f.member, l.bytes
FROM v$log l, v$logfile f
WHERE l.group# = f.group#
ORDER BY l.group#;
```

If you really want to, you can work on creating a SQL-generating SQL script to generate the statements needed to build your database. This can include the basic CREATE DATABASE command, including the SYSTEM tablespace definition, or it can be just for the additional tablespaces required by your production database. The latter is particularly useful if you want to change the datafile names (including locations, if you use full path names rather than operating system links), tablespace sizes, default storage parameter values, or auto-extensible characteristics. If you allow Import to create the tablespaces for you, they will be defined exactly as in your Oracle7 database.

No matter how you build the script to create your Oracle8*i* database, you should ensure that it will meet all your requirements. For example, as well as the tablespace changes just mentioned, you might want to rename your database, use a different character set, or change the sizes of your online redo log files. You might even want to make some, or all, of your non-SYSTEM tablespaces locally managed.

The other components of your new database that you might want to build are the rollback segments. This will allow you to change their original characteristics, such as size of extents, tablespace allocation, and so on. If you don't need to make such changes, you can allow Import to rebuild them just like your Oracle7 rollback segments. To change them, it is once again easier if you have a script that you used for your production Oracle7 database. You can then make a copy of this script and edit it to contain the new definitions you want to use. If you need to reconstruct such a script, you can run the script in Listing 6.2 against your Oracle7 database to generate the required statements.

LISTING 6.2   SQL*Plus Script to Generate Rollback Segment Creation Statements

```
REM Script to build CREATE ROLLBACK SEGMENT
REM commands for all rollback segments in
REM the database except the SYSTEM rollback
REM segment.
REM
REM The commands will be stored in the file,
REM RS_BUILD.SQL, which should be executed
REM in the Oracle8i database after the
REM required tablespaces have been built.
REM

REM Turn off headings and row count feedback, and open output
REM script file

SET PAGESIZE 0 FEEDBACK OFF
SPOOL rs_build.sql
```

```
REM Execute query to build required CREATE statements

SELECT 'CREATE ' || DECODE(owner,'SYS',' ',owner) || ' ROLLBACK SEGMENT ',
   segment_name || ' TABLESPACE ' || tablespace_name,
    ' STORAGE (INITIAL ' || initial_extent || ' NEXT ' || next_extent,
    ' MINEXTENTS ' || min_extents || ' MAXEXTENTS ' || max_extents || ');'
FROM dba_rollback_segs
WHERE segment_name <> 'SYSTEM';

REM Close output script file

SPOOL OFF

REM You may want to reset page size and feedback values to show
REM query headings, make page breaks, and report row counts
```

The script will produce a file, called RS_BUILD.SQL, which you can run to create the same rollback segments as were found in your original database, other than the SYSTEM rollback segment that was built as part of the original database creation. You should run this script file after you have created the tablespaces used by the original rollback segments, unless you first edit the script to rename either the segments or their tablespaces.

You should be aware that, until the rollback segments are created, the database might not open using the original Oracle7 initialization parameter file. If this occurs, you might need to remove, or comment out, the rollback segment-related parameters from your original parameter file. When you have run the script, you can restore the parameters to their original status. However, until the instance is restarted, the rollback segments will remain offline because this is the default status of newly-created rollback segments. Of course, you can edit the RS_BUILD.SQL script before running it to add the commands to bring the rollback segments online. The command to do this is

```
ALTER ROLLBACK SEGMENT segment_name ONLINE
```

This command will work for both private and public rollback segments. To check the status of your rollback segments, simply issue the query

```
SELECT segment_name, status FROM dba_rollback_segs;
```

You can, of course, pre-build any other database objects that you want to create with different characteristics than they were given in your Oracle7 database. This includes user definitions, their tables, indexes, and other related objects such as constraints and privileges. Anything you do build prior to running Import will require the same database structures as they would need in any other database. For example, to create a table for a user, the user must first exist along with a tablespace to store the table. If you plan to partition the table, you might want more than

one tablespace to store the segments. You might also need at least one non-SYSTEM rollback segment to be online in order to create certain types of segments in tablespaces other than SYSTEM—and you shouldn't be creating segments in the SYSTEM tablespace.

As with the tablespace and rollback segment creation scripts, if you don't have your equivalent Oracle7 scripts to copy and modify to build any of these other objects, you might want to use your original database to get you started. Data dictionary views are available, either alone or in joins, to show you the components of any of your database objects that you will need to rebuild them. Of course, you might want to change some of the values displayed by the Oracle7 data dictionary, otherwise you might as well allow Import to rebuild them just as they are in your current database. If you are up to it, you can build SQL-generating SQL scripts rather than just queries to help you with this work. Just don't forget to make the required changes before running such scripts.

> **NOTE**
>
> If you do build parts of the database prior to running the import command, you should expect to receive errors, unless you set the IGNORE option to NO, as discussed in the next section.

When you have built a database with your required redo log, tablespace, and rollback segment changes to support the contents—and the loading of them—of your Oracle7 database, you can complete your migration by importing the export file(s) you created. The next section discusses how to use the Export/Import utilities, optionally supplemented with unload/reload programs, to complete this migration.

Perform the Export/Import

You are ready to perform the migration from Oracle7 (or even Version 6). Some of you might even have your Oracle8*i* database already built and waiting for the contents of the Export dump file. The rest of you have extracted any data you need to prepare your Oracle8*i* database, including any contents such as tablespaces, users, and tables, and you can begin the export cycle with no users active on the system. As mentioned earlier, although Export can function while users continue to work, any changes they make are probably not going to end up in the new database.

Throughout this section, we will concentrate on two types of migration. The first type will use only the Export/Import tools and the second will use additional tools to migrate the table contents only. If you want to use other tools to create rollback segments, tablespaces, users, and

other objects, you need to do this using techniques similar to those described in the previous section, "Prepare the Oracle8*i* Database." Note that such objects need to be created prior to the import step, and I will point out some special considerations for you to be aware of when you run Import with such objects in place.

When you run Export, you will need to specify certain parameters. There are three ways you can do this: interactively, with command line parameters, or with a parameter file. My discussion of the features of each of these options should help you choose which one to use for your database.

Interactive Export

In this mode, Export prompts you for values of the parameters. Although this might seem to be the simplest method, it doesn't offer all the flexibility of the other two methods because you can only set values for a subset of the available parameters. However, if you are using an early release of version 6 of Oracle, this might be your only option. Also, if you are using a version earlier than release 7.3 and your production database is not very large, you might want to choose this method.

The primary drawback of this method for Oracle7, release 7.3 users is that you cannot use the direct path mode of the Export program, an option that generally speeds up the process by at least a factor of two. Earlier releases did not have this option, and a small database—no matter what release—might not benefit from the speedup anyway. For large, current release databases, you should consider one of the other methods and take advantage of direct mode Export.

To run an Export session interactively, you simply need to enter the name of the executable at a system command prompt. On Windows NT, this will require you to identify the name of the program, typically EXPxx.EXE, where the xx reflects the database release number, as in EXP73.EXE for Version 7.3. You can look in the BIN directory under your Oracle home directory to find the program if you can't figure out its name. When you know it, you can click the Start button and then the Run button, enter the name in the Open space, and click OK, or you can open an MS-DOS window and type the program name at the prompt. Either way, you will be using an MS-DOS window to interact with the program. On UNIX, you simply enter the command

```
exp
```

at the operating system prompt, regardless of what version of Oracle your production database is running.

Export will first prompt you for a username and a password. You should refer to the section "Export and Import Parameters" to determine what values to use to answer this and the other prompts for the parameter values that you can set during your interactive session.

Export with Command Line Parameters

Using Export with its parameter values as part of the command allows you to control every single available parameter. You need only to include values for those parameters for which you don't want to accept the defaults, however. As well as letting you choose values for any parameter, this method of running Export is frequently used in scripts—something that can't be done with the interactive approach. You simply include the command in an operating system script file and then, when the script is executed, the export program will execute, using values you provided.

Not only are scripts a convenient way to run your Exports, but they also allow you to easily repeat or fine tune an export without having to enter all of the same values over and over again. If you plan to test your migration using Export/Import, you should consider using a script with the Export command embedded in it. That way, you can modify the script until you build an appropriate Export dump file and then be sure that you use the correct, tested values when you perform the actual migration export.

One problem you can run into if you use a number of the parameters is the length of your command line. Should this be the case, look at the next section, "Export with a Parameter File," to find out how you can enjoy all the benefits of a command line Export without needing to put all the parameters into your command.

As with interactive mode, to use Export with command-line parameters, you need to know the name of the executable on Windows NT. This was discussed in the previous section, "Interactive Export," and you should refer back to this information if you don't know the command name. However, you will need to execute it using a Command Prompt window rather than the Start, Run option. If you don't, it will close the window in which it executes before you have a chance to read any final messages it displays. On UNIX, the basic command is still exp, as with the interactive mode.

> **NOTE**
>
> If you need to open a Windows NT Command Prompt window and don't have the necessary icon on your desktop, use Start, Run and type cmd. When you have finished your work, type exit at the prompt and the window will close.

On either operating system, you must also include the required parameters and values as part of the command. A very simple Export command could look like this on UNIX:

```
exp system/manager full=y
```

In this example, two parameters are given in the command. The first is the USERID parameter, which is not named because it is included in the correct default position. Only the parameter value, in this case system/manager, is included. Rather than try to get them in the right order, however, you will probably find it easier to list the keyword for each parameter and then give its value. The parameter name and value are separated by an equal sign as shown in the example for the FULL option, FULL=Y, where the Y, which is the abbreviation for Yes, is the value.

See the section "Export and Import Parameters" for detailed information on how to set each of the available parameters.

Export with a Parameter File

Running Export with a parameter file is very similar to running it with all the parameters on the command line. In fact, you start the program in exactly the same way that you would in the previous section. You should also use this approach for the same reasons I discussed in that section. The only difference between using the command line for all the parameters and their values and using a parameter file is this: The parameter names and values are stored in a separate file instead of being entered with the command. To make this work, the Export command contains the name of the parameter file as its only required parameter.

For those of you who like the benefits of having a file to edit as you refine your tests, or as a way to guarantee being able to repeat the export the same way over and over again, this option has one benefit that you might find appealing. To use an operating script to hold your Export command, as discussed in the section "Export with Command Line Parameters," you had to include the userid information in the script as one of the required parameters. This can be a security hazard because the name and password are both required to be in the scripted command.

Using a parameter file, you can store the optional parameters in a separate file, or even a series of separate files if you want to have different options available, but not include the user information in any of them. Then, when you are ready, you run the Export command dynamically, providing just the userid information and the parameter filename. This way, you have the benefit of stored values without the potential of a security problem should someone find the file. You also have the benefit of being able to include as many parameters as you want without being concerned about the length of the command-line string.

As with the command-line parameter mode, you need to run the Export command from an operating system prompt. The following example shows a possible Windows NT command being run from a Command Prompt window to run Export using a parameter file called MIGPARS.EXP stored in a directory on the C drive:

```
exp73 system/manager PARFILE=C:\oracle_73\migpars.exp
```

For information on how to identify the components of this command, see the previous section, "Export with Command Line Parameters." The contents of the MIGPARS.EXP file consist of a series of rows, each with a parameter name and value for that parameter, separated by an equal sign, just like the PARFILE parameter and filename in the example of the Export command. You will need to review the section "Export and Import Parameters" for the list of possible parameters and my suggestions on how to set them, but Listing 6.3 shows an example of how a small parameter file might look if displayed.

LISTING 6.3   Listing the Contents of a Sample Export Parameter File

```
C:\oracle_73> type migpars.exp

FULL=Y
FILE=PROD73.DMP
INDEXES=Y

C:\oracle_73>
```

> **NOTE**
>
> It is possible to include the USERID parameter, along with the username and password in a parameter file. This can compromise your database security, however, and we recommend against including such sensitive information in a nonencrypted form.

When you have completed the Export using the command option of your choice, you will have what is known as an Export dump file. You will then need to apply this file to your new Oracle8*i* database. If you have already installed Oracle8*i* and prepared your new database, you can simply run the Import command. On the other hand, you might need to go back and perform the steps discussed in the earlier sections "Install Oracle8*i*" and "Prepare the Oracle8*i* Database."

Should you build your new database on a different machine than your Oracle7 database, you should move the Export dump file to the new machine. If you exported to a tape, this should be an easy process—you just have to mount the tape(s) on the other machine. If you built a disk file, you should use a utility, such as FTP, to move the file. Although you can run Import across a network using SQL*Net or Net8, this is a very slow process and we discourage you from attempting it. If both versions of your database are on the same machine, you can use the dump file from its current location if you want.

When you have your Oracle8*i* database ready for the contents of the Export dump file, you can begin the Import. This time, you will use the import program from your Oracle8*i* binary directory. To ensure that you do this correctly, you should change your environment variables. You need to set your environment to point to the Oracle8*i* Oracle home. This will involve setting some or all of the following variables or registry entries to the appropriate values:

- LD_LIBRARY_PATH
- ORA_NLS
- ORACLE_BASE
- ORACLE_HOME
- ORACLE_PATH
- PATH

If you need help with setting these values, you should refer to your operating system specific Installation Guide or installation Read Me files.

As with the Export program, you have the option of running Import interactively, with command-line parameters, or with a parameter file. The reasons to use or not use each of the modes are almost the same as for Export and are covered earlier in this section. The major difference is that there is no direct mode Import, so this removes one of the disadvantages of the interactive option. The only other possible difference is that because you are now in the Oracle8*i* environment, you won't be forced to use the interactive option because the other modes are not yet supported. Table 6.2 summarizes the pros and cons of each method.

TABLE 6.2 Choosing Oracle8*i* Import Methods

Method	Benefits	Disadvantages
Interactive	Easy	Inflexible
Command Line Parameters	Flexible	Long commands
	Can be scripted	If scripted, password is exposed
Parameter File	Flexible	Have to maintain a separate file
	Don't have to expose password	

When you have chosen your method of running the Import, you should identify the name of the executable. This should be imp on both UNIX and Windows NT. If you can't get it to run with this name, check the bin directory in your Oracle8*i* home directory structure for the correct name of the program. You might also need to run the CATEXP.SQL script if, for some reason, the CATALOG.SQL script didn't run successfully in your new database.

To run an interactive Import session, enter

```
imp
```

at the operating system prompt. To run an Import with command line parameters, enter

```
imp username/password parameter_list
```

where *username/password* are the values for the USERID parameter and *parameter_list* contains pairs of parameter names and values as in this example:

```
imp system/manager full=y ignore=y
```

To run the Import program using a parameter file, your command at the operating system prompt would look something like this:

```
imp system/manager PARFILE=C:\oracle_81\migpars.imp
```

The contents of the parameter file, MIGPARS.IMP, would be formatted just as they would be for an Export parameter file: that is, a series of rows, each containing a parameter name, an equal sign, and the value for the parameter. Listing 6.3 shows a sample listing of the contents of such a parameter file.

The next section identifies the parameters that you can specify in the command line or parameter file. These also include the parameters for which you will be prompted by the interactive mode of Import. I also provide you with suggested guidelines for setting the values of these parameters in both the Export and Import steps, as well as pointing out which parameters are particularly important for migrations where you are building some or all the objects in your Oracle8*i* database before running Import.

Export and Import Parameters

In Table 6.3, I list the keywords associated with all the parameters used by Export, Import, or both. The value in the Default columns is the value the parameter will use if not reset when the associated command is run. The word None in these columns indicates that the parameter is valid for the specific operation, Export or Import. However, it doesn't have a default value, or the default is operating system specific. A value of n/a in a Default column indicates that the parameter is not valid for the specific operation.

TABLE 6.3 Oracle Export/Import Parameter Options

| | Default Values | | |
Keyword	Export	Import	Note
USERID	None	None	
BUFFER	None	None	
FILE	EXPDAT.DMP	EXPDAT.DMP	
SHOW	n/a	N	1

Keyword	*Export*	*Import*	*Note*
		Default Values	
COMPRESS	Y	n/a	
IGNORE	n/a	N	1
GRANTS	Y	Y	
INDEXES	Y	Y	2
INDEXFILE	n/a	None	2
ROWS	Y	Y	2
CONSTRAINTS	Y	Y	
LOG	None	None	
DIRECT	N	n/a	
FULL	N	N	
OWNER	None	n/a	
FROMUSER	n/a	None	
TOUSER	n/a	None	
TABLES	None	None	
RECORDLENGTH	None	None	
INCTYPE	None	None	
RECORD	Y	n/a	
COMMIT	n/a	N	
PARFILE	None	None	
DESTROY	n/a	N	1
CONSISTENT	None	n/a	
CHARSET	n/a	NLS_LANG	
STATISTICS	ESTIMATE	n/a	
ANALYZE	n/a	Y	
FEEDBACK	n/a	0	
FILESIZE	n/a	None	
VOLSIZE	n/a	None	
TOID_NOVALIDATE	n/a	None	
RECALCULATE_STATISTICS	n/a	N	
SKIP_UNUSABLE_INDEXES	n/a	N	

The final column of Table 6.3, Note, is flagged with a 1 for any parameter to which you should pay special attention if your Oracle8*i* database will contain more than the default SYSTEM tablespace contents when you perform the Import. Additionally, this column contains a 2 if the parameter is relevant to a migration process in which you intend to move the table data using an unload/load pair of processes.

Table 6.3 does not include information about parameters that were introduced for Oracle8*i* Exports because you will not be able to use these to Export your Oracle7 (or version 6) database. Similarly, the default values are those for Oracle7 Export and for Oracle8, version 8.1, Import parameters. The parameters associated with the keywords are described in detail in the following sections in alphabetical order.

ANALYZE

This parameter determines whether objects which had statistics at the time of the export will be re-analyzed during the import. The statistics are generated by executing either the ANALYZE...COMPUTE STATISTICS or ANALYZE...ESTIMATE STATISTICS, as explained under the STATISTICS parameter. Both the STATISTICS parameter for the export and the RECALCULATE_STATISTICS parameter for the import have to be set to Y for this parameter to have any impact. If you did not request statistics in your export dump file, or you want the Import utility to regenerate them, you can leave this parameter at its default setting. Should you have requested statistics but decide not to apply them during the import, you need to set the value of ANALYZE to N in your import command.

BUFFER

During Export and Import, this parameter defines the amount of array space used to hold rows that are being transferred between the database and the dump file. The more rows per array, the faster the program is likely to run. The buffer size should be calculated in bytes as the maximum row size times the number of rows per array.

> **NOTE**
>
> If the buffer size is set to 0, or a table contains a LONG or LONG RAW column, only one row will be fetched into the buffer at a time.

We recommend that you make the buffer as large as you can to speed up the process and avoid dynamic expansion of the buffer space that can be caused by tables with LONG or LONG RAW columns.

CHARSET

This parameter is only provided to allow you to import an Oracle6 database dump file if its character set is different from the character set in your Oracle8*i* database. If you are in such a situation, you need to set the parameter value to the character set of your Oracle6 database. All others can leave this parameter at its default value.

COMMIT

This parameter determines whether Oracle Import performs a commit after moving the contents of the buffer into the database, as well as after loading each table. We recommend that you set this parameter to Y in order to generate the additional commits. This reduces the amount of rollback segment space that might be needed—the larger your database, the more useful this becomes.

COMPRESS

When set to Y or Yes, this parameter will cause the Export process to modify the original storage clause in order for exported tables to create an initial extent that will be large enough to hold the entire table. This will slow down the Export process because it must calculate the required space as it executes. If you are planning to build the tables yourself prior to the Import, in which case you will define the storage clauses, you should avoid the unnecessary by setting this parameter to N.

> **NOTE**
>
> Even if you are going to enable the Export/Import programs to process all your objects for you, you still might want to avoid slowing down your migration by allowing Export to compute new initial extent sizes for you. In many cases, the calculation, which is based on current extent sizes and not overall data requirements, might overestimate the requirements if rows have been deleted and the space not reclaimed. This can lead to poor usage of space in your new database before your users even start working in it.

CONSISTENT

You should need only to concern yourself with this parameter, which defaults to being turned off, if you have other users executing DML statements on your database while you are performing the Export. When set to Y, this parameter will cause the export to attempt to build a dump file containing records that have the same values as they had when the export started. In other words, the export process will roll back any changes made by users while the export is processing. Obviously, this means that your export will not contain the most current contents

of the database. It is therefore unlikely that you will want to use this option for your actual migration, but it could be useful for testing. The big benefit of a consistent export is that any parent-child relationships between tables will be preserved. During a nonconsistent export, you can end up with child records in a table exported early in the process that no longer have a parent record in a table exported later. To ensure that your export dump file is consistent when you execute your final export for the migration, you should really ensure that your database has no other active users rather than rely on the CONSISTENT parameter.

CONSTRAINTS

You should not plan to alter this parameter from its default value of Y in either the Export or Import steps unless you are migrating your data using a combination of unload and load processes, as discussed in the section "Define System Resource Requirements." In such a case, you might want to disable the parameter during your Import until after the tables have been built and loaded. You can then run Import once again with all the other options turned off, including the ROWS parameter, in order for the constraints to be loaded. Of course, you will want to run this Import with the IGNORE parameter set to Y to avoid the errors that would occur as Import tries to create objects that you cannot control with the Import parameters. Of course, you can still use the unload/load approach and leave the CONSTRAINTS parameter alone. It is likely that you will have to perform some manual enabling of the constraints after you load your table data, however, if you do this.

DESTROY

This parameter determines whether the REUSE command will be included in the CREATE TABLESPACE commands that a full database Import will issue. If the clause is included, any existing datafiles will be overwritten and their contents lost. If the clause is not included, the import will fail if any files already exist. The default value, N, causes the CREATE TABLE-SPACE commands to be executed without the REUSE clause. Most of you will be building your Oracle8*i* database on the same machine as your current production database, and you will want to use the same tablespace structure. Unless you have already removed your original database prior to executing the Import to complete your migration, you must ensure that this parameter is set to N. Of course, this also means that you will have to prebuild the tablespaces in your Oracle8*i* database. Otherwise, the import will try to build them and will fail. If you are unsure how to do this, you should review the earlier section, "Prepare the Oracle8*i* Database," to find out how you can automate most of this process using your current database's data dictionary.

DIRECT

This parameter determines whether the process will execute a conventional path or a direct path export. During a conventional path export, the Export process works just like any other database user and issues the queries necessary to obtain the records required to build the dump

file. This means that the data has to be loaded from disk into the database buffer cache just as for any query. In direct path mode, the data is loaded into a private memory area dedicated to the Export process, and the required information is extracted without needing a normally-formulated SELECT query.

If your current database is release 7.3, we recommend that you use DIRECT=Y when you execute your migration Export because this will result in much faster processing. For the rest of you, this option does not exist and you will have to use a conventional export. To use a direct path export successfully, there are a couple of steps you need to take that are slightly different than for conventional path exports:

1. Ensure that the CATEXP.SQL script for release 7.3 has been run against your database.

2. Confirm that you have sufficient space on your dump file location; a direct path export will fail with an unusable file if it runs out of space.

3. Set the COMPATIBLE parameter in your init.ora file to a value of 7.1.5 or later release number.

4. Set the RECORDLENGTH parameter correctly in your export command or parameter file; this parameter, and not BUFFER, determines how much data is accumulated between each write to the dump file.

FEEDBACK

Feedback refers to the generation of dots by the Import facility to indicate how many rows it has imported for a table. It can help you judge how fast the process is running and, if you know how many rows a table contains, how much longer the import of the rows will take. Although this can be useful for single table imports—the additional processing that occurs when you are importing a full database to complete a migration—the feedback is not likely to be very meaningful. This is particularly true if you don't intend to sit around and watch your computer screen for the duration of the import. By default, the parameter value is 0 (zero), which turns off the feedback feature. If you do decide to use it, for example, as a way to monitor whether the import process is still doing something, we recommend setting its value to a high number, such as five or ten thousand (5,000 or 10,000), so you don't generate large log files full of dots. This value represents the number of additional rows that are imported between the display of each new dot.

FILE

This parameter defines the name of the dump file to be written by Export or to be read by Import. If a full pathname is not included in the parameter value, the file location will default to the current directory. Although the filename is quite immaterial to the migration activity, we suggest that you use a meaningful name to avoid the possibility of accidentally overwriting a file with the default name or using a file with the default name during your import.

FILESIZE

I have included this parameter because it is an option with Oracle8*i* exports and imports. However, it has no meaning on Import unless your export was performed using the parameter. Because you are reading this in order to migrate to Oracle8*i* from an earlier release, your export could not have used the parameter, so you must leave it at its default setting.

FROMUSER

This parameter is used to identify which user or users objects will be imported and is very similar to the OWNER parameter of the Export command. Unless you have specific reasons to limit the import to some subset of the user community, you should leave this parameter at its default value, which will allow the objects belonging to all schemas in the Export dump file to be imported. However, for a migration project, there should be no reason to use anything but the default value.

FULL

When you run an Export command, you must determine under what mode the export will run. Only one mode can be selected for each export and FULL is one of these export modes. The other modes you can choose are USER and TABLE. Although these modes are useful for various management options of a production database, the FULL mode is the only one you should consider using for a database migration. If you choose one of the other modes, your dump file, and, as a consequence, your Oracle8*i* database will not include a number of system level objects. For example, your export will not include user definitions, database roles, profiles, or system privilege grants. To set this parameter correctly, you need to include the keyword name, FULL, and the value Y in your export commands. For your Import, you will also probably need to set FULL=Y in your command in order to process the entire contents of your Export dump file. If you have some specialized testing in mind, you might want to use other options, leaving FULL at its default value of N. However, we do not consider such options as being relevant to an Oracle7 or Oracle8*i* migration.

GRANTS

This parameter determines whether grants should be exported during Export or imported during Imports. Unless you have a very good reason not to do so, we recommend that you leave this parameter enabled with its default value of Y.

IGNORE

This parameter determines how the Import program will handle objects that it is trying to import if they already exist. If the value is set to Y or Yes, it will not report any errors should the object exist and will bypass any processing associated with that object, other than tables. In the case of an existing table, with IGNORE enabled, the error will not be reported and any rows in the dump file will be added to the table. With IGNORE set to N or No, the default,

Import will report errors if an object already exists and, in the case of a table, no rows will be added to it.

If you are using a database in which you have created any objects prior to running the Import, you should set this parameter value to Y to enable it. This includes rollback segments, table-spaces, users, tables, and any other objects.

> **NOTE**
>
> If you are building your Oracle8*i* database on the same machine as your original database and you want to protect your original datafiles, you need to build your required tablespaces in the Oracle8*i* database and set IGNORE to Y and DESTROY to N in your import processing. This will prevent Import from attempting to recreate the tablespaces with the REUSE option for their datafiles. If it were to succeed at this, it would overwrite the current contents of these datafiles.

INCTYPE

This parameter is used when you are using Export/Import as part of you overall backup and recovery strategy for your production database. It allows you to set levels of Export/Import based on how much data you will need to transfer during the given process. This parameter is completely irrelevant for your migration process, and we refer you to your Oracle documentation if you want to use it for other purposes.

INDEXES

This parameter determines whether indexes should be exported during Export or imported during Imports. Unless you have a very good reason not to do so, we recommend that you leave this parameter enabled with its default value of Y during the Export. For the Import, you might choose to set it to N or No so that the indexes are not built during the import itself. You can use the INDEXFILE option of Import, during a separate run, to create a script file containing the commands necessary to build them. You can then modify this file to perform faster index builds by adding parallel clauses and setting better storage values. If you don't want to bother with the separate run and the script file, however, you should leave the parameter at its default value.

If you are planning to load your tables using SQL*Loader rather than Import, you should disable this parameter and use the INDEXFILE option to build a script file that can be used after the data is loaded.

INDEXFILE

Running Import with a filename defined for this parameter will prevent the program from importing anything into the database. Instead, Import will build a script file, with the name specified, containing the commands needed to create the indexes defined in your original database. You can edit this file and use it to build the indexes after you have loaded the Oracle8*i* database during an additional run of the Import program with the INDEXES parameter set to N. This will allow you to perform faster index builds by adding parallel clauses and setting better storage values. You can even break the script file into separate files and run the index creation scripts concurrently.

We suggest that you use this option to speed up your overall migration process, particularly if you have a large database with many or with large indexes. For smaller databases, or in cases when time is not critical for you, you might want to avoid the effort of running the Import program twice and editing a script file.

If you are planning to load your tables using SQL*Loader rather than Import, you should use this parameter to build a script file that can be used after the data is loaded. Remember to set the INDEXES parameter to N, as well during your regular Import.

LOG

This parameter determines whether the Export and Import tools will simultaneously write the information they display to the screen into a log file. Unless you have a very good reason not to do so, we recommend that you save the results of your migration's export and import steps in a log file. This will let you check messages that might have scrolled across the screen too quickly for you to read or research an issue if a subsequent step reports a problem. The default value of this parameter is not to create a log file. To change this in order to obtain a log, you need to define a file name. By default, the file will be created in the current directory in which you are running the Export or Import utility. You can specify a full path name if you want the log to be created elsewhere.

OWNER

This parameter, which has an undefined default value, determines whether the Export runs in USER mode. By providing one or more usernames for this parameter, you cause a USER mode Export and identify the userid for which objects will be exported. As discussed under the FULL parameter, this is not a useful option for the Export you will run to migrate a complete database because it cannot be used with the FULL option.

PARFILE

This parameter provides the full path and filename of a parameter file that contains keywords and values for any other parameter which is valid for the command being executed, Export or Import. You can include all the required parameters in a parameter file or just some of them.

Our recommendation is to use parameter files for your migration, one for the Export and one for the Import and include all the parameters in them for each operation except for the USERID. You can then execute your migration commands with a command like the following:

```
exp system/manager parfile=exp73.par
```

Listing 6.3 contains a display of the contents of a simple parameter file.

RECALCULATE_STATISTICS

This parameter determines whether the statistics will be added back to the objects that had them during the export when they are imported. The statistics are generated by executing either the ANALYZE...COMPUTE STATISTICS or ANALYZE...ESTIMATE STATISTICS as explained under the STATISTICS parameter. Both the STATISTICS parameter for the export and the ANALYZE parameter for the import have to be set to Y for this parameter to have any impact. If you did not request statistics in your export dump file, or you have decided that you don't want the Import utility to regenerate them, you can leave this parameter at its default setting. Should you have requested statistics and want to process them during the import, you need to set the value of RECALCULATE_STATISTICS to Y in your import command.

RECORD

This parameter is of use only if you are performing incremental Exports as part of a database backup/recovery strategy. This parameter is completely irrelevant for your migration process and we refer you to your Oracle documentation if you want to use it for other purposes.

RECORDLENGTH

This parameter is needed only when you are transferring your database contents between two different operating systems or if you are using a direct path export. Most of you will not be migrating your database to Oracle8*i* at the same time that you are changing system architectures. However, for the few of you who might be doing this, you will need to consult your operating system documentation for each system—the one where your original database is running and the one where you are building your Oracle8*i* database—to determine the values you'll need to supply for this parameter. They are likely to be different for the Export and for the Import.

The rest of you who need to set this parameter are those performing direct path exports. In this case, you should set the RECORDLENGTH value to the maximum of

- the default value for your operating system (which you can find in your operating system specific documentation)
- the operating system read/write buffer size
- the Oracle database block size (DB_BLOCK_SIZE)

If you have records that span multiple blocks in some of your tables, you might want to increase RECORDLENGTH to an integer multiple of the value selected previously so that it is as large as your longest database record. If this proves to be too large and Export will not run, try smaller integer multiples until you can successfully run the Export.

ROWS

This parameter determines whether table rows should be exported during Export or imported during Import. If you intend to perform your complete migration using just Export and Import, you should leave this parameter enabled with its default value of Y. However, if you intend to migrate your table data by unloading it into one or more flat files and then loading it into your Oracle8*i* database with Oracle's SQL*Loader, or similar tool, you should set the value to N for both operations. You will not need the rows for the Import, so you don't need to waste the time and space to Export them. You certainly don't need to Import them, but if you don't have them in your dump file anyway, you can't accidentally import them twice.

> **NOTE**
>
> In case you missed it, the section "Define System Resource Requirements" covers the topic of data unloading and reloading for the migration process.

> **CAUTION**
>
> You should take great care if you decide to use an alternate method to migrate your data. If you don't export the rows and something happens to your original database, either by design or by accident, you will have to rebuild it from your backups. You won't be able to use the export dump file to restore it in this case because it will be incomplete. This does not mean that you shouldn't use such an approach, but you should make very certain that you have a good backup before you begin the migration.

SHOW

If the value of this parameter is set to Y or Yes, the Import will not move anything into the database. Instead, it will list the SQL statements that would be executed where the Import is to be run with the default value of SHOW, which is N.

SKIP_UNUSABLE_INDEXES

I have included this parameter because it is an option with an Oracle8*i* import. However, it has no meaning on Import unless your export was performed on a database containing partitioned

tables or other objects that can produce unusable indexes that were not introduced until Oracle8. Because you are reading this in order to migrate to Oracle8*i* from an Oracle7, or earlier database, your export could not have contained such objects, and so you should leave this parameter at its default setting.

STATISTICS

If you are using the cost-based optimizer in your current database, your migrated database will need to have the appropriate statistics generated before it will work the same way with the optimizer. You can ask the Import program to do this for you, but you can do it by setting the STATISTICS parameter in your Export command. By default, the parameter will cause the ANALYZE…ESTIMATE STATISTICS command, with the default sample size, to be run on the segments that require it following the Import. You can also set the value to be COMPUTE, which will substitute the COMPUTE STATISTIS clause in place of the ESTIMATE STATIS-TICS clause. In either case, the command will be run only if the segment already had statistics when the Export occurred. Note that it doesn't matter how the segments were originally analyzed, COMPUTE or ESTIMATE, nor what sample size was used in the case of the latter, the same ANALYZE command will be used on them all. If you don't want statistics to be computed, you can set the parameter value to NONE. Of course, if you have been using the rule-based optimizer and there are no statistics, it really doesn't matter what setting you use; nothing will be analyzed during the import. If you are happy with the options provided by this parameter, you should use it with the setting you prefer. Some of you might prefer to execute your own ANALYZE commands in order to choose different options for different segments. In such cases, you should set the parameter to NONE in order to prevent unnecessary time being used for analyses you are likely to replace.

TABLES

This parameter, which has an undefined default value Export and a default value of NONE for Import, determines whether the Export or Import runs in TABLE mode. By providing one or more table names for this parameter, you cause a TABLE mode Export or Import and identify the tables that will be processed. As discussed under the FULL parameter, this is not a useful option for the Export/Import you will run to migrate a complete database because it cannot be used with the FULL option.

TOID_NOVALIDATE

I have included this parameter because it is an option with an Oracle8*i* import. However, it has no meaning on Import unless your export was performed on a database containing object TYPE definitions that were not introduced until Oracle8. Because you are reading this in order to migrate to Oracle8*i* from an Oracle7, or earlier database, your export could not have contained such objects, and so you should leave this parameter at its default setting.

TOUSER

This Import parameter is used only with Exports that involve one user or with Imports that specify the FROMUSER parameter. It defines the schema into which the objects in the Export dump file will be loaded. Unless you have specific reasons to limit the import to some specific user, you should leave this parameter at its default value, which will allow the objects in the Export dump to be imported back into their original schema. Changing the value of this parameter, therefore, allows you to change ownership of objects by performing an Export/Import. However, for a migration project, there should be no reason to use anything but the default value.

USERID

Required in every Export/Import execution, this parameter defines which user will connect to the database to execute the steps involved in running the process. The value consists of the username and the user's password, separated by a forward slash (/). You should not need any other possible configurations for your migration, but the USERID value can optionally contain a TNSNAMES.ORA connect string if the database is on a remote node, as in scott/tiger@hq. Further, it can use an AS SYSDBA clause, but this is only in unusual circumstances and typically with the help of Oracle Customer Support.

VOLSIZE

I have included this parameter because it is an option with an Oracle8*i* export and import. However, it has no meaning on Import unless your export was performed using the parameter. Because you are reading this in order to migrate to Oracle8*i* from an earlier release, your export could not have used the parameter, so you must leave it at its default setting.

> **NOTE**
>
> Although many of the parameters can be left to default for Export and Import during your migration, you might want to take the precaution of setting them specifically to their default values, just in case you are running a version in which the defaults are not as previously documented. This will also ensure that you consider each one and determine how it will impact your overall migration. We recommend that you use a parameter file to simplify this task.

Troubleshooting and Abandoning the Migration with Export/Import

If you have problems creating an export dump file, you might need to refer to the *Server Utilities* manual, provided by Oracle, which is where the Export and Import utilities are documented. The most common problem you are likely to run into, when you get your Export syntax correct, is running out of space. If this occurs, you have some options to try:

- Find a way to increase the space available. For example, by adding disks.
- Use an operating system pipe and a compression utility to reduce the size of the dump file before it is stored.
- Export your database in pieces. For example, first without any rows, and then user by user, or table by table.

If you have performed the proper tests, you should not run out of space unexpectedly during your actual migration. When you have added as much disk space as you can, you might have to implement either, or both of the other options if you still have insufficient space. Should you still not have enough room, you might have to consider another migration method.

As with the Export step, you might need to refer to the documentation in Oracle's *Server Utilities* manual if you run into unexpected problems with the Import step. As long as you have created your Oracle8*i* database with sufficient room in the SYSTEM tablespace and provided enough space for remaining tablespaces, you shouldn't have problems unless the export dump file has errors. This can occur if the disk drive has a bad spot, or you didn't notice errors being logged while the Export utility was running.

Other types of problems have been discussed as I covered each topic. These include allowing Import to rebuild tablespaces using the files that belong to your original database, using incompatible character sets, and forgetting to set the IGNORE parameter if you are importing into a database in which you have already created objects that are included in the export dump file. You should always check the log file—which we recommend you use for both the export and import processing—after you complete each step to confirm that there were no errors, problems, or warnings reported. Both utilities can terminate with a successful completion message, even if there were warnings generated during the run.

Summary

The Export/Import utilities provide a time-honored way to migrate Oracle databases between releases, as well as between operating systems, hardware platforms, and different physical structures, such as block size, character sets, and so on. It is also a technique to compress the segments and the free space in fragmented tablespaces.

Although not as efficient as some of the more recent tools, these utilities allow you to make some of the other changes to the database, as well as completing the migration in a single step. The utilities can be used in combination with other tools to gain some of the benefits of Export/Import while reducing the overall time taken to perform the migration.

You should consider using the Export/Import utilities for your migration if you can't achieve everything you need to accomplish with the Oracle tools provided specifically for an Oracle8*i* migration. Before committing to this migration approach, you should determine if you have the resources needed to complete it.

Migration Using Data Copying

IN THIS CHAPTER

Data copying is not considered a particularly useful method to migrate a database and has been given less and less coverage in the Oracle documentation over the years until, with the Oracle8*i* documentation, it is not even mentioned as a migration strategy. However, we discussed some techniques in Chapter 6, "Migration Using Export/Import," that can be combined with this method to make it a very useful option. In fact, the methods used to perform migration with Export/Import and with data copying can vary by only a few steps. The reason we believe it is important to discuss this technique is because it might be more efficient than Export/Import for some of you, while not necessarily being any more difficult to accomplish.

Traditionally, this method of migration was referred to as migration using the SQL*Plus COPY command. Although this technique will still work for your Oracle7 to Oracle8*i* migration, it is not necessarily going to give you good performance. However, you can also copy data using straightforward SQL commands after you have built the requisite structures, which takes very little more work than configuring the databases for the COPY command. What is more, the option to use parallel operations with Oracle's I/O slaves can substantially improve the overall processing time needed to complete the migration. It is the use of these I/O slaves that makes this option an attractive one to consider in certain circumstances.

The two major drawbacks of Export/Import are the time it takes to complete the transfer of data and the space required for the Export dump files. These result from the fact that the process is a two-step process. First, you create the Export dump file and then you load it to your new database using the Import utility. We also discussed an alternative approach in the previous chapter in which you unloaded and reloaded the data with tools other than Export/Import. This still requires two steps and some form of intermediary storage.

The data copying approach avoids both of these problems by moving the data directly from the old to the new database with a single command for each table. Of course, for this to be able to occur, both your Oracle7 database and your Oracle8*i* database must be online concurrently, something that is not the case with Export/Import and its variants. The storage for the second database, however, can be substantially less than the formatted files used to hold the intermediate version of the data. If you can create and open your Oracle8*i* database while your Oracle7 database is still open and running, you have sufficient space to use this technique—no additional space should be needed.

As you might have read in the previous chapter, Export/Import can be used to move just the database definitions from the old to the new database. The remainder of the database—that is, the contents of the tables themselves—is then moved using a different tool set. In Chapter 6, the tools included some form of data unload utility and either Oracle's SQL*Loader or an equivalent load program. Using data copying, we simply substitute the steps performed by an unload/reload pair of programs when using that approach with a series of SQL commands or, if you want, SQL*Plus commands.

We recommend using this technique if your migration would have been amenable to this hybrid approach, but you want to avoid the overhead of intermediate data storage or the time taken to move the data twice. As with Export/Import, you gain some of the other benefits that are not available with the migration tools. These benefits include the ability to migrate just portions of your database and to restructure the physical layout of the data. Even if you intend to migrate your entire database, the option to migrate just parts of it can be useful for testing purposes prior to a complete migration.

One decision you need to make after you have decided to try the data copying approach to migration is the specific command you will use to copy the data. There are a number of options to choose from:

- The SQL*Plus COPY command
- The SQL command CREATE TABLE...AS SELECT
- The SQL command INSERT INTO...SELECT

The SQL*Plus COPY command allows you to move Oracle7 data into a nonexistent or a preexisting table, or a table that might or might not exist, depending on which option you choose. The CREATE TABLE...AS SELECT command will work only if executed on the Oracle8*i* database because a database link cannot be used to execute a data definition language (DDL) SQL statement. The subquery, however, can execute against your original database using a database link. It will work only if the table does not already exist in your Oracle8*i* database. The INSERT INTO...SELECT command will work only if the table already exists in the Oracle8*i* database, but it can be run from either your old or new database. Of course, you really should know whether the table already exists or not in your new database, so the issue is really whether the SQL*Plus or the SQL command will work better. We suggest that the SQL is the better choice because it allows the commands to run in parallel using I/O slaves. This should make the process run more quickly in most cases. Only if you have the datafiles for the corresponding tablespaces in both databases on the same disk drive as each other would you be unlikely to gain any benefits from parallel execution.

Define System Resource Requirements for Data Copying

As with the Data Migration Assistant, you will need to have both the Oracle7 and Oracle8*i* versions of the software installed to complete the process. Unlike the Data Migration Assistant process, however, you will have to have both versions of the database running concurrently. The Data Migration Assistant converts one to the other, so you don't need two copies of your database files at the same time. These duplicate copies of your Oracle home directory and your database files are the only significant space requirement for migrating with data copying.

You will not need any intermediate file storage as you would with Export/Import, but, of course, you cannot substitute tapes for this disk storage, an option you do have with Export (or even unloaded) files.

There will be some space needed if you do use Export/Import to transfer the database definitions. For this, you can use disk, tape, or a mixture of both. Of course, disk will be faster, but tape generally offers greater capacity. You can reduce disk space requirements if you use some form of compression. This can be done efficiently by using a pipe, if your operating system supports it, to direct the Export output to the compression tool. If you have scripts that will create everything in your database, you could even run those against your new Oracle8i database and save yourself the work and space needed for an Export/Import. Such scripts, however, are probably not going to be that much smaller than an Export dump file that contains no table data.

Besides the running Oracle8i database, with the files to support it, of course, the other resource you will need is a Net8 or SQL*Net configuration that will support both your Oracle7 and Oracle8i databases. If you are expecting to use Net8 with your new database, you might want to take this opportunity to configure and test it. This way you will have a chance to put it through some of its paces before turning it over to your users.

NOTE

If you are using an older version of Oracle, you might have to build a database at an intermediate version to provide the SQL*Net/Net8 communication between your current system and Oracle8i. Specifically, versions prior to 7.1.6 communicate only via SQL*Net version 1, and Oracle8i communicates only with version 2 or Net8. To migrate from a version earlier than 7.1.6 using the data copying method, therefore, you have to transfer the data through SQL*Net version 2. This requires an intermediate database of at least version 7.1.6. If you want to use Net8 as the second step in this two-phase migration, you need your intermediate database to be at release 7.3 or higher.

Another resource you might want to add to your product lineup to complete the migration is a script to perform the actual data copying for you. In Chapter 6, we included a SQL*Plus script, shown in Listing 6.1, to build a generated SQL*Plus script that when executed would copy the rows into a flat file. You can modify this script to generate a data copying script. There are a couple of options you need to consider before you build your script.

First, you have to decide whether the script will be executed on the Oracle7 or the Oracle8i database. This decision will determine which tables will be identified using a database link, and which will be presumed to be local because no link is involved in naming them.

Second, you have to decide whether you are going to transfer the table definitions to the Oracle8*i* database using Export/Import, or if your script will both build and populate the tables. In the former case, the commands in the script file will be INSERT INTO...SELECT * FROM commands. In the second case, you will need to use a CREATE...AS SELECT command. However, because this is a data definition language command, it can only be executed on a local, not a remote, database. You have to run this on your new Oracle8*i* database and your database links must be defined in this database.

Listing 7.1 contains the basic SQL*Plus statements to build a command to process a single table for each of the three possible options. Of course, if you want to use the SQL*Plus COPY command, you will have to modify the commands for the option you choose accordingly. If you want to automate the process even further, you can combine these statements with the other commands shown in Listing 6.1 from the previous chapter. The important options in Listing 6.1 are those that limit what ends up in the script file for use in the migration itself, the SPOOL commands, and those that identify the tables you want to migrate. You can use the comments in Listing 6.1 to determine what changes you can make in order to identify the tables to be included in the migration.

LISTING 7.1 SQL*Plus Options for Data Copying Script Generation

```
REM SQL*Plus commands to build SQL statements to run on an
REM Oracle8i database and copy a table's contents into an
REM existing table from the equivalent Oracle7 table using a
REM database link, <link_name>, defined in the Oracle8i database.

ACCEPT table_name PROMPT "Name of table to copy > "

SELECT 'INSERT INTO ' ¦¦ '&table_name'
       ¦¦ ' SELECT * FROM '
       ¦¦ '&table_name' ¦¦ '@<link_name>;'
FROM dual
/

REM SQL*Plus commands to build SQL statements to run on an
REM Oracle8i database and to build a table and copy its contents
REM from the equivalent Oracle7 table using a database link,
REM <link_name>, defined in the Oracle8i database.
ACCEPT table_name PROMPT "Name of table to copy > "

SELECT 'CREATE TABLE ' ¦¦ '&table_name'
       ¦¦ ' AS SELECT * FROM '
       ¦¦ '&table_name' ¦¦ '@<link_name>;'
FROM dual
/
```

continues

LISTING 7.1   Continued

```
REM SQL*Plus commands to build SQL statements to run on an
REM Oracle7 database and copy a table's contents into the
REM equivalent existing table on an Oracle8i database using a
REM database link, <link_name>, defined in the Oracle7 database.

ACCEPT table_name PROMPT "Name of table to copy > "

SELECT 'INSERT INTO ' || '&table_name' || '@<link_name>'
       || ' SELECT * FROM '
       || '&table_name' || ';'
FROM dual
/
```

The commands in Listing 6.1 also include output to list the names of the tables to be migrated. This is important for a script that has to create flat files to be processed later. This is not necessary for a script that interactively performs the migration, hence you can omit the query from DUAL. For reference, Figure 7.1 shows you a sample execution of the script in Listing 6.1 and the results stored in the generated SQL script file, UNLOAD.SQL. For this run of the script, it was stored in a file called LISTING6_1.SQL and only two tables were selected to be processed: CUSTOMERS and BILLINGS.

```
SQL> @listing6_1.sql
Enter value for list_of_tables: 'CUSTOMERS','BILLINGS'
old    5: WHERE table_name IN (&list_of_tables)
new    5: WHERE table_name IN ('CUSTOMERS','BILLINGS')
SELECT 'BILLINGS' FROM dual;
SELECT * FROM BILLINGS;

SELECT 'CUSTOMERS' FROM dual;
SELECT * FROM CUSTOMERS;

SQL> get unload.sql
  1  Enter value for list_of_tables: 'CUSTOMERS','BILLINGS'
  2  old    5: WHERE table_name IN (&list_of_tables)
  3  new    5: WHERE table_name IN ('CUSTOMERS','BILLINGS')
  4  SELECT 'BILLING_DATES' FROM dual;
  5  SELECT * FROM BILLING_DATES;
  6  SELECT 'CUSTOMERS' FROM dual;
  7* SELECT * FROM CUSTOMERS;
  8

SQL>
```

FIGURE 7.1

Sample execution of the script in Listing 6.1.

The comments in Listing 6.1 tell you how to remove these file headings as well as how to add a list of tables based on a coded list of table names, or on the schema they belong to, or any other selection criteria you can code. For example, the following query will select only tables belonging to user ACCTING with no foreign key constraints:

```
SELECT table_name
FROM dba_tables
WHERE owner = 'ACCTING'
AND table_name NOT IN
  (SELECT table_name FROM dba_constraints
    WHERE constraint_type = 'R');
```

You could substitute the WHERE clause from the preceding query, or any other clause you want, into the WHERE clause of the table selection options when you combine your option from Listing 7.1 with a query from Listing 6.1.

Prepare the Oracle7 Database for Data Copying

One of the characteristics of data copying to perform a migration is that you have to work on one table at a time. This means if there are dependencies between tables, you will need to ensure there is no activity on these tables between the times you start and end the migration of those tables. If you are using the Export/Import option to move the object definitions between the two databases, the database needs to be frozen from the time the Export dump is created to the time when the data is finally transferred to the new database. We recommend, therefore, that you make your database unavailable during the complete migration process just to guarantee that nobody makes any changes that could compromise data integrity. This is most easily done by shutting down the database normally, to avoid causing users the inconvenience of having aborted transactions, and then restarting it in RESTRICTED mode. When the database is open in this mode, only users with the RESTRICTED SESSION system privilege will be able to connect to it.

Although your data copying commands will not modify the contents of your original production database, it is still a good idea to make a clean, cold backup before you begin. You can use this backup in case something unexpected occurs, such as a change to a table made by a batch program running with DBA privileges, between the time you begin and end the migration. Such a backup will also provide you with a repeatable starting point should your testing uncover problems that require a fresh migration to resolve.

If you have decided to perform your data copying by using database links in your Oracle7 database, you must create the necessary links. If you want to be able to repeat the migration using the data copying technique, or possibly using some other approach, you should add these links after stabilizing your database and making your backup. That way, the link definitions,

which might have been part of a migration problem, will not be part of any repeated migration attempt.

The next step in preparing your database is to make sure that your database links work. This will require configuring either SQL*Net version 2 or Net8 to connect to your Oracle8*i* database. To test this, you will have to have your Oracle8*i* database up and running, as described in the following section, "Install Oracle8*i* for Data Copying." We recommend using a sample schema, such as the SCOTT demo schema, to check that you can read and write records between your two database versions.

If you are going to migrate only a part of your database for test purposes, you might not need to be as rigorous in your preparations. For example, unless you need your data to be consistent to a single point in time, you don't have to worry about preventing user access while testing. Similarly, your copy commands and scripts should not change the contents of the production database, so you should not need to perform a preliminary backup. Of course, you should make sure you have a database backup if you are not certain that your scripts will not change any database contents.

The export you use to move object definitions to the test database can include the entire database, even if you are only going to test on a subset of the tables, as long as you have sufficient space for the required Export dump file and the resulting Data Dictionary contents in your test database.

Install Oracle8*i* for Data Copying

You will have to complete this step before you can perform a database migration using data copying. If you use the Export/Import approach, as we suggest, to transfer the database object definitions between your databases, naturally, the new database will have to be built before you can execute the Import. You can go ahead and perform the Export, however, as long as no subsequent changes will be made to the production database. If you want to try the migration using some method to move objects other than tables, you will almost certainly need your Oracle8*i* database ready for the whole migration process.

To begin the software installation, you need to follow your operating system–specific directions to start up the Oracle Universal Installer, provided as part of your Oracle8*i* distribution. Then, respond to the installation prompts using the suggested items listed in Table 7.1.

TABLE 7.1 Installation Options for Oracle8*i*

Installer Screen	*Your Response*
Welcome Screen	Click the "Next" button
File Locations Screen	Select a directory path separate from your Oracle7 Oracle Home

Installer Screen	Your Response
Available Products Screen	Select the Oracle8*i* Enterprise Edition or the Oracle8*i* option
Installation Types Screen	Select the Custom or Minimal installation to avoid creating a starter database
Custom Installation Screens	If you selected Custom on the previous screen, choose the options you used in Oracle7 and want to continue to use in Oracle8*i*
Upgrading or Migrating an Existing Database Screen	Click the Next button *without* selecting the Upgrade or Migrate an Existing Database selection box
Create Database Screen	Select the No radio button, and then click the Next button
Summary Screen	After confirming all the settings are correct, click the Install button, and then click the Exit button after the installation completes

NOTE

If you are using Oracle Parallel Server and want to use this option in Oracle8*i*, you must choose the Oracle8*i* Enterprise Edition from the Available Products screen and the Custom option from the Installation Types screen. You will also be presented with a Cluster Node Selection screen. You should select the nodes on which you want to install Oracle8*i*.

As you might already know, the installation process can take a little time, so you should have time to read more of this book or to prepare the scripts to build your Oracle8*i* database while you are waiting for it to complete. Our suggestions for the installation process are based on the assumption that your Oracle7 database was not built using the defaults that the Oracle installer provides. If this is not the case, you should locate the script that built your Oracle7 database, which you will find in your Oracle7 home directory, to build your Oracle8*i* database. Otherwise, you should proceed to the next section, "Prepare the Oracle8*i* Database for Data Copying," to create your new database.

Prepare the Oracle8*i* Database for Data Copying

Your Oracle8*i* database should reflect the same physical structure as your current production database unless you only plan to migrate a subset. Either way, you need to create your SYSTEM tablespace to be roughly 50% to 70% larger than in your Oracle7 database to hold the larger Data Dictionary required by Oracle8*i*. Similarly, tablespaces holding indexes and rollback segments should be increased by about 10% due to the increase in the length of the ROWID fields. Your other Oracle8*i* tablespaces shouldn't need to be any larger than they are in

your Oracle7 database, and can be proportionately smaller if you are only migrating some of their contents. If you have a script that you used to build and maintain your current database, you can use it to build its Oracle8*i* equivalent after making any necessary tablespace size changes.

If you don't have a script to build your equivalent database structure, you can obtain the information you will need for it from your Oracle7 database. The following statement will produce a listing of the names and sizes of the datafiles that comprise your various tablespaces:

```
SELECT tablespace_name, file_name, bytes
FROM dba_data_files
ORDER BY tablespace_name;
```

Similarly, you can find the names and sizes of the members of each of your online redo log groups using this query:

```
SELECT l.group#, l.thread#, f.member, l.bytes
FROM v$log l, v$logfile f
WHERE l.group# = f.group#
ORDER BY l.group#;
```

If you really want to, you can work on creating a SQL-generating SQL script to generate the statements needed to build your database. This can include the basic CREATE DATABASE command, including the SYSTEM tablespace definition, or it can be just for the additional tablespaces required by your production database. The latter is particularly useful if you want to change the datafile sizes or names (including locations, if you use full path names rather than operating system links), default storage parameter values, auto-extensible characteristics, or tablespace management from dictionary to local.

The other components of your new database you might want to build are the rollback segments. This will allow you to change their original characteristics, such as size of extents, tablespace allocation, and so on. If you don't need to make such changes and you are using Export/Import, you can allow Import to rebuild them just like your Oracle7 rollback segments. To change them, it is once again easier if you have a script that you used for your Oracle7 production database. You can then make a copy of this script and edit it to contain the new definitions you want to use. If you need to reconstruct such a script, you should use Listing 6.2 from Chapter 6. This script will produce a file, called RS_BUILD.SQL, that will construct the same non-SYSTEM rollback segments as in your current database. You should run this script file after you have created the tablespaces used by the original rollback segments unless you first edit the script to rename these tablespaces.

Finally, if you are going to use the SQL INSERT statement with a subquery to copy data between the databases rather than the SQL*Plus COPY command, you will need the tables to be built in your Oracle8*i* database ahead of time. You can do this manually, by using a script

similar to the one we discussed to build the tablespaces and so on, or through the use of the Export/Import utility. Unless you have very few tables, the manual option is probably not practical. For a larger number of tables, you will probably want to build a script. As we have discussed before, you should plan on using SQL*Plus's ability to spool to an output file to build this script using SQL queries against your Data Dictionary.

Listing 7.2 contains a SQL*Plus script that will build an output file, which can be executed to build a chosen table using the same column definitions, storage parameters, and space utilization parameters as the original tables. You really need to use such a script only if you are going to use the SQL statement INSERT INTO...SELECT to copy the table data. If you are adventurous, you can modify this script to build all the tables from a given schema or even from the whole database (although you need to avoid trying to duplicate SYS's tables if you do this). You will probably have to use an external file rather than simple spool commands if you need to create a lot of output lines. After you've create your script file, you need to run it against the prepared Oracle8*i* database.

LISTING 7.2   SQL*Plus Script to Build Table Creation Script

```
REM SQL*Plus script to generate a CREATE TABLE command for an existing
REM table which will include the table and column names along with
REM the current storage options, and space utilizations options.

ACCEPT tname PROMPT "Table definition to be built > "

SET PAGESIZE 0 SERVEROUTPUT ON ECHO OFF VERIFY OFF FEEDBACK OFF

SPOOL x

DECLARE
  CURSOR c1 IS SELECT
    column_name, data_type, data_length, data_precision, data_scale, nullable
    FROM dba_tab_columns WHERE table_name = UPPER('&tname');
  cname dba_tab_columns.column_name%TYPE;
  dtype dba_tab_columns.data_type%TYPE;
  dleng dba_tab_columns.data_length%TYPE;
  dprec dba_tab_columns.data_precision%TYPE;
  dscal dba_tab_columns.data_scale%TYPE;
  vnull dba_tab_columns.nullable%TYPE;
  dattr VARCHAR2(100);
  v1 VARCHAR2(50);
  v2 VARCHAR2(50);
  v3 VARCHAR2(50);
  v4 VARCHAR2(50);
  v5 VARCHAR2(50);
```

continues

LISTING 7.2   Continued

```
 v6 VARCHAR2(50);
 v7 VARCHAR2(50);
 v8 VARCHAR2(50);
 v9 VARCHAR2(50);
 v10 VARCHAR2(50);
 v11 VARCHAR2(50);
 v12 VARCHAR2(50);
BEGIN
  dbms_output.put_line ('CREATE TABLE &tname (');
  OPEN c1;
  FETCH c1 INTO cname, dtype, dleng, dprec, dscal, vnull;
  LOOP
    IF c1%NOTFOUND THEN
      CLOSE c1;
      EXIT;
    END IF;
    dattr := cname || ' ' || dtype;
    IF dtype = 'DATE' OR dtype = 'LONG' THEN
      NULL;
    ELSIF dtype = 'NUMBER' THEN
      IF dprec IS NOT NULL THEN
        dattr := dattr || '(' || TO_CHAR(dprec);
        IF dscal IS NOT NULL THEN
          dattr := dattr || ',' || TO_CHAR(dscal);
        END IF;
        dattr := dattr || ')';
      END IF;
    ELSE
      dattr := dattr || '(' || TO_CHAR(dleng) || ')';
    END IF;
    IF vnull = 'N' THEN dattr := dattr || ' NOT NULL'; END IF;
    FETCH c1 INTO cname, dtype, dleng, dprec, dscal, vnull;
    IF c1%FOUND THEN
      dattr := dattr || ',';
    ELSE
      dattr := dattr || ' )';
    END IF;
    dbms_output.put_line(dattr);
  END LOOP;
  SELECT 'TABLESPACE '|| tablespace_name,
    'PCTFREE '|| TO_CHAR(pct_free),
    'PCTUSED ' || TO_CHAR(pct_used),
```

```
    'INITRANS ' || TO_CHAR(ini_trans),
    'MAXTRANS ' || TO_CHAR(max_trans),
    'STORAGE (INITIAL ' || TO_CHAR(initial_extent),
    'NEXT ' || TO_CHAR(next_extent),
    'MINEXTENTS '|| TO_CHAR(min_extents),
    'MAXEXTENTS ' || TO_CHAR(max_extents),
    'PCTINCREASE ' || TO_CHAR(pct_increase),
    'FREELISTS ' || TO_CHAR(freelists),
    'FREELIST GROUPS ' || TO_CHAR(freelist_groups) || ');'
  INTO v1,v2,v3,v4,v5,v6,v7,v8,v9,v10,v11,v12
  FROM dba_tables
  WHERE table_name = upper('&tname');
  dbms_output.put_line(v1);
  dbms_output.put_line(v2);
  dbms_output.put_line(v3);
  dbms_output.put_line(v4);
  dbms_output.put_line(v5);
  dbms_output.put_line(v6);
  dbms_output.put_line(v7);
  dbms_output.put_line(v8);
  dbms_output.put_line(v9);
  dbms_output.put_line(v10);
  dbms_output.put_line(v11);
  dbms_output.put_line(v12);
END;
/

SPOOL off
```

7

MIGRATION USING DATA COPYING

If you choose to use Export/Import to create your table definitions, you might as well use it to create your entire Oracle8*i* database structure, only omitting the transfer of the table contents. To prepare your Oracle8*i* database for this type of migration, you should refer to the section "Perform the Export/Import" of Chapter 6. In particular, use the instructions for a migration using tools for the data migration. Table 6.3 shows the Export/Import parameters that are of particular relevance to this process—they are the parameters identified with a 2 in the Notes column.

Initially, you might want to use the same parameter file for your Oracle8*i* database as your Oracle7 database. There might be some changes you have to make, however. These can include rollback segment names, if you changed them, or the COMPATIBLE parameter, if you want to use Oracle8*i* features such as locally managed tablespaces, materialized views, and so on. After you have your Oracle8*i* database ready, including any table definitions you wanted, you can proceed with the final steps of the migration.

Completing the Migration with Data Copying

We mentioned earlier that now that you have your Oracle8*i* database up and running, and have all the necessary tablespaces, rollback segments, and the like in place, your migration at this point will require database links to allow you to issue commands that will partially execute on both databases. You can build your database links on either the Oracle7 or the Oracle8*i* database unless you want to use the CREATE TABLE...AS SELECT command. In this case, you have to build your links on the Oracle8*i* database because you cannot issue CREATE commands from one database that execute on another.

Although you might not want to maintain database links that access your DBA accounts on a production system, you will probably find them very useful for this migration step. Your databases should both be running in restricted mode so that only privileged users can connect, whether directly or through a database link. This mode will also prevent users from making unexpected changes to the data that you are trying to transfer. We will show you how to build and use database links that belong to one of your DBA accounts.

If you have a favorite DBA account you have created, we suggest you use that one. Just remember you will need an identical account on the other database, using the same password as on your current account. If you are using one of the Oracle-supplied accounts, SYS or SYSTEM, both databases should have them set up correctly. You might need to change the password for the account on the Oracle8*i* database, if you haven't done so already. This assumes you are not still using the default password(s) on your Oracle7 database. After you are sure you have the passwords set correctly and you are connected to the database where you want your links built, issue a command such as the following:

```
CREATE DATABASE LINK link_name USING 'database_alias';
```

The `link_name` in this command is any name you choose, although it will have to include the domain name of the other database if you did not put both databases in the same domain. The domain is included after the link name using the dot notation to separate components. For example, a link called "kitten" that needs to connect to a database in the "cat.animal.kingdom" domain would be defined as

```
CREATE DATABASE LINK kitten.cat.animal.kingdom . . .;
```

The `database_alias` is the name taken from the TNSNAMES.ORA file on the local server or an Oracle Names Server on your network. The TNSNAMES.ORA file is one of the files that is configured as part of the Oracle networking product, SQL*Net or Net8. Listing 7.3 shows a sample set of files from an NT system that could be used for a simple migration to a database with an instance name of KITTEN in the cat.animal.kingdom domain.

LISTING 7.3   Oracle Network Files for Migration

```
# SQLNET.ORA

TRACE_LEVEL_CLIENT = OFF
sqlnet.authentication_services = (NTS)
names.directory_path = (TNSNAMES, HOSTNAME)
names.default_domain = cat.animal.kingdom
name.default_zone = cat.animal.kingdom
automatic_ipc = on

# LISTENER.ORA

LISTENER =
    (ADDRESS_LIST =
        (ADDRESS=
            (PROTOCOL= IPC)
            (KEY= cat.animal.kingdom.world)
        )
        (ADDRESS=
            (PROTOCOL= IPC)
            (KEY= kitten)
        )

    )

STARTUP_WAIT_TIME_LISTENER = 0
CONNECT_TIMEOUT_LISTENER = 10
TRACE_LEVEL_LISTENER = 0
PASSWORDS_LISTENER = (mypass)
SID_LIST_LISTENER =
  (SID_DESC =
    (SID_NAME = kitten)
  )


# TNSNAMES.ORA

KITTEN.CAT.ANIMAL.KINGDOM =
  (DESCRIPTION =
    (ADDRESS = (PROTOCOL = IPC)(KEY = EXTPROC0))
    (CONNECT_DATA = (SID = kitten))
  )
```

A full link definition for your user could, therefore, be

```
CREATE DATABASE LINK kitten USING kitten;
```

Note that the link name must match the instance name and that we have used the instance name as the alias as well. The domain names are not needed in this link definition as long as the database you are building it in also belongs to the cat.animal.kingdom domain.

> **NOTE**
>
> If you are not sure how to set up the Oracle networking tools, SQL*Net, which is provided with Oracle7, or Net8, which is provided with Oracle8i, you might need to work with your Network Administrator to help you. For a migration between two databases on the same server, the setup should be very simple. If you are migrating to a new server, you will need a more complex setup. In either case, someone with network knowledge should be able to help you answer the questions that the Oracle configuration tools will ask you. Additionally, someone should be able to assist you if you need to distribute files to a new server location. If you are completely unsure of how to do this, we recommend that you use another migration method.

With your database links in place, you should be ready to start copying the tables from one database to the other. You can refer to the commands in Listing 7.1 for a way to accomplish this. You might want to build a script of your own using the appropriate sample from this listing for your method of copying. We do suggest that you consider adding a PARALLEL clause to the command. Even if you only have a single CPU machine, you might well benefit from using a degree of two in this process. You should make sure you have started sufficient query slaves in each of your instances, however. Use the parameter PARALLEL_MIN_SERVERS with a value of twice the number of CPUs on your server in your parameter file for each instance, and set the degree of parallelism to this value in your SQL command. For example, on a dual-CPU server, your parameter should have a value of four.

Similarly, adding a NOLOGGING clause to your command will speed up the command because time will not be taken to create and store redo log vectors. Additionally, this will save the time that would normally be taken to write the redo log information from the log buffer to the redo log files. If you use the CREATE TABLE...AS SELECT option, the NOLOGGING clause is part of the CREATE syntax. If you want to use the INSERT INTO...SELECT option, you should create the table with the NOLOGGING and PARALLEL options. This will cause any subsequent INSERTs to be performed in parallel without redo logging.

> **NOTE**
>
> Prior to Oracle8, the NOLOGGING option keyword was UNRECOVERABLE. You can use this keyword if you build your tables on the Oracle8*i* database before you copy the data. However, unless you are moving already-existing scripts that include the UNRECOVERABLE option, you should use the newer keyword in order to ensure the scripts will still be valid for any future use.

With these considerations in mind, you could use commands similar to the following on your Oracle8*i* database to copy your tables. This example presumes you have a dual-CPU server and that you have built a database similar to our example on your Oracle8*i* database. It simply copies SCOTT's EMP table from the Oracle7 database to your new database. If you are using a DBA account to do this work, the command will have to include a TABLESPACE clause to override the default tablespace assigned to this user. If you don't want to use the default space utilization and storage parameters for a table, you also have to include the necessary parameters to set them—they will not be carried forward from your Oracle7 database—and this example includes a TABLESPACE clause to illustrate this:

```
CREATE TABLE scott.emp
NOLOGGING PARALLEL (DEGREE 4)
TABLESPACE user01
AS
SELECT /*+ PARALLEL (e,4) */ *
FROM scott.emp@kitten e;
```

If you decide to include these additional options in your commands, you should alter any scripts—and SQL-generating scripts—you build for performing the migration to include them.

Troubleshooting and Abandoning the Migration with Data Copying

Should you have problems with the Export/Import step of your migration, assuming you use this step, you might need to refer to the Server Utilities manual, provided by Oracle, which is where the Export and Import utilities are documented. Unlike a migration performed entirely using Export/Import, you are unlikely to run out of space—the most common problem with these utilities—while only transferring database definitions.

As for the copying step, any problem you encounter should only impact the one table you are copying. In most cases, you can simply drop the table, if the system didn't already do that for you, and try it over again. If there was an error message associated with the failure, it should

give you pointers as to what you might need to fix before retrying the copy. Once again, the most likely errors you will run into are associated with running out of space.

A final issue of which you should be cognizant is that the NOLOGGING option, should you decide to use it, will make any table created using it unrecoverable in the event of an instance or media failure requiring application of redo. This is because the extents allocated for the table are controlled by recursive SQL statements that are logged regardless of the NOLOGGING setting. The rows themselves are not logged, however, so a recovery process will re-create the segment, but it will be completely empty. So, if you suffer some sort of failure during the migration, you should consider dropping any tablespaces containing unrecoverable tables and repeating the steps necessary to rebuild them.

Of course, following the migration, you should back up the new database, just as we recommend for every newly migrated database, regardless of the method used. This will also prevent any problems that might occur due to using the NOLOGGING option if there is a subsequent failure.

Summary

In its traditional form, which uses the SQL*Plus COPY command, the data copying method of migrating a database has fallen out of favor. However, using the options provided with Oracle8*i*, you can complete a migration using this method about as easily as you can using the Export/Import utility. These options include the ability to execute the transfer of data from your current database to your Oracle8*i* database in parallel and without generating any redo overhead.

Many of the steps you might use to complete a migration using data copying are very similar to those used with a more traditional Export/Import method. These include the creation of scripts to transfer the data and the use of export dump files to build some of the basic structures minus the data.

The major benefit of this approach over a pure Export/Import is that you don't need to create and manage intermediate files. This saves physical resources as well as reduces the number of times the data has to be handled to just one. However, it is still a more intensive process than a migration using Oracle's migration tools but, like Export/Import, allows you more flexibility in how your resulting database is configured.

Post-migration Issues

IN THIS CHAPTER

We hope that, now that you've reached this chapter, you are ready to receive our congratulations on a successful migration to Oracle8*i*. They are well-deserved if indeed you do have a running Oracle8*i* database. If you are reading ahead, however, let us hope those congratulations will soon be deserved. Of course, although you should be happy with your accomplishment so far, you still have more work to face.

There are a number of tasks you need to address before you can consider the migration complete. Some of these you might need to attend almost immediately, the others you can work on over time. I have listed the key tasks in the following, and you will see a section of this chapter devoted to each of these topics:

- Back Up the Migrated Database
- Execute Test Procedures
- Review Initialization Parameters
- Tune the Database
- Introduce New Features as Needed
- Modify/Add Administrative Procedures

Although I have tried to show these tasks in the order in which you should complete them, you might have circumstances that don't allow you to follow this strictly. For example, if your initialization file contains parameters that have become obsolete or acquired new functionality in Oracle8*i*, you might have to change them before you can successfully complete your test procedures. Similarly, if changes to the Oracle optimizer cause some of your SQL statements to run with a different execution plan, you might need to perform some tuning steps before you can complete your stress testing and obtain satisfactory response times. Such an optimizer change could be to use hash joins in place of another join methodology but, if the HASH_AREA_SIZE is not set appropriately for the tables involved, they will not necessarily be more efficient.

Back Up the Migrated Database

The very first thing you should do after you complete your migration, whatever method you use, is to make a backup of your new Oracle8*i* database. Even if your new database is only for test purposes, you should still make this backup. The only possible exception to this would be if you never intend to touch this database again, but only performed the migration to measure the resources needed, the time taken, or some other characteristic of the process. If you don't make the backup and you start your testing, you could be very disappointed if you run into a problem and need to start over. Instead of just restoring your Oracle8*i* database, you will have to revert back to your premigrated database and perform the migration again.

This first backup should be a full cold backup, including the datafiles, the online redo log files, and the control files. To begin the cold backup, you should shut down the database using the NORMAL or IMMEDIATE option. If, for any reason, you shut it down with the ABORT option, you should restart it and then shut it down again with one of the required options. Although you could use Oracle's Recovery Manager utility for this backup, you might want to make this first backup with whatever methodology you are familiar with from your Oracle7 database. This way, you are unlikely to make any mistakes that could render this backup unusable.

For a full record of the database at this juncture, you should also backup the parameter file and any scripts and files, such as export dump files, you used to create and migrate the database. Even though they would not be needed to perform a database restore, they could provide useful documentation should you run into problems with your testing or, should it be necessary, to repeat the migration using your last Oracle7 backup.

Should you prefer to use an export rather than perform a backup, you should perform it before allowing any users to connect to the database. This way, you don't have to be concerned about any read consistency and referential integrity issues. Because an export does not include the control files, you will need to execute the ALTER DATABASE BACKUP CONTROLFILE command to complete a database backup. You should use the TO TRACE option to build a text file containing a script to re-create them, or using the TO *'file_name'* option to build a point-in-time binary copy. You cannot back up your online redo logs while the database is open, but you should include the other files previously mentioned, such as script and any related dump files used to build the database initially.

Execute Test Procedures

In Chapter 2, "Premigration Issues," we described how to build a test program for your migration project. It is now time to put that program to use. You might recall from the earlier chapter that we recommended testing your migration process on a copy, or a representative subset, of your production database. The first time you use your testing procedures, therefore, it should not be on your production system. And if your tests reveal some serious problems, you might have to try a new migration strategy on your test system, in which case you'll be using your testing process once or more on a nonproduction database. In fact, you might end up having to try a number of migrations before you achieve acceptable test results. Hopefully, you will have been following our advice on migration, and you will encounter no more than a few problems.

Let us quickly review the testing steps we recommended you follow. You should turn back to the section "Build a Test Plan" in Chapter 2 if you need more details about any of these plans.

Migration Test

First, you should perform a migration test. This test is intended to show that the database can be opened successfully, that the users can connect to their appropriate schemas, and that these schemas contain the proper objects and data. The easiest way to conduct this test is to connect to each valid userid in turn and query the data dictionary table, USER_OBJECTS. The list of objects for each user should contain the same object names and types as premigrated database. Of course, if you have performed a test migration using just a subset of the production data, you should only check for the existence of the objects you know you were supposed to migrate.

You might also want to run a query to determine whether the tables that comprise each schema contain the same number of rows as they did prior to the migration. This can be done by issuing the command SELECT COUNT(*) FROM *table_name* for each table in the schema. Of course, for this test to be meaningful, you must have recorded the same information prior to the migration. In some cases, your applications might already contain some simple processing steps that can perform the equivalent type of test, in which case you can use them for the migration test. In most cases, the minimal test or functional test is where you test the application processing and logic.

Minimal Test

The minimal test requires not only the database to be migrated, but also needs you to make the applications available to the Oracle8*i* database. In some cases, this might require relinking the applications.

> **NOTE**
>
> Linking applications requires commands that are specific to the operating system and the type of application. For this reason, we do not attempt to provide any details here, but refer you instead to the *Installation and Configuration Guide* (IUG) that is part of the Oracle documentation set for your installation. In some cases, your platform-specific documentation might contain two or more manuals with different titles, but they are collectively known as the IUG.

If you are running third-party applications, you might need to install updated versions to run on Oracle8*i*, or the vendor might have to provide you with instructions if they have to be relinked.

After you have your database and applications ready, you should run them to ensure that

- They can complete the same tasks as in your Oracle7 database
- They produce the same results when run against the same data as in your Oracle7 database

Once again, if you have only migrated part of your database in order to perform an initial round of testing, you might not be able to run the full suite of applications. Be aware which parts of the application you do and don't expect to work so that you don't ascribe an actual problem to unmigrated data.

Do not get concerned with any performance issues during the minimal testing phase; you simply need to find out if the applications will all start and run to completion.

Functional Test

During functional testing, you need to check that the applications are performing correctly and producing the correct results. This test is a natural follow-up to your minimal test, but requires that you have results from your Oracle7 database to compare with the Oracle8*i* output. If your company has a standard test suite, either developed in house or purchased from an outside vendor, this test would be a good place to use it.

This test is more difficult to complete successfully if you have not migrated your complete database. If you have carefully controlled what you selected to migrate, you should be able to build a test to compare the results of the pre- and post-migration versions of the database. Should your partial migration have been less controlled, you might have trouble interpreting any discrepancies you uncover. You might not be able to tell which are caused by your partial database migration and which are the result of a problem with the migrated database contents.

Ultimately, no matter how restricted you make your initial testing, you should ensure that you complete the functional test on the full database before you proceed beyond this point with your production system. Any failure with this test is an indication that the data did not migrate cleanly, or that the application is not compatible with the new Oracle version. In the former case, you will need to determine what caused the data problems. In the latter case, you might have to jump ahead to some of the other post-migration tasks and make the changes necessary to support the application under Oracle8*i*.

If you are only migrating part of your Oracle7 database, your original test suite might not be an appropriate tool for evaluating the reduced data and functionality of your migrated database. In such a situation, we recommend that you construct an Oracle7 database that contains the subset you intend to migrate and build a set of test results from that database. You can then have confidence that when you compare the results from the two versions, any differences are caused by problems with the migrated database. Once again, you should not move on with further tests until you have determined that your migrated database is valid.

8

Integration Test

Integration testing examines the migrated database in the context in which it will normally run. This includes the network components that support client/server connections, 3- or n-tier architectures, and distributed database connections. It also includes tests of the user interfaces, which might be GUI, browser-based, or character mode. This test should also include any interfaces to the application that do not necessarily access the database directly, but which use data extracted from it or provide data to it.

Network connections, including Oracle's SQL*Net and Net8 tools, should be used just as they would in your production environment. This includes subjecting them to a load similar to those that you expect when the system is in production. This is not to stress the application, but to make sure that the connections are still sufficiently fast to handle the new types of messaging performed by Oracle8*i*.

Performance Test

You should complete a performance test to examine the behavior of the key SQL statements that comprise your applications. The intent of the test is to check that they either use the same execution plan and consume the same resources as they did in the Oracle7 database, or they select better plans and perform with greater efficiency. In some cases, you can tell that the statements are working well just by the speed at which you observe them running. If you want to be more systematic, you can use the Oracle tools, SQL_TRACE and TKPROF, or, in Oracle8*i*, the SQL*Plus AUTOTRACE option.

You should not expect all your statements to run with exactly the same execution plans as they did in Oracle7. However, some of the changed plans might be chosen because they are making use of new options available in Oracle8*i*. You should examine the performance of such statements to determine if the new execution is really helping before trying to force them to run the old way. As mentioned earlier, the use of the newer options might require you to set some initialization parameters before they work properly. You might want to skip ahead to the next section, "Review Initialization Parameters," to see how to use the new parameters. Of course, if you want the application to execute exactly as it did under Oracle7 until you complete the rest of your tests, you might have to modify the SQL statements with hints, change your indexing strategy, or make other changes to your application.

Volume/Load Stress Test

During the volume and load stress testing, you need to subject the Oracle8*i* database to the same level of activity that it will face during a normal processing cycle. This involves the interactive work performed by the online users as well as the batch processing that occurs on a cyclical basis—daily, weekly, monthly, and even annually.

To complete these tests, you need the assistance of your users and application developers, or else a sophisticated workload emulation package. It is assumed that—by the time you attempt these tests—the processing is accurate and producing the correct results, and, therefore, these tests are simply validating that the workload can be supported. In some, rare cases the volume/stress test will cause data to be processed incorrectly. One of the common causes of such situations is when interprocess communication channels become overloaded and an occasional message is lost. It is therefore important to validate the data being generated as well as confirming that the system can support the actual or simulated workload during these tests.

One way to fully validate the migrated system is to run the old version and the new version of the database concurrently for a period of time and confirm that they are both producing identical results. This type of parallel system testing is very resource intensive, however, particularly if it requires users to enter their work on both systems instead of just one. You will have to make sure that any expectations on the part of the personnel involved are fully understood during the planning phase of the migration and that a commitment to provide the required resources has been agreed to by all the participating parties. Even so, it is unlikely that you will be able to support such a test for any significant length of time. You will still need to simulate the workload for the periodic processing outside of the parallel test period if you want to be certain that the new system can support such things as quarterly and annual processing.

You should also be aware that maximum volumes, which is the amount of data being manipulated, and maximum loads, which is the amount of processing being performed, do not necessarily occur simultaneously. Your tests might artificially need to force a maximum volume and maximum load to occur at the same time to verify that the new system can continue to function under a maximum stress situation. Benchmarks and extrapolations are rarely able to predict the physical impact of a real-life load on the system. You shouldn't consider your testing complete until you are reasonably convinced that your database can withstand a full load of interactive users, batch jobs, and administrative tasks.

Review Initialization Parameters

A number of parameters have become obsolete since Oracle7, and your Oracle8*i* database will not be able to use them. You can check the Oracle migration manual for lists of obsolete parameters. In most cases, your database will start up even if you don't remove these parameters from your initialization file, but the database will give you a warning message such as

```
ORA-25138: <parameter_name> initialization parameter has been made obsolete
```

with the obsolete parameter named. The same warning will be posted to your database alert log. In some cases, however, parameters might have been made obsolete before this feature was enabled to trap them, and your database is unlikely to start up if your initialization file contains them. Instead, the Oracle8*i* instance will fail to start with the following message

```
ORA-01078: failure in processing system parameters
```

Of course, this message will also appear if you have misspelled a parameter name, so you might have to check your Oracle8*i* Reference Manual for the valid parameters. If you see the ORA-01078 message rather than the ORA-25138 message, you will need to remove the obsolete parameters before you can start your Oracle8*i* database.

A number of new parameters exist, as well as parameters whose default values have been impacted by other changes in the initialization file, that might be of more significance to the performance of your new database. Unlike the obsolete parameters, these changes will not cause your instance to fail to start or give you other warning messages. Instead, they can change the behavior of certain statements, background processes, and resources acquired by the instance.

A number of parameters exist that you might need to consider changing in order to avoid processing performance changes until you are prepared to tune the new features in a controlled fashion. In Table 8.1, I have grouped these new parameters according to the type of resource or activity they might impact without you realizing it.

TABLE 8.1   Oracle8*i* Features and Related Parameters

Feature	*Related Parameters*
Sorts and Joins	sort_multiblock_read_count, always_anti_join, always_semi_join, hash_join_enabled, hash_area_size, hash_multiblock_io_count
Control File Size	control_file_record_keep_time, db_files
Checkpoints	fast_start_io_target
Parallel Server	gc_releasable_locks, gc_rollback_locks, gc_files_to_locks, lm_procs, lm_ress, lm_locks, max_commit_propagation_delay
SGA Size	db_block_buffers, shared_pool_size, java_pool_size, lm_procs, lm_ress, lm_locks, large_pool_size, processes
PGA Size	open_cursors
Multi-Threaded Servers	mts_servers
Optimizer	optimizer_percent_parallel, optimizer_features_enable, optimizer_index_caching, optimizer_index_cost_adj, optimizer_max_permutations, fast_full_scan

You should consult your *Reference Manual* and *Installation and User Guide* for the specific values to which your database will set these parameters and to learn what they will do if you leave them at that value rather than change them.

Note that Table 8.1 does not contain a complete list of the new features and new parameters introduced since Oracle7, release 7.3. There are a number of new features that can significantly improve performance in your Oracle8*i* database, and we discuss these in detail in Part II ,"Using the Oracle8*i* Features." Table 8.1 only identifies those features that might be a problem for you if you have simply tried to migrate to Oracle8*i* without trying to take advantage of the any of the new features. As a simple example, even if you have no interest in supporting Java in your database, the JAVA_POOL_SIZE parameter will default to 20MB—space you might not want to dedicate to a feature you are not using.

One other option you should be aware of during this phase of your migration is the parameter called COMPATIBLE. This parameter allows you to start up an instance as if it were running against a different version of Oracle than the one currently present in your Oracle Home directory. Although this parameter will let you start up your instance without initiating the new features of Oracle8*i*, you cannot use it to simulate your Oracle7, or earlier, database setup. This is because you can only set the parameter to the lowest release number of the current version of Oracle that, for Oracle8*i*, is the first logical release of Oracle8, namely, 8.0.0.

CAUTION

If you decide to use the COMPATIBLE parameter to change the behavior of your database from the default behavior of Oracle8*i*, you should be careful what values you choose. In particular, it is not recommended that you ever set the value to a lower release number than you have used in the past for the database. So although you can gradually increment the release number as you perform testing against your migrated database, you should not set the parameter down to a lower level. Oracle Support has issued warnings that this can potentially damage your database.

Tune the Database

In general, your migrated database should perform as well as, if not better than, your Oracle7 database. You might have to adjust a few initialization parameters in order to achieve this should they cause different behavior from your old database. For example, the SGA will be larger if you leave all the new parameters, as well as some of the old ones, at their default values. If the overall size is large enough to cause parts of the SGA to be paged, or swapped, out of memory, when before it was able to stay in memory, you might well see a decrease in performance.

> **CAUTION**
>
> The default size of the SGA for an Oracle8*i* database is significantly larger than for previous releases.

The types of performance problems caused by changes in parameter default settings, or by the introduction of new parameters, should be addressed during your performance and volume/load stress testing. The parameters to which you should have paid particular attention during these tests are listed in Table 8.1 in the previous section, "Review Initialization Parameters."

Following the testing, you might want to review some of the parameters you modified to ensure that your tests were run against a similar instance and reset them to their Oracle8*i* values. Additionally, you might want to perform some standard performance tuning techniques to your new database to see if you can improve performance. Even if you don't consider this necessary as an immediate task, you should plan the groundwork for later tuning efforts.

One of the keys to successful database tuning is to be able to tell what aspect of the system is becoming the most stressed and how quickly it is running out of resources. To do this, you need a baseline against which to measure the performance changes. If you have been in the habit of running statistical reports against your production database, you could use these to provide a starting point for your Oracle8*i* database. We suggest that you don't rely on these statistics if you can avoid it, however, because of the number of changes in the new release and their impact on overall performance. Ideally, you should apply whatever statistics collection tools—such as Oracle's UTLBSTAT/UTLESTAT reports, Enterprise Manager statistics, or any home-grown or third-party products—to your migrated database as soon as it is stable and begins supporting production again. You can then use these new statistics for your Oracle8*i* baseline.

By comparing your baseline data with current data, you can see changes in resource utilization over time and, from that, be able to predict when you will need to perform more tuning or even to acquire new resources. You might find that Oracle8*i* does not follow the same trends as your previous database version because of changes in the kernel code that reflect a more contemporary mix of resources and cost of upgrades.

The baseline will also indicate if the new database version is already approaching some of the limits in your current system. Although you should have used the sizing suggestions provided in the earlier chapters prior to migrating, in order to confirm that you had sufficient resources for a successfully migration, these were only approximations. After your database is in place, you need to confirm that these calculations were reasonably accurate, and that you are not on the verge of saturating part of the system.

After you start collecting performance statistics on a regular basis, you can use the tuning guidelines for Oracle database documented in the Oracle8*i* Tuning manual as well as in numerous other publications about Oracle. You should make sure that any tuning advice you read is applicable to your current version of Oracle, however. A number of changes were made between Oracle8, release 8.0 and Oracle8*i*, release 8.1 that require some modifications in how to go about making adjustments to your parameter file. Oracle7 tuning guidelines are even less useful, and could even be counterproductive, if applied to your migrated database.

One final word before you move on. Although many of the new features in Oracle8*i* can help improve performance overall, some of them do use resources in different ways. We suggest that you always keep in mind unless you add more people, more disks, more or faster CPUs, faster networks, and so on, you cannot increase the total amount of work that can be completed by the system. So any tuning exercise will simply increase the use of one or more resources in order to reduce the load on another resource or set of resources. In particular, those features that simplify the work of the DBA, the application developers, or the end users, will almost certainly increase the work done by the automated portions of the system. We therefore recommend that you perform any necessary tuning and record a new baseline before moving on and making any more changes, such as introducing the use of new features, as discussed in the next section.

Introduce New Features as Needed

Your Oracle8*i* database offers a wide range of new capabilities in many areas. The most widely known is the support of Java- and Internet-based applications. This alone has created a number of related new features, such as different levels of security within the database as well as in the network connections to the database and the servers supporting it. Another major feature of Oracle8 databases is that they are really Object Relational Database Management Systems (ORDBMS) that provide support for objects within a standard relational model. Another goal of the Oracle8 improvements, which have been introduced or improved from Oracle8 to Oracle8*i*, is to support "big" databases. This does not just refer to the size of the database, but also the size of the segments and other objects inside it, the number of users concurrently connected, and the number and size of transactions.

Part II of this book discusses the various features that have been added to support these goals. As mentioned at the very beginning of this book, some of you might be embarking on a migration to Oracle8*i* because you have a specific need for one or more of these new features. Others of you might be migrating for other reasons and don't need any of these features immediately. Some of these features might be ones you never see directly because they will be implemented by the application developers whose programs run against your database.

For the majority of you, therefore, will have no immediate needs to make changes just in order to implement one of the new Oracle8 or Oracle8*i* features. This should not stop you from examining the capabilities of your migrated database to see if anything new could help, either in its performance or its management. Those DBAs among you who have some specific requirements of Oracle8*i* might find it useful to review what other features are available. Even if you still don't find a pressing need, you will at least have some knowledge of capabilities should your environment change in the future. You might even consider building a test database to see just how some of these features work for yourself. Some of them might prove surprisingly beneficial and change your mind about how quickly you might want to adopt them.

NOTE

Many DBAs overlook the tools that can make database management easier when they consider their database performance. We believe this is a mistake. The less time you spend on the mundane tasks associated with your database, the more time you have to monitor its behavior, to help identify performance bottlenecks, and to predict future needs. Further, the more you automate the routine tasks, the less likely you are to make mistakes, to skip steps, or to have to scramble to cover any absence you might take from work, either planned or otherwise. The time you free up can be used to help others in your organization to do their work better—for example, by teaching developers how to interpret SQL*Plus AUTOTRACE results to help them write more efficient SQL—as well as to learn how to use new tools and features yourself.

This step in the migration process, adding new features, should be considered an ongoing project unlike many of the other steps that have a specific function in the overall process, and when they are done, the step is no longer applicable. The various tests fall into this category. Do not fall into the trap of reading over this section and then moving on if you don't think it applies to you right now. A good DBA should always be comparing current and predicted needs with the tools available to achieve them.

Modify/Add Administrative Procedures

This is another of those steps in the migration process that you might not be able to perform at a specific point in the process and then move on. In some cases, you might have to address key scripts almost immediately after you complete the migration. In others, you might be able to make changes to your procedures along the lines of how you introduce new features into your database and applications—after identifying a new need for them. This approach to adding features was discussed in the previous section, "Introduce New Features as Needed."

An example of a procedure that you might need to modify immediately is your backup and recovery strategy. For those of you using Oracle's Enterprise Backup Utility (EBU) in Oracle7, you will have to plan to convert to a new strategy immediately—EBU is not supported under Oracle8*i*. You can either convert to Oracle's Recovery Manager, the replacement product for EBU, or fall back on the manual techniques for handling backups. In either case, you might also want to build scripts to automate the procedures to at least the level you had achieved with EBU.

If you were using the manual backup and recovery mechanisms—that is, hot or cold system backups of your database files—you can continue to use the same procedures. However, in this case, you might want to explore whether Recovery Manager could be a better method for you. You could approach this in much the same way you would when examining other new features to see if they would benefit you or your users.

Other types of procedures you might want to review in light of the new version of Oracle are your monitoring and performance reporting procedures. You might find that there are new Data Dictionary views and Dynamic Performance tables (commonly known as "V$-tables") that give you better information than you had before. In some cases, existing tables and views might have additional columns that could also be useful to you. You might also find out that you are not getting the results you were expecting because some of the views and tables have undergone subtle changes in what they report. Of course, you might have some procedures that fail completely because they referenced a table or view which has became obsolete in or before your current release of Oracle8*i*.

I mentioned in an earlier section, "Review Initialization Parameters," that there is a new message, ORA-25138, in Oracle8*i*. If you have any procedures that examine files or even react interactively to Oracle codes and messages, you might also have to examine these to ensure that they are still responding appropriately. A number of new messages in Oracle8*i* are simply informative rather than being an indication of problems, either errors or warnings. For example, a typical database backup using Recovery Manager can generate 20 or 30 messages: Each of which simply reports on the successful completion of a particular step or process.

Other areas where you might want to review your procedures include

- Jobs managed by Enterprise Manager that now have options to branch based on results of preceding steps and better management of events reporting.
- Free space coalescing; you should consider locally-managed tablespaces if this is a common activity for you.
- Loading data from outside the database; indexes and constraints are no longer so tightly tied together, and the Partitioning Option provides you with a lot more flexibility in loading, and removing, sets of data.

We refer you to Part II of this book for details on the various features mentioned in the previous list.

Summary

A number of activities exist that you should consider part of the migration process, even though you don't have to work on them until after the actual database migration is complete. In some cases, you might not be able to get any use out of your migrated database without performing some of these steps. At the other extreme, some of these procedures might be ongoing for as long as your database remains a production database. In this summary, I have divided these post-migration steps into three categories—those that might have to be done in order to continue work; those which are not essential, but we would consider it irresponsible not to complete; and those that are useful but not a high priority.

The activities that you might be forced to complete to get your database to work are to review the initialization parameters and to modify or add new administrative procedures. Some obsolete parameters might have to be removed before you can start your database and others might need to be changed to allow it to work at a satisfactory performance level. In particular, space allocation to the System Global Area (SGA) might be very different under Oracle8*i* and cause performance degradation if the SGA will no longer fit into real memory. Administrative procedures you might have to modify would be those that rely on obsolete tools, such as Oracle Enterprise Backup Utility, or obsolete Data Dictionary tables or views.

Not every parameter or procedure will need to be addressed immediately after the migration. However, you should consider those that you don't examine to belong to the third category discussed here and include a procedure to evaluate them as one of those that are useful but not a high priority.

The procedures that we believe you should complete as soon as possible after the migration are to backup your new Oracle8*i* database and to perform the validation tests you should have outlined in your preparation phase. The backup gives you a place to restart the testing from if you have problems, and the testing will help give you and your users a level of confidence that the new database will continue to perform as accurately and as efficiently as the previous version. Moving ahead into production without performing these two steps could result in the loss or corruption of all work subsequent to the migration, as well as requiring a return to your Oracle7 database. Of course, you would then have to perform the migration one more time.

The useful, but not urgent, procedures are to tune the database and to introduce any new features that appear useful. Although it might not be possible to tune the database immediately, it would be prudent to begin collecting performance statistics as soon as possible to act as a baseline for comparisons during future performance monitoring. Similarly, unless there are one or more new features that prompted your migration in the first place, you do not need to attempt to incorporate any of them into your database or applications. However, over time, you should evaluate what is available and make any changes you deem beneficial as time and resources permit.

Upgrading from Oracle8 to Oracle8*i*

IN THIS CHAPTER

This section is included for those of you who have already taken the step of migrating from an earlier release to Oracle8, but who now need to upgrade from release 8.0 to release 8.1. You do not face as complex a task as you did moving to Oracle8 in the first place, but you might want to look at some of the chapters covering post-migration tasks just in case your scripts, applications, initialization parameters, and so on, need to be adjusted to run optimally with Oracle8*i*. In particular, you might want to preview Chapter 8, "Post-migration Issues;" Chapter 10, "Issues with Compatibility;" Chapter 11, "Upgrading Applications;" and Chapter 12, "Issues with ROWIDs."

This chapter assumes that you are upgrading from a supported, not a beta, release of Oracle8. If you have a release earlier than 8.0.3, or if you happen to be running release 8.0.4S (a special, 64-bit, version of Oracle8), you need to upgrade to Oracle8, release 8.0.5 before attempting an upgrade to Oracle8*i*. Also, this chapter assumes that you are upgrading a single-instance database on one server. For users of Oracle Parallel Server, we will not identify those actions that need to be repeated on more than one node. You should also review the section "Parallel Server Upgrade Issues" for a discussion of some specific post-upgrade steps you will need to execute.

> **NOTE**
>
> This book does not address the special needs of Oracle Beta customers running pre-production releases of Oracle8*i*. If you are running a release earlier than 8.1.5 and want to upgrade to a production version of Oracle8*i*, we refer you to the Oracle8*i* Migration manual. This manual contains specific steps to taken when performing an upgrade from preproduction to production status.

This chapter is divided into the following sections:

- Pre-upgrade Issues
- Upgrading with Oracle Data Migration Assistant
- Performing an Upgrade Manually
- User-Defined Datatype Upgrades
- Recovery Manager Upgrades
- Advanced Queuing Upgrade Issues
- Snapshot Upgrades
- Advanced Replication Upgrades

- Parallel Server Upgrade Issues
- PL/SQL Validation
- Post-Upgrade Actions

Pre-Upgrade Issues

You should address a few issues before attempting to upgrade your release 8.0 database to release 8.1. We will look at these items in this section.

DB_DOMAIN Parameter

In Oracle8*i*, the initialization parameter, DB_DOMAIN, has a default value of NULL. If you are using a specific value in your current database, you should continue to use it in your upgraded database. However, if you have not set this parameter, it is currently defaulting to the value WORLD. Before beginning any upgrade steps, you should explicitly set this parameter to its default value so that anything which depends on the domain value will continue to function in Oracle8*i*.

OUTLN User or Role

Oracle8*i* creates a new user, called OUTLN, if you or one of the database users implement the Optimizer Plan Stability capability introduced with this release. In order to avoid potential conflicts with this username, you should ensure that your database does not include either a username or a role with the name OUTLN.

To check for a user with this name, issue the following command in a Server Manager or SQL*Plus session while you are connected as a user with the DBA role:

```
SELECT * FROM dba_users WHERE username = 'OUTLN';
```

If no rows are returned, you don't have a user with this name. If you do have a row returned, I advise you to drop this user before continuing. If the user owns objects you don't want to lose, you should move him to an alternate schema. You can do this most easily with the Export/Import utilities, using the FROMUSER to TOUSER options of the Import command. If you want to use an existing user for the OUTLN objects, you can skip the steps listed in the next paragraph. Otherwise, you should create an alternate user.

Use the tablespace names from the preceding query to define the default and temporary tablespaces for this new user, unless you have reason to change them. Remember to grant the new user the necessary quotas on the tablespaces in which the OUTLN has segments stored. Also, you might have to grant the roles and quotas currently assigned to OUTLN to your new user. To find the quotas, privileges, and roles involved, query the views DBA_TS_QUOTAS,

DBA_SYS_PRIVS, DBA_TAB_PRIVS, and DBA_ROLES. After this is done, you can export the OUTLN user with the following command:

```
exp system/manager owner=outln
```

on UNIX, or

```
exp80 system/manager owner=outln
```

on Windows NT. You then perform the import to the alternate user. If this user is called NEWOL, the command you would need is

```
imp system/manager fromuser=outln touser=newol
```

on UNIX, or

```
imp80 system/manager fromuser=outln touser=newol
```

on Windows NT. When this has completed successfully, you can drop the user OUTLN with the Server Manager or SQL*Plus command

```
DROP USER outln CASCADE;
```

> **CAUTION**
>
> Should you be running a preproduction version of Oracle8*i*, you must not drop the OUTLN user from your database.

Add Space to Key Tablespaces

You might want to add more space to your SYSTEM tablespace and any tablespaces in which you have rollback segments stored. The new release might require more room for the segments stored in these tablespaces. If you have lots of free space in these tablespaces, you might not need to do anything, but if these tablespaces are almost full, you should consider adding a new datafile to each of them. The following sample SQL command will add a UNIX file to the SYSTEM tablespace:

```
ALTER TABLESPACE system
  ADD DATAFILE '/u1/oracle/prod/system02.dbf'
  SIZE 50M;
```

Alternatively, you can alter the tablespaces to automatically grow in size. Here is an example of a command to perform this operation on the SYSTEM tablespace:

```
ALTER TABLESPACE system
  AUTOEXTEND ON NEXT 1M;
```

If you choose this option, make sure that you have room on the current disk drives in which the tablespace's datafiles are stored to allow them to grow. You should not use this command if the datafiles are stored on raw partitions unless, of course, your operating system has the option to extend the partitions.

Choose an Upgrade Method

You can choose from two methods to upgrade your Oracle8, release 8.0 database to Oracle8*i*, release 8.1. The simplest method is to use the Oracle Data Migration Assistant because this tool will perform the complete process. It uses a GUI tool that will execute the necessary steps in the correct order and offer extensive help if needed. The tool will remove any obsolete parameters from your initialization file, and it can reconfigure your *listener.ora* file if you desire.

You can also perform the upgrade manually. This approach allows you more flexibility than the Data Migration Assistant, such as the ability to modify your initialization parameters and replace obsolete ones with new ones, if appropriate. Of course, even if you use the Data Migration Assistant, you can make some of these changes after the upgrade is complete.

We recommend that you use the Data Migration Assistant if you are not familiar with upgrade and migration processing. If you are not certain which method to use, you should read ahead and study the next two sections, "Upgrading with Oracle Data Migration Assistant" and "Performing an Upgrade Manually," to see what each approach entails.

One note for those of you running Oracle Parallel Server. You cannot perform an upgrade using the Data Migration Assistant for the upgrade from release 8.0 to release 8.1. Instead, you must use just one instance to upgrade your database manually.

Make a Backup

The last step you should complete before performing the upgrade is to make a full backup of the database. We strongly recommend that you make this a cold backup by performing a normal (or immediate) shutdown of the database first. The backup should include all the datafiles, all the online redo log files, and at least one control file copy. You might also want to backup your initialization file, or make a copy you can refer to after the upgrade, particularly if you are planning to use the Data Migration Assistant for your upgrade.

Upgrading with Oracle Data Migration Assistant

If you have decided to upgrade to Oracle8*i* using the Oracle Data Migration Assistant, you must first install the Migration Assistant using the Oracle Universal Installer supplied with the Oracle8*i* distribution. We recommend that you read the installation documentation provided for your operating system to ensure that you can successfully start the Migration Assistant.

When the Data Migration Assistant starts, it opens a Welcome screen. You can press the Help button on this, or any other screen, should you need assistance at any step of the migration process. To proceed with the migration at this point, just press the Next button on the Welcome screen.

The next screen you see will ask you to provide the full pathname the home directory for your Oracle8*i* installation. This should be a different directory than the one you are currently using for your release 8.0 Oracle home because the Data Migration Assistant cannot use the same Oracle home for the two releases. When you have entered the pathname in the Files Location box, click the Next button.

The following screen will ask you to choose the standard or the Enterprise Edition of Oracle8*i*. For details on these two options, see Chapter 3, "Installing and Configuring Oracle8*i*." When you have made your selection, press the Next button.

On the next screen, you will choose whether you want the standard installation or a custom installation. Once again, I refer you back to Chapter 3 for information on what these options provide. Whichever you choose, you should ensure that you include all your current options unless you have decided to discontinue using one or more of them. The number of screens you have to complete at this point will depend on the installation method you have chosen. Eventually you will arrive at the Upgrading or Migrating an Existing Database screen. Check the Upgrade or Migrate an Existing Database box and select the name of the database you are upgrading. Then click the Next button.

A summary screen will now appear and offer you a chance to confirm all your settings. When you have verified that these values are correct, you can click the Install button to begin the installation of the Oracle8*i* software. After the installation is completed, which might take some time, the Oracle Data Migration Assistant will be started. It will begin with a Welcome screen, and you should press the Next button to begin the upgrade. As with the Universal Installer, you also have the option of pressing the Help button on any screen to get assistance with the upgrade process.

The first screen following the Welcome screen is the Before You Upgrade or Migrate screen. Just make sure that your database meets all the conditions listed and then press the Next button. Then you will have to select the name of the instance you use to start up the Oracle8 database that you are upgrading on the Select a Database Instance screen. Note that you must enter the instance name, not the database name, on this screen, and then press the Next button.

The following screen, Database Password and INIT.ORA, will need you to verify or modify the following data:

- The full pathname to the new Oracle8*i* home directory
- The full pathname and filename of the initialization file for the database you are upgrading
- The full pathname to your current Oracle8, release 8.0, database's Oracle home directory

When you have done this, you should press the Next button for the Choose Migration or Upgrade Type screen. If you choose the Custom option, you will have to respond to a number of additional questions that are dependent on your operating system; otherwise, you can allow the Data Migration Assistant to handle your migration for you. When you have answered these questions, or if you choose the standard option, you will be presented with the Confirm Backup screen.

Assuming that you have followed my preliminary steps, you will have a backup of your database, and you can press the Next button. If you didn't make a backup, you should use the Cancel button to terminate the process and make a cold backup. You can then restart the Data Migration Assistant to repeat the upgrade process. If you are running your database on UNIX, you need to execute the following command at a system prompt:

```
odma
```

If you are using Windows NT, select

```
Start > Programs > Oracle8i > Oracle Data Migration Assistant
```

Follow the same steps listed previously until you reach the Start the Migration or Upgrade screen. You should check the values on this screen for correctness. If anything is invalid, you should click the Back button until you can modify the incorrect settings. When you have everything ready, you can click the Next button on the Start the Migration or Upgrade screen to execute the upgrade.

The Oracle documentation notes that you might see a series of error messages related to the Advanced Queuing feature while the upgrade is progressing. The sample set of messages they publish include ORA-000604, ORA-00001, and ORA-06512. These are benign messages and can safely be ignored.

After the upgrade to your database completes, the Oracle Data Migration Assistant will update your *listener.ora* file if you want. The Listener.ora Migration Information screen allows to select a Yes or a No button depending on whether or not you want these updates to be performed. You should choose Yes if you are planning to use Oracle Enterprise Manager with your

upgraded database. If you click the Yes button, the Data Migration Assistant will shut down your Oracle8 and Oracle8*i* listeners and add an entry to your Oracle8*i* *listener.ora* file wherever you have a SID_DESC entry for the instance you named on the "Select a Database Instance" screen. The new entry will look like this:

```
(SID_DESC =
    (GLOBAL_NAME = database_name.domain_name)
    (ORACLE_HOME = oracle_home_directory)
    (SID_NAME = database_name)
)
```

where the *database_name* will be replaced with the name of your database, *domain_name* will replaced with the value for the DOMAIN_NAME parameter in the initialization file confirmed on the Database Password and INIT.ORA screen, and *oracle_home_directory* will be replaced with the Oracle8*i* home directory you confirmed on that same screen.

If you already had a SID_DESC entry with a GLOBAL_DBNAME clause, the Data Migration Assistant also adds the value from the GLOBAL_DBNAME entry and adds it to the values in the SERVICE_NAMES parameter in the *listener.ora* file. On the Windows NT platform, the assistant will also remove the old entries for the database. When all the changes are complete, the Data Migration Assistant will restart your Oracle8*i* listener using the updated file.

This completes the upgrade of your database and you should perform any of the additional upgrades you need for the products you support. You can then proceed with the general post-migration steps described in the "Post-Upgrade Actions" section of this chapter.

Performing an Upgrade Manually

If you decided that you want to upgrade your database manually, you should execute the tasks that I discuss in this section. If you are required to perform a manual upgrade because you have Oracle Parallel Server installed, you should also read the documentation provided by Oracle in the *Oracle8i Parallel Server Setup and Configuration Guide*. Additionally, if you are running Parallel Server on Windows NT, you also need to review the instructions about the Operating System Dependent (OSD) layer described in the *Oracle Parallel Server: Getting Started for Windows NT* manual. Remember that you only need to perform the installation and upgrade on one node of your Parallel Server cluster. I will point out any specific steps that must be executed on more than one node.

Your first task is to install Oracle8*i* on your system. This process is described in Chapter 3. Unlike an upgrade using the Oracle Data Migration Assistant, do not select the Upgrade or Migrate an Existing Database checkbox on the Upgrading or Migrating an Existing Database screen. It is this option that causes the Universal Installer to start the assistant for you automatically following the installation.

After the installation is complete, you will need to modify your initialization parameter file. First, it must be moved out of the directory for the 8.0 release of the database and into the release 8.1 directory. If you were using the default locations for this file, it will be found in the `$ORACLE_HOME/dbs` directory on UNIX and in the directory `$ORACLE_HOME\database` on Windows NT. You should move the file to the corresponding default directory under Oracle8*i*. If you used an Oracle Flexible Architecture (OFA) installation, your default location for the initialization under Oracle8*i* will be `$ORACLE_BASE/admin/instance_name/pfile`. You don't have to use the default location or even the default name, `initinstance_name.ora`, if you don't want to, but you should still move the file out of its release 8.0 location.

> **NOTE**
>
> If you are running Oracle Parallel Server and use a different initialization file for each instance, you should move and modify the files on every node in accordance with the instructions given in this section. You should also review your Parallel Server documentation for additional information on parallel server-related parameters that changed between release 8.0 and 8.1.

If you are using an included file with the IFILE parameter in your initialization file, you should also move it out of the old Oracle home directory structure. When you have relocated your initialization file, or files, you need to remove or modify parameters that changed between release 8.0 and 8.1. The Oracle migration manual for Oracle8*i*, release 8.1, lists about sixty parameters that became obsolete and another ten or so which have changed default values or function. In addition, there is a list of another twenty or so new parameters to support the features introduced in this release. Rather than repeat this information here, I advise you to turn to Appendix B of the *Oracle8i Migration* manual for the complete details of these changes. The specific changes you will have to make to complete your upgrade are as follows:

- Modify the value for any IFILE parameter that identifies an include file which you have moved out of the old home directory. The parameter needs to provide the full path and filename for the relocated include file.

- Comment out the parameters JOB_QUEUE_PROCESSES and AQ_TM_PROCESSES. You should not remove or change these parameters because you can uncomment them and use them normally again after you complete your upgrade.

- If you are short of memory, you might want to add the parameter PARALLEL_AUTOMATIC_TUNING and set its value to TRUE. This will avoid allocation of an oversized shared pool in the System Global Area.

- If you are using Oracle Parallel Server, you must temporarily change the value of the PARALLEL_SERVER parameter to FALSE on any node where you will be executing upgrade steps.

When you have modified and saved your initialization file or files, you need to prepare your operating system to identify the new release of Oracle. This involves changing the environment variables that apply to your system as shown in the following list:

- ORACLE_HOME names the Oracle8*i* home directory.
- PATH includes the BIN directory of the Oracle8*i* installation.
- ORA_NLS defines the National Language Support value used for your old database.
- ORACLE_BASE names the base directory if you performed an OFA installation of Oracle8*i*.
- LD_LIBRARY_PATH on UNIX systems includes the LIB subdirectory under Oracle8*i* home directory.
- ORACLE_PATH, if used, should name the equivalent 8.1 directory as you used in release 8.0.

You will need to change the environment variables on all nodes for Oracle Parallel Server.

You are now ready to complete the upgrade of your database. Use an operating system command to make your default directory the new Oracle8*i* ADMIN subdirectory, where you will find a number of SQL scripts with names that begin U08. You can use this substring in a wildcard search of the Oracle8*i* directory if you can't locate the correct subdirectory.

When you have changed to the ADMIN directory, start up a Server Manager or a SQL*Plus session and connect as INTERNAL. Then start the database with the following command

```
STARTUP RESTRICT
```

You might also need to include the PFILE option if you didn't use the default values for your initialization file's name and location. If your instance will not start because of obsolete parameters, perform a shutdown, remove or comment the problem parameters, and repeat the startup steps.

Before proceeding, I advise you to open a log file to record the output from the following activities in case there are problems that you will need to address. You can do this be issuing the SPOOL command and naming the file you want to use for logging. You can also issue the SET ECHO command to determine whether you will see the output on the screen—use a value of YES if you want to see the output and a value of NO if you don't.

Execute the upgrade script appropriate for the old release of Oracle8 you were running. I list the Oracle8 releases in Table 9.1, along with the name of the script you need to run to upgrade each specific release.

CAUTION

> If you don't find your current Oracle8 release number listed in Table 9.1, you are attempting to upgrade a nonproduction release, or the special release, 8.0.4S, which cannot be upgraded directly. If you have an 8.0 release, you need to upgrade to 8.0.5 before upgrading to Oracle8*i*. If you have an 8.1 release, you are running a beta version that is not addressed in this book, and you need to obtain specific instructions from the *Oracle8i Migration* manual.

TABLE 9.1 Oracle8*i* Upgrade Scripts

Oracle 8.0 Release	Upgrade Script Name
Release 8.0.3	u0800030.sql
Release 8.0.4	u0800040.sql
Release 8.0.5	u0800050.sql

You can use the commercial "at" character (@) as a shortcut to execute the script from your Server Manager or SQL*Plus prompt. For example, to upgrade from release 8.0.4, you would issue the command:

```
@u0800040.sql
```

The script creates and updates certain Data Dictionary objects to be compatible with Oracle8*i* and then executes the CATALOG.SQL and CATPROC.SQL scripts to complete the upgrade of the system catalog and the packages used by PL/SQL. If you have ever run these scripts yourself, you know that they can take some time to complete.

After the scripts finish, turn off the logging by issuing the SPOOL OFF command and check the log file for any errors. You might see some errors related to attempts to drop objects that did not exist, as well as a series of errors related to Advanced Queuing (with error numbers ORA-000604, ORA-00001, and ORA-06512). You can simply ignore these. However, if there are errors about failure to find space to create an object, or which indicate that a script failed to complete successfully, you should perform the necessary corrective action and re-run the script. It is safe to run any of the scripts invoked by the upgrade script, as well as the upgrade script itself, as many times as you need to complete the upgrade successfully.

> **NOTE**
>
> The most common errors we have encountered when performing upgrades are related to space limitations in a key tablespace. The SYSTEM tablespace is the one that causes the majority of the problems, but tablespaces containing rollback segments might also be the culprits in an upgrade to Oracle8*i*. We do not have space here to list all the possible error messages you might encounter when running the upgrade script, but refer you to the *Error Messages* manuals published by Oracle for an explanation of them and recommendations on how to resolve them.

When your upgrade script has completed successfully, you need to issue the following two commands to allow the database to perform certain internal housekeeping tasks in readiness to be opened as a strictly Oracle8*i* database:

```
ALTER SYSTEM DISABLE RESTRICTED SESSION;
SHUTDOWN IMMEDIATE;
```

You can execute these commands from the same session you used to run the upgrade script. Be sure to use the IMMEDIATE option so that any user who might have logged in after you turned off the restricted session limitation doesn't have time to complete any work. Do not use the ABORT option, however, or else you will prevent Oracle from completing the necessary housekeeping.

Your database is now ready to be opened under Oracle8*i*. Make sure that you don't accidentally open it using the older version of Oracle. We strongly recommend that you make a backup of it before you re-open it so that you can recover from such an accident. This backup will also allow you to recover your Oracle8*i* version of the database if you suffer a media failure. If you suffer a media failure without it, you might have to restore the database backup taken before you performed the upgrade, and then repeat the process. Before you open your database for your users, you might also want to perform the specific upgrades for the products you support as well as complete the general post-upgrade activities: all described in the next few sections of this chapter.

User-Defined Datatype Upgrades

If you have made use of user-defined datatypes in your Oracle8, release 8.0, database, you can benefit from some enhancements provided in Oracle8*i*. Specifically, the representation format of user-defined types—created with the CREATE TYPE SQL command—and of nested tables

and varrays, has changed in the new release. The new format makes better use of disk space and provides better performance as a result of reduced disk accesses. If you are not concerned about disk space or performance characteristics of your database, you don't need to make any changes. Oracle8*i* can handle user-defined objects with either the old or the new format.

Should you decide to upgrade your user-defined datatypes after your database upgrade, you need to execute the following steps:

1. Use the Export utility to export any tables built in your release 8.0 database that contain a user-defined object type, a nested table, or a varray.

2. Connect to the database using Server Manager or SQL*Plus and drop the tables you successfully exported in step 1.

3. Check the value of the COMPATIBLE parameter of your database by issuing the command

   ```
   SHOW PARAMETER compatible
   ```

   or the query

   ```
   SHOW PARAMETER compatible WHERE name = 'compatible';
   ```

4. If the value of the parameter is 8.1.0 or higher, you can continue with step 5; otherwise, you need to change your initialization file and add or change the COMPATIBLE parameter, providing a value of 8.1.0 or higher. When you have done this, you need to shut down and restart your database.

5. Use the Import utility to import the file you exported in step 1. Confirm that all the tables were imported successfully or else fix any problems and re-run the Import. Your imported tables will be built using the new representation format.

Recovery Manager Upgrades

This section covers the issues you need to address if you used Recovery Manager with a recovery catalog in your 8.0 database. If you didn't use a recovery catalog, your database upgrade will not impact Recovery Manager, and you can start using the new version of the executables without making any further changes. However, if you did use a recovery catalog, you need to ensure that your catalog will be compatible with the current release of Recovery Manager.

If your original database was release 8.0.3, you will not be able to use the recovery catalog after you complete your upgrade. You will need to create a new recovery catalog, ideally in an Oracle8*i* database, and rebuild your backup scripts and files. For later releases, you can use your original recovery catalog, but you will need to upgrade it so that it will work with the Oracle8*i* Recovery Manager executable. Of course, you can also upgrade the database holding your recovery catalog to Oracle8*i* in the same way that you upgraded your production database.

Whether you have upgraded the database holding your recovery catalog, you will need to update the previous version of the catalog to an Oracle8*i* version. To do this, implement the steps listed as follows:

1. Connect to the recovery catalog with Recovery Manager—your environment variables should still be set to ensure that you are using the Oracle8*i* version.

2. You should see an ORA-06186 error message if you have not yet updated your recovery catalog. The text of the message will be similar to the following:

   ```
   ORA-06189: PL/SQL package rcat.DBMS_RCVCAT version
   08.00.05 in RCVCAT is too old
   ```

   If you don't see this message, you probably don't need to perform an update to the recovery catalog or else your recovery catalog is not a valid version to be updated. You should continue with step 3 if you do receive the message.

3. Issue the command `upgrade catalog` at the next RMAN prompt. This should generate a few RMAN messages, the last one of which should be

   ```
   RMAN-06442: enter UPGRADE CATALOG command again to
   confirm upgrade
   ```

4. Enter the `upgrade catalog` command as directed to process the upgrade command. You should receive an RMAN-06408 message, confirming that the upgrade is complete and the catalog version is 8.1.5 or higher.

Advanced Queuing Upgrade Issues

If you plan to use Advanced Queuing in your Oracle8*i* database, you need to upgrade any components installed in your database to the current release. This section addresses the upgrade process and is divided into two parts. The first part discusses an initial upgrade that needs to be performed if your upgrade to Oracle8*i* was made directly from a release 8.0.3 database. The second part discusses the upgrades required by any release prior to 8.1.5, including the 8.0.3 databases that have had the initial upgrade applied. If you did not upgrade from 8.0.3 directly, you should skip the next section and continue with the section entitled "Upgrade Advanced Queuing Tables." If you did upgrade from 8.0.3 directly, you should continue with the next section "Upgrade Advanced Queuing Datatypes" before addressing the material in the "Upgrade Advanced Queuing Tables" section.

Upgrade Advanced Queuing Datatypes

In this section, I tell you how to update an Advanced Queuing AQ$_AGENT datatype to hold an extended address field for better performance. If you have not upgraded from Oracle8, release 8.0.3, you have previously run these steps on a later release of your database, or you

don't intend to use Advanced Queuing, you don't need to apply the changes discussed in this section. If you need to process the update, implement the following steps:

1. Shut down your database using the IMMEDIATE or NORMAL option. If you are running Parallel Server, shut down all your instances and change the initialization parameter, PARALLEL_SERVER, to FALSE for the instance you will be using for this task.

2. Comment out the parameters AQ_TM_PROCESSES and JOB_QUEUE_PROCESSES in the initialization file you plan to use for this task. You will be able to remove the comment characters after you complete the upgrade.

3. Change your session's default directory to the ADMIN subdirectory under your Oracle8*i* home. Confirm that you are in the correct directory by locating the files CATQUEUE.SQL and CATNOQUEUE.SQL.

4. Start up your database with the STARTUP RESTRICT command in Server Manager or SQL*Plus. You might optionally include the PFILE option if you need to.

5. Still connected as INTERNAL (or SYS), begin a log file with the SPOOL command and set the ECHO option to a TRUE or FALSE value, depending on whether you also want the output displayed on your screen.

6. Issue the query

```
SELECT owner, queue_table FROM dba_queue_tables;
```

to identify the queue tables stored in your database.

7. Host out to the operating system, using the HOST command, and run the Export utility to export the tables identified in step 6 as well as the two tables, SYSTEM.DEF$_AQCALL and SYSEM.DEF$_AQERROR.

NOTE

If you are not certain how to export Advanced Queuing table contents, you should refer to the *Oracle8i Application Developer's Guide—Advanced Queuing* manual for further details.

8. Exit back from the operating system into your Server Manager or SQL*Plus session and drop the tables you exported in step 7, including the two tables that belong to SYSTEM. Use the DBMS_AQADM.DROP_QUEUE_TABLE procedure to achieve this as shown in the following example:

```
EXECUTE dbms_aqadm.drop_queue_table (
➥queue_table => 'SYSTEM.DEF$_AQCALL');
```

9. Execute the script, CATNOQUEUE.SQL, which will remove the Advanced Queuing Data Dictionary tables, and then execute the CATQUEUE.SQL script to rebuild them for release 8.1.

10. Again, host out to the operating system and use the `Import Utility` command to re-import all the tables you exported in step 7. Ensure that the import completes without errors.

11. Exit back into your Oracle session and re-execute the query you used in step 6. You should see the two tables owned by SYSTEM, named in step 7, as well as the other tables you identified in step 6.

12. Turn off the logging by issuing the `SPOOL OFF` command and examine your log file to ensure that there were no errors when you ran the scripts in step 9. Also, you can double check that you included all the tables when you ran step 8.

13. You can now drop the restricted session mode of your instance by issuing the command:

    ```
    ALTER SYSTEM DISABLE RESTRICTED SESSION;
    ```

    and you should be ready to continue with the remaining upgrades for the Advanced Queuing feature.

Upgrade Advanced Queuing Tables

A number of features are added in Oracle8*i* to enhance Advanced Queuing functionality that is supported through additional columns in the queue tables. If you want to use these advanced features, such as rule-based subscriptions and storing the sender's ID along with each message, you need to upgrade the tables. You can do this by implementing the steps described as follows:

1. Ensure that your instance is running with the COMPATIBLE parameter set at a value of 8.1.0 or higher. In the earlier section, "User-Defined Datatype Upgrades," I describe how you can do this.

2. Issue the query

    ```
    SELECT owner, queue_table FROM dba_queue_tables;
    ```

    to identify the queue tables stored in your database.

3. Execute the DBMS_AQADM.MIGRATE_QUEUE_TABLE procedure for each of the queue tables you want to upgrade. In the following example, I upgrade the table, CUST_QUEUE, owned by the SALES schema, to release 8.1 compatibility. You should execute similar commands for each of your queue tables.

    ```
    EXECUTE dbms_aqadm.migrate_queue_table (
        queue_table => 'sales.cust_queue',
        compatible => '8.1');
    ```

Snapshot Upgrades

Oracle8*i* has introduced a new concept called Materialized Views. These objects are created using the same syntax as is used to create snapshots. In fact, "snapshot" and "materialized view" are considered to be synonyms in Oracle8*i*. One of the key characteristics of snapshots in this release is that queries can be rewritten by the optimizer to use a snapshot which is based on the tables named in the query. If you want to enable this capability on any snapshots you created in your Oracle8, release 8.0, database, you need to specifically grant it on each snapshot. To do this, you need to execute the following two steps on each snapshot in turn:

1. Grant the QUERY REWRITE system privilege to the owner of the snapshot.

2. Issue the command

    ```
    ALTER SNAPSHOT table_name ENABLE QUERY REWRITE;
    ```

    for each table, substituting the actual table name for *table_name*.

Advanced Replication Upgrades

If you have installed Advanced Replication, you need to execute the following steps to upgrade it to Oracle8*i*:

1. Change your default directory to the ADMIN subdirectory in your Oracle8*i* home directory structure. You should locate the script file CATREP.SQL in the subdirectory to confirm that you are in the correct one.

2. Connect to your database as INTERNAL using Server Manager or SQL*Plus and execute a SHUTDOWN command with the NORMAL or IMMEDIATE option. Note that if you are running Parallel Server, you need to shut down all instances and modify your initialization file to start up with the PARALLEL_SERVER parameter set to FALSE.

3. Restart the database with the STARTUP RESTRICT command, using the PFILE option if necessary.

4. You should open a log file to record the results of the remaining steps, so you can confirm that they completed successfully or determine what needs to be done to correct the problem for a subsequent attempt. Use the SPOOL command with an appropriate filename.

5. Run the CATREP.SQL script:

    ```
    @catrep.sql
    ```

6. Execute the replication upgrade script appropriate for the old release of Oracle8 you were running. I list the Oracle8 releases in Table 9.2, along with the name of the replication upgrade script you need to run for each specific release.

> **CAUTION**
>
> If you don't find your current Oracle8 release number listed in Table 9.2, you are attempting to upgrade a nonproduction release, or the special release, 8.0.4S, which cannot be upgraded directly. If you have an 8.0 release, you need to upgrade to 8.0.5 before upgrading to Oracle8*i*. If you have an 8.1 release, you are running a beta version that is not addressed in this book, and you need to obtain specific instructions from the *Oracle8i Migration* manual.

TABLE 9.2   Oracle8*i* Advanced Replication Upgrade Scripts

Oracle 8.0 Release	Upgrade Script Name
Release 8.0.3	r0800030.sql
Release 8.0.4	r0800040.sql
Release 8.0.5	r0800050.sql

7. Use the SPOOL OFF command to terminate the logging and review the file to confirm that the scripts all completed successfully.

8. Remove the restricted session mode from the instance to make the database, with upgraded Advanced Replication, available to all users:

   ALTER SYSTEM DISABLE RESTRICTED SESSION;

Parallel Server Upgrade Issues

If your database has the Oracle Parallel Server option installed, you will need to upgrade the Data Dictionary to support Oracle8*i*. Implement the following steps to complete this upgrade:

1. Change your default directory to the ADMIN subdirectory in your Oracle8*i* home directory structure. You should locate the script file CATPARR.SQL in the subdirectory to confirm that you are in the correct one.

2. Shutdown all your instances with the NORMAL or IMMEDIATE option.

3. For the node on which you are performing the upgrade, modify the value of the initialization file parameter, PARALLEL_SERVER, to FALSE.

4. Restart the database with the STARTUP RESTRICT command, using the PFILE option if necessary.

5. I recommend that you open a log file to record the results of the remaining steps, so you can confirm that they completed successfully or determine what needs to be done to correct the problem for a subsequent attempt. Use the SPOOL command with an appropriate filename.

6. Run the CATPARR.SQL script:

    ```
    @catparr.sql
    ```

7. Use the SPOOL OFF command to terminate the logging and review the file to confirm that the script completed successfully and the PL/SQL routines compiled successfully.

8. Shut down the instance and modify the initialization file again to set the PARALLEL_SERVER parameter back to TRUE. You can then restart all your instances with the Parallel Server upgraded to Oracle8*i*.

PL/SQL Validation

A number of your PL/SQL modules might have become invalid during the upgrade to Oracle8*i*. These will be automatically recompiled when they are next used. However, rather than allow your users to incur the cost of these recompilations, even possibly encountering an error if there is a problem with your upgrade, I recommend that you recompile them yourselves. You can do this by executing the UTLRP.SQL script. Use the following steps to complete this task:

1. Change to the ADMIN directory in the Oracle8*i* home directory structure. You should find the required script, UTLRP.SQL, in the directory.

2. Start Server Manager or SQL*Plus, and connect as INTERNAL.

3. Execute the script:

    ```
    @utlrp.sql
    ```

Post-Upgrade Actions

You might need to perform a number of additional tasks following your database upgrade. I suggest that you review this list of tasks and note those in which you believe are appropriate for your database.

Environment Variables

You should remember to modify any script files you use to set your environment variables so that they point to the correct Oracle8*i* values as described in the earlier section, "Performing an Upgrade Manually." This needs to be done for all user accounts who will be using your upgraded database.

listener.ora Entries for Oracle Enterprise Manager

If you want to use Oracle Enterprise Manager to manage objects in your Oracle8*i* database, you will need to add a special database entry in your *listener.ora* file. This entry is added automatically by the Data Migration Assistant if you use it to perform your upgrade. If you performed a manual upgrade, you need to add an entry with the following format:

```
SID_LIST_LISTENER_NAME =
    (SID_LIST =
        (SID_DESC =
            (GLOBAL_NAME = database_name.domain_name)
            (ORACLE_HOME = oracle_home_directory)
            (SID_NAME = instance_name)
        )
    )
```

where *database_name* and *domain_name* are from the initialization parameters DB_NAME and DOMAIN_NAME respectively; *oracle_home_directory* is the home directory for Oracle8*i*; and *instance_name* is the ORACLE_SID environment variable value.

Parameter File Issues

Initialization parameters typically change between releases, and Oracle8*i* is no exception. Some of the parameters from your 8.0 version might have become obsolete and others might have changed function or default values. Additional parameters are also available to help you take advantage of the new features in release 8.1.

We recommend that you study Appendix B in the Oracle8*i* Migration manual to determine if you have any parameters that you should consider changing. We suggest that you pay special attention to the following issues.

COMPATIBLE Parameter

If you used the Oracle Data Migration Assistant to perform your upgrade, you might need to check the COMPATIBLE parameter in your initialization file. If it was included prior to the upgrade, it will have been retained with its old value. If was not set, it will have been added with a value of 8.0.5. In either case, you might need to modify it in order to take advantage of any of the new release 8.1 features.

Parallel Execution Parameters

Oracle8*i* provides a pair of parameters that allow parallel processing to be managed by the database using information from the server itself and the amount of work being performed at the time a statement is executed. These parameters—PARALLEL_AUTOMATIC_TUNING

and PARALLEL_ADAPTIVE_MULTI_USER—impact a number of other parameters, such as SHARED_POOL_SIZE and LARGE_POOL_SIZE, which can have significant impact on the performance of your database. You should review the discussion of the parallel execution parameters in the Migration manual for specific details to help you decide how to set these parameters.

Bad Date Constraints

Constraints involving date checks that do not reference the century can cause problems in the year 2000. To find such constraints, you can run the script UTLCONST.SQL. Specifically, you should implement the following steps to identify the potential problems:

1. Change to the ADMIN directory in the Oracle8*i* home directory structure. You should find the required script, UTLCONST.SQL, in the directory.

2. Start Server Manager or SQL*Plus and connect as INTERNAL.

3. Execute the following commands:

```
SPOOL const_check.log
@utlconst.sql
SPOOL OFF
```

4. Use the contents of the CONST_CHECK.LOG to identify the constraints with date problems. The script will have made them invalid, and you should drop them or modify them to remove the potential problems before validating them again.

LONG to LOB Conversions

Oracle Corporation is making strong recommendations that customers convert any LONG datatypes to LOBs because of the improved support for available for this newer datatype. In order to help you with the conversion, a new SQL operator, TO_LOB, was introduced in Oracle8*i*. Data can be moved from a column built with the LONG datatype to an appropriate LOB column using this operator. In the following example, data from the ID column, a NUMBER datatype, and the DATA_TEXT column, a character LONG column in the OLD_TAB table, is moved into the corresponding NUMBER and CLOB columns in the NEW_TAB table:

```
INSERT INTO new_tab
  SELECT id, TO_LOB(data_text)
  FROM old_tab;
```

If you want, you can convert any of your tables with LONG columns to LOBs in the same way, and then use synonyms on the replacement table—after you drop the original—to make the change transparent to the applications.

OUTLN User Password

The Oracle8*i* installation creates a new user, OUTLN, with a password of OUTLN, to manage stored outline functions. This user has DBA privileges, and so you should change the password before your database integrity is compromised.

Summary

In this chapter, I have shown you how to upgrade a database running against a production version of Oracle8, release 8.0. You can choose from two methods to accomplish this, and I have explained how to use each one. The Oracle Data Migration Assistant is a GUI tool that guides you through the upgrade and performs many of the detailed steps for you. Alternately, you can perform a manual upgrade after installing Oracle8*i*, release 8.1.

The chapter also discusses specific upgrade steps you need to complete for individual products you might have installed. These include user-defined datatypes, Recovery Manager, Advanced Queuing, snapshots, Advanced Replication, and Parallel Server. Finally, the chapter explains a number of additional tasks you might have to complete following the upgrade in order to take advantage of the new features and capabilities of Oracle8*i*.

This chapter only covers upgrades from production versions of Oracle8, release 8.0, to a production Oracle8*i* database. When appropriate, readers are directed to other sources, which cover upgrades from and to Beta releases of the Oracle products.

Issues with Compatibility

IN THIS CHAPTER

Your Oracle8*i*, release 8.1, database has certain features and characteristics that are unique to this particular release. Although this is generally a good thing—new facilities and performance enhancements have to start somewhere and can't be back-ported to earlier releases—it does mean that your database might not be able to work smoothly with other databases and the tools used against them. In this chapter, I will show you some of the issues raised when your Oracle8*i* database has to work with different versions. One of the first times you might face this situation is during your migration to Oracle8*i*. If you are using one of the migration techniques that require you to transfer information between your Oracle7 and your Oracle8*i* database, the Export/Import utilities, for example, you will be using tools from one release to work with a database running under a different release.

I have divided up this chapter into sections to help you find any information on this topic that might be of specific interest. If you are interested in this subject in general, I suggest that you read these sections in the order in which they are presented.

The COMPATIBLE Initialization Parameter

The COMPATIBLE parameter is one of the parameters that you set in your initialization file, init<*sid*>.ora. It determines which version of Oracle the instance will appear to run. It can therefore prevent features from the installed release from being used if it is set lower than that release. On the other hand, such a lower setting can help guarantee that the database will interface successfully with a database which is running against a lower release of Oracle.

In your Oracle8*i*, release 8.1 database, you can set the parameter to a value between 8.0.0, or 8.0.0.0.0, and 8.1.x, or 8.1.x.y.z, where x, y, and z are no higher than your current release and patch numbers. You cannot set the value to a higher number than your installed Oracle release. By default, Oracle8*i* uses a value of 8.0.0, although the Oracle Universal Installer might change it to a higher value if you choose to install a product that requires a later release. You can query the V$PARAMETER view, using the SHOW PARAMETER command if you are connected to SQL*Plus or Server Manager, to see how it is set in your current instance. You can also inspect the initialization file built by the Installer to see what value it assigned.

CAUTION

A problem existed in version 7.3 related to bitmap indexes and certain SQL statements. The most common was the use of the ALTER TABLE command to add either a primary key or a NOT NULL constraint to a table with a bitmap index, although other statements could also cause the problem. When one of these commands was issued, the bitmap index could become invalidated, requiring you to drop and re-create it. These problems with bitmap indexes have been resolved in Oracle8*i*. Should you decide to use the COMPATIBLE parameter to run your database at an earlier release level of Oracle8, however, you can reintroduce this problem.

You can set your COMPATIBLE value to a higher release than its current setting without any serious implications. We do recommend that you backup your database before making the change, however. This way, just in case you need to be able to return to an earlier compatibility level, you will have a copy of the database that allow you to do this. To set your COMPATI-BLE value to a lower value requires a few more steps. These steps are covered in detail in Chapter 13, "Downgrading." Briefly, they describe which objects you will have to remove from your database and some special commands you need to run to re-set the physical structures to the appropriate release.

By now, it should be obvious to you that you cannot change the compatibility level of your database dynamically. You have to change the value of the COMPATIBLE parameter in your initialization file and then restart your database, using the SHUTDOWN and STARTUP commands in Server Manager or SQL*Plus.

In most cases, you need to make changes to other parameters in order to realize the changes to the database compatibility. But Oracle does make some physical changes to support the releases as you increase the value of the parameter. Most of these will not be that obvious to you, but you might find that SQL statements perform a little differently. In some cases, this is because other parameters take on different defaults, but also because setting the COMPATIBLE parameter to 8.1.0 or higher might enable the optimizer to use a new column, AVGCLN, in the HIST_HEAD$ Data Dictionary table to determine its choice of execution plan.

Oracle8*i* Features Requiring COMPATIBLE=8.1.x

In this section, I briefly describe the features introduced in Oracle8*i* that require the COMPATIBLE value to be 8.1 or higher. The detailed descriptions of these features are covered in Part II, "Using the Oracle8*i* Features," of this book. You will also find features described there that are not listed here. This is because not every Oracle8*i* feature requires a compatibility setting higher than 8.0. The features are organized by major topics so that you can more readily find them, even if this sometimes results in features being listed twice.

Applications

The application features that require a COMPATIBLE value of at least 8.1 include the following:

- Enterprise JavaBeans—A server-oriented Java extension that allows transactional applications to be written as Java modules.
- Java code in stored procedures—Allows PL/SQL to access the Java engine.
- SQLJ translator—An extension to Java that allows SQL to be embedded in a Java block of code.
- OCI Call Interface—An extension to OCI that allows notification call to the client.

Tablespaces

The tablespace options and characteristics that require a COMPATIBLE value of at least 8.1 include the following:

- Locally managed tablespaces—Tablespaces that use bitmaps within their datafiles, rather than data dictionary tables, to manage their extents.

- Online read-only tablespaces—The ability to make a tablespace read-only without waiting for the database to be quiesced.

- Transportable tablespaces—A feature that allows a tablespace to be extracted from one database and plugged into another.

Schema Objects

The cluster, table, and index characteristics that require a COMPATIBLE value of at least 8.1 include the following:

- Drop column—Support for the DROP COLUMN option of the ALTER TABLE command.

- Temporary tables—Tables that are available only for the length of a transaction or a session.

- Key compression support for index-organized tables—An internal modification to improve performance of index-organized tables.

- Secondary indexes on index-organized tables—Allows indexes to be added to index-organized tables to support access other than through the primary key.

- Support for LOBs in and partitioning of index-organized tables—This feature allows index-organized tables to include large objects (LOBs) and to be partitioned.

- Bitmap index protection—Prevents bitmap indexes from being invalidated when ALTER TABLE commands are executed on the parent table.

- Extensible indexing—A feature that allows each column in a multi-column index to be defined as either ascending or descending.

- Function-based indexes—Indexes that contain functions on one or more columns.

- Index segment coalescing and key compression—Internal modifications to improve index performance.

- Online index rebuild—An improvement to the algorithm that allows increased concurrent access to indexes during the rebuild operation.

- Single table hash clusters—Hash clusters defined with the SINGLE TABLE option for faster retrieval.

Partitioning

Partitioning of tables with the following characteristics requires a COMPATIBLE value of at least 8.1:

- Index-organized tables
- Tables with LOBs
- Object tables
- Tables with user-defined types, including REFs, VARRAYs, and nested tables
- Tables with hash and composite partitions
- Hash clusters with hash partitions

Built-in Datatypes

The built-in datatypes that require a COMPATIBLE value of at least 8.1 include the following:

- Partitioning of tables with LOBs—Tables with large objects can be partitioned.
- Temporary LOBs—Large objects can be created temporarily.
- Varying-width character sets for CLOBs and NCLOBs—Support for large character objects with variable width characters, including those with National Language Character support characters.
- Universal ROWIDs (UROWIDs)—Support for UROWIDs in a database object, such as a table.

User-defined Datatypes

The user-defined datatypes that require a COMPATIBLE value of at least 8.1 include the following:

- Collection locators—Internal support for nested table management
- Nested tables in index-organized tables—Support to create index-organized tables containing nested tables
- Triggers on nested table view columns—Support for triggers on view columns in nested tables
- User-specified storage clauses for nested tables—Allows support for users to define storage clauses on nested tables
- User-defined object identifiers—Allows users to define their own object identifiers (OIDs)
- Referential integrity constraint on a REF column—Provides for foreign key constraints to be defined on REF columns

- Storage parameters for storing varrays as LOBs—Allows you to define storage parameters when storing varrays as large objects
- Varray data in index-organized tables—Provides support to store varrays in index-organized tables

Parallel Server

A COMPATIBLE value of at least 8.1 is required to support Parallel Server instance affinity for jobs that allow the DBMS_JOB package to select which instance will run a job.

Data Protection

The data security features that require a COMPATIBLE value of at least 8.1 include the following:

- Application context—Allows you to choose whether a stored PL/SQL procedure will run under the security schema of the creator or the user
- Fine-grained access control—Provides low-level security to defined groups of users
- N-tier authentication and authorization—Support for complex network connections with minimal need for users to provide connection authorization information
- Fast-start, on-demand rollback—Reduces the amount of work performed by user-processes during the rollback activity of an instance recovery operation to just the blocks they need to access
- Proxy copy support for the Oracle Media Management API—Simplifies coding for third-party vendors interfacing with Oracle Media Management access

Distributed Databases

The distributed database features that require a COMPATIBLE value of at least 8.1 include the following:

- Column level snapshot subsetting for updatable snapshots—Supports use of subqueries in columns used for snapshot replication
- Agent self-registration—Allows agents for heterogeneous services to self-register

Data Warehousing

The data warehousing features that require a COMPATIBLE value of at least 8.1 include the following:

- Dimensions schema object—Provides for ways to generate grouped results from one or more tables using definitions outside of the base tables
- Query rewrite and related privileges—Provides the optimizer the capability to modify a user query to make use of alternate tables containing pre-processed copies of the data

Data Access

The features of data access that require a COMPATIBLE value of at least 8.1 include the following:

- Autonomous transactions—The ability to run a PL/SQL block that contains its own transaction, independent of the transaction executing it.
- Bulk binds—The use of arrays to perform DML on multiple rows with a single call.
- C call specifications and CALL statement—An improved interface between PL/SQL and C.
- Native dynamic SQL—A simplified method to run dynamic SQL statements from within PL/SQL code.
- NOCOPY parameter passing mode—The use of parameter passing by reference instead of by value.
- The utlchain1.sql and utlexcpt1.sql scripts—Versions of the scripts to build CHAINED_ROWS and EXCEPTIONS tables using UROWID instead of ROWID columns.
- DBMS_REPAIR package—An Oracle-supplied package to allow DBAs to identify corrupted blocks and mark them to be bypassed during current work and to be corrected later.
- Disable validate constraint state—Allows constraints to be disabled, but prevents any changes because they could violate them.
- Object OutBinds in Triggers—Improved management of objects in trigger code.
- Triggers on nested table view columns—Allows you to add triggers to view columns in nested tables.
- Triggers on DATABASE and SCHEMA—Allows triggers to be activated based on database activity, such as CONNECT or DISCONNECT, or schema changes.
- Triggers with a CALL to a procedure as the trigger body—Allows trigger code to be embodied in a procedure.
- Extensible optimizer—Allows you to define how the optimizer should handle user-defined objects.
- Optimizer plan stability—Allows you store a defined execution plan to ensure the same execution path regardless of other changes to the database.
- Database resource manager—Provides the ability to assign different levels of database resources to different groups of users at different periods of time.

Advanced Queuing

The advanced queuing features that require a COMPATIBLE value of at least 8.1 include the following:

- Additional columns—New columns in the advanced column tables to identify original message ID for propagated messages and sender's ID.
- Database event publication—Enhancement to status notification.
- Instance affinity for queue tables—Capability of Parallel Server to move work associated with queues to the most appropriate instance.
- Non-persistent queues—A property that allows messages to last only as long as the instance rather than to persist across instances.
- Queue-level and system-level privileges—The DBA can create queue managers and allow them to manage their own queues and the related privileges.
- Rules-based subscriptions—Provides alternate subscription methods for advanced queuing.
- Separate storage of history management information—Allows queue management information to be stored in a separate data structure.

Spatial and Visual Information

The spatial data and visual data characteristics that require a COMPATIBLE value of at least 8.1 include the following:

- Spatial indextype and operators—New structures to improve the performance of spatial data
- VIR indextype and operators—New structures to improve the performance of the Visual Information Retrieval (VIR) processes

Application Compatibility and Interoperability

For most of your applications, you should not need to make any changes to the code itself if you do not change the underlying database objects. You should pay attention to some specific items, and I will identify them for you in this section, organized by topic.

PL/SQL

A number of features in version 2 of PL/SQL are not supported in Oracle8, including Version 8.1.5. You can continue to use these features by changing the compatibility level at which the code runs. As a DBA, you can set the PL/SQL compatibility level to version 2 for the instance, either with an initialization parameter or with a CHANGE SYSTEM command. Additionally, a user or an application can change the compatibility level for the current session only.

To use PL/SQL Version 2 functionality, you need to set PLSQL_V2_COMPATIBILITY. You can set this parameter value to TRUE in your initialization file or use the ALTER SYSTEM or ALTER SESSION commands to change it for an instance or a session, respectively. If you don't set it, the Oracle8*i* default value for the instance and for the session is FALSE, which results in PL/SQL running at the same version level as your database installation.

The characteristics of PL/SQL that require version 2 compatibility, some of which violate correct syntax and might only have been coded inadvertently, are as follows:

- Declaring a PL/SQL table or a PL/SQL record prior to its type being declared
- Using an expression in the RETURN clause of a function instead of variable type
- Modifying or deleting elements of an index table passed to a procedure using an IN parameter
- Returning fields, using OUT parameters, from records passed to a procedure using an IN parameter
- Returning fields, using OUT parameters, from record variables that have been used in expression contexts such as dot-qualified names in the right-hand side of an assignment statement
- Using OUT parameters in the FROM clause of a SELECT list

Some other changes to PL/SQL cannot be modified by setting version compatibility. The first of these is a slight change in the error code returned if you incorrectly used one of the following keywords as a function name in a SELECT list without a qualifying schema name:

```
CHARACTER, COMMIT, DEC, FALSE, INT, NUMERIC, REAL, SAVEPOINT, TRUE
```

In Oracle7, the error codes returned were ORA-06552 and PLS-222. In Oracle8*i*, they have become ORA-06550 and PLS-00222, respectively. Programs that trap these particular messages by code number will need to be changed.

The second change that is not impacted by the compatibility parameter is that a number of new key words will generate the preceding errors if used in a SELECT list without a schema qualifier. These words could be used in Oracle7 without causing errors:

```
BFILE, BLOB, CAST, CLOB, DEREF, NCHAR, NCLOB, NVARCHAR2, REF, SYS_OP_NTCIMG,
➥ VALUE
```

Precompiler Applications

In this section, I will describe the changes you might need to make to your precompiled programs so that they will execute under Oracle8*i*.

10

First, the SYSDBA privileges are no longer available by default when making database connections using Pro*C/C++ or Pro*COBOL. If you need these privileges for your precompiled applications, you will have to modify the CONNECT statements. In Pro*C/C++, your Oracle8*i* CONNECT statements should like this:

```
EXEC SQL CONNECT :sys IDENTIFIED BY :sys_passwd IN SYSDBA MODE;
```

In your Oracle8*i* Pro*COBOL, they need to be changed to look like this:

```
EXEC SQL
  CONNECT :sys IDENTIFIED BY :SYS-PASSWD IN SYSDBA MODE
END-EXEC.
```

Second, Oracle discontinued support for Pro*ADA as of Oracle7, release 7.3. If you need to run your ADA programs against your database in Oracle8*i*, you will have to upgrade them to SQL*Module for ADA 8.1. You should be aware that SQL*Module for ADA 8.1 does not support all the features introduced in Oracle8, such as objects. Of course, your Oracle7 Pro*ADA code will not be impacted by these exclusions because they wouldn't contain calls to Oracle8 features anyway.

Third, if your precompiled programs contain PL/SQL blocks that fail because of any of the problems discussed in the previous section, "PL/SQL," you can either modify the code or set the precompiler environment to its version 2 compatibility. The latter is achieved by adding the following option to the DBMS precompiler command line:

```
DBMS=Oracle7
```

The actual precompiler command is language and platform specific, and we advise you to consult your documentation set for details.

OCI Applications

You need to consider a few issues if your database supports applications coded in OCI after you have migrated to Oracle8*i*. Some of these relate to changed calls and others to interoperability with other versions of Oracle. I will discuss the latter first in this section.

If you have migrated from a version 6 client/server environment, you will have to upgrade your code completely because the version 6 OCI library is not supported against an Oracle8*i* client. Your current version 6 OCI client code, therefore, will not run reliably.

If you have migrated from a version 7 client/server environment, you might not need to upgrade your client code. You will have to make some specific changes to your OCI calls, as discussed later in this section. Of course, not all Oracle8*i* features are available if you use version 7 calls. In particular, shared structures are not supported at all if you use version 7 OCI

clients. Additionally, the following functionality is fully enabled only if the log in and the related calls are made using Oracle8*i* OCI calls:

- failover
- prefetch
- piggybacked commit or cancel
- client-side conversions

These functions are discussed in the Oracle8*i* documentation, particularly the Concepts manual.

The call changes you have to make are related to thread safety. Specifically, the ORLON and OLON calls are no longer supported for thread safety in Oracle8*i* OCI; although, the OLOG call is still required for multithreaded applications.

Finally, a number of changes exist in the Oracle8*i* link command line. We direct you to the demo_rdbms.mk file in the Oracle8*i* Oracle Home's demo subdirectory for examples on how to compile and link your OCI applications for your migrated database.

General Application Issues

In this section, I discuss three other issues related to application compatibility and Oracle8*i* in the areas of index-organized tables, XA calls, and the VALIDATE STRUCTURE option of the ANALYZE TABLE command.

Should you decide to convert one or more of your tables to indexed organization as part of your migration processing, you might need to make some changes to the applications that reference them. This will be the case only if your applications use ROWIDs to reference the tables, and they might need to access Universal ROWIDs (UROWIDs) instead. This is because a UROWID, used by secondary indexes built on an index-organized table, contains not only just the ROWID itself, but also the contents of the primary key column(s) of the related row.

The specific application areas you might need to address are related to the following issues:

- If you use the DESCRIBE command, the application will have to accommodate the new SQLT_RDD datatype.
- If you use the SQLT_RID host variable types, you must replace them with ROWID descriptors—recommended by Oracle—or VARCHAR host variables.
- If you use CHARACTER host variables, they must be long enough to contain the primary key and be variable in length; fixed size 18 character strings must be replaced with longer variable strings or OCI descriptors.

If you have migrated from release 7.1 and any of your applications involve XA calls, you will have to relink them with the Oracle8*i* XA libraries. You do not have to relink, although we recommend that you do, applications migrated from release 7.2 and 7.3 databases.

The final type of change you might have to make to your applications is associated with the error-handling behavior of the ANALYZE TABLE VALIDATE STRUCTURE command. In earlier releases, the command would return an error message and stop running when it encountered its first error. In Oracle8*i*, it will still report errors as it finds them, but will not stop running. Should you have applications that depend on the earlier behavior, you will need to modify them to respond to this new functionality.

Startup and Shutdown Compatibility and Interoperability

The STARTUP and SHUTDOWN commands can now be run from a SQL*Plus session because Oracle prepares to discontinue support for Server Manager. If you are building new scripts to start and stop your database, we recommend that you use SQL*Plus in readiness for the disappearance of the Server Manager product. To support this change, you can connect to SQL*Plus using the INTERNAL key word.

You should be aware of a few subtle differences in the behavior of the STARTUP and SHUT-DOWN commands when using SQL*Plus instead of Server Manager. First, the connection to the database is likely to be lost following a SHUTDOWN or an implicit shutdown using STARTUP FORCE. Your SQL*Plus session will still be active, but it might not allow you to reconnect to the database, and you will need to exit the session and start a new SQL*Plus session if you need to process other commands. Second, because of this loss of connectivity, the STARTUP FORCE command will restart only the instance to the NOMOUNT level. You will need to issue the commands ALTER DATABASE MOUNT and ALTER DATABASE OPEN to reopen your database.

In addition, whether you use Enterprise Manager, Server Manager, or SQL*Plus to manage your database, you might have to modify your Oracle7 initialization parameter file to startup an Oracle8*i* instance. I discussed the COMPATIBLE parameter and its implications earlier in this chapter, as well as in the section "Review Initialization Parameters" in Chapter 8, "Post-Migration Issues." You can also find complete lists of parameters added to and dropped from each of the releases in Oracle8, including Oracle8*i*, in the *Oracle8i Server Migration* manual provided as part of Oracle's documentation.

Also, the actions of the SHUTDOWN IMMEDIATE operation have changed slightly, again independent of which tool you use to initiate it. The end result is that idle server processes are killed during the shutdown and consequently return a different error message than before to the users. The new message might need to be trapped in any exception handlers written to manage idle sessions.

Tablespace and Datafile Compatibility and Interoperability

Some of the tablespace characteristics available in Oracle8*i* were not part of Oracle7 and have resulted in changes to the Data Dictionary and the behavior of some commands. You might have scripts or database management routines that will be impacted by these changes, and you should confirm that they will still work as expected—or else make changes to them based on the following information.

The introduction of the new file type, tempfile, for use with temporary tablespaces, has made queries against the DBA_DATA_FILES, and similar views, not as comprehensive as before. Information about tempfiles, as opposed to datafiles, is stored in a separate set of Data Dictionary tables and dynamic performance views. In order to obtain a complete picture of your database files, if you begin to use tempfiles, you need to include the appropriate information from the following objects:

- DBA_TEMP_FILES
- V$TEMPFILE
- V$TEMP_EXTENT_MAP
- V$TEMP_EXTENT_POOL
- V$TEMP_SPACE_HEADER
- V$TEMPSTAT
- V$TEMP_PING

You should also be aware that a tempfile and a datafile can have the same file ID number as each other.

The behavior of the ALTER TABLESPACE...READ ONLY has changed in Oracle8*i* to simplify the processing of transportable tablespaces. In prior releases, if you issued the command while the database had any active transactions, it would fail with the following error:

```
ORA-01640: cannot make tablespace read only with active transactions
```

In a similar situation in Oracle8*i*, the command will simply wait until all current transactions complete. During this period, new transactions will continue to be allowed, so the process attempting to change the tablespace status might be blocked for a very long time. You should therefore avoid including the ALTER TABLESPACE...READ ONLY command in any time-sensitive scripts or programs.

I conclude this section with one final note about tablespace incompatibilities concerning transportable tablespaces. Such tablespaces currently do not support the advanced queuing feature that allows multiple recipients when using 8.0-compatible queues.

Data Dictionary Compatibility and Interoperability

I will not list every Data Dictionary item from earlier releases that are incompatible with Oracle8i because most of them are readily found in the Oracle8i Migration manual. In particular, lists of obsolete views can be found in two of the appendices for that manual, Appendix C, "Changes to Static Data Dictionary Views," and Appendix D, "Changes to Dynamic Performance Views." However, there are two data dictionary-related topics to which I want to draw your attention in case you have applications or scripts that might be impacted.

First, the use of the SYS schema for user tables and access to the SYS schema objects by other users is being made more difficult in order to improve security. Some commands that might have worked in the past might need new privileges. For example, DML that worked against a SYS scheme object as a result of owning the appropriate ANY system privilege might no longer work. One specific item is the SYS table used to store audit records, AUD$. You can no longer purge records from this table using the DELETE ANY TABLE system privilege, but you must also have the DELETE_CATALOG_ROLE granted to you.

Second, if you want to provide users with the ability to use the SYS userid, you should create a userid for each of them and grant them the DBA role and the SYSDBA system privilege. The users can then connect using their assigned userids as SYSDBA. This avoids the need to distribute the password for SYS to these other users. Note that you must have created a password file in order to grant the SYSDBA privilege.

Finally, in some releases of Oracle8*i*, you can use the initialization parameter, O7_DICTIONARY_ACCESSIBILITY, to maintain the Oracle7 Data Dictionary behavior. You should not depend on this parameter, however—even if it is available in your database—because it is intended only to be a short-term solution to help you transition to the Oracle8*i* features and behavior.

National Language Support Datatype Compatibility and Interoperability

If your applications are running in a client/server environment, and you are using Oracle's National Language Support (NLS) capabilities, you should be aware of some of the changes in Oracle8*i* that could affect how the client and server interact. I outline these changes in the following paragraph.

If your clients are running with any release at or higher than 7.1, any output from the national character set (NCHAR) in the server is transparently modified by OCI, as it passes through a bind variable or a define handle, to match the client's database character set. If NCHAR data is needed to be input to the server through a bind variable, and it is used in such a way that only

an NCHAR string is allowable, the bind variable must be used as part of the SQL or PL/SQL code accessing the server. The call will then perform a conversion from the client's databases character set to the national character set for the server. This restriction, which allows only the client's database character set, is because of the method in which conversion is performed for input bind variables. It might cause a problem if the client's database character set does not contain the complete NCHAR set. Should the complete NCHAR set be needed, you will have to upgrade the applications to version 8.1.

A version 6 or Oracle7 client can perform a remote procedure call (RPC) to a subprogram with ANY_CS parameters, which will interpret their actual argument as having the server's database character set. On the other hand, a version 6 or Oracle7 client cannot RPC to either of the following:

- A subprogram with a parameter declared as using the NCHAR set.
- A function with a return result using the NCHAR set.

These invalid calls will not be identified when the client application is compiled, but only when the RPC is executed. Applications from these earlier releases might, therefore, begin to experience runtime failures after your migration. These errors might require an application upgrade to fix them.

The technique used by Oracle to make the conversion for an input bind variable passed by SQL or PL/SQL is to call the CSCONVERT() function. This function, like the CHR() function with a second argument, does not exist in version 6 or Oracle7, so it cannot be coded directly in a SQL statement called from a version 6 or Oracle7 PL/SQL block. If you want to correct this and allow your code to make these calls directly, you will need to add two stored functions to your database server. Listings 10.1 and 10.2 contain the code to create both of the required functions, to_nchar_cs and to_char_cs, respectively.

LISTING 10.1   Create Function TO_NCHAR_CS to Support NCHAR Calls Across Releases

```
REM Create Function TO_NCHAR_CS
REM Used when executing NCHAR functions CHR(), with two arguments, or
REM CSCONVERT() between pre-Oracle8i clients and Oracle8i server.

CREATE OR REPLACE FUNCTION to_nchar_cs(t VARCHAR2)
  RETURN NCHAR VARYING IS
BEGIN
  RETURN TRANSLATE(t, nchar_cs);
END;
/
```

LISTING 10.2   Create Function TO_CHAR_CS to Support NCHAR Calls Across Releases

```
REM Create Function TO_CHAR_CS
REM Used when executing NCHAR functions CHR(), with two arguments, or
REM CSCONVERT() between pre-Oracle8i clients and Oracle8i server.

CREATE OR REPLACE FUNCTION to_char_cs(t nchar varying)
  RETURN VARCHAR2 IS
BEGIN
  RETURN TRANSLATE(t, char_cs);
END;
/
```

Executing these scripts allows the pre-Oracle8*i* client database calls to act as if they had an Oracle8*i* package STANDARD.

You should also ensure that your environment variables match your NCHAR and NLS settings. For any version 8 environment, set the ORA_NLS33 environment variable. Similarly, set the environment variable ORA_NLS32 for a release 7.3.x environment. An error will be generated if the client tries to load an incompatible character set.

SQL and PL/SQL Compatibility and Interoperability

A number of features have been dropped from or added to SQL and PL/SQL in Oracle8*i*. In most cases, you will not have to be concerned about what the differences are because your code will run solely in your migrated database. However, if you support a distributed database environment, you might find that you have code which is written at one release level accessing a database at another level. We will examine the specific cases in which you should be aware of the type of interoperability that is allowed or disallowed. Once more, I have divided this section into labeled topic areas for your convenience:

- De-Supported Built-In PL/SQL Functions
- Native Dynamic SQL in PL/SQL
- Versions of SQL Scripts Provided by Oracle
- Changes in PCTAS Behavior

De-Supported Built-In PL/SQL Functions

If you use Trusted Oracle, you need to be aware of the following changes. The PL/SQL functions, GREATEST_LB, LEAST_UB, and TO_LABEL, which were used to manipulate labels in Trusted Oracle, have been de-supported and are not available in Oracle8*i*. If any calls are made to these previously built-in functions, they will receive an error.

> **NOTE**
>
> Trusted Oracle is a special version of the product that is certified to meet govern-
> ment-defined security requirements. It provides security at the row level, uses destruc-
> tive deletes, and supports similar capabilities to ensure that data can be seen only by
> users with the required security level. Trusted Oracle is used only on servers and net-
> works that also have similar security capabilities.

Native Dynamic SQL in PL/SQL

In Oracle8*i*, a simplified method was introduced to execute dynamic SQL inside PL/SQL
blocks. The new method, known as native dynamic SQL, uses the command EXECUTE
IMMEDIATE <*sql_statement*> to execute the SQL statement provided in a string literal or character variable. This replaces a series of calls to the DBMS_SQL package required in earlier
releases. Despite the different syntax, native dynamic SQL can be used for commands in
distributed environments.

Specifically, if a native dynamic SQL command references a remote database via a database
link, the target database can be any version of Oracle. In the Listing 10.3 example, the anonymous procedure is running on an Oracle8*i* database, but the database link, *hq1*, could connect
to an Oracle6, an Oracle7, or an Oracle8, version 8.0 or 8.1 database to execute the query.

LISTING 10.3 Anonymous Procedure Executing Native Dynamic SQL Against a Remote
Database

```
REM Anonymous PL/SQL block to insert a row into the DEPT
REM table in the remote database defined by the HQ1 database
REM link, using native dynamic SQL.

BEGIN
  INSERT INTO dept@hq1 (deptno, dname, location)
    VALUES (110,
      'Executive Office of Database Administrators',
      'Boston');
END;
/
```

Similarly, when a procedure executing on any release of Oracle calls a remote procedure running on an Oracle8*i* database, the called procedure can include native dynamic SQL commands.

10

ISSUES WITH
COMPATIBILITY

Versions of SQL Scripts Provided by Oracle

Oracle introduced the Universal ROWID (UROWID) structure in Oracle8*i* to support secondary indexes on index-organized tables. UROWID values cannot be stored in columns defined with the ROWID datatype, and Oracle has frequently cautioned its customers not to build tables containing columns of this datatype because of potential changes to the structure. This has already occurred twice in Oracle8: first with the introduction of the extended ROWID in version 8.0, and second with the UROWID just discussed.

In order to support the database, Oracle has provided commands that rely on tables containing information about ROWIDs: the ANALYZE TABLE...LIST CHAINED ROWS and any command that uses the EXCEPTIONS INTO clause when defining or enabling constraints. Oracle also ships a script to build each of the tables used by default when these commands are executed: CHAINED_ROWS and EXCEPTIONS. With Oracle8*i*, there are two versions of each of these scripts, one for databases running with a compatibility level of 8.1 or greater and one for databases running with a lower compatibility level. Table 10.1 shows the script name to create each table under each compatibility level.

TABLE 10.1   Script Options for Oracle Tables with ROWID Data

Table Name	*Script for Compatibility < 8.1*	*Script for Compatibility >= 8.1*
CHAINED_ROWS	utlchain.sql	utlchain1.sql
EXCEPTIONS	utlexcpt.sql	utlexcpt1.sql

You will find both versions of each script in the ADMIN directory in your Oracle Home directory structure along with the other Oracle-provided script files.

Changes in PCTAS Behavior

A change exists in how Oracle allocates extents to a table that you create with a parallel CREATE TABLE...AS SELECT (PCTAS) command. This change was introduced in version 8.0, but the behavior is retained in Oracle8*i*, version 8.1, so you might need to be aware of it. In Oracle7, when you issued a PCTAS command, extent sizes were based on the INITIAL and NEXT values provided in the table definition or, failing that, in the default storage clause of the tablespace where the table was built. When you issue the same command in Oracle8*i*, the INITIAL value is ignored completely, and the first extent will be sized based on the value of the NEXT storage parameter.

If you have scripts that create tables using PCTAS commands, you might want to ensure that they will continue to execute in your migrated databases. They could allocate extents of sizes you don't expect and consequently run out of space or cause other space management problems later.

Advanced Queuing Compatibility and Interoperability

The Advanced Queuing capabilities of Oracle were enhanced in Oracle8, version 8.0, and again in Oracle8*i*, version 8.1. To make use of some of these features, you will need to set your database compatibility to 8.1.0 or higher, using the COMPATIBLE parameter. In some cases, if two databases communicate with remote procedure calls, they will both need a compatibility level of at least 8.1.0. Other new features cannot be used if the complete client/server or distributed database environment is not appropriate for them. Following are the new features that have compatibility issues and how they respond in different circumstances.

Queue-level and system-level privileges are differentiated in Oracle8*i*. The queue level privileges are granted and revoked through the GRANT_QUEUE_PRIVILEGE and the REVOKE_QUEUE_PRIVILEGE procedures, respectively, of the DBMS_AQADM package. To use these procedures successfully, your database must be running with a compatibility level of 8.1.0 or greater.

In Oracle8*i*, the sender's ID is mapped as an attribute of the message properties in addition to the other attributes defined in earlier releases. If the release 8.1 database is communicating with a release 8.0 database, the sender's ID attribute is ignored no matter in which direction the data is being processed. For client/server applications coded in OCI, a new attribute is available in the message properties descriptor to handle the sender's ID attribute. For clients using release 8.1, there is a new RPC code to pass message properties, including the sender's ID, between the application and the server.

Oracle8*i*'s message streaming functionality between two databases is supported only if both are Oracle8*i* databases at release 8.1.0 or higher. This Advanced Queuing feature is always available when the source and target databases are both at the required release level, even if their COMPATIBLE parameter values are set to an 8.0 level.

Procedure and Package Compatibility and Interoperability

A few packages require specific compatibility levels to be set in order to make use of their full capabilities in your Oracle8*i* database. The first of these is the DBMS_LOB package, introduced with release 8.0, into which a NOCOPY option has been introduced. You should not

attempt to execute the dbmslob.sql script provided with your Oracle8*i* installation nor use the NOCOPY syntax unless you have set your database compatibility level to 8.1.0 or higher.

The second package is DBMS_REPAIR that is new with Oracle8*i*. This package will work only if the compatibility level is 8.1.0 or greater.

The third, and final, procedure that has specific version dependencies is the DBMS_APPLICATION_INFO.SET_SESSION_LONGOPS procedure. This procedure was introduced in Oracle7, release 7.3, to support the tracking of recovery operations and similar system activities. However, some users were able to manipulate the procedure to track their own long-running queries and estimate completion times. Oracle8 has made this procedure available for tracking many other types of operation and provided the script, dbmsapin.sql, to define the parameters. If you want to use this procedure to track your own operations in Oracle8*i*, you should refer to the script for documentation on how to use its parameters.

Oracle Parallel Server Compatibility and Interoperability

Two major areas exist in which Oracle Parallel Server's compatibility has changed with Oracle8*i*. The first is the interpretation of the INSTANCES clause in SQL statements, and the second is a relaxation on the requirements concerning multiple instances supporting Parallel Server databases on a single server.

The changes to the interpretation of the INSTANCES clause are a precursor to the eventual obsolescence of the INSTANCES keyword in the PARALLEL clause of the CREATE or ALTER statements for tables, indexes, and clusters, as well as the ALTER DATABASE...RECOVER command. The use of the implicit INSTANCES keyword in SQL statement hints will also be discontinued at the same time.

In Oracle8*i*, the PARALLEL clause can be coded in one of two ways. The preferred method is to use the keyword PARALLEL with or without a value, as in

```
CREATE TABLE...PARALLEL
```

or

```
CREATE TABLE...PARALLEL
```

Using this syntax, which is new in release 8.1, the number of parallel threads will be the integer you provide, as in the previous first example, or an optimum number computed by Oracle if you don't provide a value, as in the second example.

The second version of the syntax is the syntax supported by earlier versions of Oracle. It consists of the keyword PARALLEL followed by a parallel clause in parentheses. The clause can

contain either or both the keywords DEGREE and INSTANCES, each of which is followed by an integer or the keyword DEFAULT. In the earlier versions of Oracle, the number of parallel threads was either the number following the keyword DEGREE or a value computed for DEFAULT that was based on other parameters. The INSTANCES keyword determined the number of distinct instances on which a command would attempt to acquire this number of parallel threads. Once again, if you included an integer, this was the specific number of instances that a statement would attempt to acquire, and if you included the keyword, the number of instances would be determined from other parameters.

When using this second version of the syntax in Oracle8*i*, INSTANCES no longer determines the number of instances that will be used by the statement, but simply modifies the value provided by DEGREE. Oracle will execute the statement just as if you had used the first version of the syntax but supplied the modified value in the PARALLEL clause. The number of instances used by either version of the statement will be determined by Oracle at runtime, based on the availability of parallel slaves and the load on each running instance.

In this second version of the syntax, if either of the keywords is omitted, a value of 1 is used for the missing value. Table 10.2 shows how the values of DEGREE and INSTANCES interact in release 8.1 to compute the modified value for the number of parallel threads that will be used to execute a statement. To save space, I show values of Not Set—for a missing keyword—and values of 1 in the same cells.

TABLE 10.2   Interpretation of DEGREE and INSTANCES Keywords in Oracle8*i*

Value for DEGREE	*Value for INSTANCES*	*Degree Requested*
Not Set or 1	Not Set or 1	1
Not Set or 1	DEFAULT	DEFAULT
DEFAULT	Not Set or 1	DEFAULT
Integer x	Not Set or 1	x
Integer x	DEFAULT	x
Not Set or 1	Integer y	y
DEFAULT	Integer y	y
Integer x	Integer y	x * y

Because this behavior differs from the behavior in earlier releases, we encourage you to convert to the new syntax to avoid having your statements execute in unexpected ways. For example, a value greater than 1 for INSTANCES can result in the statement executing on a single instance, whereas a value of 1 for DEGREE might still result in multiple parallel threads running on one or more instances.

The second major change to Parallel Server in Oracle8*i*, as mentioned previously, concerns the limitations on multiple parallel instances running on a server. The 8.1 release has removed some of the restrictions governing multiple instances, from different Parallel Server databases, running on a single server. In earlier releases, many platforms would not support two or more instances from different databases on a single node in a cluster. Also, instances for databases with different word sizes could not be supported concurrently. Some limitations still exist: These are platform dependent and might change with each new version. Your platform-specific documentation will provide the details as to how many different databases are supported on a server and whether different Parallel Server databases might run using different word sizes.

Database Security Compatibility and Interoperability

New password management features were introduced in Oracle8, version 8.0, and these continue to be available in Oracle8*i*. They include the ability to expire a password and lock the account until it is changed, as well as other features to prevent the use of a simplistic password or the reuse of a password. Compatibility issues arise when using a mix of Oracle8 and Oracle7, or earlier, clients and servers, and the password management features are enabled.

When a password expires, certain Oracle tools, such as SQL*Plus, provide the user a message to provide a new password and allow it to be reset. If you want your Oracle7, or earlier, applications to do the same thing, you must include the OCI call, OCISessionBegin(), to connect to the server and check for the password status. If the password has expired, you can use the call OCIChangePassword() to allow the user to change the password, if you want. If the password has expired, and you do not use this call to change it, the check for password reuse will not be made. Using the higher release log in call will enable the other password management features in Oracle7, or earlier release, clients.

The higher level log in calls can also be used when an Oracle8 client connects to an Oracle7, or earlier, database server. The Oracle8*i* Migration manual provides an example of the code used for this.

Database Backup and Recovery Compatibility and Interoperability

A number of compatibility issues exist between Recovery Manager recovery catalogs in Oracle8, release 8.0 and Oracle8*i*, release 8.1. These are outside the scope of this book, and we refer you to the Oracle8*i* Migration manual for the specific details if you are upgrading your database from release 8.0 to release 8.1. The compatibility issues that are related to Oracle7 and Oracle8*i* are covered in this section.

For those of you who have used Oracle's Enterprise Backup Utility (EBU), you should note that Recovery Manager has completely replaced EBU. Although both EBU and Recovery Manager use the same low-level language to communicate with third-party storage subsystems, so you can continue to use the same products as before to store your backups, the scripting languages of the two products are completely different. You will therefore need to rewrite your backup and recovery scripts for Oracle8*i*.

The following restrictions apply to datafile backups taken with Oracle7 after you have migrated to Oracle8*i*:

- If the backup was taken after running the Migration Utility, you can use it to restore and to recover your Oracle8*i* database.
- If EBU was used to backup the database, you must use EBU to restore the datafiles before using them for recovery under Oracle8*i*.
- If you used operating system commands for the Oracle7 backup and you have room for them on your disks, you can register the files with Recovery Manager (using the `catalog datafilecopy` command).

If you are using a standby database in Oracle7, you know that it must run the same maintenance release as the primary database. After you migrate to Oracle8*i*, you must therefore upgrade your standby database to the same release level (for example, release 8.1.5). The six steps to do this are documented in the Oracle8*i* migration manual and are summarized here for your convenience:

1. Apply all archived logs from the pre-migrated primary database.
2. Migrate and test the primary database.
3. Migrate the standby database.
4. Create a control file for your standby database.
5. Copy this control file to the standby database server.
6. Copy the file with ID number equal to 1 from the primary to the standby database.

Should you choose to make use of Oracle8*i*'s capability to archive to multiple destinations, you should be aware that automatic archiving will not stop if an archive destination becomes unavailable as it did in earlier releases. You define which destinations are mandatory and the total number of destinations to which archives must be successfully written. Unless there is a violation of these requirements, the archive process will write messages to the alert log regarding any failed destinations, but will continue to run. Therefore, unlike previous releases, you might not know of archiving problems unless you monitor the alert log.

Distributed Database Compatibility and Interoperability

Three areas of interest exist regarding compatibility and interoperability of Oracle8*i* databases included in distributed systems and using replication features: changes to basic snapshots, advanced replication between different Oracle versions, and interoperability of heterogeneous service agents.

In Oracle8*i*, snapshots are generally created with one underlying object: the snapshot base table that is given the same name as the snapshot. This differs from earlier releases in which the base table was given a derived name and an additional object, a snapshot view, was created with the name of the snapshot. However, a view will still be added to a snapshot in Oracle8*i* in the following situations:

- The COMPATIBLE parameter is set to a value less than 8.1.0.
- The snapshot is derived from ROWIDs rather than primary keys or the snapshot is defined for a fast refresh and contains a subquery.
- The snapshot was imported from a database release prior to 8.1.

Advanced replication changes in Oracle8*i* include the internalization of previously-external packages and some enhancements to the replication code. In order to support n-way master sites that are at a lower release level than 8.1, you must set the GENERATE_80_COMPATIBLE flag to TRUE, or leave it to default to TRUE, in the following procedures: GENERATE_REPLICATION_SUPPORT, CREATE_SNAPSHOT_REPOBJECT, and GENERATE_SNAPSHOT_SUPPORT. If your master sites are all Oracle8*i* databases, you should set GENERATE_80_COMPATIBLE to FALSE in order to use the enhanced algorithms. You should also note that if you have different releases of Oracle in the distributed environment, you cannot replicate objects from a higher release to a lower release that does not support those objects.

Oracle8*i*, release 8.1, is the first release to support multithreaded Heterogeneous Service agents. If you want any existing agents to use the multithreaded features, you need to use the Agent Control Utility to create the agent initialization files and explicitly start the agents. Of course, if you have servers at different release levels, the Heterogeneous Service agents are limited to the functionality of the lower release.

SQL*Net and Net8 Compatibility and Interoperability

Oracle8*i* requires connections from clients or from distributed databases to use either SQL*Net V2 or Net8; SQL*Net V1 connections are not supported. If you still have SQL*Net V1 running, you will need to upgrade it using the following steps:

1. Install SQL*Net V2 or Net8 on the client or server in question.
2. Update the connect strings to appropriate syntax as described in relevant network Administrator's Guide from Oracle.
3. Relink any precompiled programs and Oracle executables, such as SQL*Plus, which you need to use the upgraded connections.
4. Optionally add parameters to the network files to support connection load balancing as described in Oracle's Net8 Administrator's Guide.

Export/Import Compatibility and Interoperability

The compatibility issues between Oracle versions related to Export/Import haven't changed with the Oracle8*i* release. Any export dump file higher than release 5.1.22 can be imported into the current release, 8.1.5, or any release between them. Exports from the current release cannot, in general, be imported into earlier releases other than the previous production release. To perform such an import, the export must be made using the previous release's Export utility. In some cases, this will require running a script in the current database to reset the Export utility tables to be compatible with the earlier release.

Whenever you use the Export utility from an earlier release in order to import into a database running under that release, the dump file will not contain any objects that are not supported in the target database. If you need the data from such objects, you will have to convert them to a supported object type prior to the export.

Miscellaneous Compatibility and Interoperability Topics

In this section, I discuss two final compatibility and interoperability issues: multiple Oracle versions and files greater than 2GB.

Oracle8*i* can be installed on a computer system that already has other Oracle versions installed unless your operating system specifically precludes this. However, each release of Oracle can only execute against databases running under that same release.

In most cases, Oracle8*i* can support datafiles that are larger than 2GB. In some cases, use of files larger than 2GB is restricted by the operating system. For example, on some UNIX systems, only files on raw devices can exceed 2GB. Some operating systems might have different levels of support for files larger than 2GB in different versions. Also, the system might require firmware upgrades to allow the disk subsystems to handle files that exceed 2GB in size. Therefore, you need to confirm with your hardware vendor that you have valid versions of the operating system and firmware patches installed before attempting to use files greater than 2GB.

Finally, you might not want to use files over 2GB if the operating doesn't provide full functionality for them. On some systems, for example, asynchronous I/O is not available for such large files. If performance can be compromised by using files over 2GB, you might want to reconsider using them.

Summary

This chapter covers a lot of ground and a multitude of topics and features. The main point of the chapter is to highlight the features in your Oracle8*i* database that might cause you some problems if you try to use it in conjunction with other databases, tools, applications, and network components, which are running at a lower version level. This can make this chapter appear to be very negative about the components and features of Oracle8*i*. It is an unfortunate fact that as the product is improved, it moves further and further away from its previous versions and becomes less and less compatible with them.

If this chapter has left you with the feeling that the new release isn't worth the effort needed to get it running in your environment, we invite you to skip ahead to Part II of this book. There we discuss the benefits and primary uses of the new features in Oracle8*i*. You will see that the advantages of Oracle8*i* make the few issues you made to address for the sake of compatibility seem trivial. Some of you might even find that to implement your Oracle8*i* upgrade and meet your current needs, very little in this chapter impacts you. Even so, we do recommend that you scan the main topics in this chapter following your upgrade just to make sure that there are no issues that could impact your database and the way you intend to use it.

Upgrading Applications

IN THIS CHAPTER

This chapter describes the changes you will need to make to various types of application if you want to make use of new features available to you in Oracle8i, release 8.1. Of course, if you were migrating just to stay current with the product and don't need to use any of the new features, you will not have to touch your applications. Even if you don't, you might find that some new features are being used automatically, and as a result, your applications might possibly run better than they did under your Oracle7 release.

In order to evaluate your applications' probable performance following the migration of your production database, you might want to migrate the applications as part of your testing procedure. As you finish testing the migration process against a copy of your production database, you can use the resulting databases to run your applications. This will give you a chance to investigate whether you will want to make any changes following the migration and, if so, the extent of these changes.

Overview

We are assuming that you are migrating to Oracle8i from an Oracle7 database and will need to know about changes you could make to enable all the features in Oracle8i, even if they were introduced in Oracle8, release 8.0. For those of you who might have upgraded to Oracle8 in the past, you might already have incorporated some of the features discussed in this chapter and be ready for just the release 8.1 features. You will need to identify which changes do and don't apply to you.

I have also included a section that is outside of any specific application or tool, but which can make a significant difference to your application code. This section, "Copying LONGs to LOBs," discusses how you can convert columns defined with the LONG datatype to one of the large object (LOB) datatypes. Again, this is not a required change, but one recommended by Oracle because of the greater flexibility offered by LOBs and the intention to support LOBs rather than LONGs in later versions of the database.

You should be aware that there are some required changes to your applications and tools that you will have to make in order to run them successfully against your Oracle8i database. Those topics are discussed in Chapter 10, "Issues with Compatibility," rather than in this chapter. You should review Chapter 10 before you try making the optional changes discussed in the following.

Upgrading OCI Applications

You can choose to migrate your Oracle7 OCI applications without making any changes to incorporate new Oracle8i programmatic interfaces. Your applications will continue to function, but probably without any change in performance and no change in functionality. If you want to improve your applications' performance, you might have to replace some of the Oracle7 calls

with release 8.1 calls. To gain the functionality offered in Oracle8*i*, you should rewrite the applications completely to use only the calls offered in release 8.1. In this section, I identify the key changes you might want to incorporate.

In order to ensure that constraints are properly enabled when running your Oracle7 applications against your migrated database, you should re-link your applications with the release 8.1 runtime OCI library, OCILIB. You can choose which Oracle8 deferred mode to use when you relink: nondeferred mode or deferred mode linking. With the nondeferred mode, you will maintain your Oracle7 performance levels and functionality. Using deferred mode linking, you will obtain a performance improvement, but you might see a change in bind and define error reporting. Instead of the application being notified immediately of bind and define errors, the errors might not be reported until a later DESCRIBE, EXECUTE, or FETCH call.

To enable OCI applications to take advantage of Database Event Notification and Advanced Queuing features, Oracle8*i* has added support for client notification using the publish/subscribe interface. In order to use this interface, you must link your client applications with the release 8.1 client libraries.

Another change in Oracle8*i* to help OCI applications work with Advanced Queuing is the support of the LISTEN call to monitor a set of queues for a message. Again, to enable this feature, you have to link your client applications with the release 8.1 client libraries.

A new feature in Oracle8*i* is the support of batch error mode when performing array processing of DML statements with the OCIStmtExecute call. If you want your applications to use batch error mode, you need to modify the application to include the necessary calls and set the mode parameter to OCI_BATCH_ERRORS. You will then need to recompile and relink the application with the release 8.1 client libraries.

If you should happen to still be using the Oracle6 OCI library, you will have to upgrade your applications because this library is not supported against the Oracle8*i* database. In fact, no Oracle8 versions can process Oracle6 OCI calls.

Upgrading Precompiler Applications

As with your OCI applications, you can choose to migrate your Oracle7 precompiler applications without making any changes to incorporate new Oracle8*i* programmatic interfaces. Similarly, as with OCI applications, the programs will continue to function, but probably without any changes in performance or functionality. In fact, you don't need to re-precompile or to recompile an Oracle7 precompiler application for it to run against an Oracle8*i* database.

Further, if you have upgraded your applications to use an Oracle8*i* precompiler, you can use them to execute against an Oracle7 database as long as they don't use any release 8.0 or greater

features, such as object capabilities. In fact, within a Pro*C or a Proc*COBOL program, you can include Oracle7 and Oracle8*i* function calls: They can even be mixed in the same transaction.

Your choices for handling your Oracle7 client applications are as follows:

- Make no changes and execute the programs against your Oracle8*i* database.
- Re-link, but do not recompile, your programs without making any changes to the applications; this will upgrade your clients to Oracle8*i,* but won't allow you to use any Oracle8 or Oracle8*i* features.
- Upgrade your applications to Oracle8*i* and incorporate new performance and functional capabilities by rewriting them to use the new precompiler calls; this approach will require you to relink the modified program.

For details about the calls provided in Oracle8*i* for Pro*C/C++ and Pro*COBOL, we direct you to the relevant Precompiler Programmer's Guide provided by Oracle.

Upgrading Forms and Developer/2000 Applications

If you use Developer/2000 extensively, you should consider upgrading the current release of this product along with your database migration. If you decide not to make this change, your Forms applications should run exactly the same against your Oracle8*i* database as they did against your Oracle7 database. Of course, as with your OCI and your precompiler programs, you might want to upgrade them to take advantage of the features and performance improvements available in release 8.1. If you decide that your Forms applications could benefit from some Oracle8*i* enhancements, you should consult Volumes 1 and 2 of the Oracle Forms 4.5 documentation.

Upgrading SQL*Plus Scripts

Your current SQL*Plus scripts will run against an Oracle8*i* database without requiring any changes. However, you might want to take advantage of the new capabilities of SQL*Plus provided in Oracle8*i*. The most important of these capabilities are related to the deprecation of the Server Manager product and the inclusion of its capabilities into SQL*Plus. See the section following, "Server Manager and SQL*Plus," for details on these changes.

As with many other application products, you can choose not to make any changes to your SQL*Plus scripts and their execution environment. Your scripts, including any embedded PL/SQL blocks, will continue to run and will behave in exactly the same way as they did when run against your Oracle7 database.

If you want to upgrade your SQL*Plus scripts so that you can include new options provided in releases 8.0 and 8.1, you must ensure that there are no obstacles to the scripts running against the preferred release level. These obstacles would be the SQL*Plus SET COMPATIBILITY VERSION command included in the script or in a local LOGIN.SQL or a global GLOGIN.SQL file where the version value is a number less than 8. By default, the version value is NATIVE.

Upgrading Server Manager and SQL*Plus

In this section, I discuss the new options in SQL*Plus that allow you to execute Server Manager line mode commands and show you how to modify any existing scripts you use with Server Manager line mode, so that they will run with SQL*Plus. Oracle recommends that you make these changes because Server Manager will not be supported in future releases. In fact, Server Manager is only being supported in current releases of Oracle8*i* for backward compatibility.

> **NOTE**
>
> For the remainder of this section, I will refer to Server Manager line mode simply as Server Manager. The context in which this term is used will make it clear whether I am referring to the product name itself or Server Manager line mode.

A number of commands are available in both SQL*Plus and Server Manager. You should not need to modify these commands when using a Server Manager script in an Oracle8*i* SQL*Plus session. However, the format of the output from some of these commands might differ slightly when used with the two different tools. For example, the default file extension for the SPOOL command is not necessarily the same in SQL*Plus as in Server Manager. If you have a script that depends on the full name of the output file, you should change the SPOOL command to include the full filename with the extension used by your version of Server Manager, or else change the reference to the filename to use the SQL*Plus file extension.

These are the commands that should work without any changes, except as just noted, if they are coded in the Server Manager scripts which you'll run using SQL*Plus:

    CONNECT
    DESCRIBE
    REMARK
    SET COMPATIBILITY
    SET ECHO
    SET NUMWIDTH

SET SERVEROUTPUT
SET TERMOUT
SHOW ALL
SHOW ERRORS
SPOOL

The first key difference between SQL*Plus and Server Manager is how you start up the tool and connect to the database. In SQL*Plus, the default behavior is to require you to provide a username and password. You can do this either by providing one or both of them as part of the command to start SQL*Plus, or in response to prompts it provides before it lets you connect. Server Manager, on the other hand, starts up when you enter the product name at the operating system prompt and requires you to enter a CONNECT command once the tool has started.

Using `sqlplus` as the name of the SQL*Plus executable and `svrmgrl` as the name of the Server Manager program, the following examples show some of the different ways you can connect to each of the two tools. For simplicity, the examples in this section all use the greater than symbol, >, for the operating system prompt and omit the banner information from the output.

Example #1

Invoke SQL*Plus without entering a username or password and respond to the prompts for these two items individually. Note that when you connect to SQL*Plus this way, your password will not be echoed on the screen.

```
> sqlplus

Enter user-name: scott
Enter password: tiger

SQL>
. . .
```

Example #2

Invoke SQL*Plus as well as providing the username and password. When you connect to SQL*Plus this way, your password is echoed on the screen and, on UNIX systems, it will appear as part of the process name visible with the *ps* command.

```
> sqlplus scott/tiger

SQL>
. . .
```

Example #3

Invoke Server Manager, and then issue a *CONNECT* command. This causes the prompts for the username and password to appear. By responding to each prompt individually, your password will not be echoed on the screen. Note that Server Manager does not accept a username and password on the command line and does not automatically request them when the product is started.

```
> svrmgrl

SVRMGR> connect
Username: scott
Password: tiger
Connected.
SVRMGR>
. . .
```

Example #4

Invoke Server Manager, and then issue a *CONNECT* command that includes the username and password. Note that when you enter the password as part of the command, it will be echoed on the screen.

```
> svrmgrl

SVRMGR> connect scott/tiger
Connected.
SVRMGR>
. . .
```

If you are working with the tools interactively, you probably aren't aware of this difference. But if you have scripts that include the connection to Server Manager, they will not work with SQL*Plus without modification. You need to use the NOLOG option with the SQL*Plus

command you use to replace the Server Manager command. The following example shows two possible ways you can log into SQL*Plus with this option in place:

```
> sqlplus /nolog

SQL> connect
Enter user-name: scott
Enter password: tiger
Connected.
SQL>
. . .

> sqlplus /nolog

SQL> connect scott/tiger
Connected.
SQL>
. . .
```

Another subtle change in Oracle8*i*'s version of SQL*Plus is in the use of the INTERNAL keyword. In previous versions of SQL*Plus, you generally could not connect with the username INTERNAL unless you had already defined a password file. If you tried, it would prompt you for a password but because one didn't exist, your login attempt would fail. In Oracle8*i*, SQL*Plus will accept a login as INTERNAL, using any of the following formats:

1.
```
> sqlplus internal
```
2.
```
> sqlplus
Enter user-name: internal

SQL>
. . .
```
3.
```
SQL> connect internal
Connected.
SQL>
. . .
```

After you have modified the scripts to ensure that you can log in to SQL*Plus, you will need to change any commands in your scripts that are not supported in SQL*Plus. Table 11.1 lists Server Manager commands that have SQL*Plus equivalents and describes how to substitute them.

TABLE **11.1**   Server Manager Commands with SQL*Plus Equivalents

Server Manager Command	SQL*Plus Command	Notes
SET CHARWIDTH	COLUMN... FORMAT	SET CHARWIDTH defines the column width for all character fields, whereas COLUMN...FORMAT defines the column format for just the named column. You will have to include one COLUMN command for every character field you want to format.
SET DATEWIDTH	COLUMN... FORMAT	SET DATEWIDTH defines the column width for all date fields, whereas COLUMN...FORMAT defines the column format for just the named column. You will have to include one COLUMN command for every date field you want to format.
SET LONGWIDTH	COLUMN... FORMAT	SET LONGWIDTH defines the column width for all numeric fields, whereas COLUMN...FORMAT defines the column format for just the named column. You will have to include one COLUMN command for every LONG field you want to format.
SET STOPONERROR	WHENEVER SQLERROR/ WHENEVER OSERROR	SET STOPONERROR ON will cause a Server Manager session to terminate when an error is encountered; you will have to include both WHENEVER SQLERROR EXIT and WHENEVER OSERROR EXIT to have a SQL*Plus session act the same way.

NOTE

When substituting SQL*Plus COLUMN...FORMAT commands for the Server Manager SET CHARWIDTH/DATEWIDTH/LONGWIDTH commands, you should be aware that the format of the output will not be the same. Server Manager truncates the output to the width defined by the SET command; SQL*Plus will wrap any characters that exceed the defined format length to a new line.

If you need any further information on the SQL*Plus equivalent commands, you should refer to your Oracle8*i* SQL*Plus documentation.

Other commands used in Server Manager do not have any true equivalents in SQL*Plus: SET TIMING ON, SET MAXDATA, and SET RETRIES. The SET TIMING ON command will

usually display a condensed trace report, including the elapsed and CPU time used for the Parse and the Execute and Fetch steps, of every SQL statement or PL/SQL block processed. The SQL*Plus command, SET TIMING ON, will show only one value—the total elapsed time—after each statement or PL/SQL block, rather than providing a formatted breakdown. You can choose whether to leave any SET TIMING commands in your Server Manager scripts, but there isn't a convenient way to make them produce the equivalent output when they are run with SQL*Plus.

The SET MAXDATA command, used in Server Manager, might appear to be similar to the SET ARRAYSIZE command in SQL*Plus. However, the former restricts the amount of data that can be retrieved in a single fetch and will return an error if a single row is too long. The latter sets the number of rows that will be processed in a single fetch and will not cause a single row query to fail. The No SQL*Plus option will duplicate the behavior of the SET MAXDATA command.

The SET RETRIES command limits the number of times an instance in a Parallel Server database will attempt to startup if the RETRY option is used with the STARTUP command. This command is not currently supported, and has no equivalent, in SQL*Plus.

The final set of command changes related to SQL*Plus in Oracle8*i* is the support for the database management commands. These commands, which will not work with any previous release of SQL*Plus, have been added to allow you to perform the same database operations as you can in Server Manager. Table 11.2 describes these commands that will run unchanged in either Server Manager or SQL*Plus.

TABLE 11.2   New SQL*Plus Commands

Command	Description
ARCHIVE LOG	Starts or stops automatic archiving of online redo log files, manually (explicitly) archives specified redo log files, or displays information about archives.
RECOVER	Performs media recovery on one or more tablespaces, one or more datafiles, or the entire database.
SET AUTORECOVERY	ON causes the RECOVER command to automatically apply the default filenames of archived redo log files needed during recovery. No interaction is needed when AUTORECOVERY is set to ON, provided the necessary files are in the expected locations with the expected names.
SET INSTANCE	Changes the default instance for your session to the specified instance path. Does not connect to a database. The default instance is used for commands when no instance is specified.

Command	Description
SET LOGSOURCE	Specifies the location from which archive logs are retrieved during recovery. The default value is set by the LOG_ARCHIVE_DEST initialization parameter. Issuing the SET LOGSOURCE command without a pathname restores the default location.
SHOWAUTORECOVERY	Shows whether autorecovery is enabled.
SHOW INSTANCE	Shows the connect string for the default instance. Returns the value LOCAL if you have not used SET INSTANCE, or if you have used the LOCAL option of the SET INSTANCE command.
SHOW LOGSOURCE	Shows the current setting for the archive log location. Displays DEFAULT if the default setting is in effect, as specified by the LOG_ARCHIVE_DEST initialization parameter.
SHOW PARAMETERS	Displays the current values for one or more initialization parameters. The SHOW PARAMETERS command, without any string following the command, displays all initialization parameters.
SHOW SGA	Displays information about the current instance's System Global Area.
SHUTDOWN	Shuts down a currently running Oracle instance, optionally closing and dismounting a database.
STARTUP	Starts an Oracle instance with several options, including mounting and opening a database.

The last set of changes you might have to make to your Server Manager scripts, to allow them to run with SQL*Plus, are syntactical. These required changes are described in Table 11.3.

TABLE 11.3 Server Manager Syntax Not Supported in SQL*Plus

Syntax	Description and Changes Required for Use in SQL*Plus
/*...*/	This SQL comment delimiter syntax is valid in both Server Manger and SQL*Plus, but in SQL*Plus it is not valid following the semicolon at the end of a SQL statement. If you have such a construction in a Server Manager script, you need to move the comment to a new line by itself or replace the semicolon with a slash (/) on the following line.
—	This SQL comment delimiter is valid in both Server Manger and SQL*Plus, but in SQL*Plus it is not valid following the semicolon at the end of a SQL statement. If you have such a construction in a Server Manager script, you need to move the comment to a new line by itself or replace the semicolon with a slash (/) on the following line.

continues

TABLE 11.3 Continued

Syntax	Description and Changes Required for Use in SQL*Plus
blank lines	A blank line can be inserted between any two lines in a SQL statement when using Server Manager, but in SQL*Plus, a blank line acts as a statement terminator. You will need to remove any blank lines from your Server Manager scripts if they occur between the lines of a single SQL statement.
-	The hyphen character is interpreted as a continuation character if it occurs at the end of line in a SQL*Plus script. In Server Manager, it can be a valid part of a statement or part of a comment as in:

```
SELECT col1 -
col2 FROM table1;
or
REM ----------------------
SELECT * FROM table2;
```

	You will have to change such uses of the hyphen before running these scripts in SQL*Plus; otherwise, you will get unexpected results. The first example will treat col2 as a column alias and the second will interpret the SELECT statement as a continuation of the comment.
&	The ampersand is used by SQL*Plus to identify a substitution variable, even if it appears in a comment, whereas Server Manager always treats it as a normal character. If you find ampersands in your scripts, you have a number of options:
	(a) You can delete them if that doesn't change the meaning of the script
	(b) You can precede them with an escape character that you define with the SET ESCAPE command; however, this does not work for every type of statement.
	(c) You can change the character used to prefix substitution variables with the SET DEFINE command; this allows your script to contain substitution variables while preserving the Server Manager interpretation of ampersands.
	(d) You can turn off the use of substitution variables completely with the SET DEFINE OFF command.
; with CREATE TYPE	SQL*Plus interprets a CREATE TYPE command as a PL/SQL block instead of a SQL command unless you omit the semicolon at the end of the command and place a slash (/) on the next line of the script. Server Manager will interpret the CREATE TYPE command correctly as a SQL command even if it is terminated with a semicolon. If your scripts contain CREATE TYPE commands formulated in this manner, you must remove the semicolon and create a new line containing a single slash (/).

Syntax	Description and Changes Required for Use in SQL*Plus
; with CREATE LIBRARY	SQL*Plus interprets a CREATE LIBRARY command as a PL/SQL block instead of a SQL command unless you omit the semicolon at the end of the command and place a slash (/) on the next line of the script. Server Manager will interpret the CREATE LIBRARY command correctly as a SQL command even if it is terminated with a semicolon. If your scripts contain CREATE LIBRARY commands formulated in this manner, you must remove the semicolon and create a new line containing a single slash (/).
unterminated COMMIT	Server Manager will process a COMMIT command whether or not it is followed by a semicolon. SQL*Plus will not execute the command without a semicolon or a slash (/) on the next line of input. You must therefore add one or the other of these terminators to any COMMIT commands without a semicolon that you find in your scripts.

Copying LONGs to LOBs

Oracle8*i* supports various types of large object (LOB) datatypes: character (CLOBs), binary, or raw (BLOBs), national language support character (NCLOB), and external files (BFILE). If you are migrating from Oracle7 to Oracle8*i*, your database might contain LONG and LONG RAW column datatypes. Oracle recommends that you convert these columns to CLOB and BLOB datatypes, respectively. The easiest way to do this is to build a copy of each table containing a LONG or LONG RAW column, but substitute the appropriate LOB datatype in the copy of the table. You can then transfer the rows from the original to the new table using the TO_LOB function. Listing 11.1 contains a series of SQL statements that

- Build a table with a LONG RAW column
- Build an equivalent table with a BLOB column
- Copy the data from the original table to the new table using the TO_LOB function

LISTING 11.1   Sample Transfer of Data from LONG to LOB datatype

```
REM Script to demonstrate the transfer of LONG (LONG RAW) data
REM to one of the LOB datatypes.

REM Create the original table with LONG RAW column.

CREATE TABLE original_source (
    id NUMBER,
    long_col LONG RAW);
```

continues

LISTING 11.1   Continued

```
REM Create a new table using the original table's definition, but
REM substituting the CLOB datatype for the LONG RAW tabletype.

CREATE TABLE modified_target (
    id NUMBER,
    clob_col CLOB);

REM Copy the data from the source to the target table.

INSERT INTO modified_target
    SELECT id, TO_LOB(long_col)
        FROM original_source;
```

After you have confirmed that the new table has stored the data successfully, you need to use it to replace the original table. We recommend that you use the following steps to complete this task:

1. Export the original table using a table-level export.
2. Drop the original table.
3. Rename the new table to the original table's name.
4. Import the full dump file, choosing the option to ignore the Create Error Due to Object Existence and the option to not import table data.
5. Modify the applications, and any scripts, which used the LONG data to use the new datatype in the replacement copy of the table.

Step 1 should ensure that the objects based on the original table's existence will be included in the export dump file and step 4 will re-create them when the import is executed.

Summary

Your applications might or might not have to be upgraded after you migrate to Oracle8*i*, with the majority of them not needing any changes if you don't want to take advantage of any of the new features available in the current release. In some cases, you might need to re-link the current application code in order for it to work with your Oracle8*i* database. If you decide to incorporate new functionality, or even if you just want to benefit from some of the performance enhancements available in Oracle8*i*, you might have to do more work. Sometimes this can be as simple as modifying a few specific statements or calls. In other cases, you might have to make some extensive revisions. In the case of OCI, you might need to rewrite the application completely in order to benefit from all the features and functional changes made in release 8.1.

11

Those of you who migrated to Oracle8*i* in order to take advantage of a specific capability of this release should be able to identify which type of changes you need to make to your applications. The rest of you should take a look at Part II of this book before you make any decisions about how much effort you want to put into your applications after your migration. Some of the new features could provide substantial benefits and save you a lot of time and effort trying to improve your database performance. We remind you of the conventional wisdom, which claims that eighty to ninety percent of database performance problems are the fault of the applications, not the database.

Finally, you should also look at Chapter 10, "Issues with Compatibility," before you decide how much work you are going to put into migrating your applications and before you do any work on them. In some cases, you might find that you will have to complete some modifications just to allow them to work in a heterogeneous environment. If this is the case, you should combine the changes, recompilations, and the re-links for your applications to complete the compatibility modifications and the upgrades all at once. Of course, this will not prevent you from making further changes later, as the needs arise, but it will reduce your workload during the migration process.

Issues with ROWIDs

IN THIS CHAPTER

A new ROWID format was introduced in Oracle8, release 8.0, to support relative file numbers (which allow more datafiles to be added to a database and provide some of the functionality for transportable tablespaces) and partitioned tables. Release 8.1, and subsequent releases, will continue to use this new format. Although ROWIDs are mainly used for internal database activities, such as index construction and access, there are some cases where you might need to use them and handle their transition from Oracle7 to Oracle8*i*.

In this chapter, I will explain the structure of the ROWIDs used in Oracle8*i* and show you how you might have to modify your applications and data to support them following your database migration.

ROWID Structures

Internally, Oracle8*i* maintains two types of physical ROWIDs: restricted and extended. The physical ROWIDs are used internally and are not formatted for display. The restricted ROWID is structured just like an Oracle7 ROWID. It consists of three basic components:

- Absolute datafile ID number
- Relative block address within a file
- Row number within a block

Restricted ROWIDs are stored in 6-byte fields and are compatible with Oracle7 databases. Extended ROWIDs require 10 bytes of storage and consist of four basic pieces:

- Data object number
- Relative datafile ID number
- Relative block address within a file
- Row number within a block

NOTE

Until Oracle8, all releases of Oracle supported a maximum of 1,022 datafiles in a database, but—with the introduction of release 8.0—this limit was removed. Your Oracle8*i* database can support a maximum of 1,022 datafiles in each tablespace, with up to 65,533—depending on your operating system—allowed for the whole database. Oracle8*i* also introduced the ability to move tablespaces between different databases. In order to support these two enhancements without complicating the algorithms used to manipulate ROWIDs and file numbers, a secondary type of datafile number, relative file numbers, was introduced. Relative file numbers are used

when a tablespace is transported or the database is comprised of more than 1,022 datafiles. Relative file numbers are sequentially numbered, beginning with 1 for each tablespace. The traditional type of datafile ID number is now called an absolute file number to differentiate it from a relative file number.

To see the contents of a ROWID, you will use one of the external formats: character or binary. The external character format is the most common and is the one used when you issue a command such as

```
SELECT rowid FROM sales WHERE rownum = 1;
```

It is returned in a host variable type of DTYCHR and consists of 18 printable characters representing a special base-64 encoding. The output from the preceding query produced the following row in our database:

```
ROWID
-----------------
AAAMxQAADAAABQ+AAA
```

Each of the characters represent a base-64 value, where A = 0, B = 1, Z = 25, a = 26, z = 51, 0 = 52, 1 = 53, 9 = 61, + = 62, and / = 63. The first six characters, AAAMxQ, represent the data object number. This is the number stored in the DATA_OBJECT_ID column of the DBA_OBJECTS Data Dictionary table. The next three characters, AAD, represent the relative file number. The block number within the datafile is represented by the next six characters, AAABQ+, and the last three characters, AAA, store the representation of the row number, or slot number, within the block.

NOTE

If you have regularly used to the Oracle7 Data Dictionary table, DBA_OBJECTS, you are probably familiar with its column, OBJECT_ID. This column still exists in the Oracle8*i* version of the table in addition to the new column, DATA_OBJECT_ID. The OBJECT_ID column contains the invariant object ID number just as it did in Oracle7. The DATA_OBJECT_ID column contains this same ID number when a segment is created, but it will change as you perform certain operations, such as a TRUNCATE command on a table. It is the value in this new column, DATA_OBJECT_ID, which is used in extended ROWIDs.

The external binary ROWID format is used to return a value into a host variable of DTYRID format. It contains the same components as the character format but in a compressed form. Generally, only Oracle-provided utilities will use this format.

The DBMS_ROWID Package

Oracle has provided a new package, called DBMS_ROWID, which allows you to use information from the new ROWID format without having to perform any complicated conversions from the base-64 representation. You can also use the package to convert any ROWID data you might have stored for your Oracle7 records. In Table 12.1, I briefly describe the procedures and functions available in the DBMS_ROWID package.

TABLE 12.1   DBMS_ROWID Components

Component Name	Procedure or Function	Description
ROWID_BLOCK_NUMBER	Function	Returns the database block number for the supplied ROWID
ROWID_CREATE	Function	Allows you to build your own Oracle8*i* ROWIDs from component parts that you can then use for testing purposes
ROWID_INFO	Procedure	Provides the decimal value associated with each component of a ROWID, whether restricted or extended
ROWID_OBJECT	Function	Returns the data object ID number for the supplied ROWID
ROWID_RELATIVE_FNO	Function	Returns the relative file number for the supplied ROWID
ROWID_ROW_NUMBER	Function	Returns the row number for the supplied ROWID
ROWID_TO_ABSOLUTE_FNO	Function	Returns the absolute file number for a specific row in a table
ROWID_TO_EXTENED	Function	Translates a restricted ROWID for a specific row in a table to its extended format
ROWID_TO_RESTRICTED	Function	Translates an extended ROWID to its restricted format
ROWID_TYPE	Function	Returns a value to indicate what type of ROWID is input—a zero for restricted and a one for extended

Component Name	*Procedure or Function*	*Description*
ROWID_VERIFY	Function	Returns a value to indicate if a restricted ROWID for a specific row in a table can be converted to extended format—a zero if it can be converted and a one if it cannot

You can use the SQL*Plus DESCRIBE command, or refer to the Oracle8*i* Supplied Packages Reference manual, for a list of the parameters and their datatypes needed for each of the DBMS_ROWID package components described in Table 12.1. Note that the ROWID_INFO component is the only procedure in the DBMS_ROWID package and therefore can only be used within a PL/SQL block. The other components are functions that can be used in PL/SQL statements, but more importantly, they can be used in standalone SQL statements. Therefore, anywhere your applications use a SQL statement that includes a ROWID reference, you can modify it with the appropriate function, from DBMS_ROWID, to return the information required by the statement.

Migrating Applications and Data

Following your database migration, you might need to address your applications and your data if they include ROWID references. I describe these issues in the next two sections.

ROWIDs and Migrated Applications

If you have applications or scripts containing SQL statements that reference the ROWID pseudocolumn, you should check them to ensure that they will continue to work with the new character ROWID format. If you are simply displaying the ROWIDs on an output device, you should not need to make any changes. Similarly, if your applications don't need any of the component parts of the ROWIDs, such as the file number, they might continue to work unchanged. However, if your applications or scripts extract the component parts, you might need to make some changes. The following examples show you how to replace the typical SQL statements accessing Oracle7 ROWIDs with the equivalent commands in Oracle8*i* using the DBMS_ROWID package.

To find out on how many different blocks the rows of a table start, such as the CUSTOMERS table in the SALES_DEPT schema, you could use this query in Oracle7:

```
SQL> SELECT DISTINCT SUBSTR(rowid,1,9) ¦¦ SUBSTR(rowid,15,4)
FROM sales_dept.customers;
```

This query extracts the block number and the file number substrings from the ROWID and concatenates them. By applying the DISTINCT operator, one entry for each used block is returned. The data returned from this query could look something like this:

```
0000209E.0003
0000209F.0003
000020A0.0003
. . .
```

You would have to rewrite this query in Oracle8*i* using functions from the DBMS_ROWID package. One of the possible versions, and one that preserves the dot between the block and file numbers, would be

```
SELECT DISTINCT DBMS_ROWID.ROWID_BLOCK_NUMBER(rowid) ¦¦ '.' ¦¦
¦¦ DBMS_ROWID.ROWID_TO_ABSOLUTE_FNO(rowid,'SALES_DEPT','CUSTOMERS')
FROM sales_dept.customers;
```

The data returned by this query would begin like this:

```
8350.3
8351.3
8352.3
. . .
```

Note that the values are decimal, not hexadecimal, and so they are not the same as the values returned by the Oracle7 query. However, if you were simply trying to find the number of different blocks being used, it is unlikely you will care if the numbers are not the same. However, your application might have been relying on the Oracle7 format of the output so that you could use it easily in later statements. To obtain this format, you would have to use the LPAD function to include any required leading zeroes, as shown in the following:

```
SELECT DISTINCT LPAD(DBMS_ROWID.ROWID_BLOCK_NUMBER(rowid),8'0')
¦¦ '.' ¦¦ LPAD(
DBMS_ROWID.ROWID_TO_ABSOLUTE_FNO(rowid,'SALES_DEPT','CUSTOMERS'),4,'0')
FROM sales_dept.customers;
```

The first few lines of output now look like this:

```
00008350.0003
00008351.0003
00008352.0003
. . .
```

Another reason you might use ROWIDs is to find out how many rows are stored on a specific block. Oracle7 and the Oracle8*i* versions of a possible query are shown in the following:

```
REM Oracle7

SELECT COUNT(*)
FROM sales_dept.customers
```

```
WHERE SUBSTR(rowid,1,8) = '0000209E'
AND SUBSTR(rowid,15,4) = '0003';

COUNT(*)
--------
       8

REM Oracle8i

SELECT COUNT(*)
FROM sales_dept.customers
WHERE DBMS_ROWID.ROWID_BLOCK_NUMBER(rowid) = 8350 AND
DBMS_ROWID.ROWID_TO_ABSOLUTE_FNO(rowid,'SALES_DEPT','CUSTOMERS') = 3;

COUNT(*)
       8
```

A final example of an Oracle7 and an Oracle8*i* difference is a query that will return the three parts of an Oracle7 ROWID: the file number, the block number, and the row number. I show you two different versions of the Oracle8*i* query, one of them using the absolute file number, which is the Oracle7 file ID, and the other using the new relative file number.

```
SELECT
    SUBSTR(dbms_rowid.rowid_to_restricted(rowid,1),15,4) AS "File",
    SUBSTR(dbms_rowid.rowid_to_restricted(rowid,1),1,8) AS "Block",
    SUBSTR(dbms_rowid.rowid_to_restricted(rowid,1),10,4) AS "Row"
FROM sales_dept.customers
WHERE rownum = 1;

File Block     Row
---- --------- ----
0003 0000209E 0000


SELECT
    DBMS_ROWID.ROWID_TO_ABSOLUTE_FNO(rowid,'ME','X') AS "File",
    DBMS_ROWID.ROWID_BLOCK_NUMBER(rowid) AS "Block",
    DBMS_ROWID.ROWID_ROW_NUMBER(rowid) AS "Row"
FROM sales_dept.customers
WHERE rownum = 1;

     File     Block       Row
--------- --------- ---------
        3      8350         0
```

If you should need the hexadecimal values for the results from the various DBMS_ROWID calls, you can use the function, DEC_TO_HEX, which I show you how to create in Listing 12.1. The function is constructed in a package to allow you to define the pragma that allows it to be used in external SQL statements.

LISTING 12.1 Package and Function to Convert Decimal to Hexadecimal Values

```
CREATE PACKAGE dectohex AS

/***************************************************************\
*                                                               *
*   DECTOHEX:                                                   *
*   Packaged function to convert numbers between one base decimal *
*   and hexadecimal.                                            *
*                                                               *
*   USAGE:                                                      *
*   dectohex.dec_to_hex(input value)                           *
*   where the input value is a decimal value and the returned  *
*   value is a VARCHAR2 value.                                 *
*                                                               *
*   HISTORY:                                                    *
*   20-Nov-97 DAUSTIN Initial version                          *
*                                                               *
\***************************************************************/

  FUNCTION dec_to_hex (decin IN NUMBER) RETURN VARCHAR2
  PRAGMA RESTRICT_REFERENCES (dec_to_hex,wnds,rnds,wnps,rnps);
END dectohex;
/

CREATE PACKAGE BODY dectohex AS

FUNCTION dec_to_hex (decin IN NUMBER) RETURN VARCHAR2 IS
  v_decin NUMBER;
  v_next_digit NUMBER;
  v_result varchar(2000);
BEGIN
  v_decin := decin;
  WHILE v_decin > 0 LOOP
    v_next_digit := mod(v_decin,16);
    IF v_next_digit > 9 THEN
      IF v_next_digit = 10 THEN v_result := 'A' || v_result;
      ELSIF v_next_digit = 11 THEN v_result := 'B' || v_result;
      ELSIF v_next_digit = 12 THEN v_result := 'C' || v_result;
      ELSIF v_next_digit = 13 THEN v_result := 'D' || v_result;
      ELSIF v_next_digit = 14 THEN v_result := 'E' || v_result;
      ELSIF v_next_digit = 15 THEN v_result := 'F' || v_result;
```

```
      ELSE raise_application_error(-20600,'Untrapped exception');
      END IF;
    ELSE
      v_result := to_char(v_next_digit) || v_result;
    END IF;
    v_decin := floor(v_decin / 16);
  END LOOP;
  RETURN v_result;
END dec_to_hex;

END dectohex;
/
```

ROWIDs and Migrated Data

Oracle will automatically make certain changes during the migration process, no matter which method you use, to handle the differences between the Oracle7 and the Oracle8*i* ROWID structures. This includes modifying the size of any columns defined with the ROWID datatype, including the internal definitions for indexes and snapshot log files, as well as any data tables defined by you or your users.

The data in the indexes isn't changed if you use Migration Utility and the Data Migration Assistant, but each entry will be modified to the new format when its underlying row is updated. The other migration methods will use the new internal format for index entries as they are rebuilt by the Import utility or the alternate load routines.

Similarly, the Import or data store routines, which are part of a migration by Export/Import or by data copying, will build the snapshot logs in the new Oracle8*i* databases with the new format. The Migration Utility and the Data Migration Assistant simply invalidate any snapshot logs that are part of the database. This will cause them to be rebuilt when the next refresh is requested, even if the request is for a fast refresh.

The format of ROWID columns defined in the tables that were built by you or your users will be modified to support the longer format by any of the migration methods. However, if they contained values that were valid ROWIDs in your Oracle7 database, they will no longer function as such under Oracle8*i* because they will not be upgraded. You can convert them, however, using the ROWID_TO_EXTENDED function of the DBMS_ROWID package. The following example shows the current contents of the CUSTOMER_CHANGE_LOG table and of its use of this function in upgrading the column with the ROWID datatype:

```
SQL> DESCRIBE customer_change_log
 Name                             Null?    Type
 -------------------------------- -------- --
 CUSTOMER_ID                      NOT NULL NUMBER(10)
 CUSTOMER_ROWID                            ROWID
```

```
SQL> SELECT customer_id, customer_rowid
  2  FROM customer_change_log;

CUSTOMER_ID CUSTOMER_ROWID
----------- ------------------
        712 000013EA.0000.0003
        414 000013EB.0001.0003
. . .


SQL> UPDATE customer_change_log
  2  SET customer_rowid = DBMS_ROWID.ROWID_TO_EXTENDED
  3  (customer_rowid, 'SALES_DEPT', 'CUSTOMER_CHANGE_LOG', 0);
. . .


SQL> SELECT customer_id, customer_rowid
  2  FROM customer_change_log;

CUSTOMER_ID CUSTOMER_ROWID
----------- ------------------
        712 AAAMxPAADAAAABPqAAA
        414 AAAMxPAADAAAABPrAAB
. . .
```

If you have tables that have stored ROWIDs in columns not defined with the ROWID datatype, you will also have to run the ROWID_TO_EXTENDED function on each of the rows. You might also need to change the format of the columns if you didn't define them to contain all 18 characters of the Oracle7 display format (for example, by omitting the periods). You will need the 18 characters to hold the character display format of the Oracle8*i* ROWIDs, so you will have to modify the column width before updating the contents.

There might be cases when ROWIDs cannot be updated by the ROWID_TO_EXTENDED function. This typically happens when the row referenced by the ROWID no longer exists. Although this didn't matter in your Oracle7 database—except to a program that tried to use the referenced row, of course—the construction of the extended ROWID requires locating the row in order to identify the data object number. If the segment no longer exists, none of the ROWIDs would be valid, but if only a few rows are missing, you could convert all but those ROWIDs.

To identify which rows are invalid, you can use the ROWID_VERIFY function. Should the UPDATE to the CUSTOMER_CHANGE_LOG table in the previous example have failed, you could identify the rows causing the problem with the following query:

```
SELECT customer_id
  FROM customer_change_log
  WHERE DBMS_ROWID.ROWID_VERIFY
    (customer_rowid, NULL, NULL, 0) = 1;
```

Any row in the CUSTOMER_ID table returned by this query has a row with a ROWID that cannot be successfully converted to an extended ROWID format for Oracle8*i*. If the query returns the row for customer 439 and this is still a valid customer, you can simply update this row in the CUSTOMER_CHANGE_LOG table by storing the ROWID again:

```
UPDATE customer_change_log
  SET customer_rowid =
    (SELECT rowid FROM customers
     WHERE customer_id = 439)
  WHERE customer_id = 439;
```

If customer 439 is no longer a valid customer, you will need to delete the row in the CUSTOMER_CHANGE_LOG table.

Client Compatibility Issues

If a client of an Oracle8*i* database, whether an application or another database using database links, sends binary or character data from a ROWID pseudocolumn or a field defined as a ROWID datatype, it will be in the restricted format. Such ROWID information might have to be converted with the ROWID_TO_EXTENDED function if it has to be used to access a row in the Oracle8*i* database. To do this, you must store the ROWID in an appropriate variable in the Oracle8*i* first because the pre-Oracle8 application or database does not contain the DBMS_ROWID package.

If ROWID information has to be passed out of your Oracle8*i* database to an Oracle7 client or database, you must first convert it to restricted format so that it can be processed as a ROWID by the recipient. If you pass it without converting it first, the client or linked database will not be able to interpret it. You should also make sure that if you send data back to a pre-Oracle8 database, you reference the correct file ID number. Oracle7 file ID numbers were all absolute file numbers, and Oracle8*i* file numbers can be absolute or relative.

Even though the migration process will force master and snapshot sites to perform complete refreshes following a migration to update the ROWIDs, Oracle8*i* is not compatible with snapshots in a database with a release earlier than version 7.1.4.

Universal ROWIDs

I discussed some of the issues associated with Universal ROWIDs (UROWIDs) in Chapter 10, "Issues with Compatibility." I will summarize the key points associated with this new ROWID type here for completeness.

- UROWIDs are a combination of an extended ROWID and a primary key value.
- UROWIDs are used for secondary indexes on index-organized tables.

- If you need to store a UROWID, you will need a larger variable than for regular ROWIDs.
- UROWIDs were introduced, along with secondary indexes on index-organized tables, with release 8.1 and cannot be interpreted by any pre-Oracle8*i* database or client.

If you need more detailed information about these topics, we refer you to the following sections in Chapter 10: "General Application Issues" and "Versions of SQL Scripts Provided by Oracle."

You should consider one additional point regarding UROWIDs. The DBMS_ROWID package cannot interpret UROWIDs. It is therefore not possible to send a UROWID value to a pre-Oracle8*i* database or application and have it interpreted by the recipient. Finally, because the UROWIDs are new with Oracle8*i*, you don't have to be concerned about them during migration from any other, earlier, release of Oracle.

Summary

ROWIDs are used internally by Oracle to support indexed access to tables and some types of snapshots and materialized views. For most users, they are a completely transparent feature of the database. They can be seen, however, with the pseudocolumn ROWID and can also be stored in character type or ROWID type variables, as well as in columns of a table.

The ROWID formats, both internal and external, changed between pre-Oracle8 and Oracle8 releases. Some of the conversions necessitated by this change, both value and format related, are handled by the migration processing, but some are not. A few conversion issues are dependent on the migration method you use.

Although Oracle does not recommend storing ROWID values, you might have some tables in your database that contain them in a CHAR, VARCHAR2, or ROWID column. You will need to modify the contents of such columns to reflect the new, extended ROWID format after your migration to Oracle8*i*. Oracle provides the DBMS_ROWID package, containing a variety of functions and a single procedure, to help you handle such conversions as well as to interpret the contents of the new extended ROWID format.

When comparing Oracle7 restricted ROWID values with Oracle8*i* extended ROWID values returned by the DBMS_ROWID package, remember that the Oracle7 values for the various elements represented by the ROWID—file number, block number, and row number—are in base 16 (hexadecimal), whereas the values returned by DBMS_ROWID are in base 10 (decimal). You should also realize that there are two possible file ID numbers in Oracle8—an absolute file number and a relative file number.

Downgrading

IN THIS CHAPTER

In this chapter, I will briefly discuss what you need to do if you want to downgrade your Oracle8*i* database to an earlier release or to an earlier version. I will only discuss downgrades to production releases of Oracle8, namely 8.0.3, 8.0.4, and 8.0.5, or to Oracle7, release 7.3. If you want to downgrade to a Beta release of Oracle, you will need to read the documentation provided by Oracle. I suggest using the Oracle8*i* Migration manual and the release README files as your sources if you need this type of information.

> **NOTE**
>
> Oracle Corporation makes a careful distinction between the terms *version* and *release*. *Version* refers to a product set related with the first number in the database identifier, such as Oracle7 or Oracle8. *Release* refers to the major products belonging to each version and identified with the second number in the identifier. For example, 7.2 and 7.3 are releases of version 7, and 8.0 and 8.1 are releases of version 8. We have tried to follow Oracle's usage of these terms throughout this discussion.

I begin this chapter with a section covering the general tasks you need to complete before you start a downgrade. I then cover the particular steps you need to downgrade to earlier version 8 releases. Finally, I address the topic of downgrading to version 7.

Prepare to Downgrade

Just as I recommended you make a backup before you begin a migration or an upgrade, I make the same recommendation regarding a downgrade. The only exception to this is if you are content to revert to the version of your database you were using before you began your migration or upgrade. In this case, you can simply restore the backup you made of the unmodified database.

> **NOTE**
>
> Even if you are planning to use a backup from your previous version of Oracle to complete the downgrade, you might still want to make a backup of your Oracle8*i* version before you begin. Unless it is completely unusable, you might want to return to it if your downgrade doesn't prove as useful as you expected.

To make your backup, you should perform a normal (or immediate) shutdown of your database and include all the datafiles, the online redo log files, and at least one copy of your control file. You might also want to save a copy of your current parameter file as part of this backup.

The second key task you need to address before you downgrade is to ensure that you have the required release of Oracle installed, or available to install. Your Oracle8*i* executables will not run if your downgrade is successful.

When you have completed these steps, you need to continue with either the "Downgrade to Oracle8, Release 8.0" or the "Downgrade to Oracle7" section.

Downgrade to Oracle8, Release 8.0

This section contains three major components:

- Remove Incompatibilities
- Reset Database Compatibility
- Downgrade the Database

You should follow the instructions in these components in the order given for a successful downgrade from Oracle8*i* to release 8.0.3, 8.0.4, or 8.0.5.

Remove Incompatibilities

Before you can downgrade to an earlier release of Oracle8, you must first remove any objects or features that are from a later release than the one to which you are downgrading. You can quickly determine if you have any incompatible features for a release level by issuing the following query while connected to the database with the DBA role active:

```
SELECT release, description
  FROM v$compatibility
  WHERE release <> '0.0.0.0.0';
```

The RELEASE column of the resultset will identify the lowest release number at which you can run your database while retaining the feature described in the related DESCRIPTION column. For example, in the sample output shown in Listing 13.1, you would not be able to downgrade to release 8.0.3 or 8.0.4 successfully before addressing the two redo issues shown with a RELEASE value of 8.0.5.0.0.

LISTING 13.1 Sample Output from the V$COMPATIBILITY Table

```
RELEASE        DESCRIPTION
------------   ----------------
8.0.0.0.0      Control file
8.0.0.0.0      Compatibility segment
8.0.5.0.0      Redo contents
8.0.0.0.0      Undo contents
8.0.0.0.0      bootstrap$
```

continues

LISTING 13.1   Continued

```
8.0.0.0.0    Log structure
8.0.0.0.0    Data file structure
8.0.0.0.0    Recovery redo
8.0.0.0.0    Backup set
8.0.5.0.0    redo for transaction auditing
```

The output in Listing 13.1 does indicate that the database has no release 8.1 features activated and so it could be successfully downgraded to release 8.0.5 without any compatibility problems.

NOTE

You might not need to concern yourself with incompatibility issues if your database is running with a suitable compatibility setting. Execute the command

```
SHOW PARAMETER COMPATIBLE
```

or

```
SELECT value FROM v$parameter WHERE name = 'COMPATIBLE';
```

to determine the current value.

If your database's COMPATIBLE parameter is currently set to the value of the release to which you want to downgrade, or to an earlier release number than that, you don't need to perform any checks for incompatibilities. You can begin your downgrade immediately as described in the section "Downgrade the Database."

If the results of your query don't include any rows with a RELEASE value higher than the targeted release for your downgrade, you can skip the steps described in the remainder of this section. Continue your downgrade with the information in the next section, "Reset Database Compatibility."

If your query indicated one or more areas where your current database is using features from a release higher than the one to which you want to downgrade, you will need to remove the problem items before proceeding. First you should run the script UTLDST.SQL to downgrade image formats in readiness for the release 8.0 downgrade. After you have done this, the easiest way for you to identify any remaining incompatibilities is to use a script provided in Oracle8*i*, UTLINCMPT.SQL. This script executes a series of queries against your Data Dictionary and the dynamic performance tables. It is designed so that an empty resultset indicates that no incompatibilities exist with Oracle8, release 8.0, whereas any queries that return one or more rows allow you to identify a feature which needs to be addressed before your downgrade.

I recommend that you change your current directory at the operating system prompt to the ADMIN subdirectory in your Oracle8*i* home directory structure before continuing. Confirm that you can find the files named UTLDST.SQL and UTLINCMPT.SQL in your current directory and then connect to Server Manager or SQL*Plus as INTERNAL. When connected, issue the following commands:

```
@utldst.sql
SPOOL incmpt.log
@utlincmpt.sql
SPOOL OFF
```

> **NOTE**
>
> If you don't start your Server Manager or SQL*Plus session from the ADMIN subdirectory as suggested, you will have to include the full pathname to this directory as part of any script name you are instructed to run throughout the remainder of this section.

If you use the HOST command to shell out of your session to the operating system, you can examine the contents of your INCMPT.LOG file. If you observe any queries that have returned one or more rows rather than the message no rows selected, you will need to address an incompatibility issue. Find the appropriate section that follows using the topic in the first REM statement, which precedes the query in the output listed in INCMPT.LOG. I repeat the query from UTLINCMPT.SQL at the beginning of each of these sections, so you can double-check that you have associated the query with the correct incompatibility feature. Note that you do not need to re-run the query in order to proceed with the steps to solve the incompatibility issue.

Transported Tablespaces

Transported tablespaces are identified by the following query from UTLINCMPT.SQL:

```
select tablespace_name, plugged_in
    from dba_tablespaces
    where plugged_in = 'YES';
```

If you don't need the contents of any of the transported tablespaces, you can simply drop them, one at a time, with the command

```
DROP TABLESPACE tablespace_name
    INCLUDING CONTENTS CASCADE CONSTRAINTS;
```

If you do need the contents of a specific tablespace, you can transport it to another Oracle8*i* database or export the contents and import them back into a regular tablespace. After you have done this, you should drop the transported tablespace using the command shown previously.

After you have dropped all your transported tablespaces, you need to remove special temporary tables from the SYSTEM tablespace by issuing the following command:

```
EXECUTE dbms_tts.downgrade
```

Locally Managed Tablespaces

Locally managed tablespaces are identified by the following query from UTLINCMPT.SQL:

```
select tablespace_name, extent_management
    from dba_tablespaces
    where extent_management = 'LOCAL';
```

If you don't need the contents of any of the locally managed tablespaces, you can simply drop them, one at a time, with the command

```
DROP TABLESPACE tablespace_name
    INCLUDING CONTENTS CASCADE CONSTRAINTS;
```

If you do need the contents of a specific tablespace, you need to convert it to a dictionary-managed tablespace by executing the following command:

```
EXECUTE dbms_admin.tablespace_migrate_from_local
    ('tablespace_name')
```

Temporary Tables

Temporary tables are identified by the following query from UTLINCMPT.SQL:

```
select owner, table_name from dba_tables
    where temporary = 'Y' and
        table_name not like 'RUPD$%' and
        table_name not like 'ATEMPTAB$';
```

You will have to drop all these tables using the

```
DROP TABLE owner.table_name;
```

command for each one.

Key Compression on Indexes

Key compressed indexes and index-organized tables are identified by the following query from UTLINCMPT.SQL:

```
select index_name, index_type, table_owner, table_name
    from dba_indexes where compression = 'ENABLED';
```

To remove key compression from an index, use the command

```
ALTER INDEX index_name REBUILD NOCOMPRESS;
```

To remove key compression from an index-organized table, use the command

```
ALTER TABLE table_owner.table_name MOVE NOCOMPRESS;
```

If an incompatible index-organized table is a nested table, the preceding command will fail. If you do not need the data in the nested column, you can drop the column with the command

```
ALTER TABLE owner.table_name DROP COLUMN column_name;
```

If you need the data in the nested column, you will have to re-create the table using the CREATE TABLE...AS SELECT syntax and specify the nested column table with heap, not index, organization. After creating the new table, drop the original one and either rename the new one to the original name or create a synonym for it, using the original name. Also make sure that you duplicate any views, constraints, privileges, and triggers as well as validate any references to the original table from stored procedures.

LOBs in Index-Organized Tables

Index-organized tables containing LOBs are identified by the following query from UTLINCMPT.SQL:

```
select column_name, t.owner, t.table_name
    from dba_lobs l, dba_tables t
    where l.table_name = t.table_name
        and l.owner = t.owner
        and t.iot_type = 'IOT';
```

If you do not need the contents of one of these tables, you can simply drop it with the command

```
DROP TABLE owner.table_name;
```

If you need to preserve the contents of one of these tables, you will have to re-create it using the CREATE TABLE...AS SELECT syntax. After creating the new table, drop the original one and either rename the new one to the original name or create a synonym for it, using the original name. Also make sure that you duplicate any views, constraints, privileges, and triggers as well as validate any references to the original table from stored procedures.

Varrays in Index-Organized Tables

Index-organized tables containing varrays are identified by the following query from UTLINCMPT.SQL:

```
select v.parent_table_column, t.owner, t.table_name
    from dba_varrays v, dba_tables t
    where v.parent_table_name = t.table_name
        and v.owner = t.owner
        and t.iot_type = 'IOT';
```

If you do not need the contents of one of these tables, you can simply drop it with the command

```
DROP TABLE owner.table_name;
```

If you need to preserve the contents of one of these tables, you will have to re-create it using the CREATE TABLE...AS SELECT syntax. After creating the new table, drop the original one and either rename the new one to the original name or create a synonym for it, using the original name. Also make sure that you duplicate any views, constraints, privileges, and triggers as well as validate any to the original table from stored procedures.

Secondary Indexes on Index-Organized Tables

Secondary indexes on index-organized tables are identified by the following query from UTLINCMPT.SQL:

```
select index_name, i.owner, t.table_name
   from dba_indexes i, dba_tables t
   where i.index_type = 'NORMAL'
       and i.table_name = t.table_name
       and t.owner = i.table_owner
       and t.iot_type = 'IOT';
```

You will have to drop these indexes using the command

```
DROP INDEX index_name;
```

Nested Table Features

Nested tables with user-defined storage specifications or locators are identified by the following query from UTLINCMPT.SQL:

```
select owner, parent_table_name
   from dba_nested_tables
   where storage_spec like '%USER_SPECIFIED%'
   or return_type like '%LOCATOR%';
```

If you do not need the contents of one of the parent tables containing a nested table with an incompatible storage characteristic, you can simply drop it with the command

```
DROP TABLE owner.parent_table_name;
```

If you need to preserve the contents of one of the parent tables, you will need to issue the ALTER TABLE command, using the NESTED TABLE...STORE AS syntax without specifying any object or physical properties and with no RETURN AS clause.

Unused Columns

Tables containing unused columns are identified by the following query from UTLINCMPT.SQL:

```
select * from dba_unused_col_tabs;
```

You must drop the unused columns from each table listed in the resultset by issuing the command

```
ALTER TABLE owner.table_name DROP UNUSED COLUMNS;
```

Partially Dropped Columns

Tables containing unused columns are identified by the following query from
UTLINCMPT.SQL:

```
select * from dba_partial_drop_tabs;
```

You must remove the partially dropped columns from each table listed in the resultset by issuing
the command

```
ALTER TABLE owner.table_name DROP COLUMNS CONTINUE;
```

Single Table-Only Hash Clusters

Clusters defined with the SINGLE TABLE option are identified by the following query from
UTLINCMPT.SQL:

```
select cluster_name, single_table from dba_clusters
    where single_table like '%Y%';
```

You can identify the name of the tables associated with each of these clusters by issuing the
query

```
SELECT t.owner, t.table_name, c.owner
    FROM dba_tables t, dba_clusters c
    WHERE c.cluster_name = cluster_name
        AND t.cluster_name = c.cluster_name;
```

If you do not need the contents of one of these tables, you can simply drop it with the command

```
DROP TABLE owner.table_name;
```

You can then drop the incompatible cluster with the command

```
DROP CLUSTER owner.cluster_name;
```

If you need to preserve the contents of one of these tables, you will have to re-create it using
the CREATE TABLE…AS SELECT syntax before issuing these commands. If you don't need
the table to be stored in a cluster, simple rename it or create a synonym for it, using the original name. If you want it to be stored in a cluster again, you should create a new cluster without
including the SINGLE TABLE clause. You can then issue another CREATE TABLE…AS
SELECT statement that uses the original table name and the new cluster name in the CREATE
clause and names the re-created table in the SELECT clause.

Whether you have clustered the new table or not, make sure that you duplicate any views, constraints, privileges, and triggers as well as validate any references to the original table from
stored procedures.

8.1 Varray Features

Tables containing varrays with user-defined storage specifications are identified by the following query from UTLINCMPT.SQL:

```
select owner, parent_table_name
   from dba_varrays
   where storage_spec like '%USER_SPECIFIED%';
```

If you do not need the contents of one of the parent tables containing a nested table with an incompatible storage characteristic, you can simply drop it with the command

```
DROP TABLE owner.parent_table_name;
```

If you need to preserve the contents of one of these tables, you will have to re-create it using the CREATE TABLE...AS SELECT syntax. After creating the new table, drop the original one and either rename the new one to the original name or create a synonym for it, using the original name. Also make sure that you duplicate any views, constraints, privileges, and triggers as well as validate any references to the original table from stored procedures.

Refresh on Commit Mode

Although the UTLINCMPT.SQL script might identify materialized views (snapshots) with an ON COMMIT refresh mode—an unsupported refresh mode in Oracle8, release 8.0—you do not need to make any changes to materialized views identified by this query:

```
select owner, name, refresh_mode
   from dba_snapshots
   where refresh_mode = 'COMMIT';
```

After downgrading, Oracle will convert these materialized views automatically to an ON DEMAND refresh mode.

Never Refresh Mode Materialized Views

Materialized views (snapshots) defined with the NEVER REFRESH option are identified by the following query from UTLINCMPT.SQL:

```
select owner, name, type
   from dba_snapshots
   where type = 'NEVER';
```

After downgrading, Oracle will drop these materialized views automatically. If you want to continue to use the named materialized views, you will need to create them with a different refresh mode either before or after you perform the database downgrade.

Bitmapped Indexes

Bitmapped indexes might be protected from undesired invalidations in release 8.1, and these will be identified by the following query from UTLINCMPT.SQL:

```
select o.name index_name, u.name index_owner
   from sys.user$ u, sys.obj$ o, sys.ind$ i, sys.tab$
   where t.obj# = o.obj#
      and i.bo# = t.obj# and t.spare1 > 32767
      and i.type# = 2 and o.owner# = u.user#;
```

These indexes will be invalidated automatically during the downgrade. Although you can do nothing to change this behavior, you might want to note the names of these indexes so that you can revalidate them following the downgrade.

Function-Based Indexes

Function-based indexes are identified by the following query from UTLINCMPT.SQL:

```
select distinct index_owner, index_name
   from dba_ind_columns
   where column_name is null;
```

You will need to drop every index listed by this query, one by one, using the command

```
DROP INDEX index_owner.index_name;
```

Domain Indexes

Domain indexes are identified by the following query from UTLINCMPT.SQL:

```
select owner, index_name, index_type
   from dba_indexes
   where index_type = 'DOMAIN';
```

You will need to drop every index listed by this query, one by one, using the command

```
DROP INDEX owner.index_name;
```

Indextypes

Indextypes are identified by the following query from UTLINCMPT.SQL:

```
select owner, indextype_name from dba_indextypes;
```

You will need to drop every indextype listed by this query, one by one, using the command

```
DROP INDEXTYPE owner.indextype_name;
```

Operators

Operators are identified by the following query from UTLINCMPT.SQL:

```
select owner, operator_name from dba_operators;
```

You will need to drop every operator listed by this query, one by one, using the command

```
DROP OPERATOR owner.operator_name;
```

Dimensions

Dimensions are identified by the following query from UTLINCMPT.SQL:

```
select * from dba_dimensions;
```

You will need to drop every operator listed by this query, one by one, using the command

```
DROP DIMENSION owner.dimension_name;
```

Partitioned IOT

Partitioned index-organized tables are identified by the following query from UTLINCMPT.SQL:

```
select table_name, tablespace_name,
  iot_type, partitioned
    from dba_tables
    where partitioned = 'YES' and iot_type = 'IOT';
```

You should identify the owner of any tables listed by this query by executing it in your session with the OWNER column included in the SELECT clause. If you do not need the contents of one of these tables, you can simply drop it with the command

```
DROP TABLE owner.table_name;
```

If you need to preserve the contents of one of these tables, you will have to re-create it using the CREATE TABLE…AS SELECT syntax. You can create it using either an ORGANIZATION INDEX or a PARTITION BY RANGE clause, but not both. You can also create it as a regular, nonpartitioned table. After creating the new table, drop the original one and either rename the new one to the original name or create a synonym for it, using the original name. Also make sure that you duplicate any views, constraints, privileges, and triggers as well as validate any references to the original table from stored procedures.

Partitioned Object Tables

Partitioned object tables are identified by the following query from UTLINCMPT.SQL:

```
select unique t.table_name, t.owner
    from dba_part_tables t, dba_tab_columns c
    where t.table_name = c.table_name
```

```
and c.data_type in
(select type_name
    from dba_types
    where predefined = 'NO');
```

If you do not need the contents of one of these tables, you can simply drop it with the command

```
DROP TABLE owner.table_name;
```

If you need to preserve the contents of one of these tables, you will have to re-create it using the CREATE TABLE...AS SELECT syntax without including the PARTITION BY RANGE clause. After creating the new table, drop the original one and either rename the new one to the original name or create a synonym for it, using the original name. Also make sure that you duplicate any views, constraints, privileges, and triggers as well as validate any references to the original table from stored procedures

Partitioned Tables That Use Composite Methods

Tables with hash or composite partitions are identified by the following query from UTLINCMPT.SQL:

```
select owner, table_name from dba_part_tables
    where partitioning_type != 'RANGE'
        or subpartitioning_type !='NONE';
```

If you do not need the contents of one of these tables, you can simply drop it with the command

```
DROP TABLE owner.table_name;
```

If you need to preserve the contents of one of these tables, you will have to re-create it using the CREATE TABLE...AS SELECT syntax. You can create it without any partitions or with range partitions. You can also move its contents into a series of nonpartitioned tables using the EXCHANGE option of the ALTER TABLE command. After saving the contents using one of these methods, drop the original table. You might need to rename the new table, create a synonym for the new table, or create a view with the UNION operator if you created a series of tables in order for your applications to find the data with the original table name. You might also need to duplicate any views, constraints, privileges, and triggers as well as validate any references to the original table from stored procedures.

Universal ROWID

Tables with columns of the UROWID datatype are identified by the following query from UTLINCMPT.SQL:

```
select owner, table_name, column_name
    from dba_tab_columns
```

```
where data_type = 'UROWID'
order by owner, table_name;
```

If you do not need the contents of one of these tables, you can simply drop it with the command

```
DROP TABLE owner.table_name;
```

If you need to preserve the contents of one of these tables, except for the UROWID data, you should drop its UROWID column or columns with the command

```
ALTER TABLE owner.table_name DROP COLUMN column_name;
```

or the command

```
ALTER TABLE owner.table_name DROP (column_name_list);
```

where `column_name_list` is a comma-separated list of nonduplicated column names.

> **NOTE**
>
> If you created either of the tables EXCEPTIONS or CHAINED_ROWS using the Oracle8*i* versions of the Oracle-supplied scripts—UTLEXCPT1.SQL and UTLCHAIN1.SQL—they will contain columns of the UROWID datatype. You should drop them before downgrading to release 8.0 and re-create them with the regular versions of the scripts— UTLEXCPT.SQL and UTLCHAIN.SQL.

Stored Procedures with UROWID Arguments

Procedures defined with arguments of the UROWID datatype are identified by the following query from UTLINCMPT.SQL:

```
select owner, object_name, package_name, argument_name
    from all_arguments where data_type = 'UROWID'
        and package_name not in ('STANDARD')
    order by owner, object_name, package_name;
```

If you are not certain what type of object is referenced by any row returned by this query, you can execute the command

```
SELECT owner, object_name, object_type
    FROM dba_objects
    WHERE owner = owner AND object_name = object_name;
```

If you decide you don't need one of the objects listed, you can drop it with the appropriate DROP PACKAGE, DROP PROCEDURE, or DROP FUNCTION command. If you still need

one of the objects listed, you will have to re-create it and either omit the arguments defined as UROWID datatypes or replace them with ROWID or VARCHAR2 arguments.

CLOBS and NCLOBS in Table with Varying-Width Characterset

All tables containing LOB columns are identified by the following query from UTLINCMPT.SQL:

```
select table_name, column_name from dba_lobs
    where dba_lobs.owner != 'SYSTEM'
        and table_name not in
            ('KOTAD$', 'KOTMD$', 'KOTTB$', 'KOTTD$');
```

If your database is not using a varying-width characterset, you can ignore this section no matter how many rows this query returned. If your database has a varying-width characterset, you need to determine whether your tables contain any CLOB or NCLOB columns because these will have to be removed before you perform your downgrade. You can identify any such columns by issuing the DESCRIBE command for each of the tables listed in the query.

If you find any columns defined as CLOB or NCLOB, you need to drop the columns before you downgrade. Be careful not to drop any tables belonging to the SYS schema that you can identify from the $ character included in their names, such as those named in the query previously.

Finally, if you use the Advanced Replication feature—and your database uses a varying-width characterset—you need to execute the following commands to remove a potential problem:

```
DECLARE
    rc NUMBER;
BEGIN
    rc := dbms_defer_sys.push();
END;
/
DROP VIEW deflob;
```

LOB Columns in Partitioned Tables

Partitioned tables containing LOB columns are identified by the following query from UTLINCMPT.SQL:

```
select table_name, lob_name from dba_part_lobs;
```

If you do not need the contents of one of these tables, you can simply drop it with the command

```
DROP TABLE table_name;
```

13

DOWNGRADING

Similarly, if you don't need the LOB data in a specific table, you can preserve the table and remove the LOB column with the command

```
ALTER TABLE table_name DROP COLUMN column_name;
```

If you do need to preserve all the data from a table listed by the query, you will have to move it to individual tables before you perform your downgrade. To do this, you need to execute a CREATE TABLE command to create a nonpartitioned table for every partition defined in the table, including the LOB column. Then execute an ALTER TABLE...EXCHANGE PARTITION command for every partition in the original table, naming a different table from the set you just created with each command. You can then drop the original partitioned table. Note that this will allow you to downgrade your database, but you will no longer have any of the views, constraints, privileges, and triggers defined on the original table, and any references to the table will be invalid.

User-Defined Datatypes to 8.1 Format

User-defined datatypes in the 8.1 format are identified by the following query from UTLINCMPT.SQL:

```
select u.name as USER_NAME, o.name as TABLE_NAME,
  c.name as COLUMN_NAME
from sys.user$ u, sys.obj$ o, sys.tab$ t,
  sys.col$ c, sys.coltype$ ct
where bitand(ct.flags, 128) != 128
and o.obj# = c.obj# and o.obj# = ct.obj#
and t.obj# = o.obj# and c.intcol# = ct.intcol
and bitand(t.property, 8192) = 0
and /* not a nested table */ u.user# = o.owner#
and o.type# = 2
and /* must be a base table */
  bitand(c.property, 32) = 0
and /* not a hidden column */ (c.type# = 123
  or /* varray column */
    /* non-virtual ADT column */
  (c.type# = 121 and bitand(c.property, 8) = 0)
  or /* nested table column with adt columns in the storage table */
 (c.type# = 122 and exists
   (select * from sys.ntab$ n1, sys.col$ c1,
     sys.coltype$ ct1
   where n1.obj# = c.obj# and n1.intcol# = c.intcol#
   and n1.ntab# = ct1.obj#
   and bitand(ct1.flags, 128) = 0
   and ct1.obj# = c1.obj# and ct1.intcol# = c1.intcol#
   and bitand(c1.property, 8) = 0)));
```

To successfully downgrade your database and preserve your user-defined datatypes, you must export the objects containing them using the release 8.1 Export utility and then use the release 8.1 Import utility to re-import them after you have completed your downgrade to release 8.0.

User-Defined Object Identifiers

Tables with user-defined object identifiers are identified by the following query from UTLINCMPT.SQL:

```
select table_name from dba_object_tables
    where object_id_type = 'USER-DEFINED';
```

You must drop every table identified by this query with the command

```
DROP TABLE table_name;
```

REF Columns Based on User-Defined Objects

Tables with REF columns that are based on user-defined object identifiers are identified by the following query from UTLINCMPT.SQL:

```
select table_name, column_name from dba_refs
    where object_id_type = 'USER-DEFINED';
```

You must drop every table identified by this query with the command

```
DROP TABLE table_name;
```

Nonpersistent Queues and Queue Tables

Advanced Queuing nonpersistent queues and the tables that contain them are identified by the following query from UTLINCMPT.SQL:

```
select owner, queue_table from dba_queue_tables
    where queue_table = 'AQ$_MEM_MC'
        or queue_table = 'AQ$_MEM_SC';
```

You need to drop every table identified by this query with the command

```
EXECUTE dbms_aqadm.drop_queue_table (
    ➥queue_table => 'owner.queue_table', force => TRUE);
```

8.1 Compatible Queue Tables

Queue tables that are incompatible with release 8.0 are identified by the following query from UTLINCMPT.SQL:

```
select queue_table, compatible from dba_queue_tables
    where compatible like '8.1%';
```

You will need to downgrade all the tables retrieved by this query using a two-step process. First, you need to disable the propagation schedules for all the queues in each table. To do this, you run the following command for each such queue:

```
EXECUTE dbms_adadm.disable_propagation_schedule (
    ➥queue_name => 'queue_name')
```

Second, you run the following command for each queue table:

```
EXECUTE dbms_aqadm.migrate_queue_table (
    ➥queue_table => 'queue_table',
    ➥compatible => '8.0');
```

Object-Level and System-Level Privileges

Advanced Queuing object-level and system-level privileges are identified by the following queries from UTLINCMPT.SQL:

```
select owner, table_name, privilege
    from dba_tab_privs where privilege like '%QUEUE';
```

and

```
select * from dba_sys_privs where privilege in
    ('MANAGE ANY QUEUE', 'ENQUEUE ANY QUEUE',
        'DEQUEUE ANY QUEUE');
```

If any rows are returned by the first query, your DBMS_AQADM package should include the REVOKE_ACCESS_PRIVILEGES that you should execute for each privilege listed. If any rows are returned by the second query, your DBMS_AQADM package should include the REVOKE_SYSTEM_PRIVILEGE procedure that you should execute for each privilege listed using a command like the following:

```
EXECUTE dbms_aqadm.revoke_system_privilege (
    ➥privilege => privilege_name,
    ➥grantee => grantee)
```

Disable Validate

Constraints in the DISABLE VALIDATE state are identified by the following queries from UTLINCMPT.SQL:

```
select constraint_name, status, validated
    from dba_constraints
    where status = 'DISABLED'
    and validated = 'VALIDATED';
```

You must either invalidate or drop any constraint returned by this query. To do this, you should first re-execute the preceding query but include the TABLE_NAME and OWNER columns in the SELECT clause. You can then use the following command to drop each constraint in turn:

```
ALTER TABLE owner.table_name
    ➥DROP CONSTRAINT constraint_name;
```

Alternatively, you can invalidate each constraint with the command

```
ALTER TABLE owner.table_name
    ➥DISABLE CONSTRAINT constraint_name;
```

Triggers on Nested Table View Columns

Triggers on nested table view columns are identified by the following query from UTLINCMPT.SQL:

```
select trigger_name, table_name, column_name
    from dba_triggers
    where column_name is not null;
```

You need to drop every trigger identified by this query with the command

```
DROP TRIGGER trigger_name;
```

Triggers That Will Be Dropped Automatically

Event triggers are identified by the following query from UTLINCMPT.SQL:

```
select trigger_name, base_object_type, action_type
    from dba_triggers
    where base_object_type like '%DATABASE%'
    or base_object_type like '%SCHEMA%'
    or action_type like   '%CALL%';
```

You must drop any trigger returned by this query with a BASE_OBJECT_TYPE value of 'SCHEMA' or 'DATABASE' with the command

```
DROP TRIGGER trigger_name;
```

You can either drop the triggers with a value of 'CALL' in the BASE_OBJECT_TYPE column or make them compatible with release 8.0 by enclosing the CALL statement in a BEGIN...END PL/SQL block.

Extensible Optimizer

Extensible optimizer associations are identified by the following query from UTLINCMPT.SQL:

```
select object_owner, object_name, column_name,
  object_type
    from dba_associations;
```

You will need to remove the statistics associated with each object returned by the preceding query using the appropriate version of the following commands:

```
DISASSOCIATE STATISTICS FROM object_type
    object_owner.object_name;
```

```
DISASSOCIATE STATISTICS FROM object_type
    object_owner.object_name.column_name;
```

Optimizer Plan Stability

Stored outlines are identified by the following query from UTLINCMPT.SQL:

```
select owner, name from dba_outlines;
```

You need to drop every outline identified by this query with the command

```
DROP OUTLINE name;
```

Application Contexts

Application contexts are identified by the following query from UTLINCMPT.SQL:

```
select * from dba_context;
```

You need to drop every application context identified by this query with the command

```
DROP CONTEXT namespace;
```

User-Defined Security Policies

User-defined security policies, used for fine-grained access control, are identified by the following query from UTLINCMPT.SQL:

```
select object_owner, object_name, policy_name
    from dba_policies;
```

You need to drop every policy identified by this query with the command

```
EXECUTE dbms_rls.drop_policy (
    object_schema => object_owner,
    object_name => object_name,
    policy_name => policy_name)
```

Proxy Users

Proxy users with CONNECT THROUGH privileges are identified by the following query from UTLINCMPT.SQL:

```
select * from proxy_users;
```

You need to revoke the CONNECT THROUGH privileges identified by this query with the command

```
ALTER USER client REVOKE CONNECT THROUGH proxy;
```

Object Groups at the Top Flavor

Advanced replication object groups not at the top flavor are identified by the following query from UTLINCMPT.SQL:

```
select gname, fname from dba_repgroup
    where fname is not null;
```

Any object groups listed must be converted to the top flavor before you downgrade your database.

Temporary Updatable Snapshot Logs

Temporary updatable snapshot logs are identified by the following query from UTLINCMPT.SQL:

```
select owner, table_name from dba_tables
    where temporary='Y' and
    table_name like 'RUPD$%';
```

If any rows are returned by this query, your database contains temporary updatable snapshot logs that you'll need to remove before downgrading. The Oracle8*i* Migration manual contains a PL/SQL block to accomplish this, which is reproduced in Listing 13.2.

13

LISTING 13.2 PL/SQL Block to Remove Temporary Updatable Snapshot Logs

```
DECLARE
  sql_cur BINARY_INTEGER;
  dummy BINARY_INTEGER;
  new_flag BINARY_INTEGER;
  CURSOR mv_logs IS
    SELECT '"'||mowner||'"."'||temp_log||'"' temp_log,
      flag, mowner, master
    FROM mlog$ m
    WHERE temp_log IS NOT NULL
    FOR UPDATE;
BEGIN
  sql_cur := dbms_sql.open_cursor;
  FOR alog IN mv_logs LOOP
    new_flag := alog.flag;
    IF dbms_ijob.bit(new_flag, 64) THEN
      new_flag := new_flag - 64;
    END IF;
    BEGIN
      dbms_sql.parse(sql_cur, 'DROP TABLE ' ||
        alog.temp_log, dbms_sql.v7);
      dummy := dbms_sql.execute(sql_cur);
      UPDATE mlog$ m
```

continues

LISTING 13.2   Continued

```
        SET flag = new_flag, temp_log = NULL
        WHERE m.mowner = alog.mowner
        AND m.master = alog.master;
    EXCEPTION WHEN others THEN
      NULL;  — - Ignore the error
    END;
  END LOOP;
  dbms_sql.close_cursor(sql_cur);
  COMMIT;
EXCEPTION WHEN others THEN
  IF dbms_sql.is_open(sql_cur) THEN
    dbms_sql.close_cursor(sql_cur);
  END IF;
  RAISE;
END;
/
```

DBMS_REPAIR

Objects that the DBMS_REPAIR package have marked as skip corrupt enabled are identified by the following query from UTLINCMPT.SQL:

```
SELECT owner, table_name from dba_tables
    where skip_corrupt = 'ENABLED';
```

You need to disable the skip_corrupt attribute for each table listed in the output of this query by issuing the command

```
EXECUTE dbms_repair.skip_corrupt_blocks (
    schema_name => 'owner',
    object_name => 'table_name',
    flags => DBMS_REPAIR.NOSKIP_FLAG);
```

System-Generated REF Columns That Have a Referential Constraint Defined on Them

The final query in UTLINCMPT.SQL will identify the remaining objects that might not be valid to downgrade to release 8.0:

```
select u.name as USER_NAME, o.name as TABLE_NAME,
  decode(bitand(c.property, 1), 1, ac.name, c.name)
  as COLUMN_NAME
    from refcon$ r, coltype$ ct, obj$ o, user$ u,
      col$ c, attrcol$ ac
    where bitand(r.reftyp, 4) != 4
                        /* not a user-defined ref */
```

```
      and ct.obj# = r.obj#
      and ct.intcoL# = r.intcoL#
      and ct.intcols = 1
      and c.obj# = r.obj#
      and c.intcol# = r.intcol#
      and o.obj# = r.obj#
      and o.owner# = u.user#
      and c.obj# = ac.obj#(+)
      and c.intcol# = ac.intcol#(+);
```

If you have problems with any tables listed by this query, you can export them with the release 8.1 Export utility, drop them, and then, following the downgrade, try to re-import them with the 8.1 Import utility. In case this does not work, you should save the contents of the tables involved using CREATE TABLE…AS SELECT commands.

Reset Database Compatibility

After you have removed any of the features from your database that are incompatible with the release to which you are downgrading, you should alter its compatibility level to match the new release level. Implement the following steps to reset your database compatibility level:

1. Remove any parameters from your initialization file that were introduced in a release later than the one to which you are downgrading. You can find a list of parameters associated with each database release in the Oracle Migration manuals.

2. Start a SQL*Plus session and connect to the database with a userid that has SYSDBA privileges to start up your database. If it is already running, you should shut it down and then restart it after you have completed the modifications in step 1.

3. Issue the commands

   ```
   ALTER DATABASE RESET COMPATIBILITY;
   ```

   and

   ```
   SHUTDOWN IMMEDIATE
   ```

4. Modify the initialization file parameter, COMPATIBLE, to match the release to which you are downgrading.

5. Restart the database using the modified parameter file. If it fails to open, it is because you have not removed all the incompatible features. You should reset the COMPATIBLE parameter to its previous setting and open the database again. You can then locate and remove the incompatibilities using the techniques discussed in the previous section, "Remove Incompatibilities."

6. Repeat steps 2–5 until you successfully start up the database with the COMPATIBLE parameter value set at the release value to which you downgraded. You should not set this parameter to a higher value release value after completing this step.

13

DOWNGRADING

After you have finished step 6, you are ready to perform your downgrade to release 8.0. The following section explains how to complete this process.

Downgrade the Database

I am now ready to help you downgrade your database to release 8.0. If you have not removed all the release 8.1 components of your database that are not compatible with the release to which you are downgrading, one or more of these steps might fail. If this occurs, you will have to remove these components and start this process again. Should the database integrity have been compromised at such a time, you will need to restore the backup I recommended you create in the "Prepare to Downgrade" section earlier in this chapter. When you are ready for your downgrade, complete the activities I describe in the following steps. Note that Step 6—Downgrading Your Options contains instructions for you to use only if the specific options and conditions are in use in your database.

Step 1—Save Files

Before you start the downgrade process, you should shut down your database using the IMMEDIATE or NORMAL option. If your database is already shut down and you don't know what option was used, you should restart it so that you can shut it down with one of the correct options. You also need to move certain files out of the Oracle8*i* home directory's ADMIN subdirectory. These files are

- catlog803.sql
- utlip.sql
- utlrp.sql

and you should move them to a location where you can find them later if needed. I suggest that you create a working subdirectory in your own home directory rather than relying on a system temporary directory that could be emptied before you are finished. This subdirectory will be useful for other files you need to relocate in later steps.

Step 2—Run Downgrade Script

The downgrade commands used in step 2 should be completed in SQL*Plus and not in Server Manager. I suggest that you switch to the ADMIN subdirectory in the Oracle8*i* home directory and start up SQL*Plus using the NOLOG option with the command

```
sqlplus /nolog
```

If you have not switched to the suggested subdirectory, you will need to include full pathnames to any script files required in the following steps. Begin the downgrade by issuing the following commands in your SQL*Plus session:

```
CONNECT internal
STARTUP
```

```
SPOOL downgrade1.log
@downgrade_script.sql
SPOOL OFF
SHUTDOWN IMMEDIATE
EXIT
```

When executing the preceding commands, you might have to include the PFILE option with the STARTUP command, and you will need to select the correct downgrade_script.sql script from Table 13.1.

TABLE **13.1**   Scripts for Downgrading from Oracle8*i*

Release to Which You Are Downgrading	*Script to Be Run in Step 2 (downgrade.sql)*
8.0.5	d0800050.sql
8.0.4	d0800040.sql
8.0.3	d0800030.sql

If you want to see the commands being executed by the script, you need to issue the command

```
SET ECHO ON
```

before executing the downgrade.sql script. If you see any errors when running the script, or when you examine your log file, DOWNGRADE1.LOG, you should fix the problem and re-run step 2. You can re-run the downgrade.sql script as many times as you need.

13

DOWNGRADING

NOTE

If you are running Oracle Parallel Server, you must shut down every instance to complete step 2.

Step 3—Install the Downgrade Version

If you already have the release to which are downgrading installed on your server, you can skip to step 4. If your intended downgrade release is not installed, you should use the installation media and documentation for that release to complete the installation. Ideally, you should use a separate Oracle home directory from your Oracle8*i* release. You might need to re-set one or more of the following environment variables to identify the 8.0 release as part of this step:

- ORACLE_HOME
- PATH

- ORA_NLS
- ORACLE_BASE
- LD_LIBRARY_PATH
- ORACLE_PATH

Step 4—Prepare the Downgrade Environment

If you did not need to set your environment variables to point to your downgrade release's directories in step 3, you should do that now. Use the list of environment variables provided at the end of step 3 that you might need to re-set if they are already in use for your Oracle8*i* release.

Move the initialization parameter file and any files referenced by IFILE parameters out of the Oracle8*i* home directory structure. If you created a working directory in step 1, this would be a good place to locate them; otherwise, choose a location where you can readily identify them later.

> **NOTE**
>
> If you are using Oracle Parallel Server, you need to move the initialization files out of the Oracle8*i* home directory structure on every node. You should also change the PARALLEL_SERVER parameter value to FALSE at this time, too.

Copy the files you moved in step 1 into the ADMIN subdirectory of the Oracle home directory structure of the release to which you are downgrading—CATLG803.SQL, UTLIP.SQL, and UTLRP.SQL.

Step 5—Complete the Database Downgrade

The downgrade commands used in step 5 should be completed in Server Manager and not in SQL*Plus. I suggest that you switch to the ADMIN subdirectory in the Oracle8, release 8.0, home directory to which you are downgrading and start up Server Manager. If you do not make this switch, you will need to include full pathnames to any script files required in the following steps. The following commands assume that you are executing them in a Server Manager session started in the ADMIN subdirectory:

```
CONNECT INTERNAL
STARTUP PFILE=initialization_file
SPOOL downgrade2.log
@utlip.sql
@catalog_script
@catproc.sql
@utlrp.sql
```

For the *initialization_file* in your STARTUP command, use the full path and filename of the parameter file you relocated in step 4. If you are downgrading to release 8.0.3, you need to run

the special catalog script, CATLG03.SQL, so use this name for *catalog_script*. If you are downgrading to a higher release of 8.0, you can use the standard catalog script for that release, so use CATALOG.SQL in place of *catalog_script*.

Step 6—Downgrading Your Options

If you have Parallel Server installed, execute the script CATPARR.SQL.

If you have Advanced Replication installed, execute the script CATREP.SQL. Then regenerate Advanced Replication Support for your downgraded database. If the database supports one or more object groups, do the following:

1. Quiesce each of the object groups.
2. Generate replication support for each replicated table in each group.
3. Resume master activity for each object group.

If the database is a snapshot site, you need to generate replication support for each updatable snapshot.

If you have downgraded to release 8.0.4 and if you used the UTL_REF package in your Oracle8*i* database, you need to reinstall the package.

If you have downgraded to release 8.0.3 and if you used Recovery Manager release 8.0.4, or higher, before you downgraded, you need to execute the following scripts:

- dbmsrman.sql
- prvtrmnu.plb
- dbmsrvct.sql
- prvtrvct.plb

Step 7—Check for Errors

Close your log file using the SPOOL OFF command. Check your DOWNGRADE2.LOG file for any errors that occurred while running the scripts in steps 5 and 6. If you find errors, correct the problems and repeat steps 5 and 6. When you complete these steps without errors, your database is downgraded and ready for use. You might want to make a backup, however, before opening it for your users.

Downgrade to Oracle7

Oracle doesn't supply any tools or facilities to help you with a downgrade from Oracle8*i* to Oracle7. If you are performing a downgrade very soon after you have completed a migration to Oracle8*i*, you might find it easier to simply restore your Oracle7 database from the last backup you made before you performed the migration. You should ensure that you use your Oracle7 parameter file and environment variables if you decide to use this approach to downgrading.

If you have data changes that you want to preserve from your Oracle8*i* database, you should move it all to tables that are supported in Oracle7. For example, if you have partitioned any of your tables, you need to move the contents of each partition into a separate table using the ALTER TABLE...EXCHANGE PARTITION command. Similarly, if you have data in index-organized tables, you need to move it into a normal table with a CREATE TABLE...AS SELECT command.

Should you have stored data in datatypes that are not supported on Oracle7, such as CLOBs and BLOBs, you will need to find a way to unload it into supported datatypes or to external files that can be used to reload it into the restored Oracle7 database.

After you have identified the data you want to preserve and ensured that it is stored in objects supported by Oracle7, you need to run the CATEXP7.SQL script from your Oracle8*i* home directory's ADMIN subdirectory. This will allow you to perform an Oracle7 export.

Perform an export of the objects you want to preserve, using the Export utility from your Oracle7 installation against your Oracle8*i* database. You should then be able to use the Oracle7 Import utility to import the dump file into your restored Oracle7 database.

If you have a large amount of changed data to downgrade or aren't in possession of a usable Oracle7 backup, you will need to move the entire contents of your Oracle8*i* database to a new Oracle7 database. A number of methods are available for you to use. These are, basically, the same options you had to perform your migration from Oracle7 to Oracle8—Export/Import and data copying—minus the Oracle tools that do not support downgrades to earlier "versions. We suggest that you examine Chapters 6, "Migration Using Export/Import," and 7, "Migration Using Data Copying," which describe the available options for an upward migration, to determine whether you can adapt the methods detailed there for your downgrade. As with readers who do have an available backup, you might have to convert some of your data before you attempt a downgrade so that it is in a format supported by Oracle7.

Summary

In this chapter, I have discussed the issues you need to address if you decide to downgrade your database from Oracle8*i* to either Oracle8, release 8.0, or to Oracle7. These include the various changes you have to make to remove incompatible components from the later release and the steps you need to perform to recover the functionality of the earlier release.

I describe how to perform a downgrade to release 8.0 using the Oracle Data Migration Assistant that automates many of the steps. For those of you who might want to customize some of the steps, I also cover the required tasks you will need to perform to complete a manual downgrade to release 8.0.

The chapter concludes with a discussion of the options available to you if you need to downgrade to an Oracle7 release.

Troubleshooting the Migration Process

IN THIS CHAPTER

In the chapters that discuss the specific methods to migrate your Oracle7 database, Chapter 4, "Migration Using the Migration Utility;" Chapter 5, "Migration Using the Oracle Data Migration Assistant;" Chapter 6, "Migration Using Export/Import;" and Chapter 7, "Migration Using Data Copying," we mentioned some of the problems you might encounter and gave suggestions on how you might need to fix them. If you are using Export/Import or the data copying method, any errors you encounter are likely to be related to the specific operation you are performing and should help you identify what needs to be corrected. If you are using either of the Oracle migration tools, the Migration Utility, (which I will refer to as the utility throughout this chapter) or the Data Migration Assistant (which I will refer to as the assistant throughout this chapter), however, a number of procedures and processes are performed without any specific action on your part. In this chapter, I will try to help you determine what you need to do if you run into problems or receive errors while migrating, using the utility or the assistant.

I list the error messages you might receive from either the utility or the assistant in alphabetical order of the message text. Some errors have not been included because they are typically caused by a system problem that you are unlikely to be able to address. One such message would be

```
file <filename> is too large for DBA conversion
```

If you receive a message that is not covered in the following section, you should contact your Oracle Customer Support representative.

Migration Utility and Data Migration Assistant Messages and Corrective Actions

The following alphabetical list of error messages that can be generated by the utility and the assistant includes suggestions on the steps or methods you should use to correct the problems. This list does not include purely informational messages that might be returned, nor messages which indicate problems for which you will need assistance from your Oracle Customer Support Representative.

Terms in this list that are enclosed in curly braces ({...>}) will be replaced with an actual value or with a generic term indicating the type of field in actual error messages; angle brackets (<...>) are part of the error text and will appear as shown.

If you are using the assistant, you should restore your Oracle7 backup, fix the problems as indicated, and then re-run the program. If you are running the utility, you can restart the program without restoring the Oracle7 database, unless the problem requires modifications to the database that need a restore or recovery operation.

cannot create control file {name}

You did not rename or remove your Oracle7 control files before issuing the ALTER DATABASE CONVERT command. Retry the command after renaming or removing your old control files.

cannot create conversion file, records exceed {number} bytes

The Oracle7 control file is probably corrupted. Try to open the Oracle7 database with the control files you are using during the migration or execute the command ALTER DATABASE BACKUP CONTROLFILE TO TRACE to confirm that the control files are valid. Restore the control files from a backup if any problems are found, or else contact your Oracle Customer Support Representative.

cannot use system rollback segment for non-system tablespace '{name}'

You will receive this message only if your initialization file has the value of DB or TRUE set for the AUDIT_TRAIL parameter or if the SYS.AUD$ table is not in the SYSTEM tablespace. In the former case, reset the parameter value to NONE; in the latter case, you will have to reverse whatever steps you took to move the SYS.AUD$ table from the SYSTEM tablespace and put it back there. After you have taken the corrective action, you can re-run the program.

CHECK_ONLY and NO_SPACE_CHECK are mutually exclusive options

You have included two incompatible command-line options when running the utility. Remove either the CHECK_ONLY or the NO_SPACE_OPTION keywords: Remove the former if you are trying to complete a migration and remove the latter if you are attempting to determine whether you have sufficient space in the SYSTEM tablespace for a migration.

client nls_characterset does not match server nls_characterset – check that nls_lang environment variable is set

If you are using a client-server environment, this error indicates that a mismatch between the National Language Support settings is in PROPS$ and in NLS_LANG. You should set the latter to match the former and re-run the program.

command-Line argument value must be TRUE or FALSE ({*string*})

You have included an argument in a utility command line that requires a TRUE or FALSE value, but have provided neither. The option in the error is either CHECK_ONLY or NO_SPACE_CHECK. Check them both and correct the one in error. Note that one of these options must be TRUE and the other FALSE whenever you execute the migrate command.

command line arguments must be of the form <keyword>=<value>

You have violated the proper syntax of the utility command line, which requires a keyword, an equal sign (=), and a value. Correct the syntax of the command line and re-execute the command. Table 14.1 lists the valid options and the datatype of the argument for your convenience.

TABLE **14.1**   Migration Utility Command Line Options

Option Keyword	Value Datatype
CHECK_ONLY	Boolean (TRUE or FALSE)
DBNAME	String
MULTIPLIER	Integer
NEW_DBNAME	String
NLS_CHAR	String
NO_SPACE_CHECK	Boolean (TRUE or FALSE)
PFILE	String (on UNIX systems; must be enclosed in double quotes, each of which is preceded by the backslash escape character)
SPOOL	String (on UNIX systems; must be enclosed in double quotes, each of which is preceded by the backslash escape character)

When entering the command, you must not leave any blank space between the option keyword, the equal sign, and the value.

command name not found ({*string*})

Usually, this error occurs because incompatible versions of the utility, the MIGRATE.BSQ file, or the target Oracle8*i* software exist. If there are not any incompatibility errors, you should check for any errors in the MIGRATE.BSQ file, which is used to build to new Oracle8*i* Data Dictionary. If you can determine the cause of the error, you should fix the problem and re-run the program; otherwise, you should contact your Oracle Customer Support Representative.

command name not of form CMD(ARG1, ARG2, …)

Usually, this error occurs because incompatible versions of the utility, the MIGRATE.BSQ file, or the target Oracle8*i* software exist. If there are not any incompatibility errors, you should check for any errors in the MIGRATE.BSQ file, which is used to build to new Oracle8*i* Data Dictionary. If you can determine the cause of the error, you should fix the problem and re-run the program; otherwise, you should contact your Oracle Customer Support Representative.

controlfile: {name}

You did not rename or remove your Oracle7 control files before issuing the ALTER DATABASE CONVERT command. Retry the command after renaming or removing your old control files.

convert file not found: name

Your convert file, needed to complete the ALTER DATABASE CONVERT command, must be located in its expected location and have its expected name. You can determine what these are from your platform-specific Installation and Configuration guide.

copy long command must be of form COPYLONG(U1,T1,C1,U2,T2,C2,K1<,K2>)

Usually, this error occurs because incompatible versions of the utility, the MIGRATE.BSQ file, or the target Oracle7 database exist. If there are not any incompatibility errors, you should check for any errors in the MIGRATE.BSQ file, which is used to build to new Oracle8*i* Data Dictionary. If you can determine the cause of the error, you should fix the problem and re-run the program; otherwise, you should contact your Oracle Customer Support Representative.

corrupt block detected in controlfile: (block num, # blocks num)

You did not rename or remove your Oracle7 control files before issuing the ALTER DATABASE CONVERT command, or else you are trying to execute it without the database being in NOMOUNT mode. Retry the command after renaming or removing your old control files or restarting the instance in NOMOUNT mode.

could not find single contiguous extent of {number} bytes for {string}

Your SYSTEM tablespace is not large enough to hold the Data Dictionary components needed to complete the migration. Use the utility command-line option, CHECK_ONLY, to determine

how much space you need and then query the DBA_DATA_FILES table to see how much space you have:

```
SELECT SUM(bytes)
  FROM dba_data_files
  WHERE tablespace_name = 'SYSTEM';
```

Add one or more datafiles to your SYSTEM tablespace to provide the additional space required, as determined by the difference between the values shown by the utility and the Data Dictionary table, and then re-run the program.

could not translate logical name {*name*}

You have probably not defined a system variable or a datafile link name correctly, or you have an invalid Windows NT registry entry. After correcting the problem, re-run the program.

current version: {*str*} — Database must be version 7.1 or later

Your current database release is too early for the utility or assistant to migrate successfully. You must choose another migration method or else perform an initial migration or upgrade to Oracle7, release 7.1, or later, and then re-run the program.

data type must be long for column {*name*}

Some form of corruption probably exists in your MIGRATE.BSQ file, or else the version of the file or the utility is not compatible with your Oracle7 database. You should check for file corruption and confirm that you are running the correct version of the utility for the database releases you are converting to and from.

database name {*name*} in control file is not {*name*}

A mismatch exists between one of the following:

- the DB_NAME parameter in the initialization file and the instance name in the *sid* portion of the conv*sid*.dbf file
- the instance name set in the UNIX ORACLE_SID environment variable and in the *sid* portion of the conv*sid*.dbf filename

You need to alter the name in whichever of these places the names are incorrect or inconsistent.

datafile is offline while tablespace is online — apply media recovery and bring datafile online before migration — {*datafile*}

You have an inconsistency in the status of at least one tablespace and datafile. The datafile named in the message is the first one encountered by the program. You need to perform a database recovery process to bring the tablespace and its datafiles to a consistent state. At that point, you can convert the tablespace and datafiles to an online or to an offline normal status before beginning the migration again.

datafile {*name*} — failed verification check datafile name: {str}

You might encounter this error if you have attempted to run the ALTER DATABASE CONVERT command more than once. You might be able to continue your migration process by issuing the ALTER DATABASE OPEN RESETLOGS command, or you might have to restore your Oracle7 database and begin the migration over again.

dictionary constant not found - {*name*}

Usually, this error occurs because incompatible versions of the utility, the MIGRATE.BSQ file, or the target Oracle8*i* software exist. If there are not any incompatibility errors, you should check for any errors in the MIGRATE.BSQ file, which is used to build to a new Oracle8*i* Data Dictionary. If you can determine the cause of the error, you should fix the problem and re-run the program; otherwise, you should contact your Oracle Customer Support Representative.

entries found in system.def$_call, def$_calldest or def$_error — push all deferred transactions before migration

You have outstanding transactions because of incomplete distributed processing calls or replication job queue entries. These must be resolved and then you can re-run the program.

error calling slgtd

You have an inconsistency in the status of at least one tablespace and datafile. The datafile named in the message is the first one encountered by the program. You need to perform a database recovery process to bring the tablespace and its datafiles to a consistent state. At that point, you can convert the tablespace and datafiles to an online or to an offline normal status before beginning the migration again.

14

TROUBLESHOOTING THE MIGRATION PROCESS

error closing file {*name*}

The file named in the error message has physical corruption or does not have the correct permissions, sufficient physical space, or a high enough quota limit to complete the migration. You need to fix the specific problem by restoring the data to an undamaged disk, modifying the file permissions, adding another datafile to the tablespace to which the datafile belongs, or changing the quota for the user performing the migration. When that is done, you should be able to re-run the program successfully.

error occurred at recursive SQL level {*num*}

You will receive this message only if your initialization file has the value of DB or TRUE set for the AUDIT_TRAIL parameter or if the SYS.AUD$ table is not in the SYSTEM tablespace. In the former case, reset the parameter value to NONE; in the latter case, you will have to reverse whatever steps you took to move the SYS.AUD$ table from the SYSTEM tablespace and put it back there. After you have taken the corrective action, you can re-run the program.

error while writing to audit trail

You will receive this message only if your initialization file has the value of DB or TRUE set for the AUDIT_TRAIL parameter, or if the SYS.AUD$ table is not in the SYSTEM tablespace. In the former case, reset the parameter value to NONE; in the latter case, you will have to reverse whatever steps you took to move the SYS.AUD$ table from the SYSTEM tablespace and put it back there. After you have taken the corrective action, you can re-run the program.

failed to extend rollback segment (id = 0)

This problem can occur if your SYSTEM rollback segment had shrunk to its OPTIMAL size from a larger maximum size prior to the migration. The migration programs take all rollback segments, except SYSTEM, offline and freeze the SYSTEM rollback segment at its current size. If you have an OPTIMAL value set, you need to remove it by issuing the command

```
ALTER ROLLBACK SEGMENT system STORAGE (OPTIMAL NULL);
```

You might then need to execute a few commands to allow it to grow to a larger size. You can check its size by querying the view V$ROLLSTAT.

file header does not fit in {*number*} bytes

The Oracle7 control file is probably corrupted. Try to open the Oracle7 database with the control files you are using during the migration or execute the command ALTER DATABASE BACKUP CONTROLFILE TO TRACE to confirm that the control files are valid. Restore the control files from a backup if any problems are found, or else contact your Oracle Customer Support Representative.

fixed portion of control file does not fit in {*number*} bytes

The Oracle7 control file is probably corrupted. Try to open the Oracle7 database with the control files you are using during the migration or execute the command ALTER DATABASE BACKUP CONTROLFILE TO TRACE to confirm that the control files are valid. Restore the control files from a backup if any problems are found, or else contact your Oracle Customer Support Representative.

found NULL SQL statement

Usually, this error occurs because there are incompatible versions of the utility, the MIGRATE.BSQ file, or the target Oracle8*i* software. If there are not any incompatibility errors, you should check for any errors in the MIGRATE.BSQ file, which is used to build to new Oracle8*i* Data Dictionary. If you can determine the cause of the error, you should fix the problem and re-run the program; otherwise, you should contact your Oracle Customer Support Representative.

incomplete write

The database contains a file that has physical corruption or does not have the correct permissions, sufficient physical space, or a high enough quota limit to complete the migration. You need to fix the specific problem by restoring the data to an undamaged disk, modifying the file permissions, adding another datafile to the tablespace to which the datafile belongs, or changing the quota for the user performing the migration. After that is done, you should be able to re-run the program successfully.

insufficient space for new dictionaries, {*number*} bytes needed, {*number*} found

Your SYSTEM tablespace is not large enough to hold the Data Dictionary components needed to complete the migration. Use the utility command-line option, CHECK_ONLY, to determine how much space you need and then query the DBA_DATA_FILES table to see how much space you have:

```
SELECT SUM(bytes)
  FROM dba_data_files
  WHERE tablespace_name = 'SYSTEM';
```

Add one or more datafiles to your SYSTEM tablespace to provide the additional space required, as determined by the difference between the values shown by the utility and the Data Dictionary table, and then re-run the program.

internal error code, arguments: [kzsrsdn: 1], [32]

This ORA-600 error will occur if you are attempting to use an Oracle7 password file after you have migrated and converted your database. To fix this problem, you need to shut down your database and set the initialization parameter REMOTE_LOGIN_PASSWORD value to NONE. You must then restart your database, using an Oracle8*i* instance, to the MOUNT state, and open it with the ALTER DATABASE OPEN RESETLOGS command. You should now be able to continue your migration process by executing the Oracle8*i* database conversion script, u0703040.sql. Note that you will have to re-create the password file if you need it for your Oracle8*i* database.

invalid NLS_NCHAR value specified

You have included an invalid value for the National Language Character set of your migrated database in the utility command line. Either omit the NLS_CHAR parameter—which will cause your Oracle8*i* database to be built with the same characterset as your Oracle7 database—or replace the value with a valid characterset name, and then re-run the program.

max # extents (%s) reached in index %s.%s

This error is generated when the MULTIPLIER value, which increases the size of the base Data Dictionary table to support indexes, is set too low for the increased size of the ROWIDs in your database's indexes. You can reset it in the utility's command line or by choosing the Custom migration option in the assistant. If you had not explicitly set its value when you received this error, you need to make it larger than 15, which is the default value.

migration can't proceed – database blocksize is less than Oracle8's minimum block size 2k

An Oracle8*i* database requires a minimum block size of 2KB. If your Oracle7 database has a smaller block size, you cannot use the utility or assistant to migrate it as is. You must either rebuild your Oracle7 database with a new block size, or use the Export/Import, or data copying method to migrate your database to an Oracle8*i* database built with a valid block size.

migration can't proceed with datafile online while tablespace offline – {*datafile*}

You have an inconsistency in the status of at least one tablespace and datafile. The datafile named in the message is the first one encountered by the program. You need to perform a database recovery process to bring the tablespace and its datafiles to a consistent state. At that point, you can convert the tablespace and datafiles to an online or to an offline normal status before beginning the migration again.

migration cannot proceed with active transaction or offline tablespace with outstanding undo

Your database contains at least one tablespace that was taken offline with the IMMEDIATE or the TEMPORARY option. You must either bring the problem tablespaces online or else drop them, and then re-run the program. If the problem still persists, check for outstanding transactions because of incomplete distributed processing calls or replication job queue entries. These must be resolved, and then you can re-run the program.

MULTIPLIER value must be at least

You have included an invalid value for the MULTIPLIER value in the utility command line. This parameter determines how many times larger, compared to your Oracle7 database, the basic Data Dictionary table that stores ROWID information for indexes will be in your Oracle8*i* database. It must have a value equal to, or greater than 2, or else be omitted. Re-run the program with a valid value.

NEW_DBNAME {*name*} too long – maximum length 8 characters

You have included an invalid value for the NEW_DBNAME value in the utility command line. This parameter determines the new name for your Oracle8*i* database. It must be a character string with no more than eight characters. Re-run the program with a valid name or omit the parameter to give your migrated database the same name as your current database.

Oracle7 data file is not from migration to Oracle8i

You might encounter this error if you have attempted to run the ALTER DATABASE CONVERT command more than once. You might be able to continue your migration process by issuing the ALTER DATABASE OPEN RESETLOGS command, or you might have to restore your Oracle7 database and begin the migration over again.

ORA-NLS33 environment variable is not set or incorrectly set

Your ORA_NLS33 environment variable is not correctly set to point to your Oracle8*i* character-set files. Check your platform-specific Installation and Configuration guide to see whether this variable is required on your operating system and how to set it correctly. Modify the environment variable value and re-run the program as required.

ORA – {*number*}

If you encounter a standard Oracle message code, use the Oracle8*i* Error Messages manual to help you determine the nature of the problem and make the necessary corrections.

> **NOTE**
>
> Some of the messages that are likely to occur when running the utility or the assistant are already included in this alphabetical list, so you should check for migration-specific problems in this chapter first.

parameter buffer overflow

Your initialization parameter file is too large. This is probably because you added new parameters for Oracle8*i* without removing the obsolete Oracle7 parameters. Reduce the size of your parameter file by removing any unnecessary entries and re-run the program. If you cannot reduce the size sufficiently to avoid this error, you should contact your Oracle Customer Support Representative.

parameter file exceeds {*number*} bytes

Your initialization parameter file is too large. This is probably because you added new parameters for Oracle8*i* without removing the obsolete Oracle7 parameters. Reduce the size of your parameter file by removing any unnecessary entries and re-run the program. If you cannot reduce the size sufficiently to avoid this error, you should contact your Oracle Customer Support Representative.

seek error in file {*name*}

This error is generally an indication of a logically or physically corrupt file. You should restore, and possibly recover, the file and then re-run the program. If this is not possible, you might have to re-create the file, either before or after the migration, using techniques described in the Oracle Backup and Recovery manuals, or else drop the tablespace associated with the damaged file.

short read, {*number*} bytes requested, {*number*} bytes read

The Oracle7 control file is probably corrupted. Try to open the Oracle7 database with the control files you are using during the migration or execute the command ALTER DATABASE

BACKUP CONTROLFILE TO TRACE to confirm that the control files are valid. Restore the control files from a backup if any problems are found, or else contact your Oracle Customer Support Representative.

shut down database (abort)

This message is typically one of a series of messages that appear when Oracle performs a non-checkpointed database shutdown. The other messages should help you identify the cause of the shutdown and suggest methods to fix the problem. You should re-run the program when they are fixed.

skgfrcre: file exists

You did not rename or remove your Oracle7 control files before issuing the ALTER DATABASE CONVERT command. Retry the command after renaming or removing your old control files.

string argument is too long, maximum length {*number*}

You have violated the proper syntax of the utility command line by providing a value that is too long for its associated function, as determined by its keyword. Correct the syntax of the command line (see Table 14.1) and re-execute the command.

tablespace of datafile not taken offline normal. Bring tablespace online, offline normal or drop before migration — {*tablespace*}

You brought the named tablespace offline with either the IMMEDIATE or the TEMPORARY option, which means it requires recovery to be brought online again. You must perform this action before you migrate the database, not after. If you cannot complete this action, you will have to drop the tablespace in order to migrate your database. After the tablespace is online or dropped, you can re-run the program.

too many args in command ({*number*} max)

You have violated the proper syntax of the utility command line by providing too many arguments. Correct the syntax of the command line (see Table 14.1) and re-execute the command.

unable to allocate buffer space to copy longs

The program required temporary buffer space to migrate LONG columns, but the system had insufficient memory to allocate for this purpose. You will need to reduce the memory used by other applications, or by your database's SGA, and then re-run the program.

unable to extend temp segment by {*size*} in tablespace SYSTEM

Your SYSTEM tablespace is not large enough to hold the Data Dictionary components needed to complete the migration. Use the utility command-line option, CHECK_ONLY, to determine how much space you need and then query the DBA_DATA_FILES table to see how much space you have:

```
SELECT SUM(bytes)
  FROM dba_data_files
  WHERE tablespace_name = 'SYSTEM';
```

Add one or more datafiles to your SYSTEM tablespace to provide the additional space required, as determined by the difference between the values shown by the utility and the Data Dictionary table, and then re-run the program.

unable to obtain file status

Your convert file, needed to complete the ALTER DATABASE CONVERT command, must be located in its expected location and have its expected name. You can determine what these are from your platform-specific Installation and Configuration guide.

unable to open file {*name*}

The file named in the error message does not exist in the defined location, or else it has physical corruption, does not have the correct permissions, sufficient physical space, or a high enough quota limit to complete the migration. You need to fix the specific problem by restoring the data to an undamaged disk, modifying the file permissions, adding another datafile to the tablespace to which the datafile belongs, or changing the quota for the user performing the migration. After that is done, you should be able to re-run the program successfully.

unable to read file {*name*}

The file named in the error message does not exist in the defined location, or else it has physical corruption, does not have the correct permissions, sufficient physical space, or a high enough quota limit to complete the migration. You need to fix the specific problem by restoring the data to an undamaged disk, modifying the file permissions, adding another datafile to the tablespace to which the datafile belongs, or changing the quota for the user performing the migration. After that is done, you should be able to re-run the program successfully.

unable to write file {*name*}

The file named in the error message has physical corruption or does not have the correct permissions, sufficient physical space, or a high enough quota limit to complete the migration.

You need to fix the specific problem by restoring the data to an undamaged disk, modifying the file permissions, adding another datafile to the tablespace to which the datafile belongs, or changing the quota for the user performing the migration. After that is done, you should be able to rerun the program successfully.

V8 catalog space requirement: {*number*}

Your SYSTEM tablespace is not large enough to hold the Data Dictionary components needed to complete the migration. Use the utility command-line option, CHECK_ONLY, to determine how much space you need and then query the DBA_DATA_FILES table to see how much space you have:

```
SELECT SUM(bytes)
  FROM dba_data_files
  WHERE tablespace_name = 'SYSTEM';
```

Add one or more datafiles to your SYSTEM tablespace to provide the additional space required, as determined by the difference between the values shown by the utility and the Data Dictionary table, and then re-run the program.

wrong incarnation of this file – wrong creation time

You might encounter this error if you have attempted to run the ALTER DATABASE CONVERT command more than once. You might be able to continue your migration process by issuing the ALTER DATABASE OPEN RESETLOGS command, or you might have to restore your Oracle7 database and begin the migration over again.

Summary

This chapter identifies the errors that have commonly occurred when running the Oracle8*i* Migration Utility or the Data Migration Assistant. I have tried to provide you with the option, or options, you have to use to recover from these errors.

If you are using other methods to complete your migration, you should use the Oracle7 or the Oracle8*i* Error Messages manual to identify the nature of the problem.

Migrating from Non-Oracle Databases

IN THIS CHAPTER

More and more companies have realized the benefit of using Oracle databases and would like to move their existing non-Oracle databases to Oracle8*i*. Prior to Oracle8*i*, the migration path was complex and involved manual intervention. As a result, large corporations were not willing to make decisions about migration to Oracle and continued using their inefficient systems. Clearly, people want to use Oracle8*i* due to the tremendous benefit they would achieve, and they would easily decide to move to Oracle8*i* provided a simple and easy method was available. In this chapter, I will discuss the process of migration from MS SQL Server databases, as well as from MS Access databases, to Oracle8*i*.

The extent of planning and testing that will be required will be directly proportional to the number of different applications deployed. The migration can become more complex when you are moving many of your legacy systems to Oracle8*i*. Planning such a migration can be very stressful, and you should be aware of the impact it will have on the user community. A DBA performing migration from non-Oracle databases to Oracle8*i* should have several considerations:

- The production environment must be least affected.
- The user community must not be affected.
- Performance must be improved by making use of the additional capabilities provided by Oracle8*i*.

The following checklist of tasks can help you to ease the migration process:

1. Become familiar with the new capabilities available by using Oracle8*i*.
2. Determine the hardware and software required by Oracle8*i*.
3. Make the choices regarding the migration process. These choices involve the following:
   - Determine the migration method you will use.
   - Determine and make sure that you have the necessary resources available.
   - Become familiar with the similarities and differences between the source DBMS and Oracle8*i*.
   - Develop a plan for testing the migrated database.
   - Decide on a backup and recovery strategy so that you can quickly fall back to the source DBMS in case the migration fails.
4. Perform a test migration.
5. Using the testing strategy developed in step 1, test the migrated test database.
6. Prepare the database for migration. This step involves taking a backup of the database, scheduling downtime for the database, changing the application in a desired manner so that the post-migration changes are minimized and the migration occurs smoothly.

7. Migrate the database by using the strategy decided in step 1.

8. Back up the migrated database.

9. Tune the migrated database by using the new Oracle8*i* features, and tune the initialization parameters as desired.

10. Migrate the applications.

Migrating from MS SQL Server

Both MS SQL Server and Oracle are relational databases and share some common characteristics. However, they have notable differences in architecture, client/server communication methods, data load methods, data retrieval methods, and data storage concepts. Also, administration tasks, such as managing multiple databases, are different. In addition to these differences, the migration process should consider the differences mentioned in Table 15.1:

TABLE 15.1   Differences Between MS SQL Server and Oracle8*i* That Affect Migration from MS SQL Server to Oracle8*i*

Feature	MS SQL Server	Oracle8i
ANSI SQL compliance	ANSI compliant, but uses Transact-SQL.	ANSI compliant, but uses PL/SQL.
Cursors per session	Stream-based and uses only one cursor per session.	Connection-based and can use multiple cursors per session.
Locking	Page-level locking.	Row-level locking.
Result set manipulation	Results are automatically placed in a stream to the client.	A cursor variable is returned to the client. This cursor variable is a handle to SGA resident cursor and allows the client to fetch data.

The relational nature of both MS SQL Server and Oracle8*i* allows them to have common characteristics (see Table 15.2):

- Schema objects, such as tables and views
- Datatypes
- Use of logical transactions
- Use of triggers and stored procedures
- Use of referential integrity
- Use of constraints

- Access to system information (system catalog in MS SQL Server and data dictionary in Oracle) using SQL
- Security at the server level

TABLE 15.2 Analogous Components in Oracle8*i* and Microsoft SQL Server 6.x

*Oracle8*i	*MS SQL Server 6.*x
Database	Database
Schema	Database and database owner (DBO)
Tablespace	Database
User	User
Role	Group
Table	Table
Cluster	N/A
N/A	Temp tables
Column-level check constraint	Column-level check constraint
Column default	Column default
Unique constraint	IDENTITY property of column
Primary key constraint	Primary key constraint
Foreign key constraint	Foreign key constraint
Index	Index
PL/SQL procedure	Transact-SQL procedure
PL/SQL function	Transact-SQL function
Packages	N/A
Before triggers	Rules
After triggers	Triggers
Synonyms	N/A
Snapshot	N/A
DATE[1]	DATETIME
BLOB	BINARY
View	View

1 The DATE datatype of Oracle has a precision of one second and can't be used as a primary key. On the other hand, the DATETIME datatype of MS SQL Server has a precision of 1/100th of a second and can be used as a primary key.

Migration from MS SQL Server to Oracle8*i* can be performed using several methods:

- Write a program that connects to both SQL Server and Oracle8*i* databases, retrieves from MS SQL Server, processes the data as needed to make sure that there are no datatype conflicts, and then inserts into Oracle8*i*.

- A gateway can be used to perform a distributed query to transfer information from MS SQL Server to Oracle8*i*.

- Use flat files. This method makes use of the Bulk Copy Program (BCP) provided by MS SQL Server to unload the data into flat files. These flat files can then be loaded in Oracle8*i* using Oracle's SQL*Loader utility.

- Use Oracle's GUI Migration Workbench.

Oracle Migration Workbench Parser Issues

The current version of the Migration Workbench has several parser issues that might prevent the migration of some views and triggers, and you should consider these during the migration process:

- The parser places * in the package definition if it cannot perform name resolution.

- You will have to manually take care of SQL statements that use aliased columns with ORDER BY clauses because they will fail during parsing. The parser generally puts aliased columns in quotes, making them unrecognizable by the ORDER BY clause:

  ```
  Select total=sum(cost) from orders order by total;
  ```

  This clause parses to the following Oracle statement:

  ```
  Select sum(cost) "total" from orders order by total;
  ```

- The parser cannot migrate individual stored procedures.

- The SYSOBJECTS table in MS SQL Server contains information that is equivalent to the ALL_OBJECTS table in Oracle.

- Oracle Migration Workbench sometimes does not consider the interdependencies between the objects; as a result, creation of views, triggers, and packages sometimes fails because the objects are created in the wrong order. The Migration Wizard can be rerun to resolve this issue.

- Oracle does not use temporary tables in the same manner as MS SQL Server, and therefore creation of temporary tables results in an error.

- EXEC *(exec string)* are converted to PL/SQL procedure calls, except EXEC ("*exec_string*"), which are treated as dynamic SQL and sent to an EXEC_SQL PL/SQL stored procedure for execution.

- The parser cannot process LOAD and DUMP commands of MS SQL Server.

- MS SQL Server DDL commands are ignored.

15

MIGRATING FROM
NON-ORACLE
DATABASES

NOTE

You should check the log window of the Oracle Migration Workbench for errors and warnings that occur during the migration process.

- SQL statements containing LIKE clauses that use regular expressions result in an error.
- Manipulation of result sets and dynasets is performed by adding an argument of type REF CURSOR. You can make use of PL/SQL or Oracle JDBC to manipulate REF_CURSORs.

NOTE

Oracle ODBC driver doesn't support REF CURSORs, and therefore you will have to modify the client code. However, third-party ODBC drivers (such as from Intersolv) are available that can support REF_CURSORs.

For example, parsing the following MS SQL Server stored procedure:

```
CREATE PROCEDURE byroyalty @percentage int
AS
Select au_id from titleauthor
Where titleauthor.royaltyper = @percentage
GO
```

generates the following Oracle package and stored procedure:

```
PACKAGE BYROYALTYpkg AS
TYPE RECTYPE IS RECORD (
    au_id       titleauthor.au_id%TYPE
);
TYPE RCTYPE IS REF CURSOR RETURN REC1;
END;

PROCEDURE         byroyalty( percentage IN integer,
RC1    IN OUT byroyaltypkg.rctype)
AS
O_selcnt    INTEGER;
O_error     INTEGER;
O_rowcnt    INTEGER;
O_sqlstatus     INTEGER;
```

```
O_errmsg    VARCHAR2(255);
BEGIN
    OPEN RC1 FOR
    SELECT au_id FROM titleauthor
     WHERE titleauthor.royaltyper = :percentage;
END byroyalty;
```

Issues with Logical Transactions

The transactions in MS SQL Server are explicit, whereas in Oracle they are implicit. This difference in transaction models can cause problems if you simply take the result of migration as is.

Explicit transactions in MS SQL Server means that by default an individual SQL statement is not treated as part of a logical transaction, and it is committed on completion. The SQL statement can be made part of a logical transaction by placing it in a logical transaction that begins with BEGIN TRANSACTION (or BEGIN TRAN) and ends with a corresponding COMMIT TRANSACTION (COMMIT TRAN) or ROLLBACK TRANSACTION (ROLLBACK TRAN) statement.

On the other hand, transactions in Oracle are implicit, and therefore an individual statement by default is part of a logical transaction that ends with a COMMIT or ROLLBACK. Individual SQL statements are not committed upon completion, but rather are completed when the logical transaction completes with a COMMIT or a ROLLBACK statement.

NOTE

The ANSI standard is to use implicit transactions.

As a result of this difference, the migration process is simplified by making the transaction-handling constructs part of the client procedures instead of the server procedures.

Migrating DATETIME Datatypes

The MS SQL Server DATETIME datatype stores values with a different precision than the DATE datatype of Oracle8*i*. The DATETIME datatype stores date and time to a precision of 1/100 of a second. Many applications use this datatype for generating unique IDs. On the other hand, the Oracle DATE datatype stores date and time to a precision of one second. Applications might need a precision that is higher than one second even if they are not using it for generating unique IDs.

15

Conversion of SQL Server DATETIME values to Oracle8*i* will need manual intervention and can be done using several strategies:

- The (GET_TIME) function of the DBMS_UTILITY package returns the time in 1/100ths of a second. A higher precision can be obtained in Oracle by replacing the DATETIME datatype with a combination of DATE and NUMBER columns such that the NUMBER column is populated using the GET_TIME function.

- The SQL Server table using DATETIME datatype can be recreated with an additional column of integer datatype and NULL values. After this table is migrated to Oracle, you should create a sequence on this column such that the sequence starts with 1 and increments by 1.

> **NOTE**
>
> User-defined types are migrated to their base types.

Issues with Exception Handling

Exception handling in MS SQL Server is different from Oracle. When a SQL statement generates an error in MS SQL Server, control is passed to the next statement and the developer is responsible for handling the error. On the other hand, Oracle PL/SQL checks for errors with each SQL statement and will pass control to an exception handler instead of the next statement. Oracle developers don't have to perform error checking for each SQL statement.

The Oracle procedure resulting from the migration of a SQL Server procedure can be made to behave the same way as the SQL Server procedure (control is passed to the next statement irrespective of any errors) by enclosing each SQL statement in a PL/SQL block and performing all error handling for the SQL statement in that block.

RAISERROR Statement

Processing of a SQL Server procedure is different from an Oracle procedure after an error has been raised. The RAISERROR statement in SQL Server passes the error code and message to the client and continues further with the stored procedure. On the other hand, the Oracle RAISE_APPLICATION_ERROR statement returns to the calling routine.

By following RAISERROR with a RETURN statement, you can make its behavior similar to that of Oracle's RAISE_APPLICATION_ERROR statement.

NOTE

Don't use the SQL Server system procedures to add customized error messages because there is no Oracle equivalent for them. Instead, a user-defined error messages table should be used, which should be maintained by writing routines to insert and retrieve from it.

NOTE

Developers make use of database-specific SQL constructs to improve the performance of the system and also simplify the coding that is needed. However, I would not encourage you to do this if you are planning a migration from MS SQL Server to Oracle because the migration will be much easier and smoother if you follow the ANSI-standard SQL.

For example, the SQL Server DELETE construct allows the joining of tables:

```
DELETE titles
FROM publishers, titles
WHERE publishers.pub_id = titles.pub_id
AND publishers.pub_name = 'IPUBLISH.COM'
```

Instead, you should code it as

```
DELETE
FROM titles
WHERE pub_id IN
(SELECT pub_id
FROM publishers
WHERE pub_name = 'IPUBLISH.COM')
```

Issues with Migrating Temporary Tables

Coding can be simplified by breaking a complex query into multiple queries and making use of temporary tables to store the result of a query so that it can be used by another query. Also, a temporary table can be used like a regular table and be joined with other tables. MS SQL Server frequently makes use of temporary tables for various purposes, such as

* Improving the performance of multitable joins
* Consolidating data

- Simulating cursors while processing results coming from multiple tables
- Performing UNION operations

Oracle does not use temporary tables very efficiently, and therefore you should use multitable joins to convert SQL Server codes that use temporary tables to Oracle code. In general, multitable joins are not very efficient, but you can use parallel execution (described in Chapter 17, "Parallel Executions") to improve the performance of multitable joins. Also, UNION operations should be used where possible in order to improve performance. The following example demonstrates how a temporary table is used to store information about items that are in stock, the quantity, and their expiry:

In Microsoft SQL Server:

```
INSERT #ITEM_EXP
SELECT inventoru.item_id,
       inventory.quantity,
       inventory.exp_date
FROM   inventory, stores
WHERE inventory.item_id = stores.item_id
AND       stores.stor_loc = 'SEATTLE'
AND        inventory.exp_date BETWEEN @startdate AND @enddate

INSERT INTO #ITEM_EXP
VALUES (555, getdate(), NULL)

SELECT * FROM #ITEM_EXP
```

In Oracle8*i*:

```
SELECT inventoru.item_id,
       inventory.quantity,
       inventory.exp_date
FROM   inventory, stores
WHERE inventory.item_id = stores.item_id
AND       stores.stor_loc = 'SEATTLE'
AND        inventory.exp_date BETWEEN :startdate AND :enddate
UNION
SELECT 555, SYSDATE, NULL
FROM dual
```

Issues with Object Names and Reserved Words

SQL Server is case-sensitive, whereas Oracle is not case-sensitive. In other words, SQL Server objects such as TITLES and titles would map to the same Oracle object, causing problems during migration. The solution to this problem is to use quoted names for the objects, such as 'TITLES' and 'titles', which will be treated as separate objects.

You should be aware of the reserved words in Oracle so you don't use them in MS SQL Server. If the source databases make use of Oracle reserved words in naming objects, those objects will not be migrated.

TIP

During the migration process, you might receive

```
Failed to create a user: java.sql sql exception: ora-01017
invalid username/password' logon denied
```

The error indicates that a SQL Server user conflicts with an existing Oracle user with the same name. This problem can be resolved by changing the password of the username being migrated to be the same as the password of the Oracle username.

Migration Using the Oracle Migration Workbench

Oracle provides a graphical tool—Oracle Migration Workbench—that can be used to migrate MS SQL Server databases to Oracle. The Oracle Migration Workbench is available free with the Oracle Server, and future releases of the Workbench will support other non-Oracle databases. Oracle Migration Workbench can be installed on a Windows NT 4.0 or Windows 95/98 machine. The machine on which you install Oracle Migration Workbench should be able to access an Oracle 8.0.5 database or higher.

Oracle Migration Workbench has the following hardware requirements for the Windows NT/95/98 clients:

- Intel 80486 or higher processor
- 64MB RAM minimum
- VGA video (recommended SVGA)
- CD-ROM drive
- 180MB free hard disk space

NOTE

The Oracle Migration Workbench uses Oracle's JDBC driver, which in turn depends on the Oracle Net8 client. You cannot install Oracle Migration Workbench into a non-default Oracle home because Oracle Net8 client cannot be installed in a nondefault Oracle home.

The Migration Workbench has several important characteristics:

- A complete application system that includes the database schema, users, stored procedures, views, triggers, and embedded SQL can be migrated. The current version, however, does not allow the migration of individual objects.
- Multiple SQL Server databases can be migrated to a single Oracle8*i* database.
- Reserved words are automatically mapped between SQL Server and Oracle8*i*.
- Provides a GUI interface and wizards to simplify the migration process.
- Storage parameters for the objects can be manipulated during the migration.
- Dependencies among the components being migrated is automatically considered. The current version has several bugs regarding this feature, and you might have to rerun the migration if errors result during the first run.
- Provides logs that record the actions performed during the migration.
- The Migration Workbench can be launched from the Oracle Enterprise Manager.
- Projects can be unloaded and loaded using eXtensible Markup Language (XML) files.

NOTE

The current version of Oracle Migration Workbench v1.0.4.0.0 supports migration from only MS SQL Server.

The other methods to perform migration that I mentioned earlier will require a lot of manual intervention and make use of multiple scripts to unload and load the data dictionary and convert application files. Oracle also provides the Workbench Software Development Kit (WSDK) to provide support for the databases that are being migrated.

Using the Oracle Migration Workbench, you can perform migration of multiple databases. You can manage multiple migrations from a single console. A migration project is defined for each migration to specify the various database and application components to be migrated. After a migration project is defined, you can use various wizards that can help you to perform the migration.

Each migration project is associated with a repository that contains information about the migration, such as object dependencies. Unfortunately, you cannot migrate individual users or objects with the current version of the Migration Workbench, and the entire database is migrated. If you want to migrate only certain objects, manual intervention is required.

NOTE

The migration repository can be queried to obtain valuable information about the migration process.

The New Project Wizard is used to create a new project that describes the source and target databases by displaying the information in three panes:

- The Navigator pane

    Allows you to navigate between the various database components in a hierarchical format. The navigator pane contains information in two tabs:

    - Source model (SQL Server database being migrated)
    - Oracle model (Equivalent Oracle model)

- The Property pane

    Shows the properties of the database component currently chosen in the Navigator pane.

- The Logging pane

    Actions performed during the migration are logged here.

When the migration is performed, the following steps occur:

1. Users are created.
2. Tables are created.
3. Data is loaded into the table.
4. Table constraints are created.

The Migration Workbench uses JDBC/ODBC to read data from the SQL Server database and JDBC/OCI8 to load data into the Oracle database.

Three log files are associated with the migration process that can be used for troubleshooting. Information recorded in the log files include

- CREATE and ALTER statements
- DROP and ALTER statements
- SQL statements that are not executed

15

MIGRATING FROM
NON-ORACLE
DATABASES

> **NOTE**
>
> By default, the migration logs are placed in %ORACLE_HOME%\mwb\log. This default can be changed by using the Log File Directory setting on the Logging page of the Options dialog box.

Migrating from MS Access

MS Access is commonly used to develop prototypes that are eventually migrated to a high performance DBMS, such as Oracle8*i*. Moving your prototype to Oracle8*i* is not a trivial matter. The migration might involve several considerations such as schema changes, resource issues, and query and database tuning.

> **NOTE**
>
> MS Access database applications can be moved as is to Oracle8*i*, but I strongly discourage that because you are essentially not taking advantage of the Oracle8 features, and performance will suffer in the long run.

Benchmarking

While you make major changes to an application, you should benchmark the results so a comparison can be made to determine whether the changes are beneficial. Choose a benchmark routine with the following considerations:

- It should use at least one long, resource intensive query
- It should use at least one common query
- It should generate database statistics
- It should generate operating system statistics
- Run the script when the system has very low load
- Run the script when the system has very high load
- Run the script when the system has normal load
- Get feedback from the users to see whether they are experiencing any performance or response time gain

You should make sure that the statistics on the table are analyzed and kept up-to-date so the optimizer can choose the best execution plan. This can be done by running the analyze command on all the tables initially, and then again when significant changes (addition/deletion of many records) are made to the tables.

Database statistics must be generated on a regular basis to obtain a baseline for measuring performance and diagnosing problems with the performance of the system.

> **NOTE**
>
> BSTAT/ESTAT reports can be generated to obtain database performance statistics.

Considerations During Migration

In a single-CPU database system, the goal is to eliminate fragmentation so the CPU can perform operations, such as table scans, by reading the data sequentially and not jumping around reading multiple disks. On a multiple-CPU system, the goal is just the opposite: You try to spread the data across disks and minimize I/O bottlenecks.

Administration tasks in Oracle systems can be complex, and you should try to simplify them by changing the number of object owners. In other words, determine whether the object ownership in the current model can be simplified by changing the ownership of objects from multiple users to fewer (if possible, a single user) users. You should also revisit the security model to use the Oracle features such as roles.

A database migrated from MS Access will not perform very well if you do not increase the system resources. System resources that can help include

- Using faster CPUs
- Using faster disks
- Using more disks and reorganizing the data on the drives to take advantage of additional disks
- Using additional memory

The initialization parameters for Oracle8*i* should be increased to reflect the additional system resources. For example, after adding more memory, you should modify the init.ora parameters, such as

- Increase DB_BLOCK_BUFFERS to increase the database buffer
- Increase SHARED_POOL_SIZE to increase the shared pool
- Increase CPU_COUNT to take advantage of the additional CPUs

15

MIGRATING FROM
NON-ORACLE
DATABASES

Oracle recommends using the Optimal Flexible Architecture (OFA) to organize your data. Use of OFA simplifies the process of future upgrades and also helps during day-to-day maintenance.

> **NOTE**
>
> MS Access CHAR columns should be changed to VARCHAR2 columns in Oracle8*i*. This will save space by removing white space, and also improve performance by reducing the time to retrieve data and transmit it across the network.

> **NOTE**
>
> Most queries involving primary and foreign keys perform comparison operations, and therefore it would be beneficial to change the primary and foreign keys from CHAR to integer.

Query Tuning

Tuning queries is a major process when a migration from a prototype or a small database, such as MS Access, to an enterprise database, such as Oracle8*i*, is performed. It has been found that the biggest performance gains (75–80%) can be obtained by tuning your applications. Oracle8*i* allows you to obtain a SQL_TRACE of queries being run to determine the execution plan of the query. One of the most important things to consider is make sure that the indexes are used properly. Applications in MS Access make use of forms and queries (which can be generated by example). You can take a look at the Oracle dynamic view V$SQLTEXT to determine the SQL being executed. Tracing can be set on the statement and timing statistics generated to determine the execution plan for the query and the time it takes to execute it.

MS Access databases are commonly used as prototypes and might not use traditional database structures such as constraints. Also, indexes might not be used properly. You should make sure you are using primary and foreign keys in the database. Also, make sure the primary keys are not nulls. All the mandatory columns should have "NOT NULL" constraints so columns that do not have any data cannot contain blanks.

NOTE

Microsoft Access databases are identified by files with the extension .mdb.

The primary keys can be of any datatype, but the most efficient primary keys are integers. Applications can commonly be of the character or date datatype, or even composite consisting of several columns. Integer comparisons are straightforward, but character columns have to be compared character by character, and therefore index lookups are much faster on integer columns. Date datatypes are worse for primary keys because they use date ranges for comparison instead of equality operations. Instead of composite keys, you can obtain better performance by using a sequence to generate unique values.

Prototypes are more than likely not normalized and might contain redundant data. You should revisit the design of your database to make sure that any denormalization is for performance reasons and not due to improper design.

Performance gains can be achieved by using the SGA of Oracle and minimizing the parsing of similar SQL statements. This indicates you should make sure the SQL statements are similar for the different users, and variables should be passed as parameters. The SGA will cache the statements and recognize frequently executed SQL statements and avoid parsing them.

Client-side caching can be used in client/server applications. Data that remains fairly stable can be stored in the client cache and used on subsequent calls to reduce network traffic because the application does not have to wait for a response from the database server.

Identify SQL statements and program logic that can benefit from the use of stored procedures and triggers. Stored procedures are already parsed and minimize network traffic. The program logic can be placed in stored procedures and parameters can be passed as needed.

MS Access applications generally perform sequentially. The user clicks on a button on a form, the code behind the button is executed, the client waits for a response, and the results are displayed. You will benefit by taking advantage of the parallel executions allowed by Oracle8*i*. Parallelism can be used for operations such as running jobs in the background, full tables scans, large sorts, asynchronous communication between client and server, concurrent users, and summary data.

Query Tuning Using SQL Trace and TKPROF

When a SQL statement does not perform well, you can use SQL Trace and TKPROF to gather performance statistics and then rewrite the query to improve its performance. When SQL*Trace is used on a SQL statement, it generates a trace file (.trc) with the following information:

- Parse, execute, and fetch counts
- Number of rows processed by the statement
- CPU and elapsed times
- Disk statistics that include physical and logical reads
- Library cache statistics

The following steps can be used to tune a SQL statement that doesn't perform satisfactorily:

1. Set the following parameters in the init.ora file:
   - MAX_DUMP_FILE_SIZE (specifies the maximum size of the trace file generated)
   - USER_DUMP_DEST (specifies the destination of the trace file generated)

   Timing information can be obtained at the instance level or at the session level. Similarly, SQL_TRACE can be set at the instance or at the session level. If you plan to set them at the instance level, you can also set the following init.ora parameters to TRUE:
   - TIMED_STATISTICS
   - SQL_TRACE

   In this example, you will use the settings at the session level.

2. Start the database instance using Server Manager.
   ```
   C:\>svrmgrl
   SVRMGR>startup pfile=<location of init.ora>
   ```

3. Set SQL_TRACE and TIMED_STATISTICS at the session level.
   ```
   SVRMGR>alter session set SQL_TRACE=TRUE
   SVRMGR>alter session set TIMED_STATISTICS=TRUE
   ```

4. Run the problem SQL statement.

5. Turn off SQL_TRACE and TIMED_STATISTICS.
   ```
   SVRMGR>alter session set SQL_TRACE=FALSE
   SVRMGR>alter session set TIMED_STATISTICS=FALSE
   ```

6. Format the trace file by using TKPROF.

7. Interpret the trace file and take appropriate action to improve the performance of the SQL statement.

The TKPROF utility is provided by Oracle to format the trace file generated by SQL_TRACE to be more readable. You can refer to the Oracle server tuning manual for detailed information about the syntax and interpretation of the TKPROF output file. Table 15.3 shows the most commonly used TKPROF parameters.

TABLE 15.3 TKPROF Options

TKPROF Option	*Purpose*
TRACEFILE	The trace file to be formatted.
OUTPUTFILE	The formatted output file.
EXPLAIN=user/password	TKPROF connects to Oracle using the specified username and password, and generates execution plans by running EXPLAIN PLAN in this schema. The specified user must have CREATE SESSION privileges.
TABLE=schema.tablename	By default, the execution plan is placed in the table 'plan_table'. This option is used to specify an alternative table to use. If the table exists, the user must be able to INSERT, SELECT, and DELETE from this table. If this table does not exist, TKPROF creates, uses, and then drops the table. In this case, the user must be able to CREATE and DROP table in addition to inserting, selecting, and deleting from the table. This option allows multiple individuals to run TKPROF concurrently using the same user in the EXPLAIN PLAN, but a different value of TABLE option so that their results are separated.
SYS=NO	Ignore recursive SQL run as SYS.
SORT=option	Specifies the order in which to sort the SQL statements.

The following example makes use of TKPROF to format a trace file called 'megh_trace.trc' to an output file called 'megh_trace.out'. Recursive SQL statements will be omitted, and the explain plan generated by using the schema SCOTT is placed in the table megh.plan_table.

```
C:\> TKPROF megh_trace.trc megh_trace.out SYS=NO
```

➡ EXPLAIN=SCOTT/TIGER TABLE=megh.plan_table

The TKPROF option SYS can be set to NO, which will prevent the SQL statements run as user SYS from being displayed, in turn making the output file small and easy to interpret.

You can also make use of the sort option of TKPROF to sort the SQL statements in the order of resource intensive statements. This can help you in quickly identifying the most inefficient statements and concentrating on improving their performance. For example, the sort option 'fchela' will order the output by elapsed time fetching. The sort options available for use can be obtained by typing **tkprof** at the command prompt.

TKPROF will display important statistics for each SQL statement as shown in Table 15.4.

15

> **NOTE**
>
> In order to obtain timing statistics for the SQL statements, you will have to set TIMED_STATISTICS to TRUE.

TABLE 15.4 Statistics Displayed by TKPROF for Each SQL Statement

TKPROF Statistics	Usage
Call	Activities of each cursor are divided into three areas: • Parse statistics (statistics for parsing the cursor, including plan generation and so on) • Execution statistics (statistics for the execution phase of the cursor) • Fetch statistics (statistics for fetching the rows)
Count	Indicates the number of times a particular activity was performed on this cursor
CPU	CPU time in seconds used to perform each phase
Elapsed	Elapsed time in seconds
Disk	Number of physical blocks read
Query	Logical buffers read for read consistency (usually used by SELECT statements)
Current	Logical buffers read for current mode (usually used for DML statements)
Rows	Number of rows processed

Let us consider an example of an output from TKPROF that shows such statistics:

```
|call    |count  |cpu   |elapsed |disk |query |current |rows |
|------- |-------|----- |--------|-----|------|--------|-----|
|Parse   |   8   | 211  |  3.95  | 398 | 428  |  19    | 0   |
|Execute |   8   | 0.04 |  0.07  |  0  |  0   |   0    | 0   |
|Fetch   |   6   | 1.12 |  3.53  | 198 | 904  |   8    | 5   |
```

The above output can be interpreted as follows:

- The particular SQL statement returned five rows after reading 904 blocks and performing eight parses. Also, the CPU utilization is high (211 seconds) compared to the execute times (0.04 and 0.07). This indicates overparsing and you should consider tuning your library cache.

- The hit ratio can be determined:

  Logical Reads = Consistent Gets + DB Block Gets
  Logical Reads = query + current
  Logical Reads = (0+904) + (0+8)
  Logical Reads = 912
  Hit Ratio = 1–(Physical Reads/Logical Reads)
  Hit Ratio = 1–(198/912)
  Hit Ratio = 1–(0.217)
  Hit Ratio = 0.7829 or 78.29%

You can improve the hit ratio by increasing the DB_BLOCK_BUFFERS init.ora parameter.

Using the Oracle Migration Assistant for Microsoft Access

MS Access databases can be migrated to Oracle8*i* using a GUI tool provided by Oracle—
Oracle Migration Assistant for Microsoft Access. The wizard it provides will give you
step-by-step help during the migration process. Most of the migration is automatic; however
there might be several post-migration tasks, such as verifying that the datatypes and macros are
converted without problems. The following steps show how you can perform such a migration
on Windows NT:

1. Choose Start, Programs, Oracle for Windows NT, Oracle Migration Assistant.
2. The database that you want to migrate can be chosen in the Select Database dialog box
   by clicking the Add Database button.
3. Click Next.
4. Click the Customize button and customize the mapping of Access datatypes to Oracle
   datatypes.
5. Click Next.
6. The portions of the database that you want to migrate can be chosen. Tables, indexes,
   relationships, default values, validation rules, or entire databases can be migrated.
7. Click Next.
8. Now you can choose to migrate the database structure only or both the structure and the data.
9. Click Next.
10. Now choose the Oracle schema and the tablespace into which you want to migrate the data.

NOTE

Multiple MS Access databases can be migrated into the same Oracle database.

11. Supply a valid DBA account and password.

12. The migration proceeds and this will be indicated by a progress bar. Upon completion, a migration log will be generated. View this log for any error generated during the migration process.

Summary

Database applications are moved from one DBMS to another for a variety of reasons such as performance enhancement, cost effectiveness, and politics. When migrating a non-Oracle database such as MS SQL Server or MS Access to Oracle8*i*, you should understand very well the differences as well as the similarities between the DBMSs.

No matter which DBMS you are trying to migrate to Oracle8*i*, there is no inherent performance benefit unless you take advantage of the inherent features of Oracle8*i*. You should also prepare the source database for migration by making any changes necessary so that the migration occurs smoothly and the post-migration steps are minimal.

Using the Oracle8*i* Features

IN THIS PART

Partitioning

IN THIS CHAPTER

Partitioning relies on the concept of divide-and-conquer. A large object is broken down into smaller pieces that can be managed separately and more efficiently. Very large databases have certain special needs that cannot be satisfied by using the "standard" strategies for databases. When dealing with very large databases, you encounter unique challenges when it comes to availability and performance of the database. This is purely because of the amount of data involved. Oracle7 attempted to simplify the problem by means of partition views. However, partition views are not easy to manage and are also inefficient. Oracle8 introduced the partitioning feature to help DBAs deal with this problem. Oracle8*i* provides more features to make the use of partitioning simple and efficient.

Understanding Partitions

Oracle8 allows you to use partitioned tables and indexes. Partitioning a table consists of specifying a number of discrete files or partitions that will be used to store the table data in such a way that each partition stores a certain range of data as determined by a key value (partition key).

As an example, consider a table that stores the sale of products. This table stores sales only for the year 1997. A possible partitioning scheme consists of splitting the table into partitions based on the quarter in which the sale was made:

```
SQL> create table sale_1997
2 (order_id number not null,
3 prod_id number not null,
4 quantity number,
5 sale_date date)
6 partition by range (sale_date) (
7 partition sale97_q1
8 values less than ('04-01-1997')
9 tablespace sale97_q1,
10 partition sale97_q2
11 values less than ('07-01-1997')
12 tablespace sale97_q2,
13 partition sale97_q3
14 values less than ('10-01-1997')
15 tablespace sale97_q3,
16 partition sale97_q4
17 values less than ('01-01-1998')
18 tablespace sale97_q4);
```

The following guidelines should be used to determine whether to partition a table:

- When you are migrating from Oracle7 to Oracle8*i*, look for objects that are defined in Oracle7 as UNION VIEWs and make them partitioned tables in Oracle8*i*. The number of partitions might not necessarily match, but the reason for using a partition table in Oracle8*i* is not very different from using a UNION VIEW in Oracle7.
- Tables greater than 2GB should be partitioned.
- Tables used to perform parallel data manipulation language (PDML) operations.
- Historical tables or other large tables where most of the data is read-only. Only a portion of the data in the table is "current".
- Tables in a parallel server environment that are accessed by multiple instances.
- Tables on which parallel index scans are to be performed.
- Tables containing data that might need to be offlined for maintenance or some other reason.

Partitioned indexes can be one of four types (also refer to Table 16.1):

- Local Prefixed Index—A local index is prefixed if it is partitioned on a left prefix of the index columns. *Left prefix* refers to the index column that is used by the optimizer. For example, if a composite index is based on (order_id, prod_id, state_id) then the left prefix for this index is 'order_id'. Local prefixed indexes can be unique or non-unique.
- Local Non-Prefixed Index—A local index that is not partitioned on a left prefix of the index columns is called *non-prefixed*. A local non-prefixed index can be unique only if the index key is a subset of the partitioning key.
- Global Prefixed Index—When data in the underlying partitioned table is moved or deleted, all partitions of a global index are affected. Likewise, recovering a partitioned table to a point-in-time requires that the global index be recovered to the same point in time.
- Global Non-Prefixed Index—These are not supported in Oracle8*i*.

TABLE **16.1**   Partitioned Indexes in Oracle8*i*

Index Type	*Is Index Equi-partitioned with Underlying Table?*	*Is Index Partitioned on Left of Index Columns?*	*Can the Index Be Unique?*
Local Prefixed	Y	Y	Y
Local Non-Prefixed	Y	N	N
Global Prefixed	N	Y	Y
Global Non-Prefixed	Not Supported	Not Supported	Not Supported

In a local index, all keys in the index partition are mapped to corresponding rows in the table partition. There is no overlap of keys from any other table partition resulting in the simplification of the index maintenance process. This kind of independence makes it possible to perform multiple operations simultaneously on different partitions. For example, for the same partitioned table, all the following might be happening at the same time:

- Index rebuild on partition p1
- Direct path load on partition p2
- Offline maintenance on partition p3
- Standard SQL queries running against partition p4

A global index might include more than one partition in its range. A global index is created with the "global" attribute and is normally not equipartitioned with the underlying table. For example, suppose that we have a table "phone_list" that contains the phone numbers of various people:

```
SQL> create table phone_list
2 (lastname     varchar2(20),
3 firstname     varchar2(20),
4 phone1_prefix     number(3),
5 phone1_num     number(10),
6 phone2_prefix     number(3),
7 phone2_num     number(10))
8 partition by range(phone1_prefix)
9 (partition p1 values less than (400)
10 tablespace p1_tab storage
11 (initial 1m, next 1m, pctincrease 0),
12 partition p2 values less than (600)
13 tablespace p2_tab storage
14 (initial 1m, next 1m, pctincrease 0),
15 partition p3 values less than (800)
16 tablespace p3_tab storage
17 (initial 1m, next 1m, pctincrease 0),
18 partition p4 values less than (maxvalue)
19 tablespace p4_tab storage
20 (initial 5m, next 5m, pctincrease 0);
```

You can now create a local prefixed index on this table using the area codes as a partition key:

```
SQL> create index phone_local_idx
2 on phone_list(phone1_prefix)
3 local
4 partition by range(phone1_prefix)
5 (partition idx_p1
6 tablespace p1_idx storage
```

```
7 (initial 1m, next 1m, pctincrease 0),
8 partition idx_p2
9 tablespace p2_idx storage
10 (initial 1m, next 1m, pctincrease 0),
11 partition p3_idx
12 tablespace p3_idx storage
13 (initial 1m, next 1m, pctincrease 0),
14 partition p4_idx
15 tablespace p4_idx storage
16 (initial 5m, next 5m, pctincrease 0);
```

A global index can be created on the phone_list table using the last_name column. This index would span multiple partitions and is not going to be as easy to manage as the local index on the phone1_prefix column. Further, when using a global index, the optimizer will not be able to eliminate partitions from the query plan.

> **NOTE**
>
> Oracle treats non-partitioned indexes as global indexes.

The following things should be understood when dealing with a partitioned object:

- NULL values are placed in the last partition of a table.
- All partitions must have the same logical attributes such as number of columns, datatypes, and constraints, but they can have different physical attributes such as initrans, pctused, and pctfree.
- Partitioning can be done on numbers as well as character values.
- It is possible to have multi-column partition keys.

> **NOTE**
>
> It is more difficult to manage global indexes than it is to manage local indexes.

> **NOTE**
>
> Unique prefixed indexes enable you to access the desired data by accessing only one index partition, whereas non-unique prefixed indexes ensure that you will access only one index partition if the entire partition key is specified in the WHERE clause of the query.

When working with partitioned tables, the following things should be considered:

- The layout of the tablespace for a specific partitioned table should be such that it provides optimal access to the partitioned table.
- The size of a tablespace should be large enough to hold the volume of data belonging to the associated table partition.
- Plan enough separation between all the partitioned objects in the table such that they do not interfere with each other in terms of space usage and performance impact.
- Determine the optimal backup strategy based on your application environment such that partitions can be offlined as needed without affecting other partitions in the system. It is important to realize that offlining a partition will cause queries that try to access this partition to fail.

The possibility of tables being partitioned as well as non-partitioned, along with indexes being partitioned and non-partitioned, adds a bit of complexity to their usage and Table 16.2 tries to simplify this relationship.

TABLE **16.2**   Using Partitioning with Tables and Indexes

	On Partitioned Table	*On Non-partitioned Table*
Partitioned Index	Allowed	Allowed
Non-Partitioned Index	Allowed	Allowed
Bitmap Index	Must be a local index	Cannot be partitioned

When working with partitioned indexes, the following should be considered:

- Should I use a global index or a local index for a particular situation?
- If using local index, should I use a prefixed or a non-prefixed local index?
- How do I choose the best approach for simplifying the management of global indexes?
- How do I partition the underlying tables to exploit the parallel query capabilities of Oracle8*i*?

NOTE

For OLTP systems, a global index might provide better performance than a local index because of the minimal number of index probes involved in such environments.

It is possible for an index in a partitioned environment to be marked as "Index Unusable" (IU). The main reasons for an index to become unusable are as follows:

- Actions, such as "alter table move partition", that change the ROWIDs of local or global indexes.
- Actions, such as "alter table truncate partition", that remove rows from a table.
- An unsuccessful direct path SQL*Loader operation.
- An IMPORT PARTITION or a conventional path SQL*Loader operation that bypasses the management of local indexes.

Before attempting to use an index marked as IU, you must rebuild the index.

NOTE

The following maintenance operations are the common causes of an index becoming unusable:

- Alter table split partition
- Alter table truncate partition
- Alter table move partition
- Alter index split partition
- A direct path SQL*Loader operation that fails
- An import partition used with the option to bypass the index

Partition Views

In Oracle7, partitioning was implemented with the help of partition views. Using partition views involved physically breaking up the table into smaller parts and storing it on different disks according to some user-specified criteria such as the employees of a company based upon the location of the employee—north, south , east, and west. This can be implemented using check constraints that enforce the requirement that there is no overlapping between rows in different "partitions."

Instead of manually splitting the table, another alternative is to set the initialization parameter 'partition_view_enabled' to TRUE. This informs the optimizer that there might be tables that are partitioned in such a way that the WHERE clause could restrict the search to a subset of

the table. The resulting increase in efficiency greatly benefits full-table scans and large index scans. The following example shows how a partition view can be created:

```
SQL> create table q1_sales_curyear
2 (order_id     number(5),
3 cust_id     number(5),
4 item_id     number(5),
5 quantity     number(5),
6 price number(4),
7 sale_day     number(2),
8 sale_month number(2));

SQL> create table q2_sales_curyear
2 (order_id     number(5),
3 cust_id     number(5),
4 item_id     number(5),
5 quantity     number(5),
6 price number(4),
7 sale_day     number(2),
8 sale_month number(2));

SQL> create table q3_sales_curyear
2 (order_id     number(5),
3 cust_id     number(5),
4 item_id     number(5),
5 quantity     number(5),
6 price number(4),
7 sale_day     number(2),
8 sale_month number(2));

SQL> create table q4_sales_curyear
2 (order_id     number(5),
3 cust_id     number(5),
4 item_id     number(5),
5 quantity     number(5),
6 price number(4),
7 sale_day     number(2),
8 sale_month number(2));

SQL> alter table q1_sales_curyear
2 add constraint chkmonth check
3 (sale_month between 1 and 3);

SQL> alter table q2_sales_curyear
2 add constraint chkmonth check
3 (sale_month between 4 and 6);

SQL> alter table q3_sales_curyear
2 add constraint chkmonth check
```

```
3 (sale_month between 7 and 9);

SQL> alter table q4_sales_curyear
2 add constraint chkmonth check
3 (sale_month between 10 and 12);

SQL> create view sales_curyear as
2 select * from q1_sales_curyear union all
3 select * from q2_sales_curyear union all
4 select * from q3_sales_curyear union all
5 select * from q4_sales_curyear;
```

As seen from the preceding example, Oracle7 implemented partitioning with the help of an initialization parameter, constraints, and views. However, the various horizontal fragments of the partition view are actual tables. This kind of partitioning scheme requires you to manage each underlying table individually.

Oracle8*i* takes partitioning to a much higher level by introducing a new physical layer in the database storage architecture. In Oracle8*i*, a partitioned table is mapped to a set of partitions that are each mapped one-to-one to a set of extents. Each extent is mapped to a tablespace that contains one or more datafiles. In addition, partitioning is now part of the SQL Data Definition language (DDL), making it possible for the optimizer to exploit this feature without the need to use any initialization parameter.

Maintenance Operations on Partitions

Partitioning is a very powerful feature that can be used to simplify management of very large tables. However, you will have to periodically revisit your partitioning strategy and make any necessary adjustments to reflect your current environment. There are two statements—alter table and alter index—that can be used to perform most of the partition management tasks that you might need to perform.

The following extensions to the 'alter table' statement can be used for partitions:

- Add partition
- Drop partition
- Rename partition
- Truncate partition
- Modify partition
- Move partition
- Split partition
- Exchange partition

The following extensions to the 'alter index' statement can be used for partitions:

- Drop partition
- Rename partition
- Modify partition
- Split partition
- Rebuild partition
- Parallel
- Unusable

The following example makes use of the 'phone_list' table to demonstrate some of these operations:

- Split the table 'phone_list' to break up the 800 and the 900 area code phone numbers.

```
SQL> alter table phone_list
2 split partition p4
3 at (900)
4 into (partition p4, partition p5);
```

- The 800 numbers have increased dramatically, and you need to move the partition p4 into a new tablespace 'p4_tab_big'.

```
SQL> alter table phone_list
2 move partition p4
3 tablespace p4_tab_big;
```

An exchange operation can be used to convert a partition to a non-partitioned table or convert a non-partitioned table to a partition of a partitioned table.

- In our phone_list table, we currently do not have any phone number for area codes in the range 400 through 600, but we have created a dummy partition. Now we have a table 'ph400600' with the same structure as the phone_list table, but that is non-partitioned and contains only area codes 400 through 600. The following command can be used to exchange this table and "merge" it into our partitioning scheme:

```
SQL> alter table phone_list
2 exchange partition p2
3 with table ph400600
4 including indexes;
```

NOTE

By default, the exchange operation does not include indexes but performs validation.

16

As objects become bigger, the administrative effort to manage the object, perform backups and restores, build indexes, and perform operations such as querying the object becomes increasingly difficult. Partitions provide the following advantages:

- Improved availability—In a partitioned table, even if one or more partitions are unavailable because of system failure or scheduled maintenance, it is still possible to access the rest of the table.
- Fast recovery—If you need to restore portions of a table, you can do so without affecting the rest of the table. In addition, the entire recovery can be performed in parallel.
- Load balancing—I/O load can be balanced by mapping the different partitions to different disks.
- Improved query performance—Partitioning allows you to narrow the focus of query processing to particular partitions. This can have considerable performance improvement provided the table is well partitioned.
- Ease of maintenance—Table maintenance operations such as export, import, and index rebuilding can be much faster and easier because the operations can be performed independently on each partition.

NOTE

Only tables and indexes can be partitioned.

The following objects cannot be partitioned:

- Clusters
- Nested tables
- Index-organized tables
- Snapshots
- Snapshot logs
- Tables that are part of a cluster
- Tables that contain columns of the long, LOBs, long raw, or object datatypes
- Cluster indexes
- Indexes defined on a cluster table

> **NOTE**
>
> Local bitmap indexes cannot be created on individual partitions of a partitioned table.

Partitioning Models

Three types of partitioning models are supported by Oracle8*i*: range partitioning, hash partitioning, and composite partitioning. These methods basically differ in the manner in which they partition the data in the table. Prior to Oracle8*i*, partitioning techniques were very limited (only partition views in Oracle7, and the addition of range partitioning in Oracle8), but Oracle8*i* provides significant enhancements to this important feature.

Range Partition

Range partition is used to partition a table and map its rows to a partition, based on a range of values in a column. When partitioning a table or index by range, the following clauses are used:

- Partition by range (column_list)—column_list specifies the list of columns whose values are used in the range partitioning scheme.
- values less than (value_list)—This clause specifies for a particular partition the range of values that it contains. Each value in the value_list is either a literal, a to_date(), or rpad() function with constant arguments.

> **NOTE**
>
> For each partition, its bound must compare less than the partition bound for the next partition. Also, unless it is the first partition, all the partition key values in a given partition must be greater than or equal to the partition bound of the previous partition.

Historical tables are examples of where range partitioning can be used.

Hash Partitioning

Hash partitioning is an alternative technique that can be used to partition a table by applying a hash function on the partitioning columns. Hash partitioning is better suited than range partitioning for the following cases:

- The amount of data that is mapped to a given range is not known beforehand.
- The size of partitions would not be very uniform if range partition is applied.
- You want to perform extensive partition pruning.
- You want to make extensive use of partition-wise joins.

> **NOTE**
>
> Partition pruning refers to the process of eliminating parts of a table for access by a SQL statement by using the knowledge that they are partitioned.

The biggest benefit of hash partitioning is seen when the number of partitions is a power of 2. Local indexes on hash partitions are equipartitioned and hash partitions allow you to name and store the partitions in specific tablespaces. Hash partitions are created using the 'partition by hash' clause. The following example hash partitions the customers table:

```
SQL> create table customers
2 (cust_id    number(10),
3 cust_name    varchar2(40),
4 cust_addr varchar2(60),
5 cust_bal    number(20),
6 credit_limit    number(20))
7 storage (initial 5M)
8 partition by hash (cust_id)
9 ( partition cp1 tablespace th1,
10 partition cp2 tablespace th2,
11 partition cp3 tablespace th3,
12 partition cp4 tablespace th4);
```

The following operations cannot be performed on hash partitions:

- Splitting partitions
- Merging partitions
- Dropping partitions

Composite Partitioning

Composite partition gives the best of both range and hash partitioning in one scheme. It uses range partitioning to partition the table. Each partition is then further sub-partitioned using hash partitioning. Composite partitioning provides the following advantages:

- Ease of management of range partitioning
- Parallel operations enhancement of hash partitioning
- Capability of storing subpartitions in specific tablespaces
- Ability to build range partitioned global indexes
- Ability to build local indexes that can be stored in the same tablespace as the table subpartition

The following example uses composite partitioning to break the table into partitions based on range of area codes, and then each partition is sub-partitioned using lastname:

```
SQL> create table phone_list
2 (lastname     varchar2(20),
3 firstname     varchar2(20),
4 phone1_prefix     number(3),
5 phone1_num     number(10),
6 phone2_prefix     number(3),
7 phone2_num     number(10))
8 partition by range(phone1_prefix)
9 subpartition by hash (lastname) subpartitions 4
10 store in (t1, t2, t3, t4)
11 (partition p1 values less than (400)
12 tablespace p1_tab storage
13 (initial 1m, next 1m, pctincrease 0),
14 partition p2 values less than (600)
15 tablespace p2_tab storage
16 (initial 1m, next 1m, pctincrease 0),
17 partition p3 values less than (800)
18 tablespace p3_tab storage
19 (initial 1m, next 1m, pctincrease 0),
20 partition p4 values less than (maxvalue)
21 tablespace p4_tab storage
22 (initial 5m, next 5m, pctincrease 0);
```

Using Partition and Sub-partition Names

In Oracle8*i*, query processing can be optimized by focusing on particular partitions and sub-partitions. Extensions to DDL and DML statements are provided by the ability to name partitions and sub-partitions.

NOTE

The partitioning key can consist of up to 16 columns and not include any of the following:

- A LEVEL or ROWID pseudocolumn
- ROWID datatype
- nested table, VARRAY, object, or REF
- LOB column (BLOB, CLOB, NCLOB, or BFILE datatype)

Partition-extended and Sub-partitioned Extended Table Names

Oracle8*i* allows you to name partitions and sub-partitions. These names must conform to the following guidelines:

- The name of a table partition or sub-partition must be unique to all partitions and sub-partitions belonging to the same table.
- The name of an index partition or sub-partition must be unique to all partitions and sub-partitions belonging to the same index.

NOTE

Partition and sub-partition can be renamed, but you cannot create synonyms based on the names of partitions and sub-partitions.

Partition and sub-partition names can be referenced in DDL and DML statements, as well as utilities such as import/export/sql*loader, but they are associated always with the context of their parent. For example,

```
SQL> Select *
2 from customers
3 partition (sp2) csp2
4 where csp2.balance > 10000;
```

Oracle8*i* allows you to perform bulk operations on specific partitions or sub-partitions only. This is achieved by allowing you to specify the partition to be affected by the operation. The specification of the following DML statements contains an optional PARTITION specification

for partitioned tables and an optional PARTITION or SUBPARTITION specification for composite partitioned tables:

- Select
- Insert
- Update
- Delete
- Lock table

Using such extended table names allows you to focus on particular partitions only and improves the performance of your statements. However, it does require you to be familiar with the logical structure of the database a bit more than usual and also become aware of the data distribution. The following example operates only on the 3rd quarter of the sales table:

```
SQL> select *
2 from megh.sales partition sq3;
```

> **NOTE**
>
> For auditing partitioned tables, you don't need to do anything special. The normal audit setting for 'alter table' command would work just fine.

Equipartitioning

Equipartitioning allows you to perform partition-wise joins. *Partition-wise join* refers to the process of splitting a large join operation into smaller join operations based on the partitions.

> **NOTE**
>
> Partition-wise joins might be performed sequentially or in parallel.

Two tables of indexes are equipartitioned when all the following is true:

- They use the same partitioning method.
- They have the same partitioning columns.
- They use the same number of partitions.

- If they use range partitioning, they must use the same partition bound.
- If one or both are composite partitioned, they must be equipartitioned on at least one method (range or hash).

NOTE

Equipartitioned objects do not have to be the same type. For example, a table and an index can be equipartitioned.

Equipartitioning makes it easy to perform point-in-time recovery because you can recover the corresponding partitions of associated objects to a point-in-time.

Data Dictionary Views

A variety of Data Dictionary views are available for information about the partitioned objects in your database. The most commonly used views are mentioned as follows:

- all_ind_partitions—For each index partition, it describes the partition information, storage information, and partition statistics gathered by the ANALYZE command. This information is for the current user.
- all_ind_subpartitions—For each index subpartition, it describes the partition information, storage information, and partition statistics gathered by the ANALYZE command. This information is for the current user.
- all_part_col_statistics—Provides column statistics and histogram information for all table partitions that can be accessed by the current user.
- all_part_indexes—Provides information about all partitioned indexes that can be accessed by the current user.
- all_part_key_columns—Provides information about the partition key columns belonging to the partitioned objects that can be accessed by the current user.
- all_part_tables—Provides information about all partitioned tables that can be accessed by the current user.

NOTE

For each of the preceding dictionary views, there are corresponding DBA views with the prefix 'dba_'.

Summary

Very large databases present significant challenges to the Oracle DBA because of the amount of data that needs to be managed while maintaining the performance and availability of the system. One of the biggest features provided by Oracle8*i* is the ability to partition the tables and indexes using range-based as well as hash-based techniques.

Partitioning results in several advantages including ease of management, performance improvement, and high availability. Partitioning allows you to use techniques such as partition pruning and partition-wise joins to eliminate access to unnecessary data and simply focus on the relevant data.

Parallel Executions

IN THIS CHAPTER

When you submit SQL statements to Oracle, by default they are executed sequentially. Performance of SQL operations can be greatly improved by executing them in parallel. Oracle8*i* allows you to perform not only queries but also DML operations in parallel. The operations that can be performed in parallel include

- Table scans
- Create table as select (CTAS)
- Create index
- Rebuild index
- Update
- Insert
- Delete
- Star transformation
- Partition management, such as moving and splitting of partitions
- Order-by operations
- Group-by operations
- Select distinct
- Union operations
- Join operations, such as hash joins, sort merge joins, and nested loop joins

In order to effectively use parallel execution, you should make sure that all the following are true for your system. Otherwise, you might actually find a degradation in performance due to the additional load that will be placed on your system by parallel executions.

- You should be using symmetric multiprocessors (SMP), clusters of massively parallel systems.
- Sufficient bandwidth to support the additional I/O occurring in the system.
- Under-utilized CPUs that can take the additional load. This is especially useful if you are planning to use adaptive tuning (discussed later).
- A large amount of memory to support the additional memory-intensive processes, such as sorts and hashing.

Parallel executions are ideal for Decision Support Systems (DSS) because the complex queries being run can be optimally run in parallel. However, Online Transaction Processing (OLTP) systems are not ideal for parallel operations because they are usually comprised of short transactions, which would not benefit from parallel executions (especially after you factor in the additional system requirements that are imposed by parallel executions).

> **NOTE**
>
> All the components of a SQL statement—query as well as DML—can be parallelized.

In this chapter, we will discuss various aspects of parallel operations, such as

- The parallel query architecture
- Parallel DML operations
- Enabling parallel operations
- Disabling parallel operations
- How to troubleshoot parallel operations
- How to perform parallel data loads
- How to perform database recovery in parallel
- The initialization parameters that affect parallel operations
- Data Dictionary views that can be used to obtain information on parallel operations

> **NOTE**
>
> In order to use all the parallel operations described in this chapter, you will need the enterprise edition of Oracle8*i*.

> **NOTE**
>
> You don't have to use the Oracle Parallel Server feature in order to use intra-instance parallelism.

Parallel DML Versus Manual Parallelism

Manual parallelism can be achieved by issuing multiple DML statements simultaneously, such that each of these DML statements uses a different range of ROWIDs. Using parallel DML instead of manual parallelization has several advantages:

- Parallel DML is easier to use because the parallelism is performed by Oracle.
- Each parallel DML is a separate transaction, and all the query slaves will work on a read-consistent snapshot of the target object and commit simultaneously.
- Load balancing can be achieved by using an efficient algorithm.

17

PARALLEL EXECUTIONS

Parallelization Methods

Several methods can be used to parallelize SQL operations:

- *Parallelize by means of ROWID*

  A range of ROWIDs is generally used to parallelize SELECTs and subqueries that are part of a DML or DDL statement. This method dynamically splits a table or index on which the operation is performed into ranges of ROWIDs, and the operation is performed in parallel on different ranges.

> **NOTE**
>
> Parallel operations by means of ROWIDs can be performed on partitioned as well as non-partitioned tables and indexes, but the range of ROWIDs cannot span partitions.

- *Parallelize by using partitions*

  This method is used to perform parallel operations on partitioned tables and indexes. Different parallel query server processes are assigned to the various partitions comprising a table or index. This method is used only when the following is true; otherwise parallelization by using range of ROWIDs is performed:

  - ALTER SESSION ENABLE PARALLEL DML command must be executed.
  - More than one partition is affected by the operation and more than a predetermined number of table or index pages are being accessed.

  When this method is used, a parallel server process can span partitions but there is no intra-partition parallelism. Therefore, the efficiency of this method is dependent upon how well the tables and indexes are partitioned.

- *Parallelize by using slave processes*

  This method is used for insert operations on nonpartitioned tables. New rows are inserted into the free space by using slave processes.

Restrictions on Using Parallel Operations

It would be nice if all SQL operations could be parallelized, but unfortunately that is not the case. There are several restrictions on the use of parallel operations that you should consider. Keep in mind, however, that in the worst case the operations will be performed sequentially:

- A parallel DML (PDML) must be the only statement in a transaction. If a parallel DML is placed after a sequential statement in a transaction, the PDML will be executed sequentially.

- Each PDML is considered to be a transaction on its own.

- A commit or rollback should immediately follow a PDML statement otherwise an error will occur. Oracle can use multiple rollback segments during a parallel DML. A two-phase commit mechanism is used to commit or roll back the transaction in all rollback segments in order to achieve data consistency.

- PDML can't be performed on tables that have Long Objects (LOBs) or abstract datatypes.

- PDML can't be used on clustered or replicated tables or on bitmap indexes.

NOTE

Setting SERIALIZABLE = TRUE in the init.ora file causes all PDML operations to be serialized.

- Global indexes are ignored by parallel updates.

- Remote tables can't be referenced by PDML.

- PDML doesn't allow the use of embedded functions that read or write database or package state.

NOTE

Inserts can perform intra-partition parallelism, but updates and deletes cannot.

Parallel Query Architecture

Each Oracle user session in a dedicated (non-MTS) environment uses a single, dedicated server thread. The client requests are processed by the corresponding shadow process. Communication between the client and the shadow process occurs by means of some inter-process communication method. Parallel operations make use of a query coordinator and several slave processes. The query coordinator (QC) performs several tasks:

- Divide the workload between PQ slave processes (as explained below) and perform load balancing

- Manage the work performed by the various slave processes

- Return the query results back to the client

The initialization parameter PARALLEL_MIN_SERVERS determines the number of parallel query slave processes that are started when an Oracle instance is started. The query coordinator (also called the master query process) coordinates these slave processes. The slave processes run as background processes waiting for work. Additional slave processes can be spawned by the master query process as needed by parallel operations, up to the maximum limit specified by PARALLEL_MAX_SERVERS. The dynamic view v$pq_sysstat can be used to obtain information about usage of the slave processes. For example, the following query will return the number of slave processes that are busy and the number that are idle for the current instance:

```
SQL> select nvl(b.value,0) pq_busy_cnt,
2> nvl(i.value,0) pq_idle_cnt
3> from sys.v$pq_sysstat b,
4> sys.v$pq_sysstate I
5> where b.statistic like 'Servers Busy%'
6> and i.statistic like 'Server Idle%';
```

The algorithm detailed in the next paragraph is used to balance the workload amongst the slave processes.

The query coordinator divides the target table into roughly equal-sized partitions so that the number of partitions equals the degree of parallelism. Each partition is then further subdivided into three subpartitions: one is 9/13ths of the original, another is 3/13ths of the original partition, and the remaining is 1/13th of the original partition. Figure 17.1 shows a table on which a full table scan is being performed with a degree of parallelism of six. The table is divided into six almost-equal-sized partitions. Each partition is further subdivided into three subpartitions sized 9/13, 3/13, and 1/13. Each slave process is initially assigned to one of the large (size 9/13th of the original partition size) subpartitions. After a slave process is finished working on its assigned subpartition, it starts working on a smaller (size 3/13th of the original partition size) subpartition. After all the 3/13th sized subpartitions are finished, the 1/13th sized subpartitions are worked on, and eventually the table is scanned in parallel with efficiently load balancing among the slave processes.

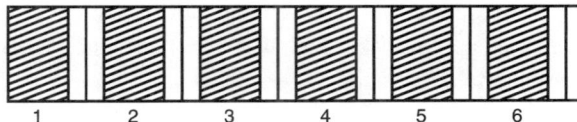

FIGURE 17.1

Table ABC is partitioned into six almost-equal-sized partitions and then further divided into 9/13th, 3/13th, and 1/13th sized subpartitions.

Using Initialization Parameters with Parallel Operations

The parallel DML features of Oracle8*i* don't require any particular option or cartridge to be installed, and can be used right after the installation of Oracle8*i* Server Enterprise Edition. However, you will need to set several initialization parameters (see Table 17.1) in order to use this feature efficiently.

TABLE 17.1   Initialization Parameters Affecting Parallel Operations

Parameter	Default Value	Purpose
Parallel_min_servers	0 (indicates that the slave processes will be started on demand	Specifies the number of parallel slave processes to start when the Oracle instance is started.
Parallel_max_servers	Depends on the values of cpu_count, parallel_automatic_tuning, and parallel_adaptive_multi_user	Specifies the maximum number of parallel slave or recovery processes that can be spawned.
Parallel_min_percent	0 (indicates that the parameter is not used)	Specifies the minimum percent of threads required for parallel execution, and prevents operations from being executed sequentially if enough resources are not available.
Parallel_automatic_tuning	FALSE (user-defined hints are used)	When set to TRUE, Oracle tunes the parallel operations. The target tables should be set to PARALLEL and user-defined hints will be ignored.
Parallel_adaptive_multi_user	Parallel_automatic_tuning	When set to TRUE, Oracle makes use of an adaptive algorithm to tune the operations automatically in a multiuser environment.
Parallel_threads_per_cpu	2	Specifies the number of threads that a CPU can handle while executing a parallel operation.
Fast_start_parallel_rollback	Low	Determines the maximum number of processes that may be used for performing parallel rollback. The valid values are • False: Disables parallel rollback. • Low: At the most, 2*CPU_COUNT number of processes are used.

continues

17

TABLE 17.1 Continued

Parameter	Default Value	Purpose
		• High: At the most, 4*CPU_COUNT number of processes are used.
Dml_locks	4*Transactions	Specifies the maximum number DML locks. One DML lock is used for each table that is modified in a transaction.
Large_pool_size	0	Specifies the size of the large pool allocation heap that is used by the message buffers during parallel execution. Message buffers are allocated if parallel_automatic_tuning is TRUE.
Parallel_broadcast_enabled	False	Used to improve the performance of hash and merge joins involving a large result set and a small resultset.
Parallel_execution_message_size	2048 (if parallel_automatic_tuning is false) or 4096 (if parallel_automatic_tuning is true)	Specifies the size of messages used for parallel execution operations.
Processes	Depends upon parallel_max_servers	Specifies the maximum number of operating system user processes (including parallel execution processes) that can simultaneously connect to an Oracle instance.
Recovery_parallelism	Operating system dependent	Specifies the number of parallel processes used during instance or media recovery.
Shared_pool_size	Operating system dependent	Specifies the size of the shared pool. Among other things, the shared pool contains the parallel message buffers if parallel_automatic_tuning is False.

Parallel DML requires many locks compared to a serial execution and you should increase the value of DML_LOCKS and ENQUEUE_RESOURCES parameters appropriately using the following guidelines.

The coordinator acquires

- One table-level SX lock

- One partition lock X per partition (unless a parallel update or parallel delete includes a where clause that limits the partitions involved)

and each slave process acquires

- One table-level SX lock
- One partition-level NULL lock per partition
- One partition-wait lock X per partition

For example, the number of locks held by a parallel update (degree two) on a table with six partitions are determined as follows:

- The coordinator has one table lock SX and six partition locks X
- The slave processes have two table locks SX, six partition NULL locks, and six partition-wait locks X

A total of 1+6+2+6+6 = 21 locks.

17

PARALLEL
EXECUTIONS

NOTE

Decrease the value of parallel_threads_per_cpu if the machine appears to be over-loaded, and increase its value if the system appears to be I/O bound.

NOTE

Parallel_max_servers is used to determine the size of large pool and other memory structures, and therefore you should not set it too high. Otherwise, you might have memory problems under heavy system loads.

NOTE

Adaptive tuning reduces the degree of parallelism when the number of users increases so that the resources are more evenly spread.

You can make use of various data dictionary views (see Table 17.2) in order to obtain information about parallel operations.

TABLE 17.2   Data Dictionary Views Providing Information on Parallel Operations

Data Dictionary View	Usage
V$pq_sesstat	Displays the statistics of parallel execution for the current session.
V$pq_sysstat	Displays the statistics of parallel execution for the entire system.
V$pq_slave	Displays the information about active parallel query slaves.
V$session	Determines whether PDML is enabled for a session.
V$transaction	Displays the status of a transaction.
V$pq_tqstat	Displays detailed information about the execution of each parallel query slave. It is useful in identifying skewed data.

Degree of Parallelism

The number of query processes used by a parallel execution operation is referred to as its *degree of parallelism*. Obviously, the degree of parallelism will play a crucial role in the eventual performance gain that will be realized. The degree of parallelism is dependent upon several factors:

- Hints specified in the parallel operation
- Initialization parameters
- The number of CPUs in the system
- The distribution of the target object over disks or files

The degree of parallelism can be specified at various levels:

- *At the SQL statement level*

  The degree of parallelism at the SQL statement level is specified by using hints:

  ```
  SELECT /*+ PARALLEL (employees,2) */ *
  FROM employees
  ```

- *At the object level*

  The CREATE and ALTER statements can be used to set the degree of parallelism at the object level for tables, clusters, indexes, and so on:

  ```
  Svrmgr> Alter table employees parallel(degree,4);
  ```

- *At the instance level*

  The default degree of parallelism for an instance depends on your system resources, such as CPU, memory, I/O bandwidth, initialization parameters, and distribution of data across the available disks.

Using Hints

Hints can be used to improve the performance of parallel executions. It should, however, be understood that if you are not familiar with the system peculiarities, you should use automatic tuning and let Oracle perform the tuning of parameters for you. However, knowledge of the system can help you in manual tuning by providing hints. The following hints can be used with parallel executions:

- PARALLEL specifies the degree of parallelism for parallel operations. The syntax for a parallel hint is

```
PARALLEL (table,x,y)
```

table is the table on which the parallel operation is to be performed, *x* is the desired degree of parallelism, and *y* is used only for a parallel server environment, specifying the number of instances that should run the SQL statement.

For example, the following can be executed from Server Manager to specify that you want to use a degree of parallelism of four when selecting from the emp table:

```
Svrmgr> select /*+PARALLEL(emp,4)*/ *
        From emp;
```

The PARALLEL clause in the CREATE INDEX statement can be used to create indexes in parallel. You can also use the NOLOGGING clause to prevent the generation of redo. However, NOLOGGING will make the index unrecoverable in case of index corruption, and therefore, you should export the table or back up the index after creation. For example, the following creates an index on the part_tab table with a degree of parallelism of four, and redo is not generated:

```
CREATE INDEX part_tab_idx
ON part_tab (col1)
        PARALLEL (degree, 4) NOLOGGING;
```

- NOPARALLEL specifies that the operation is to be performed serially. The degree of parallelism, if any, associated with the target object is ignored.

- APPEND specifies that an insert operation should use new free blocks to insert the data. Existing free blocks are ignored.

- NOAPPEND specifies that an insert operation should use existing free space in the blocks.

- PARALLEL_INDEX specifies that index range scans on a partitioned index should use parallel execution.

> **NOTE**
>
> The number of query slaves working on a partitioned table can't exceed the number of partitions.

Let us consider an example to verify that the number of slave processes cannot be more than the number of partitions and that a slave process can span multiple partitions:

1. Start Server Manager and connect as SCOTT:

```
C:\> svrmgrl
Svrmgr> connect scott/tiger
```

2. Create a table 'part_tab' with six partitions:

```
Svrmgr> CREATE TABLE part_tab (col1 number)
        PARTITION BY RANGE (col1)
        PARTITION P1 VALUES LESS THAN (5),
        PARTITION P2 VALUES LESS THAN (10),
        PARTITION P3 VALUES LESS THAN (15),
        PARTITION P4 VALUES LESS THAN (20),
        PARTITION P5 VALUES LESS THAN (25),
        PARTITION P6 VALUES LESS THAN (maxvalue);
```

3. Before you can perform parallel DML operations, you need to enable parallel DML for the session:

```
Svrmgr> alter session enable parallel dml;
```

4. Using v$session, verify that parallel DML was enabled:

```
Svrmgr> select username, pdml_enabled
        From v$session
        Where username = 'SCOTT';


USERNAME      PDM
--------      ----
SCOTT         YES
```

5. Insert sample rows into 'part_tab' from the dept table:

```
svrmgr> insert into part_tab
        select dept_id from dept;
```

6. Commit the insert operation:

```
      Svrmgr> commit;
```

7. Use parallel update to modify the part_tab table:

```
Svrmgr> update /*+parallel (part_tab,8) */ part_tab
        Set col1 = col1 * 2;
```

8. Commit the parallel update:

   Svrmgr> **commit;**

9. Determine the degree of parallelism:

   Svrmgr> **select * from v$pq_sysstat**
   **   Where statistic in ('Servers Busy','Server Sessions');**

   ```
   STATISTIC          VALUE
   --------------     -------
   Servers Busy       4
   Server Sessions    8
   ```

   The output shown verifies that although you specified eight parallel query slaves, only four are busy—one for each partition.

10. Use parallel delete to remove the values from the table:

    Svrmgr> **delete /*+parallel (part_tab,2) */ part_tab;**

11. Commit the parallel delete:

    Svrmgr> **commit;**

12. Determine the degree of parallelism:

    Svrmgr> **select * from v$pq_sysstat**
    **   Where statistic in ('Servers Busy','Server Sessions');**

    ```
    STATISTIC          VALUE
    --------------     -------
    Servers Busy       2
    Server Sessions    2
    ```

    The output shows that only two slave processes are used for all the four partitions, indicating that slave processes can span partitions.

NOTE

A parallel slave process can work on multiple partitions, but a particular partition can't be worked on by multiple slaves at the same time.

When using an insert...select operation, the following rule is used to determine the degree of parallelism:

Insert hint directive > parallel directive on insert Table > max query directive

17

PARALLEL
EXECUTIONS

Consider an example that demonstrates how to perform parallel insert operation on a partitioned table and to determine the degree of parallelism of such an insert...select operation. You will use the same partitioned table 'part_tab' used in the preceding example:

1. Connect to server manager as SCOTT and enable parallel DML (if it is not already enabled).

2. Perform parallel insert operations and insert rows from the emp table into the part_tab table:

```
Svrmgr> insert /*+parallel (part_tab,4) */ into part_tab
        Select /*+parallel (emp,8) */ emp_id from emp;
```

3. Commit the parallel insert so that all the rollback segments involved will be simultaneously committed:

```
Svrmgr> commit;
```

4. Determine the degree of parallelism used in this insert...select operation. According to the equation we mentioned earlier, the degree of parallelism should be 4 (the degree of the insert):

```
Svrmgr> select * from v$pq_sysstat
        Where statistic in ('Servers Busy','Server Sessions');


STATISTIC               VALUE
- - - - - - - - - - -   - - - - - -
Servers Busy            4
Server Sessions         4
```

> **NOTE**
>
> When using parallelism with join operations, the number of query slaves used is based on the maximum number specified in a query hint or the maximum degree of parallelism of all the tables in the particular SQL statement.

Managing Contention

Choosing the correct number of parallel server processes is very important to make sure that the system memory is utilized properly. The following statistics from the v$pq_sysstat dictionary view can be used to identify contention for parallel server processes:

- SERVERS BUSY
- SERVERS IDLE

- SERVERS STARTED

- SERVERS SHUTDOWN

```
Svrmgr> SELECT STATISTIC, VALUE
     2> FROM v$pq_sysstat
     3> WHERE statistic in ("Servers Started ",
     4> "Servers Shutdown", "Servers Busy");
```

```
STATISTIC          VALUE
================   ======
Servers Started    48
Servers Shutdown   39

Servers Busy         10
```

```
Svrmgr> show parameter parallel_min_servers
```

```
PARAMETER            VALUE
```

```
PARALLEL_MIN_SERVERS    10
```

These statistics indicate that parallel server processes are started and shut down very frequently. Also, you can see that most of the server processes are busy, therefore you should consider increasing the value of PARALLEL_MIN_SERVERS.

Parallel Data Load

Data can be loaded into a table or a partition in parallel using the direct path SQL*Loader option. When performing parallel SQL*Loader operations on a partitioned table, make sure there are no local or global indexes on the table, otherwise the parallel load will fail. You should make use of the FILE and STORAGE options in the controlfile to control the storage parameters during parallel load because each SQL*Loader session loads data into a new extent. Each SQL*Loader session loads data into a new extent and therefore you should make sure that the INITIAL extent size is set appropriately. The following example shows how you can run multiple SQL*Loader sessions in parallel to load a table:

```
C:\>Sqlload scott/tiger control=control1.ctl parallel=TRUE direct=TRUE
C:\>Sqlload scott/tiger control=control2.ctl parallel=TRUE direct=TRUE
C:\>Sqlload scott/tiger control=control3.ctl parallel=TRUE direct=TRUE
C:\>Sqlload scott/tiger control=control4.ctl parallel=TRUE direct=TRUE
```

17

PARALLEL
EXECUTIONS

> **NOTE**
>
> Local and global indexes on a partitioned table should be dropped before performing parallel load operations on a partitioned table.

Parallel Recovery

The redo log records changes made to a block and it can be used during media recovery to restore the blocks to their state prior to media failure. Very large databases cannot afford to be down for a long time (if at all) and usually the amount of data involved is large. The media recovery on such databases should be done very quickly, or at least a part of the database should be recovered quickly, so that the database can be used as soon as possible.

The initialization parameter RECOVERY_PARALLELISM or the PARALLEL clause of the RECOVER command can be used to perform recovery in parallel. The following steps occur during parallel recovery:

- The redo logs are read sequentially by the query coordinator
- Information read from the redo logs is passed to the slave processes
- The slave processes read the datafiles in parallel and apply the changes suggested by the redo log

Transaction Recovery and Rollback Segment Issues

Oracle makes use of rollback segments to record "undo" information for transactions. Rollback segments serve two purposes:

- Roll back uncommitted transactions during system failure or user-issued rollback
- Read consistency of transactions

When running parallel DML operations, you should create rollback segments in a tablespace with enough space to extend and also set the MAXEXTENTS for the rollback segments to UNLIMITED, otherwise you might have problems if a lot of undo information is generated by the parallel DML. In order to prevent contention for rollback segments, you should have enough rollback segments so that no more than two parallel transactions are assigned to the same rollback segment.

A parallel DML statement can potentially use multiple rollback segments. Each slave process generates its own undo information and can potentially use a different rollback segment. Oracle uses a two-phase commit mechanism to commit the transactions in each participating

rollback segment. In order to achieve this, you should issue a COMMIT or ROLLBACK statement after each parallel DML statement, otherwise an error is generated.

Oracle8*i* provides a feature—parallel transaction recovery—to improve the performance of transaction recovery. During parallel transaction recovery, SMON makes use of multiple server processes to roll back multiple transaction in parallel. A special feature of parallel transaction recovery, called intra-transaction recovery, allows the rollback of parallel DML to occur in about the same time as a forward operation. Intra-transaction recovery rolls back parts of a long-running transaction. The number of processes used during transaction recovery is determined by setting the initialization parameter PARALLEL_TRANSACTION_RECOVERY.

Diagnosing Parallel Query Performance Problems

Insufficient system resources can lead to performance problems when performing parallel operations. Performance problems with parallel query can be evidenced by the occurrence of ORA-12800. The solution to this problem is to use a lower degree of parallelism for the operation or to perform the operation at a later time. More detailed information about the parallel operation can be obtained by setting event 10046. Setting this event performs a SQL_TRACE on the parallel operation and generates a trace file that contains information based upon the level set for the event. The various levels that can be set for the event 10046 are

- Level 1 (default)

  It enables standard SQL tracing for the operation.
- Level 4

  It traces bind values in addition to displaying the SQL_TRACE information generated by level 1.
- Level 8

  It provides information about wait events in addition to the SQL_TRACE information generated by level 1. It can be used to determine whether the operation is waiting on some event.
- Level 12

  The most detailed level (generates a very large file, beware!), which includes SQL_TRACE information, trace bind values, and wait events.

Event 10046 can be set at the instance or at the session level:

- To set event 10046 at the instance level, set the following line in init.ora, and restart the database instance:

  ```
  Event="10046 trace name context forever, level X"
  ```

  X is the level that you want to set for the event.

- To set event 10046 at the session level, use

```
Svrmgr> alter session set events '10046 trace name
    2> context forever, level X'
```

X is the level you want to set at the session level.

You should set event 10046 at the session level just before executing the parallel operation. Setting it at the instance level has the potential of generating a huge file mixed with information about other operations also.

Interpreting the Output of Event 10046

When you execute a parallel operation after setting event 10046, a trace file is generated, containing information as specified by the level of the event. You should send the generated trace file to Oracle Support Services for a thorough diagnosis. If level 8 is specified for the event 10046, the trace file will contain wait information, which can be interpreted as follows:

```
WAIT#A: nam="B" ela=C p1=D p2=E p3=F
```

In this interpretation,

- A is the wait event number.
- B is the event being waited on.
- C is the time elapsed for the operation.
- D is the file number of the file in use.
- E is the block number in use.
- F is the number of blocks read by the operation.

For example,

- A wait for full table scan is as follows:

```
WAIT #1: nam="db file scattered read"
     ela= 8 p1=5 p2=1321 p3=32
WAIT #1: nam="db file scattered read"
     ela= 8 p1=5 p2=1354 p3=32
```

Waits for "db file scattered read" indicates that full table scans are being performed. The two lines indicate that you're reading the number of blocks specified by the db_file_multiblock_read_count parameter.

- A wait for index scans is as follows:

```
WAIT #1: nam="db file sequential read" ela= 8 p1=3 p2=1281 p3=1
WAIT #1: nam="db file sequential read" ela= 8 p1=3 p2=2378 p3=1
WAIT #1: nam="db file sequential read" ela= 8 p1=3 p2=3097 p3=1
```

Waits for "db file sequential read" indicates that index scans are being performed. The three lines indicate that only one block is being read at a time.

Parallel Executions in a Parallel Server Environment

The performance improvement that you can obtain by using a parallel server can be dramatically increased by combining it with parallel operations. For example, if your OPS environment consists of two instances and you perform a parallel operation with a degree of parallelism of six, a total of 12 parallel query slaves are used, six in each instance.

Oracle8*i* allows you to specify the instances used in parallel execution by using setting the initialization parameter PARALLEL_INSTANCE_GROUP. This parameter allows you to group instances and then specify the instance groups that you want to involve in a parallel operation.

Suppose you have four instances in an OPS environment with the following specifications:

- Instance 1 has instance_groups = g_12, g_13, g_14.
- Instance 2 has instance_groups = g_23, g_34.
- Instance 3 has instance_groups = g_34.
- Instance 4 has instance_groups = g_14, g_24, g_34.

Suppose that you are connected to instance 1 and want to perform a SQL operation in parallel on instances 1 and 4; you should log on to instance 1 and execute the following from Server Manager before performing the parallel operation:

```
Svrmgr> alter session set parallel_instance_group g_14;
```

Summary

Parallel executions can greatly enhance the performance of SQL statements provided you have enough system resources to meet the additional demands placed by the parallel server processes. It is equally important to configure the initialization parameters that affect parallel executions.

The degree of parallelism is influenced by several factors, such as the default degree on the table or index, hints specified by the user, and the number of CPUs, partitions, and disks available. If you are unsure of the manner in which your system is used, you should leave the optimization of parallel operations to Oracle by setting PARALLEL_AUTOMATIC_TUNING to TRUE.

Object Relational Features

IN THIS CHAPTER

Since their advent more than a decade ago, relational databases have been the database of choice. Generally in such systems, you end up writing applications using a 3GL, such as C++, or you use complex queries to get the information you need. Data storage has not been a real problem with relational databases; however, access and manipulation of the stored data can be a challenge. This is due to the fact that relational databases are not very efficient in capturing the logic along with the data. As a result, developers usually place the application logic in the front-end applications. The explosion and widespread use of the Internet has placed a lot of demand on the databases, which now must be able to store and manipulate complex data, such as hypertext, image, and audio data, in addition to traditional scalar data.

An object-relational DBMS such as Oracle8i stores not only the data, but also the logic. Oracle8i allows you to use objects to capture the data and logic associated with the entities being represented; this is in addition to traditional data. Use of objects allows Oracle8i to handle such complex needs and at the same time retain the scalability, robustness, and ease of use found in relational databases.

One of the main goals of Oracle8i was to simplify the management of all types of data—structured as well as unstructured. Oracle8i provides the flexibility to store data in a form that is most appropriate for your applications and environment.

In this chapter, we will look at the object features of Oracle8i including:

- Object types
- Object methods
- Nested tables
- VARRAYs
- Converting from a relational model to an object model
- Object cache

NOTE

The object relational features described in this chapter are enabled only in the enterprise edition of Oracle8i.

Objects in Oracle8*i*

Oracle8*i* allows you to use several object-relational characteristics during the design and implementation of your database. The type system is extended to include collection of objects in addition to the traditional data types:

- The OBJECT type allows the implementation of structured objects.
- The REF type allows objects to be referenced.
- The LOB type allows the use of large unstructured objects.
- The TABLE type allows the use of unordered collections of objects.
- The VARRAY type allows the use of ordered collections of objects.

In addition, extensions have been made to SQL, DDL, and DML to facilitate the creation, retrieval, and modification of objects and collections.

Using Object Types to Model Real-World Entities

Real-world entities can be modeled into the object-relational paradigm by using object types. Table 18.1 compares standard database tables and object types.

18

TABLE **18.1** Comparing Database Tables and Object Types

Oracle8i Table	Oracle 8i Object Type
Stores data	Doesn't store data
Can't be used as a template for creating objects	Can be used as a template for creating objects
Can't contain procedural code	Can contain procedural code
Can't have a body	Can have a body that's separate from the specification
Contents of the table can be accessed by granting DML privileges to users or roles	Users or roles must be granted EXECUTE privilege

OBJECT RELATIONAL FEATURES

There are several advantages to using object types:

- Application development can be standardized.

   Standardization of applications simplifies the sharing of data and merging of applications. For example, consider a large corporation that makes use of many departments that run autonomously. Each department is responsible for managing its own applications and data. Suppose that the manufacturing department uses product_id with the datatype number(5), and the sales department uses product_id with the datatype varchar2(8). These nonstandard data definitions can create problems when the two departments try to share data. Such problems can be avoided by creating object types that are used as standards in the corporation, thereby simplifying cross-department data sharing.

- Application development is fast and efficient by making use of methods.

  Methods allow you to use abstraction and object encapsulation. These features allow you to hide the complexities of the data, and allow data manipulation using a well-defined interface.

- Object types make it easy to model real-world entities because they can contain structured, as well as nonstructured data, as desired.

Object types have the following features:

- One or more attribute.

  An *attribute* represents a characteristic of the entity being defined. Various datatypes can be used to represent attributes such as scalar (number, char), collection (nested table or variable-size array), REF (reference to an instance of object type), LOB (large object), text, video, spatial, image, and user-defined.

- Zero or more methods.

  Methods are used to specify the actions that can be performed on the entity being represented. Not all methods are made public. The public methods form the interface that encapsulates the object. Object methods can be written in PL/SQL or in a 3GL, such as C++ or Java. Every object has several predefined methods associated with it, such as constructor (instantiates and creates object instances) and destructor (destroys the object when the object is removed from the system).

- Object types can be used to define a column's datatype.

- SQL, DDL, and DML extensions are available to store and manipulate object types.

- Database features, such as indexes and triggers, are also available to object types.

Object types can be created by using the CREATE TYPE command (refer to the *Oracle SQL Language* manual for the complete syntax of the CREATE TYPE statement). Let us consider an example of a company, such as Macmillan Computer Publishing, that publishes books. Information that needs to be stored includes author and book details. Object types can be used to represent authors and books. A table can then be used to store information about the book sales. Relational databases would represent the many-to-many relationships between authors and books by using a third table. However, in the object model such a relationship can be represented by using object types as column datatypes, as shown below:

1. An object type author_type can be created to represent author information such as last_name, first_name, royaltyper, city, state, and zip:

```
SQL> CREATE OR REPLACE TYPE author_type as object (
  2    Last_name    varchar2(20),
  3    First_name   varchar2(20),
  4    Royaltyper   number,
```

```
  5    City          varchar2(10),
  6    State         varchar2(2),
  7    Zip           varchar2(5));
  8 /
```

2. Using the SQL*PLUS DESC command, verify the details of the object type author_type:

```
SQL> desc author_type
```

NAME	NULL?	TYPE
LAST_NAME		VARCHAR2(20)
FIRST_NAME		VARCHAR2(20)
ROYALTYPER		NUMBER
CITY		VARCHAR2(10)
STATE		VARCHAR2(2)
ZIP		VARCHAR2(5)

3. An object type book_type can be used to represent information about books. We can also use author_type in a column to represent the authors of a particular book:

```
SQL> CREATE OR REPLACE TYPE book_type as object (
  2    ISBN          varchar2(20),
  3    title_name    varchar2(30),
  4    author        author_type,
  5    category      varchar2(10),
  6    price         number(5));
  7 /
```

4. Verify the creation of the book_type:

```
SQL> desc book_type
```

NAME	NULL?	TYPE
ISBN		VARCHAR2(20)
TITLE_NAME		VARCHAR2(30)
AUTHOR		AUTHOR_TYPE
CATEGORY		VARCHAR2(10)
PRICE		NUMBER(5)

5. Create a book_sales table by using the book_type datatype:

```
SQL> CREATE TABLE book_sales (
  2    Order_id      integer,
  3    Customer_id   integer,
  4    Book          book_type,
  5    Quantity      number(10));
  6 /
```

6. Insert rows into the book_sales table:

```
SQL> insert into book_sales
     Values(111111,999999,
     Book_type('0-123-45678-9','Oracle8i demystified',
     Author_type('Thakkar','Megh',20,'Orlando','FL','12345'),
     'Database',50),20);
SQL> insert into book_sales
     Values(222222,888888,
     Book_type('0-987-65432-1','Windows NT demystified',
     Author_type('Thakkar','Megh',20,'Orlando','FL','12345'),
     'Operating System',30),10);
SQL> insert into book_sales
     Values(333333,999999,
     Book_type('0-987-65432-1','Windows NT demystified',
     Author_type('Thakkar','Megh',20,'Orlando','FL','12345'),
     'Operating System',30),40);
```

7. You want to find the price of all the books that were ordered by customer_id '999999'. The price information is a part of the book_type, and to reference an element of an object type, you have to prefix the element with the object_type. This can be achieved as follows:

```
SQL> SELECT order_id, x.book.price, x.book.title_name
     FROM   book_sales x
     WHERE customer_id = '999999';

order_id    book.price    book.title_name
----------  ----------    ---------------
111111         50          Oracle8i demystified
333333         30          Windows NT demystified
```

> **NOTE**
>
> Constraints cannot be specified in type definitions. You have to use an 'alter table' command to assign constraints.

Object References

A REF type is used to reference an object and it can be used to uniquely identify and locate objects. Oracle generates a unique identifier for every object stored in a reference table. REF types can be used in relational columns as well as attributes of an object type. Object references serve as pointers to the object and simplify the access and manipulation of the object.

> **NOTE**
>
> Only objects stored in an object table can be referenced using the REF operator.

Using REFs in Columns

A REF type can be used in columns of a table to reference objects of the declared object type, regardless of the object table in which the object is stored. When used as a column of a table, a REF type can be scoped such that it contains references only to objects from a specified object table. REFs are different from foreign key columns as indicated in Table 18.2.

TABLE 18.2 Comparing REFs with Foreign Keys

REF Columns	*Foreign Key Columns*
Provide navigational access to the referenced object.	Provide a data value that can be used to join to the referenced table.
Can only reference a table of abstract datatypes (ADT).	Can reference tables that have real datatypes.
Can have "dangling" references to nonexistent objects.	"Dangling" references are not allowed. The referenced table must exist.

In the following example, the ACCOUNTS table references the CUSTOMERS table:

1. Create an object type customer_type for customers:

```
SQL> CREATE OR REPLACE TYPE customer_type AS OBJECT
2    (cust_no         CHAR(5),
3     cust_lastname   varchar2(10),
4     cust_firstname  varchar2(10));
5  /
```

2. Create the CUSTOMERS table by using customer_type:

```
SQL> CREATE TABLE customers OF customer_type;
```

3. Create the ACCOUNTS table to reference the customers:

```
SQL> CREATE TABLE ACCOUNTS as (
     ACCTNO number,
     ACCTYPE char(4),
     BALANCE number,
     CUST ref CUSTOMERS
     );
```

A REF is said to be "dangling" if the REF value points to a nonexistent object. Dangling REFs are different from NULL REFs; you should use the predicate IS [NOT] DANGLING to find dangling REFS and use IS [NOT] NULL to find NULL REFs. The following example uses the same ACCOUNTS and CUSTOMERS tables described earlier. The following SQL statement demonstrates the identification of accounts with valid customers:

```
SQL> SELECT a.cust.cust_no, a.cust.cust_lastname, a.cust.cust_firstname
     FROM accounts a
     WHERE a.cust is NOT DANGLING;
```

Using REF and DEREF Operators

REF operators can be used in SQL to reference objects in an object table. On the other hand, DEREFs are used to perform the complimentary operation of obtaining the object by making use of its reference. The following example demonstrates the use of REF and DEREF operators to manipulate objects within an object table:

1. Create a type emp_type for the employees:

```
SQL> CREATE OR REPLACE TYPE emp_type as object (
  2    Emp_id          integer,
  3    Lastname        varchar2(20),
  4    Firstname       varchar2(20),
  5    City            varchar2(10),
  6    State           varchar2(2),
  7    Country         varchar2(20),
  8    Zip             integer);
  9  /
```

2. Create a table by using the type:

```
SQL> Create table employees OF emp_type;
```

3. References need to be declared as variables referring to the object table so that they can refer to the objects in an object table:

```
DECLARE reftomegh REF emp_type;
```

4. Insert an object into the object table, and at the same time, obtain a reference to the object. A transaction is generally ideal to achieve both the tasks at the same time.

```
BEGIN
    INSERT INTO employees empref
    VALUES (emp_detail(12345,'Thakkar','Megh',
    ➥'Boston','MA','USA',55555))
    RETURNING REF(empref) INTO reftomegh;
END;
```

REFs cannot be used to navigate within PL/SQL procedural statements. A DEREF operator is used in SQL statements to obtain the object value by means of its reference. A DEREF operator takes as its argument a reference to an object and returns its value. The following example uses the reference reftomegh to update a column in the projects table:

1. Create the projects table that uses the emp_type abstract type to refer to employees:

```
SQL> Create table projects(
Proj_info      integer,
Emp_info     emp_type,
Proj_details     varchar2(40));
```

2. Update the projects table:

```
SQL> UPDATE projects
SET emp_info = DEREF(reftomegh)
WHERE proj_id = 99999;
```

Collections in Oracle8*i*

A *collection* is an ordered group of elements of the same data type. Collections have the following characteristics:

- Collections work similar to arrays except that they can have only one dimension and they are integer-indexed.

   Elements within a collection are determined by using a unique subscript.

   Collections can store instances of an object type and therefore can be used as attributes of an object type.

- Collections can be passed as parameters and therefore they can be used to move data into and out of database tables.

- Collection types can be defined and used in PL/SQL.

Oracle8*i* provides two types or collections (also see Table 18.3):

- *Nested tables* are unbounded and don't retain the order in which elements are added to the collection. Nested tables can therefore be also referred to as one-column database tables. Nested tables can be stored in a database column, hence the name. Nested tables can be retrieved into a PL/SQL variable and then accessed like an array. When used in this manner, each row is assigned a subscript that starts with 1. When using nested tables, a store table must be specified to store their records.

> **NOTE**
>
> Store tables associated with nested tables inherit the physical attributes of the corresponding nested table.

> **NOTE**
>
> Nested tables can have nonconsecutive subscripts; therefore, you can delete elements from a nested table and leave gaps in the index.

> **NOTE**
>
> Nested tables are unbound and their size can increase out of control if not used properly.

Let us consider an example that uses nested tables to implement a one-to-many relationship between projects and employees. The employees table is created using an abstract type emp_type and then it is nested as a column of the projects table:

1. Create an object type emp_type for the employees:

```
SQL> CREATE OR REPLACE TYPE emp_type AS OBJECT
        (emp_id              integer,
        emp_lastname    varchar2(20),
        emp_firstname   varchar2(20),
     emp_city      varchar2(10),
     emp_state     varchar2(10),
     emp_country    varchar2(10),
     emp_zip         varchar2(5),
        emp_position   varchar2(20));
    /
```

2. The abstract data type (ADT) emp_type is used to create an object table employees:

```
SQL> CREATE OR REPLACE TYPE employees
        AS TABLE OF emp_type;
```

3. Using the DESC command, verify the creation of the employees table:

```
SQL> desc employees

Employees TABLE OF EMP_TYPE
```

```
NAME                     NULL?   TYPE
---------------------    ------- -------------
EMP_ID                           INTEGER
EMP_LASTNAME                     VARCHAR2(20)
EMP_FIRSTNAME                    VARCHAR2(20)
EMP_CITY                 VARCHAR2(10),
EMP_STATE                VARCHAR2(10),
EMP_COUNTRY              VARCHAR2(10),
EMP_ZIP                  VARCHAR2(5),
EMP_POSITION                     VARCHAR2(20)
```

4. Create a nested table projects by using the object table employees:

```
SQL> CREATE TABLE projects(
     Project_id     number(5),
     Project_name   varchar2(20),
     Proj_emps      employees)
     Nested table proj_emps store as employees_table;
```

As shown earlier, the nested table is stored as a separate table employees_table.

5. Using the DESC command, verify that the nested table has been created:

```
SQL> desc projects
```

```
NAME                     NULL?   TYPE
---------------------    ------- -------------
PROJECT_ID                       NUMBER(5),
PROJECT_NAME                     VARCHAR2(20),
PROJ_EMPS                        EMPLOYEES
```

6. SQL DML extensions are provided in Oracle8*i* to manipulate the nested tables. Let us insert several records into the nested table:

```
SQL> insert into projects
     Values (11111,'Saturn',
             Employees(
                  Emp_type(123,'Thakkar','Megh','Manager',
                  ➥'Boston','MA','USA',55555),
                  Emp_type(007,'Moore','Roger','Developer',
                  ➥'Orlando','FL','USA',32817)));
```

```
SQL> insert into projects
     Values (22222,'Jupiter',
             Employees(
                  Emp_type(123,'Thakkar','Megh','Manager',
                  ➥'Boston','MA',55555),
                  Emp_type(700,'Connery','Sean','Systems Analyst',
                  ➥'Sacramento','CA',90320)));
```

18

OBJECT
RELATIONAL
FEATURES

7. Query the projects table to determine the manager of the 'Saturn' project. You can use the THE function to achieve this result:

```
SQL> SELECT emp_list.emp_lastname, emp_list.emp_firstname
     FROM THE
     (select proj_emps from projects
     where project_name = 'Saturn') emp_list
WHERE emp_list.emp_position = 'Manager';
```

- Variable-size arrays, also referred to as VARRAYs, are bounded and retain the order in which elements are added to the collection. Table columns specified as a VARRAY cannot be indexed. VARRAYs allow you to associate a single identifier with an entire collection, and each individual element is referenced by using a subscript that starts with 1. The size of a VARRAY is specified during its type definition, but the upper bound is extensible. VARRAYs can commonly be used to represent relationships between objects where all the elements of an object are processed as a group.

> **NOTE**
>
> Tables that make use of nested tables or VARRAYs cannot be partitioned.

Let us consider an example that makes use of VARRAYs. This example also shows that it is trivial to insert values into a VARRAY. However, retrieving information from a VARRAY requires the use of PL/SQL of OCI. Also, VARRAYs cannot be directly compared in SQL.

1. Create a VARRAY that stores dimensions of various items:

```
SQL> CREATE or REPLACE TYPE dimension_t AS VARRAY(3) of NUMBER;
```

2. Create an items table that uses the VARRAY:

```
SQL> CREATE TABLE items
     (itemno          integer,
     item_desc    varchar2(30),
     dimensions   dimension_t,
     price        number
     primary key  (itemno));
```

3. Insert values into the tables:

```
SQL> insert into items
     Values (111, 'Microwave', dimension_t(3,2,3),150);

SQL> insert into items
     Values (112, 'Refrigerator', dimension_t(10,6,8),800);

SQL> insert into items
     Values (113, 'Washing Machine', dimension_t(8,4,6),400);
```

4. Write a PL/SQL block to retrieve the dimensions of item 112:

```
Declare
Isize dimension_t;
Begin
    Select dimensions into isize
    From  items
    Where itemno = 112;
    Dbms_output.putline('Item is ' ||
                    To_char(isize(1)) || '*'
                    To_char(isize(2)) || '*'
                    To_char(isize(3)));
End;
/
```

5. Update the dimensions of item 111 to (4,4,4):

```
Declare
    New_dimensions    dimensions_t := dimensions_t(4,4,4);
Begin
    Update items
    Set dimensions = new_dimensions
    Where itemno = 111;
End;
/
```

6. Delete the item 113 along with its dimensions:

```
Begin
    Delete from items
    Where itemno = 113;
End;
/
```

TABLE 18.3 Comparing Nested Tables and VARRAYs

Nested Tables	*VARRAYs*
Do not have a maximum size	Have a maximum size
Can be sparse and allow individual elements to be deleted	Can only be dense and do not allow individual elements to be deleted

continues

18

OBJECT RELATIONAL FEATURES

TABLE 18.3   Continued

Nested Tables	VARRAYs
Data is stored in a separate store table that is system-generated and associated with the nested table	Data is stored in the same tablespace
Do not retain the ordering of elements	Retain the ordering of elements
Better suited for large collections because you can manipulate a subset of the collection	Better suited for small collections and are efficient for manipulating an entire collection

---

NOTE

A nested table or a VARRAY cannot contain a nested table or a VARRAY as an attribute.

Working with Object Methods

A *method* is the code associated with an object such that it defines the actions that can be performed on the object. Not all methods are made public, but those methods that are made public determine the object interface. Methods can be written in PL/SQL, Java, or a 3GL language such as C++. Oracle8*i* supports different methods:

- *Constructor*

  Every object has a predefined method called a *constructor*. This method is executed when an object is created, and it can be used to perform initialization and other DML with that object at creation-time. An object's constructor method has the same name as the object and it uses the object's attributes as its parameters. For example, in the following insert statement, book_type and author_type are the constructor methods:

  ```
  SQL> insert into book_sales
      Values(111111,999999,
      Book_type('0-123-45678-9','Oracle8i demystified',
      Author_type('Thakkar','Megh',20,'Orlando','FL','12345'),
      'Database',50),30);
  ```

- *Member*

  Member methods are non-predefined methods associated with an object. As mentioned earlier, a member method can be created by using PL/SQL or Java, or as external functions created by using a 3GL, such as C++. The CREATE TYPE or ALTER TYPE statement can be used to associate methods with objects.

The following example makes use of member methods to determine the value of an order:

1. Create an object type order_item_t with member methods. This object type will represent individual order items, and the member method is used to determine the value of each order item:

```
SQL> CREATE OR REPLACE TYPE order_item_t as object (
     Order_id       number(5),
     item_id        number(5),
     item_desc      varchar2(20),
unitprice       number(5),
     quantity       number(5),
     member function item_value return number,
     PRAGMA RESTRICT_REFERENCES(item_value, WNDS,WNPS));
```

PRAGMA RESTRICT_REFERENCES is a compiler directive that indicates the restrictions on the specified attribute while executing the method. Also, see Table 18.4 for the various ways in which you can restrict the information manipulation.

TABLE 18.4 Using PRAGMA_RESTRICT_REFERENCES to Restrict the Manipulation of Object Attributes

Value	Interpretation
WNDS	Write no database state
RNDS	Read no database state
WNPS	Write no package state
RNPS	Read no package state

2. Using the DESC command, verify the methods associated with an object type:

```
SQL> desc order_item_t

NAME                   NULL?   TYPE
---------------------  ------  -------------
ORDER_ID                       NUMBER(5)
ITEM_ID                        NUMBER(5)
ITEM_DESC                      VARCHAR2(20)
UNITPRICE                      NUMBER(5)
QUANTITY                       NUMBER(5)

METHOD
--------------
MEMBER FUNCTION ITEM_VALUE RETURNS NUMBER
```

3. Define the body of the member method using PL/SQL:

```
SQL> CREATE or REPLACE TYPE BODY order_item_t AS
     Member function item_value
     Return number IS
     Begin
          Return self.unitprice * self.quantity;
     End item_value;
     End;
/

Type body created.
```

4. The following PL/SQL code demonstrates how the member functions are used:

```
Declare
item1 order_item_t := order_item_t(11111, 10001,
➥"CD-ROM drive", 10, 200);
item2 order_item_t := order_item_t(11111, 10002,
➥"Floppy disk drive", 5, 100);
item3 order_item_t := order_item_t(11111, 10003,
➥"NetComm Modem", 20, 25);
x,y,z,s integer;

begin
    x := item1.item_value;
    y := item2.item_value;
    z := item3.item_value;
    s := x + y + z;
     dbms_output.put_line('Item value for' ¦¦
     ➥item1.item_desc ¦¦ ' is :'¦¦to_char(x));
     dbms_output.put_line('Item value for' ¦¦
     ➥item2.item_desc ¦¦ ' is :'¦¦to_char(y));
     dbms_output.put_line('Item value for' ¦¦
     ➥item3.item_desc ¦¦ ' is :'¦¦to_char(z));
     dbms_output.put_line('The total value of the order is : '¦¦
     ➥to_char(s));
end;
/

Item value for CD-ROM drive is :2000
Item value for Floppy disk drive is :500

Item value for NetComm Modem is :500

The total value of the order is : 3000
```

Working with Object Views

Object views provide a mechanism to implement object features in a relational database. Using an object view, you can map relational data to structured data and thereby retrofit object types and collection types into a relational database system. This approach is very useful during the migration process from relational to object models. Object views are based upon relational base tables. Object views contain objects in their rows, hence the name. Objects comprising an object view are identified by a unique identifier which is usually derived from the primary key of the base tables.

Object views allow relational applications and data to coexist with object-oriented applications and data because they allow you to manipulate the base tables as well as the object views. This results in improved performance because you can manipulate the data in the most efficient manner.

NOTE

Object views can be updated.

The following demonstrates how an object view can be built on top of a relational table. You also see how easy it is to manipulate the object views.

1. Any relational table can be used as a base table. Let us use the following projects table for the purpose of this demonstration:

```
SQL> desc projects
```

NAME	NULL?	TYPE
PROJID		NUMBER(5)
PROJ_DESC		VARCHAR2(30)
MGR_ID		NUMBER(5)
DEPTID		NUMBER(3)
PROJ_BUDGET		NUMBER(7,2)
PROJ_START_DATE		DATE
PROJ_END_DATE		DATE
PROJ_CITY		VARCHAR2(10)
PROJ_STATE		VARCHAR2(2)
PROJ_ZIP		VARCHAR2(5)

2. Define an object type that will represent the objects in the object view:

```
SQL> CREATE TYPE proj_t as OBJECT (
  2 PROJID              NUMBER(5),
  3 PROJ_DESC           VARCHAR2(30),
  4 MGR_ID              NUMBER(5),
```

```
 5 DEPTID                    NUMBER(3),
 6 PROJ_BUDGET               NUMBER(7,2),
 7 PROJ_START_DATE           DATE,
 8 PROJ_END_DATE             DATE,
 9 PROJ_CITY                 VARCHAR2(10),
10 PROJ_STATE                 VARCHAR2(2),
11 PROJ_ZIP                   VARCHAR2(5));
```

3. Create an object view based upon the projects table:

```
SQL> CREATE VIEW projects_ov OF proj_t
   2 WITH OBJECT OID (projid)
   3 AS
   4 SELECT p.projid, p.proj_desc, NULL, NULL,
   5    p.proj_budget, p.proj_start_date, p.proj_end_date,
   6    p.proj_city, p.proj_state, p.proj_zip
   7 FROM    projects p;
```

As shown in the preceding example, objects in an object view are based upon some attribute of the base tables. The WITH OID clause specifies how unique object IDs (OIDs) are generated.

4. DML operations can be performed on object view similar to an object table:

```
SQL> Insert into projects_ov
   2 Values (proj_t(11111,'Operation Oracle8i',12345,999,
   3 90000.00,'1/1/99 00:00:00','3/15/99 00:00:00',
   4 'MIAMI','FL','55555');
```

Oracle8i provides the MAKE_REF operator to convert a foreign key in a relation to a REF attribute in an object view.

> **NOTE**
>
> The MAKE_REF operator is used to convert a foreign key to a REF attribute in an object view. Therefore, its number of columns should match the number of attributes used in the WITH OID clause of the object view being referenced.

Case Study: Purchase Order System

Let us consider an example of a purchase order system to understand how to convert a relational model to an object-relational model. Such a system can be very complex, but we will consider the basic elements of this system and use a simplified relational model.

The system can be represented by a relational model consisting of several tables:

- customers contains customer-specific information, such as address and phone number. Information in this table does not depend upon other tables.
- orders contains information specific to the orders placed by a customer. A customer may place zero or more orders.
- line_items contains details of each order placed.
- inventory contains information about the various items that can be purchased by a customer. Information in this table is independent of the customers and the orders they place.

In a relational model, the following DDL statements can be used to create the tables:

```
SQL> Create table customers (
  2    custno          number,
  3    custname        varchar2(50),
  4    address1        varchar2(100),
  5    address2        varchar2(100),
  6    city            varchar2(40),
  7    state           char(2),
  8    zip             varchar2(10),
  9    phone1          varchar2(20),
 10    phone2          varchar2(20),
 11    primary key     (custno));

SQL> create table orders (
  2    pono            number,
  3    custno          number references customers(custno),
  4    orderdate       date,
  5    shiptoaddress1  varchar2(100),
  6    shiptoaddress2  varchar2(100),
  7    shiptocity      varchar2(40),
  8    shiptostate     char(2),
  9    shiptozip       varchar2(10),
 10    primary  key    (pono));

SQL> create table inventory (
  2    itemno          number,
  3    itemdesc        varchar2(100),
  4    price           number,
  5    primary  key    (itemno));

SQL> create table line_items (
  2    lineitemno      number,
  3    pono            number references   purchase_order(pono),
```

```
4     itemno          number references    inventory(itemno),
5     quantity        number,
6     primary key     (pono,lineitemno));
```

You can easily see that you will have to perform multitable join operations on these tables in order to obtain meaningful report from this database. Also, a change in the system, such as the format in which addresses are stored, might require changes in more than one table (customers and orders both use address information and need to be updated with the same address format).

An object-based approach can significantly improve the performance of this system. The following observations can be helpful in converting the system to an object model:

- Data formats such as address formats that are used in multiple tables and those that are static can make use of object types.
- When the number of elements is few and fixed in number, such as phone numbers, you can use VARRAYs to represent them.
- When there are many elements or the number is not known, it is more efficient to use nested tables.
- REFs can be used to represent many-to-one relationships. A REF can only reference one object and therefore REFs point from the dependent table to the primary table (the many-to-one side).

It is a good idea to standardize the naming convention used for the object model. I will use the following conventions for this model:

- All object TYPES end in "_t".
- All nested tables end in "_list".
- All VARRAYs end in "_v".
- All REFs end in "_r".
- Native datatypes are uppercase, but user-defined datatypes are lowercase.

The corresponding DDL statements using the object model are as follows.

The format of items is static, therefore, I will use object types to describe them:

```
SQL> create or replace type item_t as object (
2     itemno          number,
3     itemdesc        varchar2(100),
4     price           number);
```

Similarly, addresses are represented in a common format throughout the database and can be represented by using object types:

```
SQL> create or replace type address_t as object (
2     address1        varchar2(100),
```

```
3      address2        varchar2(100),
4      city            varchar2(40),
5      state           char(2),
6      zip             varchar2(10));
```

Each customer and order can have multiple addresses, and you can use a nested table to represent a list of addresses:

```
SQL> create or replace address_list as table of address_t;
```

Each customer is allowed a finite number of phone numbers. Therefore, you could use VARRAYs to represent phone numbers:

```
SQL> create or replace type phone_v as varray(10) of varchar2(20);
```

The line_items are dependent upon the orders table and such dependent relational tables can be changed to nested tables:

```
SQL> create type line_item_t as object (
2      lineitemno      number,
3      itemref         ref  item_t,
4      quantity        number);
```

```
SQL> create type line_item_list_t as table of  line_item_t;
```

Create the customers object table:

```
SQL> create or replace type customer_t as object (
2      custno          number,
3      custname        varchar2(50),
4      address         address_list,
5      phone_list      phone_v);
```

```
SQL> create table customers of customers_t;
```

Create the inventory object table:

```
SQL> create table inventory of item_t;
```

Create the orders object table:

```
SQL> create or replace type order_t as object (
2      pono            number,
3      custref         ref customers_t,
4      orderdate       date,
5      line_item_list  line_item_list_t,
6      shipto_addr     address_list);
```

```
SQL>create table orders of order_t;
```

Working with the Object Cache

The object cache is a client-side memory buffer that stores and tracks objects that have been fetched from the server by an OCI application. The client-side cache provides lookup and memory management functions for the fetched objects. Objects that are fetched through an OCI application or using SQL SELECT are copied into the object cache. These objects can be are referenced and can be pinned. On the other hand, objects that are fetched using direct SELECT statements cannot be referenced and they cannot be pinned. The advantage of using client cache is that objects pinned in the cache and for which a valid version is available will not need to be fetched again from the server.

> **NOTE**
>
> The object cache is used by every OCI application that dereferences REFs to retrieve objects.

There is a client-side cache available for each OCI environment handle initialized. The object cache is created when the OCI environment is initialized in the object mode. This is achieved by using the function OCIInitialize(). This OCI environment handle can be shared by multiple threads belonging to a process. For each connection, there is only one copy of an object that can be referenced in the cache. Therefore, dereferencing the same or equivalent REF multiple times will return the same object (the one stored in the cache).

When an object copy in the cache is modified, you need to flush the changes to the server before other processes can see the changes. However, association between object copies in the cache and the objects in the server is maintained by the object cache.

> **NOTE**
>
> You should unpin or free the objects no longer needed in order to save memory.

It should be noted that Oracle8*i* does not support automatic cache coherency, and it is the responsibility of the application to make sure that its object copy is up-to-date. In other words, when an application makes changes to an object in the cache, the changes are not automatically reflected in the corresponding object in the database and vice versa. The application is responsible for performing operations such as flushing a modified object copy to the database and refreshing the object copy with changes from the database object.

Object cache has two important parameters that affect the usage of cache memory. These parameters are set by using the OCIAttrSet() function and their values retrieved by using the OCIAttrGet() function.

- OCI_ATTR_CACHE_OPT_SIZE

OCI_ATTR_CACHE_OPT_SIZE specifies the optimal cache size. If the memory occupied by cached objects exceeds the high-water mark, the object cache automatically starts freeing unmarked objects with a pin count of zero until the cache size becomes optimal as specified by this parameter, or until it runs out of objects that can be freed. The default value is 200KB.

- OCI_ATTR_CACHE_MAX_SIZE

OCI_ATTR_CACHE_MAX_SIZE is used to determine the maximum cache size. It is specified as a percentage of the optimal cache size. The default value is 10%. The maximum cache size is determined as follows:

Maximum cache size =
OCI_ATTR_CACHE_OPT_SIZE(1+0.01*OCI_ATTR_CACHE_MAX_SIZE)

Object Cache Operations

18

There are several operations that you can perform on objects in the object cache. It should be kept in mind, however, that the application is responsible for making sure the object cache coherency is maintained.

OBJECT RELATIONAL FEATURES

Pinning Objects in the Cache

Applications can call OCIObjectPin() to dereference a REF and pin the associated object in the cache. Pinning an object guarantees that the object is accessible to the application and the object can be manipulated only by that application. You can also make use of OCIObjectPinArray() to dereference an array of REFs and pin the objects in the cache. The following options can be used while pinning objects:

- ANY: This option is used for read-only objects or those objects for which a change in the object will not affect the overall application. For example, lookup objects such as regions, vendors, and so on. This option will return the object copy in cache if one exists, or it will load the latest object copy from the database.

- LATEST: This option should be used for objects that change frequently, such as orders, and you need to work with the latest copy of the object. When this option is used, it will load the latest copy of the object from the database unless the object cache contains a marked copy. In that case, it returns the marked copy from the cache.

- RECENT: When this option is used, there are two possibilities:
  - If the object was pinned in the same transaction using the latest or the recent option, the recent option behaves like the ANY option.
  - If the preceding is not true, the RECENT option behaves like the LATEST option.

When pinning objects, the application can specify the duration of the pinning to be session (object remains pinned until the end of the session/connection or until explicitly unpinned) or transaction (object remains pinned until the end of the transaction or until explicitly unpinned).

When loading an object in the cache, a separate SELECT statement is effectively executed by the cache:

```
SELECT VALUE(t) FROM t WHERE REF(t) = :r
```

Where T is the object table that stores the object, R is the REF, and the fetched value becomes the copy of the object in cache.

NOTE

Object copies are not guaranteed to be read-consistent in the cache because the objects are loaded by executing individual SELECT statements.

Unpinning Objects from the Cache

An object copy should be unpinned when it is no longer needed. Unpinning and unmarking will make the object eligible to be freed.

NOTE

An object that has been pinned *N* times must be unpinned *N* times so that it is completely unpinned.

Applications can unpin objects by using OCIObjectUnpin() or OCIObjectPinCountReset(). OCICacheUnpin() can be used to unpin all the objects from the cache.

NOTE

Object that are unpinned but are still marked are not eligible for implicit freeing by the object cache.

Freeing Objects from the Cache

Objects that are no longer needed should be freed so they are removed from the cache and their memory is freed for reuse. Objects can be freed in one of two ways:

- Explicitly by an application by calling OCIObjectFree() or OCICacheFree()
- Implicitly by the object cache when it is running low on memory

Marking Cache Objects

Objects can be created, updated, or deleted locally in the cache. The process of marking is used to identify to the cache to update the object in the database server when the cache is flushed. New objects created in the cache by using OCIObjectNew() are marked for insert, objects updated in the cache are marked for update by using OCIObjectMarkUpdate(), and objects deleted from the cache are marked for delete by using OCICacheMarkDelete(). When the object copy is flushed, the server copy is updated with the marked changes.

NOTE

If an attribute of an object copy is modified multiple times, the final value of the attribute is used to update the server copy.

Unmarking Cache Objects

Unmarking an object copy prevents the changes made to it from being flushed to the server. However, unmarking does not undo the local changes made to the object copy. Unmarking object copies can be done by using OCIObjectUnmark() or OCICacheUnmark() (to unmark all the object copies for a specific connection).

Flushing Object Copies to the Server

Flushing is the process of updating the server with the changes from the object copy. After an object copy is flushed, it is unmarked. Flushing can be achieved by using OCIObjectFlush() or OCICacheFlush() (for all the objects in the cache).

Refreshing Object Copies

Refreshing an object loads it with the latest copy from the server. The refreshed copy may contain changes made to the server by other committed transactions of directly by any transaction.

> **NOTE**
>
> Direct changes to the server can be made by using SQL DML, triggers, or stored procedures.

Marked copies must be unmarked before they can be refreshed. When an unpinned object is refreshed, it is freed. Refreshing is achieved by using OCIObjectRefresh() or OCICacheRefresh() (to refresh all the objects).

Locking Object Copies in the Cache

Object copies can be locked in the cache so that the application is guaranteed that no other transaction will change the object while it is updating the object copy. This can be achieved by using OCIObjectLock(), which locks an object for update. All locks are released automatically at the end of the transaction.

If an application tries to lock an object that is currently locked by another transaction, it will be blocked. The NOWAIT option can be used to avoid this. Using a OCIObjectLockNoWait() call instead of OCIObjectLock() returns an error if the transaction is unable to lock an object immediately because it is locked by another user.

Committing and Rolling Back Transactions

When a transaction is committed by using OCITransCommit(), all the marked objects are flushed to the server and object copies pinned with the transaction duration are unpinned. When a transaction is rolled back, all the marked objects are unmarked and object copies pinned with the transaction duration are unpinned.

Summary

The explosive growth of the Internet has placed unprecedented demands on the type of data stored. Also, data processing complexity has increased tremendously. Oracle8*i* has several features that can provide efficient and cost-effective solutions to such problems by using the object model instead of the traditional relational database model.

In this chapter, I discussed the object features available in Oracle8*i,* such as the use of object types, methods, collections, and the object cache. I also discussed how you can convert relational database models to the object-oriented approach, which results in efficient systems.

Create and Manage Large Objects (LOBs)

IN THIS CHAPTER

Oracle8 has introduced many new LOB datatypes that make it very easy to manage picture, video, audio, or large character data sets. Prior to Oracle8, the datatypes available for storing such information were LONGs and LONG RAWs. LONGs and LONG RAWs have a lot of restriction in their usage. Therefore, it was better to place the information in external files and use Oracle as an indexing mechanism to use the external files.

The Oracle8*i* LOB datatypes can be used to store large and unstructured data such as text, image, video, and spatial data up to 4GB in size. Oracle8*i* allows LOBs to be one of two types depending upon their location in relation to the database: internal LOBs and external LOBs. In addition to providing these LOB datatypes, Oracle8*i* also provides procedures, cartridges, and other development tools to manipulate the LOBs.

Internal LOBs

Internal LOBs are stored within the database, allow efficient access, and optimize space usage. Internal LOBs behave in a manner similar to other datatypes, and they participate in the transactional model. Changes in the value of LOB columns can be committed or rolled back. All of the internal LOB datatypes can be stored either inline (up to a maximum of 4000 bytes) or in an external LOB storage area that is specified by the LOB storage declaration.

NOTE

Internal LOBs can be recovered in the case of transaction or event failure. External LOBs, however, do not participate in transactions, and their integrity is the responsibility of the operating system.

Internal LOBs can be defined using three datatypes:

- BLOB is a type of LOB that consists of unstructured binary raw data.
- CLOB is a type of LOB that consists of character datatype, as defined by the database character set of the database.
- NCLOB is a type of LOB that consists of character datatype, as defined by the national character set of the database.

External LOBs (BFILE)

External LOBs are stored outside the database in operating system files. They correspond to large binary data objects and can be located on secondary storage media such as hard disks, or tertiary storage media such as CD-ROMs, PhotoCDs, and DVDs. BFILEs contain binary raw data. Access to BFILEs is possible only if the underlying operating system supports a stream-mode access to these files. External datatypes can be of any format, such as text, graphic, GIF,

TIFF, JPEG, MPEG, and so on, but when read into a database they have to be moved into a compatible internal LOB datatype. BFILE datatypes are stored as a pointer or locator for the actual external data files. The locator consists of two parts:

- Filename
- Internal alias for the full path directory where the file resides. This alias is defined with the CREATE DIRECTORY command:

```
CREATE or REPLACE DIRECTORY jpeg_dir AS
'/usr/graphics/jpeg';
```

> **NOTE**
>
> Users are granted access to a directory alias by using the GRANT command:
>
> ```
> GRANT READ ON DIRECTORY jpeg_dir TO scott;
> ```

> **NOTE**
>
> Internal LOBs use copy semantics, wheareas external LOBs use reference semantics.

> **NOTE**
>
> A BFILE cannot be spread across multiple devices.

> **NOTE**
>
> BFILEs can be up to 4GB in length or up to the maximum file size allowed by the system, whichever is smaller.

Currently, BFILEs are only capable of piece-wise read operations. In order to perform an operation on a BFILE, the following steps must be performed:

1. Open the BFILE physical file using the BFILE locator.
2. Read the contents of the BFILE physical file into an internal LOB using the DBMS_LOB package.

3. Write the contents of the LOBs back to the physical file using either the server image cartridge or a Java interface.

> **NOTE**
>
> The BFILENAME() function can be used to initialize a BFILE column or attribute for a particular row by associating it with the physical file of a BFILE.

When creating a table that uses a LOB datatype, you specify tablespace and storage parameters for the LOB to be different from that of the table. The following example shows how you can create a table with LOB datatypes:

```
Svrmgr> CREATE TABLE employees(
2 employee_id      NUMBER(5),
3 last_name      VARCHAR2(20),
4 first_name     VARCHAR2(20),
5 dept_id        NUMBER(5),
6 address1        VARCHAR2(20),
7 address2        VARCHAR2(20),
8 city           VARCHAR2(10),
9 state           VARCHAR2(10),
10 country        VARCHAR2(20),
11 zip            NUMBER(5),
12 resume        CLOB,
13 picture        BLOB);
```

Values can be inserted into the above employees table using regular INSERT statements:

```
Svrmgr> INSERT INTO employees
2 VALUES (10001, 'Thakkar', 'Megh', 11111,
3 '555 Quest Parkway','Suite# 555','Melbourne', 'Victoria'
4 'Australia', 30000, EMPTY_CLOB(), EMPTY_BLOB());

Svrmgr> INSERT INTO employees
2 VALUES (10002, 'Smith', 'Scott', 11111,
3 '555 Quest Parkway','Suite# 555','Melbourne', 'Victoria'
4 'Australia', 30000, EMPTY_CLOB(), EMPTY_BLOB());
```

LOBs Versus LONGs/LONG RAWs

LONGs and LONG RAWs have several restrictions that prevent them from being used efficiently. I recommended that you use LOBs instead of LONGs/LONG RAWs. Table 19.1 shows the difference between LOBs and LONG/LONG RAWs.

TABLE **19.1**   Comparing LOBs and LONG/LONG RAWs

LOBs	*LONG and LONG RAW*
Multiple LOBs can be stored in a row	Only one LONG or LONG RAW is allowed in a row
Can be used as an attribute of a user-defined type	Can't be used as an attribute of a user-defined type
One or more LOB attributes can be defined in an object (except NCLOBs)	Only one LONG or LONG RAW attribute can be defined in an object
It is easy to insert a new row or update an existing row that contains one or more LOB columns and/or an object with one or more LOB attributes (internal LOBs can be set to NULL, empty, or replaced with some other data; external LOBs can be set to NULL or made to point to a different file)	It is difficult to insert or update LONG and LONG RAW columns
It is easy to update a LOB row/column intersection or a LOB attribute with another LOB row/column intersection or LOB attribute	It is very difficult to update a LONG or LONG RAW row/column intersection
LOB columns and LOB attributes can be selected	Cannot be selected
Only LOB locator is stored in the table column	Entire value is stored in a LONG column
The LOB locator is returned when a LOB column is accessed	The entire value is returned when a LONG or LONG RAW column is accessed
Limited to 4GB	Limited to 2GB
Can be accessed in random offsets	Must be accessed from the beginning to the desired location
Can be replicated in local and distributed environments	Can't be replicated
Can't be converted to LONG columns	Can be converted to LOBs by using the to_lob() function
Can be used to store large objects	Can be used to store large objects
Can be stored inline as well as external to the database	Stored only within the database
Cannot be distributed	Cannot be distributed

There are several restrictions associated with the use of LOBs:

- The bind variable for an internal LOB column may be of type SQLT_CHR or SQLT_LBI (limited to 4KB) only.
- Distributed LOBs are not supported. Therefore, a remote locator cannot be used in the SELECT and WHERE clauses.
- LOBs can't be used in clustered tables.
- LOBs can't be used with certain SQL clauses:
  GROUP BY
  ORDER BY
  SELECT DISTINCT
  Aggregate functions
  Joins
- UNION, MINUS, and SELECT DISTINCT are allowed on LOB attributes only if the object type has a MAP or ORDER function.

NOTE

UNION ALL operation can be used with tables containing LOBs.

- Analyze Compute/Estimate Statistics commands don't analyze LOB columns.
- LOBs can be used with nonpartitioned, index-organized tables, but not with partitioned, index-organized tables.
- LOBs can't be used in VARRAYs.
- OCI functions or DBMS_LOB routines used to update LOB values or LOB attributes on object columns will not fire the triggers defined on the tables containing the columns or attributes.
- NCLOBs can't be used as attributes in object types, but can be used as method parameters.
- LOB columns and attributes can be used in trigger body with certain restrictions:
  In a before-row trigger, only the :old value of a LOB can be read.
  In an after-row trigger, both the :old and :new values of a LOB can be read.
  In INSTEAD OF triggers on views, both the :old and :new values of a LOB can be read.
  :old and :new values are read-only.

Creating LOBs

BLOBs and CLOBs are created similar to any other built-in datatype using CREATE TABLE, ALTER TABLE, CREATE TYPE, and ALTER TYPE commands, except that LOB creation also makes use of the LOB storage clause. If the size of a BLOB doesn't exceed 4000 bytes, it can be stored inline with the other data in the tablespace. However, if the length of a BLOB exceeds 4000 bytes, it must be stored in either the storage defaulted from the table it resides in or in an explicitly defined LOB storage area.

> **NOTE**
>
> A LOB storage area doesn't need to be specified if the BLOB is less than 4000 bytes.

> **NOTE**
>
> Always specify the LOB storage area to avoid the datafile fragmentation that might result if the BLOB exceeds 4000 bytes and uses the default system-specified storage. Performance will improve by using LOB storage area.

The following example makes use of a BLOB datatype to create a table that stores information about products. The LOB storage area is used to store LOB data:

```
SVRMGR> CREATE TABLE inventory (
2 product_id              number,
3 product_desc            varchar2(50),
4 product_pict            blob,
5 product_category        varchar2(5))
6 lob (product_pict) store as ppict-store(
7 tablespace blob_data
8 storage ( initial 500K next 500K pctincrease 0 )
9 chunk
10 INDEX ppict_index( tablespace blob_index ))
11 tablespace user_data
12 storage ( initial 1M next 1M pctincrease 0 );
```

19

CREATE AND MANAGE LARGE OBJECTS (LOBs)

> **NOTE**
>
> BLOBs and CLOBs are very similar in terms of their creation and usage, except that BLOBs are used for binary data, whereas CLOBs are used for single-byte character storage.

The following example shows how you can use the BLOB datatype in TYPE creation:

```
SQL> CREATE OR REPLACE TYPE item_type (
2 item_id      NUMBER,
3 item_desc    VARCHAR2(30),
4 item_pict    BLOB);

SQL> CREATE TABLE item_table OF item_type
2 LOB (item_pict) STORE AS blob_store (
3 TABLESPACE blob_data
4 STORAGE (INITIAL 200K NEXT 200K PCTINCREASE 0)
5 CHUNK
6 PCTVERSION
7 INDEX blob_index (
8 TABLESPACE blob_index))
9 TABLESPACE users_data
10 STORAGE (INITIAL 1M NEXT 1M PCTINCREASE 0);
```

> **NOTE**
>
> LOB storage is specified only when the BLOB or CLOB is associated with a table and not during type specification.

LOB Storage Clause

If a LOB attribute size exceeds 4000 characters and a LOB storage is not specified, the overflow will be placed in the default storage specified for the table that it belongs to. Using the default will cause performance problems due to fragmentation and contention for disk resources.

LOB storage is defined with the CREATE or ALTER TABLE command and the LOB storage clause is used to specify the LOB storage profile. The LOB storage clause makes use of the LOB parameters section to specify

- LOB tablespace
- Storage in row
- CHUNK settings
- PCTVERSION settings
- CACHE or NOCACHE
- LOGGING or NOLOGGING
- LOB index specification

> **NOTE**
>
> The LOB storage clause is the same format for BLOBs, CLOBs, and NCLOBs.

> **NOTE**
>
> The index specification for LOBs can be the same as any other index and include INITRANS and MAXTRANS parameters.

Manipulating LOBs

Basic operations, such as SELECT, INSERT, UPDATE, and DELETE, can be performed on the entire value of an internal LOB using SQL DML. On external LOBs, only read-only operations can be performed. However, if you want to work with parts of internal LOBs or update and write to external LOBs, you will have to use one of the following interfaces:

- PL/SQL language by means of the DBMS_LOB package
- C language by means of the Oracle Call Interface
- C++ language by means of the Pro*C/C++ precompiler
- COBOL language by means of the PRO*COBOL precompiler
- Visual Basic language by means of the Oracle Objects for OLE (OO4O)
- Java language by means of the JDBC Application Programmers Interface (API)

Using DBMS_LOB Package

The DBMS_LOB package provided by Oracle8 can be used to access and manipulate both internal and external LOB data. DBMS_LOB package consists of several useful utilities that can be categorized into

- Routines that can be used to modify BLOB, CLOB, and NCLOB values
- Routines that can be used to read and examine LOB values
- Routines that can be used to read BFILEs

The DBMS_LOB routines make use of datatypes that can be of the following types:

- INTEGER—Used to specify the size of a buffer or LOB, offset into a LOB or the amount of a LOB value to access.
- VARCHAR2—Used for a source or destination character buffer that is used with CLOBs and NCLOBs

- RAW—Used for a source or destination raw buffer that is used with BLOBs
- BLOB—Used for a source or destination binary LOB
- CLOB—Used for a source or destination character LOB (including NCLOB)

Routines to Modify BLOB, CLOB, and NCLOB Values

Several routines can be used to modify BLOB, CLOB, and NCLOB values:

- Append()—Append() accepts two input parameters—src_lob (BLOB or CLOB) and dest_lob (BLOB or CLOB)—and appends the contents of the source LOB to the destination LOB. If either the source or the destination LOB is null, it generates the VALUE_ERROR exception.

- COPY()—COPY() takes five input parameters—src_lob (BLOB or CLOB), dest_lob (BLOB_CLOB), amount (INTEGER), src_offset (INTEGER), and dest_offset (INTEGER)—and copies the source LOB starting from the src_offset to the destination LOB, starting from the dest_offset. The amount parameter specifies how much to copy. The following exceptions are generated by this procedure:

    VALUE_ERROR (one or more of the input parameters are NULL or invalid)

    INVALID_ARGVAL, if any of the following is TRUE:

    > amount <
    >
    > amount > LOBMAXSIZE
    >
    > src_offset or dest_offset <
    >
    > src_offset or dest_offset > LOBMAXSIZE

- ERASE()—ERASE() takes three input parameters: lob_loc (BLOB or CLOB), amount (INTEGER), and offset (INTEGER). Erases all or part of the LOB specified by lob_loc by the amount specified starting at the specified offset. It generates the following exceptions:

    VALUE_ERROR (one or more of the input parameters are NULL or invalid)

    INVALID_ARGVAL, if any of the following is TRUE:

    > Amount <
    >
    > Amount > LOBMAXSIZE
    >
    > Offset <
    >
    > Offset > LOBMAXSIZE

- LOADFROMFILE()—Loads BFILE data into an internal LOB

- TRIM()—It accepts two input parameters—lob_loc (BLOB, CLOB, BFILE) and newlen (INTEGER)—and trims a LOB value into a desired shorter size. The following exceptions are raised:

  VALUE_ERROR (lob_loc is NULL)

  INVALID_ARGVAL (newlen < 0 or newlen > LOBMAXSIZE)

- WRITE()—It accepts four input parameters: lob_loc (BLOB, CLOB, BFILE), amount (BINARY_INTEGER), offset (INTEGER), and buffer (RAW, VARCHAR2). It writes a specified amount of data from the buffer parameter to the LOB starting from the specified offset. WRITE overwrites any existing data at the specified offset up to the specified length. The amount parameter returns the actual number of characters written. The following exceptions are raised:

  VALUE_ERROR (lob_loc, amount, or offset parameter is NULL, out-of-range, or invalid)

  INVALID_ARGVAL if any of the following is TRUE:

  > amount <
  >
  > amount > LOBMAXSIZE
  >
  > offset <
  >
  > offset > LOBMAXSIZE

Routines to Read or Examine LOB Values

Several routines can be used to read LOB values:

- GETLENGTH()—Obtains the length of a LOB value. It returns an integer value corresponding to the length of a LOB unless one of the following is TRUE in which case another value is returned:

  NULL is returned if the input LOB is NULL

  For BFILEs, GETLENGTH() returns NULL if any of the following occurs:

  > lob_loc is NULL
  >
  > lob_loc is not a valid open file
  >
  > lob_loc doesn't have sufficient directory or OS privileges
  >
  > lob_loc cannot be read due to OS errors

- COMPARE()—It accepts five input parameters—lob_1 (BLOB), lob_2 (BLOB), amount (INTEGER), offset_1 (INTEGER), and offset_2 (INTEGER)—and returns an integer value determined as follows:

  zero if the comparison succeeds

nonzero if the comparison fails

NULL if any of the following is true:

> amount <
>
> amount > LOBMAXSIZE
>
> offset_1 or offset_2 <
>
> offset_1 or offset_2 > LOBMAXSIZE

The following exceptions are generated for BFILE operations:

> UNOPENED_FILE (file is not opened)
>
> NOEXIST_DIRECTORY (directory doesn't exist)
>
> NOPRIV_DIRECTORY (sufficient privileges don't exist for this directory)
>
> INVALID_DIRECTORY (directory is no longer valid)
>
> INVALID_OPERATION (file doesn't exist or insufficient privileges)

- INSTR()—INSTR() takes four input parameters: lob_loc (BLOB, CLOB or BFILE), pattern (RAW), offset (INTEGER), and nth (INTEGER). INSTR()returns the matching position of the nth occurrence of the pattern in the LOB starting from the specified offset.

NOTE

For BFILEs, the INSTR function requires that the file be already successfully opened using FILEOPEN().

The following return values are possible:

Integer value corresponding to the offset of the start of the matched pattern

0 if the pattern is not found

NULL is returned if any of the following is TRUE:

> One of more of the input parameters is NULL or invalid
>
> offset <
>
> offset > LOBMAXSIZE
>
> nth <
>
> nth > LOBMAXSIZE

The following exceptions are generated:

UNOPENED_FILE (file is not opened)

NOEXIST_DIRECTORY (directory doesn't exist)

NOPRIV_DIRECTORY (sufficient privileges don't exist for this directory)

INVALID_DIRECTORY (directory is no longer valid)

INVALID_OPERATION (file doesn't exist or insufficient privileges)

- READ()—READ() takes three input parameters—lob_loc (BLOB, CLOB, BFILE), amount (BINARY_INTEGER), and offset (INTEGER)—and has one output parameter: buffer (RAW, VARCHAR2). READ() reads data from the LOB starting at the specified offset. The following exceptions are generated:

  VALUE_ERROR (lob_loc, amount, or offset is NULL)

  INVALID_ARGVAL if any of the following is TRUE:

  > amount <
  >
  > amount > LOBMAXSIZE
  >
  > offset <
  >
  > offset > LOBMAXSIZE
  >
  > amount > buffer

  NO_DATA_FOUND (end of the LOB is reached and there are no more bytes or characters to read from the LOB)

  For BFILEs, the following exceptions are raised:

  UNOPENED_FILE (file is not opened)

  NOEXIST_DIRECTORY (directory doesn't exist)

  NOPRIV_DIRECTORY (sufficient privileges don't exist for this directory)

  INVALID_DIRECTORY (directory is no longer valid)

  INVALID_OPERATION (file doesn't exist or insufficient privileges)

- SUBSTR()—SUBSTR() accepts three input parameters—lob_loc (BLOB, CLOB, BFILE), amount (INTEGER), and offset (INTEGER)—and returns part of the LOB value starting at the specified offset. The return value of the function can be as follows:

  RAW (for BLOBs and BFILEs)

  VARCHAR2 (for CLOBs)

NULL if any of the following is TRUE:

Any input parameter is NULL

amount <

amount > 32767

offset <

offset > LOBMAXSIZE

The following exceptions are raised for BFILEs:

UNOPENED_FILE (file is not opened)

NOEXIST_DIRECTORY (directory doesn't exist)

NOPRIV_DIRECTORY (sufficient privileges don't exist for this directory)

INVALID_DIRECTORY (directory is no longer valid)

INVALID_OPERATION (file doesn't exist or insufficient privileges)

Routines to Read BFILEs

There are several routines that can be used to read BFILE values:

- FILECLOSE()—Closes the file specified by its input parameter: file_loc (BFILE). It generates the following exceptions:

  VALUE_ERROR (the input file_loc is NULL)

  UNOPENED_FILE (the file is not opened)

  NOEXIST_DIRECTORY (directory doesn't exist)

  NOPRIV_DIRECTORY (sufficient privileges don't exist for this directory)

  INVALID_DIRECTORY (directory is no longer valid)

  INVALID_OPERATION (file doesn't exist or insufficient privileges)

- FILECLOSEALL()—Closes all the open files. It generates the following exception:

  UNOPENED_FILE (file is not opened)

- FILEEXISTS()—Checks for the existence of the file on a server. The file is specified by its input parameter file_loc (BFILE). It returns an integer value depending upon the outcome:

  1 if the physical file exists

  0 if the physical file doesn't exist

NULL if any of the following is TRUE:

> file_loc is NULL

> file_loc doesn't have the necessary directory or OS privileges

> file_loc can't be read due to OS error

- FILEGETNAME()—Returns the directory alias and filename of the specified input parameter file_loc (BFILE). This function indicates only the directory alias name and filename assigned to the locator and not whether the physical file or directory exists. It generates the following exceptions:

  VALUE_ERROR (input parameter is NULL or invalid)

  INVALID_ARGAL (directory alias or filename is NULL)

- FILEISOPEN()—Checks whether the file was opened using the input BFILE locators. It returns an integer value depending upon the outcome:

  1 if the file is open

  0 if the file isn't open

  It raises the following exceptions:

  UNOPENED_FILE (the file is not opened)

  NOEXIST_DIRECTORY (directory doesn't exist)

  NOPRIV_DIRECTORY (sufficient privileges don't exist for this directory)

  INVALID_DIRECTORY (directory is no longer valid)

  INVALID_OPERATION (file doesn't exist or insufficient privileges)

- FILEOPEN()—It accepts two input parameters—file_loc (BFILE) and open_mode—and opens the specified file. Currently the file can only be opened for reading. It raises the following exceptions:

  VALUE_ERROR (file_loc or open_mode is NULL)

  INVALID_ARGVAL (open_mode is not equal to FILE_READONLY)

  OPEN_TOOMANY (the number of open files in the current session exceeds the init.ora parameter SESSION_MAX_OPEN_FILES)

  NOEXIST_DIRECTORY (directory doesn't exist)

  INVALID_DIRECTORY (directory is no longer valid)

  INVALID_OPERATION (file doesn't exist or insufficient privileges)

19

CREATE AND MANAGE LARGE OBJECTS (LOBs)

Restrictions on DBMS_LOB Package

> **NOTE**
>
> The DBMS_LOB package is created with the dbmslob.sql file.

The following rules apply to the functions and procedures found in the dbms_lob package:

- For routines operating on BLOBs and BFILEs, the length and offset parameters are specified in terms of bytes.
- For routines operating on CLOBs, the length and offset parameters are specified in terms of characters.
- When specifying values for parameters, certain restrictions must be adhered to; otherwise, the functions and procedures will raise an INVALID_ARGVAL exception:

  Only positive offsets from the beginning of the LOB data are allowed.

> **NOTE**
>
> Negative offsets from the tail of the LOB data are not allowed.

  Parameters that specify size and positional quantities such as amount, offset, newlen, and so on must be nonzero positive values.

  The value of offset, amount, newlen, and nth must not exceed the maximum size of a LOB in any procedure or function.

  The maximum value of the parameters for CLOBs must not exceed (LOBMAXSIZE/CHARACTER_WIDTH) characters.

- For BFILEs, the external file must be opened with FILEOPEN; otherwise, the routines COMPARE, INSTR, READ, and SUBSTR will raise exceptions.
- RAW and VARCHAR2 parameters used in DBMS_LOB routines use an upper limit of 32,767 bytes.
- If the value of amount+offset exceeds (LOBMAXSIZE + 1) for BLOBs and BFILEs and (LOBMAXSIZE/CHARACTER_WIDTH) + 1 for CLOBs, update routines such as APPEND, COPY, TRIM, and WRITE will raise access exceptions.

- If the value of amount+offset exceeds (LOBMAXSIZE + 1) for BLOBs and BFILEs and (LOBMAXSIZE/CHARACTER_WIDTH) + 1 for CLOBs, read routines such as READ, COMPARE, INSTR, and SUBSTR will read until the End of LOB or the End of File is reached.

- Functions with NULL or invalid input parameter values will return a NULL.

- Procedures with NULL or invalid input parameter values for destination LOB parameters will raise exceptions.

- Operations such as COMPARE, INSTR, and SUBSTR that take patterns as parameters do not support regular expressions or special matching characters.

- The READ procedure makes use of NO_DATA_FOUND exception to indicate the End of LOB condition.

- In order to have consistent LOB updates, the user is responsible for locking the row containing the LOB data before calling procedures that modify LOB data.

Privileges for DBMS_LOB package are associated with the caller of the functions and procedures as follows:

- If the DBMS_LOB function or procedure is called by an anonymous PL/SQL block, the function or procedure is run with the privilege of the current user.

- If the DBMS_LOB function or procedure is called by a stored procedure, the function or procedure is run with the privilege of the stored procedure owner.

Several constants are used by the DBMS_LOB functions and procedures:

- FILE_READONLY is a binary integer with a value of zero.

- LOBMAXSIZE is an integer with a value of (4GB −1).

NOTE

If an argument that is expecting a non-null, valid value receives a null, invalid, or out-of-range value, an INVALID_ARGVAL exception is raised. This exception will have a value of 21560 and displays the message argument %s is null, invalid or out of range.

Loading LOBs

There are two methods of loading BLOBs and CLOBs:

- Using PL/SQL (DBMS_LOB package). I will discuss this method in this chapter.

- Using Oracle Call Interface (OCI). Discussion of this method is beyond the scope of this chapter.

Using DBMS_LOB to Load LOBs

Loading external LOB data into internal LOB using PL/SQL makes use of a table containing BFILE locators as shown below:

```
SQL> create table bfile_table (
2 bfile_id      number,
3 bfile_desc     varcahr2(20),
4 bfile_loc     bfile)
5 tablespace users_data
6 storage (initial 1M next 1M pctincrease 0);
```

The preceding statement doesn't use a LOB storage clause because only the BFILE locators are stored in the table. BFILE locators are loaded using the BFILENAME function of the DBMS_LOB package as shown in the following:

```
SQL> INSERT INTO bfile_table
2 VALUES (111,'March Sales Report',
3 bfilename('GIF_FILES','MARCH.JPG'));

SQL> INSERT INTO bfile_table
2 VALUES (111,'June Sales Report',
3 bfilename('GIF_FILES','JUNE.JPG'));

SQL> INSERT INTO bfile_table
2 VALUES (111,'September Sales Report',
3 bfilename('GIF_FILES','SEPT.JPG'));

SQL> INSERT INTO bfile_table
2 VALUES (111,'December Sales Report',
3 bfilename('GIF_FILES','DEC.JPG'));
```

After the BFILE locators are set in the BFILE table, the DBMS_LOB package can be used to read the BFILE into an internal LOB.

The Server Image Cartridge and LOBs

The Server Image Cartridge allows you to manipulate LOB values and perform several functions, including

- Conversion between image formats
- Cropping
- Compression

The image cartridge consists of two TYPES and their associated methods: ORDIMGB (used for BLOBs) and ORDIMGF (used for BFILEs). Image files in the supported formats contain

information about itself such as size and compression (also see Table 19.2). Methods associated with the image types are shown in Table 19.3. One of the most important methods is the PROCESS method that allows the processing of images using the commands shown in Table 19.4. The image types are owned by ORDSYS if installation is performed as specified in the installation guide.

TABLE 19.2   Attributes Associated with Image Cartridge Types ORDIMGB and ORDIMGF

Attribute	Definition
CONTENT	The BLOB value
CONTENTFORMAT	MONOCHROME, 4BITGRAYSCALE, 8BITGRAYSCALE, 1BITLUT, 2BITLUT, 4BITLUT, 8BITLUT, 16BITRGB, 24BITRGB, 32BITRGB, 24BITPLANER
CONTENTLENGTH	Size of the image "on disk"
COMPRESSIONFORMAT	JPEG, SUNRLE, BMPRLE, TARGARLE, LZW, LZWHDIFF, FAX3, FAX4, HUFFMAN3, Packbits, GIFLZW
FILEFORMAT	TIFF, JFIF, PICT, PCXF, RASF, CALS, TGAF, JFIF, BMPF
HEIGHT	Height of the image in pixels
WIDTH	Width of the image in pixels

TABLE 19.3   Methods Associated with Image Types

Method Name	Method Usage
CopyContent	Copy BLOB content
Process	Perform processing commands on the BLOB contents (ORDIMGB only)
ProcessCopy	Perform processing command and copy the results to a second BLOB
SetProperties	Read properties from BLOB file and write them into the TYPE attributes

TABLE 19.4   Commands That Can Be Processed by Images

Command	Usage
ByteOrder	Endian format
BitOrder	Bits number 1-to-N
BmpOrder	Bitmap order
BmpFormat	Bitmap format
Cut	Window to cut or crop

continues

19

CREATE AND MANAGE LARGE OBJECTS (LOBs)

TABLE **19.4**   Continued

Command	Usage
ContentFormat	Image/pixel/data format
CompressionFormat	Compression type
CompressionQuality	Compression quality
FileFormat	Change file format of image
Scale	Scale factor (such as 0.5 or 2)
XScale	X-axis scale factor
Yscale	Y-axis scale factor

Data Dictionary Views

The data dictionary provides several views that can be used to obtain information about LOBs:

- DBA_LOBS—Displays the information about tables containing LOBs. It consists of the following columns:

  OWNER specifies the owner of the table containing LOB columns

  TABLE_NAME specifies the name of the table containing LOB columns

  COLUMN_NAME specifies the name of the LOB column

  SEGMENT_NAME specifies the name of the LOB segment

  INDEX_NAME specifies the name of the LOB index

  CHUNK specifies the size in bytes of the LOB chunk as a unit of allocation/manipulation

  PCTVERSION specifies the maximum percentage of the LOB space used for versioning

  CACHE specifies whether the LOB is accessed through the buffer cache

  LOGGING specifies whether the changes to the LOB are logged

  IN_ROW specifies whether the LOB is stored with the base row

NOTE

For LOBs, the default logging attribute is obtained from the tablespace in which the LOB value resides unless the CACHE attribute is specified, in which case the LOB changes are logged.

- DBA_LOB_PARTITIONS—Displays the information about LOB partitions. It consists of the following columns:

  TABLE_OWNER specifies the owner of the table

  TABLE_NAME specifies the name of the table

  COLUMN_NAME specifies the name of the LOB column

  LOB_NAME specifies the name of a partitioned LOB item

  PARTITION_NAME specifies a table partition name

  LOB_PARTITION_NAME specifies a LOB data partition name

  LOB_IN specifies the corresponding LOB index partition name

  PARTITION_POSITION specifies the position of the LOB data partition in the LOB item

  COMPOSITE specifies whether the partition is composite

  CHUNK specifies the size in bytes of the LOB chunk as a unit of allocation/manipulation

  PCTVERSION specifies the maximum percentage of the LOB space used for versioning

  CACHE specifies whether the LOB is accessed through the buffer cache

  IN_ROW specifies whether the LOB is stored with the base row

  TABLESPACE_NAME specifies the name of the tablespace containing the LOB data partition

  INITIAL_EXTENT specifies the size of the initial extent of the LOB data partition

  NEXT_EXTENT specifies the size of the next extent of the LOB data partition

  MIN_EXTENTS specifies the minimum number of extents in the segment of a LOB data partition

  MAX_EXTENTS specifies the maximum number of extents in the segment of a LOB data partition

  PCT_INCREASE specifies the percentage increase in the size of extents for the LOB data partitions

  FREELISTS specifies the number of freelists associated with the segment of the LOB data partition

  FREELIST_GROUPS specifies the number of freelist groups associated with the segment of the LOB data partition

  LOGGING specifies whether the LOB actions are logged

  BUFFER_POOL specifies the buffer pool of a LOB data partition

- DBA_LOB_SUBPARTITIONS—Displays the information about LOB subpartitions. It consists of the following columns:

TABLE_OWNER specifies the owner of the table

TABLE_NAME specifies the name of the table

COLUMN_NAME specifies the name of the LOB column

LOB_NAME specifies the name of a partitioned LOB item

LOB_PARTITION_NAME specifies the lob data partition name to which this LOB data subpartition belongs

SUBPARTITION_NAME specifies the name of a table subpartition to which this LOB subpartition corresponds

LOB_INDSUBPART_NAME specifies the corresponding LOB index subpartition

SUBPARTITION_POSITION specifies the position of the LOB data partition in the LOB item

CHUNK specifies the size in bytes of the LOB chunk as a unit of allocation/manipulation

PCTVERSION specifies the maximum percentage of the LOB space used for versioning

CACHE specifies whether the LOB is accessed through the buffer cache or not

IN_ROW specifies whether the LOB is stored with the base row

TABLESPACE_NAME specifies the name of the tablespace containing the LOB data partition

INITIAL_EXTENT specifies the size of the initial extent of the LOB data partition

NEXT_EXTENT specifies the size of the next extent of the LOB data partition

MIN_EXTENTS specifies the minimum number of extents in the segment of a LOB data partition

MAX_EXTENTS specifies the maximum number of extents in the segment of a LOB data partition

PCT_INCREASE specifies the percentage increase in the size of extents for the LOB data partitions

FREELISTS specifies the number of freelists associated with the segment of the LOB data partition

FREELIST_GROUPS specifies the number of freelist groups associated with the segment of the LOB data partition

LOGGING specifies whether the LOB actions are logged

BUFFER_POOL specifies the buffer pool of a LOB data partition

- V$TEMPORARY_LOBS—Displays information about temporary LOBs. It consists of the following columns:

SID specifies the session ID

CACHE_LOBS specifies the number of cache temp LOBs

NOCACHE_LOBS specifies the number of nocache temp LOBs

Summary

Starting with Oracle8, the preferred datatype for use with multimedia data is LOBs. LOBs are similar to LONGs and LONG RAWs, but LOBs allow more flexibility and have more enhanced support in Oracle8*i*. There are two types of LOBs: internal LOBs and external LOBs. You have examined the differences between these LOB types and also seen how the DBMS_LOB package can be used to manipulate LOB data.

In this chapter, you looked at the enhanced support provided by Oracle8*i* for the LOB data types. You looked at both SQL and PL/SQL approaches as well as the procedures and cartridges available for use.

Advanced Queuing

IN THIS CHAPTER

Workflow applications perform deferred processing of work in which transactions are buffered for a particular time period before undergoing further processing. Such applications process as a set of messages and use queues as the mechanisms for processing. Oracle8*i* offers an integrated messaging support for workflow applications.

To understand how advanced queuing might be useful for workflow applications, consider an application, such as a distributed sales order processing system, in which messages come from and are sent to multiple clients. Order processing is an example of a workflow application in which the use of queues for storing and retrieving messages is required. For example, there could exist a business requirement specifying that all new orders submitted over a particular day are not processed until after 5:00 p.m. daily. In this case, a sales order would represent a message. The order entry application, therefore, would need to be able to provide *enqueuing* of new orders during the day, and the order processing application would need to be able to *dequeue* the newly created orders after 5:00 for subsequent processing.

Overview of Advanced Queuing

Oracle Advanced Queuing (AQ) integrates workflow message processing with the Oracle8*i* database, effectively enabling it as a message-enabled database. Using AQ, you can build and maintain queues within the database. Processes are able to enqueue and dequeue messages to and from these queues. In addition, using Oracle8*i*'s robust recoverability features using archived redo logs, recovery of queues, and their data is provided as well. Figure 20.1 illustrates the basic concepts behind AQ.

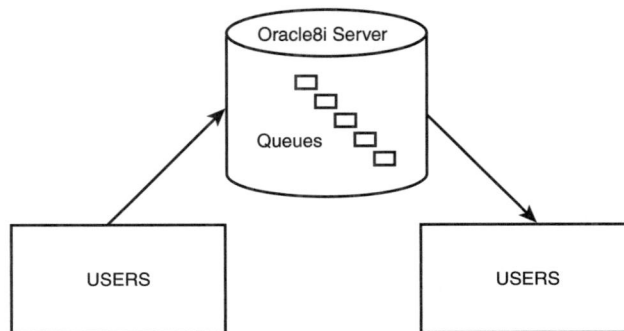

FIGURE 20.1
Advanced Queuing.

All message support is enabled through queues that are built and maintained by the database administrator. A single message is placed into a queue by a server process, and the message is later dequeued by another process. A *message* is the fundamental unit of workflow processing and contains data and control information. Messages are placed into rows of a database table (called a queue table), and therefore can be queried using standard SQL. This means that you can use SQL to access the message properties, the message history, and the payload (that is, the message text). All available SQL technology, such as indexes, can be used to optimize the access to messages. Standard database features such as recovery, restart, and enterprise manager are supported.

Because Oracle8*i* queues are implemented in database tables, all the operational benefits of high availability, scalability, and reliability are applicable to queue data. If a queue table is lost by media failure (such as disk failure), standard recovery mechanisms are able to recover all queue entries up to the point of failure. In addition, database development and management tools can be used with queues. For instance, queue tables can be imported and exported.

Essential Features of Advanced Queuing

Advanced queuing offers numerous significant features for use by workflow applications. Developers can specify that an enqueue/dequeue is part of the current transaction, or a transaction by itself, making the result immediately visible to other transactions. When creating queues, several time-related options can be set. For example, a message can be required to be dequeued within a specific time window. Also, when a message is dequeued, it can be browsed (nondestructive read), locked, or removed from the queue. A message can be delivered to multiple recipients based on subscriber properties, message properties, or message content.

Messages can be related to each other. All the messages produced in a single transaction can optionally be grouped to form a set that can only be consumed (that is, dequeued) by one user at a time. Messages are stored as database rows, so you can use SQL to query the message properties, the message history, and the payload directly. Also, we can set up exception queues to handle business rules. For example, if a new sales order is not dequeued within 24 hours for internal processing, it can be moved to an exception queue in order to find out why that sales order has not yet been processed.

You can create either persistent or non-persistent queues. Messages in persistent queues persist until they are removed from the queue, whereas messages in non-persistent queues do not persist beyond the failure of the instance.

AQ offers a number of features to provide effective queue security. The owner of a queue can grant or revoke queue-level privileges on the queue. DBAs can grant or revoke new AQ system-level privileges to any database users. The new system-level privileges supported are 'ENQUEUE ANY QUEUE', 'DEQUEUE ANY QUEUE', and 'MANAGE ANY QUEUE'. In addition, two new predefined roles exist in the Oracle8*i* database for AQ security:

- AQ_ROLE (for application users)
- AQ_ADMINISTRATOR_ROLE (for DBAs)

Both of these roles can be seen in the dba_roles dictionary view. Additionally, you can query the dictionary views dba_sys_privs and dba_tab_privs to view which privileges are contained in each of these roles. Figure 20.2 shows how to obtain information from the data dictionary regarding these two roles.

```
SQL> select substr(grantee,1,25) "ROLE",substr(table_name,1,25) "OBJECT",
  2  substr(privilege,1,20) "PRIVILEGE"
  3  from dba_tab_privs
  4  where grantee like 'AQ%'
  5  order by grantee;

ROLE                      OBJECT                     PRIVILEGE
------------------------- -------------------------- -------------------
AQ_ADMINISTRATOR_ROLE     DBMS_RULE_EXIMP            EXECUTE
AQ_ADMINISTRATOR_ROLE     AQ$_PROPAGATION_STATUS     SELECT
AQ_ADMINISTRATOR_ROLE     DBA_QUEUE_TABLES           SELECT
AQ_ADMINISTRATOR_ROLE     DBA_QUEUES                 SELECT
AQ_ADMINISTRATOR_ROLE     DBA_QUEUE_SCHEDULES        SELECT
AQ_ADMINISTRATOR_ROLE     V_$AQ                      SELECT
AQ_ADMINISTRATOR_ROLE     GV_$AQ                     SELECT
AQ_ADMINISTRATOR_ROLE     DBMS_AQ                    EXECUTE
AQ_ADMINISTRATOR_ROLE     DBMS_AQADM                 EXECUTE
AQ_ADMINISTRATOR_ROLE     DBMS_AQ_IMPORT_INTERNAL    EXECUTE
AQ_ADMINISTRATOR_ROLE     DBMS_AQIN                  EXECUTE
AQ_USER_ROLE              DBMS_AQ                    EXECUTE
AQ_USER_ROLE              DBMS_AQIN                  EXECUTE

13 rows selected.
```

FIGURE 20.2

Database roles for Advanced Queuing.

AQ is able to retain statistics about the current state of the queuing system, the history of messages, and propagation. Queues are imported or exported by importing or exporting the underlying queue tables and related dictionary tables. Import and export are done at queue table granularity. Because a single queue table can store multiple queues, multiple queues can be exported for a single queue table.

Support for Oracle Parallel Server (OPS) environments is provided by AQ.

When AQ is used in conjunction with parallel server and multiple instances, instance affinity options are used to partition the queue tables between instances for queue-monitor scheduling.

Setting Up Advanced Queuing

The structures for use by applications for advanced queuing are set up by the database administrator. The database administrator must possess the role AQ_ADMINISTRATOR_ROLE in order to set up advanced queuing in an Oracle8*i* database. Advanced Queuing is available only with Oracle8 Enterprise Edition or Oracle8*i* Enterprise Edition. For Oracle8 Enterprise Edition, the objects option is required in order to have (1) a structured payload (otherwise, a RAW datatype must be used to define the message payload), (2) multiple message recipients, or (3) message propagation to other destinations. In addition, because AQ uses the large pool structure of the SGA, for extensive workflow application usage, it is recommended to have the large pool configured with at least 20–50MB of physical memory.

The chief tasks of building and using an AQ environment are as follows. First, the DBA configures the instance to enable queue management. Next, the DBA creates the AQ Administrator who will configure and manage the AQ environment. The AQ Administrator then uses the DBMS_AQADM package to create queuing objects and to grant the necessary privileges to AQ users. Finally, AQ users use the DBMS_AQ package through applications to enqueue and dequeue messages.

Configuring the Instance

Message timing in the Oracle8*i* instance is enabled by creating AQ time monitoring (QMN) processes. These processes are responsible for such tasks as purging expired messages, scanning queues for messages that are able to be dequeued, and moving messages to exception queues. The init.ora parameter AQ_TM_PROCESSES specifies how many AQ time monitoring processes will be created. If this parameter is set to 1, one queue monitor process will be created as a background process to monitor the messages. This parameter is able to specify up to 10 QMN processes, and it can be dynamically set via the ALTER SYSTEM command, shown in the following:

```
SQL> alter system set AQ_TM_PROCESSES = 10;

System altered.
```

Unlike the QMN processes, Oracle8*i* uses job queue (SNP) processes to perform the actual message propagation. The SNP processes perform all movement of messages between application queues. In order for message propagation to occur, you must start the job queue processing by setting the `init.ora` parameter JOB_QUEUE_PROCESSES to at least 1 (you can set up to 36 SNP processes). You can set this parameter to higher values via the ALTER SYSTEM command if there are multiple queues from which the messages have to be propagated, or if there are many destinations to which the messages have to be propagated.

Setting Up Security

In Oracle8*i*, the DBA uses procedures GRANT_SYSTEM_PRIVILEGE and REVOKE_SYSTEM_PRIVILEGE (both in the DBMS_AQADM package) to grant or revoke ENQUEUE_ANY, DEQUEUE_ANY, or MANAGE_ANY privileges to users or roles. In Oracle8*i*, these three privileges—the ENQUEUE_ANY, DEQUEUE_ANY, or MANAGE_ANY— as well as the EXECUTE privilege on DBMS_AQADM and DBMS_AQ are already granted to the role named AQ_ADMINISTRATOR_ROLE. Hence, granting this role to the administrator provides him with the necessary basic security privileges to set up and maintain an AQ environment.

Note that several significant security-related differences exist for AQ administration between Oracle8 and Oracle8*i*. In Oracle8, the procedure GRANT_TYPE_ACCESS is executed, instead of GRANT_SYSTEM_PRIVILEGE. User SYS executes GRANT_TYPE_ACCESS to grant access for AQ object types to the AQ administrator. The AQ administrator can then execute this procedure to grant access for AQ object types to other AQ users. GRANT_TYPE_ACCESS is obsolete in Oracle8*i* because all AQ objects are now accessible to PUBLIC. Additionally, in Oracle8 the AQ_ADMINISTRATOR_ROLE allows the user to maintain queues in any schema, and the AQ_USER_ROLE allows enqueues and dequeues from any queue in any schema.

However, the finer-grained security in Oracle8*i* provides significantly more flexibility when granting privileges. First, the AQ_ADMINISTRATOR_ROLE in Oracle8*i* allows the user to maintain queues in any schema, and the AQ_USER_ROLE only allows enqueues and dequeues from queues in the user's schema. This role does not allow enqueues and dequeues from any queue. Second, the execute privilege on DBMS_AQADM allows the user to maintain AQ objects in his schema only. Use this technique to allow the user to administer queues in his own schema. The chief benefit of this approach is that it provides localized management of queueing structures by specific users rather than by the DBA.

Third, the execute privilege on the package DBMS_AQ only allows enqueues and dequeues from queues in the user's schema. However, the user cannot maintain these queues without the

execute privilege on the package DBMS_AQADM. Fourth, use the procedures
GRANT_SYSTEM_PRIVILEGE and REVOKE_SYSTEM_PRIVILEGE in package
DBMS_AQADM to grant or revoke the ENQUEUE_ANY, DEQUEUE_ANY, or
MANAGE_ANY privileges. Finally, use the procedures GRANT_QUEUE_PRIVILEGE
and REVOKE_QUEUE_PRIVILEGE in package DBMS_AQADM to grant or revoke the
ENQUEUE_ANY, DEQUEUE_ANY, or ALL privilege on individual queues.

Creating Queue Tables and Supporting Structures

Building the fundamental AQ structures is performed by using the package DBMS_AQADM.
Queue tables are the physical storage structures for queues, and a single queue table can
contain one or more queues. To create the necessary structures for advanced queuing, the following steps must be applied. First, queue tables must be created. Second, queues must be created in the specified queue tables. Third, the queues must be started in order to allow enqueues
and dequeues to be performed.

DBMS_AQADM is created by running the script `dbmsaqad.sql`, found in the directory
`$ORACLE_HOME/rdbms/admin`. Only the designated queue administrator and privileged users
should be granted execute privilege on this package. Initially, only SYS has the execution privilege to the procedures in DBMS_AQADM. Table 20.1 summarizes the procedures that can be
called through DBMS_AQADM.

TABLE 20.1 DBMS_AQADM Procedures

Procedure Name	Description
CREATE_QUEUE_TABLE	Creates a queue table, and allows specifying properties of the queue table (tablespace, storage clause properties, message sort properties, and so on).
DROP_QUEUE_TABLE	Drops an existing queue table.
CREATE_QUEUE	Creates a queue, and allows specifying properties of the queue (queue table for storage of queue, max retries, and so on).
DROP_QUEUE	Drops an existing queue.
ALTER_QUEUE	Alters properties of a queue (such as max retries, message retention time, and retry delay).
START_QUEUE	Enables a queue for enqueuing and dequeueing by applications.
STOP_QUEUE	Disables a queue for enqueuing and dequeueing by applications.
START_TIME_MANAGER	Causes the time manager process to start executing its opera-tions. This operation takes effect when the call completes and does not have any transactional characteristics.

continues

20

ADVANCED
QUEUING

TABLE 20.1   Continued

Procedure Name	Description
STOP_TIME_MANAGER	The command causes the time manager to stop executing all its operations. The physical process is not terminated. This operation takes effect when the call completes and does not have any transactional characteristics.
ADD_SUBSCRIBER	Adds a default subscriber to a queue. This operation takes effect immediately, and the containing transaction is committed. Enqueue requests that are executed after the completion of this call will reflect the new behavior.
REMOVE_SUBSCRIBER	Removes a default subscriber from a queue. This operation takes effect immediately, and the containing transaction is committed. All references to the subscriber in existing messages are removed as part of the operation.
QUEUE_SUBSCRIBERS	The function returns a PL/SQL table of aq$_agent. This can be used to get the list of all subscribers for a queue.
GRANT_SYSTEM_PRIVILEGE	Grants the ENQUEUE_ANY, DEQUEUE_ANY, or MANAGE_ANY privileges to users or roles.
REVOKE_SYSTEM_PRIVILEGE	Revokes the ENQUEUE_ANY, DEQUEUE_ANY, or MANAGE_ANY privileges from users or roles.
GRANT_QUEUE_PRIVILEGE	Grants the ENQUEUE_ANY, DEQUEUE_ANY, or ALL privilege on individual queues.
REVOKE_QUEUE_PRIVILEGE	Revokes the ENQUEUE_ANY, DEQUEUE_ANY, or ALL privilege on individual queues.

Figure 20.3 illustrates the basic steps of setting up advanced queuing. The example, developed by Bruce Ernst of Oracle Corporation, sets up basic queuing structures for the purpose of capturing and enqueuing PL/SQL exceptions raised in an application code block and then allowing another procedure to dequeue the exceptions. First, we create an object type (error_log_type) and an object table (error_log) for defining the basic structure of the queue table. Second, we build a single queue table (error_log_q), and a single queue (error_queue) in the queue table. We then start the queue in order to enable application users to access the queue.

```
SQL> create or replace type error_log_type as object
  2    ( user_name  varchar2(30),
  3      error_date  date,
  4      module        varchar2(60),
  5      code          number(6),
  6      msg   varchar2(500) );
  7  /

Type created.

SQL> create table error_log of error_log_type
  2     tablespace demo_data;

Table created.

SQL> exec sys.dbms_aqadm.create_queue_table -
>    ( 'error_log_q',    -
>      'error_log_type' );

PL/SQL procedure successfully completed.

SQL> exec sys.dbms_aqadm.create_queue -
>    ( 'error_queue',   -
>      'error_log_q' );

PL/SQL procedure successfully completed.

SQL> exec sys.dbms_aqadm.start_queue('error_queue');

PL/SQL procedure successfully completed.
```

FIGURE 20.3
Creating essential queuing structures.

Internal Objects Built via CREATE_QUEUE_TABLE

When the CREATE_QUEUE_TABLE procedure is executed to create a queue table, the
following objects are created. AQ$<queue_table_name> is a read-only view that is used for
querying queue data. AQ$_<queue_table_name>_E is the default exception queue for the

queue table. AQ$_<queue_table_name>_T is an index for queue monitor operations.
AQ$_<queue_table_name>_I is an index or an index organized table for dequeue operations on
multiple consumer queues. AQ$<queue_table_name>_S contains subscribers for queues in the
queue table. Finally, AQ$<queue_table_name>_R contains only the rule-based subscribers for
queues in a queue table including the text of the rule defined by each subscriber.

Using Basic Queue Structures for Message Management

The package DBMS_AQ is used to enqueue and dequeue messages. This package is
created via the Oracle-provided script dbms_aq.sql, found in the directory
$ORACLE_HOME/rdbms/admin. Table 20.2 summarizes the procedures that are called via
DBMS_AQ. Also, in order to enqueue or dequeue messages, users must be granted execute
privileges to DBMS_AQ. This is accomplished by granting the role AQ_USER_ROLE to the
specified users.

TABLE 20.2   DBMS_AQ Procedures

Procedure	Description
ENQUEUE	Adds a message and its payload to a queue specified by the user.
DEQUEUE	Dequeues a message from a queue. The payload that was enqueued is copied into the payload parameter at dequeue. The message properties are also set.
LISTEN	Used to listen on one or more queues on behalf of a list of agents. This is a blocking call that returns when there is a message ready for consumption for an agent in the list. If there are no messages found when the wait time expires, an error is raised.

We show the use of DBMS_AQ by means of our earlier example for logging application
exceptions. Figure 20.4 shows a simple stored procedure named log_error that, when called,
enqueues exceptions into error_queue for later processing.

```
SQL> create or replace procedure log_error
  2    ( p_module in varchar2, /* Module causing the exception */
  3      p_code in number,
  4      p_msg in varchar2 )
  5  is
  6    enqueue_options sys.dbms_aq.enqueue_options_t;
  7    message_properties sys.dbms_aq.message_properties_t;
  8    message_handle RAW(16);
  9  begin
 10    enqueue_options.visibility := sys.dbms_aq.immediate;
 11    sys.dbms_aq.enqueue
 12      ( 'error_queue',
 13        enqueue_options,
 14        message_properties,
 15        error_log_type
 16   ( user,
 17     sysdate,
 18     p_module,
 19     p_code,
 20     p_msg),
 21        message_handle );
 22  end;
 23  /

Procedure created.
```

FIGURE 20.4
Message enqueuing procedure.

Figure 20.5 shows a stored procedure named copy_errors, which is used to remove exceptions from error_queue and then copy them into the object table error_log. This procedure, when called, loops continually until error_queue is empty. It then inserts all dequeued messages into error_log.

```
SQL> create or replace procedure copy_errors
  2  is
  3    dequeue_options sys.dbms_aq.dequeue_options_t;
  4    message_properties sys.dbms_aq.message_properties_t;
  5    message_handle RAW(16);
  6    error_entry  error_log_type;
  7    no_error_entries exception;
  8    pragma exception_init (no_error_entries, -25228);
  9  begin
 10    dequeue_options.wait := sys.dbms_aq.no_wait;
 11    loop
 12      sys.dbms_aq.dequeue
 13        ( 'error_queue',
 14          dequeue_options,
 15          message_properties,
 16          error_entry,
 17          message_handle );
 18      insert
 19        into error_log
 20        values (error_entry);
 21      commit;
 22    end loop;
 23  exception
 24    when no_error_entries then null;
 25    when others then
 26      log_error
 27        ( 'copy_errors',
 28      sqlcode,
 29      sqlerrm );
 30      rollback;
 31      raise;
 32  end;
 33  /

Procedure created.
```

FIGURE 20.5

Message dequeuing procedure.

Figure 20.6 shows the usage of the two stored procedures discussed previously. An anonymous PL/SQL code block is executed to generate "no data found" exceptions by twice selecting from an empty table (sales_aq). The code block inserts two messages into error_queue, one per exception raised. Next we show, by querying error_log_q, that two messages are in fact enqueued. We then call copy_errors, which dequeues both messages, followed by verifying that error_log_q is empty. Finally, we select both exceptions from the object table error_log.

```
SQL> create table sales_aq (acct_no number, amount number)
  2  /

Table created.

SQL> declare
  2     v_acct_no number;
  3  begin
  4    begin
  5      select  acct_no
  6        into  v_acct_no
  7        from  sales_aq;
  8    exception
  9      when others then
 10         log_error
 11  ( 'select accts',
 12      sqlcode,
 13      sqlerrm );
 14    rollback;
 15     end;
 16    begin
 17      select  acct_no
 18        into  v_acct_no
 19        from  sales_aq
 20        where acct_no = -1;
 21    exception
 22      when others then
 23         log_error
 24  ( 'select accts',
 25      sqlcode,
 26      sqlerrm );
 27    rollback;
 28     end;
 29  end;
 30  /

PL/SQL procedure successfully completed.

SQL> select count(*) from error_log_q;

 COUNT(*)
---------
        2

SQL> exec copy_errors
```

continues

```
continued
PL/SQL procedure successfully completed.

SQL> select count(*) from error_log_q;

 COUNT(*)
_ _ _ _.
       0

SQL> select user_name, substr(msg,1,40) "MESSAGE" from error_log;

USER_NAME                       MESSAGE
- - - - - - - - - - - - - - - - - - - - - - - - - - - - - - - - - - - - - - - -
MATTHEW                         ORA-01403: no data found
MATTHEW                         ORA-01403: no data found
```

FIGURE 20.6

Enqueuing and dequeuing messages.

Data Dictionary Views for Advanced Queuing

New data dictionary views exist to support Advanced Queuing. DBA_QUEUE_TABLES describes the names and types of all queue tables created in the database. DBA_QUEUES contains operational characteristics for every queue in a database. DBA_QUEUE_SCHEDULES describes the current schedules for propagating messages. QUEUE_PRIVILEGES describes queues for which the user is the grantor, grantee, or owner, or access to the queue is granted to an enabled role or PUBLIC.

Programmatic Interfaces for Working with Advanced Queuing

Oracle now offers you five different environments for working with queues.

- You can use the PL/SQL interface using the DBMS_AQADM and DBMS_AQ packages, discussed earlier in this chapter.
- An interface to C++ is provided by means of the Oracle Call Interface (OCI).
- You can use either C or C++ to access AQ by means of the Pro*C/C++ precompiler.
- Visual Basic interface is provided by means of the Oracle Objects For OLE (OO4O), as well as any other languages that use OO4O.
- Finally, a Java interface is provided by means of the SQLJ translator. When developing Java programs for messaging applications, you can use JDBC to open a connection to the database and then use the Java AQ API for message queuing.

Summary

Advanced Queuing offers significant advancement in workflow processing by allowing Oracle8*i* to message-enable a database. The DBA is able to set up and administer all the necessary queuing structures to be used by workflow applications. Because all queues physically reside within the Oracle8*i* database, workflow applications benefit from the improved scalability and recoverability features of the queueing structures.

Recovery Manager (RMAN)

IN THIS CHAPTER

Chapter 28, "Performing Backups and Recovery," discusses the importance of a good backup strategy. In this chapter, I will discuss the Recovery Manager (RMAN), a valuable tool provided by Oracle8 to simplify and automate the process of performing database recovery on a backup under a variety of scenarios. RMAN is available both as a command-line interface and a GUI interface (integrated with the Oracle Enterprise Manager [OEM]). I will focus on the command-line interface of RMAN and discuss the following:

- RMAN components
- Perform database backups using RMAN
- Perform database recovery using RMAN
- RMAN commands and scripts

NOTE

The Enterprise Backup Utility (EBU) provided in Oracle7 has been replaced in Oracle8 databases with RMAN. RMAN is not compatible with EBU.

You need to understand several terms in order to work with RMAN:

- *Whole backup*: A backup consisting of all the datafiles and the control file.
- *Full backup*: A nonincremental backup of one or more datafiles.
- *Incremental backup*: A backup of one or more datafiles that includes only those blocks that have changed since the last incremental backup. A level 0 incremental backup of a datafile will backup all the blocks belonging to that datafile.
- *Operating system level backup*: Backup of one or more datafile obtained by using operating system utilities.
- *Closed backup*: Backup of a complete database, or a part of it, with the database closed.
- *Open backup*: Backup of a complete database, or a part of it, with the database open.

NOTE

Open backups are different from hot backups because open backups allow the backup of individual objects, whereas hot backups copy redo log files to archive log files.

RMAN has several important features that simplify the process of backup and recovery:

- It can be used to perform four levels of incremental backups.
- During backup and restore, RMAN can perform checks for block corruption so that there are no surprises during database recovery. Information about corrupt blocks detected is placed in alert logs, trace files, and data dictionary views, such as v$backup_corruption and v$copy_corruption.

> **NOTE**
>
> RMAN cannot detect all types of database corruption.

- It allows the backup of archived redo logs.
- The size of a backup piece can be limited, allowing easy backups of VLDBs (Very Large Databases).

> **NOTE**
>
> RMAN is not compatible with Oracle database prior to Oracle 8.

- There is no need to place the tablespaces in hot backup mode because RMAN does this for you automatically.
- Several enhancements are provided over traditional backup and recovery using scripts: automatic parallelization of backup, restore, and recovery operations; limiting the number of reads per file; multiplexing of file backups; and not generating extra redo logs during backups.
- When used with an Oracle Parallel Server configuration, it can perform load balancing while performing backups, restores, and recoveries across the clustered nodes.
- RMAN scripts can be written to automate or repeat backup and restore processes.

RMAN Components

Recovery Manager consists of four main components (see Figure 21.1):

- RMAN executable (rman)
- Target database
- Recovery catalog or the database's control file
- Channel (disk or tape)

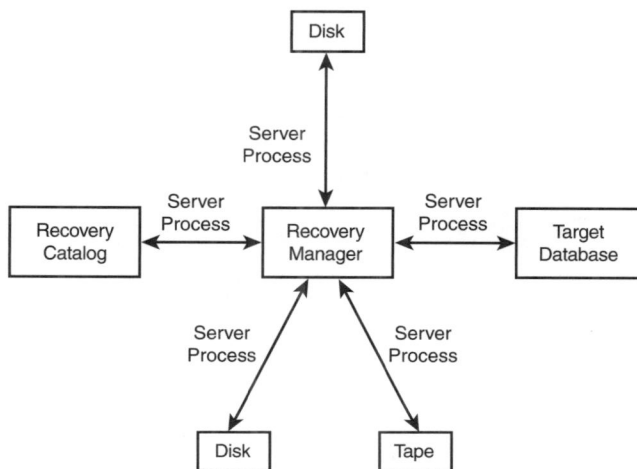

FIGURE 21.1

RMAN components.

Let's discuss each of these components and understand how each fits in the overall RMAN strategy.

RMAN Executable

The RMAN executable is a PRO*C application that takes RMAN commands as input and translates them into an equivalent sequence of PL/SQL calls that can be interpreted by Oracle. RMAN makes use of several PL/SQL packages for this purpose:

- dbms_backup_restore performs backup and restore operations on the target database by interfacing between the Oracle server and the operating system. This package is created by the dbmsbkrs.sql and prvtbkrs.plb scripts. It is automatically installed when the catproc.sql script is run.

- dbms_rcvman obtains the information used to perform backup and restore operations by querying the recovery catalog or the database's control file. It is created by the create catalog command.

- dbms_rcvcat updates the recovery catalog (if one is used). It is created by the create catalog command.

Target Database

The database on which the RMAN operation—such as backup, restore, and recovery—is performed is referred to as the *target database*. If the recovery catalog is not used, the target database's control file contains the necessary information used by RMAN.

Recovery Catalog

The *recovery catalog* is a repository of information stored in an Oracle database. Information in the recovery catalog is used by RMAN. The recovery catalog is an optional component, and in its absence, the necessary information is derived from the target database's control file. When the recovery catalog is not used, you might have several disadvantages:

- The control file must be first recovered in case of the loss of all the control files.
- It is very difficult to perform point-in-time recovery.
- You cannot make use of stored RMAN scripts.
- Usually the restore of a database is very slow.

The recovery catalog is a set of tables, views, indexes, and packages created and maintained under a schema known as the *recovery catalog owner*. Information stored in the repository includes

- Physical schema of the target database
- Backup sets and pieces
- Copies of datafiles
- Archived redo logs
- Backup history of the target database
- Reusable stored scripts

NOTE

Usually the recovery catalog is stored in a database separate from the target database.

Channel

In order to perform backup, restore, and recovery operations on a target database, you need Oracle server processes. RMAN initiates these Oracle server processes by allocating channels. Channels allow you to specify several characteristics of the RMAN operation:

- The type of media used—disk or SBT_TAPE
- Size of the backup piece
- Read rate
- Degree of parallelism

Starting RMAN

Depending on how RMAN has been configured—whether it is using a recovery catalog or not—you can start it in one of two ways:

- Without the recovery catalog

Suppose that you have a user called rdba with the SYSDBA role and RMAN isn't using a recovery catalog, the following steps can be used on Windows NT. (On a UNIX platform, the steps are similar except that the commands are executed from the UNIX prompt.)

1. Set the oracle_sid to the target database prod:

   ```
   C:\> set oracle_sid=prod
   ```

2. Start RMAN without the catalog:

   ```
   C:\> rman nocatalog
   ```

3. Connect to the target database:

   ```
   RMAN> connect target rdba/rdba
   ```

> **TIP**
>
> Steps 2 and 3 can be combined:
>
> ```
> C:\> rman target rdba/rdba nocatalog
> ```

- With the recovery catalog

Supposing that you have a user rdba with the SYSDBA role and the recovery catalog is stored in the database rcat, the following steps can be used on Windows NT:

1. Set the oracle_sid to the target database prod:

   ```
   C:\> set oracle_sid=prod
   ```

2. Start RMAN and connect to the recovery catalog:

   ```
   C:> rman rcvcat rman/rman@rcat
   ```

3. Connect to the target database:

   ```
   RMAN> connect target rdba/rdba
   ```

> **TIP**
>
> Steps 2 and 3 can be combined:
>
> ```
> C:> rman target rdba/rdba@prod rcvcat rman/rman@rcat
> ```
>
> where prod is the TNS alias of the target database.

When RMAN is started, the following occurs:

1. An RMAN user session starts on the client.
2. Two default server sessions are created that connect to the target database.
3. A channel is allocated for each disk or tape used for I/O.
4. If a recovery catalog is used, a server session is created on the recovery catalog database.

> **NOTE**
>
> Each allocated channel corresponds to a server session.

> **NOTE**
>
> RMAN performs backup, restore, and recover operations on the target database using server sessions through a PL/SQL interface.

Performing Database Backups with RMAN

RMAN can be used to take backups of open as well as closed databases. However, you should make sure that the closed database is mounted, but for open databases the tablespaces should not be placed in the hot backup mode because RMAN does it for you. Backups performed using RMAN make use of different server processes and allow files to be backed up in parallel. RMAN can be used to back up a whole database or a part of it, including tablespace, datafile, control file, and archived redo logs. Using RMAN, you can perform two types of backups: file copy backups and backup sets.

> **NOTE**
>
> RMAN automatically places tablespaces in the hot backup mode and therefore you should not use the ALTER TABLESPACE BEGIN BACKUP command to place tablespaces in backup mode.

Incremental Versus Cumulative Backups

An incremental backup copies only those Oracle blocks that have changed since the previous incremental backup. Incremental backups, as the name suggests, are incremental and build upon other backups; they are always in reference to a level 0 backup set or a level 0 file copy. An incremental backup at level N (where N is greater than 0) backs up all Oracle blocks that have changed since the last incremental backup at level less than or equal to N. The following guidelines can be used to perform incremental backups until you become more familiar with your environment and its requirements:

- Level 0 backup every quarter
- Level 1 backup every month
- Level 2 backup every week
- Level 3 backup every day

> **NOTE**
>
> Incremental backups can reduce the amount of backup done each time.

On the other hand, cumulative backups take longer and are larger than incremental backups. A cumulative backup of level N contains all the Oracle blocks changed since a prior backup at a level less than N.

> **NOTE**
>
> Only one incremental backup of any particular level is needed to perform recovery because a cumulative backup of level N supersedes all incremental backups of the same level.

File Copy Backups

A *file copy* makes an image copy of the file and is like an operating system backup. File copies can be used as part of an incremental level 0 backup. The advantage of file copy backups is that they can be used immediately without requiring a restore. The disadvantage of file copy backups is that they can be written only to a disk and can contain only one file as input. Therefore, you cannot take advantage of parallelism unless you make use of multiple channels.

The following example shows how to perform file copy backups. At the RMAN prompt, type the following:

```
Run {
    Allocate channel dk1 type disk;
    Copy
        Level
        Datafile 1 to 'c:\backups\data1prod.ora';
}
```

The following example shows how file copy operations can be parallelized. At the RMAN prompt, type the following:

```
Run {
    Allocate channel dk1 type disk;
    Allocate channel dk2 type disk;
    Allocate channel dk3 type disk;
    Allocate channel dk4 type disk;
    Allocate channel dk5 type disk;
    Allocate channel dk6 type disk;
    Allocate channel dk7 type disk;
    Allocate channel dk8 type disk;
Copy
    Datafile 1 to 'c:\backups\data1prod.ora',
    Datafile 2 to 'c:\backups\data2prod.ora',
    Datafile 3 to 'c:\backups\data3prod.ora',
    Datafile 4 to 'd:\backups\data4prod.ora',
    Datafile 5 to 'd:\backups\data5prod.ora',
    Datafile 6 to 'd:\backups\data6prod.ora';
    Datafile 7 to 'd:\backups\data7prod.ora';
    Datafile 8 to 'd:\backups\data8prod.ora';
        Sql 'alter system archive log current';
}
```

Backup Sets

A *backup set* is a logical set consisting of one or more physical files called *backup pieces*. Backup sets can be written to a disk or sbt_tape. The benefit of backup sets is that they can

easily take advantage of parallelism. The drawback of backup sets is that unlike file copies, they need to be restored before recovery can be performed. RMAN allows two types of backup sets:

- Datafile backup sets that can include datafiles and control files
- Archive log backup sets that can only include archive logs

NOTE

Archive log backup sets can only be full backups.

Backup sets can be taken as demonstrated in the following. At the RMAN prompt, type

```
Run {
    Allocate channel tp1 type 'SBT_TAPE';
    Backup
        Format 'c:\backups\df_%t_%s_%p'
        (database);
}
```

Parallelism of backup sets is demonstrated in the following:

```
Run{
    Allocate channel tp1 type 'SBT_TAPE';
    Allocate channel tp2 type 'SBT_TAPE';
    Allocate channel tp3 type 'SBT_TAPE';
    Allocate channel tp4 type 'SBT_TAPE';
    Allocate channel tp5 type 'SBT_TAPE';
    Allocate channel tp6 type 'SBT_TAPE';
    Allocate channel tp7 type 'SBT_TAPE';
    Allocate channel tp8 type 'SBT_TAPE';
    Backup
        Filesperset
        Format 'c:\backups\df_%t_%s_%p'
        (database);
        sql 'alter system archive log current';
}
```

In the preceding example, the filesperset parameter specifies the degree of parallelism. The name of the output file is determined using the format specification described in Table 21.1.

TABLE 21.1 Formatting of Output Files in RMAN

Substitution Variable	Specification
%d	Database name
%p	Number of the backup piece within the backup set
%s	Number of the backup set
%t	Timestamp
%u	A value obtained from the backup set number and the time of its creation

Archive log backup sets are demonstrated in the following example. Note that it can only be a full backup. At the RMAN prompt, type the following:

```
Run {
    Allocate channel tp1 type 'SBT_TAPE';
    Backup
        Filesperset
        Format 'c:\backups\al_%t_%s_%p'
        (archivelog all delete input);
}
```

Performing Database Restores with RMAN

File copies do not need to be restored and can be immediately used. Backup sets, however, need to be restored. RMAN can be used to restore or extract an original file from a backup set. The restore command of RMAN can be used to restore any logical unit such as a tablespace, datafile, control file, archive redo log file, or even the entire database from a backup set.

NOTE

Archive redo log files are automatically restored by RMAN during recovery as needed or you can restore them manually.

The following guidelines determine how much restoration can be performed on a database using RMAN:

- For an open database, you can restore only offline datafiles or tablespaces.
- For a database instance in the MOUNT state, you can restore the system tablespace or the entire database (but not the control file).
- For a database instance in the NOMOUNT state, you can restore the entire database (including the control file).

RMAN takes several things into consideration when determining the backup that should be restored:

- The type of channel allocated: disk or SBT_TAPE?
- Availability of file copies?
- Availability of backup sets?
- Incremental or cumulative backup sets? What level?

Restore of a database backup is performed by querying the recovery catalog or the control file of the target database.

If a database is being moved from one machine to another, you might need to restore the entire database (including control files). The following steps show how this can be done using RMAN on Windows NT. I will assume that the database is called dev.

1. Set oracle_sid to the target database dev:

   ```
   C:\> set oracle_sid=dev
   ```

2. Connect to Server Manager as internal:

   ```
   C:\> svrmgrl
   Svrmgr> connect internal
   ```

3. Shut down the database:

   ```
   Svrmgr> shutdown immediate
   ```

4. Startup nomount the database instance:

   ```
   Svrmgr> startup nomount
   ```

5. Exit Server Manager:

   ```
   Svrmgr> exit
   ```

6. Using RMAN at the command prompt, connect to the recovery catalog and the target database:

   ```
   C:> rman target internal/oracle@dev rcvcat rman/rman@rcat
   ```

7. Restore the database and control file using the following commands from the RMAN prompt:

   ```
   RMAN> run {
         Allocate channel tp1 type 'SBT_TAPE';
         Allocate channel dk1 type disk;
         Restore controlfile to 'c:\prod\ctr1prod.ctl';
         Replicate controlfile from 'c:\prod\ctr1prod.ctl';
         Sql 'alter database mount';
         Restore (database);
         }
   ```

21

After the database is restored, you might or might not have to perform recovery, depending upon the consistency of the backup.

> **NOTE**
>
> The log command-line option can be used to log the output of RMAN to a file.

Point-In-Time Recovery Using RMAN

Point-in-time recovery is the process of recovering the database to a particular point specified by an event, such as

- A specific time
- A log sequence number
- An SCN (system change number)

    Usually point-in-time recovery is used either to recover to a database state that is known to be good or to recover an object that has been accidentally dropped. Point-in-time recovery makes use of an until clause to specify the event that is used during recovery to indicate the end-point of the recovery. The following commands can be executed at the RMAN prompt to perform point-in-time recovery for the dev database used earlier. We will recover until 5PM, April 15th, 1999.

```
RMAN> run {
        Set until time '1999/04/15 17:00:00';
        Allocate channel tp1 type 'SBT_TAPE';
        Allocate channel dk1 type disk;
        Restore controlfile to 'c:\prod\ctr1prod.ctl';
        Replicate controlfile from 'c:\prod\ctr1prod.ctl';
        Sql 'alter database mount';
        Restore (database);
}
```

Performing Database Recovery Using RMAN

RMAN can automate the task of recovering a database and can be used to perform complete as well as incomplete recovery. When performing complete database recovery, all changes to the database (including those recorded in the online redo log files) are applied. Incomplete recovery is performed by stopping the recovery procedure before all the database changes are applied. Even though incomplete recovery does not apply all the database changes, it does recover all the files to the same point in time, making them consistent. Let us consider some examples of how recovery is performed.

- You need to perform the recovery of tablespaces data1_tblspc and data2_tblspc. The target database is dev on the Windows NT platform and it is open.

NOTE

Tablespace recovery can be performed while the database is open.

1. Connect to Server Manager as the internal account.

   ```
   C:\> svrmgrl
   SVRMGR> connect internal/oracle
   ```

2. Offline the tablespaces (if they are not already)

   ```
   SVRMGR> ALTER TABLESPACE data1_tblspc OFFLINE IMMEDIATE;
       SVRMGR> ALTER TABLESPACE data2_tblspc OFFLINE IMMEDIATE;
   ```

3. Connect to the recovery catalog and the target database:

   ```
   C:\> rman target internal/oracle@dev rcvcat rman/rman@rcat
   ```

4. Type the following commands at the RMAN prompt:

   ```
   RMAN> run {
       Allocate channel tp1 type 'SBT_TAPE';
       Allocate channel tp2 type 'SBT_TAPE';
       Restore tablespace data1_tblspc;
       Restore tablespace data2_tblspc;
       Recover tablespace data1_tblspc;
       Recover tablespace data2_tblspc;
       Sql 'alter tablespace data1_tblspc online';
       Sql 'alter tablespace data2_tblspc online';
       }
   ```

You can create RMAN scripts that contain the necessary RMAN commands and then run those scripts from the RMAN prompt. Those scripts can later be modified as needed. The following example shows how the recovery of two tablespaces, data1_tblspc and data2_tblspc, can be parallelized by using RMAN scripts:

1. Connect to the recovery catalog and the target database through RMAN:

   ```
   C:> rman target internal/oracle@dev rcvcat rman/rman@rcat
   ```

2. Create the stored RMAN script reco_2tblspc_par:

   ```
   RMAN> create script reco_2tblspc_par {
       Allocate channel dk1 type disk;
   ```

```
        Allocate channel dk2 type disk;
             Sql 'alter tablespace data1_tblspc offline immediate';
        Sql 'alter tablespace data2_tblspc offline immediate';
        Restore tablespace data1_tblspc;
         Restore tablespace data2_tblspc;
      Recover tablespace data1_tblspc;
         Recover tablespace data2_tblspc;
      Sql 'alter tablespace data1_tblspc online';
         Sql 'alter tablespace data2_tblspc online';
    }
```

3. Edit the init.ora file and set the RECOVERY_PARALLELISM parameter to TRUE.

4. The RMAN script reco_2tblspc_par is stored in the recovery catalog and is associated with the target database dev. The script can be executed at any time:

```
RMAN> run {
      Execute script reco_2tblspc_par;
      }
```

> **NOTE**
>
> The RMAN command-line option cmdfile can be used to execute stored RMAN scripts:
>
> ```
> C:> rman target internal/oracle@dev rcvcat rman/rman@rcat
> ➥cmdfile reco_2tblspc_par
> ```

> **NOTE**
>
> The recovery catalog view RC_STORED_SCRIPT can be used to obtain information about stored RMAN scripts.

Sample Scenarios for Using RMAN

Let us consider the following schedule for our examples:

- Level 0 full backup on Sunday
- Level 2 incremental backup on Monday
- Level 1 incremental backup on Tuesday

- Level 2 incremental backup on Wednesday
- Level 1 incremental backup on Thursday
- Level 2 incremental backup on Friday
- Level 2 incremental backup on Saturday

Case 1: Failure Occurs on Tuesday Before Backup

The following steps demonstrate how to recover the database if the database failure occurs on Tuesday before a backup is taken:

1. Apply the level 0 backup from Sunday.
2. Apply the level 2 backup from Monday.

You will lose the work done on Tuesday.

Case 2: Failure Occurs on Wednesday Before Backup

The following steps demonstrate how to recover the database if the database failure occurs on Wednesday before a backup is taken:

1. Apply the level 0 backup from Sunday.
2. Apply the level 1 backup from Tuesday.

You will lose the work done on Wednesday.

Case 3: Failure Occurs on Friday Before Backup

The following steps demonstrate how to recover the database if the database failure occurs on Friday before a backup is taken:

1. Apply the level 0 backup from Sunday.
2. Apply the level 1 backup from Thursday.

You will lose the work done on Friday.

Case 4: Failure Occurs on Sunday Before the Full Backup

The following steps demonstrate how to recover the database if the database failure occurs on Sunday before a full backup is taken:

1. Apply the level 0 backup from the previous Sunday.
2. Apply the level 1 backup from Thursday.
3. Apply the level 2 backup from Friday.
4. Apply the level 2 backup from Saturday.

You will lose the work done on Sunday.

Useful RMAN Commands

There are several RMAN commands that can be useful in day-to-day operations to obtain information from the recovery catalog as well as to troubleshoot problems while using RMAN. RMAN commands are basically one of two types:

- Standalone commands that are self-contained (except change, crosscheck, and delete)
- Job commands that must appear within the brackets of a run command

After connecting to the target database and optional recovery catalog, most of the RMAN commands can be executed within the run command.

Standalone RMAN Commands

Standalone RMAN commands are not executed as subcommands within run. Some useful standalone commands include

- catalog—catalog adds information about a datafile copy, archived redo log, or control file to the recovery catalog and the control file. The following example catalogs a datafile as an incremental level 1 backup:

  ```
  Catalog datafile '/disk1/datafiles/data1.f' level 1;
  ```

- change—change is used to change the status of backup pieces, image copies, or archived redo logs. For example, to make an archive log unavailable, use this command:

  ```
  RMAN> change archivelog 'c:\backups\al_prod_1.rdo' unavailable;
  ```

  Catalog validation can be used to synchronize the recovery catalog and control file with the disk. For example, if you delete many archive logs from disk and want to make sure that the catalog is aware of this, use this command:

  ```
  RMAN> change archivelog all validate;
  ```

  The preceding command verifies that the files the catalog believes to exist really do exist on disk. Files that do not exist are marked as deleted.

- create catalog, upgrade catalog, and drop catalog—Manage the recovery catalog schema.

- create script, replace script, and drop script—Manage RMAN scripts.

- crosscheck—crosscheck can be used to check the recovery catalog to verify that a backup piece listed as available in the recovery catalog is really available.

- delete expired backup set—This command deletes backup sets marked as EXPIRED by the crosscheck command and removes their reference from the recovery catalog and control file.

- list—list is used to query the recovery catalog or the target control file to produce a detailed report about a specified group of backup sets or copies. To obtain a list of all databases the recovery catalog is aware of, use this command:

```
RMAN> list incarnation of database;
RMAN-03022: compiling command: list
RMAN-06240: List of Database Incarnations
RMAN-06241: DB Key Inc Key DB Name DB ID       CUR  Reset SCN
Reset Time
RMAN-06242:------- ------- ------- ----------- ---- ---------
---------
RMAN-06243: 127    128     PROD    1957829059  YES
17-JAN-99
RMAN-06243: 133    134     DEV     1850267933  YES
18-JAN-99
```

To obtain a list of file copies containing a backup of any datafile that's a member of a tablespace, use this command:

```
RMAN> list copy of tablespace user_data1;
RMAN-03022: compiling command: list
RMAN-06210: List of Datafile Copies
RMAN-06211: Key    FILE  S Completion time Ckp SCN  Ckp Time
NAME
RMAN-06212: ------- ------- ------- ----------- ---- ---------
--------------
RMAN-06213: 212    1     D 17-JAN-99       389120   17-JAN-99
C:\ORANT\DATABASE\PROD\USER1PROD.ORA
RMAN-06213: 219    1     D 17-JAN-99       389120   17-JAN-99
C:\ORANT\DATABASE\PROD\USER1PROD.ORA
RMAN-06213: 232    1     D 17-JAN-99       389120   17-JAN-99
C:\ORANT\DATABASE\PROD\USER1PROD.ORA
RMAN-06213: 239    1     D 17-JAN-99       389120   17-JAN-99
C:\ORANT\DATABASE\PROD\USER1PROD.ORA
```

List the backup sets that contain archive logs within the sequence 131–138 with this command:

```
RMAN> list backupset of archivelog
from logseq 131 until logseq 138 thread 1;

RMAN-03022: compiling command: list
RMAN-06220: List of Archived Log Backups
RMAN-06221: Key  Thrd  Seq  Completion time
RMAN-06222: ---- ----- ---- --------------
RMAN-06223: 160  1     131  17-JAN-99
RMAN-06223: 209  1     132  17-JAN-99
RMAN-06223: 311  1     133  17-JAN-99
```

Recovery Manager (RMAN)

CHAPTER 21

439

21

RECOVERY
MANAGER
(RMAN)

```
RMAN-06223: 313   1      134    17-JAN-99
RMAN-06223: 325   1      135    17-JAN-99
RMAN-06223: 342   1      136    17-JAN-99
RMAN-06223: 357   1      137    17-JAN-99
RMAN-06223: 362   1      138    17-JAN-99
```

- report—report performs a detailed analysis of the contents of the recovery catalog. For example, to find the files that need to be backed up, use this command:

```
RMAN> report need backup
```

To find obsolete backups that can be deleted, use this command:

```
RMAN> report obsolete
```

> **NOTE**
>
> Some of the standalone RMAN commands might need to be preceded by the allocate channel for maintenance command.

- resync catalog—This command compares the recovery catalog to the control file of the target database or a snapshot control file and updates the recovery catalog with new or changed information. This command should be executed once daily or at least when the physical database structure changes, such as when a new tablespace is created.

- setlimit channel—This command controls the usage of resources for a channel. One or more of the following limitations can be placed on a channel:

readrate	Prevents disk contention by controlling the read I/O rate
kbytes	Limits the maximum size of the output files created during a backup operation
maxopenfiles	Limits the max number of files that can be concurrently opened by a channel

Job Commands

RMAN job commands are executed as subcommands with the run command. The run command defines a unit of command execution and executes all its subcommands sequentially. If one of its subcommands fails, it stops the processing of further commands within the block. Some useful job commands include

- allocate channel—allocate channel is used to establish a link between RMAN and the target database. A single channel can work on only one file copy or backup set at any

given time. Multiple channels will need to be allocated in order to achieve parallelism. Several parameters can be specified when allocating channels:

connect	Specifies the connect string to use when connecting the target database
format	Specifies the format of the filenames used by this channel
name	Specifies the name of the device to be used to perform the backup or restore
parms	Specifies the port-specific parameters for the device
type	Specifies the type of device, such as "disk" or "SBT_TAPE"

The following example allocates two disk channels for a database backup:

```
Run{
Allocate channel dk1 type disk format '/disk1/backups/%U';
Allocate channel dk2 type disk format '/disk2/backups/%U';
Backup database;
}
```

NOTE

Before executing a change or a crosscheck command, you need to execute an allocate channel for maintenance command.

- backup—backup can be used to backup a database, tablespace, datafile, or archived redo log file.

- copy—This command creates an image copy of a file. The following example copies the control file to a good disk and gives it the tag of good_controlfile:

```
Run{
Allocate channel dk1 type disk;
Copy current controlfile to '/disk1/copies/control1.f'
tag = 'good_controlfile';
}
```

- deallocate channel—This command deallocates or releases the channel that was allocated with the allocate channel command.

- duplicate—duplicate creates a duplicate database by using the backups of the target database.

- restore—This command restores files from the backup sets or copies on disk to the current location by overwriting existing files.

- recover—recover is used to perform database recovery.
- set duplex—This command can be used to create up to four copies of the same backup set concurrently. By default, it makes only one copy of the backup set.
- switch—switch specifies that the datafile pointed to by the control file is current. The following example shows how you can perform tablespace recovery by using the switch command to point to the current datafiles to use:

```
Run{
Allocate channel dk1 type disk;
Sql "ALTER TABLESPACE tb1 OFFLINE IMMEDIATE";
Set newname for datafile '/disk1/db1.dbf'
to 'disk2/db1.dbf';
restore tablespace tb1;
switch datafile all;
recover tablespace tb1;
sql "ALTER TABLESPACE tb1 ONLINE";
}
```

> **NOTE**
>
> The following RMAN commands can be executed as standalone or job commands: @, @@, host, send, startup, shutdown, and sql.

> **NOTE**
>
> When you open a database with reset logs, the recovery catalog should be updated with the reset database command before further attempts to back up the database using RMAN are made. The reset database command creates a new incarnation of the database in the recovery catalog and marks the new incarnation as current.

Let us consider an example where we are using an older incarnation of a database. Suppose that you are performing an incomplete database recovery and open the database with the reset-logs option. The following steps can be performed to update the recovery catalog:

1. Query the recovery catalog to determine the incarnation to use:

   ```
   RMAN> list incarnation of database identifier;
   ```

   where *identifier* represents the database SID.

2. Reset the database to an older incarnation:

   ```
   RMAN> reset database to incarnation;
   ```

TIP

In order to troubleshoot problems during RMAN operations, you should run RMAN in the debug mode and redirect the output of the debug operation to a trace file, instead of the log file or screen output. In the debug mode, RMAN provides useful information, such as

- The PL/SQL generated
- Indications of where RMAN is hanging
- Detailed information about the problem

The following example demonstrates how RMAN can be used in the debug mode and a trace file generated on Windows NT:

```
C:\> rman target internal/oracle@prod rcvcat rman/rman@rcat
➥debug trace rmantrc1.log
```

NOTE

The Media Manager library in use can be determined by querying the comments field in v$backup_piece.

NOTE

You can query v$session_longops to determine the progress of a backup operation performed using RMAN.

Summary

RMAN is an Oracle tool that simplifies and automates your automates your backup and recovery needs. It can be used to perform backups with a variety of strategies and also eliminates most of the manual intervention that might be needed during a database recovery.

RMAN is neither compatible with Oracle databases prior to Oracle8 nor with the Enterprise Backup Utility (EBU). RMAN makes use of server sessions on the target database to perform backup, restore, and recover operations. The recovery catalog is an optional but recommended component of the RMAN strategy and contains information used by RMAN.

Password Management

IN THIS CHAPTER

Oracle provides passwords as a mechanism to control the access to the database. Users are authenticated when they attempt to connect to the database by using the information stored in the data dictionary in an encrypted format. Prior to Oracle8, the abilities to define password composition/complexity, aging, expiration, history, and account locking are features that were available and performed using the operating system. The password management features available through the database were very limited, and you had to rely on the operating system security for protecting your database. In such a situation, a lot of interaction was needed between the system administrators and database administrators. For small corporations and systems, this was not a problem because the database and system administrators might be the same person, or the bureaucracy in the company would not make it difficult for them to interact easily. However, this is not the case for large corporations or systems.

Oracle database administrators needed a mechanism to control the security of the database using the database account/password feature. With the advent of Oracle8, the password management features have been enhanced. In this chapter, you will understand and use various password management features provided by Oracle8*i*, such as

- Password composition/complexity
- Password aging and expiration
- Password history
- Account locking
- Data dictionary views

The password management functions mentioned previously can be defined by using the CREATE PROFILE statement. Password management can be enabled by executing the utlpwdmg.sql script from the server manager while connected as SYS, as shown in the following:

NOTE

The script utlpwdmg.sql can be found in $ORACLE_HOME/rdbms/admin on UNIX and Windows NT platforms.

```
C:\>svrmgrl
SVRMGR>connect SYS/change_on_install
SVRMGR>@$ORACLE_HOME/rdbms/admin/utlpwdmg.sql
```

Password Composition/Complexity

Password composition allows the Oracle DBA to describe how a password must look. The physical composition, as described by the DBA, must be satisfied by all the passwords used in the system. Oracle also provides a mechanism to verify the complexity of passwords to ensure that the passwords chosen by users are complex enough, and they cannot be easily guessed by someone who is trying to break into the system. Oracle provides a PL/SQL function to verify the complexity of passwords. If you want more complexity in the database passwords, you can write your own function and make sure that it is owned by SYS.

> **NOTE**
>
> The password verification function must be owned by the SYS account.

The default PL/SQL function used for password verification ensures some basic rules for the passwords used. Each password

- Must contain a minimum of four characters
- Must not be the same as the username
- Must contain at least one alpha, one numeric, and one punctuation mark
- Must differ from the last password used by the username by at least three characters
- Must not match any word on an internal list of common words such as welcome, database, and so on

> **NOTE**
>
> Password verification can be disabled by setting PASSWORD_VERIFY_FUNCTION to NULL. For example,
>
> ```
> ALTER PROFILE myprofile LIMIT PASSWORD_VERIFY_FUNCTION NULL;
> ```
>
> The above SQL statement will disable password verification for the profile 'myprofile'.

If you are not satisfied by the default password verification function, you can write your own function using the following format:

- Password_routine_name(username_parameter in VARCHAR2(30), Password_parameter in VARCHAR2(30), Old_password_parameter in VARCHAR2(30))
  RETURN BOOLEAN

After the function is created, you must assign the routine to the user either by using the user's profile or the system default profile. The parameter PASSWORD_VERIFY_FUNCTION of the CREATE/ALTER PROFILE statement can be used for this purpose.

> **NOTE**
>
> The CREATE PROFILE statement can be used to assign the password complexity verification function to a specific user or a group.

If you are using your own password verification routine, you should take the following into consideration:

- An appropriate error message should be returned if the password verification routine raises an exception.
- An appropriate error message should be returned if the password verification routine becomes invalid.
- The password verification routine should be owned by SYS and functions in the system context.

Password Aging and Expiration

Password aging is a mechanism to make sure that users will periodically change their passwords. Password aging and expiration will increase the security of the data. No matter how careful you are in making sure that the password is not revealed to people who are not supposed to know them, passwords have a way of somehow becoming vulnerable to hackers over time. Changing passwords periodically is therefore a good practice and can be enforced using this mechanism. Oracle8*i* extends the password aging and expiration provided by operating system to the database level.

> **NOTE**
>
> The password lifetime can be set for an individual user or a group.

When password aging is enabled and the life of a password ends, Oracle provides a grace period in which the user will be notified that he should change the password. If the user does not change the password during the grace period, the account will be locked and further logins on this account will not be allowed until it is unlocked by a DBA.

The DBA can explicitly set passwords to expire so that new accounts are forced to change the passwords, and also existing accounts will have to change passwords when the lifetime of the password is reached.

For example, suppose that the PASSWORD_LIFE_TIME is set to 90 days and the PASSWORD_GRACE_TIME is set to 7 days. When the user logs in anytime after day 89, she will be notified that the password has expired and she has 7 days to change the password. If she does not change the password in those 7 days, the account will be locked and she will not be allowed to log in until a DBA unlocks it.

Password History

Password history is a mechanism to ensure that a password is not reused until a specified amount of time has elapsed. Password history is another mechanism to increase the security of the database. The whole exercise of changing passwords periodically is to make sure that you prevent someone from guessing the password over time. This would be meaningless if the user keeps choosing the same password again and again. Password history forces the user to choose a different password. The following parameters are used together to enforce password history and define how much time must elapse before a password can be reused:

- PASSWORD_REUSE_TIME—This parameter defines the number of days before a password can be reused.
- PASSWORD_REUSE_MAX—This parameter defines the maximum number of times that a password can be reused, after which it cannot be used again.

The following must be taken into consideration when setting the previous password history parameters:

- When you set one of the parameters—PASSWORD_REUSE_TIME or PASSWORD_REUSE_MAX—the other parameter must be set to UNLIMITED.
- Both the parameters can be set to UNLIMITED. This effectively disables password history checking.

Account Locking Feature

Prior to Oracle8, the only way to lock an account was to revoke the connect privilege from the user.

```
SVRMGR> REVOKE CONNECT FROM <username>;
```

Oracle8 server allows you to enable account locking under several conditions:

- Oracle8 will automatically lock an account after a number of failed attempts (specified by FAILED_LOGIN_ATTEMPTS) have been made to access that account. When a user successfully logs in, the number of failed attempts is automatically set to zero for that user. Also, if an account is re-enabled, the number of failed attempts is reset to zero.

22

PASSWORD
MANAGEMENT

- If a password has expired and the user has not set a new password before the grace period is over.
- The DBA can explicitly lock an account. This can be done if it is suspected that the password has been compromised or the account is not needed for a specified amount of time. For example, if you are going on vacation and want to make sure that your account is not accessible for a certain number of days, the account can be locked for the duration and then unlocked upon your return. The account can be set to unlock after a specified amount of time by using the parameter PASSWORD_LOCK_TIME.

> **NOTE**
>
> The number of failed attempts before an account is locked can be set for an individual or a group.

The following things should be considered when using account lockout:

- The account will not unlock automatically after a specified period of time has elapsed if the account was locked by a DBA explicitly.
- If a user makes a specified number of failed attempts (FAILED_LOGIN_ATTEMPTS) and the account is locked, the account will automatically unlock after the PASSWORD_LOCK_TIME has been reached.
- Setting PASSWORD_LOCK_TIME to UNLIMITED prevents the account from automatically unlocking. In this case, the DBA has to manually intervene to unlock the account.

> **NOTE**
>
> The password management features described in this chapter cannot be easily disabled even if the resource limitations are disabled through the parameter RESOURCE_LIMIT or the ALTER SYSTEM command.

Consider an example of how password management can be set by using the CREATE PROFILE statement:

```
SVRMGR> CREATE PROFILE test_profile
2> LIMIT
3> FAILED_LOGIN_ATTEMPTS 4
4> PASSWORD_LOCK_TIME 1
5> PASSWORD_LIFE_TIME     60
```

```
6> PASSWORD_REUSE_TIME 30
7> PASSWORD_GRACE_TIME 7
8> PASSWORD_VERIFY_FUNCTION     test_passwd_func;
```

The following is true for the *test_profile* created previously:

- The account will be automatically locked after four failed attempts to login.

- If the account is locked because of failed attempts, it will automatically unlock after 24 hours (one day).

- The password will expire after 60 days, and there will be a seven day grace period to change the password. The grace period starts with the time at which the account is accessed after the 59th day.

- The same password cannot be used within 30 days.

- A DBA-created function *test_passwd_func* is used to enforce password complexity verification.

NOTE

Profiles are assigned to a user using the CREATE USER or ALTER USER statement.

Now you can make use of the profile created to associate it with a user account:

```
SVRMGR> CREATE USER megh
2> IDENTIFIED BY r2_d2_g1
3> DEFAULT TABLESPACE users
4> TEMPORARY TABLESPACE temp
5> PASSWORD EXPIRE
6> PROFILE test_profile;
```

The previous example creates a user megh with a password that satisfies the complexity specified by the function test_passwd_func. The user makes use of the default tablespace users and temporary tablespace temp. The password is set to pre-expire and the profile test_profile is in effect for the user.

Data Dictionary Views for Password Management

The data dictionary views have been enhanced in Oracle8*i* to include information about the password management features described in this chapter.

- USER_USERS and DBA_USERS views have several additional columns:
  ACCOUNT_STATUS indicates the status of the account: locked, expired, or open.
  GRACE_DATA indicates when the account will expire.

LOCK_DATE indicates when the account was locked.

EXPIRY_DATE indicates when the account will expire.

- DBA_PROFILES has the following new columns:

RESOURCE_TYPE indicates the type of resource: KERNEL or PASSWORD.

LIMIT indicates the limit placed on the resource for this profile.

- USER_PASSWORD_LIMITS indicates the name of the password resource and its limit

- V$PWFILE_USERS view can be used to obtain information about the users that have been granted SYSDBA and SYSOPER system privileges for a database. The following columns are useful:

USERNAME shows the name of the user that the password file recognizes.

SYSDBA can be TRUE of FALSE depending upon whether the user can log in with SYSDBA system privileges.

SYSOPER can be TRUE of FALSE depending upon whether the user can log in with SYSOPER system privileges.

Managing Profiles

A profile is a set of limits on database resources and password usage. When a profile is assigned to a user, the user cannot exceed these limits. You must have the CREATE PROFILE system privilege to create a profile.

> **NOTE**
>
> If a profile that is explicitly assigned to a user does not put a limit for a particular resource or password parameter, the user is subject to the limits on that resource as defined by the DEFAULT profile.

The syntax of the CREATE PROFILE statement is as follows:

```
CREATE PROFILE <profile_name>
LIMIT [<resouce_parameters>][, <password_parameters>];
```

Where,

- Profile_name is the name of the profile to create

- Resource_parameters can be used to set the following:

sessions_per_user limits a user to the specified number of concurrent sessions.

cpu_per_session limits the CPU time used by the session (in 1/100th of a second).

cpu_per_call limits the CPU time per call (parse, execute, or fetch) (in 1/100th of a second).

connect_time limits the total elapsed time for a session (in minutes).

idle_time limits inactive time (continuous) for a session (in minutes).

logical_reads_per_session limits the number of data blocks (memory and disk) read in a session.

logical_reads_per_call limits the number of data blocks read for a call (parse, execute, or fetch).

private_sga limits the amount of private space that can be allocated in the shared pool by a session.

composite_limit limits the total resource cost for a session (in service units that are calculated as a weighted sum of CPU_PER_SESSION, CONNECT_TIME, LOGICAL_READS_PER_SESSION, and PRIVATE_SGA).

NOTE

Setting a resource or a password parameter to UNLIMITED indicates that no restriction has been placed on the usage of that parameter.

- password_parameters can be used to set the following:

    failed_login_attempts limits the number of failed attempts to log in after which the account is locked automatically.

    password_life_time limits the number of days for which the same password can be used.

    password_reuse_time limits the number of days, after which the password cannot be reused.

    password_reuse_max specifies the number of password changes required, after which the current password can be reused.

    password_lock_time specifies the number of days for which an account will remain locked after automatically locking because of failed login attempts.

    password_grace_time specifies the number of days in the grace period during which the password must be changed or the account will be locked.

    password_verify_function specifies the password complexity checking function to use.

22

PASSWORD
MANAGEMENT

> **NOTE**
>
> Resource parameters must be enabled by using the ALTER SYSTEM statement or the init.ora parameter RESOURCE_LIMIT. However, password parameters are always enabled.

In order to drop a profile, you must have the DROP PROFILE system privilege. When a profile that is assigned to users is dropped, the DEFAULT profile gets assigned to the users. Profiles can be dropped by using the DROP PROFILE statement with the following syntax:

```
DROP PROFILE <profile_name> [CASCADE];
```

Where,

- Profile_name is the name of the profile to drop.
- Cascade indicates that you want to de-assign the profile from users before dropping it.

> **NOTE**
>
> The DEFAULT profile cannot be dropped.

The following example drops the *test_profile* and also assigns the DEFAULT profile to the users currently assigned the *test_profile*:

```
DROP PROFILE test_profile CASCADE;
```

> **NOTE**
>
> The DEFAULT profile sets the following password parameters when you run the utlpwdmg.sql file to enable the password features:
>
> - PASSWORD_LIFE_TIME is set to 60.
> - PASSWORD_GRACE_TIME is set to 10.
> - PASSWORD_REUSE_TIME is set to 1800.
> - PASSWORD_REUSE_MAX is set to UNLIMITED.
> - FAILED_LOGIN_ATTEMPTS is set to 3.
> - PASSWORD_LOCK_TIME is set to 1/1440.
> - PASSWORD_VERIFY_FUNCTION is set to verify_function.

The ALTER PROFILE statement can be used to add, modify, or remove a resource or password limitation from an existing profile. Altering a profile affects only subsequent users who are assigned the profile (not current users). Changing resource parameters requires that you have the ALTER PROFILE system privilege, whereas changing the password parameters requires that you have the ALTER PROFILE and the ALTER USER system privilege. A limit cannot be removed from the DEFAULT profile. The syntax of the ALTER PROFILE statement is as follows:

```
ALTER PROFILE <profile_name>
LIMIT [resource_parameters] [password_parameters];
```

Where,

- Profile_name is the name of the profile to modify.
- Resource_parameters are the resource parameters to modify.
- Password_parameters are the password parameters to modify.

Consider the following examples of altering profiles:

- Modify the profile test_profile so that the account becomes locked for two days after four unsuccessful login attempts.

```
ALTER PROFILE test_profile
FAILED_LOGIN_ATTEMPTS 4
PASSWORD_LOCK_TIME 2;
```

- Set the PASSWORD_LIFE_TIME and the PASSWORD_GRACE_TIME to their value set in the DEFAULT PROFILE.

```
ALTER PROFILE test_profile
PASSWORD_LIFE_TIME DEFAULT
PASSWORD_GRACE_TIME DEFAULT;
```

Profiles can be assigned to users with the CREATE USER or ALTER USER statement. You need the CREATE USER system privilege in order to be able to create a user and the ALTER USER system privilege in order to be able to alter a user. The syntax of the CREATE USER statement is as follows:

```
CREATE USER <user_name>
IDENTIFIED [BY password¦ EXTERNALLY ¦ GLOBALLY AS 'external_name']
DEFAULT TABLESPACE <default_tablespace>
TEMPORARY TABLESPACE <temp_tablespace>
QUOTA <value> ON <tablespace_name>
PROFILE <profile_name>
DEFAULT ROLE <role_specification>
PASSWORD EXPIRE
ACCOUNT [LOCK¦ UNLOCK];
```

> **NOTE**
>
> After creating a user, you must at least give the user CREATE SESSION privilege so that he can connect to the database.

where,

- user_name specifies the username that is being created.
- IDENTIFIED specifies the authentication method used for this account:

  BY password indicates that the user is a local user and must specify the password to log in.

  EXTERNALLY indicates that the user is an external user and must be authenticated externally by the operating system or a third-party utility.

  GLOBALLY AS 'external_name' indicates that the user is a global user and authenticated by the enterprise directory service.

- DEFAULT TABLESPACE specifies the default tablespace for the objects created by the user.
- TEMPORARY TABLESPACE specifies the tablespace used for the users temporary segments.
- QUOTA specifies the maximum space that can be used by the user in the particular tablespace.
- PROFILE specifies the profile assigned to the user. If you omit this, the user will be assigned the DEFAULT profile.
- DEFAULT ROLE specifies the default role assigned to the user.
- PASSWORD EXPIRE forces the password to expire for the user. Setting this will force the user (or DBA) to change the password before he can log in to the database.
- ACCOUNT specifies whether to LOCK (and disable access) or UNLOCK (and enable access) the account.

Consider an example:

Create a user susan with the initial password of welcome, which must be changed before the user can log in to the database. The users tablespace can be used for both the default and temporary tablespace. Type the following at the server manager or SQL*Plus prompt:

```
CREATE USER susan
IDENTIFIED BY welcome
DEFAULT TABLESPACE users
TEMPORARY TABLESPACE users
PROFILE test_profile
PASSWORD EXPIRE;
```

The ALTER USER statement can be used to modify the characteristics of the user such as the password, profile, or default and temporary tablespace. The syntax is as follows:

```
ALTER USER <user_name>
IDENTIFIED [BY password ¦ EXTERNALLY ¦ GLOBALLY AS 'external_name']
DEFAULT TABLESPACE <tablespace_name>
TEMPORARY TABLESPACE <tablespace_name>
QUOTA <value> ON <tablespace_name>
PROFILE <profile_name>
DEFAULT ROLE <role_specification>
PASSWORD EXPIRE
ACCOUNT [LOCK ¦ UNLOCK]
```

Where the parameters have the same meaning as in the CREATE USER statement.

Consider the following examples:

1. Lock the account of user spy

   ```
   SVRMGR> ALTER USER spy ACCOUNT LOCK;
   ```

2. Set the DEFAULT PROFILE to the user greg

   ```
   SVRMGR> ALTER USER greg PROFILE DEFAULT;
   ```

3. Expire the password for the user mark

   ```
   SVRMGR> ALTER USER mark PASSWORD EXPIRE;
   ```

Choosing the Authentication Method

The CONNECT INTERNAL syntax of earlier versions has been replaced with two methods: OS authentication and password files. You can choose to use either of these methods based upon how you want to administer the database. The OS authentication technique is good if you are planning to administer your database locally on the same machine where the database resides. On the other hand, password files are better if you are planning to administer many different databases from a central client machine.

> **NOTE**
>
> In order to connect to Oracle over a non-secured connection, the following must be TRUE:
>
> - A password file must be used by the server to which you are connecting.
> - The SYSDBA or SYSOPER system privilege must be granted to you.
> - The connection must be made using a username and password.

22

PASSWORD MANAGEMENT

Using OS Authentication

OS authentication can be used to integrate the security of Oracle with that of the operating system. OS authentication is achieved by linking Oracle accounts with the operating system user accounts such that when the user successfully logs on to the operating system, she can use the Oracle database without supplying a username and password again: In other words, the user is not authenticated by Oracle again. Oracle user accounts are created as OPS$<os_user_accounts> and are identified externally. The Oracle bulletin #10676850.6 (found on Oracle MetaLink at http://www.oracle.com/support) can be referred to for details on setting OS authentication.

> **NOTE**
>
> Use of OS authentication requires a secure connection.

When OS authentication is used on Windows NT systems, the following result is derived:

With proper Oracle/Windows NT authentication setup in a single domain model, any domain user can be authenticated by the operating system if domain logon is successful.

With proper Oracle/Windows NT authentication setup in a two domain master-resource or master-master domain model, any domain user can be authenticated by the operating system, provided the user logs on successfully into one of the Windows NT domains.

The Oracle services and Windows NT security accounts database operate independently of the user currently logged on.

In a workgroup model, OS authentication is possible if the same username/password combination is defined locally on both the client and server machines, or a client user maps a drive to the Oracle server machine using the username/password of a local server account that is valid to both Windows NT and Oracle.

The following steps can be used to set up OS authentication:

1. Create the OS user who needs to be authenticated by the operating system

2. In the init.ora file, set the following parameters:
   - REMOTE_LOGIN_PASSWORDFILE = NONE—This setting indicates that you are not using a password file.

NOTE

REMOTE_LOGIN_PASSWORDFILE can take the following values:

- NONE—indicates that a password file is not being used.
- EXCLUSIVE—indicates that the password file can be used with only one database and can contain users who are neither SYSDBA nor SYSOPER.
- SHARED—indicates that the password file can be used by multiple databases and can contain only users who are SYSDBA or SYSOPER.

- OS_AUTHENT_PREFIX = ""—This setting indicates which prefix used in the database usernames will match with the OS names. Setting OS_AUTHENT_PREFIX to "" indicates that there is no prefix. The default prefix used is OPS$.

3. Create Oracle users with the username of <OS_AUTHENT_PREFIX><OS_username>. For example,

- With the OS_AUTHENT_PREFIX = "", the OS user fred maps with the Oracle user fred.
- With the OS_AUTHENT_PREFIX = "TEST", the OS user fred maps with the Oracle user TESTfred.
- With the OS_AUTHEN_PREFIX = "OPS$", the OS user fred maps with the Oracle user OPS$fred.

The specified users are now authenticated by the operating system.

Using the Password File

A password file can allow you to administer multiple databases from a central location and also over unsecure connections. The following steps can be used to perform authentication using a password file.

NOTE

The initial password for SYS is *change_on_install*, and the initial password for SYSTEM is *manager*.

1. Using the ORAPWD utility, create a password file.

```
C:\> ORAPWD FILE=meghpwd.pwd PASSWORD=oracle ENTRIES=10
```

TIP

The ORAPWD utility is used to create a password file. It should be executed from the OS prompt and takes the following parameters:

- file—indicates the name of the password
- password—password for SYS and internal
- entries—maximum number of distinct DBAs and OPERs

---

2. In the init.ora file, set the REMOTE_LOGIN_PASSWORDFILE parameter to EXCLUSIVE.
3. Grant SYSDBA and SYSOPER privileges to users in order to add them to the password file.

```
GRANT SYSDBA TO john;
GRANT SYSOPER TO john;
```

The specified users are now authenticated by the password file.

NOTE

The password file should be protected; otherwise, the database security can be compromised.

The password file is an important part of your security strategy, and when it is used, you have to protect it. There are several maintenance actions that you need to perform in relation to password files such as replacing, removing, or expanding it to allow more users.

NOTE

The password file should not be removed or modified if a database or instance has mounted it using the REMOTE_LOGIN_PASSWORDFILE set to SHARED or EXCLUSIVE. Otherwise, you will not be able to reconnect remotely using the password file even if it is later replaced.

Migration Problems with Password File

Migrating an Oracle7 database to Oracle8*i* needs special consideration if a password file is being used. You might encounter ORA-600 [kzsrsdn: 1] during the migration of an Oracle7 database to Oracle8*i* if the following conditions are true:

- A password file is being used by the Oracle7 database.
- The password file is not moved to the correct directory in the Oracle8*i* environment: $ORACLE_HOME/dbs (UNIX) or $ORACLE_HOME\database (Windows NT).
- The REMOTE_LOGIN_PASSWORDFILE init.ora parameter is set to EXCLUSIVE.

The following steps can be taken to continue with the migration and recover from the ORA-600 error:

1. Shut down the database.

   ```
   SVRMGR> shutdown
   ```

2. Edit the init.ora file and set the REMOTE_LOGIN_PASSWORDFILE to NONE.

3. Start up mount the database.

   ```
   SVRMGR> STARTUP MOUNT PFILE=<path of the init.ora file>
   ```

4. Reset the archive logs.

   ```
   SVRMGR> ALTER DATABASE OPEN RESETLOGS;
   ```

5. Continue with the migration process.

6. After the migration completes successfully, re-create the password file using the ORAPWD utility.

7. Edit the init.ora file to set REMOTE_LOGIN_PASSWORDFILE to EXCLUSIVE.

Summary

Oracle8*i* provides several enhancements for password management, allowing the DBA to have a lot of control over the usage of passwords in the database. Some of the features such as password complexity verification, password aging and history, password lifetime, and account lockout can be used to make sure that the passwords are periodically changed and the DBA has more control over the manner in which accounts are used. Use of these features prevents unauthorized personnel from accessing user accounts by attempting to guess the passwords.

Net8 Features

IN THIS CHAPTER

Net8 enables network connectivity between the Oracle8*i* server and remote clients. Net8 replaces SQL*Net 2.x as the underlying software providing networking services and connectivity to an Oracle8*i* database, and it runs on top of standard network protocols such as TCP/IP, SPX/IPX, and NetBEUI. Net8 has evolved considerably from SQL*Net, supporting numerous APIs, Java-enabled browsers, and advanced network security. Net8 provides complete backward compatibility with SQL*Net 2.x, and it offers a bridge to Oracle's future object-based connectivity approach.

This chapter addresses the new functionality added to Net8 in Oracle8*i*. In brief, the features I address are

- Listener enhancements: Instances are able to register themselves with the listener
- Scalability: Improvements for multithreaded server configuration and tuning
- Connectivity: Multiprotocol connectivity enhancements
- Manageability: Improvements for administration tools and enhanced dynamic discovery capabilities
- Security: Enhancements to the Advanced Security Option

Net8 and Listener Enhancements

Prior to Oracle8*i*, it was necessary to configure instance information in the `listener.ora` file (via the SID_LIST_*<listenername>* parameter) in order to register instances with the listener process upon instance startup. In Oracle8*i*, instances are able to register themselves to the listener when started. Oracle8*i* provides two new initialization parameters that allow instances to specify their instance name and the services to which they belong:

- `instance_name`: Specifies the instance name
- `service_names`: Specifies the services the instance is to be registered for (includes both database name and domain name)

By default, a background process registers an instance's information to the listener on the local machine. The chief benefit of dynamic instance registration is that it provides automatic failover of a user process's request to a different listener (that is, one listed in the `service_names` parameter) if an instance is unavailable and enables connection load balancing.

Enhanced Connectivity and Scalability

Net8 offers considerable features to enable vast scalability for high-end online transaction processing, data warehousing, and messaging driving for highly scalable servers. Net8 provides multiplexing, connection pooling, concentration, and naming services as a solution to scalability requirements. In addition, Net8 supports the Level 2 ODBC-compliant driver in order to provide enhanced connectivity to non-Oracle databases.

Connection and Client Load Balancing

Load balancing is a Net8 feature in which client connections are uniformly distributed across multiple listeners, dispatchers, instances, and nodes in order to reduce the likelihood of a single component becoming overloaded. Load balancing is accomplished at two levels: connection load balancing, and client load balancing.

Connection Load Balancing

Connection load balancing is enabled only within a multithreaded server environment. Registration of an Oracle8*i* database enables connection load balancing because of the inherent registration that occurs with remote listeners. This enables the listener to make intelligent routing decisions based on how many connections each dispatcher is currently managing and on how heavily loaded the server nodes are for running the database instances. Node load balancing is new in Oracle8*i* and enables balancing the load at two levels: dispatchers and nodes.

Figure 23.1 summarizes the fundamental scheme used for connection load balancing. A client requesting a connection to a service will randomly pick a listener from the list of listeners identified for the service in `tnsnames.ora`. If the selected listener is unavailable, the connection request fails-over to the next available listener. This capability is called client load balancing and failover. Each listener has information about the load on all available nodes (because each instance has registered with all identified listeners). For each connection request, the listener identifies which node has the least amount of CPU resource usage. The listener then identifies which dispatcher is currently handling the least number of connections on that node. The connection is then routed to that dispatcher on the chosen node.

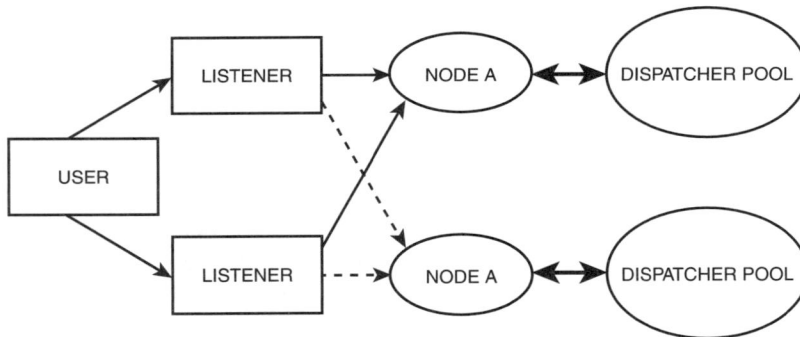

FIGURE 23.1
Connection load balancing.

Client Load Balancing

If a given database instance is serviced by more than one listener, a client would be able to select between listeners for its connections. This selection is randomized, which provides the benefit of allowing all listeners to equally share the load of connection requests.

Client load balancing and failover is enabled through new settings in tnsnames.ora. Figure 23.2 shows a sample tnsnames.ora entry that configures client load balancing. The load_balance parameter must be set to ON to enable clients to randomly select listeners when trying to connect. Additionally, it is necessary to configure multiple listening addresses for each Net8 service name. Connection failover can also be requested by setting the FAILOVER parameter to ON for your set of listening addresses.

```
CONNECT1 = (DESCRIPTION=
                    (FAILOVER=on)
                    (LOAD_BALANCE=on)
                    (ADDRESS =   (PROTOCOL=tcp)
                                 (HOST=svr1)
                                 (PORT=1521))
                    (ADDRESS =   (PROTOCOL=tcp)
                                 (HOST=svr2)
                                 (PORT=1521))
                    (CONNECT_DATA=(SERVICE_NAME=erpsvr))
          )
```

FIGURE 23.2

Sample tnsnames.ora *entry for client load balancing.*

Setting Service Names

In Oracle8*i*, service naming is able to include multiple services provided by a single database and services that span multiple instances. Although the SID identifies a database instance, it does not identify a database. Because of this limitation, prior to Oracle8*i*, a database could not have more than one service associated with it. In Oracle8*i*, a database can serve multiple instances, and the SID parameter in the connect descriptor of tnsnames.ora has been replaced by SERVICE_NAME and INSTANCE_NAME. Figure 23.3 illustrates the use of these new parameters.

```
mfg = (DESCRIPTION=
                    (ADDRESS = (PROTOCOL=tcp)(HOST=mfg-svr1)(PORT=1890)
                    (CONNECT_DATA=(SERVICE_NAME = manufac01)
                                  (INSTANCE_NAME = mfg01)
                    )
```

FIGURE 23.3
Use of SERVICE_NAME and INSTANCE_NAME parameters.

When setting service names, the parameter `service_name` is commonly set to the global database name. Additionally, setting `instance_name` is only necessary if using Oracle Parallel Server.

Connection Pooling

Connection pooling allows you to maximize the number of physical network connections across Net8 to a multithreaded server. This feature is accomplished by sharing (pooling) a dispatcher's set of connections among multiple clients. A connection pool is the maximum allowed number of connections that is shared among several clients. Because connection pooling allows Oracle to not have to maintain unused connections, performance of active user sessions is improved. Connection pooling can be used only for multithreaded servers and does not apply to dedicated server environments.

The ideal usage for connection pooling would be for networks in which many clients run interactive high idle/search time applications, such as messaging and OLAP. In this situation the clients can afford the wait time to get connected to a dispatcher.

How Connection Pooling Works

Assume that multiple connections are established to particular dispatchers. When the maximum connections are reached for available dispatchers for a given protocol, the next session that attempts to establish a connection will wait for an existing idle connection to be temporarily disconnected by the dispatcher, after which the connection is established.

The connection that was idle becomes temporarily disconnected. If the disconnected session needs to process a request, the connection is reestablished by waiting for another session to temporarily disconnect. However, if the maximum number of sessions for a dispatcher are less than configured, the processing request is carried out immediately.

Enabling Connection Pooling

In order to enable connection pooling, additional settings must be configured for the init.ora parameter `mts_dispatchers`. An example of such a configuration is shown in the following. Please note that the parameter abbreviations shown are new to Oracle8*i*.

```
MTS_DISPATCHERS =
            "(PRO=tcp)(CON=30)(DIS=8)(POO=on)(TICKS=10)(SESS=50)"
```

What do each of the parameters mean in the preceding example? POOL (POO) enables connection pooling if ON, YES, or TRUE is specified. If a number is specified for POOL, connection pooling is enabled for both incoming and outgoing network connections, and the number specified is the timeout in ticks (one tick equals one second) for both incoming and outgoing network connections. CONNECTION (CON or CONN) is the maximum number of network connections to allow for each dispatcher. Up to 255 concurrent dispatchers can be set up in Net8.

TICKS (TIC or TICK) is optional and specifies the size of a network tick in seconds. The default for TICKS is 15 seconds. SESSIONS (SESS or SES) specifies the maximum number of user processes that can work against a dispatcher.

Connection Manager

Connection Manager (CMAN) is a standalone application that works only with multithreaded servers. It takes multiple session requests from a client and multiplexes them to a server over a single transport network protocol. CMAN would be useful for many large client applications that have high response time requirements. Ideally, CMAN would be installed in a middle tier (that is, application server) of a multitier computing environment to reduce resource consumption on the server tier. Figure 23.4 illustrates the usage of Connection Manager.

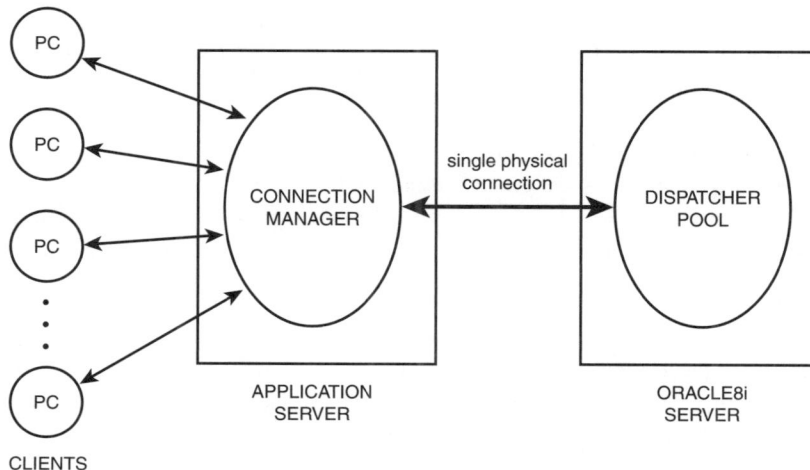

FIGURE 23.4
Connection Manager.

Uses of Connection Manager

Connection Manager transmits data from one process to another in a TNS network. It can act as a Network Access Controller, checking whether a party is authorized to transmit across it. CMAN can act as a concentrator, accepting data from multiple separate connections and multiplexing the data into one common physical transmission. Also, CMAN can act as a multi-protocol interchange, passing data from one protocol to another (say, from TCP/IP to NetBEUI). Therefore, CMAN enables a client and server with different networking protocols to communicate with each other. This capability effectively replaces the Multi Protocol Interchange used in SQL*Net 2.x.

Connection Concentration: Configuration Issues

Figure 23.5 shows the essential configuration of Connection Manager for performing connection concentration. Note again the use of CMAN in a middle tier configuration. The tnsnames.ora file resides on the clients, the listener.ora and init.ora files reside on the Oracle8 server, and the cman.ora file resides in the CMAN tier. When configuring connection concentration, it is necessary to start the connection manager process CMGW (on UNIX) or the CMGW80 service (on Windows NT). By default, the CMGW process listens on either port 1610 or 1600 (exactly which of these two port values is the default is strictly platform dependent). In addition, there is a process CMADM that maintains address information in the Oracle Names server for the SQL*Net 2.x and Net 8.x clients. Both CMGW and CMADM are started through a special control utility cmctl (on UNIX) or cmctl80 (on Windows NT).

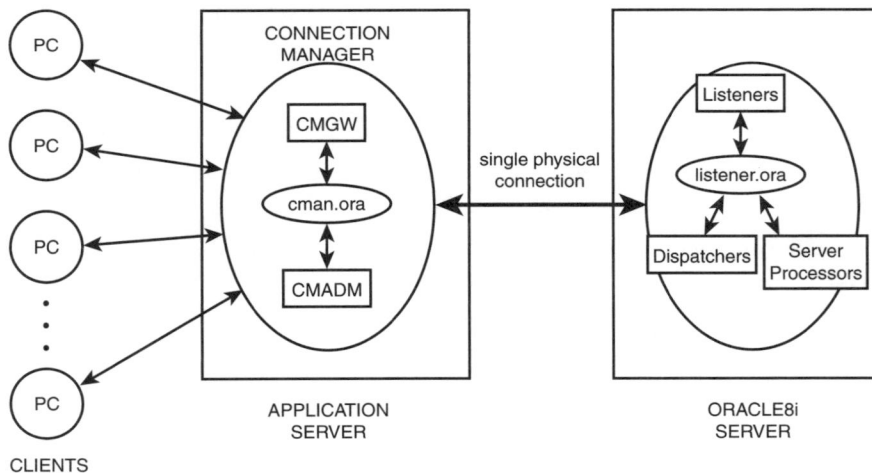

FIGURE 23.5

Connection concentration via CMAN.

Configuring the Client

In order to properly configure the clients for connection concentration, both the listener address for the Connection Manager process CMGW and the address for the destination listener need to be listed in `tnsnames.ora`. The sample output from `tnsnames.ora` illustrates these requirements:

```
# D:\ORANT\NET80\ADMIN\tnsnames.ora Configuration File
# Generated by Oracle Net8 Assistant
# for connection concentration
TEST1 = (DESCRIPTION = (SOURCE_ROUTE=yes)
            (ADDRESS = (PROTOCOL=tcp)
                    (PORT = 1600)
                    (HOST = app_server1))
            (ADDRESS= (PROTOCOL = tcp)
                    (PORT = 1521)
                    (HOST = mfg_server1))
                    (CONNECT_DATA=
                            (SERVICE_NAME=mfg))
        )
```

In the preceding output, note that we have specified the address for the connection manager process CMGW (port number 1600 on host app_server1). We specified the address for the listener on the destination machine (port number 1521 on host mfg_server1). We had to specify the SERVICE_NAME to which the connection needs to be established (mfg). Finally, in order to allow the clients to connect through Connection Manager, we had to set the value of SOURCE_ROUTE to YES.

Configuring Connection Manager

Configuration of Connection Manager is done through the file `cman.ora`. This file is placed in the `$ORACLE_HOME/network/admin` directory of the tier in which Connection Manager resides. An example of a `cman.ora` file is shown in the following:

```
# cman's listening addresses for connection concentration
CMAN = (ADDRESS_LIST=
        (ADDRESS=(PROTOCOL=tcp)
        (HOST= app_server1)
        (PORT=1600)))
# cman's configurable parameters
CMAN_PROFILE = (PARAMETER_LIST=
                        (MAXIMUM_RELAYS=1024)
                        (LOG_LEVEL=1)
                        (TRACING=no)
                        (RELAY_STATISTICS=yes)
                        (SHOW_TNS_INFO=yes)
                        (USE_ASYNC_CALL=yes)
                        (AUTHENTICATION_LEVEL=1))
```

The cman.ora file shown previously contains two important configuration sections necessary for connection concentration. The parameter entry CMAN contains the listening address for Connection Manager (in this case, app_server1 on port 1600). This entry must always be specified, unless default configuration is chosen.

The entry CMAN_PROFILE in cman.ora contains various optional CMAN configuration parameters that can be set for use by Connection Manager when administering user sessions. Table 23.1 summarizes these settings.

TABLE 23.1   Configuration Parameters for CMAN_PROFILE

Parameter Name	Description
MAXIMUM_RELAYS	Determines the maximum number of concurrent connections allowed.
LOG_LEVEL	Determines the level of logging performed by the CMAN.
TRACING	Can be specified as YES or NO. YES enables CMAN tracing to a file.
RELAY_STATISTICS	Can be specified as YES or NO. YES instructs the CMAN to maintain statistics pertaining to relay I/O activities such as Number of IN bytes, Number of OUT bytes, and so on.
SHOW_TNS_INFO	Can be specified as YES or NO. Yes instructs the CMAN to include TNS events in the log file.
USE_ASYNC_CALL	Can be specified as YES or NO. YES instructs the CMAN to use all asynchronous functions while in the answering, accepting, or calling phase of establishing a connection.
AUTHENTICATION_LEVEL	Can be specified as 0 or 1. A value of 1 instructs the CMAN to reject connect requests that are not using Secure Network Services. Secure Network Services is part of the Advanced Networking Option. 0 is the default, which means Secure Network Services is not required.

23

NET8 FEATURES

Configuring Oracle8i Server

To use connection concentration, you are required to configure the multithreaded server on the destination database. In order to enable connection concentration, you need to specify a new setting MULTIPLEX (with an abbreviation of MUL) to ON for the init.ora parameter mts_dispatchers. The following is an example of setting this in init.ora:

```
MTS_DISPATCHERS="(PROTOCOL=tcp)(DIS=3)(MUL=on)"
```

Security Features

Connection Manager offers network access control for an Internet environment. Using a predefined Net8 application proxy, administrators control how a connection request is routed on the

Internet. Connection Manager filters connections based on origin, destination, or database service names. This capability is critical for the Internet in order to restrict remote access to sensitive data.

Setting Up Access Control Rules

All access control rules are configured in the `cman.ora` file. In addition to the CMAN and CMAN_PROFILE sections of `cman.ora`, we need to add another section, CMAN_RULES. The CMAN section remains the same.

To configure for network access control, the CMAN_RULES section of the `cman.ora` needs to be configured. The following example illustrates how to configure the CMAN_RULES section:

```
# cman's listening addresses for connection concentration
CMAN=(ADDRESS_LIST=
     (ADDRESS = (PROTOCOL=tcp)
                (HOST= app_server1)
                (PORT=1600)))

# cman is used as a TCP fire wall proxy IF
# AND ONLY IF "cman_rules" exist
CMAN_RULES=(RULES_LIST=
           (RULE=(SRC=A)(DST=mfg-servers)(SRV=mfg100)(ACT=accept))
           (RULE=(SRC=B)(DST=mfg-servers)(SRV=mfg100)(ACT=reject))
           )

# cman's configurable params
CMAN_PROFILE=(PARAMETER_LIST=(MAXIMUM_RELAYS=1024)  ...

                             (AUTHENTICATION_LEVEL=1))
```

SRC is the source hostname or IP address of the session request (Client). DST is the destination hostname or IP address (Server). SRV is obtained from SERVICE_NAMES in `init.ora`. ACT can be set to ACCept or REJect based on the other three parameters.

Configuration Features

Manageability challenges involve increasing complexity and cost. Larger networks with more complex services are required. Oracle8*i* networking provides solutions to these problems with new configuration options.

Net8 Assistant is launched directly from the Windows workstation. It is found under the Network Administration program group of Oracle8*i*. Figure 23.6 shows the user interface for this tool. When launched, the administrator is able to use pull-down menus to configure the listener, names server, or TNS service names.

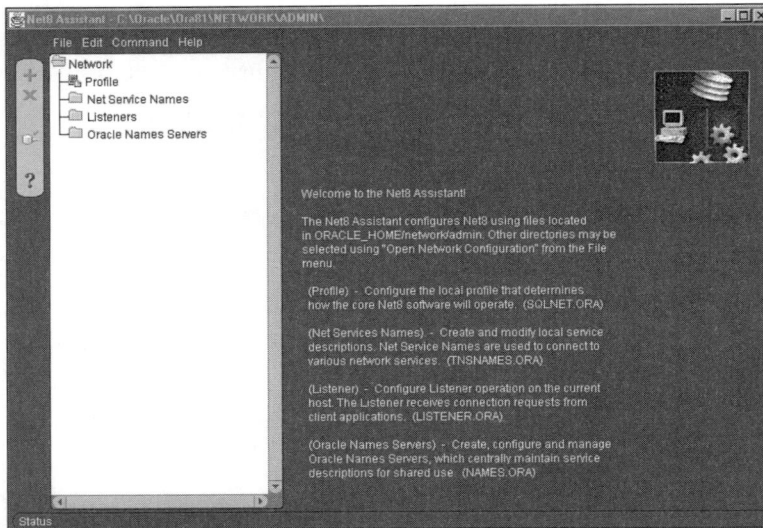

FIGURE 23.6

Net8 Assistant.

The Net8 Assistant replaces the Network Manager tool of Oracle7 and provides a wide range of network configuration and management features. It is a graphical tool that allows users to customize network preferences through a simple interface.

Wizard-like tools take users step by step through the most common network configuration tasks. It can read and configure files for both Net8 and SQL*Net V2. Net8 Assistant also allows connectivity of new (or existing) services to be tested. This tool can be used for Oracle Names. It provides a GUI with similar functionality as the names control utility namesctl that can be run from the operating system prompt to start and control the Oracle Names server. Because Net8 Assistant is written in Java, it is available on a wide variety of platforms. It also works with Oracle's directory services and Oracle Names.

In addition to Net8 Assistant, Oracle offers the Oracle Net8 Easy Config tool. This tool replaces the SQL*Net Easy Configuration tool. Net8 Easy Config is useful for configuring and testing simple networks.

Additional Net8 Features

A number of additional features have been incorporated into Net8 for Oracle8*i*. Considerable improvements have been incorporated into Net8 for administration of the Oracle Names Server, including faster name translation and more efficient client-side caching. Net8 has also been enhanced with improved tuning and troubleshooting through the Oracle Trace Assistant.

Improvements to Oracle Name Server

Oracle Names is a powerful directory service that provides name-to-address resolution for each Net8 service on the network. We recommend using Oracle Names, if you have either (1) an enterprisewide network that spans multiple geographic regions, or (2) several local area networks, each with a few servers and a few hundred clients.

Oracle Names with Net8 has three features to improve network performance and ease of administration:

- *Dynamic service resolution*: Net8 services can register themselves with a Names Server.
- *Client discovery of Names Servers*: The client can retrieve a list of Names Servers at installation.
- *Names resolution optimization (client-side cache)*: The client maintains a list of Names Servers and name query results in a local cache.

All destination services register themselves with a Names Server. After every component is registered and running, the client can find any service on the network by following these steps:

1. The client provides the service name and obtains a list of all known local Names Servers (stored in sdns.ora).
2. The service name is forwarded to each Names Server on the list until it is resolved to a destination address.
3. With the resolved destination address, the client initiates a session request to the database server.

Names Server configuration details are described in Oracle's documentation manual Oracle8i Net8 Configuration Guide. This manual is an extremely valuable source of information for setting up and configuring Names Servers.

Trace Assistant

Net8 provides a tool called Trace Assistant to assist you in understanding the information provided in your Net8 trace files by converting existing lines of trace file text into a more readable form. Trace Assistant is able to display summary statistics for complete client sessions from the client through to the server. Error messages are extracted from trace files and displayed. Trace Assistant runs against only a level 16 (SUPPORT) SQL*Net or Net8 trace file.

The Trace Assistant is invoked from the command line via trcasst, and the name of the network trace file must be passed in when starting Trace Assistant. For example, the command:

```
trcasst -o sqlnet144.trc
```

invokes Trace Assistant to analyze the file sqlnet144.trc, and the -o option enables the display of connectivity and two tasks with common information to be displayed. Other options that can

be used with Trace Assistant include -s (displays statistical information) and -e (enables display of error information).

Please refer to Oracle's documentation manual *Oracle8i Net8 Configuration Guide* for further details of the use of Trace Assistant.

Summary

Net8 offers significant benefits in Oracle network configuration administration features. Listener enhancements, scalability, improved connectivity, and configuration tools all represent vast improvements over network management support in pre-Oracle8*i* releases. The features of Net8 are designed to dramatically simplify the administrator's work in managing large, multitier Oracle environments. In addition, Net8 offers the ability of massive networks to be supported for high connectivity to Oracle databases.

23

NET8 FEATURES

Oracle Parallel Server

IN THIS CHAPTER

Oracle Parallel Server (OPS) provides high availability and scalability to allow multiple Oracle instances running on multiple nodes to access a single shared Oracle database. The same database is shared by all the nodes that have common datafiles and control files but separate SGAs, log files, and rollback segments.

This chapter discusses the Oracle Parallel Server architecture and makes you familiar with the parallel server enhancements available with Oracle8i.

Cluster Configurations

Machines can be configured in a variety of cluster configurations, depending on the manner in which resources are shared and internode interaction occurs:

- Tightly coupled systems use multiple CPUs that share memory through a common memory bus. For such systems, the performance is limited by the bus's bandwidth.

- Loosely coupled systems use multiple nodes that share disk and other resources but not memory (see Figure 24.1). Each node contains one or more CPUs and communicates with other nodes through a high-speed common bus.

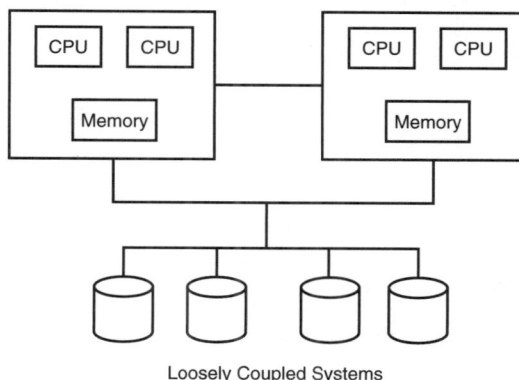

Loosely Coupled Systems

FIGURE 24.1
Loosely coupled systems.

- *Massively parallel processors* are also referred to as a *shared-nothing architecture* (see Table 24.1) because neither memory nor disk resources are shared between the nodes (see Figure 24.2). This configuration makes use of hundreds of nodes to achieve scalability. Each node usually contains an inexpensive CPU. A high-speed interconnect is used for internode communication.

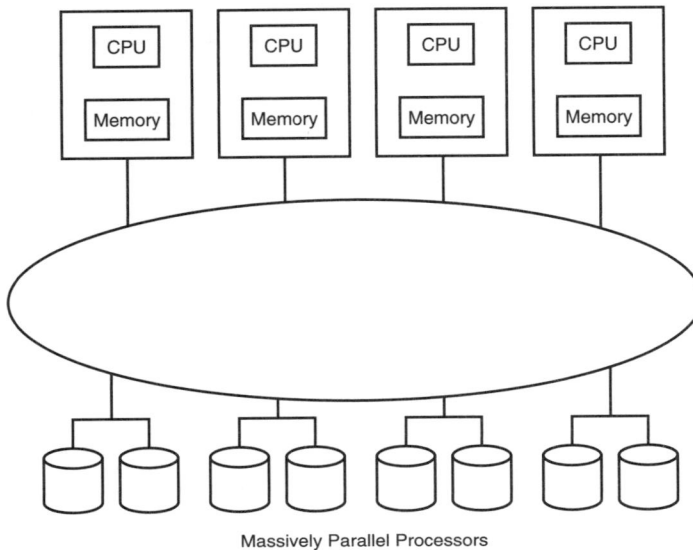

Massively Parallel Processors

FIGURE 24.2
Massively parallel processors.

> **NOTE**
>
> OPS isn't used with tightly coupled systems because of the performance problems associated with the maintenance of cache coherency and the distributed lock manager (DLM). However, OPS can be used with both loosely coupled systems and massively parallel processors.

24

ORACLE PARALLEL SERVER

TABLE 24.1   Comparing Shared-Disk and Shared-Nothing Architectures

Feature	Shared Disk	Shared Nothing
All nodes have direct access to all disks	Yes	No
Load Balancing	Yes	No
Resource allocation	Flexible	Nonflexible and results in skewed resource usage

continues

TABLE 24.1   Continued

Feature	Shared Disk	Shared Nothing
Performance dependency on the bandwidth of shared bus	High	Low
Internode communication	Can cause performance problems if the applications are not designed properly	Minimal
Uses node-to-disk affinity	No	Yes
Scalability	Low	High
Coherency control	Global coherency control provided by Distributed Lock Manager	Local coherency control provided by individual nodes
Fault tolerance	High	Low

NOTE

Oracle Parallel Server makes use of shared-disk architecture.

Several benefits can be achieved by using OPS:

- High performance and scalability—The performance of a well-designed database and applications can be improved by using OPS. It is very important to put a lot of effort into designing your database and applications because an improperly designed single instance environment that is performing poorly will perform worse in an OPS environment. Pinging should be minimized to increase scalability.

- High availability—High availability can be achieved by using the fault-tolerance and failover capabilities of the operating system and the DLM. Failure in one node doesn't affect other nodes, and they can keep running and help to recover the failed node.

- Support a large number of users—Each node has its own memory and can support users. By adding more nodes to the clusters, you can increase the number of users supported.

Oracle Parallel Server Architecture

Oracle8*i* Parallel Server architecture makes use of the shared-disk approach. Each node can run its own instance and share the same set of database files and control files. Each instance has its own shared global area (SGA) and background threads. Each instance can use a separate

init.ora file, but it must have common parameters. The redo threads of the instances are used during instance recovery, and therefore the redo thread of each instance is accessible by the other instances. Similarly, archived redo log files are available to all instances. Users can be supported by any node in the cluster.

The SGA in each instance contains the following structures:

- Database buffer cache that contains the data blocks
- Redo log buffer cache that contains redo entries
- Shared pool that contains the shared SQL and PL/SQL
- Data Dictionary cache that caches the Data Dictionary information
- Distributed lock area that contains locks used for coordinating access to shared resources

In Oracle8*i*, clients connect to the database using a service (instead of an instance name). Multiple nodes are associated with a particular service as specified by tnsnames.ora. Clients connect to a service and not any particular node. When any node fails, automatic failover is provided by connecting to another surviving node associated with the service.

Operating System Dependent Components

Oracle Parallel Server architecture makes use of several operating system dependent (OSD) components. The OSD layer consists of several modules. Some of these modules are required, whereas others are optional and used by individual vendors for competitive advantage. Oracle has defined the requirements and interfaces for the operating system dependent components to provide valuable service during the operation of OPS.

NOTE

Each hardware vendor provides its own OSD layer.

OSD layer consists of several important modules:

- Cluster Manager (CM)—Used to discover and access the cluster's state. The fault-tolerance capabilities of Oracle Parallel Server depends on the cluster resources' fault-tolerance capabilities. When a cluster node fails, the surviving nodes in the cluster are reconfigured by using the CM module. Table 24.2 shows the difference between cluster members and nonmembers.

24

ORACLE PARALLEL SERVER

TABLE **24.2** Cluster Members Versus Nonmembers

Characteristic	Cluster members	Nonmembers
Aware of one another's existence	Yes	No
Can access the shared resources	Yes	No

- Inter-Process Communication (IPC)—Provides reliable communication between instances. The performance of OPS depends heavily on the speed of the interconnect between nodes.

- Input/Output—Provides access from all nodes to a cluster disk farm. To increase performance, use fiber-channel links to connect high-speed storage devices to the nodes in the cluster.

- Startup—Initiates the OPS components in a particular order during instance startup. Vendor-specific structures are initialized by this module.

Integrated Distributed Lock Manager

The Integrated Distributed Lock Manager (IDLM) is an important component of the OPS architecture that maintains a list of system resources and provides a locking mechanism to control the access to these system resources. IDLM-controlled resources are logical structures and not actual tables. Concurrency control to resources such as data blocks and rollback segments is provided by the IDLM. The IDLM coordinates the requests for resources and grants available resources to the process or user requesting it. When resources are not available, it tracks the requests and grants them the resources when they become available.

IDLM has several important features:

- Distributed architecture is used to maintain a database of resources and locks on these resources. Each node in the cluster maintains a portion of the global locks.

- Fault tolerance is provided by means of the ability to provide continued service of lock, so long as at least one instance is active in the cluster configuration.

- Lock mastering is achieved by nominating one node to maintain all information about a resource and its locks.

- Provides automatic deadlock detection.

- Lamport SCN generation is used to generate SCNs in parallel on all the instances.

- Group-based locking allows multiple processes belonging to the same group to share a lock and minimize the amount of lock conversion performed.

- Resources are persistent, allowing them to retain their state even though the processes or groups holding them die abnormally.

IDLM is external to Oracle and resides on each node. Several functions are provided by the IDLM:

- Coordinates the requests for locks on shared resources such as data blocks, Data Dictionary entries, and rollback segments by the various Oracle processes running on the different instances.
- Keeps track of the resource owners.
- Informs the resource owner when another process requests the resource owned by it.
- Notifies the requesting process when the resource it requests becomes available.
- Communicates with Oracle via the Lock (LCK) processes.

The following formulas can be used to determine the settings for the resources, locks, and processes while configuring DLM:

```
resources = total_PCM_locks + (total_non_PCM_locks * num_instances)

locks = (total_PCM_locks * num_instances) +
        (total_non_PCM_locks * num_instances)

processes = processes * num_instances
```

IDLM makes use of the following two types of queues to keep track of resources:

- Granted queue contains lock requests that have been granted.
- Converted queue contains lock requests that are waiting for lock conversion—for example, an exclusive lock request by process A for a resource currently granted to process B as a shared lock.

Table 24.3 shows the various lock modes available through the IDLM.

TABLE **24.3**   Lock Modes Available Through IDLM

Lock Mode	Description
NULL	This is the null mode indicating that there is no lock on the resource. This is the lowest level and is used as a placeholder.
SS	Sub-shared mode. It is used for concurrent read operations. The associated resource can be read in an unprotected fashion while other processes are reading or writing to it.
SX	Shared exclusive mode. It is used for concurrent write operations. The associated resource can be read or written in an unprotected fashion while other processes are reading or writing to it.

24

ORACLE PARALLEL SERVER

continues

TABLE **24.3**   Continued

Lock Mode	Description
S	Shared mode. Multiple processes can read the resource, but no one can write the resource.
SSX	Sub-shared exclusive mode. The process holding this lock can modify the resource without others being able to modify it. Others can read the resource in an unprotected fashion.
X	Exclusive lock. Grants the holding process exclusive access to the resource. Other processes can neither read nor write to the resource.

IDLM is also responsible for communicating the status of requests to the processes. It achieves this by means of the following two types of ASTs (asynchronous traps):

- Blocking AST (BAST) is sent to processes that are currently owning the locks on the resource in an incompatible mode.
- Acquisition AST (AAST) is sent to the requesting process after the lock on the requested resource becomes available.

The following example demonstrates the use of the various queues and asynchronous traps:

1. Shared lock request for resource X is granted to process 1. Another shared lock request for resource X is granted to process 2. Both these requests are placed in the granted queue (see Figure 24.3).

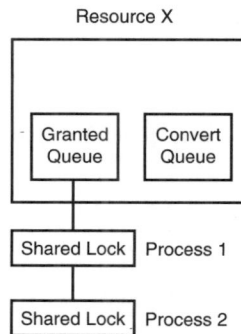

FIGURE 24.3
Process 1 and 2 holding shared lock on resource X.

2. Process 2 makes a request for exclusive lock on resource X.

3. The exclusive lock request is placed in the convert queue, and a blocking AST is sent to process 1 informing it about an exclusive request waiting (see Figure 24.4).

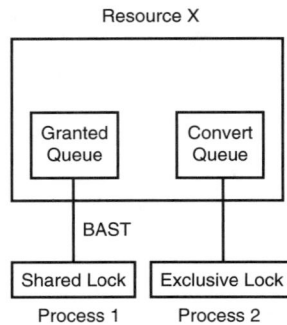

FIGURE 24.4
BAST sent to process 1.

4. Process 1 relinquishes the lock on resource X, and the lock is converted from shared to NULL.

5. An acquisition AST is sent to process 2, indicating that the requested lock is available (see Figure 24.5).

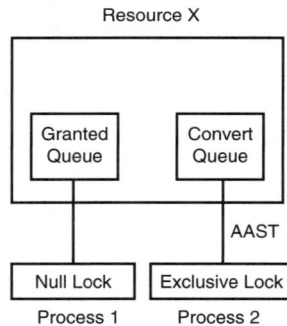

FIGURE 24.5
AAST sent to process 2.

6. The exclusive lock is granted to process 2 and placed in the granted queue (see Figure 24.6).

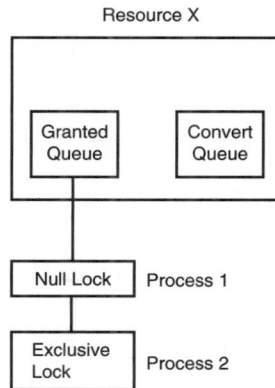

Resource X

Granted
Queue

Convert
Queue

Null Lock — Process 1

Exclusive
Lock — Process 2

FIGURE 24.6

Process 1 holding NULL lock and process 2 holding exclusive lock on resource X.

Several dynamic views provide information about the IDLM:

- V$DLM_CONVERT_LOCAL—This statistic is enabled by setting event 29700. It shows the convert time for local lock convert operations.

NOTE

Event 29700 can be set by placing the following line in the init.ora file and restarting the instance:

```
Event="29700 trace name context forever"
```

- V$DLM_CONVERT_REMOTE—This statistic is enabled by setting event 29700. It shows the convert time for remote lock convert operations.
- V$DLM_ALL_LOCKS—It contains information about all the locks currently known to IDLM.
- V$DLM_LOCKS—It contains information about all the locks currently known to IDLM that are blocking others or being blocked by others.
- V$DLM_RESS—It contains information about resources used by the locks.
- V$DLM_MISC—It contains miscellaneous DLM statistics.

Parallel Cache Management and Locking

In a shared-disk implementation such as OPS, it is very important to maintain cache coherency. Cache coherency allows the changes to data blocks synchronized across multiple memory caches. The Distributed Lock Manager is used to provide cache coherency. See Table 24.4 for a mapping of DLM locks to Oracle locks.

TABLE 24.4   Mapping DLM Locks to Oracle Locks

DLM	*Oracle*	*Interpretation*
NL	NULL	No lock acquired
CR	SS	Read concurrently
CW	SX	Write concurrently
PR	S	Read protection
PW	SSX	Write protection
EX	X	Exclusive write

In an OPS environment, the DBWR writes dirty blocks to the disk when any one of the following occurs:

- A checkpoint.
- A server process moves a buffer to the dirty list, and a threshold length is reached.
- A certain number of blocks are searched in the Least Recently Used (LRU) list without finding a free block.
- A copy of the block is requested by another instance for write purposes.

Prior to Oracle8*i*, cache coherency was achieved by writing dirty blocks by one instance to disk before reading by another instance. With Oracle8*i*, a low-cost cache coherency solution—cache fusion—is used. Cache fusion allows the transfer of requested blocks between instances via the high-speed interconnect. Cache fusion should take care of the following scenarios:

- Read/read—The user on one node wants to read a block just read by the user on another node.
- Read/write—The user on one node wants to read a block just modified by the user on another node.
- Write/write—The user on one node wants to modify a block just modified by the user on another node.

Currently cache fusion is implemented in Phase I, which takes care of only the read/write case, whereas future releases will also deal with the write/write case.

> **NOTE**
>
> Cache fusion provides high scalability for online transaction processing (OLTP) applications with a medium level of update activity.

Locking in Oracle Parallel Server

Access to shared resources is synchronized between the different instances by using various types of locks:

- PCM locks—Data blocks in datafiles are managed by using parallel cache management (PCM) locks. Before reading or writing any data block, an instance has to first acquire the PCM lock on that block. PCM locks allow only one instance to modify a block. Typically, several data blocks are covered by one PCM lock, and the locking granularity determines the amount of concurrency in the system.

> **NOTE**
>
> One data block can't be covered by more than one PCM lock, and therefore the smallest PCM lock granularity that can be achieved is one PCM lock per data block.

- Non-PCM locks—These locks aren't used for cache coherence.
- DFS (Distributed File System) enqueue locks—When running in the parallel mode, these instance locks act as global locks; otherwise they act as normal enqueues.
- DFS locks—These instance locks are used only in parallel mode.

Methods of PCM Locking

PCM locks can be used in two ways—hashed locking and fine-grain locking. You can use both hashed locking and fine-grain locking with different datafiles in the same database.

Hashed Locking

Hashed locking is a nondynamic approach that pre-allocates the PCM locks as specified by the init.ora file. Instance startup is usually slow when using this method because locks are statically hashed to blocks at instance startup. In this method, the init.ora parameter gc_files_to_locks

specifies the association between the number of locks to datafiles. Locks are released only when the instance shuts down. Read-only datafiles and well-partitioned data can benefit from the use of hashed locking.

Fine-Grain Locking

Fine-grain locking is a dynamic approach that acquires and releases locks on demand. Instance startup is faster compared to hashed locking, but performance suffers when a DLM resource is requested. Update intensive files can benefit from fine-grain locking.

Pinging

We have seen that in order to maintain cache coherency, a data block is written to disk by one instance when another instance wants to read the block. This is referred to as *pinging*. On the other hand, false pinging occurs when a block is written to disk by one instance: not because the particular block is requested, but because another block that's managed by the same PCM lock is requested. A ping is considered to be a hard ping if it results in a block being written to disk; it's considered to be a soft ping if it simply involves lock conversion.

> **NOTE**
>
> In an OPS environment, pinging cannot be completely eliminated, but it can be minimized by using well-designed applications.

You can understand false pinging by using as an example a PCM lock that manages data blocks 1 through 8:

1. Instance 1 is updating block 4.
2. Instance 2 requests block 8 for update.
3. All the blocks (including block 4) are written back to disk before being converted.
4. When the write is completed, instance 2 acquires the lock and can update block 8.

> **NOTE**
>
> Pinging activity can be monitored by using V$PING and V$LOCK_ACTIVITY dynamic view tables.

In the preceding example, false pinging occurs in step 3 because block 4 is written to disk even though it is not requested. You can see that the amount of false pinging in the system can depend on the granularity used by the PCM locks. False pinging is a bigger performance problem than true pinging.

> **NOTE**
>
> False pinging is determined by the lock granularity.

Row-Level Locking in OPS

In addition to PCM locks, OPS makes use of row-level locking. Consider an example that demonstrates how PCM locking is used in conjunction with row-level locking to achieve data consistency. For the sake of simplicity, assume that there is one PCM lock per block. I use the convention X_{ij} to indicate row i in block j:

1. Instance A requests to update X_{1n} covered by a PCM lock.
2. Instance A becomes the owner of the PCM lock that's covering block n.
3. Instance A updates row 1 in block n.
4. Instance B requests to update X_{3n}.
5. The DLM informs instance A that another instance is requesting a PCM lock owned by instance A.
6. Instance A writes the data block to disk and releases its ownership of the associated PCM lock.
7. Instance B acquires the ownership of the PCM lock covering block n.
8. Instance B updates row 3.
9. Instance A requests to update X_{4n}.
10. The DLM informs instance B that another instance is requesting a PCM lock owned by instance B.
11. Instance B writes the data block to disk and releases its ownership of the associated PCM lock.
12. Instance A acquires the ownership of the PCM lock covering block n.
13. Instance A updates row 4.

LCK processes associated with an instance perform several functions in an OPS environment:

- Manage PCM locks
- Perform lock conversion in case of hash locks
- Acquire, convert, and release fine-grained locks

NOTE

At least one LCK process is associated with each OPS instance. If multiple LCK processes are associated with an instance, they share the preceding functions.

Initialization Parameters Affecting OPS Locking

The use of PCM locks in an OPS environment can be controlled by several init.ora parameters:

- GC_FILES_TO_LOCKS specifies the mapping of hashed and database access (fine-grained) locks to datafiles.

NOTE

All instances involved in OPS must use the same value for the following parameters:

- GC_FILES_TO_LOCKS
- GC_LCK_PROCS

NOTE

The default locking method used for PCM locks is hash locking. Fine-grained locking can be used by setting a GC_ parameter to 0. For example, GC_DB_LOCKS = 0 sets fine-grained locking for data blocks, whereas GC_ROLLBACK_LOCKS = 0 sets fine-grained locking for undo blocks.

- GC_LCK_PROCS specifies the number of LCK processes used by an instance. (LCK0 through LCK10 are possible.) The default value is 1. This parameter is used only during the shared mode of operation.

24

ORACLE PARALLEL
SERVER

- `GC_RELEASABLE_LOCKS` specifies the number of locks used by fine-grained locking. The default value is the same as the value for `DB_BLOCK_BUFFERS`. Different instances can use a different value for this parameter.
- `GC_ROLLBACK_LOCKS` specifies the number of locks to control the simultaneous modification of rollback segment blocks.

> **NOTE**
>
> By default, fine-grained locks are used for rollback segments.

- `GC_FREELIST_GROUPS` specifies the number of locks to use for free-list groups.

The following parameters determine the usage of PCM resources and locks:

- `GC_DB_LOCKS`
- `GC_SEGMENTS`
- `GC_FREELIST_GROUPS`
- `GC_SAVE_ROLLBACK_LOCKS`
- `GC_ROLLBACK_SEGMENTS`

Non-PCM resource usage depends on

- `PROCESSES`
- `DLM_LOCKS`
- `TRANSACTION`
- `GC_LCK_PROCESSES`
- `ENQUEUE_RESOURCES`

Mapping Blocks to PCM Locks

Mapping of PCM locks to blocks in the datafiles is specified by the `GC_FILES_TO_LOCKS` parameter. `GC_FILES_TO_LOCKS` has the following syntax:

```
GC_FILES_TO_LOCKS = "{file_list=lock_count[!blocks][EACH][:]}..."
```

where,

- `file_list` specifies the files affected by the locks. You can specify a single file, range of files, or multiple files separated by commas.

- *lock_count* specifies the number of PCM locks to be assigned to the specified file list.
- *!blocks* optionally specifies the number of contiguous data blocks to be covered by each PCM lock.
- EACH optionally specifies that each file in the *file_list* should have *lock_count* locks.

NOTE

If both EACH and *!blocks* are omitted in the specification, the locks specified by *lock_count* are collectively allocated to the files specified by *file_list*.

When setting this parameter, the following should be considered:

- GC_FILES_TO_LOCKS should be set to the same value for all instances accessing the same database.
- "Hot" files concurrently accessed by many instances should be assigned a large number of locks to reduce pinging.
- Files not accessed simultaneously by many instances can have fewer locks to reduce the overhead associated with their management.
- Datafiles and their associated indexes should be placed in separate tablespaces and assigned PCM locks separately.
- A single PCM lock is sufficient for a read-only index.
- Specify all the datafiles in GC_FILES_TO_LOCKS in order to prevent the assignment of "leftover" locks to those datafiles.
- Undo blocks should not be assigned any locks.
- Temporary/sort blocks should not be assigned any locks.
- All read-only objects can be placed in one file, which is then covered by only one hash lock.

NOTE

The value of GC_DB_LOCKS must be greater than or equal to GC_FILES_TO_LOCKS.

24

ORACLE PARALLEL
SERVER

The following examples assume the following datafile sizes:

- Datafile 1 has 40 blocks.
- Datafile 2 has 60 blocks.
- Datafile 3 has 100 blocks.
- Datafile 4 has 160 blocks.
- Datafile 5 has 200 blocks.
- Datafile 6 has 240 blocks.

Example 1:

```
GC_FILES_TO_LOCKS = "1=40:2=30:3=0:4=40:5=50:6=40"
```

Interpretation:

- Datafile 1 gets 40 hash locks.
- Datafile 2 gets 30 hash locks.
- Datafile 3 will use fine-grain locking.
- Datafile 4 gets 40 hash locks.
- Datafile 5 gets 50 hash locks.
- Datafile 6 gets 40 hash locks.

Example 2:

```
GC_FILES_TO_LOCKS = "1=20:2-5=60:4=240"
```

Interpretation:

- In datafile 1, 20 PCM locks map to 40 blocks. Therefore, each PCM lock covers 2 blocks.
- For datafiles 2 through 5, a total of 520 blocks is covered by 60 blocks. Therefore, one PCM lock might cover eight or nine data blocks across the datafiles 2 through 5.
- In datafile 6, each PCM lock maps to a single data block.
- The total PCM locks are 20+60+240=320.

Example 3:

```
GC_FILES_TO_LOCKS = "1-2,4-6=20EACH:3=40"
```

Interpretation:

- Datafiles 1, 2, 4, 5, and 6 will have 20 PCM locks each.
- Datafile 3 will have 40 PCM locks.
- The total PCM locks are 20*5+40=140.

Application Design

Proper application design is very important to the performance of an OPS environment. If your applications are not designed properly, you might have excessive pinging. The following features, if used in your application, can cause performance problems with OPS, and you should make the necessary changes to minimize pinging:

- Multiple nodes inserting in the same table concurrently

  The insert operation will become slow because of contention for the free blocks of the table.

  Resolution: Use free-list groups and partition the table.

- Multiple nodes inserting in the same indexed table concurrently

  The insert operation will become slow because of contention for the free blocks of the index.

  Resolution: Use free-list groups and partition the index.

- Use of sequence numbers

  In an OPS environment, ordering of sequence numbers cannot be maintained because the sequence numbers aren't cached in the SGA of multiple instances.

  Resolution: Redesign your application so that it doesn't rely on the ordering of sequence numbers. Don't use sequence numbers as primary keys.

- Full table scans and updates performed at the same time on a table

  Pinging of rollback segment blocks can occur because of the necessity to provide read-consistent image of the data.

  Resolution: Redesign your SQL statements to avoid full table scans.

- Use of referential integrity constraints and triggers

  This can potentially cause pinging if the DML operation is cascaded to other tables.

  Resolution: Redesign your applications and partition the data so that the effect of cascading DML statements is localized to fewer partitions.

- Use of tables holding transient information

  Tables that hold transient information such as the state of a transaction have a lot of DML activity and would contribute to pinging.

  Resolution: Redesign your applications so that a minimum number of such tables are used.

- Performing range-based DML activity in parallel

  If the tables are not partitioned properly, range-based DML activity performed in parallel can cause a lot of pinging.

  Resolution: Make sure that the range-based DML activity conforms to the partitioning strategy in use.

Space Transaction Lock Contention

It is very common in an OPS configuration to experience contention for Space Transaction (ST) locks because of the serialization of space management.

> **NOTE**
>
> A frequent occurrence of ORA-1575 indicates contention for space management resources.

Contention for ST locks can be minimized by using the following guidelines:

- Increase SORT_AREA_SIZE.
- Disable coalescing by setting event 10269.
- Use dedicated temporary tablespaces and minimize sort space management operations.
- Set PCTINCREASE to 0.
- Perform DML operations on the same file from the same instance.
- Frequent creation and deletion of objects should not be performed.
- Enable SMON on very few instances.

Global Dynamic Performance Views

Each instance has its own set of dynamic views (V$ views) that store tuning and performance information. In an OPS environment, you can query global views (GV$ views) to obtain the V$ view information from all qualified instances. A global view contains all the columns from the corresponding V$ view and an addition column INST_ID that shows the ID of an instance.

> **NOTE**
>
> A global view is available for all V$ views except for V$ROLLNAME, V$CACHE_LOCK, V$LOCK_ACTIVITY, and V$LOCKS_WITH_COLLISIONS.

Several dynamic views can provide useful information about OPS activity:

- V$SYSSTAT contains statistics of global locks used by OPS.

NOTE

Parallel Server views are created from the catalog.sql and catparr.sql scripts.

- V$PING can be used to determine hot objects and obtain details about tables or indexes and the file and block numbers where there is significant pinging activity.
- V$CLASS_PING can be used to determine the type of blocks on which lock conversion and pinging activity is occurring.
- V$LOCK_ACTIVITY provides a summary of the lock up- and down-converts that have occurred since instance startup.
- V$SYSTEM_EVENTS contains events for which processes have waited the longest. The TIME_WAITED column shows the total wait time for each system event.

NOTE

V$SYSTEM_EVENTS shows waits for the following OPS events:

- Global cache cr request
- Library cache pin
- Buffer busy because of global cache
- Global cache lock busy
- Global cache lock open x
- Global cache lock open s
- Global cache lock null to x
- Global cache lock s to x
- Global cache lock null to s

24

Summary

Well-designed applications can benefit from the use of Oracle Parallel Server. OPS is a clustering solution that provides not only reliability, but also good scalability. Pinging is an unavoidable characteristic of OPS systems, and your goal should be to reduce the amount of pinging (True and False) that occurs in the system. Several data dictionary views and global views are provided in Oracle8*i* to identify performance problems.

Oracle8*i* makes use of cache fusion to minimize expensive disk I/Os by allowing data blocks to be shipped directly from the buffer cache of one node to the buffer cache of another node by using the low latency, high bandwidth interconnect between the nodes.

Using the Advanced Replication Option

IN THIS CHAPTER

In today's global environment, organizations have data distributed throughout the world, and they need an efficient and cost-effective method for transmitting changes made to a group of objects in one instance to be applied to the corresponding objects in another instance. Oracle provides the replication feature as a store-and-forward mechanism for transmitting the changes across database instances.

This chapter discusses among other things the various replication configurations and how conflict resolution can be performed. Issues involved in migrating an Oracle7 replication environment to Oracle8i is also discussed.

Replication Concepts

Several terms are commonly used with replication and should be understood in order to work with replication:

- Replicated object—A database object copied and maintained at multiple sites in a distributed database environment. Any replica of a replication object can be updated, and the changes propagated to all copies.
- Replicated group—A collection of replicated objects maintained as a single unit of replication. A replication group can comprise of objects belonging to different schemas, but a replicated object can belong to only one replicated group. There is a many-to-one relation between replicated objects and replicated groups.
- Deferred transaction—A deferred transaction consists of a set of RPCs executed as a single transaction at the destination site.
- Replication catalog—All the information necessary to maintain a replicated environment is stored in a set of tables referred to as the replication catalog. It contains several important views:

  repcatalog shows information about asynchronous administration requests.

  repddl shows DDL changes that have to be applied.

  repobject shows information about replicated objects.

  repgroup shows information about replicated groups.

  repprop shows propagation information about the replicated objects.

  repsite shows information about the replication groups and the master sites.

  repkey_columns shows the primary key columns for tables that use row-level replication.
- Job queue—Consists of PL/SQL code scheduled for periodic execution.
- Replication facility—A set of packages, such as DBMS_REPCAT and DBMS_DEFER_SYS, used to maintain data consistency in a replicated environment.

- Master definition site—At this site, replicated schemata and replicated objects are defined, and replicated object groups are created.

- Master site—Replicated schemata and replicated objects that are identical to the master definition site are maintained at this site.

- Snapshot site—A replicated schema name that's identical to a master site, a subset of the replicated objects, and updateable snapshots of the replicated tables are maintained at this site.

- Quiesce—While making a DDL change to a replicated object, replication must be suspended to all the sites. This process is called Quiesceing.

Row-level Versus Procedure-level Replication

Changes made to replicated objects can be propagated from one site to another using row-level or procedure-level replication. When row-level replication is used, the entire row is forwarded to all other master sites, regardless of the number of columns changed. On the other hand, procedure-level replication allows changes to be made by means of a procedure. The same procedure (and same set of arguments) is used to replicate the data to other master sites. Table 25.1 compares row-level replication with procedure-level replication.

TABLE 25.1   Row-Level Versus Procedural-level Replication

Row-level Replication	*Procedure-level Replication*
Oracle writes the underlying code to implement this technique	You must write the necessary code to implement this technique. The code includes
	$RT—Replication trigger $TP—Trigger package $RP—Replication package $RR—Replication resolution
Customization is not supported	Can be customized to control the propagation characteristics.
Conflict detection is automatic	Conflict detection must be manually implemented.
Makes use of built-in conflict resolution routines	Built-in conflict resolution routines can't be used.
Uses a direct interface	Uses a wrapper interface.
Propagates entire row even if only a few columns are changed	Uses the same procedure and arguments to propagate changes.

25

USING THE ADVANCED REPLICATION OPTION

Replication Administration Accounts

In order to administer a replication environment, you must set up several accounts with appropriate privileges:

- SYS Surrogate User

  Several replication administration activities must be performed under the SYS account and need access to remote nodes. However, this account does not need all the privileges associated with the SYS account, and therefore, you need to create a SYS surrogate user who acts as the user SYS and is used to perform DDL changes in a replicated environment. The SYS surrogate user can be created by executing the following statement from the server manager prompt while connected as internal:

  ```
  CREATE USER syssur IDENTIFIED BY syssur;
  EXECUTE DBMS_REPCAT_AUTH.GRANT_SURROGATE_REPCAT(syssur)
  ```

- Replication Administrator

  All replication commands are executed while you're connected as the replication administrator. Replication administrators can be allowed to administer any object or only the objects they own.

  To create a global replication administrator, use these commands from the server manager while connected as internal:

  ```
  Svrmgrl> CREATE USER global_rep IDENTIFIED BY global;
  Svrmgrl> EXECUTE dbms_repcat_admin.grant_admin_any_repgroup
       2> ('global_rep');
  ```

  To create a specific group administrator, use these commands from the server manager while connected as internal:

  ```
  Svrmgrl> CREATE USER specific_rep IDENTIFIED BY specific;
  Svrmgrl> EXECUTE dbms_repcat_admin.grant_admin_repgroup
       2> ('specific_rep');
  ```

Several database links must also be created:

- One public database link:

  ```
  target_database_name USING 'SQL*Net alias';
  ```

- Two private database links. One for the SYS surrogate user:

  ```
  target_database CONNECT TO surrogate_user
  IDENTIFIED BY surrogate_user_password;
  ```

  And the other for the replication administrator:

  ```
  target_database CONNECT TO rep_admin_user
  IDENTIFIED BY rep_admin_user_password;
  ```

Replication Configurations

Replication is a very popular method for data distribution providing several benefits:

- The source and destination databases can be simultaneously used.
- Provides a high-availability solution.
- A GUI tool—replication manager—can be used to easily configure and monitor a replication environment.
- Provides flexible configurations ranging from publish-and-subscribe replication to update-anywhere models.

> **NOTE**
>
> Replication should not be used with high transactional OLTP systems because the amount of data changes is large and will result in performance problems.

Replication can be symmetric or asymmetric, as shown in Table 25.2.

TABLE 25.2 Comparing Synchronous and Asynchronous Replication

Symmetric Replication	Asymmetric Replication
Transactions are executed immediately	Execution of transactions are deferred to a later time
Performance is poor because all the sites are updated at the same time	Better performance than symmetric replication
Two-phase commit is used to ensure transactional integrity	No special technique is used for committing transactions
Conflicts do not occur	Conflicts can occur
At any time, all sites have up-to-date information	Sites might be running with out-of-date data
Low data availability	High data availability

Oracle8*i* provides several replication configurations. You should carefully analyze your business needs before choosing a particular replication configuration:

- N-way replication or multiple-master replication

  This configuration uses multiple master sites and a push-push configuration. In this configuration, the entire contents of a table are replicated at all sites. For each table, database

triggers are defined and deferred Remote Procedure Calls (RPCs) are used to replicate row changes to each site. Certain procedures must be periodically executed:

Difference procedure—to check for differences between tables regarding columns and contents.

Rectify procedure—to synchronize the tables on replicated sites.

- Updatable snapshots

  Updatable snapshots use a pull-pull configuration. In this configuration, a snapshot has only one master, and it communicates with its master even though the configuration can consist of multiple master sites. Changes from the master are pulled by a snapshot by means of a snapshot refresh. Multiple snapshots can be refreshed from masters on demand. For each table, database triggers are defined, and deferred RPCs are used to replicate row changes to each site. The advantage of this configuration compared to multiple-master configuration is that it is possible to replicate subsets of tables.

- Hybrid configuration

  This configuration combines multimaster and updatable snapshots. This configuration supports both full-table as well as table subset replication.

Methods for Distributing Data

Replication allows several methods for the distribution of data. The method of data distribution used depends upon the site owning the data and the availability needs:

- Basic techniques—Primary site ownership is an example of a basic technique. It tries to avoid conflicts at the expense of some performance degradation. In this technique, only one site is allowed to update the data. This site becomes the owner of that table. Conflicts can occur in this technique if you allow different sites to own different partitions of a partition table.

- Advanced techniques—Dynamic ownership and shared ownership are examples of advanced techniques. Both of these techniques are more efficient than the primary site ownership technique but are difficult to implement.

NOTE

It is possible to have conflicts even in advanced techniques such as dynamic ownership and shared ownership models.

- Dynamic ownership model—In this technique, the ownership of data is determined by the state of the data. Ordering is used to control data. Only the site that owns the data can update the data, and furthermore, only rows with a given status can be updated. Each site updates the status to the next state and pushes ownership to the next site, which is then allowed to update the data. As seen from this technique, the ownership of data changes dynamically.

- Shared ownership model—This technique allows multiple sites to update the same data. As a result, the ownership of data is shared between the sites. Update conflicts can occur in this method, and some mechanism must be used to detect and resolve the conflicts so that eventually all the replicated data converge to a consistent state at all the sites.

  Detection of update conflicts is performed by using row-level replication to propagate before-image values of modified rows with the changed values. At the destination site, before applying changes to remote replicas, the before-image value is compared with the current value at the destination. If the values are different, an update conflict is detected, and a user-defined stored procedure is called to resolve the update conflict.

Conflict Resolution

Conflict detection and resolution are an important part of any replication configuration. You have already seen how conflicts can occur. In order to keep data consistent across all sites, you must resolve these conflicts. Several techniques are commonly used to resolve these conflicts:

- Using timestamps—This technique requires all the sites involved in replication to be at the same time zone. An example of this technique is a distributed system, such as airline ticket reservation that allows customer records to be updated from any site. Eventually the changes are replicated and only the most recent changes are applied. In other words, this technique compares the timestamp of the propagated change with the value at the destination. The propagated changes are applied only if they have a timestamp later than that at the destination site.

- Additive method—This technique adds the delta value (difference) of replicated changes to the current value. An example of this technique is an Orders table that is used to keep track of customer orders. Customer orders can be maintained from two sites. For each customer, an order_count is maintained to track the orders placed by that customer. The order_count is incremented by 1 each time an order is placed and is decremented by 1 each time an order is cancelled. Update conflicts can occur in the order_count. These conflicts are resolved by adding the delta of the replicated value to the current value.

Alternatives for Replicating Data

In addition to advanced replication, various other methods are used to replicate data in a distributed environment. Some of these methods are synchronous, whereas others are asynchronous, but none of them provide the flexibility and sophistication of using an advanced replication configuration:

- Export/Import—This is an example of an asynchronous method. It requires you to manually export the table from the source site and then import it at the destination site. In addition to requiring manual intervention, the other disadvantage of this method is that only entire tables can be replicated.

- Create Table as Select—This is an example of an asynchronous method. This method creates new tables; therefore, you should drop any existing table replicas at the destination site prior to using this method. The problem with this method is the manual intervention and also the complexity of resolving conflicts if multiple sites are allowed to change the data.

- SQL*PLUS COPY Command—This is an example of an asynchronous method. Similar to the export/import and the CTAS method described previously, it requires manual intervention and can involve complex techniques for resolving conflicts.

- Database Trigger—This is an example of a synchronous method. Database triggers are used to automatically replicate the changes. This method requires that the database and the network be highly available. Also, performance problems exist because the changes are replicated immediately.

Initialization Parameters

When using replication with Oracle8*i*, you should set several initialization parameters to the appropriate values:

- compatible—This must be set to at least 8.1.5.0.0
- job_queue_processes—Specifies the number of job queue processes that can be started
- job_queue_interval—Specifies the time interval for the execution of jobs
- shared_pool_size—Should be large enough to hold the replication packages and PL/SQL code
- distributed_transactions—Specifies the number of distributed transactions that can be simultaneously run
- global_names—Must be set to TRUE
- open_links—Specifies the number of links that individual users can have open at the same time

Replication Components

Replication consists of several components:

- Job queues—These are used to automatically execute jobs. Information about job queues can be obtained by using several Data Dictionary views:

    DBA_JOBS contains a record for each job submitted to the database.

    USER_JOBS contains a record for each job submitted by a particular user.

    DBA_JOBS_RUNNING contains a record for each job currently running.

    The DBMS_JOBS package contains several procedures to manipulate the jobs in the job queues.

- Replication catalog—It is used to perform DDL and other administrative tasks by using the DBMS_REPCAT_ADMIN package. Replication catalog can be queried by using the Data Dictionary views: DBA_REPCAT, DBA_REPGROUP, and DBA_REPOBJECT.

- RPC queue—It is used to perform DML and other RPC tasks by using the DBMS_DEFER and DBMS_DEFER_SYS package. Deferred transaction queue consists of the following tables:

    deftran contains a record for each deferred transaction.

    defcall contains the remote procedure calls used to maintain data consistency.

    deftrandest contains a list of the destinations for each transaction.

    defcalldest contains a list of destinations for each remote procedure call.

Using the Replication Manager

Replication Manager is a GUI tool that allows you to perform replication-related activities. In Oracle8*i*, it has been rewritten to integrate with the Oracle Enterprise Manager. It is Java-based and is no longer limited to the windows platform.

> **NOTE**
>
> Replication manager can be used as a standalone application or launched from the Oracle Enterprise Manager.

Replication manager has several features that make it simple to administer and troubleshoot replication environments:

- Wizards are provided to set up different replication configurations.
- It can use both asynchronous as well as synchronous modes.
- It allows the centralization of replication tasks.
- Multimaster configurations can be set up including account, schema, and link creation.
- Snapshot replication configuration can be set up including account, schema, and link creation.
- Several built-in routines for conflict resolution are provided: latest timestamp, unique, site priority, and user-defined.
- It can be used to troubleshoot errors during replication.
- It can be used to create repgroups and supporting objects.
- It can be used to create snapshots and snapshot groups.
- It allows the management of deferred transaction queues.
- It provides drag-and-drop functionality for master groups and snapshots.

Using DBMS_JOB package

The DBMS_JOB package contains several procedures that can be used to manipulate the job queues:

- SUBMIT—It can be used to submit a new job to the job queue. The job is executed by a background process (job queue process) that wakes up periodically.
- CHANGE—It can be used to change the job characteristics, such as the procedure to execute, the date of the next execution, or the execution interval.
- NEXT_DATE—It can be used to change the date of the next execution for a job.
- INTERVAL—It can be used to change the execution interval for a job.
- REMOVE—It can be used to removes a job from the job queue.
- BROKEN—It can be used to specify whether a job is broken or not. A broken job is not executed again.
- WHAT—It can be used to change the procedure that gets executed for a job.
- RUN—It can be used to force a job to be executed immediately.

Migrating from Oracle7 to Oracle8*i* Replication Environments

Several features require that you successfully migrate all sites to Oracle8*i*:

- Replication of LOB datatypes
- Parallel propagation of deferred transactions
- Use of the validate procedure
- Reduced data propagation by making use of the min_communication parameter and the send_old_values/compare_old_values procedures
- Use of global authentication and privileged database links

In addition to migrating all sites to Oracle8*i*, the following features require the use of primary key snapshots:

- Use of simple snapshots with subqueries
- Use of deployment templates
- Use of vertically partitioned snapshots
- Use of procedures that reorganize the master table

NOTE

Fine-grained quiesce and registration of snapshots will work in a mixed environment of Oracle7 and Oracle8*i*, but will have problems with Oracle8.

For small replication configurations, it is possible to migrate your environments from Oracle7 to Oracle8*i* in one step. However, for large configurations, it might be better to perform the migration incrementally. You can perform replication-related activities in a mixed Oracle7 and Oracle8*i* replication environment with certain restrictions:

- Oracle8*i* snapshot sites can interact only with Oracle7 release 7.3.3 or higher master sites
- Oracle8*i* master sites can interact only with Oracle7 release 7.3.4 or higher snapshot sites and with Oracle7 release 7.3.3 or higher master sites

> **NOTE**
>
> After migrating a master site to Oracle8*i*, you should perform a full refresh of all the relevant snapshot sites.

Migrating the Entire Multimaster Environment in One Step

You can migrate the entire multimaster environment to Oracle8*i* using the steps outlined in this section. Oracle7 snapshots can still be used, provided they are at release 7.3.4 or higher:

1. Execute DBMS_REPCAT.SUSPEND_MASTER_ACTIVITY at the master definition site for all master replication groups and quiesce the replication environment.

2. Temporarily suspend the entries in the job queue that perform propagation and automatic refreshes from the snapshot sites to the master.

3. Resolve any errors in the local error queue.

4. Migrate all the master sites from Oracle7 to Oracle8*i* using any of the methods described earlier in the book.

5. Run catrep.sql.

6. Run rold_release.sql (where old_release represents the previously installed database version).

7. Using the replication manager, create a primary master replication administrator account pm_rep_admin.

8. Grant replication administrator, propagator, and receiver privileges on all master sites to the pm_rep_admin account and set up links to connect all the sites. Refer to the section "Using Replication Manager for Multimaster Replication."

9. Using replication manager or the appropriate replication management API calls, regenerate replication support for each replication base object.

10. Resume replication activity by unquiescing the environment. This can be achieved by executing DBMS_REPCAT.RESUME_MASTER_ACTIVITY for all the master groups.

11. Make sure that all the related snapshot sites are at least release 7.3.4 or higher. Upgrade them if necessary.

12. Using the DBMS_JOB.BROKEN procedure, unbreak any job that might have been broken in step 2.

13. Perform a full refresh of all the snapshots.

> **NOTE**
>
> If procedural replication is used at snapshot sites, you also need to regenerate snapshot support on all packages and package bodies used for procedural replication.

Using Replication Manager for Multimaster Replication

The replication manager's setup wizard can be used to prepare the master sites in a multimaster replication system by performing several tasks:

- Create a database account to serve as a replication administrator/propagator/receiver
- Grant the necessary privileges to the replication administrator/propagator/receiver account
- Create new database connections to correspond to the new replication administer accounts
- Create scheduled links to all other master sites
- Schedule the purging of the deferred transaction queue for all master sites

Creating Master Sites

The following steps can be used to create master sites:

1. Launch the replication manager from the OEM console.
2. Choose File, Setup Wizard to launch the replication setup wizard.
3. When prompted to choose the type of replication environment to set up, choose Set up Master Sites.
4. Click Next.
5. In the next page, click the ADD button to add master sites.
6. In the Add Site dialog box, enter the following:

   Global database name of the master site to add

   Password for the SYSTEM account
7. Press the down arrow to add the master site.
8. Repeat steps 6 and 7 for each master site to add.
9. Click OK.
10. Click NEXT.

    This takes you to the next page where you can provide the specifications for the replication administrator, propagator, and receiver accounts. Accounts with the same name and

password are created at all master sites. You can either create an account that performs all the functions (replication administrator, propagator, receiver) or choose to create different accounts. Click NEXT.

11. The next page allows you to create schemas that will contain the replication objects. The same name and password is used to create schemas at all master sites. Click ADD.

12. In the Create Schema dialog box, enter the name and password for the account that will contain the replication objects. Click OK.

13. Repeat steps 11 and 12 for each schema to add and when finished click NEXT.

14. The next page allows you to specify the default propagation characteristics for all master sites. It creates scheduled links from each master site to all master sites. These settings can be changed anytime by using the Create Scheduled Link button on the toolbar.

15. The general and options page of the Create New Scheduled Link property sheet can be used to specify the following properties for a scheduled link:

    Link specifies the database link to use for this scheduled link.

    Next Date specifies the next time when the changes are pushed to the destination.

    Interval specifies how often to automatically push changes to the destination.

    Delay Seconds specifies the amount of time to poll the queue.

    Enabled specifies that the scheduled link is enabled, and changes are immediately pushed to the destination. You should not use this unless the destination site is available.

    Stop On Error specifies whether the propagation of the local deferred transaction queue continues or stops when an error occurs.

    Parallel Propagation specifies whether to use serial or parallel propagation for the scheduled link.

    Processes specifies the number of background processes to use for parallel propagation of the scheduled link. A value of 0 indicates serial propagation.

16. Click Next.

17. The next page allows you to specify the default purge schedule for the deferred transaction queue at each master site. After a deferred transaction is pushed to the destination site, it should be periodically purged from the deferred transaction queue so that the queue is kept manageable in size. The following settings can be specified:

    Next Date specifies the next time when the purging is applied to the local deferred transaction queue.

    Interval Expression specifies the time interval to automatically purge the applied transactions from the local deferred transaction queue.

    Rollback segment specifies the rollback segment to use for the purging process.

    Delay seconds specifies the amount of time to poll the queue.

18. Click Next.

19. The next page allows you to customize the settings made in the previous steps for each master site. After making any desired changes, click OK.

20. Click FINISH if you are now ready to complete the configuration.

21. Click OK to confirm that you want to configure the replication environment as chosen.

Performing Incremental Migration

In large systems, it might not be feasible to migrate the entire replication environment in one step, and you might be forced to perform incremental migration. When performing incremental migration, you should make sure that you fully understand the interdependencies between the sites so that they can continue to interoperate while the incremental migration is being performed. The following sequence of steps is recommended:

1. Upgrade all master sites to Oracle7 release 7.3.3 or higher

2. Incrementally migrate all snapshot sites to Oracle8*i*

3. Incrementally migrate all master sites to Oracle8*i*

NOTE

The following procedures are obsolete in Oracle8*i*:

DBMS_REPCAT.GENERATE_REPLICATION_PACKAGE

DBMS_REPCAT.GENERATE_REPLICATION_TRIGGER

DBMS_REPCAT_ADMIN.GRANT_ADMIN_REPGROUP

DBMS_REPCAT_ADMIN.GRANT_ADMIN_ANY_REPGROUP

DBMS_REPCAT_ADMIN.REVOKE_ADMIN_REPGROUP

DBMS_REPCAT_ADMIN.REVOKE_ADMIN_ANY_REPGROUP

DBMS_REPCAT_AUTH.GRANT_SURROGATE_REPCAT

DBMS_REPCAT_AUTH.REVOKE_SURROGATE_REPCAT

DBMS_DEFER_SYS.EXECUTE

Pre-Migration Steps

Before you can perform incremental migration of master or snapshot sites, you must prepare the Oracle7 master sites by making sure that

- All master sites are at Oracle7 release 7.3.3 or higher

- All replication administration and propagation activities are performed in the security context of the same user

- The replication administrator on all sites must have the same name and password
- In a multimaster replication environment, create the following links from each master site to all other master sites:

  A public database link, created as SYS, that includes a valid global database name and uses a valid TNS alias.

  A private database link, created as SYS, that includes a valid global database name and makes use of a CONNECT TO clause with the username and password of the primary master replication administrator.

  A private database link, created as the primary replication administrator, that includes a valid global database name and makes use of a CONNECT TO clause with the username and password of the primary master replication administrator.

Performing Incremental Migration of Snapshot Sites

Before performing an incremental migration of snapshot sites, the following must be true:

- The associated master site must have been upgraded to Oracle7 release 7.3.3 or higher.
- The master site must be fully prepared for migration (as described in the section "Pre-migration Steps").

The following steps should be performed to migrate Oracle7 snapshot sites to Oracle8*i*:

1. Stop all local updates to updatable snapshots at the snapshot sites.
2. Push the local deferred transactions to the snapshot's master site and empty the deferred transaction queue.
3. Stop all propagation from the snapshot site to its master by breaking (if necessary) jobs from the job queues that perform automatic propagation.
4. Migrate the Oracle7 database to Oracle8*i* using any method described in this book.
5. Run catrep.sql.
6. Run rold_release.sql (where old_release represents the previously installed database version).
7. Using the replication manager, create a primary snapshot replication administrator account ps_rep_admin.
8. Grant replication administrator propagator privileges on this snapshot site to theps_rep_admin account and create a receiver account on the associated master site. Set up links to the master site. Refer to the section "Using Replication Manager for Multimaster Replication" to see how you can customize the receiver account for the master.
9. Using replication manager or the appropriate replication management API calls, regenerate snapshot replication support.

10. Using replication manager or the appropriate replication management API calls, reschedule propagation or refresh intervals with the master site.

11. Enable local updates for the updatable snapshots.

12. Using the DBMS_JOB.BROKEN procedure, unbreak any job that might have been broken in step 3.

Performing Incremental Migration of Master Sites

Before performing an incremental migration of master sites, the following must be true:

- All other master sites in the replication environment must have been upgraded to Oracle7 release 7.3.3 or higher.

- The master site must be fully prepared for migration (as described in the section "Pre-migration Steps").

- Any associated snapshot site(s) must have been upgraded to Oracle7 release 7.3.4 or higher.

The following steps must be used to incrementally migrate master sites to Oracle8*i*:

1. Choose a master site to migrate. The master definition site should be the first one that is migrated.

2. If procedural replication is being used, record the configuration information and locations (schemas) of the procedure wrappers.

3. Stop all updates to the master site. This can be achieved by doing one of the following:

   Call DBMS_REPCAT.SUSPEND_MASTER_ACTIVITY at the master definition site for all master replication groups.

   Call DBMS_DEFER_SYS.UNSCHEDULE_EXECUTION for Oracle7 sites.

   Call DBMS_DEFER_SYS.UNSCHEDULE_PUSH for Oracle8*i* sites at every remote master site and dependent snapshot site.

4. Manually push the deferred transactions to all sites and empty the local deferred transaction queue.

5. Resolve any errors in the local error queue.

6. Stop refreshes from occurring at the snapshot sites by breaking, if necessary, any entries in the job queue at each snapshot site that control automatic propagation and refreshing of the snapshots.

7. Migrate the Oracle7 database to Oracle8*i* using any method described in this book.

8. Run catrep.sql.

9. Run rold_release.sql (where old_release represents the previously installed database version).

10. Using the replication manager, create a primary master replication administrator account pm_rep_admin.

11. Grant replication administrator, propagator, and receiver privileges on the master site to the pm_rep_admin account and set up links to connect all the sites. Refer to the section "Using Replication Manager for Multimaster Replication."

12. Execute DBMS_REPCAT.SUSPEND_MASTER_ACTIVITY at the master definition site for all master replication groups and quiesce the replication environment.

13. Using replication manager or the appropriate replication management API calls, regenerate replication support for each replication base object.

> **NOTE**
>
> When performing incremental migration of master sites, you must set the parameter min_communication to FALSE if any site is running Oracle7. After all sites have been migrated to Oracle8*i*, you should set min_communication to TRUE.

14. If procedural replication is being used, check the remaining Oracle7 master sites to determine if the wrappers have been moved (check against the list created in step 2). If the wrappers have been moved, create a synonym in their old location to the new location in the schema of the primary replication administrator. The synonym will link the old location to the new location.

15. Grant object privileges to access the new owner and location.

16. Using replication manager or the appropriate replication management API calls, regenerate snapshot replication support.

17. Resume replication activity by unquiescing the environment. This can be achieved by executing DBMS_REPCAT.RESUME_MASTER_ACTIVITY for all the master groups.

18. Reschedule the propagation between all sites.

19. Using the DBMS_JOB.BROKEN procedure, unbreak any job that might have been broken in step 6.

20. Perform a full refresh of all the snapshots.

Primary Key Snapshots

Oracle8*i* allows you to use primary key snapshots as the default, but also allows you to use the traditional ROWID snapshots. Use of primary key snapshots allows you to perform reorganization of the master tables while retaining fast refresh capability. It is possible to convert ROWID snapshots to primary key snapshots but the reverse is not possible.

> **NOTE**
>
> Oracle8*i* master logs, which have been altered to log both primary key as well as ROWID information when master rows are updated, can simultaneously support Oracle7 ROWID snapshots as well as Oracle8*i* ROWID and primary key snapshots. This allows incremental migration to be performed smoothly.

In order to use primary key snapshots, the snapshot logs for each master table must be altered to log both ROWID, as well as primary key information, when master rows are updated. This can be achieved as follows:

1. Define and enable a primary key constraint on each master table (if not already enabled).

2. Alter the snapshot log on each master table that supports fast refresh to include primary key information. The following example alters the ROWID snapshot log on the Orders table to also record primary key information:

```
ALTER SNAPSHOT LOG ON orders ADD PRIMARY KEY;
```

After the master sites have been configured to support primary key snapshots, the following can be done at the snapshot sites (Oracle8 and higher) to convert the ROWID snapshot to a primary key snapshot:

1. Stop all local updates to updatable snapshots at the snapshot sites.

2. If you have read-only ROWID snapshots that do not include all the columns of the primary key, drop and re-create them with all the primary key columns.

3. Stop all propagation and refreshes from the snapshot to the master site by breaking, if necessary, any entries in the job queue that perform automatic propagation.

4. Perform a fast refresh of all the snapshots. This will remove the need for any ROWID references in the master snapshot log.

5. Convert the ROWID snapshots to primary key snapshots by using the ALTER SNAPSHOT command. The following example converts a ROWID snapshot on the Orders table to a primary key snapshot:

```
ALTER SNAPSHOT orders_rs REFRESH WITH PRIMARY KEY;
```

6. Reschedule the propagation between all sites.

7. Using the DBMS_JOB.BROKEN procedure, unbreak any job that might have been broken in step 3.

8. Perform a full refresh of all snapshots.

25

USING THE
ADVANCED
REPLICATION OPTION

Parallel Propagation

In Oracle8*i*, a scheduled link in the replication environment can asynchronously propagate changes to the destination using either serial propagation or parallel propagation. In serial propagation, the replicated transactions are propagated one at a time in the same order in which they are committed on the source system. On the other hand, in parallel propagation, replicated transactions are propagated in parallel streams resulting in high throughput. Data integrity is maintained by ordering dependent transactions.

The following steps can be used to perform parallel propagation of a scheduled link:

1. Launch Replication Manager.
2. Expand the database node that contains the scheduled link to edit.
3. Expand the scheduling node.
4. Expand the scheduled links node.
5. Select the scheduled link to edit, and its property sheet will appear in the right side pane of the replication manager interface.
6. On the Options page, enable the parallel propagation setting.
7. Set the processes value to the desired number of parallel processes.
8. Click Apply.

You can revert back to the serial propagation by setting the processes value to 0 or by disabling the parallel propagation setting.

Oracle uses the same mechanism to perform parallel propagation in a replication environment as it used in other parallel executions such as parallel query and parallel DML. A parallel coordinator process is used to control parallel server processes. The parallel coordinator performs several functions:

Keeps track of the dependencies between the transactions

Allocates work to the parallel server processes

Keeps track of the progress of the parallel server processes

Each parallel server process remains associated with a parallel operation throughout the execution of the operation. When the operation completes, the parallel server process becomes available to execute other parallel operations.

Two initialization parameters affect the parallel propagation of transactions:

- parallel_min_servers—Specifies the minimum number of parallel server processes used for an instance
- parallel_max_servers—Specifies the maximum number of parallel server processes used for an instance

When adjusting the preceding parameters for parallel propagation, keep in mind that if all the scheduled links are set up for serial propagation, the parallel server processes are not used.

Summary

Certain Oracle8*i* features require that you migrate all your sites to at least Oracle8*i* before using them. Primary key snapshots are an example of such features. Both incremental as well as one-step migration can be performed for the entire replication environment, and in this chapter I have discussed both of the techniques.

Replication Manager provides a GUI interface to simplify the replication-related tasks. Parallel propagation of transactions make use of the same parallel processes used by other parallel executions and can be configured using the replication manager. The replication manager is Java-based and is no longer restricted to windows platforms.

Using the Internet Capabilities of Oracle8*i*

IN THIS CHAPTER

Java, an interpreted, platform-independent language, has several important characteristics that make it a very popular language for developing enterprise applications. Oracle has recognized the potential of using Java. Several important features of Java include

- It's an object-oriented language and can easily represent real-world entities and their behaviors.
- It uses an open standard for application development.
- It allows code reuse by allowing you to use JavaBeans and Enterprise JavaBeans (EJB). A Bean is a reusable software component that is written in Java. Tools such as Sun's Java Studio allow you to combine Beans and build applications.
- Compared to C++, Java is simpler to use but retains most of the object-oriented features, except multiple inheritance, pointers, and a few other error-prone features.
- It enables you to develop portable applications.
- It is widely used to develop Internet applications because it can run in browsers, application servers, and databases. This is achieved by writing *applets*, which are Java programs downloadable from the Web that can be run in Web browsers.

In this chapter, we will discuss the Internet capabilities of Oracle8*i* that include

- Java Virtual Machine
- Enterprise Java Beans (EJBs)
- Internet File System
- Java Stored Procedures
- JDBC
- SQLJ

Java is a platform-independent language by virtue of the fact that it is interpreted and not a compiled language. The machine-level code for a Java script is not generated until runtime and therefore the script is downloaded from the Web to the local machine. The Java applet that you write on your machine will run on it as long as a Java interpreter is available for your operating system. Initially, Java was provided as a toolkit language for small devices, but extensions such as JDBC (Java Database Connectivity) and SQLJ (Java SQL that can be embedded in Java applications) make it suitable as a language for interfacing between HTML pages and Web-enabled database servers such as Oracle8*i*.

> **NOTE**
>
> Java with the extensions such as JDBC and JSQL can be used as a standalone language with or without HTML wrappings.

Java in Oracle8*i*

Oracle's strategy of a network computer model makes use of Java as a key component. Java is implemented into Oracle8*i* with two major approaches:

- By providing an enterprise-class Java server platform that can be used with a wide range of applications from online transaction processing systems to decision support systems, integration with system management tools such as Oracle Enterprise Manager, to integration of a Java virtual machine (JVM) that can be used to run Java scripts.

- By providing a set of Java tools that can be used to quickly develop efficient Java applications. The Java tools provided by Oracle8*i* include JDBC drivers that provide database connectivity from Java; a SQLJ translator, which allows the use of embedded SQL in Java; JDeveloper, a complete development environment that allows the use of JDBC and SQLJ to develop Java applications; CORBA connectivity; Oracle Application Server; use of JavaBeans and EJBs to enable component-oriented development; ability to create and load Java stored procedures and triggers.

Java programs are a collection of classes. A *class* is a collection of data and methods that operate on the data. Classes are used to represent concepts that might or might not be real-world entities. Java programs use data encapsulation, which means that the only way to access the data is to use the well-defined interface (set of methods implemented by the class and made public) surrounding the class. The ability to create classes allows you to also create your own abstract data types. Unlike C++, which allows the mixing of object-oriented code with procedural code, Java requires that all code be object-oriented.

> **NOTE**
>
> Java is a good object-oriented programming language, but it does not force you to write good object-oriented programs.

A Java package allows you to group classes and interfaces. Java allows you to organize the packages in a hierarchy, and therefore, you might have subpackages. The Java Class Libraries are implemented as subpackages of the java package. JDBC is implemented as a subpackage of java called java.sql. You can use the import clause in your programs to have access to classes in packages and subpackages. For example,

```
import java.sql.*
```

indicates that you want to access all the classes in the subpackage java.sql.

> **NOTE**
>
> Java allows you to import classes selectively.

Using Java Database Connectivity (JDBC)

Developers can access and manipulate relational databases from within Java programs by making use of JDBC. JDBC is an application programming interface (API). JDBC API became a part of the Java class libraries with Java 1.1 and since then it is a part of the Java programming language. The JDK available from Sun Microsystems provides a reasonable development environment for Java applications. The JDK includes

- Java Compiler
- Java Class Libraries
- Java Virtual Machine
- Java Applet Viewer
- Java Debugger

The JDK can be downloaded from `http://java.sun.com/products/jdk/`. The JDK components are command-line driven and can sometimes be cumbersome to use. Java developers generally prefer an Integrated Development Environment (IDE) that integrates the JDK components in a GUI interface. Several popular IDEs for Java include

- Symantec Visual Café (available in Database edition—which allows database access and the Enterprise edition—which allows the development of servlets and CORBA applications)
- Oracle JDeveloper
- Borland JBuilder
- Microsoft J++

*Using the Internet Capabilities of Oracle 8*i

CHAPTER 26

523

26

USING THE INTERNET
CAPABILITIES OF
ORACLE 8*I*

- Sun Java Workshop
- IBM VisualAge for Java

JDBC supports SQL92 syntax and allows vendors to provide extensions to improve performance.

NOTE

JDBC was modeled by JavaSoft on the basis of open database connectivity (ODBC), an open standard developed by Microsoft for accessing databases.

Oracle-Supplied JDBC Drivers

In addition to a Java programming environment, you will need database drivers to allow access to the database. If database drivers for Oracle are not available from your programming environment, you can use the Oracle-supplied JDBC drivers. The Oracle-supplied JDBC drivers and the SQLJ precompiler can be downloaded from the Oracle Web site at `http://technet.oracle.com/software/download.htm`. All interactions between Java programs and a database occur through a JDBC driver. There are four different types of JDBC drivers:

- JDBC-ODBC bridge + ODBC driver

  The Java Development Kit (JDK) available from Sun Microsystems contains a driver of this type. It accesses a database through an ODBC driver and allows you to access any database for which an ODBC driver is available. The biggest disadvantages of this type of driver are that you need an ODBC driver, and the DBMS client code might have to be downloaded on each client machine.

- Native-API partly Java driver

  This driver converts Java calls into calls in the database's native client API. Oracle's JDBC/OCI driver (discussed later) is of this type. This type of driver does not require an ODBC driver, but it requires the code to be loaded on each client.

- JDBC-Net pure Java driver

  This driver communicates with a special server in the middle tier via a database independent protocol. The server then communicates with the database using a particular protocol. This driver does not require code to be downloaded on the client but makes use of an additional tier.

- Native-protocol pure Java driver

  This driver converts JDBC calls directly into the network protocol used by the database. The thin driver (discussed later) provided by Oracle is of this type. This driver does not

require software to be loaded on the client. It communicates with the database by opening a socket. This approach requires a Web server to be loaded on the same machine as a database server because Web servers allow an applet to open a socket only to the machine from which they were downloaded.

Two types of JDBC drivers are provided by Oracle that allow you to write different types of applications:

- *Thin JDBC driver*

  Thin JDBC driver is written completely in Java and is ideal for Java applets that can be used with a browser. When you download an applet from an HTML page, the thin JDBC driver is downloaded with it. The thin JDBC driver is only 300KB and does not require client-side libraries. When the applet is fired, the thin driver establishes a direct Net8 connection between the applet and the Oracle database. The Connection Manager that should reside on the same machine as the Web server multiplexes several inbound physical connections onto a single database connection, thereby saving server memory and providing scalability.

NOTE

Only Net8 running over the TCP/IP protocol is supported by the thin JDBC driver.

- JDBC/OCI driver

  The JDBC/OCI driver is also referred to as a fat driver, and it is larger in size than the thin JDBC driver. It provides access to the database by using Oracle client libraries such as OCILIB, CORE, and Net8. The driver isn't downloadable and you have to perform client installation of the JDBC/OCI driver. This driver is suitable for client/server Java applications, as well as middle-tier Java applications running in a Java application server.

NOTE

The thin driver and the JDBC/OCI driver are both JDBC 1.2.2 compliant.

Using the Internet Capabilities of Oracle 8i

CHAPTER 26

525

26

USING THE INTERNET
CAPABILITIES OF
ORACLE 8i

> **NOTE**
>
> The Java code written to access Oracle databases is not affected by the type of driver you use. The only change is the connect string used.

Both the thin JDBC driver and the JDBC/OCI driver support Oracle-specific features including

- Oracle7 and Oracle8 object-relational datatypes
- Manipulating LOBs
- Access to PL/SQL and Java stored procedures
- Support for all Oracle character sets
- Performance enhancement features such as batch SQL executions

> **NOTE**
>
> JDBC/OCI driver is not pure Java and requires software to be loaded on the client. Therefore, applications written using the JDBC/OCI driver would not qualify as being '100% Pure Java' as per the Sun Microsystems specification or standard. On the other hand, the thin driver is completely written in Java and does not require software to be loaded on the client. As a result, applications written using the thin driver will be '100% Pure Java'. Application code written in Java runs the same regardless of the JDBC driver used and, therefore, you should use the thin driver for your applications. There is no compelling reason to use the JDBC/OCI driver.

Java Scripts and Applets

Java allows you to write standalone programs called *scripts* (similar to anonymous PL/SQL blocks in PL/SQL), as well as class and method declarations called applets (similar to stored procedures and functions in PL/SQL). In addition to this, classes can be placed in packages just like PL/SQL allows you to place stored procedures in packages.

Similar to the code in other programming languages, Java code is stored in files, but the name of the file must match both the content and format of the class contained in the file. A Java code file usually ends in the extension .java,. and it must be made into a CLASS by passing it through the Java compiler (javac) before it can be used.

Two environment variables—PATH and CLASSPATH—can affect the operation of your Java programs. You will need to set these in the environment of your operating system.

- CLASSPATH is used to specify the path to user-defined classes. The directories are separated by semicolons, for example, on a Windows NT machine, .;c:\users\ classes;c:\tools\java\myclasses.

- PATH is used to specify the search path for executables.

Using SQLJ to Embed SQL in Java Programs

SQLJ, built on top of JDBC, allows application developers to embed SQL statements in Java programs. SQLJ allows you to write efficient and compact Java programs. A preprocessor can be used to translate SQLJ to Java code that makes JDBC calls to the database by using a JDBC driver from any vendor. Oracle provides JDeveloper, which is a standard Java development tool that can be used to develop and debug SQLJ programs. SQLJ provides several benefits:

- It results in Java code that's significantly more compact than JDBC (see Listings 26.1 and 26.2).

- It allows the use of typed cursors to obtain strong typed queries.

- It provides compile-time checking of SQL statements. This allows errors to be detected and applications to be debugged at an early stage.

> **NOTE**
>
> SQLJ is also commonly referred to as JSQL.

Using SQLJ instead of JDBC results in code that is concise, fast, and robust. The code is concise due to the fact that one SQLJ clause is replaced with multiple JDBC calls. SQLJ programs are fast because the statements are available to the database at precompile time instead of runtime. The robustness of SQLJ code is attributed to the extensive checks performed:

- Syntax checking to ensure that the SQLJ code contains valid SQL statements

- Type checking to ensure that the bind variables in the program are compatible with database column types

- Schema checking to ensure that the SQL statements will work against the particular schema

> **NOTE**
>
> The current implementation of SQLJ does not allow the use of dynamic SQL.

SQLJ programs can be used by following these generic steps (see Figure 26.1):

1. Write SQLJ Java programs.

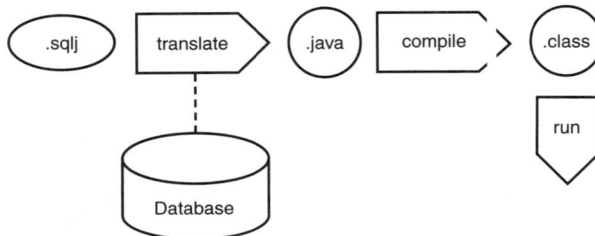

FIGURE 26.1
Developing Java applications using SQLJ.

2. Use the SQLJ translator to preprocess the SQLJ program and generate standard Java code with JDBC calls.

3. Compile the Java code.

4. Run the Java program.

Listings 26.1 and 26.2 show a JDBC program and its equivalent SQLJ program to demonstrate that using SQLJ results in compact code.

LISTING 26.1 A Sample JDBC Program

```
Java.sql.CallableStatement stmt;
Connection conn;
ResultSet res;

/* Declare the objects for a callable statement,
connection, and the result set*/

Conn = DriverManager.getConnection("jdbc:default");

/* Initialize the connection object with the default connection */
Stmt = conn.prepareStatement
```

continues

LISTING 26.1   Continued

```
("SELECT ename, ecity FROM emp WHERE deptno = ?");

/* Prepare the statement to execute */

Stmt.setInteger(1,deptno_p);

/* Use positional parameters to set the variables*/

Res = stmt.executeQuery();

/* Execute the query and store the results in the result set */
```

> **NOTE**
>
> javadoc is a program distributed with the JDK. It can be used to document Java classes. It takes as input a Java source file and produces as output an HTML file that documents the Java classes contained in the source file.

LISTING 26.2   A Sample SQLJ Program

```
ResultSet res;

/* Define an object to store the result set */

#sql res = (SELECT ename, ecity FROM emp
        WHERE deptno = :deptno_p);

/* Pass the program through the SQLJ translator and execute the program.
The result set is stored in "res" */
```

> **NOTE**
>
> A SQLJ translator is provided by Oracle8*i* as part of its Java machine.

Oracle's Java Virtual Machine

Java's philosophy is "Write once and run anywhere." The Java Virtual Machine is central to the platform independence achieved by using Java programs. Oracle's Java virtual machine (JVM)

(see Figure 26.2) is tightly integrated with the database and runs on the Multi-Threaded Server. The JVM provides high performance, scalability, and portability of Java applications. The JVM is a software program that emulates the operation of a hypothetical computer. The Java Virtual Machine is the only environment where Java code is executed. The Java Virtual Machine is automatically configured by Oracle. The following process describes how the JVM is used.

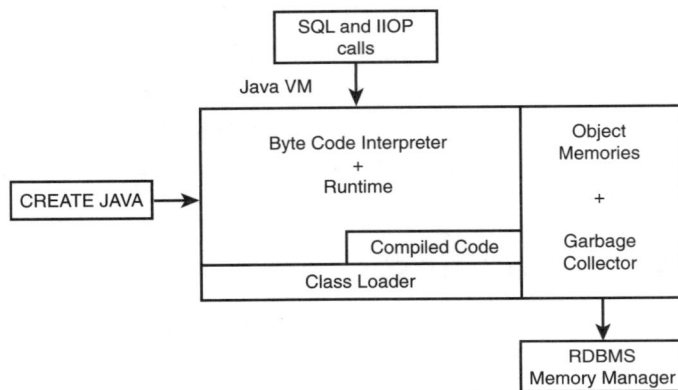

FIGURE 26.2
Components of the JVM.

- A programmer writes a Java program.
- The Java code is passed through the compiler.
- The compiler performs syntax checking and so on and generates a class file as output. The class file is unlike a platform-specific executable image or object file and it can be interpreted by the Java Virtual Machine.
- The Java Virtual Machine interprets the Java byte codes contained in the class file.

The JVM has several characteristics:

- Shared Java byte codes as well as lightweight Java threads are supported.
- It provides a well-tuned memory manager and garbage collector that optimize the use of the SGA (40KB per user session) and the operating system's virtual memory manager.
- You can store Java classes in the database as database library units.
- Java byte code can be translated to C executables by using the NCOMP Java compiler.
- Standard Java libraries such as Java.lang, Java.io, and Java.util are supported.
- Both the JDBC driver and SQLJ translator approaches are supported.

- CORBA/IIOP protocol can be used to call in and out of the database by means of a CORBA 2.0–compliant ORB (Object Request Broker) provided with the JVM.
- Utilities are provided to load and unload Java programs into the database.
- Enterprise JavaBeans (EJB 1.0 compliant) can be used by taking various approaches: pure Java clients, CORBA/IIOP clients, and DCOM clients.
- It provides mission-critical high availability and transparent application failover.
- It supports efficient load balancing on SMP and MPP architectures.
- Oracle Enterprise Manager can be used to simplify the management of Java stored procedures.
- Existing database security mechanisms, such as roles and grants, can be used with PL/SQL as well as Java stored procedures.

Java Stored Procedures

Oracle8*i* allows you to build applications in Java by using any one of three methods:

- Write Java stored procedures (see Listing 26.3) and triggers.
- Implement CORBA servers in the database in Java.
- Use Enterprise JavaBeans.

Stored procedures can be implemented in Oracle8*i* by using PL/SQL or Java. Although PL/SQL is seamless with SQL and results in very efficient code, Java provides an open general-purpose platform for developing and deploying applications. You can use SQLJ to write efficient and compact Java stored procedures.

Java stored procedures can run in different runtime contexts:

- Business logic can be implemented by writing top-level SQL functions and procedures.
- All types of Oracle triggers can be implemented in Java.
- In addition to PL/SQL and C/C++, Java can also be used to implement methods associated with objects.

NOTE

Oracle lite allows the replication of Java stored procedures from Oracle8*i* servers to mobile clients.

*Using the Internet Capabilities of Oracle 8*i

CHAPTER 26

531

26

USING THE INTERNET
CAPABILITIES OF
ORACLE 8*i*

Java stored procedures provide several benefits to OLTP applications:

- Network traffic is reduced because result sets can be processed on the database server and only the results are sent across the network.
- Java stored procedures can be replicated between Oracle8*i* servers; therefore, you can have business rules enforced centrally and then allow the Java stored procedures to be replicated to the other servers.
- Use of Java allows the stored procedures to be portable across various platforms.
- A variety of configurations such as client/server and multitier architecture can be supported.

Java stored procedures can be developed by using the following general steps:

1. Write a Java program that you want to make a stored procedure. This can be done by using any standard Java tool, such as JDeveloper provided by Oracle. You can make use of SQLJ to write efficient Java programs (see Listings 26.4, 26.5, and 26.6 that show how to create Java stored procedures using SQLJ and JDBC).

2. Load the Java program into Oracle8*i*'s Java Virtual Machine. Java source text can be loaded as standard Java .class files or as Java .jar files. The Java class files can be loaded in Oracle8*i* by issuing the `CREATE JAVA DDL` command, or by using the LoadJava utility to automate the loading process.

3. Expose the top-level entry point and register the Java programs with SQL so that SQL can call the Java program using these entry points. The exposed entry points are the only calls that SQL can make to this Java program. Subsequent Java-to-Java calls can be made within the JVM as needed.

4. Grant permissions to users so that they can run the Java stored procedure.

5. The Java stored procedure can now be called from SQL DML, PL/SQL, or triggers.

Using Java Programs in Oracle8*i*

After you have written the Java programs, you will need to load them into the database. Two input sources are accepted by Oracle8*i*:

- As a binary file at the operating system level
- As a LOB column in the database

These two input sources can be obtained in three formats:

- Standard Java source texts
- Java binaries
- Java resources

The Java Virtual Machine's class loader is responsible for loading Java from any input source in any format into a library unit (libunit). One library unit is created per Java class. Three types of libunits are available, one for each type of input.

> **NOTE**
>
> The name of the libunit is derived from the Java class. For example, if the fully qualified name of a Java class is com.oracle.sqlj.MyClass, the libunit's name is com/oracle/sqlj/MyClass.

LoadJava and DropJava Utilities

Java programs can be automatically loaded into the database by using the LoadJava utility. LoadJava uses the JDBC drivers to communicate with the database. Input to LoadJava can be in the form of Java source texts, Java binaries (.class files), or Java archives (JAR).

> **NOTE**
>
> Java resources cannot be directly loaded by LoadJava. You can archive the Java resources into JAR files and then load them using the LoadJava utility.

DropJava is a utility that can be used to drop Java binaries and archives from the libunits.

The following occurs when you run LoadJava:

1. LoadJava creates a system-generated table, `create$Java$lob$table`.
2. The Java binaries and JARs are loaded into a BLOB column of this system-generated table.
3. Java is loaded from the BLOB column into database libunits by using CREATE JAVA.

LoadJava has the following syntax:

```
LoadJava [-user connectstring] [options]
```

In this syntax,

- *connectstring* is of the form `username/password@database`. The Java is loaded into this schema.

Using the Internet Capabilities of Oracle 8i

CHAPTER 26

533

26

USING THE INTERNET
CAPABILITIES OF
ORACLE 8i

- The following options can be used with LoadJava:

  -o   Specifies that the JDBC/OCI driver should be used.

  -t   Specifies that the thin JDBC driver should be used.

  -v   Specifies that the verbose mode should be used to indicate the status of the load.

  -f   Specifies that existing classes should be replaced.

  -r   Specifies the resolver spec to use during the load.

  -s   Specifies that public synonyms should be created for the loaded classes.

  -g   Permissions are granted on the loaded classes.

  -h   Provides help on the syntax of the LoadJava utility.

The following code example loads a Java class named My.class into the schema SCOTT in the specified server using thin JDBC drivers. Only new and modified classes are loaded.

```
LoadJava -user scott/tiger@myserver:5235:ORCL -t My.class
```

Registering Java Programs

After Java procedures are loaded into libunits, you will have to register them so that they can be accessed from SQL. Unlike PL/SQL procedures, Java procedures aren't automatically available to SQL. Registering Java procedures refers to the process of publishing the Java entry points so that SQL can call the Java methods by means of these entry points.

> **NOTE**
>
> Java-to-Java calls can be made within the Java Virtual Machine.

The following steps can be used to register Java procedures:

1. A PL/SQL program that provides a type system wrapper for the Java method is created. This PL/SQL program, known as the *call descriptor*, specifies the mapping from Java types to SQL types, the mapping of the parameter modes, and other mapping from SQL to Java.
2. The wrapper program is called by the SQL and PL/SQL code.
3. The Java Virtual Machine intercepts this call and executes the Java method in the database's address space.

The PL/SQL call descriptor consists of two parts:

- The PL/SQL procedure PSEC declaration, which represents a proxy for the Java method.
- The body of the PL/SQL program, which is composed of the Java method signature.

The syntax for declaring the PL/SQL call descriptor is as follows:

```
CREATE [OR REPLACE]
PROCEDURE proc_name [(([sql_parameters])] |
FUNCTION func_name [(([sql_parameters])]
    RETURN sql_type
AS LANGUAGE JAVA NAME 'Java_fullname ([Java_parameters])
    [return Java_type_fullname]'
```

where,

```
sql_parameters := sql_type> [, sql_parameters]
Java_parameters := Java_type_fullname [, Java_parameters
```

> **NOTE**
>
> Positional mapping is used to map arguments between the proxy program and the Java method signature.

When using Java stored procedures, it is very important to correctly map Java datatypes to SQL and PL/SQL datatypes (see Table 26.1), otherwise the programs might not run as desired.

TABLE 26.1 Mapping Java to SQL and PL/SQL Datatypes

Java	*SQL and PL/SQL*
String, oracle.sql.CHAR	CHAR, VARCHAR2
Oracle.sql.DATE	DATE
Int, Integer, float, Float, double, Double, oracle.sql.NUMBER	NUMBER, DECIMAL, INTEGER, FLOAT, REAL, DOUBLE PRECISION
Oracle.sql.BLOB	BLOB
Oracle.sql.CLOB	CLOB
Oracle.sql.BFILE	BFILE
Oracle.sql.RAW	RAW and LONG RAW
Oracle.sql.ROWID	ROWID
Oracle.sql.OracleObject	Oracle8 objects
Oracle.sql.REF	Oracle8 REF

*Using the Internet Capabilities of Oracle 8*i

CHAPTER 26

535

26
USING THE INTERNET
CAPABILITIES OF
ORACLE 8*I*

NOTE

The oracle.sql package provides automatic datatype conversion between Java, SQL, and PL/SQL.

Java accepts only IN arguments by reference, whereas SQL and PL/SQL use IN, OUT, and IN OUT modes of parameter passing. This should be taken into consideration when using Java stored procedures. When using IN parameters, consult Table 26.1 to determine the datatype mapping that can be used between Java and PL/SQL types. While using OUT and IN OUT parameter modes in SQL and PL/SQL, the corresponding Java parameter should be a one-element array of the appropriate Java type.

Listing 26.3 is a sample Java stored procedure.

LISTING 26.3   A Java Stored Procedure

```
/* The Java method 'greetings' takes the firstname as a String
argument and returns another string value by appending it to 'Good Morning' */
Java Class Welcomejava:
    Public class welcome {
    Static public String
    Greetings(string firstname) {
        Return "Good Morning " + firstname;
        }
    }

/* PL/SQL proxy for welcomejava. This proxy is necessary
to register the Java program. The string datatype is mapped to SQL VARCHAR2 */
CREATE FUNCTION greetings(fname VARCHAR2) RETURN
VARCHAR2 AS
    LANGUAGE JAVA NAME
    'Welcome.Greetings(Java.lang.String)
    return Java.lang.String'
```

NOTE

Java methods called from SQL or PL/SQL execute under the definer's privileges. However, by default, Java methods called from other Java methods execute under the invoker's privileges.

The following privileges must be granted to users of Java stored procedures:

- EXECUTE rights on the PL/SQL call descriptor for the Java method
- EXECUTE rights on the Java class
- EXECUTE rights on the Java classes and resources used by the Java class being called

> **NOTE**
>
> Security of Java stored procedures is managed in the same manner as PL/SQL procedures by using Oracle GRANT and REVOKE statements.

LISTING 26.4   updjava—Writing Java Stored Procedures Using SQLJ

```
package modify_emp;

import sqlj.runtime.*;
import sqlj.runtime.ref.*;

public class update_emp {

  public static int update_emp (String name,
          int raise, String ncity, String nstate) {

    int newsal = -1;
    String newcity = "UNKNOWN";
    String newstate = "UNKNOWN";

    try{
      #sql {UPDATE emp
            SET sal = sal + :raise
            WHERE ename = :name};

      #sql {UPDATE emp
            SET city = :ncity
            WHERE ename = :name};

#sql {UPDATE emp
            SET state = :nstate
            WHERE ename = :name};

      #sql {SELECT sal INTO :newsal
            FROM emp
            WHERE ename = :name};
```

Using the Internet Capabilities of Oracle 8i

CHAPTER 26

537

26

USING THE INTERNET
CAPABILITIES OF
ORACLE 8*i*

```
        #sql {SELECT city INTO :newcity
                FROM emp
                WHERE ename = :name};

#sql {SELECT state INTO :newstate
                FROM emp
                WHERE ename = :name};


    }
    catch (Java.sql.SQLException e) {};

    return newsal;
  }
}
```

LISTING 26.5   empjava—Calling Java Stored Procedures

```
//Title:       Using SQLJ with Java Stored Procedures
//Author:      Megh Thakkar
//Description: This Java program modifies the employee record by
// giving the employee a raise and changing the employee's city and state
package modify_emp;
import Java.sql.*;
import Java.io.*;

class maintain_emp
{
  public static void main (String args [])
      throws SQLException, IOException
  {
    String cstring = args[0];
    String uname = args[1];
    String pwd = args[2];

    // Load JDBC Drivers
    DriverManager.registerDriver
        (new oracle.jdbc.driver.OracleDriver());

    // Connect to the database using the specified parameters
    Connection conn =
      DriverManager.getConnection (cstring, uname, pwd);

    // Prepare to call the stored procedure
    CallableStatement cstmt =
        conn.prepareCall ("{? = call
```

continues

LISTING 26.5   Continued

```
                modify_emp_update_emp (?, ?, ?, ?,?)}");

   // We are using positional arguments
   // The first argument is declared as an OUT parameter
   cstmt.registerOutParameter (1, Types.INTEGER);

 // The second argument is SCOTT
 //  The third argument is the raise
 // The fourth argument is the new city
 // The fifth argument is the new state
   cstmt.setString (2, "SCOTT");
   cstmt.setInt (3, 20000);
   cstmt.setString(4,"SEATTLE");
   cstmt.setString(5,"WASHINGTON");

   // Execute the command
   cstmt.execute ();

   // The first argument returns the new salary
   int new_salary = cstmt.getInt (1);

  System.out.println ("Employee record has been updated successfully");
  System.out.println ("The new salary is: " + new_salary);
  }
}
```

LISTING 26.6   Using the JDBC Driver with Java Applications

```
//Title:       Using JDBC with Java Applications
//Author:      Megh Thakkar
//Description: This Java program queries the emp table to find the
// location of each employee

package package1;

import Java.sql.*;

public class find_location

{
  public static void main (String args [])
      throws SQLException
  {
```

```java
    String cstring = args[0];
    String uname = args[1];
    String pwd = args[2];

    // Load JDBC Drivers
    try
    {
      Class.forName ("oracle.jdbc.driver.OracleDriver");
    }
    catch (ClassNotFoundException e)
    {
      System.out.println ("Unable to load driver");
    }

// Connect to the database using the connection parameters
    Connection conn =
      DriverManager.getConnection (cstring, uname, pwd);

    // Create JDBC Statement
    Statement stmt = conn.createStatement ();

    // Query the location of each employee and store
    // the output in the result set
    ResultSet rset = stmt.executeQuery
                ("select empno, name, city, state from emp");

    while (rset.next ())
    {
      // Get Employee Number
      int eno = rset.getInt(1);
      // Get Employee Name
      String ename = rset.getString(2);
      // Get Employee city
     double ecity = rset.getString(3);
    // Get Employee state
    double estate = rset.getString(4);

      System.out.println (ename + "  with employee# " + eno +
➥" lives in  " + ecity + "," + estate);
    }
    conn.close();
  }
}
```

Enterprise JavaBeans and CORBA

Java's component architecture is referred to as JavaBeans. Enterprise Java Beans (EJBs) allow the use of a component-based model for implementing Java systems. EJBs can be developed in Java and applications can be developed using tools such as Sun's Java Studio. EJBs can be deployed by using execution containers such as databases, TP-Monitors (also known as Transaction Processing Monitors), and application servers. EJBs are compatible with CORBA, DCOM, and so on. A CORBA 2.0–compliant Object Request Broker (ORB) is provided with Oracle8*i* that allows you to access Java stored procedures and EJBs through the IIOP protocol. IIOP can also be used to communicate with other ORBs.

> **NOTE**
>
> The Multi-Threaded Server configuration is required to use CORBA/IIOP with Oracle8*i*.

CORBA/IIOP can be used as follows:

1. Develop Java stored procedures and EJBs.
2. Publish the procedures and EJBs to allow access to them via Net8 and as a CORBA server.
3. The published procedures can be accessed by the client applications through IIOP.

Oracle Internet File System

The general trend in storing information is to store most of the data in file systems and only a very small percentage in a relational database system such as Oracle. In a file system, information is stored in separate data stores such as documents, Web content, and so on. Each of these data stores has its own storage and access methods. There are several problems in storing information in file systems:

- Difficult to manage diverse data stores by end users—Managing information stored in diverse data stores can be difficult because each of these data stores may require its own storage and access method.

- System administration difficulties—Maintaining security, performance, and configuration; providing access to users; and maintaining the integrity of the data, which may be spread across multiple machines and data stores can become difficult.

- Application development problems—Application developers have to understand different operating system peculiarities; understand different APIs to access files, Web content, and relational data; and keep track of all the components of the project.

The problems associated with diverse data stores can be minimized if you place all the information in one type of data store, such as a relational database system. This approach has several challenges:

- Relational databases cannot efficiently manage certain types of information, such as email and simple files.
- Placing all information in relational databases makes it necessary for everyone, including end users, to be more familiar with the use of SQL.
- Regular file systems allow you to access the contents of a file by simply double-clicking it. However, in a relational database system, you will have to download the file, edit it as desired, and then upload it back into the database. These additional steps can reduce productivity.

Oracle8*i* allows you to store all the data in a database system. This is achieved by using the Internet File System (IFS) that merges the file system with the database. IFS is a database file system (DBFS) that provides several benefits:

- IFS allows you to access the information by using multiple protocols and client interfaces. The following protocols can be used with IFS:

SMB	Windows 95, Windows 98, and Windows NT can use this protocol to edit IFS files. You can drag and drop files in IFS.
HTTP	Web browsers can use this protocol to access information in IFS.
FTP	IFS contents are viewed as FTP directories and you can get and put files via FTP.
SMTP, IMAP4, POP3	Email clients such as Microsoft Outlook and Eudora can make use of these protocols to access IFS.

- A common API can be used for programming against the database.
- SQL can be used to search the contents of the DBFS much more efficiently then searching a regular file system.
- Database-level security can be used to protect all the data.
- Check in and check out facilities can be used to simplify information management.
- Document parsing and rendering make it possible to view the same document in different formats.
- Data within the database is tightly integrated with the Oracle Enterprise Manager, ConText data cartridge, and Oracle8*i* features such as objects.
- Java stored procedures and EJBs can be used in conjunction with IFS.

- IFS messaging allows you to send emails to system administrators alerting them of important events.
- Version control allows you to use multiple versions of a file by identifying one official copy that can be used by all the users. A new version of a file is created when you copy or edit a file.
- Files can be automatic purged after a specified expiration period.
- Application development is achieved by using the programming APIs provided by Java, CORBA, and PL/SQL.

IFS contents appear in folders and subfolders, which can be easily manipulated just like a file system. Both relational and nonrelational data can be stored in the same folder. An IFS file can have multiple parent directories. For example, an email document (which appears as an IFS file) can be part of two separate folders.

NOTE

Oracle 8.1.7 (due for release in June 1999) will implement the full production features of IFS. Several features are planned, including support for NFS, portable IFS, file system tablespaces, SQL integration, and tools to develop IFS applications.

Summary

Java is an important part of Oracle8*i*'s strategy that makes it Web-enabled. The Oracle Java Virtual Machine provides an environment in which to run Java applications efficiently. In this chapter, we discussed the various Internet capabilities of Oracle8*i*, including the ability to write and use Java stored procedures. Java stored procedures provide an alternative way in which to implement object methods and result in portable and reusable code.

Oracle provides two types of drivers: the thin driver and the JDBC/OCI driver to allow access to Oracle databases from Java applications. IFS allows you to manage all your data in a common format by placing it in a single type of data store—the Oracle Database File System.

Managing Security

IN THIS CHAPTER

Oracle8*i* provides an impressive suite of new security features based on the principle of least privilege. This principle basically means that any user should be given only the permissions that are needed for him to perform his duties. A granular approach is taken to implementing security policies. The Oracle8*i* security features can be broken down into two categories:

- Database security includes security features that any database can use
- Internet database security features used by a database that performs Internet processing

A database that performs Internet processing should use security features from both of these categories.

Using Views to Secure Applications

Access to the information stored in the database can be controlled by using views.

Suppose that you have an employees table containing information about all employees. The principle of least privilege would require that any employee should be able to see only information that pertains to her. The following view can be used for this purpose:

```
Create view employees_v as
   Select * from employees
   Where emp_name = USER
```

Similarly, the following view allows a user to access only those records that are modified by him. This view assumes that we are using a column `last_modified_by` in the orders table that keeps track of the user who last modified the order:

```
Create view orders_v as
   Select * from orders
   Where last_modified_by = USER
```

When using views as a security mechanism, you might encounter several problems:

- Inflexible and difficult to maintain—For example, you might want to implement function-based security where an employee can view only his records, a manager can view the records of all employees in her department, and an HR manager can view the records of all company employees. This implementation using views only approach would require you to create different views to satisfy all these requirements. Such a solution can be very costly because it would require you to maintain a large number of views and associated synonyms or alternatively create a complex view that encompasses all the scenarios resulting in a very inefficient view.

- It is difficult to implement security based on runtime parameters. For example, you might want the nature and extent of the access to an object to be related to the time of day, the IP address of the machine, and the task currently being performed by the application.

- Views are not very secure because experienced and knowledgeable users might be able to access the information directly from the base table.

A better approach to implementing security is to make use of the Oracle8*i* features such as application contexts and fine-grained access control.

Application Contexts and Fine-Grained Access Control

Oracle8*i* allows you to implement complex security requirements by making use of application contexts and fine-grained access control.

Using Application Contexts

Oracle8*i* provides a new database object type called application context that enables you to cache session information securely. The following syntax can be used to create application contexts:

```
CREATE OR REPLACE CONTEXT namespace using package;
```

The new SQL function SYS_CONTEXT can be used to extract attributes of the application context:

```
SYS_CONTEXT(namespace,attribute);
```

Oracle makes use of a "primitive" context to store certain information for a session such as the username, session ID, and IP address. The primitive context is stored in the namespace called USERENV. SYS_CONTEXT can be used to manipulate even the USERENV namespace as demonstrated in the following:

```
SYS_CONTEXT('userenv','username');
```

The DBMS_SESSION.SET_CONTEXT procedure can be used to set nonprimitive contexts as shown in the following:

```
DBMS_SESSION.SET_CONTEXT(namespace,attribute,value);
```

Making use of attributes stored in a context can be very useful because the attribute values are stored in the private memory of the session. Attributes of a context are transient and, when set or reset, are valid for the entire duration of the user session. Access to data is controlled by using the attributes that are stored securely. Also, the context can be set only by the designated procedure. Each application can have its own context and SYS_CONTEXT() is treated as a bind variable during query execution resulting in performance improvement.

Using Fine-Grained Access Control (FGAC)

The *fine-grained access control* feature of Oracle8*i* allows you to define policies on tables and views. When an operation such as INSERT or DELETE is performed on a table or view that has a policy associated with it, the policy dynamically generates predicates on those operations. In other words, a virtual private database is created for each user. This guarantees that each user accessing the database can only access information that they have been authorized to access. Security implemented with the use of fine-grained access control is kept at the database server level, preventing it from being bypassed by the client software.

Tables and views are associated with a security policy and any access to the table or view after the policy has been implemented causes the server to call a function that is enforcing the policy. The function returns code that is added to the WHERE clause before the SQL statement is executed. The SQL statements are fully parsed and optimized and stored in the shared pool for use by other users.

NOTE

Different policies can be set for different DML statements on the same table or view.

The DBMS_RLS package contains the necessary interfaces to manage policies:

- add_policy(*object_schema*, *object_name*, *policy_name*);
  policy_function_schema, policy_function, statement_type, update_check, enable);
- drop_policy(*object_schema*, *object_name*, *policy_name*);
- enable_policy(*object_schema*, *object_name*, *policy_name*, *enable*);
- refresh_policy(*object_schema, object_name, policy_name*);

The policy function that is invoked when a DML is performed on a table or view protected by a policy is defined using the following syntax:

```
FUNCTION policy_function(schema_name VARCHAR2, object_name
        VARCHAR2) RETURN VARCHAR2;
```

NOTE

Security policies should not be used as an alternative to constraints.

Use of fine-grained access control provides several benefits:

- *Security*—The policies set for an object are stored on the server and can't be bypassed by the client software.
- *Flexibility*—Dynamic and complex security requirement can be implemented because the predicates are generated dynamically, based on the application's state.
- *Transparency*—A change in security rules associated with an object can be made by simply changing the associated policies, and no change to the applications is required.
- *Scalable*—The SQL statements are parsed, optimized, and stored in the shared pool, making them available to other users.

Consider an example of the projects table where an employee should only see the projects that he leads. The projects table has the following description:

```
(proj_id    number(5),
 proj_desc  varchar2(30),
 proj_lead  number(6))
```

The employees table has the following description:

```
(emp_id    number(6),
 emp_name  varchar2(20))
```

The following steps can be used to implement this security requirement:

1. Connect to Server Manager as internal.
2. Create the application context:
   ```
   create or replace context proj_ctx
   using sec_admin.pj_ctx;
   ```
3. Create the trusted package specification:
   ```
   Create or replace package sec_admin.pj_ctx as
      Procedure set_emp_number;
   End pj_ctx;
   ```
4. Create the package body:
   ```
   CREATE PACKAGE BODY pj_ctx IS
     PROCEDURE set_emp_number IS
       empnum NUMBER;
       BEGIN
         select emp_id into empnum
         from employees
         where emp_name = sys_context('userenv', 'session_user');
         dbms_session.set_context('proj_ctx', 'proj_lead', empnum);
       END set_emp_number;
     END pj_ctx;
   ```

5. Grant permissions to everyone to execute the package:

```
GRANT EXECUTE ON pj_ctx TO PUBLIC;
```

6. Create the policy function:

```
CREATE PACKAGE sec_admin.proj_security AS
    FUNCTION empnum_sec(owner VARCHAR2, object_name VARCHAR2)
    RETURN VARCHAR2;
    END proj_security;
```

7. Create the package body for the policy function:

```
CREATE PACKAGE BODY proj_security IS
    FUNCTION empnum_sec(owner VARCHAR2, object_name VARCHAR2)
    RETURN VARCHAR2 IS
    BEGIN
        RETURN ('proj_lead =
            sys_context("proj_ctx",  "emp_id")');
        END empnum_sec;
    END proj_security;
```

8. Add the new policy to the projects table:

```
execute DBMS_RLS.ADD_POLICY('apps','projects', 'proj_policy',
 'sec_admin', 'proj_security.empnum_sec');
```

When this policy is associated with the projects table, any access to the projects table causes the predicate 'where proj_lead = sys_context("proj_ctx", "emp_id")' to be added to the query.

Invoker Rights

By default, stored procedures and SQL methods are executed with the definer's rights. For example, suppose that we have a standalone procedure called add_project in the schema darin:

```
SQL> create procedure add_project(new_proj varchar2(10),
2 new_projdesc varchar2(20)) as
3 begin
insert into projects(proj_id, proj_name, proj_desc)
values(projno_seq.nextval, new_proj, newprojdesc);
end;
```

Suppose that another user james has been given the permission to execute this procedure and decides to execute it; then the procedure will execute with the privileges of the definer (in this case, darin). Also, the unqualified reference to the projects table is resolved in the schema darin. The result is that a new project record is inserted in the projects table in darin's schema.

If we want to have procedures that modify objects in some schema other than the definer's schema, we could either use fully qualified references or copy the same procedure in every schema that will use this procedure. Both of these solutions are undesirable because use of fully qualified references will make the procedure not portable, whereas the copying of procedure in all schema will create a maintenance nightmare.

Oracle8*i* allows the use of AUTHID clause in the procedures that can be used to specify that the procedure should execute with the invoker's rights instead of the definer's rights. Several advantages of using invoker's rights are as follows:

- The procedure becomes portable
- The definer of the procedure need not worry about who will use the procedure
- They are not bound to a particular schema
- Data retrieval can be centralized
- Easier to maintain

NOTE

The AUTHID clause can be used to specify whether references to objects outside the routine are resolved in the schema of the definer or the invoker.

The syntax for using the AUTHID clause is as follows:

- Functions
  ```
  CREATE [OR REPLACE] FUNCTION [schema_name.]function_name
  ➡[(parameter_list)] RETURN datatype
  ➡[AUTHID {CURRENT_USER ¦ DEFINER}] {IS ¦ AS}
  ```

- Procedures
  ```
  CREATE [OR REPLACE] PROCEDURE [schema_name.]procedure_name
  ➡[(parameter_list)] [AUTHID {CURRENT_USER ¦ DEFINER}] {IS ¦ AS}
  ```

- Packages
  ```
  CREATE [OR REPLACE] PACKAGE [schema_name.]package_name
  ➡[AUTHID {CURRENT_USER ¦ DEFINER}] {IS ¦ AS}
  ```

- Object types
  ```
  CREATE [OR REPLACE] TYPE [schema_name.]object_type_name
  ➡[AUTHID {CURRENT_USER ¦ DEFINER}] {IS ¦ AS} OBJECT
  ```

In all the preceding usage, the default is the `DEFINER` rights and the use of `CURRENT_USER` specifies that you want the execution to be performed with the invoker's rights.

The procedure `add_projects` can be modified as follows to specify that it should be executed with the invoker's rights:

```
SQL> create procedure add_project(new_proj varchar2(10),
2 new_projdesc varchar2(20))
AUTHID CURRENT_USER as
projects(proj_id, proj_name, proj_desc)
values(projno_seq.nextval, new_proj, newprojdesc);
end;
```

> **NOTE**
>
> `AUTHID CURRENT_USER` causes the invoker's rights to be checked at runtime, and the external references are resolved in the schema of the invoker. However, the PL/SQL compiler must resolve the references at compile time, and therefore the definer must create template objects that must match the actual invoker objects.

When the invoker's rights are used, the external references are resolved in the schema of the invoker only for the following cases:

- `SELECT`, `INSERT`, `UPDATE`, and `DELETE` statements
- The transaction control statement `LOCK TABLE`
- The cursor control statements `OPEN` and `OPEN-FOR`
- The dynamic SQL statements `EXECUTE IMMEDIATE` and `OPEN-FOR-USING`
- SQL statements that are parsed by using `DBMS_SQL.PARSE()`

Other than the preceding cases, the privileges of the definer are checked at compile time, and the external references are resolved in the schema of the definer.

Overriding Name Resolution

In some instances, you might want the procedure to execute with the invoker's rights and certain external references resolved in the definer's schema—for example,

```
SQL> create procedure max_salary (dept_id integer)
2 authid current_user as
3 max_sal real;
4 begin
5 select max(sal) into max_sal
```

```
6 from dept, emp
7 where dept.dept_id = :dept_id and
8      dept.emp_id = emp.emp_id;
9 end;
```

This procedure will execute with the invoker's rights and use the max function from the invoker's schema.

Suppose that you want the max function to be executed from the definer's schema. This can be achieved with two methods:

- Using a public synonym

  You can create a public synonym for the max function as follows:

  ```
  SQl> create public synonym max for scott.max;
  ```

  Now the max function from scott's schema will be used unless the invoker has defined a function or private synonym called max.

- Fully qualifying the external reference

  This can be done as follows:

  ```
  SQL> create procedure max_salary (dept_id integer)
  2 authid current_user as
  3 max_sal real;
  4 begin
  5 select scott.max(sal) into max_sal
  6 from dept, emp
  7 where dept.dept_id = :dept_id and
  8      dept.emp_id = emp.emp_id;
  9 end;
  ```

  This will work provided the definer has not created a package called scott with the function max.

NOTE

When invoker-rights routines are used within a view or a database trigger, the view owner (not view user) is considered the invoker.

Database Resource Manager

The database resource manager manages the amount of CPU and the degree of parallelism that can be acquired by the instances from the operating system. This new tool in Oracle8*i* allows you to control the allocation and use of CPU resources among database users and applications.

Prior to Oracle8*i*, all users and applications had equal access to the database. This tool allows you to assign more resources to the more important tasks.

The database resource manager provides several benefits:

- Improved security—It can be used to prevent denial of service attacks against a production environment used for the Internet.
- Enhanced administration—Administration is enhanced if a database used for the Internet shares system resources with other databases that are not used for the Internet.

Database resources can be managed by the following four mechanisms:

- Resource consumer groups can be assigned at the user level, and all their sessions become part of that consumer group.
- Resource plans contain resource consumer groups or other resource plans.

NOTE

A maximum of eight levels can be defined for allocating resources.

- Resource allocation methods define a policy that is to be followed by a particular resource. Resource consumer groups and resource plans make use of resource allocation methods.
- Administrators can make use of resource plan directives to assign members to a particular plan and then manage the resources used by that member.

NOTE

While managing a production environment connected to the Internet, you can create an Internet resource group and restrict the amount of resources for that group. This prevents one resource group from consuming all the operating system resources.

Changes made in the database resource manager are dynamically applied to the database without requiring a shutdown or a restart of the database. The different resource plans and resource consumer groups are all stored in the Data Dictionary.

When the database resource manager is used, the system utilization can be optimized by integrating the automatic degree of parallelism (ADOP) feature with it. This will limit the degree of parallelism for parallel query operations.

Oracle8*i* Internet Security Features

Generally, Internet applications make use of multitiered architectures and access the databases via multiple networks. For example, thin clients connect to application servers, and application servers connect to the database servers. The database servers need to be able to trust that the client is who it says it is, and the application server is who it says it is as well. Authentication is usually performed using one of two methods:

- Passwords
- Digital certificates

Using Passwords

Oracle8*i* conveniently allows you to manage and protect user passwords. You can specify several characteristics of a password such as the following:

- Password lifetime and expiration—A given password can have a specified time limit for its use, and it will expire and have to be changed. A grace period is given to the user after the password expires, and if the user does not change the password in that time, the account is locked.

> **NOTE**
>
> The database administrator can set the password for any account to an expired state.

- A password history to prevent users from choosing the same password for the specified amount of time or for the specified number of password changes.

> **NOTE**
>
> The CREATE PROFILE statement can be used to configure the rules for password reuse.

- Enforcement of password complexity verification to prevent it from being easily guessed. The default password complexity verification routine requires that each password satisfy the following:

    Contain a minimum of four characters in length

    Should not equal the UserID

Should equal at least one alphabetic character, one numeric character, and one punctuation mark

Should not equal any word on an internal list of simple words

Should differ from the previous password by at least three characters

- Account lockup after a certain number of unsuccessful attempts

---

NOTE

Don't set the number of unsuccessful attempts after which the account locks up to a very low value unless you are ready to receive many calls from users who tend to forget their password easily and frequently lock their account.

Using Digital Certificates

Users or machines can be authenticated by using digital certificates of the type X.509 version 3, an Internet standard–based public key infrastructure(PKI). The following information is contained in a digital certificate:

- Name of the certificate owner
- Name of the certificate authority
- Public key of the certificate owner
- The range of date for which the certificate is valid
- Signature of the issuer
- Certificate serial number

The digital certificates must be used with the Secure Sockets Layer protocol (SSL). SSL provides data integrity checking and data encryption across the network. This provides security for data transmission across the network. The Oracle certificate authority or another certificate authority publishes wallets in an Oracle directory server. The certificate and private key are stored in the 'Oracle Wallet'. These Oracle Wallets are managed by a centralized tool—the Oracle Wallet Manager. Use of digital certificates allows a stronger means of authentication than a password. The Oracle8*i* advanced security option allows the use of the RADIUS protocol that has become an Internet standard.

NOTE

The RADIUS protocol supports the use of passwords, tokens, biometrics, and smartcards.

Oracle8*i* also allows firewall support. A firewall is used to prevent the public Internet traffic from entering a private network of a company. By means of a firewall, you can protect the database servers that communicate with servers connected to the Internet. You can make use of firewalls that provide proxies to allow only SQL*NET and NET8 traffic to pass through the firewall.

External Authentication

External authentication refers to the authentication of the user by some means that is external to the database. The database still identifies the user, but a database password is not required for login. Usually external authentication is performed by the operating system or network authentication service. To use external authentication, set the parameter OS_AUTHENT_PREFIX in the init.ora file. Setting this parameter tells Oracle that any user who has the same prefix as this value is to be authenticated externally. For example, if OS_AUTHENT_PREFIX is set to ops$ and you have two Oracle users—ops$smith and johnson—no Oracle password is required for ops$smith, whereas johnson requires a password.

NOTE

OS_AUTHENT_PREFIX can be set to any value, even null (by setting it to " ").

The init.ora parameter REMOTE_OS_AUTHENT must be set to TRUE to enable Oracle to use the username from an insecure connection.

Oracle Advanced Security (OAS) option allows network authentication for users with the following technologies:

- Network authentication services (such as Kerberos and SESAME)

  A user is created on each database that she will use and database privileges are assigned to the user, but the password is the reserved word *external*. Oracle only identifies the user, and an external source is enabled to authenticate the user. Passwords are verified by using an authentication server that has usernames, passwords, and hostnames.

- Token Devices

  A token is a physical device that the user must have to establish connection. A commonly used method is challenge/response. When the user enters the username, a number is sent back to the user (challenge), and the user enters the number on a device. The device that is configured specifically for this user generates another number (response) that is used as the password. A different challenge/response sequence is used for each connection.

- Biometric Devices

  Biometric devices use a physical characteristic that is unique to the individual. Currently, a fingerprint scanning device can be used with the Oracle8*i* advanced security option. The fingerprint of the user must first be recorded on the system. The user specifies the Oracle service and places her finger on the fingerprint reader. The finger placed on the reader is compared with the fingerprint stored in the database, and if there is a match, the user is allowed access.

Enterprise Authentication

Enterprise authentication uses Oracle Security Service (OSS) to enable a central source for password management. The user is called a *global* user and must be created on each database that she will use with the password *globally*. Oracle will only identify the user and Oracle Security Service is enabled to authenticate the user. OSS interfaces with the Oracle Enterprise Manager to centralize security management.

NOTE

Oracle Security Service allows users to have global identities that are managed centrally.

Enterprise Roles

A global role enables you to assign authorization information to global users. Global roles are assigned to a global user in the Oracle Security Server and privileges are associated with each global role on the database server. When a global user logs on to a database, the global roles are dynamically assigned to the user.

Enterprise roles are a container for one or more global roles and are stored in an Internet directory or in a Lightweight Directory Access Protocol (LDAP)–compliant directory structure.

> **NOTE**
>
> Privileges associated with a global role can differ between databases.

> **NOTE**
>
> Default tablespace can be associated with a user so that the objects—such as tables and views created by the user—can be placed in a specific tablespace. By default, the objects will be created in the system tablespace. Similarly, a temporary tablespace should be associated with a user for temporary space requirements such as during index creation and the use of SQL statements such as ORDER BY and GROUP BY. It is also important to specify a quota for a user in a particular tablespace. This will prevent the user objects from taking excessive space.

Encrypting the Data

Data integrity can be maintained by the use of secure user connections and encryption algorithms. User passwords can be encrypted by using a modified DES (data encryption standard) algorithm. Encryption is enabled by using the following steps:

1. On the database server, set the init.ora parameter `DBLINK_ENCRYPT_LOGIN` to `TRUE`.

2. On the client machine, set the environment variable `ORA_ENCRYPT_LOGIN` to `TRUE`.

Instead of simply encrypting the password, a better solution is to encrypt all your data. This can be achieved by using Oracle's advanced security (OAS) option. Currently, OAS provides two encryption algorithms: RSA and DES with different key lengths. Different key lengths are used within the USA and Canada, and outside it:

- 56-bit RSA RC4, 56-bit DES, and 128-bit RSA are used in the USA and Canada.
- 40-bit RSA RC4, 40-bit DES40, and 3DES are available for export outside the USA and Canada.

Use of these algorithms ensures data integrity during the transmission from the client workstation to the database server.

Auditing

Database access can be monitored by using the auditing feature of Oracle8*i*. Auditing is enabled by using the AUDIT command and it is disabled by using the NOAUDIT command. The following actions can be audited:

- Login attempts
- Access to objects
- Database actions that are specific system privileges and statements without regard to the object being accessed

> **NOTE**
>
> Both successful and unsuccessful attempts can be audited.

In order to use auditing, the following steps must be taken:

1. Connect to server manager as the SYS account.
2. Run CATAUDIT.SQL.
3. In the init.ora file, set the parameter AUDIT_TRAIL to the appropriate value: DB (for database) or OS (for operating system).
4. Restart the database instance.

> **NOTE**
>
> If AUDIT_TRAIL is set to DB, all audited activity is written to the SYS.AUD$ table. Make sure that this table is placed in a tablespace that has enough space.

Auditing Logins

In order to use auditing, the AUDIT ANY privilege is required. The AUDIT SESSION command can be used to audit successful as well as unsuccessful login attempts. Auditing information about login attempts can be queried by using the DBA_AUDIT_SESSION view.

> **NOTE**
>
> To audit only successful login attempts, use the AUDIT SESSION WHENEVER SUCCESSFUL command and to audit only unsuccessful login attempts use the AUDIT SESSION WHENEVER UNSUCCESSFUL command.

For example, the query

```
Select os_username, username,
    To_char(timestamp, 'DD-MON-YY HH24:MI') logon_time,
    To_char(logoff_time, 'DD-MON-YY HH24:MI') logoff_time
From dba_audit_session;
```

can result in the following output:

```
OS_USERNAME    USERNAME    LOGON_TIME          LOGOFF_TIME
MEGHT          MEGHT    07-AUG-99 16:00    07-AUG-99 18:40
```

Auditing Database Actions

Database actions can be audited at the statement or the system privilege level without reference to any particular database object being accessed. The AUDIT statement can be used to audit specific statements for a user, session, or access. Both successful and unsuccessful attempts can be audited. Refer to Table 27.1 for a list of statement options that can be audited.

TABLE 27.1 Audit Options for Statements

Statement Option	*SQL Statements Audited*
ALTER SYSTEM	ALTER SYSTEM
CLUSTER	CREATE CLUSTER, ALTER CLUSTER, TRUNCATE CLUSTER, DROP CLUSTER
DATABASE LINK	CREATE DATABASE LINK, DROP DATABASE LINK
INDEX	CREATE INDEX, ALTER INDEX, DROP INDEX
NOT EXISTS	SQL statements that return an Oracle error that the specified object does not exist
PROCEDURE	CREATE [OR REPLACE] FUNCTION, CREATE [OR REPLACE] PACKAGE, CREATE [OR REPLACE] PACKAGE BODY, CREATE [OR REPLACE] PROCEDURE, DROP PACKAGE, DROP PROCEDURE
PUBLIC DATABASE LINK	CREATE PUBLIC DATABASE LINK, DROP PUBLIC DATABASE LINK
PUBLIC SYNONYM	CREATE PUBLIC SYNONYM, DROP PUBLIC SYNONYM
ROLE	CREATE ROLE, ALTER ROLE, SET ROLE, DROP ROLE

continues

TABLE 27.1   Continued

Statement Option	SQL Statements Audited
ROLLBACK SEGMENT	CREATE ROLLBACK SEGMENT, ALTER ROLLBACK SEGMENT, DROP ROLLBACK SEGMENT
SEQUENCE	CREATE SEQUENCE, DROP SEQUENCE
SESSION	Session connects and disconnects
SYNONYM	CREATE SYNONYM, DROP SYNONYM
SYSTEM AUDIT	AUDIT, NOAUDIT
SYSTEM GRANT	GRANT, REVOKE
TABLE	CREATE TABLE, ALTER TABLE, DROP TABLE
TABLESPACE	CREATE TABLESPACE, ALTER TABLESPACE, DROP TABLESPACE
TRIGGER	CREATE TRIGGER, ALTER TRIGGER, ENABLE OR DISABLE TRIGGER
USER	CREATE USER, ALTER USER, DROP USER
VIEW	CREATE [OR REPLACE] VIEW, DROP VIEW

Auditing DML Activity

A specific database object can be audited by using the following syntax:

```
AUDIT obj_option on schema.object
BY SESSION/ACCESS WHENEVER [NOT] SUCCESSFUL;
```

For example, the following will audit unsuccessful updates and deletes on the emp table in the scott's schema:

```
AUDIT update, delete
ON scott.emp
WHENEVER NOT SUCCESSFUL;
```

> **NOTE**
>
> The keyword ALL can be used to audit all activities on a specific database object.

Auditing can be a very space-consuming and time-consuming task and you should be selective in determining the activities that you want to audit. If the audit trail is stored in the database, you should periodically delete the records from the sys.aud$ table and also make sure that access to this table is restricted and audited as well.

> **NOTE**
>
> Audit access to sys.aud$ table by using the following command:
>
> ```
> AUDIT select, insert, update, delete
> ON sys.aud$
> BY ACCESS;
> ```

Auditing BY SESSION causes Oracle to write a single record for all SQL statements used concurrently during the same session, whereas auditing BY ACCESS causes Oracle to write one record for each audited statement.

Summary

Information stored in the database is shared by all the users. Different users have varying levels of authority, and it is important to implement a security mechanism that is easy to maintain and at the same time satisfies the complex requirements of the system. In addition to physical security for the system, you should use the various features provided by the operating system and the database to protect the data.

Prior to Oracle8*i*, you could use the Oracle features such as roles, views, and profiles to implement security. Oracle8*i* allows you to use application context and fine-grained access control to dynamically control security at runtime. In addition, the explosive growth of the Internet has created a daunting security challenge. Oracle8*i* advanced security option provides an impressive set of security features specifically designed with the Internet in mind.

Performing Backups and Recovery

IN THIS CHAPTER

An optimal backup strategy requires detailed understanding of your business process and the interaction between your system and applications. You should also consider the anticipated data growth, expected data availability requirements, and the resources available to you. The backup strategies available to you with Oracle8*i* are mentioned in Table 28.1. If you are using a particular media manager, you should also become familiar with the use of that media manager.

Types of Failure

The whole idea of making a backup of your database is to protect the data. The various types of failures that can occur in a database should be taken into consideration when choosing a backup strategy. Using an uninterrupted power supply (UPS) and mirroring the disks and the most important database files are definitely good ideas, but they should not be used as an alternative to a good backup. Database failures can be of the following types:

- *Instance failure* is usually the result of an operating system error, a hardware error, or an Oracle exception (or some other software-related error). Usually, a restart of an Oracle database instance automatically performs instance recovery by rolling forward the committed transactions and rolling back the uncommitted transactions.
- *Media failure* is usually the result of a disk drive failure, bad disk blocks, or damaged or deleted database files. A good backup strategy allows you to recover from a media failure.
- *Application/user failure* refers to the loss of data that can occur when the user or application accidentally drops a row or table. A good backup strategy can help you recover from such a loss.

Choosing a Backup Strategy

A backup strategy should allow the recovery strategy to be successful. A recovery strategy might impose requirements such as the ability to recover the database in parallel, to allow access to the critical parts of the database while other parts are still being recovered, or to perform point-in-time recovery. *Mean time to backup* (MTTB) is the average time required to back up a database so that if recovery is needed, all the required components are available. In large databases, it is very important to minimize MTTB and this can be achieved by

- Reducing the amount of data that needs to be backed up regularly
- Increasing the rate at which data is backed up each time

Increasing the Rate of Backup

The rate at which backup is performed can be increased by using the following guidelines:

- Back up to disk instead of tape.
- Parallelize the backup process.

- Use backup devices with high capacity.

- Do not perform backups over the network.

- Consider splitting the backup over several backup windows and into smaller backup sessions.

Reducing the Amount of Data to Back Up

Reducing the amount of data to backup requires that you are familiar with the database design in use so that you can decide which components are needed and which are not needed for the operation of the most important functions. The following guidelines can be useful in determining the frequency and extent of backups:

- Read-only tablespaces should be backed up only once because they should contain unchanging data. It is very important to verify the read-only status of tablespaces since the previous backup. In other words, make sure that the tablespace has remained read-only since the previous backup, and has not switched from read-only to read-write and back to read-only status. The partitioning feature of Oracle8 can be used to partition your table into read-only and read-write partitions so that the read-only partitions are backed up only once. For example, if a sales table is maintained for product sales occurring throughout the year, and only the sales record for the current month is modified while the previous months' sales are stored only for reporting purposes, then during the month of December, sales records for the months of January–November can be placed in read-only partitions and don't need to be backed up daily.

- Incremental backups can be used to back up only the changed blocks.

- Lookup tables don't change frequently and should also be backed up less frequently.

- Indexes should not be backed up because they can be quickly created (using the parallel capabilities if desired).

- Temporary tables should not be backed up because they can be regenerated easily. Summary data can be regenerated quickly using the fact tables.

Several high availability techniques are provided by Oracle8*i*:

- Using Oracle utilities such as Export/Import and SQL*Loader—This technique can be used to perform fast object-level recovery, but you should understand very well the dependencies between the objects. This technique should not be the only backup solution you use.

- Hardware redundancy—This technique can be very expensive depending upon the amount of redundancy you use. Additional hardware does not provide scalability. The data loss can, however, can be eliminated by this technique.

- Oracle standby database—In this technique, the redo logs of the primary database are maintained on the standby database. The standby database is used in case the primary

fails. This technique can be implemented easily (as shown later in this chapter), and provides a cost-effective way of providing fast recovery. It can work with all Oracle datatypes. The disadvantage of this technique is that there is a possibility of data loss. Therefore, it cannot be used to perform point-in-time recovery. Also, the databases cannot share the workload.

- Oracle Symmetric Replication (also refer to Chapter 25)—This technique makes use of Oracle's symmetric replication feature. Transactions are used to maintain data consistency. Therefore, recovery is slow and the use of two-phase commit can cause problems in database maintenance. However, there is no data loss as a result of this technique.

- Oracle Parallel Server—This technique provides fast failover and high scalability. The success of this method depends upon proper application design. Design, configuration, and tuning can be complex.

- Customized store-and-forward—This technique makes use of advanced queuing of trigger-based asynchronous replication and results in fast recovery, but the implementation is very complex.

- Oracle Fail Safe (Windows NT only)—This is a simple and cost-effective technique available only on Windows NT. Currently, only two-node clusters are supported. During normal conditions both nodes can support independent applications, but under abnormal conditions one node has to service both applications; as a result, the scalability is low.

Using Standby Databases

A *standby database* configuration makes use of a primary database and a standby database that is maintained almost up-to-date with the primary by applying the redo logs of the primary database to the standby database. Upon the failure of the primary database, the standby database can be quickly opened to continue servicing the client applications; hence the name *standby* or *hot* database.

The standby database is initially made to be in sync with the primary database by applying the cold backup of the primary to it. The standby is then kept up-to-date by periodically applying the archive redo logs of the primary database. As a result, the standby database is always in a recovery mode and cannot share the workload under normal conditions. Point-in-time recovery cannot be performed by using standby databases because the archive redo logs of the primary database are applied to it. In other words, suppose that a table is accidentally dropped from the primary database. It will also be dropped from the standby database when the redo logs are applied to it.

The following steps demonstrate how you can create a standby database:

1. Place the primary database in the archivelog mode (if it's not already in archivelog mode).
2. Back up the primary database.
3. At the primary database, execute the following at the Server Manager prompt to create a control file for the standby database:

```
Svrmgr> alter database
     2> create standby controlfile as 'control.std';
```

A standby control file will be created in the Oracle_home directory.

4. With the primary database open, force a log switch to archive the current redo log file group:

```
Svrmgr> alter system archive log current;
```

5. Transfer the following files to the system that will be used as the standby database:

The files from the backup taken in step 2

The standby control file generated in step 3

The archive log generated in step 4

6. Create an initialization file for the standby database. This initialization file should be identical to that of the primary database so that the behavior of the standby database (when used) is similar to that of the primary database.

Now the standby database is ready, but it should be kept updated with the changes in the primary database so that it can easily be brought online and used without much effort. The following steps can be used to keep the standby database updated:

1. Startup nomount the standby database:

```
Svrmgr> startup nomount;
```

2. Mount the standby database in standby exclusive mode:

```
Svrmgr> alter database mount standby database;
```

28

PERFORMING BACKUPS AND RECOVERY

3. Apply the archived redo logs received from the production database to the standby database:

   `Svrmgr> recover from location standby database until cancel;`

   where `from location` specifies the location of the archived redo logs obtained from the primary database. This clause is not needed if the archive logs are available in `LOG_ARCHIVE_DEST`.

4. Apply the archive logs as prompted by Oracle, and then cancel the recovery if the specified archive log isn't available.

> **NOTE**
>
> If you have used unrecoverable data loads and/or the no-logging features on the primary database's tables and indexes, you have to keep in mind that these operations won't generate redo and won't appear in the archived logs. The standby database will not be aware of changes made to objects using such operations and will mark the object as corrupt. In order to keep the standby database up-to-date, you will have to use Export/Import or some other method to load the data into the target objects.

> **NOTE**
>
> The standby database will become invalid if you perform an incomplete recovery of the primary database and open it with the resetlogs option.

As mentioned earlier, the standby database is always in the recovery mode. When the primary database fails, the standby can be activated using the following steps:

1. Apply all the archived and unarchived redo logs from the production database to the standby database.

2. Activate the standby database:

   `Svrmgr> alter database activate standby database;`

Performing Cold and Hot Backups

We have mentioned several backup strategies that you can use to protect your data. No matter which method you use, make sure that it is well-tested. Several Data Dictionary views provide useful information that can be used to obtain valuable information about the database state and its structure:

- v$datafile can be used to obtain information about all the data files associated with the database.

- v$logfile can be used to obtain information about your redo log files.
- v$controlfile can be used to obtain information about the control files.
- v$loghist can be used to obtain information about archive redo log files.

Using Cold Backups

Cold backups involve shutting down (normal) an Oracle database and backing up all the relevant database files, including

- Data files
- Control files
- Redo logs
- Archived redo logs
- Initialization files

Cold backups are fast and simple to use. However, they cannot be used to perform point-in-time recovery. Also, complete recovery might not be possible by just using a cold backup if the last CHANGE# is not in the online redo logs. Listing 28.1 shows a script that can be used to perform cold backups on Windows NT:

LISTING 28.1   Script to Perform Cold Backups on Windows NT

```
REM cbackup.cmd
REM Author: Megh Thakkar
REM  Script to perform cold backup of an Oracle database
REM  on a Windows NT system
REM  We will use the sample ORCL database
REM The script assumes that the database is up and running
REM  Set the ORACLE_SID to the database to back up
set ORACLE_SID=ORCL
REM Create the backup directory
mkdir c:\backup
REM Set the path to the backup directory
set O_BACKDIR=c:\backup
REM Create a script to shut down the database and start up in
REM restricted mode
echo connect system/manager; > db_restrict.sql
echo shutdown immediate; >> db_restrict.sql
echo startup restrict pfile=
➥%ORACLE_HOME%\database\init%ORACLE_SID%.ora ; >> db_restrict.sql
echo exit >> db_restrict.sql
REM Create a script to shut down the database
echo connect system/manager; > db_shut.sql
```

continues

LISTING 28.1   Continued

```
echo shutdown immediate; >> db_shut.sql
echo exit >> db_shut.sql
REM Create a script to start up the database
echo connect system/manager; > db_start.sql
echo startup pfile=%ORACLE_HOME%\database\init%ORACLE_SID%.ora ;
➥>> db_start.sql
echo exit >> db_start.sql
REM Execute db_restrict.sql to shut down the database and start up
REM in the restricted mode
Svrmgrl system/manager @db_restrict.sql
REM Create a SQL*PLUS script to create a batch file to take cold backup
Echo Creating cold.sql to perform cold backup
Echo set heading off; > %O_BACKDIR%\cold.sql
Echo set feedback off; >> %O_BACKDIR%\cold.sql
Echo spool %O_BACKDIR%\cold.cmd; >> %O_BACKDIR%\cold.sql
Echo select 'copy '^¦^¦name^¦^¦' %O_BACKDIR% from v$controlfile;
➥>>%O_BACKDIR%\cold.sql
Echo select 'copy '^¦^¦member^¦^¦' %O_BACKDIR% from v$logfile;
➥>>%O_BACKDIR%\cold.sql
Echo select 'copy '^¦^¦file_name^¦^¦' %O_BACKDIR% from dba_data_files;
➥>>%O_BACKDIR%\cold.sql
Echo spool off; >>%O_BACKDIR%\cold.sql
Echo exit; >>%O_BACKDIR%\cold.sql
REM
REM Run the SQL*PLUS script cold.sql to generate cold.cmd
REM
Sqlplus system/manager @%O_BACKDIR%\cold.sql
REM
REM Shut down the database by executing db_shut.sql
REM
Svrmgrl system/manager @%O_BACKDIR%\db_shut.sql
REM
REM Run cold.cmd to perform the cold backup
REM
Call %O_BACKDIR%\cold.cmd
REM
REM Start up the database
REM
Svrmgrl @db_start.sql
REM
REM End of cold backup
REM
Echo Cold backup is complete
```

Performing Hot Backups

Hot backup refers to the process of backing up a database while it's open and in use. Hot backups require that the database be run in the archivelog mode. Hot backups can be used to perform point-in-time recovery. The drawback of hot backups is that the database is open and it might not be easy to test your backups unless you use another system for the testing. Also, taking hot backups might incur additional overhead in CPU and I/O, and affect the overall system performance. Therefore, you should carefully schedule them.

> **TIP**
>
> The archive logs that need to be backed up during a hot backup can be determined as follows:
>
> 1. Connect to Server Manager as system/manager.
> 2. Find the oldest online log sequence number by issuing the following:
>
>   Svrmgr> archive log list
>
> | | |
> |---|---|
> | Database log mode | ARCHIVELOG |
> | Automatic archival | ENABLED |
> | Archive destination | c:\archives |
> | Oldest online log sequence | 52 |
> | Next log sequence to archive | 54 |
> | Current log sequence | 54 |
>
> All the archive logs starting from the oldest online log sequence (in this example, 52) should be part of the online backup.

Listing 28.2 shows a script that can be used to perform hot backups on Windows NT.

LISTING 28.2   Script to Perform Hot Backups on Windows NT

```
REM hbackup.cmd
REM Author: Megh Thakkar
REM  Script to perform hot backup of an Oracle database
REM  on a Windows NT system
REM  We will use the sample ORCL database
REM The database should be up and running
REM  Set the ORACLE_SID to the database to back up
set ORACLE_SID=ORCL
REM Create the backup directory
```

continues

LISTING 28.2   Continued

```
mkdir c:\backup
REM Set the path to the backup directory
set O_BACKDIR=c:\backup
REM Back up the initialization file
echo Backing up the init.ora file
copy %ORACLE_HOME%\database\init%ORACLE_SID%.ora c:\backup
REM
REM Create a SQL*PLUS script to obtain the minimum log sequence
REM number
REM
Echo set heading off; >%O_BACKDIR%\minlog.sql
Echo set feedback off; >>%O_BACKDIR%\minlog.sql
Echo spool %O_BACKDIR%\minlog.cmd; >>%O_BACKDIR%\minlog.sql
Echo select 'set minlog_value='^¦^¦min(sequence#) from v$log where
➥UPPER(status) = UPPER('INACTIVE'); >>%O_BACKDIR%\minlog.sql
Echo spool off; >>%O_BACKDIR%\minlog.sql
Echo select 'exit;' from dual; >>%O_BACKDIR%\minlog.sql
Echo exit; >>%O_BACKDIR%\minlog.sql
REM
REM Run the SQL*PLUS script minlog.sql to create minlog.cmd
REM
Sqlplus system/manager @%O_BACKDIR%\minlog.sql
REM
REM Run minlog.cmd to set minlog_value
REM
Call %O_BACKDIR%\minlog.cmd
REM
REM Create a SQL*PLUS script that can be used to generate a script
REM to back up the datafiles
REM
Echo set heading off; >%O_BACKDIR%\tblspc1.sql
Echo set feedback off; >>%O_BACKDIR%\tblspc1.sql
Echo spool %O_BACKDIR%\tblspc2.sql; >>%O_BACKDIR%\tblspc1.sql
Echo select 'connect system/manager;' from dual;
➥>>%O_BACKDIR%\tblspc1.sql
Echo select 'alter tablespace '^¦^¦tablespace_name^¦^¦'
➥begin backup;'^¦^¦ '>>%O_BACKDIR%\tblspc1.sql
Echo '^¦^¦ 'host start /wait ocopy '^¦^¦ file_name^¦^¦ '
➥%O_BACKDIR%; '^¦^¦' >>%O_BACKDIR%\tblspc1.sql
Echo '^¦^¦' alter tablespace '^¦^¦ tablespace_name^¦^¦'
➥end backup;' from dba_data_files; >>%O_BACKDIR%\tblspc1.sql
Echo spool off; >>%O_BACKDIR%\tblspc1.sql
Echo select 'exit;' from dual; >>%O_BACKDIR%\tblspc1.sql
Echo exit; >>%O_BACKDIR%\tblspc1.sql
```

```
REM
REM Run the SQL*PLUS script tblspc1.sql to create tblspc2.sql
REM
Sqlplus system/manager @%O_BACKDIR%\tblspc1.sql
REM
REM Run tblspc2.sql from server manager to back up the datafiles
REM
svrmgrl system/manager @%O_BACKDIR%\tblspc2.sql
REM
REM Create a SQL*PLUS script to obtain the maximum log sequence
REM number
REM
Echo set heading off; >%O_BACKDIR%\maxlog.sql
Echo set feedback off; >>%O_BACKDIR%\maxlog.sql
Echo spool %O_BACKDIR%\maxlog.cmd; >>%O_BACKDIR%\maxlog.sql
Echo select 'set maxlog_value='^¦^¦max(sequence#) from v$log where
➥UPPER(status) = UPPER('CURRENT'); >>%O_BACKDIR%\maxlog.sql
Echo spool off; >>%O_BACKDIR%\maxlog.sql
Echo select 'exit;' from dual; >>%O_BACKDIR%\maxlog.sql
Echo exit; >>%O_BACKDIR%\maxlog.sql
REM
REM Run the SQL*PLUS script maxlog.sql to create maxlog.cmd
REM
Sqlplus system/manager @%O_BACKDIR%\maxlog.sql
REM
REM Run maxlog.cmd to set maxlog_value
REM
Call %O_BACKDIR%\maxlog.cmd
REM
REM Create a SQL*PLUS script that can be used to generate a script
REM to back up the controlfile
REM
Echo set heading off; >%O_BACKDIR%\control1.sql
Echo set feedback off; >>%O_BACKDIR%\control1.sql
Echo spool %O_BACKDIR%\control2.sql; >>%O_BACKDIR%\control1.sql
Echo select 'connect system/manager;' from dual;
➥>>%O_BACKDIR%\control1.sql
Echo select 'alter database backup controlfile to trace ' from dual;
➥>>%O_BACKDIR%\control1.sql
Echo spool off; >>%O_BACKDIR%\tblspc1.sql
Echo select 'exit;' from dual; >>%O_BACKDIR%\tblspc1.sql
Echo exit; >>%O_BACKDIR%\tblspc1.sql
REM
REM Run the SQL*PLUS script control1.sql to create control2.sql
REM
Sqlplus system/manager @%O_BACKDIR%\control1.sql
```

28

PERFORMING
BACKUPS AND
RECOVERY

continues

LISTING 28.2   Continued

```
REM
REM Run control2.sql from server manager to back up the controlfile
REM
svrmgrl system/manager @%O_BACKDIR%\control2.sql
REM
REM Create a SQL*PLUS script that can be used to generate a batch
REM file to copy the archive logs
REM
Echo set heading off; >%O_BACKDIR%\archive.sql
Echo set feedback off; >>%O_BACKDIR%\archive.sql
Echo spool %O_BACKDIR%\archive.cmd; >>%O_BACKDIR%\archive.sql
Echo select 'copy '^¦^¦archive_name^¦^¦' %O_BACKDIR% from
➥v$log_history where sequence# between %minlog_value% and
➥%maxlog_value%+1; >>%O_BACKDIR%\archive.sql
Echo spool off; >>%O_BACKDIR%\archive.sql
Echo select 'exit;' from dual; >>%O_BACKDIR%\archive.sql
Echo exit; >>%O_BACKDIR%\archive.sql
REM
REM Run the SQL*PLUS script archive.sql to create archive.cmd
REM
Sqlplus system/manager @%O_BACKDIR%\archive.sql
REM
REM Run archive.cmd to copy the archive logs
REM
Call %O_BACKDIR%\archive.cmd
REM
REM End of hot backup
REM
Echo End of hot backup
```

Archivelog Versus Noarchivelog Mode

The function of the redo logs is to record all transactions going on in the database. The redo logs are written by the LGWR background process in a circular fashion—one redo log to another until it comes to the end of the group, and then it starts writing from the first redo log. When the database is in the noarchivelog mode, hot backup is not available as a recovery option because the LGWR writes the first redo log when the end of the circle is reached. On the other hand, when the database is in the archivelog mode, the ARCH background process is used to read redo logs when they get full and write their contents to the archived redo log, thereby allowing hot backups to be performed.

> **NOTE**
>
> When the database is in the archivelog mode, make sure that sufficient space is available in the archive log destination because if it gets full, database activity comes to a halt. If this occurs, you will have to free up space so that the archiver can finish archiving the redo log and database activity can continue.

While you're trying to perform maintenance operations on the database, you might want to place the database in the noarchivelog mode and stop the archiving of the database. This is done so that the redo generated during the maintenance is not archived unnecessarily. After the database maintenance is complete, you can place the database back in the archivelog mode. The following steps can be used for this purpose:

- To stop the archiving of a database:
    1. Start Server Manager and connect with the internal account:
       ```
       C:\ svrmgrl
       Svrmgr> connect internal
       ```
    2. Shut down the database (normal or immediate):
       ```
       Svrmgr> shutdown immediate;
       ```
    3. Mount the database in exclusive mode:
       ```
       Svrmgr> startup mount exclusive;
       ```
    4. Enable noarchivelog mode for the database:
       ```
       Svrmgr> alter database noarchivelog;
       ```
    5. Open the database:
       ```
       Svrmgr> alter database open;
       ```
    6. Verify that the database is in noarchivelog mode by checking the LOG_MODE column from v$database:
       ```
       Svrmgr> select * from v$database;
       ```

> **NOTE**
>
> The log_mode (archivelog or noarchivelog) of a database stays as it is until it is explicitly changed.

- To place a database in archivelog mode:

    1. Edit the initSID.ora file by adding the following parameters:

       Log_archive_start   Set to TRUE

       This parameter, when set to TRUE, will enable automatic archiving of filled redo logs.

       Log_archive_dest   Set to the directory where the database archived redo log files are to be written.

       Log_archive_format   Specify the format of the archived redo log filenames.

    2. Start Server Manager and connect with the internal account:
       ```
       C:\ svrmgrl
       Svrmgr> connect internal
       ```

    3. Shut down the database (normal or immediate):
       ```
       Svrmgr> shutdown immediate;
       ```

    4. Mount the database in exclusive mode:
       ```
       Svrmgr> startup mount exclusive;
       ```

    5. Enable archivelog mode for the database:
       ```
       Svrmgr> alter database archivelog;
       ```

    6. Open the database:
       ```
       Svrmgr> alter database open;
       ```

    7. Shut down the database again (normal or immediate):
       ```
       Svrmgr> shutdown immediate;
       ```

    8. Perform a cold backup of the database. This cold backup will serve as a basepoint.

    9. Start the database:
       ```
       Svrmgr> startup;
       ```

    10. Verify that the database is in archivelog mode by checking the LOG_MODE column from v$database:
        ```
        Svrmgr> select * from v$database;
        ```

Database Recovery Considerations

Database recovery should not be treated as a situation to test your backups. You should have already tested your backups for a variety of recovery scenarios. The strategy used for database recovery, however, should depend upon several considerations:

- Type of database failure
- Extent of database failure

- Acceptable downtime of the database
- The backup strategy in place
- The cost of different recovery strategies
- Mean-Time-To-Recovery (MTTR)

Reducing Mean Time to Recovery

For large databases and those that have high availability requirements, the *mean time to recovery* (MTTR) is an important consideration. MTTR for a database depends on several factors: the database size, complexity of the system, database structure, and application structure.

The following guidelines can be used to minimize MTTR:

- The impact of a failure on the overall system can be minimized by using partitioning techniques.
- Database design should be such that the components are small and autonomous. This will result in fast recovery because the recovery of one object won't depend on other objects. You might also be able to perform parallel recovery.
- The backups should be tested against dummy recovery scenarios to avoid surprises and anguish during real problem situations. You should also make yourself familiar with the backup and recovery procedures for your database.
- Backups should be easily accessible so that the recovery process is not delayed due to waiting periods to obtain the backups.
- Keep the information necessary to contact Oracle Support Services handy.

Analyzing the Extent and Type of Failure

Before you decide to use a particular recovery strategy, you should analyze the extent and type of the failure. The following checklist can be helpful:

- Which activity was being performed at the time of failure: power outage, upgrade (OS, database, hardware), routine maintenance (OS, hardware, network, database)?
- How was the failure detected: performing database operations, the database went down, error messages returned by the database or the application, at startup, at shutdown, database parameters changed?
- Can you reproduce the failure?
- What is the current state of the database? Is the database up or down? If it's down, how did it go down: shutdown abort, crash, normal shutdown? Can you startup nomount? Mount? Open the database?
- Are there are any operating system errors?
- Do the event viewer logs show any errors?

- Does the alert log show any errors?
- Are any trace files generated?
- Is this an Oracle Parallel Server configuration?
- Is this is a Multi-Threaded Server configuration?
- What activity or steps have been performed after the failure?
- Is the backup strategy in place? Tested?
- Is the database in archivelog mode? Are all archive logs available?
- Are there mirrored online redo logs?
- Are there mirrored control files?
- Is a recent full database export available?
- What are the system availability requirements?
- What's the database size?
- Can you afford the loss of data? Can it be easily re-created?

Database Recovery: Case Studies

We have already discussed the factors that affect the choice of recovery strategy: database size, extent and type of failure, availability requirements, and so on. Let us consider some recovery scenarios and step-by-step procedures to recover from those situations.

Case 1: Loss of a Datafile in the User or Index Tablespace and the Database Is Not in Archivelog Mode

Solution: In this situation, the recovery of the lost datafile will be complete if the redo to be applied is within the range of your online redo logs. Follow these steps to recover from the loss:

1. Shut down the database.
2. Restore the lost datafile from the backup.
3. Startup mount the database:

   ```
   Svrmgr> STARTUP MOUNT;
   ```

4. Using the following query, determine all your online redo log files, their respective sequence, and their first change numbers. This will be used to determine whether complete recovery is possible:

   ```
   Svrmgr> SELECT X.GROUP#, MEMBER, SEQUENCE#, FIRST_CHANGE#
        2> FROM V$LOG X, V$LOGFILE Y
        3> WHERE X.GROUP# = Y.GROUP#;
   ```

5. Determine the CHANGE# of the file to be recovered:

```
Svrmgr> SELECT FILE#, CHANGE#
    2> FROM V$RECOVER_FILE;
```

> **NOTE**
>
> You can recover the datafile if the CHANGE# obtained is greater than the minimum FIRST_CHANGE# of your online redo logs.

6. Use the online redo logs to recover the database:

```
Svrmgr> RECOVER DATAFILE 'full_path_of_datafile';
```

Supply the files that you're prompted for during the recovery until you receive the message Media Recovery complete.

7. Open the database:

```
Svrmgr> ALTER DATABASE OPEN;
```

Case 2: Loss of Datafile in the User or Index Tablespace and the Database Is in Archivelog Mode

The database is in archivelog mode; therefore, you might have good hot backups. The recovery of the datafile will be complete if the redo to be applied is within the range of your online logs. Follow these steps to recover the datafile:

1. Shut down the database.

2. Restore the lost datafile from the backup.

3. Startup mount the database:

```
Svrmgr> STARTUP MOUNT;
```

4. Using the following query, determine all your online redo log files, their respective sequence, and their first change numbers. This information will be used to determine whether complete recovery is possible:

```
Svrmgr> SELECT X.GROUP#, MEMBER, SEQUENCE#, FIRST_CHANGE#
    2> FROM V$LOG X, V$LOGFILE Y
    3> WHERE X.GROUP# = Y.GROUP#;
```

5. Determine the CHANGE# of the file to be recovered:

```
Svrmgr> SELECT FILE#, CHANGE#
    2> FROM V$RECOVER_FILE;
```

> **NOTE**
>
> Complete recovery of the datafile is possible only if the CHANGE# obtained is greater than the minimum FIRST_CHANGE# of your online redo logs. Otherwise, the file can't be completely recovered, and you have two choices:
>
> - If the data can be easily recreated since the last cold backup, you should recover the database using the last cold backup and re-create the data since that point.
> - If the data can't be easily re-created, the tablespace will have to be re-created and the data exported (if available) or re-created by applying good redo logs as described later in step 7 onward.

6. Recover the datafile by using the archived and online redo logs:

   `Svrmgr> RECOVER DATAFILE 'full_path_of_datafile';`

   Supply the files that you're prompted for during the recovery until you receive the message `Media Recovery complete` or the needed redo logfile is not available.

7. If media recovery is complete, you can open the database:

   `Svrmgr> ALTER DATABASE OPEN;`

   Otherwise, open the database by resetting the redo logs:

   `Svrmgr> ALTER DATABASE OPEN RESETLOGS;`

Case 3: Loss of a Datafile in a Read-Only Tablespace

Solution: This is probably the simplest recovery scenario that you can encounter. We are assuming, however, that the tablespace has been read-only for the entire time. The datafile isn't modified; therefore, it can be restored from its last backup to its original location. Media recovery is not needed.

Case 4: Loss of a Control File and Mirrored Control Files Are Available

Solution: Usually problems with a control file are not detected when the database is up and running unless a database structural change is being made. An ORA-205, `error in identifying control file '%s'`, along with an operating system–level error during database startup indicates a damaged or lost control file. It is recommended that you mirror your control file because the recovery procedure is greatly simplified in this situation as shown by the following steps:

1. Shut down the database (if it's running).

2. Check your hardware and fix any hardware problems (disk or controller) that could have caused the problem with the control file.

3. Copy a good copy of the control file to a good disk.

4. Edit the init*sid*.ora file and modify the CONTROL_FILES parameter to reflect the new location of the control file.

5. Start the database.

Case 5: Loss of a Control File and Mirrored Control Files Are Not Available

Solution: If all your control files are lost, or you don't have any control file that accurately reflects the current database structure, the following steps can help in the recovery:

1. Shut down the database (if it's running).

2. Startup mount the database.

3. Generate a trace file containing the statement that can be used to create the control file:

```
Svrmgr> alter database backup controlfile to trace;
```

This command creates a trace file in USER_DUMP_DEST. An example of such a trace file generated on Windows NT is shown in Listing 28.3.

LISTING 28.3   Sample Control File Creation Script

```
# The following commands will create a new control file and use it
# to open the database.
# Data used by the recovery manager will be lost. Additional logs may
# be required for media recovery of offline datafiles. Use this
# only if the current version of all online logs is available.
STARTUP NOMOUNT
CREATE CONTROLFILE REUSE DATABASE "PROD" NORESETLOGS NOARCHIVELOG
    MAXLOGFILES 32
    MAXLOGMEMBERS 2
    MAXDATAFILES 254
    MAXINSTANCES 1
    MAXLOGHISTORY 226
LOGFILE
  GROUP 1 'E:\ORACLE\ORADATA\PROD\REDO01.LOG'  SIZE 1M,
  GROUP 2 'E:\ORACLE\ORADATA\PROD\REDO02.LOG'  SIZE 1M
DATAFILE
  'E:\ORACLE\ORADATA\PROD\SYSTEM01.DBF',
  'E:\ORACLE\ORADATA\PROD\RBS01.DBF',
  'E:\ORACLE\ORADATA\PROD\USERS01.DBF',
  'E:\ORACLE\ORADATA\PROD\TEMP01.DBF',
  'E:\ORACLE\ORADATA\PROD\INDX01.DBF',
  'E:\ORACLE\ORADATA\PROD\OEMREP01.DBF'
CHARACTER SET WE8ISO8859P1
```

continues

28

PERFORMING
BACKUPS AND
RECOVERY

LISTING 28.3   Continued

```
;
# Recovery is required if any datafiles are restored backups
# or if the last shutdown was not normal or immediate.
RECOVER DATABASE
# Database can now be opened normally.
ALTER DATABASE OPEN;
# No tempfile entries found to add.
#
```

4. Edit this trace file as follows, and then save it as create_control.sql:
   - Remove the header information.
   - Make any changes desired to database settings such as MAXLOGFILES and AXDATAFILES.

5. Perform a normal shutdown of the database.

6. Take a cold backup of the database.

7. Create a new control file by executing the script saved in step 4:
   ```
   Svrmgr> @create_controlfile.sql
   ```

8. Open the database:
   ```
   Svrmgr> Alter database open;
   ```

9. Perform a normal shutdown of the database.

10. Take a full database backup.

If you are not able to mount the database, you should execute the CREATE CONTROLFILE statement with the database in the NOMOUNT state to create a new control file. After the control file is created in this manner, you should perform media recovery and then open the database. For example:

1. Start up nomount.

2. Create the control file:
   ```
   Svrmgr> Create Controlfile reuse database "PROD"
        2> noresetlogs noarchivelog
        3> Maxlogfiles  100
         4>Maxlogmembers  3
        5> Maxdatafiles  400
        6> Maxinstances  8
        7> Maxloghistory  400
        8> Logfile
        9> Group 1 'c:\orant\database\prod\log1prod.ora' size 5M,
   ```

```
10> Group 2 'c:\orant\database\prod\log2prod.ora' size 5M,
11> Group 3 'c:\orant\database\prod\log3prod.ora' size 5M,
12> Datafile
13> 'c:\orant\database\prod\sysprod.ora' size 80M,
14> 'c:\orant\database\prod\data1prod.ora' size 20M,
15> 'c:\orant\database\prod\data2prod.ora' size 20M;
```

3. Perform media recovery on the database:

   ```
   Svrmgr> Recover database;
   ```

4. Open the database:

   ```
   Svrmgr> alter database open;
   ```

Case 6: Loss of Rollback Tablespace and Database Is Up and Running

NOTE

When you lose a rollback tablespace, the recovery steps can be complex depending on the current state of the database.

Solution: In this situation, an open database can be used to your advantage—*don't shut down the database*. Creating additional rollback segments in a different tablespace will allow you to continue working with the database while recovery is being performed. The following steps can be used to recover:

1. Offline all the rollback segments in the tablespace to which the lost datafile belongs by performing the following for each rollback segment in the affected tablespace:

   ```
   Svrmgr> ALTER ROLLBACK SEGMENT rollback_segment OFFLINE;
   ```

2. By using the following query, verify that the rollback segments are offline:

   ```
   Svrmgr> SELECT SEGMENT_NAME, STATUS
       2> FROM DBA_ROLLBACK_SEGS
       3> WHERE TABLESPACE_NAME = 'tablespace_name';
   ```

   If this query is successful, skip to step 6; otherwise, continue with step 3.

3. If step 2 indicates that you have active transactions in the rollback segments, run the following query to determine the active transactions:

   ```
   Svrmgr> SELECT SEGMENT_NAME, XACTS ACTIVE_TX, V.STATUS
       2> FROM V$ROLLSTAT V, DBA_ROLLBACK_SEGS
       3> WHERE TABLESPACE_NAME = 'tablespace_name' AND
       4> SEGMENT_ID = USN;
   ```

Check the `ACTIVE_TX` column for the rollback segments that have the status of `PENDING_OFFLINE`:

- Segments with a value of zero will soon go offline.
- Segments with a non-zero value indicate that they contain active transactions that have to be committed or rolled back.

4. By using the following query, identify the users who have transactions assigned to the rollback segments being considered:

```
Svrmgr> SELECT S.SID, S.SERIAL#, S.USERNAME, R.NAME "ROLLBACK"
    2> FROM V$SESSION S, V$TRANSACTION T, V$ROLLNAME R
    3> WHERE R.NAME IN
    4> ('pending_rollback1', ... 'pending_rollbackN');
```

5. Inform these users to commit or roll back their transaction or kill their session by executing the following:

```
Svrmgr> ALTER SYSTEM KILL SESSION 'sid, serial#';
```

6. Drop all the offline rollback segments:

```
Svrmgr> DROP ROLLBACK SEGMENT rollback_segment;
```

7. Drop the tablespace, including contents.

8. Re-create the rollback tablespace.

9. Re-create the rollback segments, and bring them online.

NOTE

A good backup is an essential part of any recovery strategy for a loss of a datafile from the system tablespace. In the absence of a good backup, your only option might be to rebuild the database and potentially lose data.

CAUTION

Recovery procedures might require the use of certain undocumented parameters. Use these parameters with caution:

- _allow_resetlogs_corruption, when set to TRUE, allows the opening of the database with the resetlogs option, even if such an action can result in a corrupt or inconsistent database:

```
ALTER DATABASE OPEN RESETLOGS;
```

This parameter might be required in the worst case to force a database open in order to export as much data as possible.

- `_corrupted_rollback_segments` is used to specify the rollback segments that are corrupt and should be ignored. It is used in situations when a database doesn't start because of corrupt rollback segments. It can be used to force the database to be open without using these rollback segments. Active transactions in the specified rollback segments are not rolled back.

- `_offline_rollback_segments` prevents the rollback of active transactions in the listed offline rollback segments.

Case 7: Loss of Rollback Tablespace and the Database Is Down

Solution: In this situation, the recovery steps depend on the manner in which the database went down. The alert log can be checked to determine whether the database shutdown was clean or not. The following log entry indicates that the shutdown was clean:

```
'alter database dismount
completed: alter database dismount"
```

This might be followed by an attempt that you made to start up, resulting in the ORA errors and also a subsequent SHUTDOWN ABORT by Oracle.

Database Shutdown Was Clean

The following steps can be used to recover from this situation:

1. Edit the init*sid*.ora file to modify the ROLLBACK_SEGMENTS parameter by removing all the rollback segments belonging to the damaged tablespace. If you aren't sure which rollback segments are part of the damaged tablespace, comment out the ROLLBACK_SEGMENTS parameter by placing a # at the beginning of its line.

2. Mount the database in restricted mode:
   ```
   Svrmgr> STARTUP RESTRICT MOUNT
   ```

3. Offline drop the lost datafile:
   ```
   Svrmgr> ALTER DATABASE DATAFILE 'full_path_of_datafile'
        2> OFFLINE DROP;
   ```

4. Open the database:
   ```
   Svrmgr> ALTER DATABASE OPEN
   ```

   If you get error codes ORA-604, ORA-376, and ORA-1110, shut down the database and continue to step 5; otherwise, skip to step 6 after the statement is processed.

28

PERFORMING BACKUPS AND RECOVERY

5. This step should be performed only if step 4 resulted in errors. Edit the init*sid*.ora file as follows:

   Comment out the `ROLLBACK_SEGMENTS` parameter.

   Add the following line:

   `_Corrupted_rollback_segments = (rollback1,...,rollbackN)`

   where (`rollback1,...,rollbackN`) is the list of rollback segments that originally appeared in the `ROLLBACK_SEGMENTS` parameter.

   Now, start up the database in restricted mode:

   `Svrmgr> startup restrict mount`

6. Drop the damaged rollback tablespace:

   `Svrmgr> drop tablespace tablespace_name including contents;`

7. Re-create the rollback tablespace with all its rollback segments.

8. Bring the rollback segments online.

9. Make the database available for general use:

   `Svrmgr> alter system disable restricted session;`

10. Shut down the database.

11. Edit the init*sid*.ora file as follows:

    Uncomment the `ROLLBACK_SEGMENTS` parameter.

    If you had to perform step 5, remove the following line:

    `_Corrupted_rollback_segments = (rollback1, ...,rollbackN)`

12. Start up the database.

Database Shutdown Wasn't Clean

In this situation, the datafile might contain active transactions and therefore cannot be dropped. The following steps can be used to recover:

1. Restore the lost datafile from a backup.

2. Mount the database.

3. Bring the file online if it's not already online:

   `Svrmgr> SELECT FILE#, NAME, STATUS FROM V$DATAFILE;`

   If the file is offline:

   ```
   Svrmgr> ALTER DATABASE DATAFILE 'full_path_of_datafile'
        2> ONLINE;
   ```

4. Use the following query to determine all your online redo log files, their respective sequence, and their first change numbers:

```
Svrmgr> SELECT X.GROUP#, MEMBER, SEQUENCE#, FIRST_CHANGE#
    2> FROM V$LOG X, V$LOGILE Y
    3> WHERE X.GROUP# = Y.GROUP#;
```

5. Determine the CHANGE# of the file to be recovered:

```
Svrmgr> SELECT FILE#, CHANGE#
    2> FROM V$RECOVER_FILE;
```

> **NOTE**
>
> If the CHANGE# obtained is greater than the minimum FIRST_CHANGE# of your online redo logs, the datafile can be recovered by proceeding with step 6. Otherwise, you have two options:
>
> - Restore from a full database backup. This has the potential for data loss.
> - Force the database to open in an inconsistent state. This will require a database rebuild.

6. Recover the datafile by using the online redo logs:

```
Svrmgr> RECOVER DATAFILE 'full_path_of_the_datafile'
```

Supply the files that you're prompted for during the recovery until you receive the message Media Recovery complete.

7. Open the database:

```
Svrmgr> ALTER DATABASE OPEN
```

Case 8: Loss of Rollback Tablespace and Neither a Good Backup Nor a Good Export Is Available

As a last resort, when all else fails, you can force a database to open in an inconsistent state so that you can extract as much data as possible. This will eventually require a database rebuild. The following steps can be used for this purpose:

1. Shut down the database.

2. Take a full database cold backup.

3. Edit the init*sid*.ora file as follows:

    Add the following lines:

    ```
    _allow_resetlogs_corruption = true
    _corrupted_rollback_segments = list_of_all_rollback_segments
    ```

    Comment out the rollback_segments parameter.

4. Startup mount the database.

5. Perform an incomplete database recovery:

    ```
    Svrmgr> RECOVER DATABASE UNTIL CANCEL;
    ```

6. When prompted for the file, type CANCEL.

7. Open the database by resetting the logs:

    ```
    Svrmgr> ALTER DATABASE OPEN RESETLOGS;
    ```

The database is now open but is potentially corrupt, containing inconsistent data. You should take a full database export and rebuild the database.

Summary

A sound backup strategy is very important to protect your data. Several backup strategies can be used, but you should consider the MTTB (Mean Time To Backup), data availability, and implementation complexity, among other things to choose a strategy for your system. When a failure does occur, you should first understand the type and extent of failure before you start performing any recovery. Become familiar with the backup and recovery procedures in place and choose the best recovery procedure after considering the MTTR (Mean Time To Recovery) for each approach. We looked at several different scenarios of database failures and step-by-step procedures to recover from these situations. When a database failure occurs, you should gather all the pertinent information and follow the guidelines discussed in this chapter.

Oracle Enterprise Manager

IN THIS CHAPTER

The complexity of businesses and the demands they place on the database have increased tremendously with the global nature of applications. Database administrators need a cost-effective solution for managing their databases and monitoring the health of the system. Oracle Enterprise Manager (OEM) is an integrated and comprehensive system management platform for managing databases. OEM version 2.x makes use of a three-tier architecture and is Java-based, making it portable, and it is no longer limited to only a Windows platform. OEM version 2.x has several important characteristics:

- It allows you to administer, diagnose, and tune multiple databases from a single location.
- It provides an integrated job and event system that allows the scheduling of jobs on multiple nodes.
- It allows the use of shared repositories.
- The console and database applications are Web-enabled.
- Oracle Management Server is used to achieve load balancing and failover.
- It allows third-party tools to be integrated with other database applications.

Oracle Enterprise Manager Architecture

OEM v2.x consists of the following major components (see Figure 29.1):

- OEM console
- OEM repository
- Intelligent agents
- Common services
- Application Programming Interface (API)
- Oracle Management Server
- Integrated applications

Oracle Enterprise Manager makes use of a three-tiered architecture to provide high scalability and flexible deployment options. Figure 29.1 shows the OEM architecture with its three tiers.

First Tier

This tier consists of Java clients such as consoles or database administration applications. The first tier relies on the middle tier for its application logic, and therefore provides the same functionality for all administrative tasks irrespective of how they are deployed. Interface to all management tasks is provided at this layer with the same set of functionality whether it is an installed console or browser-based. Communication between this tier and the middle tier occurs using standard CORBA interfaces and IIOP.

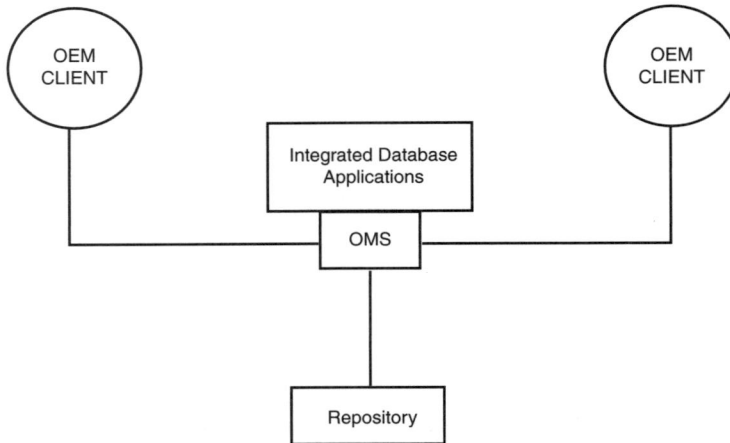

FIGURE 29.1
Oracle Enterprise Manager v2.x architecture.

Middle Tier

This tier consists of the OMS. Data-intensive business logic is moved from the first tier to the middle tier and is implemented as shared servers. Tasks are distributed by the middle tier to the intelligent agents on the third tier. OMS is responsible for the back-end application logic and services such as

>   Job system
>
>   Event system
>
>   Paging and email service
>
>   Failover and load balancing for multiple OMS

OMS connects to and communicates with the OEM repository. The OEM repository is a set of tables stored in an Oracle database that maintains system data, application data, and the state of entities that are managed by OEM. The data stored in a repository represents a domain.

Third Tier

This tier consists of managed services or targets such as databases, application servers, nodes or applications. One such application at the third tier is an intelligent agent that executes the tasks it receives from the Oracle Management Server. Intelligent agents also monitor the networked systems. Communication between this tier and the middle tier occurs using Net8.

29

ORACLE ENTERPRISE MANAGER

When a task is assigned to an intelligent agent, it will perform the task at the scheduled time. Some of the tasks that can be assigned to an intelligent agent include

Performing daily database backups

Executing SQL scripts

Monitoring database buffer cache activity

Monitoring the SQL statements taking the most CPU time

NOTE

Scalability and reliability can be increased by adding more Oracle Management Servers. They will use a collaborative peer mechanism to provide failover and load balancing.

Collaborative Peer Mechanism

When multiple Oracle Management Servers are used, each request made to an OMS is stored in the repository, and the OMS peers share the same state maintained in the repository. Each request can be processed by any OMS. When an OMS acquires an operation, it stamps the operation with its unique name and locks it so that no other OMS can work on it. Upon completion, the OMS updates the status of the work and releases the work; then it looks for more work in the work queue maintained by the repository. As a result of this, workload generated by multiple consoles and agents are balanced among the available OMS peers.

In addition to scalability, each peer OMS is responsible for communicating with other OMS servers about its status. Information about the availability of each OMS is stored in the repository. When an OMS peer is identified as being unavailable, any work in its queue is reassigned to the other available OMS peers.

Notifications such as job completion are sent by the intelligent agent to the OMS. If the OMS is not available, the notifications are retained until the OMS becomes available, and it resends the notifications that are passed by the OMS to the applications. The agent provides direct access to the Oracle database's management information base variables and also allows third-party applications to communicate with it using Simple Network Management Protocol (SNMP).

OEM Console

The OEM Console is the central framework for all management functions. The console is the GUI that acts as the primary interface to enable the launching of integrated applications and third-party applications. You can customize the console as desired.

The console consists of several components:

- Navigator window—provides a tree view of all objects in the system and their relationships.
- Group window—allows you to define the topology of services and logically group them.
- Job window—interfaces to the Job Scheduling system. Jobs can be created and managed by using this system.
- Event Management—interfaces to the Event Management system. These events can be used to monitor the health of the system.

OEM Repository

OEM repository is a set of tables in your schema that contains information used by OEM. Information placed in the repository include

Jobs and event status

Discovery cache

Tasks performed

The nature of the data stored in the repository makes it suitable to be placed in relational tables and can be placed in any Oracle database, not necessarily the database being monitored.

NOTE

In OEM v2.x, multiple repositories can be merged into one shared repository.

Large systems might be managed by a team of administrators with varying degrees of responsibility, and they need to share information with each other. The centralized repository makes this possible. OEM has a default superuser called SYSMAN that can be used to initially log in and create other superusers and administrators with different degrees of responsibility as desired. During the creation of an administrator account, you can specify the console services that can be accessed by this user such as the job system and event system.

NOTE

The default Enterprise Manager superuser is SYSMAN, with the password oem_temp.

Administrator preferences can be defined to specify:

- Password
- Pager and email settings
- Schedule how notifications are received via pager/email
- Permissions that other administrators can have on the groups you create. These permissions can be one of the following:

  NONE specifies no permissions.

  VIEW specifies that objects can be viewed and notifications received.

  MODIFY specifies that object properties can be modified. Ownership cannot be changed, and permissions for other administrators cannot be changed.

  FULL specifies that object properties can be changed, ownership can be changed, and even permissions for other administrators can be changed.

- Preferred credentials for the services managed

  Preferred credentials should be set up to avoid logging in again each time a user tries to access a service. Preferred credentials can be set up by using the Preferred credentials tabbed page as follows (see also Figure 29.2):

  1. From the console menu bar, choose System, Preferences.
  2. On the Preferences tabbed page, populate the following:

     Username

     Password

     Confirm the password, Role
  3. Click OK.

Administrators and other users connect to the Oracle Management Service that is responsible for connecting them to the repository.

It is possible to create domains that equate to a database repository schema. An administrator created in one domain can't log in to another domain, and data can't be shared between domains.

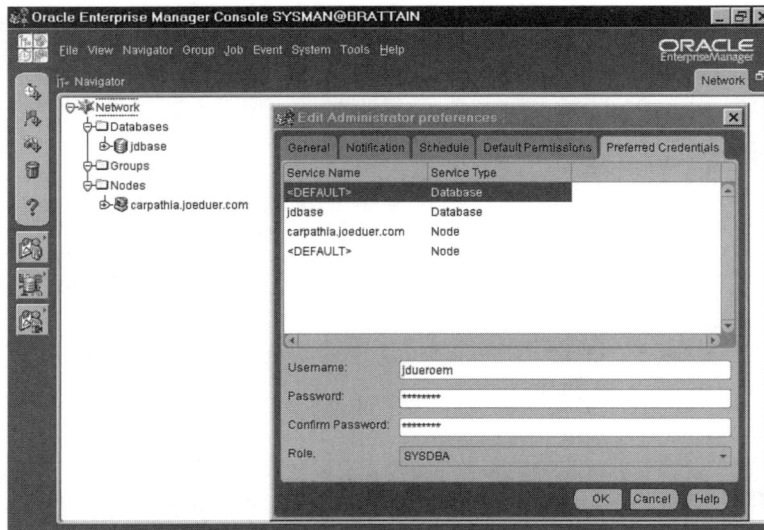

FIGURE 29.2
Setting preferred credentials.

NOTE

A user can connect to only one repository at a time.

NOTE

The intelligent agents allow automatic discovery of all services across the network. Services that are discovered are displayed in a hierarchical fashion in the navigator window and can be used by other applications.

Intelligent Agents

The intelligent agents are run on remote nodes and service requests from multiple domains. Functions performed by the intelligent agents include

- Accepting jobs or events from the console or third-party applications.
- Canceling jobs or events as directed.

- Running jobs, collecting the results, and queueing them for the Oracle Management Service.
- Handling SNMP requests.

Common Services

Several services are shared by all OEM components to perform some common tasks:

- Job services—Allow you to schedule jobs on remote sites. Job specification includes the task to perform, the start time, and the frequency of execution. When a job is created, it can be submitted for immediate execution, saved in the library for execution at a later time, or both. The job creator is, by default, the owner of the job, and anyone with full permission can manage the job.

> **NOTE**
>
> The intelligent agent should run on every database server against which jobs will be scheduled to run.

- Security services—Maintains the list of administrators that will be notified when a particular event occurs. They also manage administrative privileges for the nodes and services.
- Event services—Comprised of conditions that are checked periodically. Events are monitored, and when the specified conditions becomes true, administrators are alerted of the event occurrence and optionally fix the problem according to a prespecified criteria. Alerts can be one of several levels of severity: clear, warning, critical, or unknown. When an event is created, it can be registered, saved in the library, or both.

> **NOTE**
>
> The job and event management systems can be used together to establish a reactive management system.

- Discovery services—Maintain an up-to-date view of the nodes and services being managed.

Application Programming Interface (API)

An API is provided by OEM to allow the integration of third-party applications with the OEM database applications at the console level or the agent level. Third-party applications can be used

to analyze the data gathered by the Oracle Expert and other OEM performance-tuning tools. For additional information on this topic, refer to the book *Using Oracle8* published by Que.

Integrated Database Applications

Several integrated database applications are provided by OEM to simplify the task of administrating multiple databases. Some applications are Java based, whereas others are Win32 based. Table 29.1 shows the available applications and their use.

TABLE 29.1   Integrated Database Applications Provided by OEM

Integrated Database Application	Usage
Instance Manager	Manages database instances and initialization parameters
Storage Manager	Manages datafiles, rollback segments, tablespaces, and other storage parameters
Security Manager	Manages users, roles, profiles, and privileges
Schema Manager	Manages schema objects such as tables, views, and so on
Software Manager	Manages the distribution of software
Backup Manager	Manages database backup and recovery
Replication Manager	Manages the replication environment
SQL Worksheet	Executes SQL queries and DML
Data Manager	Performs database export/import and data loads

Two modes exist in which you can run the database applications:

- From the console, using OMS—Using this method, you can run the applications in a browser and also support multiple databases in the navigator. All the OMS functionality, such as jobs and events, are available.
- From the command line, using `oemapp tool_name oms_machine_name`—This method works like v1.x, and it cannot be run in a browser. Also, only one database is supported in the navigator, and OMS functionality, such as jobs and events, are not available.

Managing OMS

OMS is managed using the OEMCtrl utility (see Figure 29.3). For example,

1. To start OMS, execute the following from the command prompt:
   ```
   OEMCtrl START OMS
   ```

29

ORACLE ENTERPRISE MANAGER

2. To shut down OMS, use the following:

   OMSCtrl STOP OMS *emsuperuser/empassword*@domain

3. To check the status of OMS, use the following:

   OEMCtrl STATUS OMS *emsuperuser/empassword*@domain

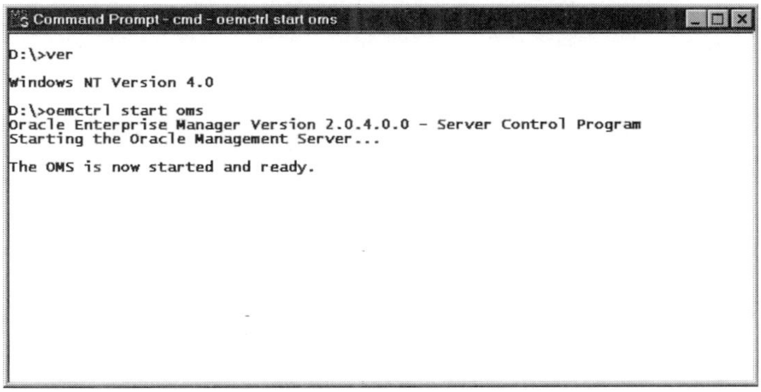

FIGURE 29.3
Managing OMS.

Using the Console to Start Up and Shut Down a Database

Using the OEM console, you can start up and shut down an Oracle database.

> **NOTE**
>
> The console can't be used to shut down the server running the repository.

The following steps can be used to start up an Oracle database (see Figure 29.4):

1. Start up and log on to the Oracle Enterprise Manager.
2. From the database folder, select the database object to start up.
3. If preferred credentials are not set up, you will have to specify the correct username and password for this host.
4. On the General page of the Database property sheet, select the Start up mode.
5. Specify the location of the INIT.ORA file.
6. Click Apply.

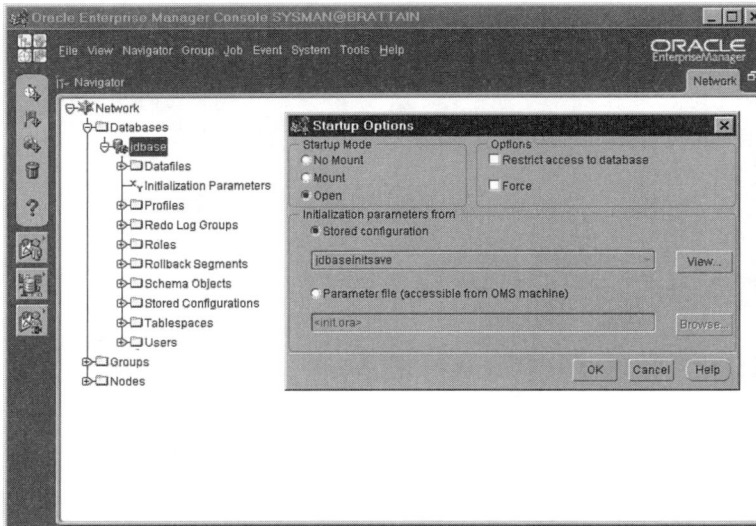

FIGURE 29.4
Starting a database.

The following steps can be used to shutdown an Oracle database (also see Figure 29.5):

1. Start up and log on to the Oracle Enterprise Manager.
2. From the database folder, select the database object to stop.
3. If preferred credentials are not set up, you will have to specify the correct username and password for this host.
4. On the General page of the Database property sheet, select the Shutdown mode.
5. Click the Shutdown button.

Managing Database Storage

Administrative tasks associated with managing database storage such as managing tablespaces, datafiles, and rollback segments can be performed by using the storage manager. As an example, use the storage manager to create a tablespace by using the following steps (see Figure 29.6):

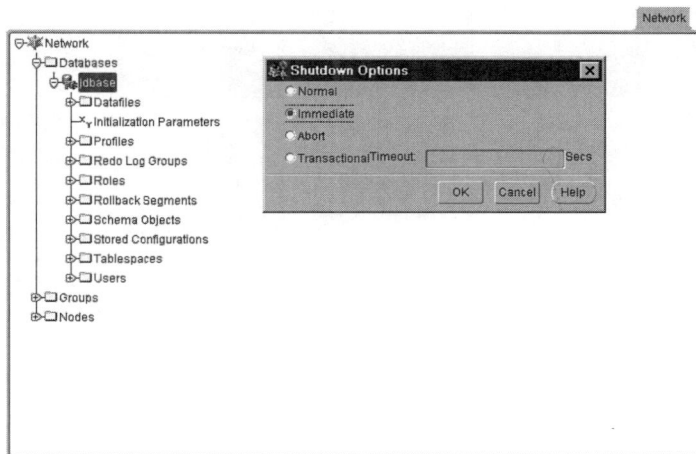

FIGURE 29.5

Shutting down a database.

1. Launch Storage Manager from the Oracle Enterprise Manager console or as a standalone, and connect to a database.

> **NOTE**
>
> Storage Manager can be launched as a standalone application by typing `oemapp` `storage` at the command prompt.

2. Choose Object, Create.

3. Choose Tablespace. This opens the Create Tablespace property sheet.

4. On the General page, specify the details of the new tablespace:

    Name   Specify the name of the tablespace (maximum 30 characters long).

    Status   Specify whether the tablespace is online or offline.

    Add, remove, or edit datafiles belonging to the tablespace.

5. On the Extents page, specify the storage parameters associated with the tablespace. These storage parameters will be used as the default for all objects belonging to this tablespace. If you want to edit the storage parameters, click the Override Default Values check box and change any of the following parameters:

    Initial Size   Specify the size of the first extent allocated to the object. Specification is in units of KB or MB.

Next Extent	Specify the size of the next extent allocated to the object. Specification is in units of KB or MB.
Minimum Size	Specify the minimum size allocated to the object. Specification is in units of KB or MB.
Minimum Extents	Specify the minimum number of extents that can be allocated to the object.
Maximum Extents	Specify the maximum number of extents that can be allocated to the object.

6. Click Apply.

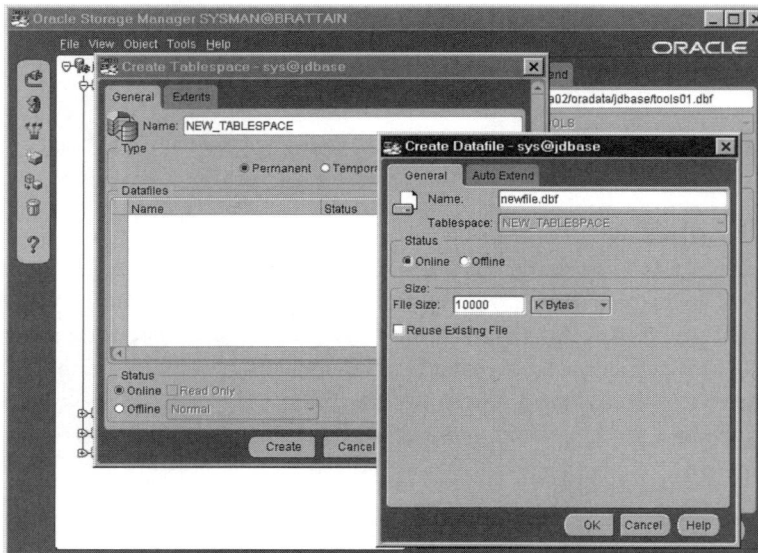

FIGURE 29.6
Using storage manager to create a tablespace.

Advanced Administration

Tuning database performance and diagnosing problems are important functions of the database administrators. Tuning the system requires thorough knowledge of the entire system: database, applications, operating system, and network. Tuning can involve a wide variety of tasks ranging from identifying and reducing contention for system resources, to tuning individual SQL statements.

OEM provides the tuning and diagnostic packs as value-added components. The tuning pack provides a variety of applications that help you in monitoring and tuning the performance of your database system by making use of performance statistics gathered over a period of time.

Oracle Tuning Pack

The Oracle tuning pack provides a useful set of tools to perform database tuning. The following tools are provided:

- Tablespace Manager for tuning database storage and correcting storage problems.
- SQL Analyze for tuning application SQL statements.
- Index Tuning Wizard for tuning database indexes.
- Oracle Expert for providing automated database tuning recommendations, using an inference engine that interprets the data collected.

The Oracle tuning pack is built upon the Oracle Enterprise Manager framework and provides effective and comprehensive tuning methods for the major sources of performance problems in Oracle.

Oracle Tablespace Manager

An Oracle database will dynamically change its storage requirements because of the addition, modification, and deletion of data. Performance problems associated with improper storage settings can be minimized by careful planning, but when you do need to perform some maintenance, it usually involves reorganizing the tables and indexes in order to reclaim unused space. For example, indexes will become inefficient if they have a lot of unused space, and you will have to rebuild the indexes to reclaim this space and improve performance.

Oracle tablespace manager helps the DBA in managing storage problems and improving the performance. It consists of four main features: tablespace viewer, proactive problem detection wizard, tablespace reorganization wizard, and tablespace analyzer wizard.

Tablespace Viewer

It provides a graphical view of the different aspects of all tablespaces belonging to an Oracle instance. Information displayed include: datafiles and segments of the tablespaces, free and total data blocks, and so on. It allows you to select all the segments for a tablespace or all the segments for a datafile and displays performance metrics for the segment such as chained rows, free data blocks, and so on. Another useful feature of the tablespace viewer is the display of segment mapping for a chosen tablespace. This can be used to determine fragmentation in the tablespace.

Proactive Problem Detection Wizard

Proactive maintenance is always better than reactive maintenance, and the problem detection wizard is used for that purpose. It analyzes tablespace objects and identifies potential space management problems because of chained rows, stagnated indexes, objects approaching their maximum extent setting, and so on.

Tablespace Reorganization

Space problems can be corrected by using the tablespace reorganization wizard that allows you to select a single segment, multiple segments or the entire tablespace for reorganization. When the tablespace reorganization is run, it checks for availability of sufficient space to perform the reorganization, presents the user with a dialog box to specify (if needed) a different set of storage parameters to use, and then uses Oracle export/import functions to reorganize the object.

> **NOTE**
>
> When performing tablespace reorganization, segments can be moved between tablespaces.

Tablespace Analyzer Wizard

The tablespace analyzer wizard works together with the Oracle job system and allows you to analyze specified objects or the entire database. Analyzing of objects makes sure that the object statistics are maintained up-to-date, and the cost-based optimizer has access to the correct information about the objects. This results in improved performance of SQL statements. The ANALYZE command can be run immediately, scheduled to run at a later time, or run periodically at specified time intervals.

Oracle Expert

Tuning a database system is an essential function of a database administrator. It is important to monitor the performance of a database system and identify contention, but it is more important to perform proactive tuning so that the performance problems can be minimized. Oracle Expert provides a flexible approach to database tuning. It can be used to correct the problems that are identified by the Oracle Diagnostic Pack and other Oracle monitoring applications. Some of the functions performed by the Oracle Expert include

- Automating the collection and analysis of data
- Making use of a rules-based inference engine to provide database tuning recommendations
- Providing scripts to implement the recommendations
- Generating reports

29

ORACLE ENTERPRISE
MANAGER

Oracle Expert allows you to focus on the tuning goals of each tuning session (refer to Figures 29.7, 29.8, and 29.9), so the amount of data that is collected and analyzed is sufficient to perform the desired tuning.

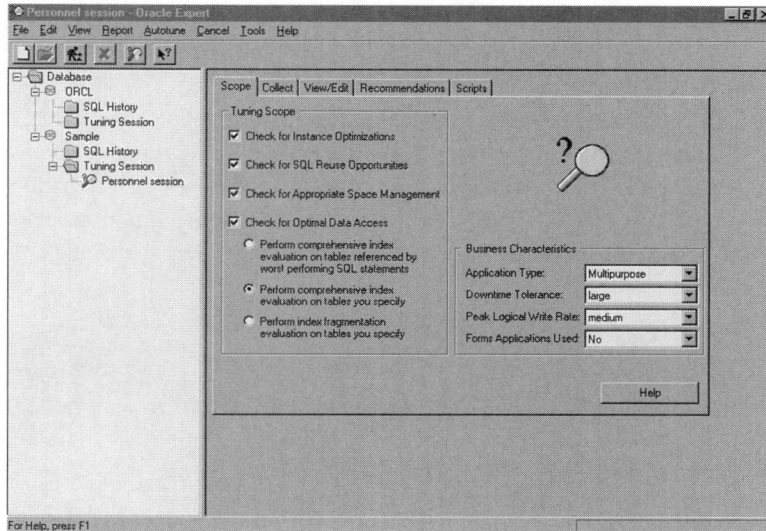

FIGURE 29.7

Specify the scope of the tuning session.

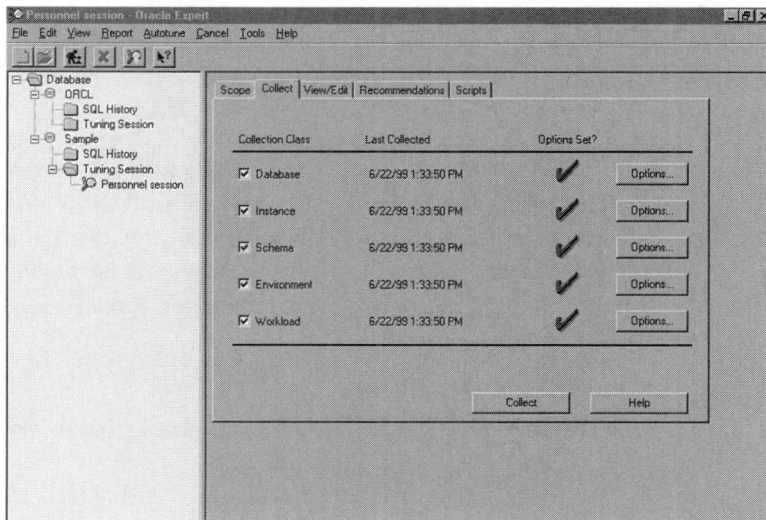

FIGURE 29.8

Specify the collection classes.

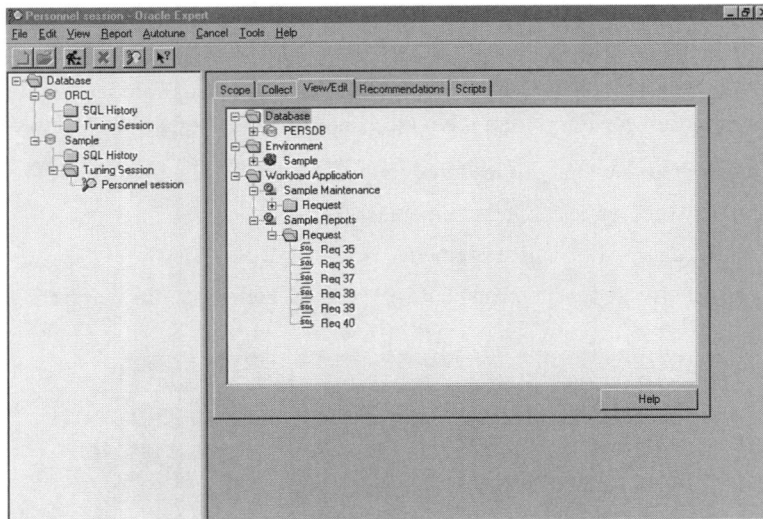

FIGURE 29.9
View the reports of the tuning session.

The tuning performed by the Oracle Expert can be broken into several categories:

- Database instance tuning—Involves tuning of the shared pool, sort operations, parallel query, and parallel server operations.
- Optimization of database access—Involves tuning of the indexes, index reorganization, and making sure that the reuse of SQL statements is done properly.
- Database structure tuning—Involves tuning of the database storage parameters, placement of database objects such as indexes, rollback segments, and temporary segments.
- Platform specific tuning—This involves tuning of initialization parameters to improve the performance of Oracle databases running on specific platforms.

29
ORACLE ENTERPRISE
MANAGER

NOTE

You can use Oracle Expert to tune several Oracle databases simultaneously or run different tuning approaches against the same database.

SQL Analyze

Application SQL statements are a major cause of performance problems in database systems. The Oracle tuning pack provides the SQL Analyze tool to identify problem SQL statements and generate suggestions for improving them (see Figure 29.10). It can be used to

- Detect SQL statements that are resource intensive
- Obtain the explain plan for SQL statements
- Perform index analysis of SQL statements
- Generate alternative SQL statements that will perform better than the current SQL statement

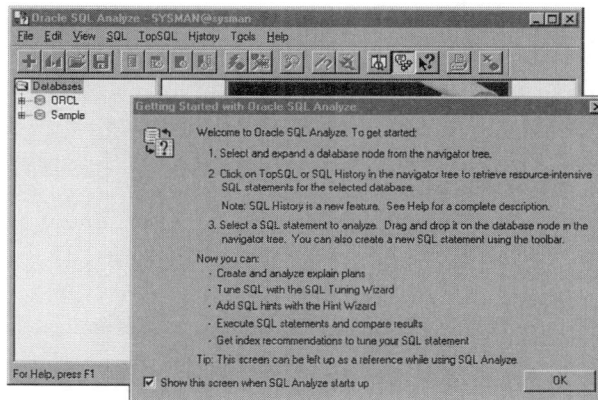

FIGURE 29.10
Analyze SQL statements using SQL Analyze.

NOTE

SQL Analyze simplifies the process of interpreting explain plans by providing a description of each step.

Oracle Diagnostic Pack

Oracle diagnostic pack is an optional set of applications that can be used to monitor an Oracle environment, diagnose problems, and plan for the future growth. It provides five different applications:

- Performance Manager is a real-time monitoring tool to determine the performance of Oracle and host operating system by means of an extensive array of performance charts that can also be customized.

- Capacity planner allows for the gathering, storing, and analyzing of historical data so that future resource needs can be planned.
- Advanced events allows the monitoring of events on remote nodes and servers.
- TopSessions allows you to perform focused diagnosis of Oracle8*i* sessions.
- Oracle Trace is an event-driven data gathering tool for tracing performance data of applications and databases.

Consider an example that shows how to perform some monitoring and diagnostic tasks using the tuning and diagnostic pack applications:

Using Oracle TopSessions, determine the top five sessions accessing the ORCL database. Information is to be displayed by using the "CPU Used by This Session" user statistic and updated automatically every two minutes.

The following steps can be used:

1. Start up, and log on to the Oracle Enterprise Manager.
2. From the Navigator window, select the ORCL database.
3. Launch the Oracle TopSessions application from the OEM toolbar.
4. In the Sort page of the Options property sheet, specify the criteria to focus on the desired sessions (see Figure 29.11):

   In the Statistics Filter list box, select USER.

   In the Sort Statistics list box, select CPU Used By This Session.

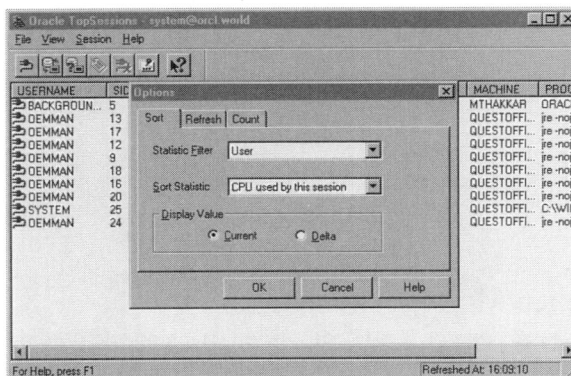

29

ORACLE ENTERPRISE MANAGER

FIGURE 29.11

Specify the sort options.

5. In the Refresh page of the Options property sheet, specify the refresh characteristics (see Figure 29.12):

Choose Automatic Refresh.

Set the Refresh Interval to 30, and re-set the Minutes and Hours text boxes to 00.

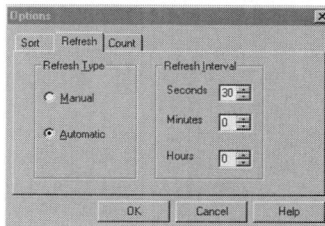

Figure 29.12
Specify the refresh options.

6. In the Count page of the Options property sheet, specify the number of sessions to display. Click the Display Top N Sessions button and change the count to 5 (see Figure 29.13).

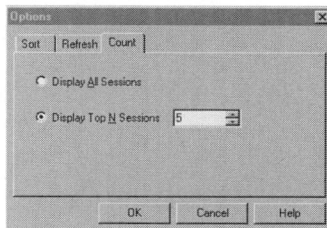

Figure 29.13
Specify the number of sessions to display.

7. Click OK.

Oracle Performance Manager Charts

The task of monitoring performance can be simplified by using the predefined charts provided by the Oracle Performance Manager. Several categories of charts are provided (see Figure 29.14):

- Contention—Charts in this category include Circuit, Dispatcher, Free List Hit %, Latch, Lock, Queue, Redo Allocation Hit %, Rollback NoWait Hit %, and Shared Server.

- Database_Instance—Charts in this category include Process, Session, System Statistics, Table Access, Tablespace, Tablespace Free Space, # Users Active, # Users Waiting for Locks, and # Users Running.

- I/O—Charts in this category include Load Buffer Gets Rate, Network Bytes Rate, Redo Statistics Rate, Sort Rows Rate, Table Scan Rows Rate, and Throughput Rate.

- Overview—Charts in this category include # Users Active, # Users Logged On, # Users Running, # Users Waiting, Buffer Cache Hit, Data Dictionary Cache Hit, File I/O Rate, Rollback NoWait Hit %, System I/O Rate, and Throughput. These charts provide a good overview of the system performance.

- User-defined—This category contains charts created by the user.

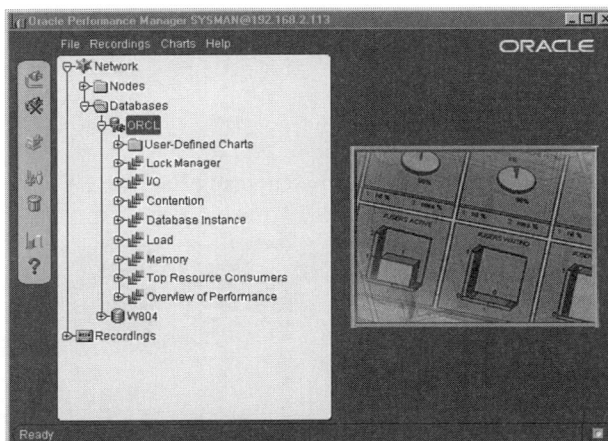

FIGURE 29.14
Predefined charts provided by Oracle Performance Manager.

If the predefined charts don't provide the information that you want, you should create your own charts. The following example demonstrates how you can monitor contention for job queue processes in the ORCL database (see Figure 29.15):

1. Start up, and log on to the Oracle Enterprise Manager.
2. Select the ORCL database from the Navigator window.
3. Launch the Oracle Performance Manager application.
4. Choose Charts, Add User-Defined Charts.
5. Specify a name for the new chart.

6. In the Script Command to Define Chart Columns text box, specify the SQL statement that will gather the statistics to display in the chart. For example, job queue contention can be identified by using the following SQL statement:

```
Select dj.due-vl.active jobs_waiting, vp.snp_processes
➥idle_jq_processes
From
(select count(*) active from v$lock where type='JQ') vl,
(select count(*) due from dba_jobs where next_date < sysdate) dj,
(select value snp_processes from sys.v_$parameter where name='
➥job_queue_processes') vp
```

7. Click the Evaluate button.

8. Verify the results in the Results field. Proceed to the next step when you are satisfied with the result.

9. On the Display Options page, specify the information for each variable to display, and click the Add button.

10. Click the Apply button and then click OK.

11. The chart can be saved in the repository by choosing File, Save Chart.

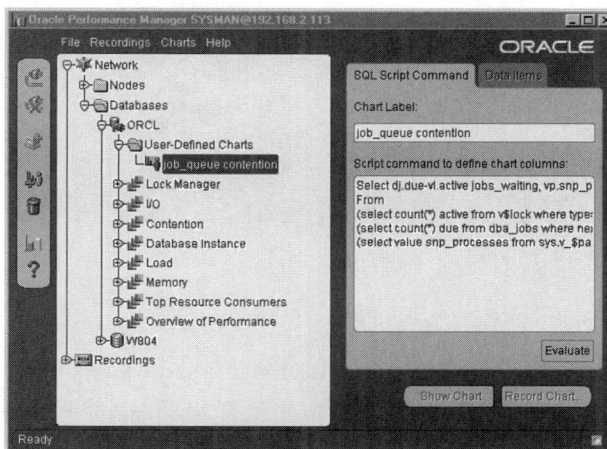

FIGURE 29.15

Create new user-defined charts.

Summary

Oracle Enterprise Manager is a comprehensive set of tools for managing Oracle databases from a centralized location. OEM 2.0.4 used with Oracle8*i* is Java-based and is not restricted to the Windows platform. It uses a three-tiered architecture and makes use of the Oracle Management Server to manage all communication with the OEM repository.

Database administration is possible with the use of an extensive range of integrated database applications. In addition, optional tuning and diagnostic packs provide a comprehensive set of applications that can be used to diagnose and tune performance problems.

29

ORACLE ENTERPRISE
MANAGER

Application Development

IN THIS CHAPTER

Oracle has always focused on simplifying the application development process, and Oracle8*i* is no exception. Several important enhancements are provided in Oracle8*i* to make this process more efficient. These enhancements include

- PL/SQL enhancements such as bulk binds and native dynamic SQL
- Optimization of Top-N analysis
- Integration with Windows NT

Optimization of Top-N Analysis

A top-n query is a query that wants to find the top N largest or smallest values of a column. Some examples of such queries include

- What are the top 25 selling books in the bookstore?
- What are the top five travel destinations in the USA?
- What are the worst 10 movies of 1998?

The basic logic of obtaining the result of top-n queries is as follows:

```
Select column_list rownum
From (select column_list
      From table
      Order by topn_column [asc¦desc])
Where rownum <= N
```

In the preceding syntax,

- column_list specifies the list of columns that you want to view in the result.
- topn_column is the column whose top N values are desired.
- order by clause is used to specify whether we want the top N largest or smallest values.
- rownum is a pseudo column that is used to assign a sequential value (starting with 1) to each of the rows returned by the subquery.

The following example makes use of a table cur_temp in the schema weather to store the names of the major cities in the USA and their current temperatures. We need to find the top 10 hottest cities in the USA. This can be achieved as follows:

```
SQL> select ROWNUM as rank, city, temperature
2 from (select city , temperature
3      from weather.cur_temp
4      order by temperature desc)
5 where ROWNUM <= 10
```

The output of the preceding query can be as follows:

Rank	City	Temperature
1	Phoenix	110
2	Miami	95
3	Orlando	92
4	Los Angeles	89
5	Dallas	82
6	Washington, D.C.	74
7	Atlanta	71
8	San Diego	69
9	San Antonio	65
10	San Francisco	60

Index Enhancements

Oracle8*i* provides several enhancements to the use of indexes that can be helpful during application development. The enhancements include

- Partitioned indexes—Indexes can be partitioned along a partition key. These partitions can be stored on separate tablespaces with separate storage parameters, as shown in the following:

```
SQL> create index sales_idx on sales(month_num)
2 partition by range (month_num)
3 (partition sp1 values less than (3)
4 tablespace sal_idx1,
5 partition sp2 values less than (6)
6 tablespace sal_idx2,
7 partition sp3 values less than (9)
8 tablespace sal_idx3,
9 partition sp4 values less than (13)
10 tablespace sal_idx4);
```

- Equi-partitioned local indexes—Oracle8*i* automatically equi-partitions a local index. Equi-partitioning means that the index uses the same partition key, the same number of partitions, and the same partition boundaries as the partition table referenced. Such equi-partitioned indexes have a one-to-one mapping with the table data. Equi-partitioned local indexes allow the optimizer to be partition-aware.

NOTE

A partition-aware optimizer can improve performance by making use of parallel operations.

An example of creating a local index follows:

```
SQL> create index dept_idx on dept(dept_id)
2 local
3 (partition dpt1 tablespace dept_idx1,
4 partition dpt2 tablespace dept_idx2,
5 partition dpt3 tablespace dept_idx3);
```

- Index-only tables—Index-only tables, also called in-place indexes, can be used to improve performance. Instead of logically sorting the table with a B*Tree, the index-only table is sorted physically. The data and index are essentially the same, and therefore it eliminates the logical reads to the B*Tree. Index-only tables are created by using the `organization index` clause during the creation of a table.

NOTE

Index-only tables normally use the primary key as the indexing column.

An example of creating an index-only table follows:

```
SQL> create table dept
2 (dept_id number(4) constraint dept_pk primary key,
3 dept_loc    varchar2(20),
4 dept_name    varchar2(10),
5 dept_budget    number(10))
6 organization index tablespace dept_indx;
```

- Reverse-key indexes—A reverse-key index is created by reversing the order of the individual column bytes. The order of columns remains the same. Reverse key indexes can be used to improve the performance in an Oracle parallel server environment.

Rewriting Queries

Queries can be rewritten to improve performance. Query rewriting is a task that should be performed with great care because it might result in efficient queries at the expense of readability. Several techniques are commonly used to improve the performance of queries including set operators and Boolean operators.

Set Operators

Performance of queries can be improved by means of MINUS or INTERSECT operators. For example, suppose that you want to find the list of all employees who live outside California. The desired result can be obtained by using both of the following queries:

```sql
SQL> select *
2 from emp
3 where emp_state not in (
4    select emp_state
5    from emp
6    where emp_state = 'CA');

SQL> select *
2 from emp
3 MINUS
4 Select *
5 From emp
6 Where emp_state = 'CA';
```

The second query results in fewer logical reads and is therefore more efficient than the first query.

Similar to the MINUS operator, the INTERSECT operator is very efficient in Oracle. However, the UNION operator is found to be quite inefficient.

Boolean Conversions

A Boolean expression is one that returns either TRUE or FALSE. The WHERE clause in an SQL statement is an example of a Boolean expression. Suppose that we are storing two different prices for an item depending upon whether it is requested as a wholesale item by corporations or a retail item by individuals. For each request, the following queries can be used to obtain the price of items:

```sql
SQL> select whole_price
2 from items
3 where request_type = 'C';

SQL> select retail_price
2 from items
3 where request_type = 'I';
```

The preceding queries require two table scans and can be improved by using the decode function as follows:

```sql
SQL> select decode(request_type, 'C', 1, 0)*whole_price +
2 decode(request_type, 'I', 1, 0)*retail_price
3 from items;
```

The preceding rewritten query is more efficient, but it is also relatively difficult to read and maintain.

Using Hints

The Oracle optimizer can be either rule-based or cost-based. A rule-based optimizer chooses the access path, based on a static vendor-specific rank ordering of access paths that are the fastest ways to the data (refer to Table 30.1 for the rank order used by Oracle). On the other hand, cost-based optimizer chooses the access path based on the data distributed statistics that are stored internally and that need to be updated periodically.

TABLE 30.1   Oracle8*i* Rank-Ordered Optimizer Access Paths

Rank	Access Method
1	Single row by ROWID
2	Single row by cluster join
3	Single row by hash cluster key
4	Single row by unique or primary key
5	Cluster join
6	Hash cluster key
7	Indexed cluster key
8	Composite key
9	Single-column indexes
10	Search indexed columns with bounded range
11	Search indexed columns with unbounded range
12	Sort-merge join
13	Indexed column using MAX or MIN values
14	Indexed columns using ORDER BY clause
15	Full table scans

Suppose that you are using the rule-based optimizer with the following query:

```
SQL> select *
2 from orders
3 where order_id > 1000
```

The preceding unbounded range search can be improved by binding the range. This can be done by using either a known maximum or a theoretical maximum as demonstrated in the following two examples:

```
SQL> select *
2 from orders
3 where order_id > 1000 and order_id < 49500
```

or

```
SQL> select *
2 from orders
3 where order_id > 1000 and order_id < 99999
```

NOTE

As seen from the ranking scheme in Table 30.1, use of the MAX function as follows can actually be slower than using an unbounded range search:

```
SQL> select *
2 from orders
3 where order_id > 1000 and order_id < max(order_id);
```

PL/SQL Enhancements

It has been rumored that Oracle might drop PL/SQL support. This is certainly not evidenced from Oracle8*i* in which a number of features have been added in order to improve the usability and performance of PL/SQL. The significant enhancements to PL/SQL include bulk binds and native dynamic SQL.

Bulk Binds

PL/SQL provides the ability to send a set of SQL statements to the server as a group. Prior to Oracle8*i*, use of such groups required a context switch between the PL/SQL engine and the SQL engine as shown in the following:

```
For I in 1..1000
Loop
    Update items set item_discount = 20 where item_id = I;
End loop;
```

A much more efficient construct is allowed in Oracle8*i*, as shown in the following:

```
FORALL I in 1..1000
    Update items set item_discount = 20 where item_id = I;
```

Context switches between PL/SQL engine and SQL engine can cause significant overhead especially if a SQL statement is used in a loop using collection elements as bind variables. Binding refers to the process of assigning values to PL/SQL variables in SQL statements. Bulk

binding refers to the binding of an entire collection in one step. Oracle8*i* allows you to improve the efficiency of bulk binds by using

- FORALL clause for bulk-binding input collections

- BULK COLLECT clause for bulk-binding output collections

Using the FORALL Statement

The FORALL statement has a construct similar to that of an iteration, but is not really a loop construct. It instructs the PL/SQL engine to bulk-bind all input collections before passing them to the SQL engine. The syntax of using the FORALL construct is as follows:

```
FORALL i IN lower_bound..upper_bound
    Sql_statement;
```

In the preceding construct,

i is used as a collection subscript and can only be used within the FORALL construct.

Sql_statement must be an insert, update, or delete statement that manipulates collection elements.

lower_bound and upper_bound refer to valid ranges of consecutive index numbers.

Several restrictions to the use of bulk binds are as follows:

- The PL/SQL engine bulk binds only subscripted collections.

- The collection subscripts cannot be expressions. The following is not valid:

```
FORALL I in itemids.lower..itemids.upper
    Delete from items where item_id = itemids(I+1);
```

- All the elements in the specified range must exist.

If a FORALL statement fails, the changes are rolled back to an implicit savepoint that is marked before each execution of the SQL statement. Any changes made prior to the execution of the failed SQL statement are not rolled back. This is illustrated in the following example:

Create a table to store the items

```
SQL> create table items
  2    (itemid    number(2),
  3     itemdesc  varchar2(15),
  4     price    number(4));
```

Insert some values into the table

```
SQL> insert into items
  2 values(1, 'Tomato', 4);

SQL> insert into items
  2 values(2, 'Potato', 6);
```

```
SQL> insert into items
2 values(3, 'Onion', 8);
SQL> insert into items
2 values(4, 'Sweet Peas', 3);
```

The following bulk bind is attempted to add the string `'frozen'` to the items `'onion'` and `'sweet peas'`:

```
Declare
    Type numtab is table of number;
    Itemt numtab := numtab(3,4);
Begin
    FORALL I in itemt.FIRST..itemt.LAST
        Update items
set itemdesc = itemdesc ¦¦ ' - frozen'
where itemid = itemt(I);
exception
        when others then
            commit;
end;
```

The use of bulk binds gives the efficiency of sending the entire collection to the SQL engine at once. The SQL engine executes the update statement once for each index value (in this case, two values). The execution succeeds for `itemt(3)` but fails for `itemt(4)` because the `itemdesc` becomes larger than the value allowed in the column (15 characters). However, the rollback only occurs for the execution of `itemt(4)` and not for `itemt(3)`.

Using BULK COLLECT

The BULK COLLECT clause informs the SQL engine to bulk bind output collections before passing it back to PL/SQL engine. It can be used with the following clauses:

- SELECT INTO
- FETCH INTO
- RETURNING INTO

The syntax for BULK COLLECT is

```
BULK COLLECT INTO collection1 [, collection 2, collection3...]
```

Each collection specified in the BULK COLLECT clause is bulk binded. The only restriction is that the corresponding columns should only store scalar values. The following example shows how you can bulk fetch from a cursor into a collection:

```
Declare
    Type itemidtab is table of items.itemid%TYPE;
    Type itemdesctab is table of items.itemdesc%TYPE;
```

```
        Type pricetab is table of items.price%TYPE;
        Ids itemidtab;
        Descs itemdesctab;
        Prices pricetab;
        Cursor c1 is select itemid, itemdesc, price
                    From items
                    Where price > 5;

Begin
    Open c1;
    Fetch c1 BULK COLLECT into ids, descs, prices;
    ..
    ..
    ..
end;
```

> **NOTE**
>
> Bulk binds from a cursor to a collection of records is not allowed. For example, the
> following is illegal:
>
> ```
> DECLARE
>     TYPE deptrectab IS TABLE OF dept%ROWTYPE;
>     dept_recs deptrectab;
>     CURSOR d1 IS select deptno, dept_name from dept where location = 'CA';
> BEGIN
>     OPEN d1;
>     FETCH d1 BULK COLLECT INTO dept_recs;
>     CLOSE d1;
> END;
> ```

Native Dynamic SQL

Prior to Oracle8*i*, developers had the ability of using dynamic SQL by means of the
DBMS_SQL package. Use of DBMS_SQL resulted in code that was not concise and required
several steps such as parsing and execution. Oracle8*i* allows you to write code that is very efficient, in addition to allowing you to be able to execute it immediately. The result is concise and
efficient code. Oracle8*i* provides the EXECUTE IMMEDIATE statement to accomplish this task as
shown in the following:

```
Procedure update_employee(eid number, etitle varchar2, esal number) is
    Sql_statement varchar2(1000);
Begin
```

```
Sql_statement := 'update emp
   set emp_title = '||:etitle||',
 emp_sal = '||:esal||'
   where emp_id = '||:eid;
execute immediate sql_statement using etitle, esal, eid;
end;
```

Using DBMS_SQL, the same procedure would require more coding:

```
PROCEDURE update_employee(eid NUMBER, etitle varchar2, esal NUMBER) IS
        l_cursor integer default 0;
        rc       integer default 0;
        sql_statement     varchar2(1000);

   BEGIN
        Sql_statement := 'update emp
   set emp_title = '||:etitle||',
 emp_sal = '||:esal||'
  where emp_id = '||:eid;
        l_cursor:=dbms_sql.open_cursor;
        dbms_sql.parse(l_cursor,stmt,dbms_sql.native);
        rc:=dbms_sql.execute(l_cursor);
        dbms_sql.close_cursor(l_cursor);
   EXCEPTION
        WHEN OTHERS THEN
            BEGIN
                dbms_sql.close_cursor(l_cursor);
            EXCEPTION WHEN OTHERS THEN NULL;
            END;

            RAISE_APPLICATION_ERROR(-20101,'Cannot update employee: '
            ➥||sqlerrm);

   END;
```

Oracle WebDB

Oracle WebDB is a complete Web development environment including an HTML server. It can be used to process HTTP requests and serve Web pages. Oracle WebDB doesn't require you to install additional software on client machines. It only makes use of a Web browser such as Netscape Navigator 3.1 or later or Microsoft Internet Explorer 4.0 or later to develop and deploy applications.

Oracle WebDB is easy to use and consists of a set of PL/SQL procedures contained in the Oracle database. It provides a lightweight listener to serve as a Web server and a PL/SQL interface to the database. Web applications can be developed by using browser-based HTML tools.

Wizards are provided to help users with development of components such as reports, charts, menus, calendars, and so on. Any new component developed is given an URL that can be added to HTML text. WebDB includes all the tools necessary to administer, manage, and configure the database.

WebDB allows for decentralization of content management without decentralizing Web site management. This is achieved by creating a Web site that is divided into sections called *corners*. Items related to a specific topic are placed in corners. The Web site administrator then assigns owners to the various corners. These owners are responsible for the contents of their corners. The corner owners can grant different privileges such as add, edit, and delete for the contents of their corner to other users. Content authors can then maintain their corner of the Web site using a point-and-click interface.

Online Data Reorganization and Defragmentation

Oracle8*i* allows you to have full access to the database while performing data reorganization and defragmentation. Maintenance operations such as index rebuilds can be performed without any interruption to DML operations being performed on the base tables. Any changes being made to the base table and the index are recorded in a journal table and applied to the new index at the end of the maintenance operation.

Index-organized tables (IOT) also can be moved and reorganized while being available to users. Changes made to these tables are recorded in a journal table and merged with the table at the end of the process. Such reorganizations of the data can be performed on the entire IOT or a single partition of a partitioned IOT.

Oracle InterMedia

Multimedia in the database can be handled by using Oracle InterMedia, which provides five management modules:

- Oracle InterMedia Text—This module is built on top of Oracle's Context technology, and it provides users with advanced search capabilities, with the help of advanced retrieval and natural language queries.

- Oracle InterMedia Image—This module can be used to manage images in a variety of formats such as TIFF, JPG, BMP, PCX, GIF, SUN, TARGA, Flashpix, PIX, and RPIX. It can be used to manage two-dimensional static digital images and to perform functions such as scaling and cropping.

- Oracle InterMedia Video and Audio—This module can be used to enable browser-based audio and video input. A variety of sources can be used for audio and video such as

Oracle VideoServer and Web sites. The following industry standard audio and video formats are supported: AIF, AIFF-C, AUFF, WAV, AVI, MPEG, QuickTime, and Real Networks.

- Oracle InterMedia Locator—This module can be used to perform location queries such as finding stores based on spatial data. It supports online geocoding facilities for locator applications and proximity queries. It allows geocoding, storage, and retrieval of geocoded data in Oracle8*i* databases. The process of geocoding makes use of points to represent addresses and locations. InterMedia can be used, along with third-party geocoding and mapping tools, to perform queries on geocoded data such as finding the nearest gas station or the shortest route to reach Las Vegas from Los Angeles.

NOTE

Oracle InterMedia is fully integrated with Oracle8*i*, and therefore applications can query and retrieve multimedia data in the same fashion as traditional relational data using standard SQL.

Oracle InterMedia Text performs searches by using text indexes. These text indexes can be created on almost any database column and are stored and managed by the database. Text queries are executed against these text indexes and return a hit list of matching documents that can be stored in the file system or at a specified URL address. A single SQL command can be used to search full text as well as structured data. Text search queries can be performed from any tool that supports SQL or PL/SQL. Several types of search capabilities are provided:

- Exact word or phrase searching
- Boolean specifications
- Proximity searches
- Wildcard searches
- Thesaurus word equivalence
- Case-sensitivity
- Section searching
- "About" searches for a particular subject or theme

  The following example searches the books table for all books that satisfy the following conditions:

  Authored by an author with the last name of "thakkar"

  Contain the word "Oracle"

30

APPLICATION
DEVELOPMENT

Written about the subject of "Internet"

```
SQL> select isbn, title, author, price
2 from books
3 where lastname like '%thakkar%' and
4 contains (btext, 'Oracle AND ABOUT (Internet)') > 0;
```

Oracle InterMedia makes use of object data types called ORDAudio, ORDImage, and ORDVideo to describe audio, image, and video data. Each instance of this datatype contains the following:

Metadata that provides information about the data. It is stored and managed in the database.

Media data that represents the actual data. It can be stored in the database as BLOBs or externally as BFILEs, HTTP server-based URLs, specialized media servers, or user-defined sources.

Methods represent the procedures that can be performed on the objects such as store and retrieve. It is stored and managed in the database.

InterMedia and the Web

Internet applications and Web e-commerce make use of a variety of datatypes. Oracle8*i* is the first real Internet database that is capable of handling all these rich datatypes. Oracle8*i* InterMedia provides the capability to manage the audio, video, image, spatial, as well as text data used in such Internet applications. Oracle InterMedia is Web-enabled by means of a clipboard and Web agent working together. The clipboard has the following functions:

- Captures multimedia objects from a variety of sources such as files, cameras, scanners, and so on.
- Retrieves multimedia objects from the Oracle8*i* database.
- Uses third-party tools such as Microsoft Word or Paint to edit objects.
- Drags and drops multimedia objects to Web authoring tools such as Microsoft Front Page.
- Uses the InterMedia Web agent to construct the URL to access the objects.

Oracle8*i* Web agent is used to decode the URL of objects to retrieve them for display by Web clients. The following servers are supported:

- Netscape Enterprise Server
- Netscape FastTrack Server
- Oracle Application Server
- Microsoft Internet Information Server

NOTE

The clipboard and Web agent of the Oracle8*i* InterMedia are not available on the distribution media, but can be downloaded from
`http://www.oracle.com/products/free_software/index.html`.

Extensible Framework

In order to support multimedia datatypes, Oracle8*i* provides an interface that allows developers to define domain-specific operators and indexing schemes that can be integrated with the Oracle database server.

A set of built-in operators are provided:

> Arithmetic operators (+, -, *, /)
> Logical operators (NOT, AND, OR)
> Comparison operators (=, <, >)
> Set operators (UNION, MINUS, INTERSECT)

The extensible framework for datatype management allows developers to create new operators. Even though the implementation of the new operators is user-defined, Oracle8*i* allows the use of these user-defined operators with standard SQL statements.

In addition to user-defined operators, Oracle8*i* also allows developers to create domain indexes. These domain indexes are implemented by the application software that is responsible for defining the index structure, maintaining the index content, and searching through the index during query processing. However, the domain indexes can be stored in the Oracle database or externally as files.

Before creating a domain index, you must first create an indextype object using the CREATE INDEXTYPE command. indextype is an object that specifies the routines that manage a domain index. In order to create an indextype object, the following privileges are required:

- Create indextype system privilege (if creating the indextype in your schema)
- Create any indextype system privilege (if creating the indextype in another schema)
- Execute privilege on the implementation type and the supported operators

indextype objects make use of operators. These operators can be the predefined Oracle8*i* operators mentioned earlier, or they can be user-defined operators. User-defined operators can be created and implemented using the create operator command. The following example creates an operator called contains in the schema megh. It searches the first varchar2 value in the second varchar2 value and returns another varchar2 result.

```
SQL> Create operator megh.contains
2 binding (varchar2, varchar2) return varchar2
3 using text.contains;
```

Refer to the Oracle8*i* SQL reference guide for the complete syntax of using the `create operator` command.

In order to use the `create operator` command, you need the following permissions:

- Create operator system privilege (if creating the operator in your own schema)
- Create any operator system privilege (if creating the operator in another schema)
- Execute privilege on the functions and operators referenced in the command

After the operators have been created, the `indextype` can be created. The following example creates an `indextype` called `textopttype` that makes use of the `contains` operator:

```
SQL> create indextype textopttype
for contains (varchar2, varchar2)
using textoptmethods;
```

In the preceding example, the USING clause specifies the type that provides the implementation of the new `indextype`. These required routines are implemented in the Oracle Data Cartridge Interface (ODCI interface).

Please refer to the Oracle8*i* SQL reference guide for the complete syntax of using the `create indextype` command.

Domain indexes have the following restrictions:

- There can be only one domain index per column.
- A domain index cannot be composite.
- The BITMAP clause cannot be used with a domain index.
- The UNIQUE clause cannot be used with a domain index.
- A local domain index cannot be created on a partitioned table.
- A domain index cannot be created on a column of datatype REF, nested table, Varray, LONG, or LONG RAW.
- A domain index cannot be created on an attribute of a column of user-defined type if the attribute is also of a user-defined type.

The following example shows how to create a domain index that can speed up the processing of user-defined data:

Create a type to define an object box

```
SQL> create type box as object
```

```
2 (length number,
3 width number,
4 height number,
5 member function volume return number);
```

Implement the member function of the user-defined type

```
SQL> create or replace type body box as
2 member function volume return number is
3 begin
4   return (length*width*height);
5 end;
6 end;
```

Create a table making use of the user-defined type

```
SQL> create table boxtab of box;
```

Create an index using the member function

```
SQL> create index boxvol_idx on boxtab bt (bt.volume());
```

This index can be used to execute the following query efficiently:

```
SQL> select *
2 from boxtab bt
3 where bt.volume() > 500;
```

Integration with Windows NT

Oracle8*i* provides several new features that allow integration with Microsoft products. Windows NT is increasingly becoming an important and viable platform for development and deployment of database applications, and, combined with Oracle8*i* features, it provides a highly scalable and secure platform for application developers.

Oracle Application Generator for MS Visual Studio

Oracle8*i* allows developers to quickly and easily develop Visual Basic, Visual C++, or Visual InterDev applications that connect to and access Oracle databases. This is done by using a GUI tool called Oracle Application Wizard (AppWizard). The AppWizard is highly graphical and intuitive and can be used to develop database applications with very little coding. The AppWizard is integrated with the Visual Studio IDE, making it very easy to develop applications on Windows 95/98/NT platforms.

Two simple steps involved in using the AppWizard are as follows:

1. It prompts the user with connection information such as

   connection string

   username

   password

Then the user can select the specific tables and columns from which data is to be retrieved.

2. Based on the user response, AppWizard will generate a Visual Studio project and the source code for an application framework. The framework generated consists of both:

Microsoft Foundation Classes (MFC) for GUI application code

Oracle Objects for OLE (OO4O) that provide the connectivity and data access

Oracle Objects for OLE

Oracle Objects for OLE (OO4O) is a COM-based database connectivity tool that can be used to access Oracle databases. It can be used in a variety of environments such as

- Two-tier client-server applications
- Application servers in n-tier environments
- Web servers such as Microsoft Transaction Server

OO4O consists of an in-process COM automation server, a C++ class library, and the Oracle data control. It can be used from any programming language that supports the Microsoft COM automation such as

- Microsoft Visual Basic
- Microsoft Visual C++
- VBA in Excel
- VBScript
- JavaScript

Oracle8*i* allows efficient management of database connections and supports connection pooling and multiplexing of user sessions. It also supports access to instances of the new datatypes introduced in Oracle8 such as

- Nested tables
- Varrays
- BLOBs, CLOBs, NCLOBs, and BFILEs
- Object References (REFs)
- Objects

In addition, it provides full support for Microsoft Transaction Server as well as advanced queuing capabilities of Oracle8*i*.

Integration with Microsoft Transaction Server

Microsoft Transaction Server (MTS) is a middle-tier application server that can be used to manage distributed transactions. Oracle8*i* is fully integrated with it and provides users the ability to create distributed transactions that are coordinated by MTS and work with Oracle databases on any platform. It also provides a runtime environment for the distribution of these applications. Oracle8*i* allows for faster execution of distributed transactions with less configuration compared to the alternative solution of using MTS coordinated transactions that are mapped to the Microsoft XA protocol.

COM Cartridge

The COM cartridge provided by Oracle8*i* allows PL/SQL developers to programmatically manipulate COM/DCOM objects using the OLE automation interface. The COM cartridge provides several benefits:

- Allows the functionality of PL/SQL to be extended to suit specific environments
- Allows the developers to reuse COM objects available from third-party vendors
- Manipulates COM objects from PL/SQL stored procedures, functions, and triggers

Summary

Return-on-investment strategies usually indicate that you must tune the application before tuning the database. Tuning the application amounts to tuning the variety of SQL statements used. Oracle8*i* provides several features that can help in increasing the productivity of application development. These include PL/SQL enhancements such as bulk binds and native dynamic SQL. Integration with Microsoft Transaction Server allows efficient use of distributed transactions, whereas the AppWizard can help tremendously in managing Web sites with minimal coding.

30

APPLICATION
DEVELOPMENT

Data Warehousing Enhancements

31

IN THIS CHAPTER

Organizations have been increasingly relying on reporting and online analytical processing tools with data warehouses and data marts to help in the decision making process. Several important enhancements are provided by Oracle8*i* by means of features such as materialized views, query enhancements such as CUBE and ROLLUP, and other performance enhancements. In this chapter, you will look at these features and also make use of the DBMS_STATS package to manipulate the optimizer statistics.

Multidimensional Analysis

Decision support systems frequently make use of multidimensional analysis. A *dimension* refers to a category of fact (event associated with a set of values that are worth tracking). Multidimensional analysis involves examining the database system from all the necessary combination of dimensions. Examples of dimensions include time, region, product, department, and so on, but it could potentially refer to anything that is worth tracking as a category and might be used in analytical questions.

The following are examples of multidimensional requests:

- Show the sales for all products with increasing aggregation levels: from individual, to department, to division for 1997 and 1998.

- Perform a cross-tabular analysis of all products showing profits by countries in Europe for 1997 and 1998.

Such multidimensional data is visualized as a data cube where fact is stored at the intersection of the dimensions. Cross tabular reports are generated from a slice of the cube. Different multidimensional requests can be satisfied by looking at different slices of the cube.

Usually such multidimensional analysis makes use of a huge amount of data (millions of rows) and might involve several complex aggregations. Efficient processing is critical in such analysis. Oracle8*i* provides the CUBE, ROLLUP, and top-n queries (discussed in Chapter 30, "Application Development") operations to enhance the performance of such queries.

To illustrate the ROLLUP and the CUBE operations, we will use the example of a store, "ANV store", that sells audio CDs and videos. ANV stores are located in several regions of the USA, and we will track the sales of audio and video for 1997 and 1998.

A sample cross-tabular report showing sales by product category and region in 1998 is shown in Table 31.1.

Data Warehousing Enhancements

CHAPTER 31

635

31

DATA
WAREHOUSING
ENHANCEMENTS

TABLE 31.1   Sample Cross-Tabular Report of the ANV Stores Sales

| | *1998* | | |
| | | *Product Category* | |
Region	*Audio Sales*	*Video Sales*	*Total Sales by Region*
Eastern	41000	23000	64000
Central	22000	31000	53000
Western	57000	19000	76000
Total Sales by product	120000	73000	193000

Such a cross-tabular report requires calculation of sub-totals and grand totals that cannot easily be calculated with query capabilities prior to Oracle8*i*.

ROLLUP Operations

ROLLUP is an extension of SQL that allows you to use a SELECT statement to calculate multiple levels of subtotals for a specified group of dimensions. It also calculates a grand total. ROLLUP is an extension of the GROUP BY function and is easy to use. It is also very efficient because it can be performed in parallel. Rollup operations are best suited to perform aggregation of data across hierarchical categories such as time and region.

The following syntax is used with the ROLLUP operation:

```
Select .. group by
    Rollup(list_of_grouping_columns)
```

The list of grouping columns specified in the ROLLUP clause is used to create subtotals that "roll up" from the most detailed level to a grand total. The "roll up" is performed by creating progressively higher subtotals from the right to the left of the grouping columns list and finally creating the grand total.

> **NOTE**
>
> ROLLUP creates subtotals at n+1 levels, where n is the number of grouping columns.

Using the example of ANV stores, we can perform ROLLUP operations as shown in the following:

```
SQL> select time, region, product
2 sum(item_sales) as item_sales
3 from sales
4 group by rollup(time, region, product)
```

The output of this query can be seen in Table 31.2.

TABLE 31.2   Output of Performing Rollup Operation

Time	Region	Product	Sales
1997	Central	Audio CDs	20000
1997	Central	Videos	33000
1997	Central	[NULL]	53000
1997	Eastern	Audio CDs	46000
1997	Eastern	Videos	43000
1997	Eastern	[NULL]	89000
1997	Western	Audio CDs	20000
1997	Western	Videos	45000
1997	Western	[NULL]	65000
1997	[NULL]	[NULL]	207000
1998	Central	Audio CDs	55000
1998	Central	Videos	36000
1998	Central	[NULL]	91000
1998	Eastern	Audio CDs	71000
1998	Eastern	Videos	20000
1998	Eastern	[NULL]	91000
1998	Western	Audio CDs	46000
1998	Western	Videos	62000
1998	Western	[NULL]	108000
1998	[NULL]	[NULL]	290000
[NULL]	[NULL]	[NULL]	497000

The preceding output shows the following values:

- Standard aggregation that would result from GROUP BY operations without ROLLUP
- Subtotals for all products across time and region
- Subtotals for all regions and products across time
- A grand total

> **NOTE**
>
> NULL values returned from ROLLUP and CUBE operations are not traditional NULL values, but they indicate that a subtotal or grand total is calculated.

The same result can be obtained by using n+1 SELECT statements and performing UNION ALL between them (where n is the number of dimensions). For example,

```
SQL> select time, region, products, sum(item_sales)
2 from sales
3 group by time, region, products
4 union all
5 Select time, region, '',' sum(item_sales)
6 from sales
7 group by time, region
8 union all
9 select time, '', '', sum(item_sales)
10 from sales
11 group by time
12 union all
13 select '', '', '', sum(item_sales)
14 from sales;
```

Compared to the rollup operation, this query is more complex and also is very inefficient because each of the preceding SELECT statements will cause table access even though the subtotals could all be calculated in a single pass (using rollup).

CUBE Operation

The ROLLUP operation previously described generates only a subset of the possible subtotals. For example, the ROLLUP operation used earlier doesn't generate the subtotals for a product across all regions or across all time categories. This would require you to perform ROLLUP operations in a different order. If you need exhaustive subtotals, the best way to do it is by using the CUBE operation. The CUBE operation extends the SELECT statement to perform subtotal calculations for all possible combinations of a specified group of dimensions, and it also provides a grand total.

> **NOTE**
>
> Both ROLLUP and CUBE operations can be performed as parallel operations, and the benefit of using them increases as the number of dimensions used increases.

Similar to a ROLLUP operation, a CUBE operation is also an extension of the GROUP BY clause and can be used with the following syntax:

```
Select .. group by
    cube(list_of_grouping_columns)
```

The CUBE operation takes the list of grouping columns and creates a cross-tabular report with subtotals of all possible combinations of the dimensions and also a grant total.

> **NOTE**
>
> Cube operation performed on n columns will result in 2^n combinations of subtotals.

Using the example of ANV stores, we can perform CUBE operations as shown in the following:

```
SQL> select time, region, product
2 sum(item_sales) as item_sales
3 from sales
4 group by cube(time, region, product)
```

The output of this query can be seen in Table 31.3.

TABLE 31.3   Output of Performing a CUBE Operation

Time	Region	Product	Sales
1997	Central	Audio CDs	20000
1997	Central	Videos	33000
1997	Central	[NULL]	53000
1997	Eastern	Audio CDs	46000
1997	Eastern	Videos	43000
1997	Eastern	[NULL]	89000
1997	Western	Audio CDs	20000
1997	Western	Videos	45000
1997	Western	[NULL]	65000
1997	[NULL]	Audio CDs	86000
1997	[NULL]	Videos	121000
1997	[NULL]	[NULL]	207000
1998	Central	Audio CDs	55000
1998	Central	Videos	36000

Time	Region	Product	Sales
1998	Central	[NULL]	91000
1998	Eastern	Audio CDs	71000
1998	Eastern	Videos	20000
1998	Eastern	[NULL]	91000
1998	Western	Audio CDs	46000
1998	Western	Videos	62000
1998	Western	[NULL]	108000
1998	[NULL]	Audio CDs	172000
1998	[NULL]	Videos	118000
1998	[NULL]	[NULL]	290000
[NULL]	Central	Audio CDs	75000
[NULL]	Central	Videos	69000
[NULL]	Central	[NULL]	144000
[NULL]	Eastern	Audio CDs	117000
[NULL]	Eastern	Videos	63000
[NULL]	Eastern	[NULL]	180000
[NULL]	Western	Audio CDs	66000
[NULL]	Western	Videos	107000
[NULL]	Western	[NULL]	173000
[NULL]	[NULL]	Audio CDs	258000
[NULL]	[NULL]	Videos	239000
[NULL]	[NULL]	[NULL]	497000

NOTE

The ROLLUP and CUBE operations can be used with all the functions available to the GROUP BY clause, such as sum, count, min, max, and avg.

Filtering Results

The HAVING clause has no effect on the use of ROLLUP and CUBE operations. The HAVING clause can be used to filter out groups (similar to the WHERE clause that is used to filter out records). By making use of the HAVING clause, you can focus on a particular group of records. Filtering

of subtotals can be performed in the same manner as filtering of nonsubtotals as shown in the following:

```
SQL> select time, region, product
2 sum(item_sales) as item_sales
3 grouping (time) as t,
4 grouping (region) as r,
5 grouping (product) as p
6 from sales
7 group by cube(time, region, product)
8 having (t=1 and r=1 and p=1)
9 or (t=1 and p=1);
```

The output of this query shows only the regional totals and the grand total as shown in Table 31.4.

TABLE 31.4   Using the HAVING Clause with the CUBE Operation

Time	Region	Product	Sales
[NULL]	Central	[NULL]	144000
[NULL]	Eastern	[NULL]	180000
[NULL]	Western	[NULL]	173000
[NULL]	[NULL]	[NULL]	497000

> **NOTE**
>
> The use of ROLLUP or CUBE operations does not impose any additional restrictions on the number of columns that can be used with the GROUP BY clause. (It can still work with up to 255 columns.)

SAMPLE Operations

A SAMPLE operation can be performed to retrieve a random set of data from a table and determine if it satisfies the WHERE clause. Sampling of records is specified by using the SAMPLE or the SAMPLE BLOCK option in the FROM clause of a SELECT statement. When the SAMPLE option is used, a specified percentage of rows is read and checked against the WHERE clause, whereas SAMPLE BLOCK option causes a specified percentage of the table's blocks to be read and each row in a block to be checked against the WHERE clause.

> **NOTE**
>
> Sample table scans involving joins or remote tables are not supported.

When you use the cost-based optimizer, the access path chosen is based upon determining the following:

1. The access paths available to it.

   The access paths available are determined by looking at the WHERE clause and the FROM clause (for SAMPLE and SAMPLE BLOCK options).

2. The estimated cost of executing the statement using those access paths.

   The cost of using an access path is derived by using the tables and index statistics available for the statement.

3. Choosing the access path with the least cost.

   The access path chosen by the optimizer can be overridden by using hints except when the SAMPLE or SAMPLE BLOCK option is used.

> **NOTE**
>
> Use of sample table scans requires the use of the cost-based optimizer.

For example,

```
SQL> select * from dba_tables;
```

The explain plan for the preceding SQL statement might look like the following:

OPERATION	OPTIONS	OBJECT_NAME
SELECT STATEMENT		
TABLE ACCESS	FULL	DBA_TABLES

Whereas, if you execute

```
SQL> select * from dba_tables sample block (2);
```

the explain plan for the preceding SQL statement might look like the following:

OPERATION	OPTIONS	OBJECT_NAME
SELECT STATEMENT		
TABLE ACCESS	SAMPLE	DBA_TABLES

The preceding statement performs a table scan using 2 percent of the rows.

Materialized Views

Oracle8*i* allows the optimization of aggregate information by using a new feature called *materialized views*. Materialized views allow you to create, maintain, and use summary tables. Summary tables are also called aggregate tables, and they are used to precompute summary and join operations and store the result in the database. Performance is improved by accessing the aggregate information from such summary tables instead of computing it every time. DBAs can specify how and when to refresh these summary tables. Oracle8*i* makes it very easy to manage materialized views by providing a collection of materialized view analysis and advisory functions in the DBMS_OLAP package. These functions can be called from any PL/SQL program and can be used to provide summary information such as the space used by each summary and summary recommendations (for example, creation and dropping of summaries).

Oracle8*i* Supplied Database Packages

In addition to the STANDARD package that gives Oracle8*i* server its basic functionality, a set of packages is provided for use by DBAs and developers. These packages are prefixed by DBMS_ or UTL_ and provide utilities that can simplify database interaction. These supplied database packages provide a variety of functionality such as manage snapshots, generate asynchronous alerts, work with the Data Dictionary, obtain tuning information about the shared pool, and so on. Table 31.5 describes the various packages available with Oracle8*i*.

TABLE 31.5   Oracle8*i* Supplied Packages

Package Name	*Usage*
Dbms_alert	Handles database events asynchronously
Dbms_application_info	Registers the application currently running
Dbms_aqadm	Works with the advanced queuing option
Dbms_ddl	Recompiles stored procedures and packages
Dbms_debug	Works with the PL/SQL debugger
Dbms_defer	Interfaces with a remote procedure call facility
Dbms_describe	Describes parameters of stored procedures
Dbms_job	Manipulates job queue processes
Dbms_lob	Manages large objects
Dbms_lock	Manages database locks
Dbms_output	Writes text to a buffer that can be retrieved later
Dbms_pipe	Performs inter-process communication using a "pipe"
Dbms_profiler	Profiles PL/SQL scripts to identify bottlenecks

Package Name	Usage
Dbms_refresh	Manages snapshot groups so that they can be refreshed together
Dbms_session	Programmatically performs alter session statements
Dbms_shared_pool	Manipulates the shared pool
Dbms_snapshot	Manages snapshots and snapshot logs
Dbms_space	Obtains information about segment space
Dbms_sql	Performs dynamic SQL and PL/SQL
Dbms_system	Enables/disables SQL tracing
Dbms_transaction	Manages SQL transactions
Dbms_utility	Provides miscellaneous utilities
Utl_file	Reads/writes ASCII-based operating system files
Utl_http	Gets an HTML-formatted page from a URL
Utl_raw	Manipulates raw datatype

Using DBMS_STATS Package

The DBMS_STATS package is provided to allow you to view modified optimizer statistics that might be placed in the dictionary or a table in a user's schema. Placing the statistics in the user's schema allows the user to experiment with "sets" of statistics without affecting the optimizer.

NOTE

If you use a table in a user's schema, the optimizer doesn't look at those statistics.

DBMS_STATS package contains a variety of procedures and most of these procedures allow the use of the following three parameters to indicate where the statistics are placed:

- stattab—This parameter specifies the name of the table that will contain the optimizer statistics. If this parameter is not specified (that is, left NULL), the statistics are placed in the dictionary.

- statown—This parameter is meaningful only when you use stattab. By default, when you specify stattab, the statistics are placed in the same schema as the object whose statistics are being collected.

- statid—This parameter allows you to place a different set of statistics in the same stattab.

> **NOTE**
>
> The DBMS_STATS package allows the gathering of statistics in parallel.

DBMS_STATS Procedures

The procedures provided by DBMS_STATS can be placed in one of the following three categories:

- Set or get statistics
- Transfer statistics
- Gather statistics

By making use of the DBMS_STATS procedures, you can have better control over how statistics are used by the cost-based optimizer. Table 31.6 shows the procedures belonging to the DBMS_STATS package.

TABLE 31.6 DBMS_STATS Subprograms

Subprogram	Category	Usage
Prepare_column_values	Set/Get statistics	Converts user-specified minimum, maximum, and histogram endpoint datatype-specific values into Oracle's internal format.
Set_column_stats	Set/Get statistics	Sets column-related statistics.
Set_index_stats	Set/Get statistics	Sets index-related statistics.
Set_table_stats	Set/Get statistics	Sets table-related statistics.
Convert_raw_value	Set/Get statistics	Converts the internal representation of a minimum or maximum value to a datatype-specific value. Essentially, this operation is the reverse of that performed by prepare_column_values.
Get_column_stats	Set/Get statistics	Gets column-related statistics.
Get_index_stats	Set/Get statistics	Gets index-related statistics.
Get_table_stats	Set/Get statistics	Gets table-related statistics.
Delete_column_stats	Set/Get statistics	Deletes column-related statistics.
Delete_index_stats	Set/Get statistics	Deletes index-related statistics.
Delete_table_stats	Set/Get statistics	Deletes table-related statistics.
Delete_schema_ stats	Set/Get statistics	Deletes schema-related statistics.

Subprogram	Category	Usage
Delete_database_stats	Set/Get statistics	Deletes the entire database statistics.
Create_stat_table	Set/Get statistics	Creates a table in the owner's schema to store statistics.
Drop_stat_table	Set/Get	Drops the statistics statistics table created by create_stat_table.
Export_column_stats	Transfer statistics	Extracts statistics for a particular column and stores them in the table identified by `stattab`.
Export_index_stats	Transfer statistics	Extracts statistics for a particular index and stores them in the table identified by `stattab`.
Export_table_stats	Transfer statistics	Extracts statistics for a particular table and stores them in the table identified by `stattab`.
Export_schema_stats	Transfer statistics	Extracts all the statistics for a particular schema and stores them in the table identified by `stattab`.
Export_database_stats	Transfer statistics	Extracts statistics for all the database objects and stores them in the table identified by `statown.stattab`.
import_column_stats	Transfer statistics	Extracts statistics for a particular column from the table identified by `stattab` and stores them in the dictionary to be used by the optimizer.
import_index_stats	Transfer statistics	Extracts statistics for a particular index from the table identified by `stattab` and stores them in the dictionary to be used by the optimizer.
import_table_stats	Transfer statistics	Extracts statistics for a particular table from the table identified by `stattab` and stores them in the dictionary to be used by the optimizer.
import_schema_stats	Transfer statistics	Extracts statistics for all the objects belonging to the schema specified by `ownname` from the table identified by `stattab` and stores them in the dictionary to be used by the optimizer.
import_database_stats	Transfer statistics	Extracts statistics for all the database objects from the table identified by `stattab` and stores them in the dictionary to be used by the optimizer.
Gather_index_stats	Gather statistics	Gathers statistics for the specified index.
Gather_table_stats	Gather statistics	Gathers all the statistics (table, column, and index) for the specified table.

continues

TABLE 31.6   Continued

Subprogram	Category	Usage
Gather_schema_stats	Gather statistics	Gathers statistics for all the objects belonging to the specified schema.
Gather_database_stats	Gather statistics	Gathers statistics for all the database objects.
generate_stats	Gather statistics	Gathers the statistics of the specified object based on previously collected statistics of related objects.

For example, suppose that a lot of modifications have been made to the orders table. It is important to keep the statistics up-to-date so that the optimizer chooses the best plan. If you are concerned that the new statistics might in fact cause the optimizer to choose a bad plan, it is advisable to experiment with the new statistics before implementing them in production. This can be achieved as follows:

```
SQL> begin
2    dbms_stats.create_stat_table ('megh', 'oldstats');
3    dbms_stats.gather_table_stats ('megh', 'orders', 5, stattab =>
     ➥'oldstats');
4    end;
```

The preceding code will store the old statistics on the orders table into the oldstats table and generate new statistics for the orders table. If you are not satisfied with the access path chosen by the optimizer with the new statistics, you can revert back to the old statistics as follows:

```
SQL> begin
2    dbms_stats.delete_table_stats ('megh', 'orders');
3    dbms_stats.import_table_stats ('megh', 'orders', stattab => 'oldstats');
4    end;
```

Parallel Query Enhancements in Oracle8*i*

Several enhancements are made in Oracle8*i* with respect to parallel operations, but these changes do not affect the manner in which parallel operations are performed. In fact, the changes are internal to Oracle and can help to automate the determination of the degree of parallelism. Oracle can now perform the tuning of parallel operations dynamically by considering the amount of system resources available.

The following parameters can help in tuning parallel operations:

* parallel_automatic_tuning—Setting this parameter to TRUE will cause Oracle to tune the parallel operations. The DBA should also set the target tables to PARALLEL. When this parameter is used, the user-specified hints are ignored.

- `parallel_adaptive_multi_user`—When this parameter is set to TRUE, an adaptive algorithm is used to tune parallel queries in multiuser environments. The free resources available in the system are considered while determining the degree of parallelism.

    Refer to Chapter 17, "Parallel Executions," for details on transaction and rollback segment issues with the use of parallel operations. Oracle8*i* also allows media recovery to be performed in parallel.

Summary

Oracle8*i* provides several enhancements to simplify and speed up the manipulation of data in a data warehousing environment. The huge amount of data involved and the complex requirements such as generation of cross-tabular reports can be easily handled with the use of SQL extensions such as the CUBE, ROLLUP, and SAMPLE operations. Performance of parallel operations can be improved by leaving the tuning aspects of such operations with Oracle, allowing the DBA to concentrate on other aspects of database management. DBMS_STATS package provides procedures that allow you to experiment with statistics in order to decide if the access path chosen by the cost-based optimizer is the best path or not.

Miscellaneous Oracle8*i* Features

IN THIS CHAPTER

When you have migrated to Oracle8*i*, you will be able to use the various new features that we have discussed in the previous chapters. The functional enhancement from Oracle7 to Oracle8*i* is much more significant than the changes from Oracle6 to Oracle7. Although the previous chapters have discussed the most important new features available to you with Oracle8*i*, several other miscellaneous features exist. Constraints, national language support (NLS), tablespace management, and so on are not discussed earlier as major enhancements, but are significant enough that we should discuss them in this chapter.

Constraints

Several enhancements are provided with Oracle8*i* in terms of the use of constraints. The usual manner in which constraint checking is performed is called *immediate* constraint checking. With immediate constraint checking, the server checks the constraint at the end of each statement. If the statement violates the constraint, the statement is rolled back but the entire transaction is not. Oracle8*i* allows you to defer the checking of constraints. With deferred constraint checking, the checking is performed at the end of the transaction instead of at the end of each statement. In other words, the server checks the constraint at commit time. When deferred constraint checking is used, it is possible for the constraint to be violated during the transaction, but not at the end of the transaction. A constraint violation will cause the rollback of the entire transaction.

Another significant enhancement with regards to constraints is that the constraints can not only be enabled and disabled, but also *enforced*. An enforced constraint ignores currently existing data (which might violate the constraint), but enforces all new modifications to satisfy the constraint.

Oracle8*i* also allows unique and primary key constraints to be handled using non-unique indexes—a feature that is not really desirable.

National Language Support Enhancements

Oracle8*i* allows you to use two new datatypes: NCHAR and NVARCHAR2. NCHAR is a fixed-width character, multibyte datatype and can hold up to 2,000 characters. NVARCHAR2 allows up to 4,000 characters. Storage and retrieval of NCHAR and NVARCHAR2 datatypes is performed by prefixing the actual value with a literal N, not in quotes.

NOTE

NVARCHAR2 is to VARCHAR2 as NCHAR is to CHAR.

SYS Security

Oracle8*i* requires that you have the SELECT_CATALOG_ROLE or EXECUTE_CATALOG_ROLE to select or execute SYS objects. Oracle7.*x* allows you to access SYS schema if you have system privileges with the ANY qualifies such as SELECT ANY TABLE. However, Oracle8*i* does not allow this. In Oracle8*i*, unless you belong to the OSDBA group or you have the SYS or internal password, you cannot connect to the SYS schema without the SYSDBA role.

LogMiner

Oracle8*i* allows DBAs to use SQL to read, analyze, and interpret the redo log files by using a new tool called the *LogMiner*. LogMiner is able to work with redo log files that are Oracle8.0 or higher. In order to use LogMiner, you need access to the Data Dictionary of the database being analyzed. LogMiner maps the redo log files to a dynamic performance view v$logmnr_contents. Each row of this table contains information about the logical operations performed in the database. A pair of REDO and UNDO SQL statements are associated with each operation such that the SQL REDO statement shows the original operation performed, whereas the SQL UNDO statement shows the statements that can roll back the changes made by the original operation.

For example, suppose that we want to find out the changes made by Megh to the orders table. The following query can be used:

```
Select sql_redo, sql_undo
From v$logmnr_contents
Where username='megh' and
Seg_name='inventory';
```

The output of this query can be as follows:

SQL_REDO	SQL_UNDO
Delete * From inventory	Insert into inventory(item_id, item_desc, quantity)
Where item_id = 100	Values(100, "Tomato",20)
Insert into inventory(item_id, item_desc, quantity)	Delete * From inventory
Values(100, "Tomato",30)	Where item_id = 100

LogMiner Restrictions

When using LogMiner for analyzing your redo log files, the following restrictions should be kept in mind:

- It can only run in Oracle8.1 or higher.
- It can be used to analyze redo log files from an Oracle8.0 or higher database with the same database characterset and hardware platform as the analyzing instance.
- A PL/SQL package is used to create a dictionary that is used by LogMiner to perform the analysis.
- DML operations on conventional tables are supported but the following are not supported:

  Index-organized tables

  Clustered tables

  Clustered indexes

  Chained rows

  Non-scalar data types

LogMiner Data Dictionary Views

LogMiner performs all its analysis by making use of Data Dictionary views created by a PL/SQL package. The following views can be used with the LogMiner for analyzing the redo log files:

- v$logmnr_contents—This view shows the contents of the redo log files being analyzed. The most important columns of this view are SQL_UNDO and SQL_REDO.
- v$logmnr_dictionary—This view shows the dictionary file being used.
- v$logmnr_logs—This view shows the details of the redo log files being analyzed.
- v$logmnr_parameters—The view shows the current parameter settings for the LogMiner.

Using LogMiner for Redo Log File Analysis

When using LogMiner, it is recommended to use a dictionary file. This dictionary file should be created from the same database that generated the redo log files you are trying to analyze. Generation of the dictionary file is performed with the database mounted; however, the LogMiner utility can be run with the database mounted or unmounted. If the dictionary file is not used, the SQL statements from the redo log files will be displayed using Oracle internal

object IDs for the object name and show column values as hex data. For example, instead of the following SQL statement:

```
Insert into projects(project_id, proj_desc)
values(1124, 'Venus');
```

LogMiner might display

```
Insert into object#1582(col#1, col#2)
Values(hextoraw('464'),hextoraw('3a68290af7106107'));
```

The following steps can be used for creating a dictionary file:

1. Specify UTL_FILE_DIR in the init.ora file so that this directory will be used by the PL/SQL procedure. For example,

   ```
   UTL_FILE_DIR = /oracle/logmnr
   ```

2. Open the database whose redo files you want to analyze.

3. Execute the PL/SQL procedure DBMS_LOGMNR_D.BUILD to create the dictionary file. Specify the following parameters:

   ```
   dictionary_filename
   dictionary_location
   ```

   For example,

   ```
   Execute dbms_logmnr_d.build(
       Dictionary_filename => 'logmnr_dict.ora',
       Dictionary_location => '/oracle/logmnr');
   ```

> **NOTE**
>
> Although LogMiner runs only on Oracle8.1 or higher, it can be used to analyze redo log files from Oracle8.0 databases.

When the dictionary file is created, the next step is to specify the redo log files to analyze. This can be done using the ADD_LOGFILE procedure as shown in step 5.

4. With the database either mounted or unmounted, connect to the database instance.

5. Create a list of redo log files by using the NEW and the ADDFILE options:

   ```
   SQL>Execute dbms_logmnr.add_logfile(
   2 Logfilename => '/oracle/logmnr/redolog1.f',
   3 Options => dbms_logmnr.NEW);
   ```

   Add more redo log files:

   ```
   SQL>Execute dbms_logmnr.add_logfile(
   ```

```
2 Logfilename => '/oracle/logmnr/redolog2.f',
3 Options => dbms_logmnr.ADDFILE);
SQl>Execute dbms_logmnr.add_logfile(
2 Logfilename => '/oracle/logmnr/redolog3.f',
3 Options => dbms_logmnr.ADDFILE);
```

NOTE

The option dbms_logmnr.REMOVEFILE can be used to remove redo log files from the analysis.

After the dictionary file is created and the redo log files specified for analysis, the LogMiner can be started and analysis performed using the options shown in Table 32.1.

TABLE 32.1   LogMiner Options for Analyzing Redo Log Files

LogMiner Option	*Usage*
StartSCN	Specifies the beginning of an SCN range.
EndSCN	Specifies the end of an SCN range.
StartTime	Specifies the start of a time interval.
EndTime	Specifies the end of a time interval.
DictFileName	Specifies the name of the dictionary file to use.

For example,

```
SQL> execute dbms_logmnr.start_logmnr(
dictfilename => '/oracle/logmnr/dict.ora',
startscn => 200,
endscn => 350);
```

The preceding example specifies that you want to use the LogMiner to analyze redo log files with the help of the dictionary file /oracle/logmnr/dict.ora and filter the data by the system change number (SCN).

The output of this analysis can then be viewed by using v$logmnr_contents.

Transportable Tablespaces

Oracle8*i* allows you to use transportable tablespaces. This allows you to move tablespaces between databases without performing a full export/import. Datafiles belonging to a tablespace can be copied between identical systems provided that the tablespaces are self-contained such that there are no references pointing from inside the tablespace to outside of the tablespace.

NOTE

A PL/SQL procedure called `transport_set_check`, provided with Oracle8*i*, can be used to check whether a particular tablespace is self-contained.

The following steps can be used to transport a tablespace:

1. The tablespace to be moved is placed in the read-only mode. This ensures that the data to be moved is in a consistent state.
2. Export the metadata of the tablespace. This step is very fast because a small amount of data is involved.
3. Using the operating system facilities, copy the datafiles belonging to the tablespace to the new system.
4. Import the metadata of the tablespace.

NOTE

Transportable tablespaces can be used to perform point-in-time recovery of a database.

Locally Managed Tablespaces

Prior to Oracle8*i*, free and used extents belonging to a tablespace were managed through the use of Data Dictionary tables. This can potentially cause excessive access to the Data Dictionary and result in inefficient space utilization. Oracle8*i* allows you to use bitmaps in a tablespace to indicate free and used extents. Use of such locally managed (bitmapped) tablespaces can result in efficient space utilization and minimize fragmentation.

Locally managed tablespaces are created with the CREATE TABLESPACE command with the EXTENT MANAGEMENT LOCAL clause. Locally managed tablespaces will automatically size all new extents at standard sizes using either an autoallocate or uniform option. The autoallocate option causes the system to automatically create variable extent sizes. After you specify the initial extent size, the system will automatically determine the size of additional extents. On the other hand, the uniform option creates all extents of the same size.

> **NOTE**
>
> If the EXTENT MANAGEMENT clause is not specified, the default is EXTENT MANAGEMENT DICTIONARY, indicating that the tablespace management is done through the Data Dictionary.

When the LOCAL clause is used with the CREATE TABLESPACE command, the following cannot be used:

- DEFAULT storage_clause
- MINIMUM EXTENT
- TEMPORARY

Suppose that you want to create a locally managed tablespace with all extents being of the same size (32K). The following command can achieve this:

```
SQL> create tablespace LM_TS
2 datafile '/u01/oracle/orcl/lmts1.dbf' size 20M
3 extent management local uniform size 32K;
```

Assuming a block size of 2K, the preceding command creates a locally managed tablespace such that each bit of the bitmap represents 16 blocks.

Temporary Tables

Oracle8*i* allows temporary tables to be created in a user's temporary tablespace. These temporary tables have the following characteristics:

- They are available only to the session that inserts data into them.
- They last only for the duration of a transaction or session.
- They cannot be partitioned.
- They cannot be index-organized.
- They cannot be clustered.
- They cannot contain columns of nested tables or varray type.
- They cannot have any foreign key constraints.

The following example creates a temporary table called population:

```
SQL> create global temporary table population
2 (country       varchar2,
3 num_people float);
```

Oracle8*i* allows you to drop an unwanted column from a table without requiring the re-creation of the table and its associated indexes and constraints. For example,

```
SQL> alter table trial drop noneed_col;
```

will remove the column `noneed_col`, the data associated with this column from each row of the trial table, indexes on this column, and constraints on this column.

Materialized Views

Oracle8*i* allows the optimization of aggregate information by using a new feature called *materialized views*. Materialized views allow you to create, maintain, and use summary tables. Summary tables are also called *aggregate tables* and they are used to precompute summary and join operations and store the result in the database. Performance is improved by accessing the aggregate information from such summary tables instead of computing it every time. DBAs can specify how and when to refresh these summary tables. A summary advisor wizard is provided to help in the creation and maintenance of summary tables.

Dealing with Data Block Corruption

Before using an Oracle data block, Oracle checks it for possible block corruption. Each Oracle data block is written in a proprietary binary format. A data block is considered to be corrupt if the format of the data block doesn't conform to this proprietary format.

Checking for data block corruption is performed at the cache and other higher layers of the Oracle code. The following information is checked:

Block type

Block incarnation

Block version

Block sequence number

Data block address

Block checksum

If an inconsistency in block format is identified at the cache layer, the block is considered to be *media corrupt*, whereas an inconsistency identified at a higher layer of Oracle code marks the block as being *software corrupt*.

When Oracle encounters corrupt blocks, you will see an error message such as ORA-1578 or ORA-600. Information in the corrupt block is more or less lost; you will have to re-create it by using some data backup or export.

In the worst case when the data cannot be easily reproduced and you cannot afford to lose the data, you should call Oracle Support Services. Oracle has several tools—such as the Data Unloader (DUL) utility, which you can use to extract the data out of bad blocks—but typically, using these techniques is very expensive, and they are not guaranteed to recover the data.

Analyze the Table

```
Analyze table table_name validate structure cascade;
```

When this command is used, the data blocks are checked at the cache and higher levels, index blocks are also checked, and the one-to-one association between the table data and its index rows is verified.

Use DB_VERIFY

DB_VERIFY is an external command-line utility that can be used to validate datafiles even when a datafile is offline or the database is unavailable. The executable of DB_VERIFY that comes with Oracle8*i* is dbverif81.exe:

```
dbverif81 parameters
```

You can use the following parameters with DB_VERIFY:

FILE	The datafile to run DB_VERIFY against.
START	The starting block address (by default, the first block of the file).
END	The ending block address (by default, the last block of the file).
LOGFILE	The name of the file that should contain the output of running DB_VERIFY.
BLOCKSIZE	The logical block size (by default, 2,048 bytes).
FEEDBACK	0 indicates that no feedback exists, but if a number *n* is used, a . is displayed for every *n* pages verified.
HELP	Indicates whether online help is needed.
PARFILE	The parameter file to use for DB_VERIFY, which contains the parameters you would have specified on the command line.

When using `DB_VERIFY` to verify a datafile on a raw partition, the nondatabase blocks on the raw partition will be unrecognized and marked as corrupt. This can be avoided by using the `START` and `END` parameters:

```
C:> deverif81 rawdata1.ora

DBVERIFY: Release x.x.x.x.x - date

Copyright........

DBVERIFY - Verification starting: FILE =  rawdata1.ora
Page 28631 is marked software corrupt
Page 28841 is marked software corrupt
Page 28842 is marked software corrupt
Page 28843 is marked software corrupt
Page 28844 is marked software corrupt
Page 28845 is marked software corrupt
Page 28846 is marked software corrupt
Page 28847 is marked software corrupt
Page 28848 is marked software corrupt
Page 28849 is marked software corrupt
Page 28850 is marked software corrupt
Page 28851 is marked software corrupt
Page 28852 is marked software corrupt
Page 28853 is marked software corrupt
Page 28854 is marked software corrupt
Page 28855 is marked software corrupt
Page 28856 is marked software corrupt
Page 28857 is marked software corrupt
Page 28858 is marked software corrupt
Page 28859 is marked software corrupt
Page 28860 is marked software corrupt
Page 28861 is marked software corrupt
Page 28862 is marked software corrupt
Page 28863 is marked software corrupt
Page 28864 is marked software corrupt
Page 28865 is marked software corrupt
Page 28866 is marked software corrupt
Page 28874 is marked software corrupt

DBVERIFY - Verification Complete

Total Pages Examined............................: 11086
Total Pages Processed....(Data)..................: 0
Total Pages Failing.........(Data)...............: 0
Total Pages Processed....(Index).................: 324
```

32

**MISCELLANEOUS
ORACLE8I
FEATURES**

```
Total Pages Failing.........(Index)..............: 0
Total Pages Empty...............................: 12396
Total Pages Marked Corrupt......................: 28
Total Pages Influx..............................: 0
```

- Set events 10210, 10211, 10212, and 10225 by adding the following line for each event in the init.ora file:

    ```
    Event = "event_number trace name errorstack forever, level 10"
    ```

    When event 10210 is set, the data blocks are checked for corruption by checking their integrity. Data blocks that don't match the format are marked as soft corrupt.

    When event 10211 is set, the index blocks are checked for corruption by checking their integrity. Index blocks that don't match the format are marked as soft corrupt.

    When event 10212 is set, the cluster blocks are checked for corruption by checking their integrity. Cluster blocks that don't match the format are marked as soft corrupt.

    When event 10225 is set, the fet$ and uset$ dictionary tables are checked for corruption by checking their integrity. Blocks that don't match the format are marked as soft corrupt.

> **NOTE**
>
> Setting _db_block_cache_protect to TRUE protects the cache layer from becoming corrupted. This is an undocumented parameter and can be set by editing the init.ora file.

Using the DBMS_REPAIR Package

The methods discussed earlier might not always be desirable and might make the entire object unusable even if only a subset of the rows are bad.

Oracle8*i* provides the DBMS_REPAIR package that contains routines to detect and repair corrupt blocks in tables and indexes. DBMS_REPAIR is owned by SYS, and the execution privileges for this package is not granted to other users.

> **NOTE**
>
> DBMS_REPAIR is intended for use by Oracle database administrators only.

DBMS_REPAIR makes use of several enumerated constants for specifying parameter values as shown in Table 32.2.

TABLE 32.2   Enumeration Types Used by the DBMS_REPAIR Package

Parameter	*Enumeration Constant*
object_type	table_object, index_object, cluster_object
action	create_action, drop_action, purge_action
table_type	repair_table, orphan_table
flags	skip_flag, noskip_flag

> **NOTE**
>
> When the table_type is repair_table, the default table is repair_table, and it is orphan_key_table when the table_type is orphan_table.

DBMS_REPAIR makes use of several exceptions that are shown in Table 32.3.

TABLE 32.3   DBMS_REPAIR Exceptions

Exception	*Interpretation*
942	A drop_action is performed on a table that doesn't exist.
955	A create_action is performed when the table already exists.
24120	An invalid parameter was passed.
24122	The block range specified is not valid.
24123	An attempt was made to use an unimplemented feature.
24124	The action parameter specified is not valid.
24125	An attempt was made to fix corrupt blocks in an object that has been dropped or truncated.
24127	Improper use of the tablespace parameter.
24128	A partition name was specified for a non-partitioned object.
24129	An attempt was made to pass a table name parameter without the proper prefix.
24130	The specified repair or orphan table doesn't exist.
24131	The specified repair or orphan table does not have the correct definition.
24132	The table name specified is greater than 30 characters long.

32

MISCELLANEOUS ORACLE8i FEATURES

DBMS_REPAIR package provides several useful subprograms (see Table 32.4) that can be used to check tables and indexes for corrupt blocks and fix the corruption.

TABLE 32.4   DBMS_REPAIR Subprograms

Subprogram	Usage
ADMIN_TABLES	Administrative functions for the repair and orphan key tables.
CHECK_OBJECT	Checks tables and indexes for corrupt blocks.
DUMP_ORPHAN_KEYS	Reports index keys that point to rows in corrupt blocks.
FIX_CORRUPT_BLOCKS	Corrupt blocks detected by check_object function are marked software corrupt by this function.
REBUILD_FREELISTS	Rebuilds the freelists of an object.
SKIP_CORRUPT_BLOCKS	Specifies whether corrupt blocks encountered during table and index scans should be ignored or reported with an ORA-1578 error.

NOTE

DBMS_REPAIR provides routines that allow you to continue working with the corrupt object while they are being repaired or rebuilt.

DBMS_REPAIR should not be used without understanding the impact of using its routines. You should also determine the extent of corruption to determine if it would be appropriate to use the DBMS_REPAIR routines that could potentially introduce logical inconsistencies and even result in the loss of data.

The following steps can be used to correct data block corruptions:

1. Determine the extent of the corruption.
2. Evaluate the advantages and disadvantages of using DBMS_REPAIR in the given situation.
3. Make the objects available for use.
4. Repair the corrupted object and rebuild any lost data.

Determining the Extent of the Corruption

Determining the extent of the corruption is a very important step in repairing a corrupt system because it will help you in choosing the appropriate method for recovering from the situation. Several techniques can be used for this purpose:

- Using block checking initialization parameters

  Block checking for an instance can be enabled by setting the initialization parameter `db_block_checking` to true (default value). When this parameter is set, it will check data and index blocks for corruption whenever they are modified.

- Analyze `table...validate` structure

  A table can be analyzed with the validate structure option, and it checks the structure of the table for corruption. If the object is corrupt, an error message is generated indicating the corruption.

- Using DB_VERIFY

  DB_VERIFY is a utility that can be used to check an offline database for corruption.

- Using DBMS_REPAIR routines

  DBMS_REPAIR package provides the `check_object` routine that can be used to check the specified object for corruption. In addition to reporting the extent of corruption similar to the `ANALYZE...VALIDATE STRUCTURE` statement, it provides the fixes that would result if `fix_corrupt_blocks` routine was subsequently run on the corrupt object. The report of corruptions and fixes is generated in a repair table that must be previously created using the `admin_tables` procedure.

Evaluating the Advantages and Disadvantages of Using DBMS_REPAIR

As mentioned previously, you should not use DBMS_REPAIR routines without first understanding its impact on the given situation. The following things should be useful in making this determination:

- What is the extent of the corruption?

  This is a very important question that needs to be answered and can help you in choosing the appropriate technique to recover from the corruption.

- What options are available under the given situation?

  Several techniques can be used to recover a corrupt object including

  Drop and re-create the object.

  `create table...as select` to create a new table by selecting the good rows from the corrupt table.

  Media recovery.

  DBMS_REPAIR routines.

- What are the side effects of using DBMS_REPAIR routines?

  You should be aware of the different side effects that can result from the use of DBMS_REPAIR such as

  A block might be marked corrupt even though it might contain rows that are valid. This will make even those good rows inaccessible.

  There is a potential for referential integrity constraints to become broken.

  Triggers on the table might need to be treated with care.

  Inconsistencies with freelists can occur if the corrupt block is at the head or tail of a freelist. This is because of the fact that the space management will reinitialize the freelist, making free blocks unavailable. This particular problem can be fixed by using the rebuild_freelists procedure of the DBMS_REPAIR package.

  Logical inconsistencies can occur between the tables and indexes. You can use the dump_orphan_keys procedure of DBMS_REPAIR package to fix this problem and rebuild the index.

- DBMS_REPAIR might result in the loss of data. Can you reproduce the data easily?

Making the Objects Available for Use

DBMS_REPAIR can be used to make objects available for use by ignoring corruptions during table and index scans. The fix_corrupt_blocks procedure can be used to mark bad blocks as software corrupt. The skip_corrupt_blocks procedure is then used to skip corrupt blocks. This setting will cause index and table scans to skip the corrupt blocks of the object.

> **NOTE**
>
> Both media and software corrupt blocks are skipped by the table and index scans when the skip_corrupt_blocks procedure is used.

You should take special consideration when working with corrupt blocks or chained rows or when SET TRANSACTION READ ONLY is being used. Different queries on the same row might return different results in the preceding situations depending on whether the corruption is being accessed.

Repair the Corrupt Object and Rebuild the Data

Several techniques are available for recovering from corruption, and we have discussed some of these earlier, such as

Media recovery

DBMS_REPAIR routines

```
create table...as select
```

The technique you use should be based on the analysis of the damage and the pros and cons of using any particular method. The DBMS_REPAIR procedures—`dump_orphan_keys` and `rebuild_freelists`—are quite useful in recovering from logical inconsistencies in the database, but they should be used with caution.

Salvaging Data from a Corrupt Database

A database can become corrupt for various reasons, such as

- Bad hardware
- Operating system bugs
- I/O or caching problems
- Running unsupported disk repair utilities
- Memory problems
- Oracle bugs
- A computer virus

Hardware and operating system problems frequently contribute to corruption in the database, and therefore these are the first things to check when a database becomes corrupt. When all the non-Oracle problems are resolved, the following steps can be used to recover a corrupt database:

1. Determine the extent of the damage.

    The information in the alert log, trace files, and the complete error message(s) reported by Oracle can provide enough information to determine the extent of database damage.

    Suppose that the error message indicates that the damage is done to `file#(F)` and `block#(B)`. The corrupt file can be identified as follows:

    ```
    SQL>   SELECT name
             FROM v$datafile
             WHERE file# = F;
    ```

    The damaged object can be identified as follows:

    ```
    SQL> SELECT owner, segment_name, segment_type
             FROM dba_extents
             WHERE file_id = F
             AND B BETWEEN block_id AND block_id + blocks - 1;
    ```

2. Run the ANALYZE command at least twice to make sure that the problem is not intermittent. At the Server Manager prompt, use the following for a table:

```
Svrmgr> analyze table owner.tablename validate structure cascade;
```

Use this command for an index:

```
Svrmgr> analyze table owner.tablename validate structure cascade;
```

Use this command for a cluster:

```
Svrmgr> analyze cluster owner.clustername validate structure cascade;
```

3. Perform the recovery.

The recovery approach depends on the segment that is damaged as identified by the preceding query. It might be as simple as recreating the index or might even involve rebuilding the entire database. Several methods are commonly used to recover from the block corruption:

- Select around the corrupt blocks as shown in the following:

    a. Create a table to contain the salvaged data:
    ```
    CREATE TABLE salvage_test AS
    SELECT * FROM test WHERE 1 = 2;
    ```

    b. Select around the corruption, and insert into the salvage table:
    ```
    INSERT INTO salvage_test
    SELECT /*+ ROWID(test) */ * FROM test
    WHERE rowid <= 'low_rowid_of_corrupt_block';

    INSERT INTO salvage_test
    SELECT /*+ ROWID(test) */ * FROM test
    WHERE rowid >= 'high_rowid_of_corrupt_block';
    ```

- Set event 10231 in the init.ora file to cause Oracle to skip software and media corrupted blocks when performing full table scans:
    ```
    Event="10231 trace name context forever, level 10"
    ```

- Set event 10233 in the init.ora file to cause Oracle to skip software and media corrupted blocks when performing index range scans:
    ```
    Event="10233 trace name context forever, level 10"
    ```

- Oracle Support Services has access to several tools, such as Data Unloader (DUL) and BBED (Block Editor), that you can use to extract data from bad blocks. These tools are costly, however, and they are not guaranteed to recover all the data.

4. Perform the analysis on the object again to make sure that it's no longer corrupt.

Several restrictions to the use of DBMS_REPAIR procedures are as follows:

- Cannot be used with index-organized tables and LOB indexes.
- The `dump_orphan_keys` procedure cannot be used with bitmap indexes or function-based indexes.
- Keys that are more than 3950 bytes long cannot be processed by `dump_orphan_keys`.
- The `check_object` procedure doesn't support clusters.
- Out-of-line columns are ignored.

Summary

Oracle8*i* provides a lot of new features that you can make use of after you have migrated to it. Some of the features allow you more flexibility with the handling of tablespaces such as the transportable tablespaces discussed in this chapter. One of the greatest benefits of using Oracle8*i* is the additional features that allow you to perform detailed diagnosis that was not possible earlier, such as the use of LogMiner to analyze the redo log files and the DBMS_REPAIR package to deal with corrupt data blocks.

INDEX

SYMBOLS

A

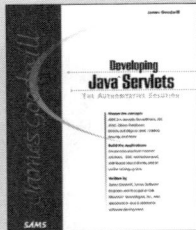

Developing Java Servlets
James Goodwill
ISBN: 0-672-31600-5
$29.99 USA/$44.95 CAN

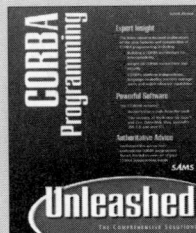

CORBA Programming Unleashed
Suhail M. Ahmed
ISBN: 0-672-31026-0
$39.99 US/$57.95 CAN

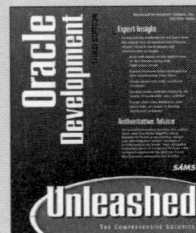

Oracle Development Unleashed, Third Edition
Advanced Information Systems, Inc.
ISBN: 0-672-31575-0
$49.99 US/$71.95 CAN

Oracle 8*i* DBA Certification Guide
William Troper and Paul Lane
ISBN: 0-672-31785-0
$99.99 US/$148.95 CAN

Sams Teach Yourself PL/SQL in 21 Days, Second Edition
Jonathan Gennick and Tom Luers
ISBN: 0-672-31798-2
$39.99 US/$59.95 CAN

Java Distributed Objects
Bill McCarty and Luke Cassady-Dorion
ISBN: 0-672-31537-8
$49.99 US/$71.95 CAN

Java 2 Certification Training Guide
Jamie Jaworski
ISBN: 1-56205-950-5
$39.99 US/$59.95 CAN

Special Edition Using Oracle Applications
BOSS Inc.
ISBN: 0-7897-1280-6
$75.00 US/$111.95 CAN